This Book is a Gift of:

FRIENDS OF THE
LAFAYETTE LIBRARY

Contra Costa County Library

D0788517

THE MESSIAH MYTH

Other books by Thomas L. Thompson

The Mythic Past
The Early History of the Israelite People
The Historicity of the Patriarchal Narratives

THE MESSIAH MYTH

The Near Eastern Roots of
Jesus and David

Thomas L. Thompson

BASIC
B
BOOKS

A Member of the Perseus Books Group
New York

3 1901 03410 3178

CONTRA COSTA COUNTY LIBRARY
LAFAYETTE BRANCH

Copyright © 2005 by Thomas L. Thompson

Published by Basic Books,
A Member of the Perseus Books Group

All rights reserved. Printed in the United States of America. No part of this book may be reproduced in any manner whatsoever without written permission except in the case of brief quotations embodied in critical articles and reviews. For information, address Basic Books, 387 Park Avenue South, New York, NY 10016–8810.

Basic Books are available at special discounts for bulk purchases in the United States by corporations, institutions, and other organizations. For more information, please contact the Special Markets Department at the Perseus Books Group, 11 Cambridge Center, Cambridge MA 02142, or call (617) 252-5298 or (800) 255-1514, or e-mail special.markets@perseusbooks.com.

Designed by Jeff Williams

Library of Congress Cataloging-in-Publication Data

Thompson, Thomas L., 1939-
    The Messiah myth : the Near Eastern roots of Jesus and David / Thomas L. Thompson.
        p. cm.
    Includes bibliographical references and indexes.
    ISBN 0-465-08577-6 (hardcover : alk. paper) 1. Jesus Christ. 2. Jesus Christ—Genealogy. 3. Jesus Christ—Historicity. 4. Bible. N.T.—Criticism, interpretation, etc. 5. Bible. O.T.—Criticism, interpretation, etc. 6. Middle East—History—To 622. I. Title.

BT303.T57 2005
220.6'7—dc22

                                                              2004028573

05 06 07 / 10 9 8 7 6 5 4 3 2 1

To
Ingrid Hjelm

CONTENTS

❧ PREFACE ❧

This book attempts to answer the question I first raised some five years ago: What is the Bible if it is not history? In *The Mythic Past*, I wrote confidently that the Bible is not a history of anyone's past and that the Bible's story of the chosen and rejected Israel presented a philosophical metaphor about mankind losing its way.[1] Our knowledge of the history of early Palestine has not been seriously altered in the intervening years and the debate about its history still deals with the question of its possibility, given the heavy commitment of biblical scholars to the idea that the Bible reflects a historical past.[2] The historical work that is being done is both interesting and promising, depending primarily on historical sources from archaeology and contemporary inscriptions.[3] But the question of what information in the Bible might be used by historians to write a history of Palestine is a false one and a distraction. Historians need evidence for their historical constructions and, without evidence, history is appropriately silent. That the Bible alone offers no direct evidence about Israel's past before the Hellenistic period is not because it is late and secondary—though surely that should give pause to the most conservative of historians—but because the Bible is doing something other than history with its stories about the past.

In discussions about both monumental inscriptions and biblical narratives, historians tend to place events in a demythologized space, which they themselves create. The intention is to displace the mythic space to which biblical and ancient texts have given voice. Whether one is dealing with an army led by God and meeting no resistance, a heroic king marching through the night to attack at sunrise or—in victory—returning the people to faithful worship and the abandoned temple to its god, absence of attention to the story's world ignores the function of ancient texts. The further failure to weigh our texts against comparable literature cripples reading by neglecting the stereotypical quality of biblical tropes. Rhetorical strategies such as the logic of retribution, reiterative echoes of legends past and ever illusive irony are lost in the historian's search for a past that shifts the reader's attention from the story to an imagined past. The assumption that the narratives of the Bible are accounts of the past asserts a function for our texts that needs to be demonstrated as it competes with other more apparent functions.

The question is whether the modern history of Palestine, Syria's southern fringe, is concerned with the same kind of questions as biblical interpretation. Are archaeologists and historians dealing with the same kind of past as the Bible does? This, I think, is the central question of the current debate about history and the Bible, rather than the questions that have dominated. Can biblical stories be used to write a modern history of the ancient past—whether of the individuals or of the events in which they participate? Even when confirmation of the historical references is available—as with inscriptions relating to Sennacherib's invasion of Palestine at the close of the eighth century BCE—our historical information is formed by the extrabiblical and archaeological sources. The Bible uses such historical information for other purposes, in the way that literature has always used what was known of the past.

The public debates on the historicity of the Bible have tended since the mid-1970s to focus on questions about the historical existence of individuals such as Abraham, Moses, David, Josiah, Ezra and Jesus, rather than on literary and theologically more significant questions of understanding and interpreting biblical texts. I, therefore, have chosen to focus on the role of the king, and in particular on his presentation as savior of his people and servant of the divine, which we meet in the myth of the messiah. Although I concentrate on the rich development of this figure in the works of the Hebrew Bible, I also stress the antiquity and continuity of this tradition. The Pentateuch and the early Jewish biblical tradition present Samaritan and Jewish versions of an ancient Near Eastern intellectual understanding of the late first millennium BCE; the gospels present and share this same intellectual and literary tradition in the Greco-Roman period of late Hellenism. I, therefore, decided to represent this ancient myth of the king through three perspectives. Part I deals with the perspective of the gospels, which builds its narrative figures on the basis of the myth drawn primarily from earlier Jewish tradition. Part II considers three of the most central figures of ancient Near Eastern royal ideology—the good king, the conquering holy warrior and the dying and rising god—and discusses their reuse in biblical tradition and especially in the Hebrew Bible. Part III describes the biblical revision of holy war ideology and the way this tradition has affected the composition of the narratives about the kings of Judah and Israel and finally the development of the messiah figure in narrative and song.

My selection of material from the ancient Near Eastern world has many gaps—the many extrabiblical traditions of early Judaism not included in the biblical collections and especially the rich literary traditions of the Mediterranean world in Greek and Latin. These occidental perspectives in the ancient world were deeply intimate with the intellectual traditions of Mesopotamia, Syria and Egypt through writers like Berossus, Philo of Byblos and Manetho. They had their own independent development and relationship to the biblical material that is profound and enlightening. However, like the ancient author, I have not been able to read everything in my library and I have made a selection from what I have read that relates to the themes of royal ideology. An as yet unfinished project ("From Gilgamesh to the Gospels"), in which I am engaged with my colleagues Niels Peter Lemche (Copenhagen) and Philip Davies (Sheffield), will adjust whatever imbalance this present research has involved.

ACKNOWLEDGMENTS

This book began in a course I presented together with Thomas Bolin at Marquette University a dozen years ago. In the discussions I shared with Thomas and the students, some of the essential perspectives of this present book first took shape. Not least among them is the recognition that the common theological principles implicit in the writing of the gospels and the Hebrew Bible hardly support the separation that is usually assumed in today's scholarship.[4] Such separation, of course, has its roots in a postbiblical development of antagonistic and separate Jewish and Christian identities during the second and third centuries CE. This literature reflects a common intellectual engagement of its writers in the Mediterranean and Southwest Asian worlds of the Persian, Hellenistic and Greco-Roman periods.

I wish to thank my students and the members of the Old Testament graduate seminar in the Department of Biblical Studies in Copenhagen, from whom I have gained much insight and advice relating to the issues of this book. My colleagues have strongly supported my efforts to understand these issues. Professor Niels Peter Lemche, with whom I share many interests, encouraged my questions about the implications of intellectual history that dominate the present study. Bodil Ejrnæs's work on the Psalms of the Dead Sea Scrolls has encouraged me to investigate the development of themes in biblical poetry. My editor, Chip Rosetti, has helped much in clarifying the book's argument, and Jim West has caught countless mistakes in my language and presentation. My copyeditor, Chrisona Schmidt, has caught many inconsistencies in my writing style. I must also thank my stepson, Andreas Hjelm, for his support and help with my computer. I am most grateful to my wife and colleague, Ingrid Hjelm, to whom I dedicate this book. She followed this book through the different stages of its development, criticizing and supporting it. She herself is responsible for central contributions to today's scholarship that have changed my thinking and helped lay the foundations for this study, particularly the figure of Hezekiah, whose tears of humility saved Jerusalem from Sennacherib's siege; an explication of the literary techniques with which the patterns of biblical stories have served to develop a never-ending chain of reiterative narrative and a historical understanding of the implicit competition between the two interrelated religious traditions of Samaria and Jerusalem during the Persian and Hellenistic periods.[5] Ingrid ever directed my attention to this historical context of the literature I wish to understand.

THOMAS L. THOMPSON
Copenhagen, November 2004

ABBREVIATIONS

Gen . . . . . Genesis
Ex . . . . . . Exodus
Lev . . . . . Leviticus
Num . . . . Numbers
Dt . . . . . . Deuteronomy
Josh . . . . . Joshua
Jgs . . . . . . Judges
1 Sm . . . . 1 Samuel
2 Sm . . . . 2 Samuel
1 Kgs . . . . 1 Kings
2 Kgs . . . . 2 Kings
1 Chr. . . . 1 Chronicles
2 Chr. . . . 2 Chronicles
Ezra . . . . . Ezra
Neh . . . . . Nehemiah
Job. . . . . . Job
Ps . . . . . . Psalms
Prv. . . . . . Proverbs
Eccl . . . . . Ecclesiastes
Song . . . . Song of Songs
Is . . . . Isaiah
Jer . . . . . . Jeremiah
Lam. . . . . Lamentations
Ez . . . . . . Ezekiel
Dan . . . . . Daniel
Hos . . . . . Hosea
Jl . . . . Joel

Am . . . . . Amos
Jon. . . . . . Jonah
Mic . . . . . Micah
Zeph . . . . Zephaniah
Zech . . . . Zechariah
Mal . . . . . Malachi

Mt . . . . . . Matthew
Mk . . . . . Mark
Lk . . . . . . Luke
Jn . . . . . . John
Eph . . . . . Ephesians
1 Th . . . . 1 Thessalonians
1 Pet . . . . 1 Peter
Js . . . . James
Rev . . . . . Revelation

1 Macc . . .1 Maccabees
2 Macc . . .2 Maccabees
1 Esd . . . . 1 Esdras
Sir . . . . . . Sirach
Jub . . . . . Jubilees
CD . . . . . Damascus Code

THE MESSIAH MYTH

PART ONE

The Kingdom of God

CHAPTER I

Historicizing the Figure of Jesus, the Messiah

An Apocalyptic Prophet?

The best histories of Jesus today reflect an awareness of the limits and uncertainties in reconstructing the story of his life. Knowledge of that life is based almost entirely on four variants of a legend-filled, highly stereotyped "biography." These four "gospels" were written many decades after the date ascribed to their stories. An exact date for them is uncertain, available to us as they are in a manuscript tradition from the second to fourth centuries CE. Whether the gospels in fact are biographies—narratives about the life of a historical person—is doubtful. Their pedagogical and legendary character reduces their value for historical reconstruction. New Testament scholars commonly hold the opinion that a historical person would be something very different from the Christ (or messiah), with whom, for example, the author of the Gospel of Mark identifies his Jesus (Hebrew: Joshua = savior), opening his book with the statement: "The beginning of the good news about Jesus Christ, God's son."

The search for a historical Jesus has not changed much during the past century.[1] While almost all modern discussion takes its departure from the Nobel laureate Albert Schweitzer's classical critique of 1906, Schweitzer's own understanding grew out of the nineteenth-century debate over history and myth.[2] As this debate largely defined the first efforts to identify a historical core in the New Testament, its themes form an implicit agenda in discussions today.

J. G. Eichhorn, professor in Jena from 1775 and in Göttingen from 1788 until his death in 1827, for example, based his history of Jesus on the Enlightenment understanding of mythology as a primitive form of thought and writing that produced narratives based in miracle and superstition from both national and personal experiences. He set himself the task of interpreting the myths of the Bible around a nucleus of historical experience.[3] Critical research tried to un- cover the historical realities hidden in the written myth. For example, Moses is identified as liberator of his people, but the stories of the Exodus were drawn from legend, oral traditions and other fabulous stories to give history impressive divine credentials. The theory was that every myth could be reduced to a histor- ical core by removing the miraculous, the fantastic and the stereotypical. That such stories in fact had a historical core was taken for granted and rarely ques- tioned. Critical attention was given to the Bible's miracles. As a remedy, scholars suggested natural explanations for events that only seemed miraculous. Mar- velous events and symbolic language were understood as hyperbole, decorating the historical and giving expression to an ideal world. Rationalist scholarship in- terpreted the gospels within a self-understanding of "ultimate values."[4]

Understanding ancient myth as hiding history encouraged a secular presenta- tion of a Bible without miracles. Such efforts, however, did not go unchallenged. David Friedrich Strauss argued that reducing biblical story to natural or histori- cal events was not an honest translation of the gospels to a modern understand- ing and violated the intention of the text.[5] Rather than fraudulent invention, myth was, Strauss argued, the spiritual product of a community's imagination. Eternal ideas and values were represented through story. The Jesus story trans- formed the Hebrew Bible's understanding of the messiah as surpassing both Moses and the prophets. The myth of God becoming man used the myth of the messiah to speak of all humanity; it did not represent an individual god-man. Strauss distinguished two kinds of myth. One reflected Jewish thought, long pre- ceding Jesus' own life. Historical myths, on the other hand, so completely rein- terpreted events in Jesus' life as messianic that nothing of a historical Jesus survived. A biography of Jesus was impossible. We had access only to the Christ, understood as an expression of the faith of the gospel writers. Strauss's arguments about the figure of Jesus were sympathetic to the philosopher Ludwig Feuerbach's effort to interpret religion as a reflection of the human predicament.[6] Feuerbach argued that myths were not rooted in experiences of the divine but rather gave ex- pression to the highest values of humanity. Similarly, Strauss understood "histor- ical myths" as symbolic and metaphoric interpretations of actual events.

Strauss's influence in biblical studies was far-reaching. At the turn of the cen- tury, it faced strong reaction. Giving greater weight to the historical Jesus behind the mythic, Johannes Weiss argued that references to the "kingdom of God" re-flected Jesus' own thoughts about the end of the world.[7] Jesus referred to and be-lieved in a future reign of God. Rather than reflecting universal truths, Jesus' understanding of the kingdom, Weiss argued, reflected the expectations of his time of the imminent end of the world. This he associated with his own death. Since, however, the end of the world did not occur, Jesus' teaching could only have relevance for an audience of his own time. They could not be attributed to the beliefs or expectations of the early church or to the authors of the gospels. Weiss's distinction between Jesus' teaching to his own audience and the writing of the gospels in support of a later audience's Christian belief underlined an im-portant critical aspect of the question. If the Jesus of history was to be associated with the teachings in the gospels, they had to be understood as contingent and relative to his experiences and his time, rather than the time of the early church, when the gospels were written. Jesus' belief in "the coming kingdom," therefore, was mistaken. With Weiss, the mythical, universal Christ gave way to the mis-taken prophet.

Weiss took the search for the historical Jesus out of the nineteenth-century discussion of myth and religion. His task distinguished the historical from its mythical interpretation. Weiss opened two avenues for historical research, cen-tering interest in the sources for the gospels, rather than in the texts themselves. The Gospel of Mark offered him an outline of the events of Jesus' life. Separated from such events were the teachings of Jesus, rooted in pregospel oral collections of sayings. These, Weiss claimed, were independently used by Matthew, Mark and Luke.

The "Jesus of history," who was thought to belong to the real past and to the gospel's sources was sharply separated from the "Christ of faith," belonging to a mythic past created in the gospels. "Authentic" sayings of Jesus and the events of his life stood apart from the interpretations that housed them. Scholarship was intensely polarized in 1901 by William Wrede.[8] His study of Jesus' self-understanding as the messiah in Mark's gospel attacked various psychological speculations of scholarship on Jesus' thought. Wrede followed Eichhorn's con-servative understanding that both the accounts of Jesus' life and genuine sayings were preserved in the gospels. Events and sayings had been two distinct aspects of the tradition and each needed independent study. In separating story from sermon in the gospel narrative, Wrede—and with him most New Testament scholarship—understood the Gospel of Mark as the first to combine and har-monize an early understanding of Jesus as human with a "postresurrection," Christian understanding of the messiah. Wrede's book undermined acceptance of Mark's account of the events of Jesus' life. Rather, the gospel was understood as a Christian document of faith. Belief in Mark's narrative structure, as holding the events of Jesus' life together in a coherent form, broke down. The gospels were thought to have been formed from small units of tradition, describing short, meaningful episodes, preserved and given coherence because of their importance to the later church.

Albert Schweitzer's critique of nineteenth-century scholarship supported Weiss and Wrede. He too concluded that Mark, assumed to be the first author of a gospel, did not try to write history. He offered, rather, a theological interpretation of Jesus' life. Schweitzer had a double argument to present: a trenchant critique of the liberal theology of his day and a historicist understanding of the life of Jesus. Every generation of scholarship and every author of a life of Jesus, Schweitzer charged, wrote more about himself than the historical Jesus. Each created a Jesus in the image of his own particular understanding of Christianity. Whether Jesus was a revolutionary of his day, a mythic representation of humanity or a teacher of rationalism, no scholar found a historical Jesus very far from his own time or values. Much in line with Strauss's and Feuerbach's critiques of myth and religion generally, Schweitzer saw scholars presenting a figure of humanity's highest ideals. Ironically true to his own historicist ideals—attempting to present Jesus as he really had been—Schweitzer's Jesus had to be a man of the first century. Nor could his Jesus be reused to support a modern, Christian faith. It needed to belong to the past and be historical. Mark's figure of a prophet preaching the end of the world was therefore attractive. Schweitzer's historical Jesus expected the end to come, at first in his own time but then delayed until his death on the cross. The world did not end at the crucifixion, which allowed Schweitzer to conclude that Jesus had misunderstood his role in God's plan. As a result, the claim of widespread Jewish messianic expectation in the first century came to dominate the figure of Jesus that was presented by twentieth-century scholarship. He was an apocalyptic prophet who made a mistake.[9]

A wary reader does well to recognize the wish fulfillment of Schweitzer's figure of Jesus. His mistaken prophet is historical primarily because he does not mirror the Christianity of Schweitzer's time. But the assumption that this mistaken prophet of the apocalypse is a figure appropriate to first-century Judaism is itself without evidence. The prophetic figure Mark presented, and the assumed expectations associated with his coming, belong to the surface of Mark's text. Schweitzer did not consider why Mark presented such a figure or such expectations. Nor did he consider whether the life of such a person and the expectations of his coming in fact belonged to the historical reality of first-century Jews in Palestine, or whether both expectations and figure were literary tropes. That the figure of the messiah might express Judaism's highest values within Mark's story does not imply that either the figure or expectations about him were to be found in early first-century historical Palestine.

Unfortunately Schweitzer drew from the texts the historical facts he needed. That his prophet was mistaken—because the world did not come to an end—hardly belongs to that text but to Schweitzer's modernist reading of it as history. If Schweitzer were correct and such a Jesus was mistaken—and therefore historical—could this historical figure have been given the role he has in Mark's gospel? Surely Mark—let alone a presumably much later John writing his gospel—would have known about the failure of Jesus' messianism. They would have found it as unacceptable as Schweitzer did. Schweitzer so understood Mark's gospel *as a text interpreting the life of Jesus* that he assumed the existence of his historical Jesus from the start. The historical presence Jesus gained in Schweitzer's reading, the gospel's author never had. The question was not whether Mark presented the figure of an apocalyptic prophet, but whether he was describing a historical figure.

The debate hardly closed with Schweitzer's famous *Quest for the Historical Jesus.* Twentieth-century scholarship, with its faith in history, assumed a historical Jesus as its starting point. It shared Schweitzer's personal dilemma: a choice between a Jesus who fits modern visions of Christianity and Mark's failed prophet. But they always assumed there was a historical Jesus to describe. One solution has been to understand the theology of the gospels as centered in the cross and the associated story of the resurrection. Unfortunately, this also tended to separate scholars' understanding of Judaism from Christianity. The historical Jesus could be understood as Jewish and not Christian, to the extent that the theological world of the gospels was understood to be Christian and not Jewish. A Jewish Jesus could be ignored and even accepted as long as the gospels remained Christian. This distinction provided Christian theology a convenient distance from its Jewish past.

Others have continued the search for historicity, seeing the disquieting failed prophet of Schweitzer's conclusions as a challenge to be answered and even overturned in a never-ending quest for the Jesus of history. By the 1960s, Western scholarship's "orientalism" permitted an easy distinction between Jesus' Judaism and early Christianity's Hellenistic roots.[10] Both the New Testament and its Jesus were compared to Hellenistic models. Many assumed that the more Hellenistic and Christian-oriented Jesus appeared the less he could be identified as the historical Jesus. Conversely, the more Jewish the gospels seemed the more likely it was assumed that they were dealing with an authentic and original Jesus. While this dichotomy between Hellenism and Judaism is now known to be false, it led to a greater concern for understanding the social context of the gospels. Other developments involved literary aspects of the New Testament, especially biography. Both fictive and pedagogical aspects of the narratives were given greater attention. Nevertheless, almost all research has remained intensely preoccupied with the figure of Jesus.

Such fragile efforts to bridge the gap that separates the gospels from the life of Jesus that historians would like to reconstruct leave great uncertainty about every presentation of the life of Jesus. Strauss's assertion that the gospel myths were about a person's life fatally confused narrative intention with form. Weiss's transference of the kingdom of God theme to a reconstruction of Jesus' self-understanding was similarly without warrant. The assumptions that (1) the gospels are about a Jesus of history and (2) expectations that have a role within a story's plot were also expectations of a historical Jesus and early Judaism, as we will see, are not justified. Even though a historical Jesus might be essential to the origins of Christianity, such a need is not obviously shared by the gospels. The worlds that words create are not always intended. Before we write the history behind a text, we must first understand the literary world of which a text is but a single, historical example.

BIOGRAPHY AND THE BIBLICAL FIGURE

Albert Schweitzer concluded unhappily that the historical Jesus was a mistaken apocalyptic prophet who died for his beliefs. His judgment that Jesus was mistaken in his belief about the imminent end of the world—a judgment that has come to dominate much of the discussion since—is not based on his often sound reading of the gospels or his reading of any other ancient sources. It comes from Schweitzer's modern—what he assumed to be privileged—view of ancient thought. His assumptions about the gospels steered his judgment. On the one hand he assumed that Jesus existed apart from the gospels and on the other that the gospels were about this historical person and reflected his beliefs. This lack of clarity in method supported the radical separation of a Jesus of history from the Christ of faith. Of even greater importance, however, was the assumption that apocalyptic prophets in literature reflect beliefs in apocalyptic scenarios. Do Jesus and John bear a message about the end of the world or does the Judgment Day metaphor express other values? One could similarly ask whether the creation story expresses a specific belief in the origins of the world.

That the stories of the gospels are about a historical person is a difficult assumption. To what extent does the figure of Jesus—like the figures of Abraham,

Moses and Job—fulfill a function in a narrative discourse about something else? Is Jesus rather—like so many other great figures of ancient literature—the bearer of a writer's parable? The question does not refer to our knowledge of a historical person. It asks about the meaning and function of biblical texts. The figure of Socrates we read about in Plato's *Dialogues* and the figure of Jesus we read of in Luke's gospel are all-dominating figures of their narratives. One could argue that the *Dialogues* and the gospel are entirely about Socrates and Jesus, in that these classical figures of wisdom, humility and salvation have been defined by the themes they give voice to. The authors may well be assured that their figures bear the weight of their central stories. Discernment is all the greater for Socrates' example, as is humility for Jesus'. Though one might conceivably pit the Socrates of Xenophon against Plato's figure, an intertextual discourse on the "Socrates of faith" would be our result, not a "Socrates of history." Even as with the biblical figures of a Moses or a David, with their authors stridently competing with each other for their heroes, such figures of literature are capable of challenging and displacing their often anonymous creators.

Before we can speak of a historical Jesus, we need a source that is independent of Matthew, Mark and Luke and refers to the figure of the early first century. Such an ideal source, of course, is hardly to be hoped for in the ancient world apart from monumental inscriptions and gravestones, business or administrative records and dispatches. The problem with using the far from ideal gospels as sources for history has attracted great attention to oral tradition. Such traditions could hardly be expected to overcome the distance between, for example, the stock trope of an itinerant prophet and the man whom tradition sends on such journeys. They could help, however, in bridging the considerable gap between the time in which the gospels were written and that earlier time in which they set Jesus.

Although Schweitzer's work closed the nineteenth-century quest for the historical Jesus, the discussion was reopened by the discovery of a large collection of early Coptic manuscripts in Nag Hammadi, Egypt, shortly after the end of World War II. One of the manuscripts, the Gospel of Thomas, which dated to about 350 CE, is a translation of an earlier Greek text. This allowed some to claim the original text had been written in Greek as early as the second century CE— as early as the latest of the biblical gospels. Thomas is a very simple form of gospel dominated by 114 sayings attributed to Jesus. They are typically presented with a short setting and lack the dramatic narrative of the Bible's gospels. Although there is much in the present Coptic text, which is gnostic and obviously belongs to third- and fourth-century philosophical and religious thought, many scholars have found some of the sayings collected in Thomas to be close variants of those in Matthew and Luke. That the author was familiar with these gospels is an obvious explanation of such similarity. Thomas, however, also supports an old nineteenth-century theory that Matthew and Luke were composed independently of each other. Each, in turn, combined Mark's "biography" of Jesus with a collection of sayings, produced in an oral tradition reaching back to the public teachings of Jesus in history. Before the Gospel of Thomas was discovered, this oral source for the sayings common to Matthew and Luke (Q) was defined by the striking similarity of Jesus' sayings in these two gospels.[11] The discovery of a written collection of such sayings in a fourth-century translation reawakened these old speculations about Q. Even more importantly, the use of this text from Nag Hammadi as corroborating evidence for an oral tradition of sayings supported the hope that a comparison of Q with Thomas could help in distinguishing earlier from later sayings. If the sayings in Thomas are earlier than the gospels, scholars would be closer to identifying the earliest of them as Jesus' own.[12] Necessity, once more, was mother to invention. Even though the Greek original of the Gospel of Thomas could hardly have been earlier than the second century, the similarities of the sayings in Thomas to Q have seduced many. Thomas can fill the gap separating a historical Jesus from the earliest of the gospels and therefore it does. This accepts the unlikely assumption that the sayings from Thomas were based on an oral tradition, rather than on the known gospels or on a tradition harmonizing them. It was also claimed that a comparison with the wisdom literature of antiquity supports the assertion that an "earliest level" of sayings, often associated with Q, could be distinguished from a later reorganization of the collection along an apocalyptic theme of judgment. The goal of this assertion was to separate a "historical Jesus" reflected in the earliest traditions of Thomas and Q from a later figure of Jesus corresponding to the apocalyptic theme and its prophetic figure. This distinction, between wisdom and apocalypse, we will see, is unwarranted.[13] Nevertheless, the work of the Jesus Seminar[14] has encouraged at least American scholars to accept Thomas and Q as providing a preapocalyptic, earliest source of the gospels, an oral tradition rooted in the life and teaching of the historical Jesus.[15]

The polemical atmosphere surrounding the research of the Jesus Seminar and the sensationalism of the American press in reporting the opposition from evangelical scholars and conservative Christian groups have grossly distorted what the seminar set out to accomplish with its research. The effort to distinguish sayings in the gospels according to their reliability as genuine sayings of Jesus, as well as the conclusion that only a minority of these sayings could be identified *with certainty* as originating in Jesus' own teaching, has received much attention.[16] Biblical scholars outside the United States find the seminar's conclusions consistently conservative. A generation ago, scholars accepted few sayings of Jesus with the unanimity the seminar could claim. Rather than presenting the more skeptical voice of international research, the Jesus Seminar encouraged startlingly optimistic claims of authenticity. Much more unfortunately, the question of authenticity—whether Jesus actually said it—has narrowed understanding of the function of the sayings. Their association with a particular historicized figure of the first century has led scholars, for example, to ignore what the gospel texts are doing with ancient literature. It is difficult enough for the Jesus Seminar to argue convincingly that the fourth-century Coptic text we have is a translation from a second-century Greek original we do not have. This fragile effort to put the Gospel of Thomas on a footing with Q cannot reasonably be used also to confirm the likelihood of Q's existence as well as date Thomas—now transformed into a source for Matthew and Luke—even earlier. Dating sayings common to Q and Thomas as an "earliest level" of sayings and suggesting a time between 30 and 60 CE for their origin is a conclusion drawn from the assumption that there was an oral tradition derived from a historical Jesus' teaching.

This chain of improbabilities, besides constituting a circular argument, can be falsified on other grounds. While Q in theory consists of sayings that occur in similar form in Matthew and Luke, both Matthew and Luke often present the same or similar saying in variant forms and in the mouths of different figures. When spoken by John, a saying can hardly be called a "saying of Jesus," whatever its original context may have been. As we will see in the following chapters, the most central sayings in the gospels were spoken by many figures of ancient literature. That they are "sayings of Jesus" is to be credited to the author who put them in his mouth. Many sayings the seminar identifies as "certainly authentic" are well-known and can be dated centuries earlier than the New Testament. The very project of the Jesus Seminar is anchored in wishful thinking. Evidence for the prehistory of these sayings is so abundant and well attested that we can trace a continuous literary tradition over millennia.

The tendency to evoke oral tradition to transmit the sayings from event to the writing of the gospels is required only by the assumption that the text is about a historical Jesus. The projected function of the sayings in Q and Thomas as *oral sayings* is to link the gospels with their text's heroic teacher. This, of course, confuses categories. If, instead of Q and the collection of sayings in Thomas, we were to consider actually existing Jewish collections of sayings, such as the proverbs of Solomon, the songs of David or the laws of Moses, would we also conclude that such sayings originated with the figure to which the Bible attributes them? Solomon as a writer of proverbs (Prv 1:1), David as the singer of Psalms (Ps 3:1, 7:1, 18:1) or Moses as the writer of law (Ex 32:32, 34:27; Jub

1:4–6) belong to the literature collecting the traditions that the proverbs, songs and laws might be transmitted, interpreted and debated. Such collections tell us nothing about a historical Solomon, David or Moses—not even whether they existed. Rather, such figures—writer, singer and lawgiver—have few historical ties apart from the collections and texts that transmit them. At the same time, these proverbs, songs and laws have oral and written forms apart from their heroes and are frequently transmitted by other heroes. Many long antedate the biblical collections.

Having distinguished the "authentic" sayings of Jesus in Thomas and Q, several members of the seminar attempted to use them to create a sketch of Jesus' life.[17] However, given the function of the figure of Jesus to epitomize Jewish tradition, there is little room for a reconstruction of Jesus' life apart from the gospels' Jewish stereotype of savior, prophet and teacher. Reducing such a figure to sayings judged "earliest" also reduces the flexibility of such typecasting.

Basing himself on the personality of the speaker he thinks implied by earliest sayings, Marcus Borg, for example, sketches Jesus as a "charismatic and subversive sage."[18] He has two reasons. The sayings he uses have a close affinity to the wisdom literature of antiquity. This leads Borg to conclude that his Jesus must be a sage. That the role of sage is already obvious and explicit in the gospels' presentation of Jesus, however, suggests that the sayings Borg has chosen are integrated with the narratives in which they are found. The claim that they are separate from the stories is inappropriate, for they were selected by Matthew and Luke to fit their stories. If the sayings in fact imply that Jesus was a sage, they reflect his role in Matthew's and Luke's gospels, not a historical figure independent of the written literature. Borg also argues against Schweitzer's presentation of Jesus as eschatological prophet—the figure of Jesus in the surface narrative of Mark's gospel.[19] As an alternative, he presents his figure of a "subversive Jesus." Borg finds such subversion implicit in a number of sayings from Q, with parallels in Thomas, that he claims do not refer to the kingdom. A subversive Jesus speaks of the world and its values turned topsy-turvy. Such a figure, Borg argues, is different from Schweitzer's and Sanders's understanding of Jesus as an apocalyptic prophet announcing the kingdom of God. Therefore he rejects the gospel's prophetic and apocalyptic roles as associated with a historical Jesus. Whether he is correct in this judgment is the subject of the next three chapters.

Borg's reconstruction, like Richard Horsley's presentation of Jesus as a revolutionary figure involved in social and political conflicts of the first century,[20] shares recent interests in anthropology.[21] Since the early 1970s, this research has provided us with a much more sophisticated understanding of Palestinian society.[22] Efforts to reconstruct a context for the earliest of the sayings also encouraged some to compare their implied figure of Jesus to cynic philosophers of the Hellenistic period. Some of the gospel sayings are comparable to what we know of this philosophical school. Caution is needed, however. A sketch of a historical Jesus, drawn by harmonizing his sayings with what we know of the cynic movement, the period and its texts, is often attractive because the harmony supports a circular argument.[23] The efforts to write a biography of Jesus as a peasant nonconformist resisting Roman exploitation, a cynic philosopher walking the hills of Galilee or a charismatic preacher—all descriptions of persons who could have existed in first-century Palestine—are more reassuring than convincing. They are more attractive to conservative theology than Schweitzer's mistaken prophet.

The Jesus of the earliest texts of Q—reduced to a few sayings reflecting a broad wisdom tradition—could find his way in any one of these roles. As soon as we notice, however, with James Horsley and John Dominic Crossan, that rural bandits and magicians might provide alternative contexts and scenarios, cracks begin to appear in the confidence that a Jesus we know only from the gospels can be reduced to human proportions and reflect a historically plausible figure of the first century.[24] Magicians can become miracle workers—or be described as such. Bandits can be thought Robin Hoods and philosophers are indeed teachers. If our philosopher and teacher speaks to crowds as well as his disciples, how far are we from a charismatic preacher, a prophet or an apocalyptic visionary? It takes little to be a revolutionary in any period, if one does not need to remain alive. Since the broad social contexts of a largely unknown first-century Palestine can fit a wide range of possibilities of individuals and their activities, only our knowledge of this period limits our choices. The projection of a biographical narrative of Jesus to epitomize such possibilities, ironically, evokes a mythic Jesus, not the historicized figure sought. Biographies and bibliographies multiply as new myths replace the one the gospels have reiterated.

The persuasiveness of the Jesus Seminar's figures of Jesus dissipates even further when it is recognized that what they use from Q—reflecting the oral tradition of Jesus' teaching—is far less than the materials Luke shares with Matthew. It was pointed out long ago that Q has little that Matthew does not and only what is described as "massive verbal agreement" of these passages as rendered in both Matthew and Luke that supports identifying them as a coherent collection of sayings with its original source in the teachings of a historical Jesus. Unfortunately, alternative explanations of such verbal similarities in the typical literary strategies of early Jewish commentary and theological discussion have not adequately compensated for the modern need to relate the gospels to a historical person.[25]

The sayings that the Jesus Seminar claims are authentic are the "earliest stage of Q," marked by wisdom content and philosophical language. These sayings are used to give substance to the Jesus Seminar's historical figure. The language this Jesus speaks is identified by a group of sayings thought to be coherent and (therefore?) earlier. But as with the events of the gospels, the sayings of Jesus are based on multiple sources and models. They reflect a broad and deep theological tradition. Their use in a story of a Jewish savior, set in a narrative context of first-century Palestine, has created a secondary reiteration of a tradition that is not centered on nor restricted to the events in the life of any historical individual. The problem of the quest for the historical Jesus is not merely the difficulty of identifying him with specific events or sayings, given the length of time between any such figure of first-century Palestine and the gospels. Nor is the problem that the sources have been revised by the theological message of the gospels. The problem is rather that the gospels are not about such a person. They deal with something else.

Stories presenting great and admirable figures of tradition as models for the good life exploded in popularity during the Hellenistic period. Not only great kings like Sennacherib, Esarhaddon and Alexander stood as model for the reader, but the lives of great thinkers, writers and speakers such as Homer, Socrates, Demosthenes and Cicero were celebrated. Among the best known today are collected in Plutarch's *Lives*. Such stories and collections had purposes other than telling their readers about the lives of great and admirable persons. The surface of the text expresses a plot capable of bearing ethical, philosophical and theological themes. As with Plato's Socrates and several biblical figures, the function they serve the author often outstrips their story. The life of Moses, for example, accomplished in a small part of a narrative five books in length, bears with it a much larger tradition. Not Moses' life but the Torah is the narrative's goal. The Torah is the identity-bearing origin story of faith and identity of those who transmit the tradition. Whether there ever was a historical Moses, the Moses we know from the Hebrew Bible is necessarily an invention—for the Torah depends on that figure.

A great figure—bearing and illustrating a tradition—is stock-in-trade of ancient literature. For example, the figure of an extraordinary teacher or king who presents his life's wisdom to his son or grandson dates as far back as the third millennium. One such collection of sayings from the seventh to sixth centuries BCE, organized in thirty chapters and put into the mouth of the Egyptian teacher Amenemopet, serves our point well.[26] A significant portion of the Amenemopet collection is transmitted in the Bible. In the Bible, however, it is not Amenemopet's sayings we read, nor is piety toward Amon-Re encouraged. In the Bible, these same sayings are presented as the words of King Solomon, exhorting his reader to trust in Yahweh:

> Incline your ears and hear the words of the wise and apply your mind to my knowledge; for it will be pleasant if you keep them within you, if all of them are ready on your lips. That your trust may be in Yahweh, I have made them known to you today, even to you. Have I not written for you thirty sayings of admonition and knowledge, to show you what is right and true, that you might give a true answer to those who sent you. (Prv 22:17–21)

Clearly Proverbs continues the tradition of Amenemopet, since it translates and expands the ancient sage's opening lines:

> Give your ears, hear what is said; give your heart to understand them. To put them in your heart is worthwhile, but it is damaging to him who neglects them. Let them rest in the casket of your belly, that they may be a key in your heart.[27]

The Egyptian text follows this introductory chapter with another collection of thirty proverbs, the second of which reads: "Guard against robbing the oppressed and against overbearing the disabled . . ." Proverbs' second saying translates for its audience as follows: "Do not rob the poor, because he is poor or crush the afflicted at the gate" (Prv 22:22). The collection of thirty sayings in Proverbs (Prv 22:22–24:20) is self-consciously transmitting a tradition, structuring it in the context of Jewish piety and presenting it as Solomon's wisdom. It offers instructions in proper behavior, and ten of the thirty sayings are also presented in the Egyptian collection. Direct borrowing or translation, however, is unlikely; rather, both texts share a common tradition and similar purpose. Some of the sayings Proverbs and the Egyptian collection share, such as, "Do not remove the ancient landmark" (Prv 22:22, 23:10) also find their way into the Pentateuch and come to us as part of Moses' Torah (e.g., Dt 19:14, 27:17). Such reiterations may take the form of a paraphrase, as in the introduction to Proverbs cited above. They can also be nearly verbatim repetition as with the instruction not to remove a landmark, though this saying is attributed variously to Amenemopet, Moses and Solomon. Sayings may also reiterate specific themes or oppositions and appear quite self-sufficient in their formulation. Such ancient words of wisdom are transmitted across languages, cultures and centuries. As with Moses and the Torah, the association of a saying with a specific teacher or a specific audience allows the saying to serve a specific function or support a specific plot. However, such plot and function tie the tradition with the figure only secondarily. In dealing with this genre of literature, one doesn't have to invent hypothetical texts like Q; one should rather think of the literature used in the schools of scribes. Ancient literature swarms in such sayings and stories to give them context.

The purpose of this book is not historical reconstruction. Nor is it centered in the problems of the historical Jesus. It is about the influence of the ancient Near Eastern figure of the king in biblical literature, and this has much to do with how figures such as Jesus are created. There is much more that can and needs to be said about the historical Jesus. I will limit my discussion, however, to two well-known recent efforts to sketch his life. I choose them because together they reflect the Jesus Seminar's attribution of authenticity to sayings that are central to the larger tradition's secondary reuse of the royal ideology of the ancient Near East.

John Dominic Crossan brings the seminar's work together with a social and historically oriented discussion of Palestine in the first century to present a socially idealistic picture of Jesus that reflects the theological interests of current U.S. liberal Catholic theology.[28] He describes Jesus as a preacher arguing the cause of the poor in Palestine. He sketches a figure he identifies as a "Galilean peasant." Much influenced by cynic philosophy, this Jesus challenges Roman oppression. While one might worry about the plausibility of Crossan's intellectual peasant, another member of the seminar, Burton Mack, is less interested in Jesus as a historical figure and more in the development of myths, especially that ever-seductive myth of Christian origins that the figure of Jesus has come to represent. Similarly to Crossan, Mack identifies his historical Jesus as a "cynic philosopher."[29] These two reconstructions are sketched from a selection of "authentic" sayings of Jesus. The figure of their sage is explicitly opposed to the figure of an apocalyptic prophet, presented a century ago by Schweitzer and more recently by Sanders. Much as Schweitzer's apocalyptic prophet competed with scholarly reconstructions of a miracle-working Jesus, Crossan and Mack draw a figure belonging to ancient wisdom literature, which they believe excludes the apocalyptic and the prophetic. Jesus is a sage, a philosopher or a peasant influenced by philosophers and, *therefore*, he is not the prophet of the gospels. He uses aphorisms, repartee and parables to talk about a kingdom of God for the poor. He is not the Christ of the gospels but a man made great by tradition.

While Schweitzer indicted the scholarship of his time for replacing the gospels' apocalyptic prophet with a teacher of morality, the Jesus Seminar set itself the task of reversing the critique.[30] The mistaken and disillusioned apocalyptic prophet was chosen by Schweitzer because he had the advantage of being very unmodern. Such a Jesus was necessary to Schweitzer's modern view of the historical. It also fit the ancient tales historians were wont to believe as historical, filling the caves of Roman Palestine with prophets. Nevertheless, such authentic flavor has not withstood the corrosive nature of a Jesus in error and disillusionment. The clay feet of Schweitzer's prophet hardly bear the weight of Christianity's origins. However historical Schweitzer's Jesus seemed in the early and mid-twentieth century, he was unacceptable to a far less critical scholarship at the end of that century.

Crossan has tried to separate Jesus' role as prophet—and particularly that apocalyptic prophetic figure of Elijah returned—from the figure of Jesus as teacher. The role of Jesus as teacher, a "past-oriented, sapiential Jesus," is opposed to and dated earlier than the "future-oriented apocalyptic Jesus."[31] His argument depends on three earlier studies that trace the oral tradition about Jesus' sayings.[32] Crossan suggests that Christian groups in the early 50s CE debated two opposing presentations of Jesus: one belonging to a tradition of wisdom and the other introducing themes of judgment. Crossan takes for granted that we have two incompatible forms of sayings. This scenario, however, begins to unravel when it is recognized that such apocalyptic sayings are not new to Paul or his communities in the early 50s; nor are they peculiar to Jesus. They are commonplace in early Jewish literature. Ezekiel's famous *Dies Irae* (day of wrath) reads:

> Behold the day! It has come. The dawn has gone forth; the rod has blossomed; pride has budded. . . . The time has come; the day draws near. Let not the buyer rejoice, nor the seller mourn, for wrath is upon all their multitude. For the seller shall not return to what he has sold, while they live. For wrath is upon all their multitude; it shall not turn back; and because of his iniquity, none can maintain his life. (Ez 7:10–13)

This passage presents motifs capable of bearing quite different meanings, depending on the contexts an author might give them (cf. Ez 2–7).[33] The passage cited is an obvious forerunner of the metaphors that Paul uses in the so-called debate that provides Crossan with his example of "sayings of Jesus" introduced in the early 50s:

> The appointed time has grown very short. From now on let those who have wives live as though they had none, and those who mourn as though they were not mourning and those who rejoice as though they were not rejoicing, and those who buy as though they had no goods and those who deal with the world as though they had no dealings with it. For the form of this world is passing away. (1 Cor 7:29–30)

Obviously rewriting and not misunderstanding Ezekiel, this passage reflects Paul's knowledge of the tradition. Crossan rather assumes that Paul was unaware of Ezekiel's metaphor and therefore misunderstood his purpose. He assumes that Paul's passage reflects fundamentalistic expectations of his own immediate future.

The book of 1 Peter offers a similar revision of the same passage in Ezekiel. Its author is fully aware of Ezekiel's theme and purpose and has no problem understanding such metaphorical language. In the scholarly manner of his day, he interprets Ezekiel's day of wrath as a vehicle of instruction for proper behavior. Implicitly, he understands his audience to be facing a *comparable* judgment: "The end of all things is at hand. Therefore, keep sane and sober for your prayers" (1 Pet 4:7). However, he hardly projects Ezekiel's judgment day into his own future; rather, like all the prophets from Amos to Malachi to 1 Enoch, 2 Macabbees and Ben Sira, he projects the realization of divine justice with his idealistic metaphor.

Crossan defines apocalyptic in terms of historical expectations concerning the end of the world, rather than as a literary or mythic trope projecting utopian ideals.[34] For Crossan, expectations are implicit in the motif of "the son of man," especially as they echo Daniel and 1 Enoch.[35] Such overtones owe much to the literary techniques of Daniel. For example, one such "apocalyptic" poem is presented in the words of the Babylonian king, Nebuchadnezzar, who speaks of his role as a servant of the "Most High God" (Dan 3:33). Both this role and references to signs, wonders and the divine kingdom echo what scholars typically refer to as apocalyptic language:

> How great are his signs; how mighty his wonders! *His kingdom is an everlasting kingdom, and his dominion is from generation to generation.* (Dan 3:33)

A second scene reiterates Nebuchadnezzar's piety in a conversion story, turning the king's hubris to humble acknowledgment and recognition. This confession of humility is set in the context of judgment:

> At the end of the days, I Nebuchadnezzar lifted my eyes to heaven and my understanding returned to me and I blessed the Most High and I praised and honored him who lives forever, *whose dominion is an everlasting dominion and his kingdom is from generation to generation.* (Dan 4:31)

This epitome of royal confession, idealistically signifying divine rule on earth and the presence of the kingdom, is reused in the Persian King Darius's Cyrus-like decree. The "apocalyptic" judgment has been transferred to a great event of this world to be fulfilled by the king's decree.

I make a decree that in every dominion of my kingdom men tremble and fear the God of Daniel. He is the living God and steadfast forever and *his kingdom is one which will not be destroyed and his dominion will be even to the end.* (Dan 6:27)

Daniel reuses his kingdom metaphor yet again, transposing and raising its mythic potential considerably by associating the kingdom of God with an Ezekiel-like "son of man," the theme of divine judgment and the possession of the kingdom. It is this aspect of Daniel's associations that finds obvious echoes in similar sayings in the New Testament:

I saw in the night visions, and behold, with the clouds of heaven there came one like a son of man and he came to the Ancient of Days [God as judge; cf. Dan 7:9–22] and was presented before him. And to him was given dominion and glory and kingdom, that all peoples, nations and languages should serve him; *his dominion is an everlasting dominion, which shall not pass away and his kingdom one that shall not be destroyed.* (Dan 7:13–14)

In the fifth and final context, possession of the kingdom is transferred to the people whom the son of man represents, much as Psalm 132 identifies the sons of David with the pious ones who sing the psalm:

The kingdom and dominion and the greatness of the kingdoms under the whole heaven shall be given to the people of the holy ones of the Most High, *whose kingdom is an everlasting kingdom.* (Dan 7:27)

Because such tropes are not unique sayings originating with Jesus, Crossan's arguments about a *late* intrusion of apocalyptic ideas in Paul's conflicts over what Jesus once taught evaporate. That we have two different kinds of sayings, one sapiential and the other apocalyptic, is contradicted by Daniel. Whether or not a saying is understood as apocalypse depends entirely on the setting the author gives it. The attempt to isolate the sayings of Jesus from their contexts in the gospels is arbitrary and mistaken. Some of the central sayings Crossan and Mack accept as authentic and belonging to the figure of a philosopher, as we will see, bear typical characteristics of the divine judgment scene. They are as "apocalyptic" as any other aspect of the Elijah tradition. Efforts to date such expectations late and to use this dating to speak of historical development are unfortunately commonplace among New Testament scholars. We will see that early Jewish texts like Job, the Psalter and Isaiah are soaked with such apocalyptic metaphors. Yet they do not reflect either the writer's or his audience's view of what will happen in the world outside their literary project.

AUTHENTIC SAYINGS OF JESUS

Among the many competing figures of a historical Jesus, the miracle worker has been, perhaps, the easiest to dismiss. While earlier scholarship struggled to find historically palatable explanations for the miracle stories of the gospels, later scholars often saw such tales as an attempt to make associations between Jesus and the fulfillment of hopes raised by the prophets. Scholarly beliefs about future-telling and miracle-working prophets in early Judaism support belief in Jesus' self-understanding as an eschatological prophet. With such expectations at the center of scholarly understanding, the structure of any biography of Jesus was not very far from the gospels' own story world.

The Jesus Seminar has argued against such reconstruction in an effort to identify sayings of Jesus as earlier than the gospels and as originating in Jesus' life and teachings. In general, different aspects of a common portrait of Jesus compete with one another, not only miracle worker and prophet, but preacher to the poor, social revolutionary, subversive sage or cynic philosopher. Crossan, for example, connected sayings of Jesus, especially ones that seem to favor the cause of the poor, with what we know of Roman economic policy in the Galilee. He concludes that Jesus was a Galilean peasant, critical of the Romans in their treatment of the poor and landless. Crossan's paraphrase of these sayings is based on a Stoic-related reading of the earliest version of Q. This is harmonized with a setting in Roman Galilee's peasant society. Burton Mack offers more than a paraphrase of what Q and the Gospel of Thomas have in common. His study associates them with theories of ancient Greek rhetoric and understands them as similar to those of a cynic philosopher. His Jesus is such a person as he might have been had he lived in Galilee.[36]

To understand the gospel stories of Jesus and his teaching in the intellectual world of antiquity, Mack seems to be aware of the need to place the teachings of the gospels within the larger intellectual and literary context from which such sayings and stories spring. He does not simply deal with the sayings of an individual. He identifies Q with what he calls a "Jesus movement," developing during the forty years between the assumed date of the death of Jesus and the writing of the Gospel of Mark, thought to be the earliest of the gospels.[37] Although for Mack, the earliest material in Q is centered on the figure of Jesus, his role of teacher is thought to have changed when Mark integrated the Jesus movement's figure of a prophet-teacher with Mark's historicized figure of a divine sovereign: "The ruler of God's world and the lord of God's people."[38]

While some might judge Mack's "prophet-teacher" as harmonizing traditions that are thematically contradictory, it is the assumed later harmonization of this figure with the Gospel of Mark's divine sovereign that is central to Mack's argument. Mack's Christ figure—the divine sovereign ruling over the kingdom of God—is not in the Q sayings. It is also distinct from the figure or figures of teacher and prophet. In opposing Q to Mark's gospel, Mack believes he has warrant to distinguish the sayings from the Gospels of Matthew and Luke from which Q has been drawn. He takes the sayings out of their contexts and projects an oral tradition going back to a historical "Jesus movement" and ultimately to the person of Jesus. We need to look at how closely linked the figure of prophet, miracle worker and royal messiah are in the biblical tradition as a whole. We need further to ask whether these, centered in the themes of the kingdom of God and judgment, are related to the role of teacher or sage; it is that role which Mack and Crossan propose as historical. They do not merely argue that the sayings are earlier than the gospels and that the voice implied by the sayings is a coherent one, reflecting a particular point of view. Also critical is their assertion that the figure of wise teacher or philosopher is earlier than and different from the figure of the prophet Schweitzer proposed. That the sayings were collected and orally transmitted as sayings of Jesus is an assumption without which the argument founders.

ON BORROWING AND DEPENDENCE

In a recent study, Antoinette Clarke Wire attempted to relate the development of heroic stories by examining the oral character of early Jewish narratives.[39] She is clearly influenced by the studies of oral tradition related to Homer.[40] She applies the insights of this research to short stories and legends in early Jewish tradition. She sees them as "apparently oral stories" preserved in literary texts.[41] Adapting the methods of folklore scholars, Clarke Wire identifies "storytelling performance" reflected in literary texts. Unfortunately, she confuses a distinction in forms of presentation—oral and written—with methods of composition and types of narrative. Moreover, she assumes that classifying the stories as legend allows her to imply that the stories have oral qualities. She also transforms known written narratives to oral with her assertion that "ancient legends" imply not only a product of storytellers but also stories that were "retold" and "written down" in the first and second centuries CE, and even later.[42] The idea that modern scholarship can distinguish originally written stories from oral stories that have been written down is hardly obvious. The task is formidable, as we have no oral narrative from this early period to examine.[43]

The claim that particular stories depend on oral traditions, which Clarke Wire shares with the Jesus Seminar, has not been argued, only assumed. It is needed to connect the gospels with the life of a historical figure some two generations earlier than the written traditions we have. The critical issue is whether we can identify some of the sayings and narratives as having been connected through oral tradition to a historical person's life or teaching. Discussions about an oral quality of the gospel stories, unfortunately, do not bring us any earlier than the actually written narratives we have, which Clarke Wire claims record oral traditions. If they did record oral traditions, they were traditions current at the time the written narratives were fixed. If there were oral traditions behind Matthew, Mark and Luke, the evidence in the gospels does not bridge the historical gap between them and the teachings they supposedly transmit. We have access only to the oral tradition of the time in which texts are made.

To speak of an oral quality in Luke's rhetoric is even more difficult. Clark Wire's discussion of the dramatic story of Mary's visit to Elizabeth in the opening chapter of Luke's gospel is fairly representative (Lk 1:39–56). Rather than oral qualities, she considers dramatic qualities of a highly polished, literary work. They may or may not be comparable to the rhetorical characteristics of what are now unknown oral traditions of the period. Clarke Wire stresses three aspects of Mary's speech to Elizabeth. (1) She points to the dramatic use of direct speech when Mary blesses God, supported by shouts of greeting and the striking account of the baby's quickening, concluding that these qualities imply an oral presentation. (2) She asserts that the dominant thematic element expressing a series of reversals, combining the personal with the political, departs from themes of high literature. Similarly, she understands the reversal of the fate and destiny of the weak and strong, humble and proud, hungry and filled—implicit signs expressing the restoration of Israel and the expulsion of the powerful—to reflect the hopes of "everyone in hard places." These, Clark Wire believes, are not qualities of a literary text of the learned and the elite, but of tales of the common people. (3) Finally, she asserts that the central roles given to women in this scene, expressed through motifs of expectant childbirth, the child leaping in the womb and the cozy country scene of women visiting, imply a context of women storytellers.[44]

However reasonable these assumptions may at first appear, Clarke Wire's is not a reading or a reflection rooted in comparative literature. Considered among the dramatic elements of Luke's tale, the rhetoric marks this story as one in a long, well-attested chain of written tradition. The tradition is hardly "folk" and hardly reflects identifiable favorites of women's lore. The scene—and the entire birth story in which it is found—is a thoroughly elitist composition, centered in the male values of warriors and imperial politics. (1) The direct and dramatic quality of Mary's announcement evokes the language and the content of a song that Hannah sang (1 Sm 2:1–10) on the comparable occasion of conceiving Israel's savior. (2) The dominance of women in the scene, the motifs of childbirth and pregnancy and the homey qualities of the narration, are not rooted in the hearth but in a specific ancient literary genre of the Bible, for which we have dozens of written examples. In the stories of the patriarchs alone, this form of tale is found in the story of Isaac, whom the aged Sarah bore to her husband when he was one hundred years old as a gift from Yahweh for their hospitality (Gen 18; 21:1–6). Sarah's daughter-in-law, the barren Rebekah, conceives as an answer to prayer and gives birth to twin nations, struggling already in her womb (Gn 25:21–26). Jacob's wives—the loved one who was barren and the fertile wife, rejected—vie with each other in bearing their children (Gn 29:15–30:24). Such clusters of motifs in birth stories occur, for example, in the story of Moses—replete with midwives, birthing stools and an ironic search for a nurse to return the child to his mother's love (Ex 1:15–2:10). The story of Samson's birth is full of rich feminine detail: his mother's infertility, secret meetings and erotically naive responses to her "man of God" (Jgs 13:1–18). The story of the barren Hannah, which Luke specifically rewrites for his birth narrative, also belongs to this tale type (1 Sm 1:1–2:10).[45] Stereotypical scenes of the home are central to this genre. They are also there with purposes other than a feminine interest. Rather than a reflection of the folklore of the countryside or of women storytellers, they belong among some of the most effective tools of high literature in court and temple. Luke's story shares the genre that the Babylonian Enuma Elish calls "the birth of a hero."[46] In a tale of the birth of the god Marduk—a story recited at the royal New Year festival—thematic elements of a child at play, of the distress of the elder gods created by the child's laughter and of the sleeplessness they suffer as a result, produce literary echoes of the same story's chaos dragon in uproar. They develop the ideologically important theme of the divine call of the hero from his birth to a king's task of creation. (3) Finally, the highly stereotyped list of reversal of fortune for the poor and oppressed has roots in this same literary world of royal and imperial propaganda. The literary tradition goes back at least to the Sixth Dynasty, and its influence in literature can be seen in several hundred ancient texts. Luke's effective reuse of this trope, as we will see, shows him to be a far more frequent visitor of books in the library than of the storytellers of the market square.

Oral tradition is not needed to explain the development of a figure embodying a tradition of ancient wisdom. The parable of Job and his suffering reflects the most typical way in which figures of wisdom function in the Bible and ancient literature. Job, the meaning of whose name ("enemy") echoes the way God treats his friend and faithful servant, is described as "the greatest among the sons of the East." The language that he and his friends use in their debates bears alliterations and overtones of Arabic. He is all things exotic: the epitome of the stranger. His foreignness serves the story's function of representing Judaism's highest values in search for a philosopher's purity of heart. He offers a model of piety where it is least expected, self-critically, apart from Judaism itself. The same role of stranger, however, exposes him all the more to assumptions about borrowing and dependence from other and older ancient Near Eastern works with similar themes. Job's deep roots at the heart of the ancient world's intellectual life have served to hide his biblical role, blunting the brilliant, critical voice he offers to biblical theology.

The book of Job is a good witness to a wide swath of themes and traditions, songs, stories and exercises of the ancient world's education system. Its roots can be traced back at least to the Sumerian song, referred to as the "lamentations to a man's god"[47] and to the Akkadian *Ludlul bel nemeqi*.[48] Job reiterates many features of the strikingly similar Babylonian Theodicy.[49] These earlier texts share themes, ideas and points of view with Job. Their style and structure belong to a shared tradition. There are many identical or nearly identical motifs and phrases. Theories of borrowing and direct citation, however, are difficult to test and unfortunately they often mislead. I would not assume direct borrowing—whether oral or written—between Job's proverbs and eighth- to seventh-century Babylonian proverbs.[50]

Even the astonishingly similar Sayings of Ahiqar, closer in language and time and, like Job, set in a context of fictive drama, has the independent voice a written text creates.[51] Known in Aramaic from the fifth century BCE, Ahiqar's sayings are placed in a far distant and legendary past during the reigns of the famous Assyrian kings, Sennacherib and Esarhaddon.[52] Ahiqar and Job take on a role for their Aramaic and Hebrew reading audiences. It is the role of the outsider who brings wisdom to the seat of empire. It is this dissonance that Job strikes for his audience—in this classic of Hebrew literature. Job has the task of epitomizing "the stranger," not as inimical or unfamiliar but as vulnerable, rejected and despised. In Hebrew literature, Job, as stranger, lies close to the center of the Torah. In the literature of the ancient Near East that has survived, this role is first taken up in the Egyptian tale of a peasant's eloquence at court. Having, like Job, successfully survived his ordeal—mistreated throughout his long search for justice from the "Lord of Justice"—our poor peasant finally comes to the end of his story and his reward. He is bound to the king and invited to sit at the king's table for the rest of his life: "I will surely eat of your bread and I will surely drink of your beer for eternity."[53] Without irony, our Egyptian Job has raised up the head of the figure of lame Mephibosheth in David's court (2 Sm 9:6–13). This foreigner's story also shares a voice with the great command of the Torah to "love the stranger and give him food and clothing" (Dt 10:18). The root by which this trope has traveled is, however, impossible to retrace.

Babylonian proverbs, Ahiqar's sayings and the Egyptian Tale of the Eloquent Peasant have many passages, identical or nearly identical to those in the book of Job. To argue for historical dependence and a direct relationship between such texts, separated from each other as they are, is more than we can do. Attempting to do so ignores many qualities of our texts and carries us beyond simple questions about whether a particular work may have been original or not. Common bonds of technique, rhetoric, function and sentiment imply a relationship that is well beyond the sharing of phrases, metaphors, motifs and themes, or even entire segments of a story or a song. An intellectual world was shared. The Bible is a collection of specific compositions that Samaritan, Jewish and other Palestinian scribes produced and contributed. They shared and transmitted a common ancient Near Eastern intellectual and cultural world created by Egyptian, Mesopotamian, Syrian, Persian and Greek writers. Each of the ancient works we draw into our comparison was formed within a common stream of tradition and opened their readers to a worldview that dominated the region for millennia.

The influence of literature in the ancient world is so widely spread—geographically and chronologically—and so unrestricted by language, social context and genre that efforts to trace the development of particular literary plots and figures within a single language or culturally identifiable body of literature, or to identify direct dependence or borrowing between any two or three specific works is not possible. Our witnesses to this literature are limited to a few surviving examples—as it always unfortunately is with the literature of antiquity. If we have—as with the gospels and other biblical texts—three or four similar texts, one is tempted to ask which came first and which used the other. We can even make such a question purposeful: How did Matthew change Mark's story? What influence did Mark's narrative have on the sayings Matthew and Luke transmit? Could the sayings in Thomas be as early as those in Matthew and Luke, though the gospel itself is much later? The strength of these and similar questions, however, is fed by our limited knowledge. If one has a more adequate representation of tales and proverbs, reflecting a broad geographical and linguistic spectrum, theories of borrowing and origins break down from the enormous press of the examples demanding consideration. Similar statements occur in texts that are many centuries apart and in quite different languages. Even within the same language or the same genre, similarities between texts are so dense that historical associations can hardly be made. The much beloved exercise among biblical scholars of reconstructing sources implied by texts and tracing the history of their subsequent redaction across centuries has not been very successful. Already in 1923, the method was stripped of its scientific credibility. The folktale scholar Walter Anderson identified eighteen separate recensions of a single short tale: the well-known medieval story of King John and the bishop.[54] He had available about 600 oral variants and 151 widely diverging written versions of the tale. But even so, the more he knew about his tale from the many examples available, the less he could speak of any as an original story. The implications of this eighty-year-old study undercut efforts to trace the prehistory of such traditions. Anderson dealt with a whole tale: a very substantial and easily traceable unit of tradition. Literary elements are transmitted in much smaller units than an entire story and persist in the history of every culture. Motifs, formulas, episodic structures and themes have an independent potential within the repertory of storytellers and writers and have a much wider mobility than whole tales.[55] The brief, simple sayings and episodes the Jesus Seminar and Clarke Wire have in mind hardly stretch the limits of the small segment of a tradition. Complex tales and chains of poetry and proverbs of great length have persisted for centuries. Those that we know display a wide range in the stability of their verbatim reiteration. One is hardly pressed to resort to fictive texts like Q or speak about a specific source to recognize what is common to Matthew and Luke.

The stability in the transmission of a collection of proverbs or repartee, one notices in comparing Job and Ahiqar, is enhanced by the use of the heroic figure as either speaker or implied author. The importance or uniqueness of a figure for an audience may increase this stabilizing effect, as when the words or deeds of an Alexander, Sennacherib or Moses are projected. Such stability does not seem affected by whether the figure is fictive or historical. The presentation of the hero as actively composing, singing or teaching about his life journey or rule can identify a particular tradition as uniquely belonging to that hero. Characteristic songs with an identifiable voice can be reserved to the songs of David. Proverbs can be appropriated by the figure of Solomon. In the Bible, laws belong to Moses and eclectic moral sayings to Jesus. The same or similar saying can be given to different figures in different narratives without disturbing the conviction that it belongs to each. Nevertheless, a particular saying out of its author's context can hardly be identified as belonging to Job, a Psalter's David or Isaiah's suffering servant.[56]

CHAPTER 2

⌒∞⌒

The Figure of the Prophet

THIS LOST GENERATION

Schweitzer's portrayal of the historical Jesus as an apocalyptic prophet who mistakenly believed that the end of the world was imminent and later came to think that his death would inaugurate the kingdom of God on earth is shared by many scholars today.[1] Since Weiss and Schweitzer, the critical issue of debate has been how much the gospels reflect Jesus' understanding of himself and his role in the kingdom of God. He is presented as belonging to a long tradition of Jewish prophets who believed they were sent to further a divine plan. God would soon enter the world, destroy the powers that rule it and establish his kingdom, where there would no longer be war, poverty or evil. Jesus is argued to have believed that this apocalyptic closure would occur in his own generation. Such a historical Jesus is in line with the doomsday prophets who have accompanied radical movements throughout the history of Christianity.[2]

The figure of a prophet announcing the kingdom of God plays a central rhetorical role in the gospel stories. This apocalyptic prophet, announcing the kingdom of God and the day of judgment, as we will see, is inseparable from not only the parables of the kingdom and the portrayal of John the Baptist, but also the miracle stories and the sayings of Jesus they illustrate. The literary template that unites them is drawn from the traditions of Elijah and Elisha in 1–2 Kings. The apocalyptic quality of the kingdom Jesus is presented as announcing involves a divinely determined day of destiny (Lk 17:24, 26–27, 30; Mt 24:27, 37–39), in which all are tested and judged (Mt 13:40–43). This prophet urges "this generation" (Mk 8:38–9:1; 13:24–27, 30) to watch day and night (Lk 21:34–36). The kingdom will come when least expected. This is also a picture presented in 1 Thessalonians (1 Th 4:15–17), a letter attributed to Paul and usually considered to be earlier than the gospels. The theme of the kingdom is so pervasive in the synoptic gospels that it is assumed to belong to the gospel's "earliest sources."[3]

Nevertheless, to make an argument that a specific theme belongs to the earliest sources of the gospels is not sufficient to associate it with history. The interrelated themes that have brought Weiss and Schweitzer—and the scholarship following them—to speak of Jesus as an apocalyptic prophet do not reflect religious movements of the first century BCE. The thematic elements of a divinely destined era of salvation, a messianic fullness of time and a day of judgment bringing about a transformation of the world from a time of suffering to the joys of the kingdom are all primary elements of a coherent, identifiable literary tradition, centuries earlier than the gospels, well-known to us from the Bible and texts throughout the entire ancient Near East.

The mythic language New Testament scholars describe as "apocalyptic" is also very old. This language is rooted in the Hebrew Bible and dominates much of Jewish literature of the second and first centuries BCE. For example, Luke's parable of the coming of the kingdom of God as a "day" of destiny, comparing the day on which the son of man comes with the "days" of Noah and Lot (Lk 17:20–37), speaks of the suddenness of the coming of the kingdom and a need to stand ever prepared for it; it also speaks of its arbitrariness. It comes and yet it does not come. It is like lightning, but first the son of man must suffer and be rejected by "this generation." A reiterated simile about the arbitrariness of death's arrival separates the one "who is taken" from the one "left behind." The parable began with a question from the Pharisees: "Does the kingdom come with signs to be observed?" Jesus' negative answer closes on the theme of the divine will, citing an ironic proverb of Job to the same effect: "Where the body lies, there vultures gather" (Job 39:30).

The similarity is obvious when we look at a thematically related discourse (Mt 13:18–43) in which Jesus offers parables of the kingdom and interprets them for his disciples, using Psalm 1 as his template. The implied reference of Matthew's "good seed" and "sons of the kingdom" are those who follow in the Psalter's path of the righteous. The weeds, those "sons of the evil one," are the "wicked" in Psalm 1, who are compared to chaff blown away by the spirit. While the implicit citation is immediate, Matthew's parable of the kingdom builds on the motif it shares with the psalm: the chaff-like weeds. Immediately after the chaff is "thrown into the furnace, where men weep and grind their

teeth" (Mt 13:42), "the righteous shine like the sun in the kingdom of their father," a paraphrase of a passage in Daniel: "Those who are wise will shine like
the brightness of the firmament; and those who turn away to righteousness,
[will shine] like the stars for ever and ever" (Dan 3:12). Matthew is not presenting a historical Jesus or anything he said to disciples or Pharisees. He is using
his figure of Jesus to discuss the book of Daniel. The stories present a metaphor
of the kingdom, much as Psalm 1 uses the related metaphor of the path of righteousness to educate the audience.

One central motif of the recurrent theme of the kingdom, which many see
as implying a historical expectation of a messianic time of apocalyptic change,
is the thematic element of this generation. The use of this theme in the Hebrew Bible is complicated, as it draws on the royal ideology of ancient Near
Eastern literature, in which the theme of the kingdom has deep intellectual
roots. The mythical perception of a time of destiny, a fullness of time or, more
simply, the use of significant numbers to mark a plot's event as implying the
divinely willed destiny of the hero, is a feature with many variations in ancient
literature. Mark, for example, has his Jesus speak of the world overturned and
of the temple destroyed on "that day." Rather than assuming that this expresses
expectations of Jews in the first century or a self-understanding of a historical
Jesus, one should understand what such language implies in the earlier traditions from which it is drawn.

In Matthew 13, Jesus is presented telling the parable of the sower, ending with
a teacher's admonishing remark: "He who has ears, let him hear." This remark
refers to Isaiah 6, identifying any without understanding to Isaiah's lost generation. Their ears were made heavy so that they could not hear (Is 6:10). The disciples—who also did not understand the parable and lacked ears of
understanding—ask him why he has to speak in parables (Mt 13:10). In answering their impatient question, Matthew gives the disciples a special role: "To you
it has been given to know the secrets of the kingdom of heaven, but to them it
has not been given" (Mt 13:11). The great crowds, to whom the parable was told
originally, do not understand at all. They are Isaiah's "evil and adulterous generation." In the preceding story, they had asked for a sign: another central thematic
element of Isaiah's narrative (Is 7:11). Matthew contrasts his generation to the
generation of Nineveh, which believed the prophet Jonah and repented, even
though it had no sign (Mt 12:39, 41, 42, 45; Jon 3:5). Jesus' generation is,
rather, Isaiah's. "Though seeing, they do not see. Hearing, they do not hear, nor
do they understand" (Mt 13:13–15; Is 6:9–10).

In telling Jesus' birth story, Matthew also draws on Jeremiah (Jer 5:21), whose
Jerusalem was rejected for not "fearing God." As in Jeremiah, the destruction of

the city—historically in 70 CE—is explained and cast in the near future, because once again "not a single man who does justice and seeks truth" can be found in Jerusalem (Jer 5:1). Having evoked Jeremiah's Jerusalem, Matthew cites a variant of Jeremiah's prophecy from Isaiah that he might present Jerusalem's fate as fulfilled in "this generation":

> You will indeed hear but never understand and you will indeed see but never perceive. For this people's heart has grown dull and their ears are heavy of hearing and their eyes they have closed, lest they should perceive with their eyes and hear with their ears and understand with their hearts and turn for me to heal them. (Mt 13:14–15)
>
> Go and say to the people: Hear and hear, but do not understand; see and see, but do not perceive. Make the heart of this people fat and their ears heavy, and shut their eyes; lest they see with their eyes and hear with their ears and understand with their hearts and turn and be healed. (Is 6:9–10)

Matthew's story about Jesus is one with the parables his prophet tells. Jerusalem's remnant—like Jeremiah's wood and Matthew's weeds—becomes Isaiah's felled oak stump surviving the fire of exile. Echoing the sacred bush of Exodus (Ex 3:2–3), which burns but does not perish, Isaiah's dead stump, lying in the ashes of an exile's flames, becomes a symbol of hope (Ex 3:2–3). Matthew's oak—become holy seed (Is 6:12–13) and promising resurrection for a new generation—defines the role the disciples play in the narrative. Matthew's reuse of the purifying quality of fire and exile reiterates the forgiveness of sins, with which Isaiah opened the story of his calling. The unforgettable scene of the burning coal that touched and purified the prophet's lips (Is 6:6–7) becomes a universal parable in Matthew's hands. He combines Jeremiah's and Isaiah's metaphor of purification and renewal to support his projection of an Isaiah-like new generation, who will hear and understand the secret of the kingdom, this generation, whose eyes and ears are blessed. The narrative has deftly set the stage for Matthew's *readers* to hear the parable in vicarious imitation of the disciples hearing Jesus' parable of the sower. Understanding, they join the righteous and "shine in the sun in their father's kingdom" (Mt 13:43).

Neither Matthew nor Mark suggests that Jesus speaks within history. Nor do they offer an account of their prophet's own thoughts or expectations. They do not speak of expectations of a cosmic apocalypse. They rather use stories as parables to deal with well-worn theological issues of the tradition they share and continue. They expand the discourse about the kingdom, the "path of the righteous" and understanding. They speak as theologians about how one understands

Torah. Neither events nor expectations of events but a specific quality of language is recognized in the stereotyped motifs of impending judgment, a lost generation, the destruction of the ungodly; Jerusalem and the salvation of the righteous reflect the hopes of the pious. All are drawn from the greater tradition's myth of the kingdom of God, which structures the book of Isaiah.

THE DAY OF JUDGMENT

Understanding the figure of Jesus as historical, as the quest for the historical Jesus has encouraged, distorts our reading. It is only in the imaginary world of scholarly speculation that we find Schweitzer's failed prophet. Of course his prophet must die mistaken; for through the nearly twenty centuries separating Schweitzer from the gospels, the kingdom transforming this world had not come. It is Schweitzer who is mistaken. No historian can be surprised by this. In the real historical world of texts and ancient literature, a prophet who speaks of a cosmic judgment that inaugurates God's kingdom is neither mistaken nor failed, but is a figure in a literary world. The prophet remains a metaphor of myth and literature, where he has a meaningful place.

The anachronism of today's quest for historicity—defining the Bible in terms not shared by its authors—has made our texts homeless. To attribute mistaken expectations about the end of the world to the gospels attributes to them meaning they do not bear.[4] The myth of the kingdom of God has its home in a long tradition of literature. Before asking whether episodes and scenes that structure the story of Jesus' life are based on events, we need to look at the function of stories in antiquity. The stories of Jesus' birth and baptism, of his teaching and miracle working, of his suffering and crucifixion—as well as the story of his resurrection—fulfill a clearly defined, coherent function. Together, they embody a well-defined tradition of discussion that formed the Judaism to which the gospels belong. That they might create expectations among the readers of the tradition does not define their intended function.

An even older tradition of Jewish literature determined how the stories about Jesus were written. One brief episode of Mark's gospel echoes Matthew's use of the parable of the sower and defines his motif of the kingdom of God. The scene in both Mark and Matthew has the disciples ask Jesus about the prophet Elijah: "Why do the scribes say that first Elijah must come?" (Mt 17:9–13; Mk 9:9–13). Mark, in fact, presents a double question. The disciples ask whether Elijah is to come, while the second question is posed by Jesus. He asks whether the "son of man" should suffer. Both questions relate to the prophet Elijah, who has "already come" and has suffered. The identification of John as Elijah is in Jesus' answer: Elijah "has come and they did to him whatever they pleased" (Mk 9:13). Reference to the suffering of the son of man, however, is a self-identifying prophecy—of the story's closure, teasing the reader, not the disciples.

In Matthew's variation, the first question of the disciples is asked much as in Mark's gospel: "Why do the scribes say that first Elijah must come?" (Mt 17:10; Mal 3:23-24). Jesus answers with a paraphrase from the prophet Malachi: "Elijah does come and he is to restore all things" (Mt 17:11). Matthew's story continues, in which Jesus not only quotes from scripture but gives an expansive interpretation, identifying the returning Elijah with John the Baptist, while his suffering is also extended to Jesus' future suffering. As Elijah, John had come and suffered because he had not been recognized. So too must Jesus suffer, like John, unrecognized (Mt 17:12–13; cf. Mk 9:11–13). At least one scholar sees the differences in Mark's and Matthew's versions of the scene as evidence for the existence of independent presentations of an original saying of Jesus.[5] This is, however, difficult to defend. While Mark implicitly distinguishes between his readers and Jesus' audience, Matthew has Jesus balance the connection between John and Elijah and between Elijah and suffering. For example, he has Jesus speak of John the Baptist in prison:

All the prophets and the law prophesied until John; and if you are willing to accept it, he is Elijah who is to come; he who has ears to hear, let him hear. (Mt 11:13–14)

Mark's version projects a similar understanding, particularly in the successful effort to expand the disciple's questions with one of Jesus' own. Nor can one argue that Matthew takes the story from Mark's gospel, as both writers use the scene to integrate other aspects of their gospels. One interesting aspect of the biblical discourse on the return of Elijah and his suffering is Matthew's use of Elijah to legitimize the suffering of the gospel's figures. Elijah is for him the first in a threefold chain of suffering prophets: Elijah, John and Jesus. Both Matthew and Mark center on Elijah's suffering, yet neither attempts to clarify or explain it. It is obviously already understood by the gospel's implied audience. The source, however, in Malachi, with which most scholars associate the disciples' question (Mal 3:23–24)[6] lacks the element of suffering entirely:

Behold, I will send you Elijah, the prophet, before the great and terrible day of Yahweh comes. He will turn the hearts of fathers to their children and the hearts of children to their fathers, lest I come and strike the land with a curse. (Mal 3:23–24)

Malachi's closure refers to Elijah's return before the Day of Yahweh comes, a scenario that is also implied in the disciples' question. Malachi's Elijah controls Yahweh's wrath and prevents the judgment altogether. The savior's role of reconciliation and restoration is also given to Elijah in the Greek version of the book of Ben Sira in the Catholic Bible, with echoes of the themes of death and resurrection:

> You who were taken up by a whirlwind of fire, in a chariot with horses of fire; you who are given to reproofs at the appointed time, it is written: to calm the wrath of God before it breaks out in fury, to turn the heart of the father to the son and to restore the house of Jacob. Blessed are those who saw you and those who have died in love, for we also shall surely live. (Sir 48:9–11; cf. Jer 8:1–9:3)

In Malachi, Elijah's function is similar. In both texts, Elijah's return reconciles the generations (Samaria and Jerusalem) in an effort to prevent Yahweh from cursing the land (Mal 3:24). The threatened curse projects a scene of judgment, in which those who fear Yahweh are blessed and those who do not are cursed. This theme dominates the entire last stanza of Malachi's poem (Mal 3:16–24). Yahweh's role is to separate the righteous from the unrighteous; those who serve God from those who do not. He prepares the fire for the ungodly, who are turned to straw. On the day to come, he will light the fire. Elijah's role, in this scenario, is to prevent this fire of judgment and transform the fate of all humanity. He brings reconciliation between the generations. Elijah is Malachi's angel, who, like the angel of Exodus 24—sent to guide the wilderness story's lost generation—prepares the way for Yahweh's kingdom.

PAIRED FIGURES

The sources for Matthew's story are found among the traditions about Elijah and Elisha, such as we find in Ben Sira, Malachi and 1–2 Kings. In creating roles for John and Jesus, Matthew's recasting of story and tradition also creates a new voice. It is not clear that Mark's more paraphrastic voice is as independent. Neither Mark nor Matthew uses a source that departs from the early written traditions we possess. In Luke, John and Jesus meet before they are born—while in the womb, echoing the Samson story (Jgs 13–16; esp. 13:5b). Luke's unique version of Elijah's return associates both John and Jesus with stereotyped echoes of the kingdom and son of God themes, in which John and Jesus are presented in a complementary pair. The rich construction of his Christmas story is a tour de force of the Bible's birth of a savior stories.[7] The heroic births of John and Jesus create an intensifying doublet, with the birth of each child reiterating earlier legends from this same genre. John is born in the image of Isaac, of a pious, childless couple, too old to have children (Gen 18; 21:1–7). The thematic element of the pious, childless couple is a close variant of the motif of the pious, barren woman in the birth story of the prophet Samuel. In fulfillment of a vow made in gratitude, she dedicated her miraculous child to the temple in a tale that opens the Saul–David narrative (1 Sm 1–2). Luke's Jesus is born of a virgin, not because it is more miraculous but because it echoes, along with a more explicit Matthew (Mt 1:23), the Greek version of Isaiah's riddle of the child Immanuel ("God with us": Is 7:14), an important theme in both Isaiah and Matthew. Also in the story of John's birth, Luke draws on this motif from Isaiah of the child as a sign of divine presence.

The full revelation of that presence awaits the child growing up: "And the child grew and became strong in spirit, and he was in the wilderness till the day of his revelation to Israel" (Lk 1:80). In the desert, John becomes an Immanuel of understanding: "He will eat curds and honey when he knows how to refuse the evil and choose the good" (Is 7:15). The details of Luke's story are filled with motifs related to Elijah's role from Malachi. In Luke's revision of Malachi 3, for example, the angel Gabriel comes to John's father. In Malachi, the messenger awakens fear: "Who can endure the day of his coming?" (Mal 3:2). In Luke, Gabriel reassures Zechariah, "Do not be afraid," and predicts that Zechariah's wife, Elizabeth, will give birth to a child. Growing up, the child will be like a Nazirite and take up his role as Elijah. He "will go before him" and, like Elisha, in possession of the "power and spirit of Elijah," he will reconcile fathers with their children and bring many in Israel back to the Lord their God (Lk 1:17 = Mal 3:24).

This story-interpreting prediction is fulfilled after Elizabeth hides her pregnancy for five months (Lk 1:24–25). In the sixth month (Lk 1:26), Gabriel appears to Mary and, now doubling the scene with Elizabeth, gives the classic opening line of a biblical theophany: "Do not be afraid." In his message, the angel describes Mary's impregnation: the "holy spirit and the power of the Most High will cover you" (Lk 1:35). She will bear a child who will be the "son of the Most High" (Lk 1:32). After this scene, and having learned from the angel of Elizabeth's parallel pregnancy, Mary goes immediately to Elizabeth to stay with her for three months, oddly returning to her own home just when Elizabeth's child is to be born. Such a social faux pas in a story built on intense family emotion draws a modern reader's attention to the chronology and the story's associated events. The months are counted much as they are in Sarah's pregnancy in the book of Jubilees version of the birth of Isaac. This is echoed in Luke's synchronism of his paired pregnancies. Elizabeth stays hidden in her home until her fifth month, much as Abraham and Sarah moved from Hebron to live in the desert until the fifth month (of the year). In Elizabeth's sixth month, the angel Gabriel visits Mary to tell her that the Holy Spirit will impregnate her. Just so, in the sixth month of the year, Yahweh visited Sarah and "did to her as he had said." Sarah, having now conceived, bears her child in the third month of the following year (Jub 16:10–13). Mary's visit to her relative Elizabeth, following the Jubilees chronology, therefore ends in her third month of pregnancy, as the story moves immediately to now separated—but still thematically paired—births.

Such anomalies reveal the character of their stories as rewritten tales. The discourse creates added significance through the parallelism of their heroes' destinies. Luke's "son of the Most High," whose role is to rule God's kingdom eternally as David's son (Lk 1:32–33 = Is 9:6), not only echoes the blessing Abraham received from the priest-king Melchizedek in Genesis 14, but also offers a variation on Isaac's role of a "new Israel," much as David had done.[8] The interplay of Jesus' story with its implied references also involves an intertextual play between the gospels, suggesting a much more creative interrelationship between them than ordinary theories of borrowing allow. In fact, the gospels reflect an independent use of the greater tradition. This is particularly clear in the meeting between the two expectant mothers described by Luke. At the sound of Mary's greeting, the child jumps with joy, filled with the Holy Spirit from her womb (Lk 1:44), an episode that echoes the story of Samson's birth dedicating the child who will be led by the Spirit "from his mother's womb" (Jgs 13:4–7; cf. 1 Sam 1:13–16; Sir 48:12–14). In Luke, Elizabeth greets Mary with a question: "Why is it granted me that the mother of my Lord should come to me?" (Lk 1:43). Her humility is a version of a motif that is found in a speech of John in Matthew's introduction to the first meeting of the sons at the Jordan (Mt 3:11–12; cf. Lk 3:15–17). In this scene, however, John is given humility's role, speaking of his baptizing with water in contrast to the spirit, with which Jesus will baptize. John plays the Elijah of Malachi and Ben Sira, while Jesus, baptizing with an unquenchable fiery spirit, is given Elisha's divine role of judgment (cf. Lk 12:49–56; Mt 10:34–36). Both authors independently present John and Jesus in twin roles, preparing the people for the kingdom in the context of the Elijah paradigm.

In their presentation of the thematic element of humility, they are not very far from the classic biblical story pattern of the "calling of the reluctant prophet" played out so strikingly in the Moses and Isaiah stories (Ex 4:10–17 and Is 6:1–8):

> Jesus came from Galilee to the Jordan to John, to be baptized by him. John would have prevented him, saying: "I need to be baptized by you, and do you come to me?" But Jesus answered him, "Let it be so now; for thus is it fitting for us to fulfill all righteousness." (Mt 3:13–15)

In the story of Elisha's call, the type of scene is at its most charming. Elijah has been instructed to anoint three messiahs to bring Yahweh's revenge against the rebellious Ahab and Jezebel. He is to anoint Hazael as king over Syria, Jehu as king over Israel and Elisha as prophet in Elijah's place. He finds Elisha plowing with twelve yoke of oxen, signifying the twelve tribes of Israel. Passing by, he throws his cloak over Elisha, who immediately leaves his oxen and runs after Elijah, asking for permission to first kiss his father and mother good-bye. Elijah refuses to acknowledge that he has called Elisha: "Go back; for what have I done to you?" Accordingly, Elisha slaughters his twelve oxen, cooks their meat and gives it to the people to eat. He then follows Elijah and becomes his servant (1 Kgs 19). This brief episode seems to be the gospels' point of departure for a number of stories of Jesus calling twelve disciples, who go on to play roles closely parallel to the roles of Elisha's disciples (Mt 9:9; Mk 2:13–14; Lk 5:27–28; Mt 10:5–15; Mk 6:7–13; Lk 9:1–6; cf. Mt 8:18–22; Lk 9:57–62).

Yet another element contributes to the elaborate coupling of the scene of John's birth with Mary's visit to Elizabeth and confirms the dual role of John and Jesus in carrying out Elijah's task of reconciliation. Songs are sung after the expectant mothers meet and after John is born. Mary sings her Magnificat to acknowledge Elizabeth's greeting. The song centers on the theme of the kingdom, reechoing a song that Hannah sang to celebrate her miraculous pregnancy at the opening of the David story (Lk 1:46–56 = 1 Sm 2:1–10). Luke uses the motif of exalting the humble as a response to Elizabeth's humble words, allowing the story not only to celebrate but to illustrate the coming of the kingdom. The second song is sung after John is born. He is the prophet, announcing and submitting his role to the service of his king. His father, Zachariah, sings this song's doublet in another version of Hannah's song to refer to John's destined future, much as Mary's song had sung of Jesus'. Zachariah expands the theme of the reconciliation of David's house and finds closure in the kingdom's coming sunrise in the face of this world's darkness, a theme drawn from Isaiah and Malachi (Lk

1:78–79 = Is 8:23–29:1; Mal 3:20). Zachariah's song returns Luke to the Elijah theme. John will be called the prophet of the most high and prepare the way of the Lord, teaching the people about forgiveness (Lk 1:76 = Is 40:3; Mal 3:1, 23–24). Through these two songs, Luke places both the apocalyptic reversal of destiny and the coming of the kingdom at the center of his theme of salvation. John and Jesus become stock savior figures of biblical tradition. This role is not based on any particular event or saying of Jesus. The two figures and the roles given them already exist. They are fully functional and dynamic, in an active and creative discourse on a series of themes, drawn from the ancient world's royal ideology.

MIRACLE STORIES AND THE LIVING GOD

Mark's gospel uses the doubling of the roles of John and Jesus and reiterates the Elijah–Elisha tradition to present the theme of the kingdom. Opening his gospel with a proclamation of "good news" (Mk 1:1) announcing a king's accession to the throne, Mark begins his gospel with the closing lines of Luke's song of Zachariah (Lk 1:68–73). Revising motifs drawn from Isaiah and Malachi (Mk 1:2–3 = Mal 3:1; Is 40:3), Mark presents John as the angel prophesied by Malachi. He is given the role of preparing the way, calming the divine wrath and bringing men to repent, while Jesus is given the idealized role of judge and ruler of the world. His judgment over the world, creating the kingdom he rules, is expressed through the stories of miracles and healing, reversing the destiny of all who suffer. It is the theme underlying the gospel stories of miracles and healing, which are lightly veiled revisions of the Elijah and Elisha tales from 1–2 Kings. In a chain of reiteration, a discussion is developed, closely related to the interpretations of the Elijah and Immanuel themes from Malachi, Ben Sira and Isaiah.[9] It reiterates a common literary tradition of the king as savior, which has roots deep in the literature of the ancient Near East. Whether the tale is of Elijah, Elisha or Jesus, a common story type can easily be recognized.

The Hebrew Bible's Elijah narrative opens with the announcement of a great drought and builds a chain of stories, whose pattern and themes the gospels imitate. Yahweh wishes to punish King Ahab for being king in Samaria, continuing the separation of the northern tribes from Jerusalem's House of David (1 Kgs 17–19). Neither dew nor rain will fall until Yahweh wishes it (1 Kgs 17:1). Yahweh sends Elijah into the wilderness to hide by the side of the brook Cherith. The brook furnishes drinking water and ravens bring him meat and bread, morning and evening (1 Kgs 17:2–6). Yahweh cares for him until the brook dries up. The story proceeds as Yahweh sends him to the town of Zarephath in Sidon, to a widow (1 Kgs 17:8–16). Elijah asks the woman for a little bread. She tells him she has only a little flour in a jar and some oil in a jug. She is just then gathering sticks to bake a last meal for her and her son before they die. Elijah tells her to make bread for him to eat first. She can make some for her and her son later. He promises that the jar will not run out of flour nor the jug of oil until the drought is over. The woman obeys him and all happens as Elijah said. As the widow passes her test, the story of the magic jar extends Yahweh's care to the widow and the fatherless.

The next tale in the chain creates continuity by intensifying the hospitality theme and offers an answer to the greater story's question: whether Elijah is a true prophet and Yahweh the living God who hears prayer (1 Kgs 17:17–24). The widow's son, whom Elijah saved from starvation, becomes sick and dies. Angered, the woman upbraids Elijah and opens a Job-like discussion about God as judge, bringing evil to the guilty and good to the righteous. Elijah, she complains, has reminded Yahweh of her guilt and caused her son to be killed. Without answering her, Elijah takes the child, lays him on his bed and asks God whether he has brought evil on the widow by killing her son. He stretches himself over the child three times and calls to Yahweh. The child comes back to life and Elijah returns him to his mother: "Your son lives." She now knows that Elijah is a man of God and that Yahweh's word in his mouth is true (1 Kgs 17:17–24). Even as the story has great emotional potential, it is hardly sentimental but holds to its theological theme. She, not understanding, had seen a dead child and a God of wrath. Elijah has shown her a living child and a God of compassion. The conclusion is inescapable that Yahweh's word in Elijah's mouth is true. The identity of truth and life, of the true prophet and his God of life and blessing, marks out an implicit debate: denying that the God of Israel is a God of judgment and wrath—a God of death—and supporting the understanding of Yahweh as the living God.

This leads into a central story about Yahweh as El Qano, the "jealous," violent God of Joshua (cf. Josh 24:19), the theme with which the chain of stories had begun. Following the resurrection plot of this introduction, the author sets his central theme of life's victory over death and of blessing over judgment. The outcome of his story's struggle is projected onto two mountain tops: Carmel (1 Kgs 18:17–46) and Horeb (1 Kgs 19:1–13), reiterating the Pentateuch tradition of Ebal as the mountain of cursing and Gerizim as the mountain of blessing (Dt 11:29). The story again chooses life over death. The first story is a heroic contest of storm and violence. Which of the Gods, Yahweh, Israel's God, or the great storm god, Baal, will hear the prayer of his prophet and end the drought (1 Kgs

18:16–46)? Who controls the storm? Not least in the story's irony is that, in the myth of the dying and rising Baal, the storm God brings the gift of rain as he rises from the dead each spring. It is this role that the Elijah story gives to Yahweh.[10] Elijah is pitted against King Ahab and the prophets of Baal. The goal is Israel's allegiance to the living God. "If Yahweh is God, follow him; but if Baal, then follow him." The author plays with the competing noise of the shouting voices of prophets calling on their god and the divine voice of thunder and storm that responds. Of course, the odds are all against Elijah, who stands like David before his Goliath in a most unpromising situation. He is the remnant of the prophets, the last left alive. Like Noah, he "found grace in Yahweh's eyes" (Gen 6:8). The main plot, however, turns on the gods, not their prophets, and on whether these gods, Baal and Yahweh, are true or empty. In Elijah's story, the contest is cast between an empty god of a world of appearances and Yahweh, the transcendent and true God. Elijah stands alone, calling on Yahweh's name. Against him, call the voices of 450 prophets of Baal and 400 of Asherah. They are the first to choose and slaughter their bull as an offering. They do not set fire to it but call on the storm god Baal to do so. From morning to noon, they call out, "Baal answer," but he does not. Elijah mocks them: "Perhaps he is asleep, shout louder!" They shout louder, they cut themselves and, bleeding, dance themselves into ecstasy, but—and here the tale's rhetoric is important—"there is no answer, *not a sound*" (1 Kgs 18:25–29).

It is now Elijah's turn, and he takes up the role of Moses. The author becomes conscious and explicit in his rhetorical strategy. Assembling the people on the mountain, the prophet rebuilds the altar first built by Moses at the foot of Mount Sinai in the wilderness story. Again, twelve stones are used: one for each of the twelve sons of Jacob, who—as explained by the narrator of 1 Kings—had become the twelve tribes of Israel by Yahweh's word (1 Kgs 18:30–32 = Ex 24:4) and whose separation had been the greatest of Ahab and Jezebel's sins. As Elijah prepares his bull for sacrifice on the altar, he has so much confidence in Yahweh that he has everything soaked down with water—three times (1 Kgs 18:34)! Only then does Elijah pray to Yahweh to send his fire onto the altar. Yahweh's fire falls and burns up even the water. Leading the people in a violent and bloody massacre of the prophets of Baal, Elijah ruthlessly orders them to be dedicated to Yahweh in holy war that leaves not one of them alive. The brutality is not careless. The theme of the living God opened with the widow's complaint against a death-bringing Yahweh. We were reassured that Yahweh is the "God of hearing" of the patriarchal stories, who answers his prophet's prayer. Yet the story has unfinished business. As the drought continues and holds the story's narrative thread, the reader has the task of dealing with a negative image, epitomizing

Baal's failure in the reiterated phrase: no voice, no answer. No one heard as his prophets called to him. Yahweh, on the other hand, heard and answered. Is that enough to carry the story safely to closure? The answer comes quickly. As soon as Elijah rids himself of his prophetic competitors, he tells Ahab to eat and drink; for there is "the voice of the roar of the rain" (1 Kgs 18:41).

But what of the violence and the widow's fear it supports? As Ahab goes to dinner, Elijah goes to the top of Carmel, curls up on the ground with his face hidden between his knees and tells his servant to look toward the sea. The servant sees nothing and Elijah tells him to go back seven times. On the seventh time, "behold a little cloud, the size of a man's hand rising from the sea." The contrast of this delicate metaphor to the roaring voice of a Baal-like storm God reintroduces the tension of the opposition of the destructive voice of divine wrath and the gentle, supportive voice of the rain's life-bringing blessing. The author pits Elijah, running on foot to bring the news of the coming rain to the town of Jezreel, against Ahab, racing in his chariot on yet another quest. In the background, the little cloud turns to a great storm and fills the sky with blackness, wind and rain (1 Kgs 18:44–46). The race is transformed as the queen, Jezebel, hears of the massacre of her prophets and seeks to kill Elijah, who now runs for his life (1 Kgs 19:1–3). We are not finished with the motif of Yahweh's greatness, nor of the greatness of his mercy in the form of a little cloud. These motifs are taken up in the next story to stress even more emphatically the deconstructive opposition between the curse and the blessing of a living God. The narrative parallels Elijah's command to Ahab to "eat and drink" to build a thematic bridge with the story of Elijah on Mount Horeb. With deepening irony, this story opposes the true God to Elijah's own self-understanding as a zealous, hardworking prophet of the God of armies. Angels care for Elijah in his flight to the mountain of God, where the voice of Yahweh waits for his new Moses (1 Kgs 19:1–12).

Elijah's flight from Jezebel closes a day's journey into the desert from Beersheva. He is in despair at his failure to convert "his fathers" and reunite Israel (1 Kgs 19:4). Like Jonah and Job in their stories (Job 7:16; Jon 4:3), Elijah sits under a tree, wishing for death—and falls asleep. A threefold scene follows, echoing Yahweh's care for Elijah at the beginning of the drought at the brook, much as he once cared for the Israelites in the wilderness of Sinai.[11] An angel awakens him with newly baked bread to eat and a jug of water to drink. He sleeps, to be awakened by Yahweh's angel a second time and given food and drink. The story of Israel in the wilderness takes over as Yahweh's food and care give him strength for a forty-day and forty-night journey through the desert to Mount Horeb. There Yahweh shows himself as he had to Moses in a cloud through forty days and forty nights on Mount Sinai (1 Kgs 19:1–13; cf. Ex 24:15–18). Elijah stays in a cave, where "Yahweh's word" asks him why he came there. This prophet of El Qano, the jealous god, who announces divine judgment and death to all who oppose him, asserts that he has been "jealous for Yahweh, the god of the armies." Ignoring his bloody victory on Carmel, he recognizes the failure of his violence. He complains that Israelites have abandoned the covenant, torn down Yahweh's altars and killed his prophets (1 Kgs 19:10). Only Elijah is left and they seek his life too. Yahweh's word tells him to stand on the mountain as Yahweh passes by. Yahweh passes by. A great wind tears at and shatters rocks, but Yahweh is not in the wind. Then an earthquake, but that is not Yahweh either. After the earthquake, comes fire, but Yahweh is not in the fire. Then—after the fire—a small, silent voice. Elijah, ever zealous for Yahweh's glory, stands confounded by the paradox of Yahweh's true face (1 Kgs 19:12; cf. Ps 107:29). If not in the wind, the earthquake and the fire, where is El Qano? The true Yahweh draws an ironic reiteration of Baal's earlier silence as the story closes.

The Elijah story lives again in the stories of Elisha, his successor and the bearer of his spirit and mantel (2 Kgs 4:1–37). Elisha's story also sets out in a three-tale chain of story. It too takes its departure with reference to a king (King Mesha) sacrificing his firstborn son (2 Kgs 3:27). Elisha's first story is a variant of Elijah's magic jar story. It too features a widow, but here—in the stories of Elisha and his disciples—she is the widow of a prophet. Her children are to be taken into slavery for debt, but she has nothing to pay the debt—save a jar of oil. Elisha instructs her to go around and borrow empty jars from her neighbors, as many as possible. Then she is instructed to close her doors and, with her sons, fill all the jars with oil from the first. She does so and the oil does not stop coming from the magic jar until all the jars she borrowed were full. Like the jars of flour in the Elijah story, the magic jar of oil fills all her needs. She sells the oil to pay her debts, and she and her sons live from the remainder (2 Kgs 4:1–7).

This magic jar tale is tied to a double story of a rich woman, the lady of Shunem. In the first story (2 Kgs 4:8–17), she feeds Elisha every time he goes by, in a minor variation of the care that the widow, the ravens and the angels gave Elijah. She and her husband even build a room for Elisha to stay in whenever he visits. On one of his stays, he rewards this generous couple—a woman, childless like Sarah with her aging husband Abraham (Gen 18:1–15)—with the promise of a child in a year's time (cf. Gen 18:10, 14). Like Sarah, standing in her doorway, the woman disbelieves, becomes pregnant and bears a child the following year (Gen 18:10–15; 21:1–7). Also like Sarah's Isaac, the child grows up (2 Kgs 4:18 = Gen 21:8) that the reader might enter his mother's second tale (2 Kgs 4:18–37), in which the narrative returns to the themes of Elijah, all the while maintaining its discourse with the Abraham narratives. The child becomes sick and dies in his mother's lap. The dead son—a grown man in the introduction—surprisingly takes on the form of a small child in the bereavement scene. This imitates the story of the grown Ishmael in Genesis 21, who is carried like a babe in the arms of the grieving Hagar. Even Abraham sets him on his mother's shoulder that she might carry him into the desert to lay him under a bush, allowing him the voice of a child to cry that Yahweh might hear him (Ishmael = God hears: Gen 21:14–17). So too the son of Elisha's rich woman is borne home to his mother by a single servant. After he dies, his mother carries him upstairs and, laying him on the prophet's bed, hurries to Elisha at Mount Carmel. Like Elijah's widow, the rich woman upbraids her prophet when she meets him. Her complaint, however, makes her own Abraham's complaint: "Did I ask for a son? Didn't I say, do not give me false hopes?" (2 Kgs 4:28; cf. Gen 15:2–3; 18:13–14). In her anger, she asks one of the classical questions of theodicy—surely a worthy mate to Abraham's challenge to the God of justice (Gen 18:24–25): Is a child born to die? This is the implied reader's intended question—filled with the anger of all mothers of their dead children and undermining pious perceptions of divine will with charges of betrayal. Elisha sends his servant to lay his staff on the child. Elisha's staff, however, doesn't work. He goes himself and, seeing the child lying on his bed, closes the door that he might be alone with the child and pray. Like Elijah, he stretches himself out over the child, not three times, but holding three points of contact: mouth on mouth, eyes on eyes and hands on hands. The child becomes warm with the dramatic emphasis of the story's emotion. The prophet has almost succeeded. Elisha gets up and walks about. In making a third effort to bring the child back to life, he stretches himself over the child (cf. 1 Kgs 17:21). The child sneezes wonderfully a full seven times and opens his eyes. Elisha then gives the child to his mother, who throws herself at Elisha's feet, takes the child up and leaves.[12]

The third story of the Elisha chain deals with the feeding of his disciples. This story is also told in two scenes, the first of which begins when Elisha orders his servant to set a pot to boil with food for his disciples. One of them puts wild squash and vines in the pot, without knowing what they are. The disciples eat and realize "there is death in the pot" (2 Kgs 4:40). Called to solve the problem, Elisha saves the day by making a gravy for the poisoned stew with a touch of the flour from Elijah's widow. The prophet's power to turn death into life is affirmed and the reader's attention returns to the theodicy of a God of judgment who turns curses into blessings. This tale of judgment and of the "food of death" averted is balanced by a story of abundance and the "food of life" (2 Kgs 4:42–44). Once upon a time, a man brought Elisha some "bread of the first-fruits, twenty loaves of barley, and fresh ears of grain" and suggests that the prophet give it to the people to eat. Elisha instructs his servant to give the food to the men for their supper. He objects: "How am I to set this before a hundred men?" Elisha assures him that Yahweh will give enough and some left over. "And so it was, as Yahweh had said."

Stories accumulate, reiterating themes of life and death. Both the Elijah and the Elisha miracle stories affirm life and struggle against the power of death. Such stories build a common trope: a prophet taken up to heaven before his death (2 Kgs 2:9–14) who has unfinished business: to reconcile the sons with their fathers, that Yahweh will bless and not curse them for their sins (Mal 3:24). This greater discourse builds gradually, each author and each story adding its voice and creating its links with the tradition: back to Abraham and Sarah, to Ishmael and Isaac and to Joshua and Moses. Elisha inherits from Elijah his spirit in word and deed, but Abraham and Moses also live in his stories. The authors of the gospels, when they take up these themes, do not look back on a closed tradition, apart from their tales—a Jewish Old Testament, interpreted in a Christian New Testament. Rather, they join and become part of a tradition that is itself a secondary tradition. It does not deal with original texts or founding events as much as it reflects a widespread literary discussion that has many other refractions than those we meet in the Bible. When the gospels present John and Jesus in the guise of apocalyptic prophet, they are not talking about contemporary ideas about the end of the world. They join Elijah and Elisha's narrative world and make their own effort to reconcile the generations, Samaria and Jerusalem, that death's judgment might be transformed to life. They confirm a day of blessing over judgment. They speak of a God who hears prayer: of the small silent voice displacing the storm, the earthquake and fire of El Qana's judgment.

THE FOOD OF LIFE

The story cycle in Luke 7 about life's power over death begins with a tale echoing the minor motif of a miracle at a distance we saw in Elisha's first, failed effort to raise the rich woman's son by sending his servant. In that story, the element of distance serves a dramatic rhetoric of delay that makes the prophet's third effort unexpected in its success. "God kills and God gives life" is ever a fragile doctrine with which to support life's victory over death. Nevertheless, having given life in the child's heroic birth, would this God of Abraham's covenant make his life meaningless? If the child was—like Isaac—a gift of God, is he to be taken back? The woman of Shunem challenges her prophet. She insists that Yahweh is the living God. In responding to the woman's just rebuke, Elisha sends his servant with his Moses-like staff to raise the child (2 Kgs 4:29). The woman, more resolute than Elisha, refuses to accept a mere servant's failure. She will have the prophet himself for her miracle. She does not leave Elisha. She forces him to go with her and take responsibility for the child. The rhetoric of this exchange is marked by the motif of the reluctant prophet. The woman's oath makes the theme of life giving life explicit: "As Yahweh lives, and as you yourself live, I will not leave you" (2 Kgs 4:30). Yahweh lives and the prophet lives, and her son will also live.

In Luke's story, the prophet Jesus is not involved in the life or the death of the person healed. Yet Jesus' response fits the one seeking help as much as in Elisha's tale. Luke's story is rhetorically expanded by stock thematic elements of the good stranger and the proper exercise of authority.[13] A centurion, whose beloved servant is deathly sick, sends Jewish elders to Jesus to argue on his behalf. They present the Roman as a worthy man: one who supports Judaism (Lk 7:3–5). As Jesus comes close to the house, the status-conscious story presents the centurion in a role that contrasts with the desperate, determined rich woman of the Elisha story. In a world of living and dying, Jesus is like a centurion. The Roman soldier gives him the respect due to one who commands. He has servants. A command suffices: "Say but the word and let my servant be healed." And so Jesus did.

The story develops in three stereotypical scenes, built on a template used in many biblical stories. (1) The beloved becomes sick (and/or dies) and the prophet is told or sent for. (2) The prophet is delayed or goes to the house and is told that the beloved is already dead. (3) The prophet acts and the child is raised from the dead. This pattern controls the story of Jairus's daughter (Mk 5:21–43) and its variants (Mt 9:18–26; Lk 8:40–56) and the story of Lazarus (Jn 11:1–57). In Luke's centurion story, the prophet is neither delayed nor does the beloved die. The differences allow the story to supplant the stock theme of victory over death with the theme of the prophet's authority. In the hierarchy of power over life and death, the soldier recognizes the authority of Jesus: an order given suffices for one who has true authority (Lk 7:6–8).

My interpretation of the Elisha story's rhetoric, in which the prophet's role is to mediate divine power, finds confirmation in the understanding implied in the Gospel of John's revision in his tale of the healing of the official's son in Capernaum (Jn 4:46–53). John's version of this healing story begins as Jesus comes through the town of Cana and the author refers to the story of Jesus' changing water to wine there (Jn 4:46; cf. Jn 2:1–12). It was also in this story that the author began his chain of seven miracle tales to illustrate Jesus' role as savior of the world (Jn 4:42), a theme that he draws from Isaiah (Is 2:3–4; 12:3, 5; 45:22; 49:6; 52:10). The healing story opens as a royal official goes to him with a request to come to Capernaum to save his dying son. Jesus' response takes us into the author's world of discourse: Jesus rebukes the man for not believing without a sign, also a well-worn theme from Isaiah. Though perfectly appropriate to the "wine from water" miracle story (Jn 2:1–11; Is 7:11–12), Jesus' rebuke seems at first displaced in this story, as it is addressed to a man who does believe and asks for his son's life. The royal official ignores the rebuke and—true to the pattern of a resurrection story—presses Jesus to come with him before his son dies. Jesus' second response provides context for his first. He tells the official his son lives. Without a sign, the man believes the life-creating word of this world's savior:

> Turn to me and be saved, all the ends of the earth! For I am God and there is no other. By myself I have sworn, from my mouth has gone forth in righteousness a word that will not return. (Is 45:22–23)

The closure of John's story echoes Luke's presentation of the centurion's faith in the power of Jesus' word (Lk 7:7). Creation by the word is a classic illustration of divine power, emphasized not only in the creation story of Genesis 1 but, even more dramatically, in the Babylonian creation story, in which Marduk demonstrates his divine power in creating by word alone.[14]

The motifs of Matthew's story (Mt 8:5–13) are close to Luke's, but less close to the Hebrew Bible variations of the story. The tale is less engaged than Luke with the miracle itself or the resurrection theme, so central to the Elijah-Elisha cycle of tales. Nor is it interested in the motif of the beloved. Matthew's officer tells Jesus that his servant lies lame at home, suffering terribly. Rather than delaying or sending a message, Jesus agrees to come to heal him. Jesus' readiness to travel opens the scene to a lecture by the officer on authority. In Jesus' response—marveling at the officer's faith—Matthew seems aware of the discourse on believing without a sign, which we find in John's version. Matthew's officer implicitly draws on the foreignness of Luke's centurion as he turns his officer's marvelous faith to a supersessionist function. He draws on an anti-Jewish apocalyptic metaphor of the kingdom, wherein the whole world comes to sit at Abraham's table, while the sons of the kingdom are cast out. The miracle caps Matthew's emphasis on faith: "Go, let it be done to you as you believed; and the servant was healed at that very moment" (Mt 8:13).

In Luke's cycle, a second scene follows the centurion's story, offering a variant of the same tale type. Jesus is on his way to Nain, accompanied by his disciples and a great crowd. When he comes to the town gate, he is met by the bier of a man who had died, the only son of a widow (Lk 7:11–17). The story is a delicate but efficient story of sentiment. It draws on the greater tradition to emphasize the kingdom's reversal of the fate of widows and orphans. Jesus meets the widow and her dead son and has compassion: "Do not cry." He "touches the bier and the bearers stood still." Jesus tells the young man to rise and the dead man sits up and begins to speak, as Jesus gives him back to his mother. As in the stories of Elijah and Elisha, Luke's tale closes with the motif of the prophet returning the child to the mother: from death to life. The scene closes as the crowd correctly interprets the event as a sign of the kingdom:

> All were filled with awe and praised God, saying: "A great prophet has arisen among us. God has visited his people." And the word spread (Lk 7:16–17).

Explicit in his dependence on the stories of the prophets, Luke's closure allows the crowd to play the role of a generation filled with the fear of God who understands.

The next scene explains the previous scene's emphasis on sentiment and the importance of Jesus' compassion (Lk 7:18–23). Two of John's disciples are sent to ask Jesus whether he is "the one who is to come, or should they wait for another." Is Jesus Malachi's Elijah? Luke continues the pairing of John and Jesus, as do Matthew and Mark's variants of this scene (Mt 17:12–13; Mk 9:11–13). Jesus offers John's disciples a sixfold list of fate reversed, each of them, individually and together, signs of the kingdom. They render understanding in his listeners, who finally have ears that hear and eyes that see and who will be healed (cf. Is 6:8–10): "The blind see, the lame walk, lepers are cleansed, the deaf hear, the dead are raised and the poor have the gospel preached to them." Healing the sick, raising the dead, compassion for the widow and the fatherless are all well-known examples of the reversal of the fortunes of the oppressed, which in Isaiah are stereotypical signs of the messiah's victory. They mark Luke's cycle as kingdom narrative, celebrating life's victory over death.

Luke's narrative joins two stories on the theme of John and Elijah. Having placed Jesus in the role of a returning Elijah in the first, he turns to the parallel role played by John. After John's disciples depart, Luke's second scene has Jesus turn to the crowds to ask what they were looking for when they went out into the desert to John (Lk 7:24). He sets a double question: "Was it a reed blowing in the wind?" "Was it a rich man in fine clothing?" No. You went out to see a prophet. And John, Jesus tells them, is that great prophet of whom it was written: "I send my messenger before your face, who will prepare the way before you" (Mal 3:1; with variations in Mal 3:23; Is 40:3–4; Ex 14:19 23:20, 32:34, 33:2). While Malachi, Isaiah and Exodus all draw their inspiration from the Near Eastern theme of the king acting with divine guidance, they reuse this trope to present Yahweh's messenger or angel as defining the way of obedience, which leads to salvation's blessing. The messenger of Exodus, who shows the way of Yahweh, is a variant metaphor of the way of the Torah, a leitmotif of the Pentateuch and one of the Bible's defining narratives, as Yahweh's messenger leads Israel through the wilderness to the promised land. Just so, all who understand themselves as children of Israel, who bear the tradition, follow the way of the Torah through the desert of life and enter the kingdom. Isaiah—with a metaphor close to what we find in ancient Near Eastern inscriptions—uses this same desert motif to reflect the exile and the way of return straightened by Yahweh's messenger. This is the way to the New Jerusalem, which in the closing chapters of Isaiah takes on idealistic form. Luke uses his questions, pairing John with Jesus as fulfilling the prophecies of Moses, Isaiah and Malachi (Ex 23:20; Is 40:3; Mal 3:1) to present his story as rewritten Torah. John is given Elijah's role of messenger, preparing the way for the kingdom (Lk 7:27). He is like Malachi (*malachi* = my messenger). He shows the way to the promised land through reconciliation, but—like the Moses of Deuteronomy—stands at the close of his story on the threshold of what is greater.

Mark's gospel closes with a similar goal. The foreigner—a Roman centurion in charge of Jesus' execution—addresses the reader's generation and explains the story he closes. Jesus calls out for the last time before dying, quoting from the Psalter in Aramaic: *Eloi, Eloi, lama sabachtani* (Ps 22:2: "My God, my God, why have you abandoned me?"). Those at the cross misunderstand. They think he is calling on Elijah to save him. Only the centurion understands. In fact, the learning of Mark's Roman soldier—turned theologian—is considerable. The author's presentation of Psalm 22's opening words allows him, through his understanding of the psalm as a whole, to recognize David in "this man." His conclusion that Jesus "surely was the son of God" (Mk 15:39) offers Mark the opportunity to close his story on the theme with which his narrative began: the "good news of Jesus Christ, the son of God" (Mk 1:1). Rather than a mistaken prophet, Jesus, in his death—like his gospel as a whole—allows the reader a glimpse of the kingdom.

NARRATIVE TECHNIQUES IN THE HEBREW BIBLE

As in the biographical tales of the prophets of the Hebrew Bible, riddles and parables, explicit and implicit, play a large role in the gospels. For example, the answer to Jesus' rhetorical question, "To what can I compare this generation?" is given with the help of a parable-creating riddle in both Luke and Matthew. This generation is like:

> Children, sitting in the market place, calling to their playmates: "We piped to you and you did not dance; we wailed and you did not mourn." (Mt 11:16–17 = Lk 7:31–32)

The demand for mourning and its call to imitate Jesus' compassion is a condition for entrance into the joys of the kingdom. In the tradition in which this story operates, a king who cannot weep cannot rule. His kingdom is taken from him. The use of flutes for both dancing and mourning is well-known. It reiterates two biblical stories in the tradition thought of as unequivocally apocalyptic. The people play on flutes and dance at the good news of Solomon's coronation so loudly that "the earth was split by their noise" (1 Kgs 1:40; similarly Is 30:29; Job 21:12; Ps 150:4). Conversely, flutes moan like "a woman in labor" in Jeremiah's lament over Moab on its final day of shame, and they offer us an essential prelude to the motif of flutes in Jesus' simile (Jer 48:36; cf. Is 24:11; Lam 5:14–15; Job 30:31; 1 Macc 3:45).[15] The flute playing motif marks the joy of entrance into the kingdom as well as the terror of judgment and exclusion.

As we read the gospels and compare one story with another, it becomes apparent that the stories draw on and revise motifs and themes from each other. For example, a story that shares far more with Luke's flutes than those of 1 Kings or Jeremiah is a story in Matthew (Mt 9:18–26), which is quite close to Luke's story of the raising of the widow's son from the dead. It also has considerable common ground with Luke's story of the centurion and his beloved servant and the more expansive tale of Jairus's daughter (Lk 8:40–56; cf. Mk 5:21–43). While Jairus is the leader, or one of the leaders, of the synagogue, his role in the story is that of the centurion, who is friendly and supportive of the Jews and their synagogue. The common ground is the positive authority figure. In Matthew's story we meet "a ruler." He tells Jesus of his daughter's death. He asks him to lay his hands on her "and she will live." This brief tale bears the kingdom theme of "from death to life" of the Elijah tradition (Mt 9:18). Jesus gets up and follows him. Using a typical technique of the chain narrative, the second scene offers a short version of a parallel story, interrupting the journey briefly. A woman suffers from a twelve-year hemmorhage (reiterating the 12 years of Jairus's daughter). In the third scene or closure, Jesus finds flute players at the ruler's house and the noise of a great crowd. Their flutes of mourning are unfitting, Jesus explains to the crowd, since the girl is not dead. They laugh at him. He takes the girl's hand and she gets up, as mourning and mockery turn to "reports" to the whole countryside. The use of flutes to stress unbelief bears echoes of Isaiah's generation without understanding, the same theme that Luke gave to the children's song scolding them for not mourning (Lk 7:31–32).

Luke's story of Jairus's daughter closes on an intriguing yet simple motif, absent to Matthew. After raising the girl from the dead, Jesus orders that she be given something to eat (Lk 8:55; Mk 5:43). This is not an empty element of plot realism; nor does it answer to the individual's hunger and it is not merely an effort to overcome a natural skepticism about miracles. Rather, it falls in the same scene pattern as the tale of Jesus sharing a meal with two disciples after his own resurrection. Their "eyes were opened" (Lk 24:18–35). "He became known to them in the breaking of the bread" (Lk 24:35). The episode is doubled. When the disciples recount their experience to the others, Jesus again shows himself, announcing peace (Lk 24:36–52). They think he must be a shade from the realm of the dead and are afraid. Jesus shows them his hands and feet to prove that he was their friend who had died. He asks for food and eats before them to illustrate that life has overcome death. Explaining what he has demonstrated, he interprets the Torah, the prophets and the psalms, explaining that his suffering and resurrection were intended by God. Their purpose is defined in an echo of the prophecy of Elijah's return, which Luke used to begin Jesus' career in his baptism by John (Mal 3; Lk 3:3). Repentance and forgiveness of sin will be preached to all nations. This scene—and Luke's gospel—close with Jesus ascending into heaven (Lk 24:36–53). Luke's story of Jesus begins and ends with the theme of heaven's victory over the realm of the dead; a new life and entry into the kingdom are one. The symbolic overtones of eating in these resurrection stories have their roots in the Exodus vision of God's kingdom on Mount Sinai. When Israel's birth as a nation is fulfilled in the revelation at Sinai, when the Torah has been delivered to them for the first time through Moses, Israel's seventy elders, having survived the crossing of the desert, climb the mountain of god. In an ecstatic theophany, they see the God of Israel standing on heaven's floor of sapphire. They "saw God, ate and drank" (Ex 24:9–11).

The narrative association of food to life's victory over death structures both the Elijah and the Elisha chain narratives. The two opening scenes of Elijah's story—of being fed and cared for by the ravens (1 Kgs 17:1–7) and of the widow and the magic jar of flour (1 Kgs 17:8–16)—are closed with the resurrection scene of the widow's son (1 Kgs 17:17–24). Similarly, the parallel narrative in the Elisha chain begins with the story of the widow and the magic jar of oil (2 Kgs 4:1–7). It is followed by the hospitality story of the wealthy woman of Shunem feeding and caring for Elisha (2 Kgs 4:8–17). These two feeding stories are then closed with the story of Elisha raising the Shunemite's son (2 Kgs 4:18–37). The association between feeding tales and the struggle between life and death is confirmed in the immediately following three short tales, even as the last uses the variant of leprosy for its figure of death, while the leper is the official himself and not his beloved son. The story of Elisha's curing the food of death with magic flour (2 Kgs 4:38–41) is joined to a brief tale of feeding one hundred men with twenty loaves of bread and having leftovers (2 Kgs 4:42–44).

The influence of rhetorical patterns, affecting the creation of narrative figures, plot development, order and structure of scenes and episodes on the gospels, is confirmed in an interesting variation on the story of the centurion's beloved servant. This story can expand our understanding of how scenes in a central figure's life story function as biblical commentary. The influence from the earlier tradition is both formal and compositional. The tale of the healing of the Canaanite woman's daughter (Mt 15:21–28; Mk 7:24–30) opens a three-tale cycle. As in the centurion's and Shunemite's stories, the theme of this story turns on the motif of "compassion for the foreigner" as a sign of the kingdom. It is highlighted by a comic debate over the woman's right to ask for compassion: "Have mercy on me, O lord, son of David." She, like Elisha's Shunemite, is so insistent in her effort to force Jesus to cure her beloved daughter that the disciples try to get rid of her. They beg Jesus to "send her away, for she is crying after us" (Mt 15:23), exposing the story to one of the most central discourses in the Hebrew Bible. Jesus treats her like an enemy who cries for help where there is no help (Ps 18:42). He tells her that he is sent only to the "lost sheep" of Israel. She, however, persists, kneeling before him and again asking his help. Again he refuses, arguing—and keeping to an animal metaphor—that "it is unjust to take food from the children [Israel] and give it to the dogs"—as good a racial slur as any you might find. In her third and decisive effort, our foreigner trumps Jesus' metaphor with her own: "Even dogs may eat crumbs from the master's table" (Mt 15:27). The homely humility of the proverb hardly disguises her scholarly commentary on the Torah. A cryptic citation of Leviticus is implicit:

> When you harvest corn on your land, you must not harvest the whole of it out to the edge of the field. What remains after you have harvested, you must not gather. Neither should you pluck your vineyard clean nor gather up the grapes that have fallen. You must leave them for the oppressed and the foreigner. (Lev 19:9–10; var. 23:22; Dt 24:19)

The Canaanite woman understands. She has "great faith," Jesus acknowledges, as he admits defeat in the debate and closes Matthew's parable (Mt 15:28). The story has a close parallel in Luke's portrayal of the centurion's love and compassion for his servant in that the foreigner epitomizes true faith, a role model that is served famously by such figures as Tamar (Gen 38), Ruth and Job.

While Mark offers a concrete example in the curing of the deaf man to create an epitomizing closure for his chain (Mk 7:31–37), Matthew presents Jesus' miracles in a fourfold summarizing list, presented in two variant formulas:

> Great crowds came to him, bringing with them the lame, the maimed, the blind the dumb and many others, and they put them at his feet and he healed them. This crowd wondered when they saw the dumb speaking, the maimed made whole, the lame walking and the blind seeing and they glorified the God of Israel. (Mt 15:30–31)

Rhetorically, this summary echoes Jesus' answer to John's disciples in Luke, as he gives a list of six signs of the kingdom.

> The blind receive their sight, the lame walk, lepers are cleansed and the deaf hear; the dead are raised up and the poor have good news preached to them. (Lk 7:22)

The miracle stories in Matthew function as illustrations of the kingdom. Just as clearly, the roles of Jesus as miracle worker and as teacher of parable are not to be separated from the figure of Jesus as prophet, announcing the kingdom. The episodes of Jesus' life serve as parables of the kingdom, while the figure of Jesus develops as a rhetorically coherent figure common to all three gospels. If this observation is correct, the foundation for Schweitzer's historical Jesus collapses, as does the scholarly distinction between a "Christ of faith" and a "Jesus of history." The figure of the gospels is one and coherent.

Matthew's list of signs of the kingdom is followed by a third scene, which closes his brief trilogy. Topping the story of Elisha feeding his hundred with twenty loaves and having something left over, Jesus turns his compassion toward the crowd. Seven loaves and a few fish are hardly enough to feed four thousand, yet seven baskets of crumbs are left over (Mt 15:32–39; Mk 8:1–10; cf. 2 Kgs 4:42–44). The story's biblical roots are exposed in its opening line. The crowd stands in Elisha's desert, while the messenger is unwilling to send them away hungry lest they faint on their journey. Much as Jesus' Sermon on the Mount echoes Moses on Mount Sinai (Mt 5:1–7:27), the story of the feeding of four thousand is placed "on the mountain," as it echoes the feeding of Elijah by angels at Horeb, while the disciples ask Jesus where bread is to be found in the desert—a place where miraculous feeding stories have been placed since the wilderness narratives. The story of feeding the four thousand has a close variant in another New Testament tale, offered in all four of the canonical gospels. Jesus feeds five thousand with five loaves and two fish (Mt 14:13–21; Mk 6:30–44; Lk 9:10–17; Jn 6:1–13). As in the story of the feeding of the four thousand in the desert, the story of the five thousand is set in an "empty place." Matthew's version of the story moves simply and directly to the closing motif, in which twelve baskets of bread bear the symbolic weight of a new Israel, fed by the five books of Torah and the two traditions of Jerusalem and Samaria.[16] The other gospels, though using a similarly interpretive rhetoric, include other supportive elements in their versions. Luke—linking the story with the sending of the twelve to spread the kingdom to a new generation (Lk 9:1–6)—uses Jesus' feeding story to illustrate the kingdom (Lk 9:11). Mark's more expansive tale reuses the empty place motif that Jesus and his disciples might be alone in the desert (Mk 6:30–32). Distance is created that they might look with compassion on the crowd, following Jesus. The crowd functions as an old Israel: "sheep without a shepherd" (Mk 6:34). Mark refers to the close of the wilderness story of the Pentateuch, when Yahweh told Moses he must remain and die in the wilderness (Num 27:12–23) and Moses asked that the people not be left alone, like "sheep without a shepherd." As in the Elijah–Elisha succession story, Joshua was given some of Moses' spirit that he might take up Moses' role and play the good shepherd of Psalm 23, leading Israel into the promised land. Mark's figure of Jesus also plays Joshua's role in Mark's next episode. He has compassion on the crowd, teaches and feeds them, though the unsympathetic disciples would send them away (Mk 6:34–36).

Matthew's use of the same scene from Numbers has quite a different function in developing the figures of Jesus and his disciples. It is used to close a series of miracle stories, similar to the threefold story of chapter 15. Like Moses, Jesus has compassion for the crowd and compares the people to "sheep without a shepherd" (Mt 9:36). The scene functions as an introduction to sending the disciples. The great crowd is likened to a harvest, for which Jesus is given the master's role, while the disciples are workers in the field. As in the commentary on the parable of the feeding of the four thousand in chapter 15, Matthew draws on Isaiah's generation that demands signs before believing in the kingdom but does not understand the signs that are given.

The Pharisees and Sadducees are given the role of Matthew's lost generation (cf. Mt 16:1–12), while the disciples think the miracle stories were in fact about bread and confuse that bread with the sourdough of the Pharisees and Sadducees. Matthew explains to his readers that "they understood that he had not told them of the leaven of bread, but of the teaching of the Pharisees and Sadducees" (Mt 16:12). The parallel scene in Mark maintains its rhetorical function as parable. The disciples are kept in ignorance and their lack of understanding is underlined. While the Pharisees play the role of this generation, who demand a sign and are to be rejected (Mk 8:11–13), the disciples play a more difficult role of ignorance. They are the deaf and blind, a generation in need of healing. They must separate themselves from the leaven of the Pharisees: "Are their hearts hardened?" Although Mark's disciples do not come as far as Matthew's in understanding, he lays a secure foundation for their conversion by asking, Do you not remember—the five loaves for the five thousand and the seven for the four thousand (Mk 8:14–21)? And just to be sure that his readers are not as dense as the disciples with whom they identify, Mark adds a parable that his reader have patience until his story is told. Jesus takes a blind man's hand and leads him out of the village to be healed. He asks, "Do you see anything?" The blind man replies, "Men, but they look like trees, walking." Again, he heals him. . . and "he saw everything clearly" (Mk 8:22–26).

One aspect of the feeding stories at first seems to clash with the empty place motif and desert motif so important in the Elijah and Moses traditions. When the story is ready for the crowd to be fed, Jesus instructs the disciples to sit the people on the *green grass* (Mk 6:39; Mt 14:19; Jn 6:10 has "much grass in the place"). The motif of green grass in the desert, like Mark's simile of the crowd as "sheep without a shepherd" (Mk 6:34), is drawn from the Joshua succession story of Deuteronomy 27. It enters the gospel narratives because of associations with Psalm 78 and 23, which are used as foundation for our narrative. The central question in Psalm 78—Can Yahweh lay a table in the wilderness?—echoes a related passage of Psalm 23. David is unafraid in his desert valley of death because Yahweh has laid a table for him in view of his enemies (Ps 23:4–5). Yahweh is the shepherd, leading David his lamb to green grass (Ps 23:2). Another text (Ez 34:17–31) offers a more cosmic portrayal of Yahweh as judge of the world and humanity as sheep shepherded by Yahweh's servant David, who feeds them. In Yahweh's presence, they are the sheep of his green grass. Ezekiel's song, which fills out the shepherd parables of Psalms 23 and 78, presents David as the shepherd keeping Yahweh's flock much as Adam is Yahweh's gardener in the story of Genesis 2. He is the prince, bringing his sheep a new covenant of peace. Staying with the sheep metaphor, he banishes wild beasts of prey that harass the shepherd's flock. While Ezekiel's simile shifts unsteadily between the world of politics and the pasture of a shepherd, his idyllic picture of the kingdom's peace also offers an ideal rain in its proper season, trees that bear fruit at the right time and a lasting freedom from the yoke which enslaves. The green grass motif in Psalm 72 (Ps 72:6) combines Moses' simile of a flock without a shepherd with the messianic figure of Yahweh's servant as king and shepherd. He feeds Yahweh's people to make them his own. This shepherd king's justice cares for and brings redemption to a fourfold humble, poor, needy and helpless. His justice is fertile rain, falling on newly harvested grass. His judgment is that of Job, shepherd of the eastern desert and philosopher-king, whose words of counsel once fell like raindrops on his people. The helpless and the weak, the widow and the father-less, the blind and the crippled, the poor and the stranger all placed their hope in him as the grass hopes for rain (Job 29:7–25). Such are the echoes surround-ing the figure of the shepherd that Mark evokes for the lost sheep of his story.

Each variation on Elisha's feeding story creates parables that draw directly on a long-established rhetoric of myth building. Three texts—one from the Psalter and two from the Pentateuch—are particularly helpful in understanding the de-velopment of such story parables. The long, historically reflective Psalm 78 opens with a thematic question in an interpretive context and closes with a vari-ation on the role of Joshua as shepherd. The song begins as a pedagogically ori-ented address, reflecting on Israel's wilderness stories. It speaks in metaphor and riddle. A future generation must learn to understand, to avoid becoming as stub-born and rebellious as the lost generation of the wilderness. The people should not be like their fathers but set their hope in God. The lost generation's rebellion and doubt is epitomized through questions: Can God spread a table in the wilderness? Can he give bread? Can he provide meat for his people (Ps 78:19–20)? With a striking double echo of Elijah and Moses, it interprets one story's manna in the desert as "bread of angels and food in abundance" for an-other (Ps 78:25; cf. Ps 105:40; 1 Kgs 19:6–8). As in the wilderness story, the feeding of Israel is recounted in an exchange of blessing and punishment. The people repented and remembered that God was their redeemer. Yet, once satis-fied, they rebelled.

The Pentateuch offers two parallel versions of the feeding in the wilderness. The Exodus tale of Yahweh providing for his people opens on the note of rebel-lion. The people complain, hungry for the full pots of meat they once had in Egypt (Ex 16:2–36). Angry at their ingratitude, Yahweh gives them meat to eat at night and bread to eat in the morning. This version of the story features quails, coming over the Israelite camp each night and *manna* ("What's that?"), provided each morning. It centers on a moralistic parable, supporting the Sabbath day's rest. Just so, the Israelites are provided with food for forty years until they come into the promised land. The parallel story of the quail (Num 11:4–35) refers to a variation of the manna story now lost to us to build a comic parable about glut-tony and retribution. The manna, for all its angelic origins, is boring. The peo-ple long for the quality and variety of Egypt's finer cuisine: fish and cucumbers, watermelons, leeks, onions and garlic. They have no appetite for manna. Yahweh—ever playing the overstressed parent in the wilderness stories and trying to satisfy an insatiable child—loses his temper. Moses echoes their complaint on his own behalf. His job as baby-sitter is too much for him. Yahweh is the one who gave birth to this people, but Moses has to take care of them, "like a stepfather to an infant." "How am I going to find meat for so many people?" As the story echoes the motif of the overburdened Moses and the seventy elders judging the people at Sinai (Ex 18), Yahweh instructs Moses to choose seventy to share his spirit. Moses will have Israel's elders to help him and Yahweh will do his part by providing meat to feed the people, not just for a day or two but for a whole month—so much that it will come out their noses. In the logic and language of biblical retribution, they will throw it up because they have thrown Yahweh up (Num 11:19–20)!

The discursive retelling of stories through reiteration and revision is clear: a cyclical, never-ending story of the imminent kingdom of divine rule to every new generation. The passing of Moses' spirit to the people, represented in their seventy elders, is reiterated in the tradition in many forms. The New Testament reiterations of this fertile motif include the quickening of John, leaping in his mother's womb (Lk 1:41), the opening clouds in the scene at the Jordan, with the spirit descending on John's chosen successor (Mk 1:10), and in the tongues of fire, bringing the spirit to a new generation of witnesses (Acts 1:8, 2:1–4). In all such scenes, the spreading of the spirit is fundamental to the tradition's understanding of piety. Intrinsically, the story line is unlimited, extending to the scene of the disciples, in an ecstasy of all the world's languages (Acts 2:1–13). Hardly drunk with the new wine of the festival, they are filled with a spirit of piety to be poured out on all nations. It is a life that conquers the realm of the dead, as Jesus enters his kingdom as lord and messiah (Acts 2:5–36; cf. 2 Sm 23:2; Jl 3:1–5; Ps 16:8–11; 110:1). This apocalyptic scene closes with pious Jews asking Peter, "What shall we do?" Peter answers with an interpretation of Jesus' role as the Elijah for his generation: "Repent and be baptized every one of you in the name of Jesus Christ for the forgiveness of your sins; and you will receive the Holy Spirit as a gift" (Acts 2:38). This interpretation answers to Moses' wish that all be prophets. It is as illustration and reiteration of earlier tradition that the gospels stress the crowd's greatness and the disciples' lack of understanding that so many could be fed.

The gospels center on the figure of Jesus. He is like Moses of Numbers and like David, the shepherd of Psalm 78. They can lay a table in the wilderness and give both meat and bread to their generations of Israel. Jesus' compassion echoes the compassion of Yahweh for his people. His fish and bread echo the wilderness story's meat and mannah, just as the crowds are organized into companies as an army of salvation in imitation of Israel's encampment in Numbers as Yahweh's army. A single, interrelated tradition shares a common intellectual world. These reiterated traditions stand together with a common message and purpose.

As the story of John the Baptist gives way to the story of his successor, Jesus, the role of Jesus' disciples is brought center stage. Jesus sends them "to preach the kingdom of God and to heal" (Lk 9:2). The question about who Jesus is is all the gossip, awakening even the king's interest. "Is he John, raised from the dead?" (Lk 9:7). Is he Elijah or another of the prophets (or Jeremiah: Mt 6:14)? The crowd presses, ever demanding to be healed. Jesus heals them and talks of the kingdom (Lk 9:11–12). The press is significant. It causes the plot to pause briefly as the crowd—now grown to five thousand—needs to be fed in the wilderness (Lk 9:12–17). Once they are fed, the author takes his story back to the plotline and takes Jesus to another deserted place, where the disciples again concentrate on the burning bush story's central question between Moses and Yahweh: Who am I?/Who are you? (Ex 3:13–18, 6:2–9).[17] The question defined Yahweh as "God with you" (Ex 3:12), a nuance that Isaiah reiterates as a child's name, "Immanuel," that it might function as a sign of Yahweh's presence in judgment (Is 7:14). In Jesus' story, Isaiah's sign is reused as God's name for Jesus as a sign for the divine presence in blessing (Mt 1:23). In the New Testament's reiteration of the question of identity, emphasis is created through repetition: Who does the crowd say I am? John? Elijah? One of the prophets? Stabilizing his story with twice-repeated gossip, each reiterating the question of John's disciples, the author turns his story's question to his audience and the interpretation of his narrative: "Who do you say I am?" Jesus asks his disciples (Lk 9:20) and Peter, superceding all the world's gossip, answers: "God's messiah." Forbidding the disciples to discuss the issue, Jesus tells them that this son of man must suffer, be rejected and killed, that—like Jonah—he might rise from the dead on the third day (Lk 9:22), clearly marking the cost of being his disciple. In returning the story to its central theme, four aphorisms are offered as a discourse on the retributive logic of saving or losing one's life:

Whoever would save his life, will lose it; and whoever loses it for my sake, will save it. What does it profit a man if he gains the whole world and loses or forfeits himself? Whoever is ashamed of me or my words, of him will the son of man be ashamed when he comes in his glory, and the glory of the father and the angels. But I tell you truly that there are some standing here who will not taste death before they see the kingdom of God. (Lk 9:24–27)

That Jesus speaks of those in his audience who "will not taste death before they see God's kingdom" (Mt 16:28; Lk 9:27; Mk 9:1) turns the narrative's center away from the figure of Jesus. The presentation of the transfiguration scene follows the template of the theophany story in Exodus 24. As Moses waited six days on Mount Sinai before Yahweh's glory showed itself as devouring fire in the sight of all the people, so Jesus' audience is described as waiting six days for the kingdom (a Sabbath festival's "eight days" in Lk 9:28; cf. Ex 24:16), until Jesus is transfigured. Jesus is on the mountain with Peter, James and John (Mt 17:1), in imitation of Moses, who went up the mountain with Aaron, Nadab and Abihu (Ex 24:1).

This close, creative association of events in Jesus' stories with similar events in the stories of Elijah and Moses is not merely implicit. The association is conscious, explicit and significant. When Jesus comes into ecstatic conversation with Elijah and Moses, he is on a mountain—his clothes white and his face shining like the sun. His face is like the face of Moses (Mt 17:2; cf. Ex 34:30) and much like the face of the man in the vision of Daniel (Dan 10:5–6) or of "one like a man" or like the clothes and the "glory" of the angels in the book of Revelation (Rev 1:12–16, 15:6). In the gospels' story, Peter's suggestion that they build three booths (Lk 9:22–36) reflects three traditions: the Samaritans' Moses, the Jews' Elijah and Jesus' own, and seems at first strikingly Christian, even supersessionist. However, the author rejects this not very bright but enthusiastic competitiveness with a citation. He compares Jesus, as in the theophany at the Jordan (Lk 3:22), with Isaiah's suffering servant Israel (cf. Lk 9:35: "a voice from the cloud saying: 'my son, my chosen [or 'my beloved']'" and Is 42:1: "my servant, whom I uphold: my chosen in whom my soul delights"). Rejecting Peter's suggestion, Luke rather gives Jesus the role of fulfilling Moses' law from Horeb that Malachi had assigned Elijah; namely, reconciling the Samaritan father with his Jewish son; uniting Israel by overcoming the divisions of Samaria's Moses and Jerusalem's Elijah: the elder and younger generations.[18]

The greater tradition explains Luke's emphasis on the glory transferred from Moses and Elijah to Jesus and hence to the disciples. Jesus has raised Jairus's daughter from the dead, allowing the narrative to turn to the theme of Jesus' own death as apocalyptic event. Although Mark and Matthew's presentation of the theophany is nearly identical, differing primarily in their presentation of Peter, Luke integrates the scene with the theme of life's victory over death. A discourse on discipleship supports the illustrative function of his narrative. The transfiguration comes during prayer (Lk 9:28–36). Jesus' face is altered and his clothing becomes dazzling white. Moses and Elijah speak with him. While Mark and

Matthew mention nothing of Jesus praying and nothing of what Moses, Elijah and Jesus discuss, Luke ties the scene to his larger narrative by telling his audience that they spoke of "his departure" to "be fulfilled in Jerusalem" (Lk 9:31). Luke's implicit biblical commentary reiterates the Moses traditions, as he plays with the nuances of veiling, yet revealing and of not knowing, yet witnessing. The transformation of Jesus' face echoes the scene in Exodus in which Moses holds a debate with Yahweh in the wilderness because he wants to "know God and find favor in his sight" (Ex 33:13). This debate immediately spills over into a discourse on the "face of God" (Ex 33:12–34, 35). It is Yahweh's presence in Israel that is their mark of his favor. It marks their difference from all other peoples of the world. When Moses, in a scene referred to earlier, asks Yahweh to show him his glory (Ex 33:18), Yahweh finds the request impossible:

> I will make all my goodness pass before you and I will proclaim before you my name, Yahweh, and I will be gracious to whom I will be gracious and show mercy to whom I show mercy, but you cannot see my face, for a man will not see me and live. (Ex 33:19)

The argument closes with a compromise. Moses will hide in a cleft in the rock while Yahweh's glory passes by. Yahweh will protect him from the revelation with his hand. In such a way—fitting the human capacity to know the past but not the future—Moses sees but the backside of Yahweh and worships (Ex 34:5–8). From this experience, Moses draws a striking conclusion, important in understanding the reuse of these tropes by Luke:

> If I have now found favor in your eyes, O Yahweh, let Yahweh go in the midst of us, though it is a stiff-necked people. Pardon our iniquities and sin and take us for your inheritance. (Ex 34:9)

This is the foundation for Elijah's role in reconciling future generations (Mal 3:22–24). In miming this theophany to Moses, Luke uses techniques of reiteration from Elijah's theophany at Horeb (1 Kgs 19). The continuous play, developing chains of traditions, is hardly exhausted by the examples given here. The covenant story (Ex 34), as it makes the covenant explicit, reiterates the Ten Commandments of Exodus 20 and Deuteronomy 5 and offers its own version of the "ten words" written on tablets of stone (Ex 34:10–28). As Moses descends the mountain with the tablets in his hands, he is the one unaware. Moses' face shone because he talked with God. The people, like Jesus' disciples, are afraid. Moses talks with the people and gives them the words of Yahweh, as the story finds closure in Moses' face veiled to protect them from its shining (Ex 34:29–35). In the context of a discourse on Jesus' coming death, Luke's gospel uses the transfiguration story to point ahead to the ascension narrative (Acts 1:8) in a chain of transference of divine glory through the generations: from Moses and Elijah to Jesus, and hence to the disciples. Couching this glory in the words of the Spirit expands the mythic base for the transmission of Yahweh's words to Israel. As in other stories of the Elijah chain, the dominant theme is life's conquest over death: the most defining motif of the myth of the kingdom.

As we develop a clearer idea of the literary and intellectual world of our texts, we need to discuss theories of borrowing and dependence. The process of often conscious referencing of one tradition by another needs a different description. Jesus should not be spoken of as a second Moses, nor should John and Jesus be too simply understood as Elijah *redivivus*. This transfers an explicit element of the plot to the expectations of the society from which the story springs. As Jesus plays roles common to and interchangeable with other characters of early story and song, we might also think of the stories and their functions as comparable. The book of Ezra or the gospels might be understood as *rewritten Torah* or rewritten Bible. The successive characters are protagonists of successive themes in a continuous, never-ending story. The Jesus story of Luke, like the Job or Moses story, speaks to us more about justice, humanity and life than they tell us about any of this tale type's often interchangeable protagonists. This issue will engage us throughout our study. The particular contribution of the Elijah tradition to myth building will, I hope, be made clearer by looking again briefly at the birth stories in Matthew, as the birth of a hero defines its narrative's central theme.

IMMANUEL AND THE KINGDOM

Cue names—identifying the function of a story's figure—are commonplace in biblical narrative. This rhetorical technique is usually implicit and it guides the progression of a narrative. Already in the garden story, for instance, the representative character of Adam's and Eve's names ("humanity" and "mother") express their role in their story, as do the names of their first two children, Cain ("creature") and Abel ("dew," "mist", reflecting the transient nature of our lives). A name can also mark a specific role a figure plays or—as with the names Isaac ("laughter") or Ishmael ("God hears")—names can be used to mark an episode with transcendent significance. Abraham's name expresses his role as "father of many nations," as Israel's reflects both the patriarch's and his nation's penchant to struggle with their God. In the book of Ruth, the names of the central figures, Ruth ("faithful one") and Boaz ("strength"), expose the value system in which the story operates. Such cue names have a similar function in the gospels, especially in the birth stories that open the gospels of Matthew and Luke.

The angel explains to Joseph, in a dream, that the child Mary will give birth to a child that must be given the cue name "Jesus" (Joshua = "savior"). The angel explains that "he will save his people from their sins" (Mt 1:20–21). In clarifying the child's Elijah role, Matthew cites Isaiah for another cue name. His story is modeled on his understanding of a prophecy (Is 7:14) that a "virgin will conceive and bear a son, whose name will be Immanuel." Matthew translates this for his audience, "God with us," and draws strongly on the Exodus tradition (Mt 1:22–23; Ex 3:12). Though the child is called Jesus, the cue name works, nonetheless. To express divine presence on earth through what Matthew calls the kingdom of heaven is his figure's primary role.

Matthew cites Isaiah's metaphor of the child "Immanuel" ("God with us"). In Isaiah, it is found in an irony-filled critique of King Ahaz of Judah, whose enemies, the kings of Israel and Damascus, threaten Jerusalem (Is 7:1–3; 2 Kgs 16:1–20). Yahweh sends Isaiah to Ahaz to reassure the king that they will not succeed.[19] His son is sent with him, bearing his cue name, Shearyashub ("a remnant will return"), as a sign of Israel's future. This becomes a leitmotif in Isaiah, referring to a return from exile of both Samaria and Jerusalem. He should not fear Samaria's king, for in sixty-five years, "Ephraim will be broken in pieces—no longer a people" (Is 7:7–9).

A second sign is given Ahaz, as the figure of another child is used to expand the message of Isaiah's son, *Shearyashub*:

> A young woman is pregnant and will bear a child and call his name Immanuel. He will eat curds and honey until he learns to reject evil and choose good. For before the child knows how to reject evil and choose the good, the land, before whose two kings you are terrified, will be made a desert. (Is 7:14–16)

The child Immanuel is not the prophecy but the sign, confirming the prophecy of Samaria's and Damascus's destruction. The birth of a third child to make the prophecy complete doubles the sign of the second child, Immanuel's prophetic projection of the divine presence in the Assyrian king who will come to turn the land into a desert. Isaiah lay with a prophetess who, like the young woman, becomes pregnant and bears a child, whom Yahweh names:

Maher-Shalal-Hash-Baz ["the spoil speeds; the prey hastens"]. Before the child learns to cry "my father" or "my mother," the wealth of Damascus and the spoil from Samaria will be carried away before the king of Assyria. (Is 8:3–4)

The coming attack by the king of Assyria is likened to a great flood that will reach from the Euphrates all the way to Jerusalem, "reaching even to the neck" (Is 8:8). With an echo of Psalm 2, Isaiah mocks the nations in uproar, making plans against Yahweh and his messiah, "for God is with us" (Is 8:9–10; cf. Ps 2:1–6). Yahweh gives Isaiah instruction. Rather than fear the kings of Damascus and Samaria, Isaiah and the children are "signs and warnings" from Yahweh of the armies. The living God is the one whom they should fear. The Assyrian king is "Immanuel," bringing judgment (Is 8:11–20). As Isaiah's song confirms the day of judgment against Samaria and Damascus, the motif of divine presence, dreaded, is reversed and transformed into a song of peace as the child becomes a sign of promise. "The people who wandered in darkness will see a great light." Immanuel continues to signify God's presence, but now as blessing. The birth of yet another child is announced, a son who will rule with the divine presence on earth. He will be named "Wonderful; Counselor, Mighty God, Eternal Father and Prince of Peace." This kingdom of David will have no end, but will be up-held with justice and righteousness (Is 9:1–6).

The utopian transformation from war to an eternal messianic peace that Isaiah's songs of the children offer, transforms a day of judgment into a day of blessing. Isaiah's thematic development of his ideal of a kingdom of peace has common ground with the idealistic role of reconciliation of the generations, which Malachi gives to the returning Elijah (Mal 3:19–24). This parallel with Malachi is suggested in the songs of "that day" of Yahweh's judgment. On the one hand: destruction, but on the other: salvation. The remnant of Israel, those who have survived the Assyrians, will no longer give their trust to those who have destroyed them. This remnant will return to Yahweh in truth (Is 10:20–21). Isaiah's book turns on the dominating metaphor of the child Israel of Isaiah's generation, growing up to see with eyes and hear with ears of understanding (Is 6:9–10), becoming the Immanuel child who chooses good and avoids evil (Is 7:16).

To understand the implications of the Immanuel riddle, transferred now to Matthew, Isaiah's metaphor is important. In citing Isaiah, Matthew uses the quotation, not only because the "young woman" (Greek, "virgin") fits his plot's demand for a heroic birth story, clearly echoing similar stories of Moses and Samson, but also because the reference helps define the role Jesus plays in Matthew's story. He will overcome the great conflict between the "fathers" and the "sons," the division of Solomon's peace in the separation of the kingdoms of Samaria and Judah.

It is not that Matthew misreads Isaiah, thinking that Isaiah had prophesied a coming savior, whom Matthew identifies with Jesus. The Immanuel cue name rather signifies the role Jesus is given to play in Matthew's story. It is the utopian role of David and his kingdom of peace that he will play for his generation. That is, he is to be Immanuel in the gospel story: a figure "for instruction and testimony." Much as in the Isaiah narrative, Immanuel marks events in Matthew's narrative with the riddle of divine presence. In Isaiah, as on Judgment Day, "God with us" is markedly ambivalent. It alternates between the catastrophic day of judgment, bringing destruction and a day of blessing, a remnant returning. Both Immanuel and Isaiah's children "are signs and warnings" of Yahweh's presence, bringing his day of judgment. Those who fear God do not need to fear the judgment (Is 8:12–13). Matthew's transference of this role to his story marks a central theme of his narrative. The child is a sign of the day of judgment, when "God is with us" (Mt 1:23) for good or for evil, for destruction or for salvation. While John's preaching in the wilderness (Mt 3:1–3) will call the people to repentance and reconciliation's forgiveness, the doubling of cue names in the story of Jesus' birth allows Matthew to interpret Jesus (savior) as an Immanuel of blessing. He is Joshua, both Yahweh's warrior and the shepherd of his people.

The old Catholic–Protestant debate about the distinction between Matthew's use of a Greek version of Isaiah, which used the word "virgin" *(parthenos)* to describe the mother of the child, instead of the word "young woman" (*'almah*) in the less distinctive Hebrew, is not helpful. Neither the particular description of the mother engaged by the narrative nor the child's divine status is at issue in Matthew's story. The myth of a hero's birth, with its motif of miraculous pregnancy, illustrates the coming of the kingdom whose inauguration the heroic birth announces. The function of the miraculous pregnancy, overturning barrenness of whatever cause, marks a divine intervention—whether or not the particular motif of a virgin is used. That is a minor element of rhetoric. It gives opportunity for the reversal of destiny and fortune, effected for a whole community's suffering and longing. The young girl or virgin, without a story of suffering of her own, does not have her own tale, as Ruth has. She plays a supportive role. In the Bible, mothers are variously described. She can be a virgin, whether metaphorical or actual, as Mary is, much as the "daughter of Jerusalem" or "the virgin of Zion" or "Israel" (Mt 1:18; Lk 1:27–28; Jer 31:21; Lam 2:13; Am 5:2). The miraculous is also signified in the role of a barren, elderly woman and her role can even be taken by a virtuous couple like Elizabeth and Zechariah (Lk 1:18) or, showing the divine stranger hospitality, as Abraham and Sarah or the rich woman and her husband in Elisha's story do (Gen 18:1, 11; 21:2–6; 2 Kgs 4:8–17). The child's mother can also be a barren woman like Rachel and Hannah or she can be a wife, meeting an angel alone as does the wife of Manoah (Gen 29:15ff.; 1 Sm 1:5–6; Jgs 13:2). She can be like Leah, married to a man who does not love her (Gen 29:31–32). In some stories the role of the mother has mythic overtones, like Eve, the mother of all living (Gen 3:20; 4:1).[20] Gods or their messengers are typically involved as fathers in both pregnancies and births. Such children signify divine presence in the story.

Matthew's story reuses several earlier motifs, such as the unknowing husband of the Samson story (Jgs 13), the virgin of Jeremiah's new covenant (Jer 31:21) and the Immanuel child, who reiterates Isaiah's own son, *Shearjashub* ("repentant remnant"), who is reborn as a new Israel after his exile's suffering.

Setting Isaiah's utopian vision of a new Israel as his context, Matthew starts his birth story amid rumor and riddle. Mary has been found with child by the Holy Spirit before she and her husband had come together. Joseph does not understand and plans to divorce her. Joseph's not understanding is, however, quickly resolved. Unlike Isaiah's generation, Joseph, like the disciples, is given to understand. In dreams, the secrets of the kingdom present him with his guardian role for the child. This delicate echo of the similar birth of Samson, in which his mother was visited by an angel of Yahweh, "when her husband, Manoah, was not with her." The author of Judges has little mercy on the husband or his wife in his comic version of the birth of a hero. The audience is allowed to laugh at the unknowing expectations of the pious husband and his less-than-pious wife. The husband hears from his wife of a man who had come "with the face of an angel of God and very terrible," to give his wife a child. He prays to Yahweh to send him again "to teach us what we are to do with the boy that is to be born" (Jgs 13:6). When this man or angel visits again, the husband asks further—and his euphemism exposes a divine presence hidden from his ignorance. "When your *word is fulfilled*, what is the child to be?" (Jgs 13:12). Having played with Manoah's ignorance, the narrator catches the audience by surprise. In answer to Manoah's third question, "What is your name?" (Jgs 13:18), the angel gives one of the divine names of Isaiah's Immanuel child: "Wonderful" (Jgs 13:19 = Is 9:5) and vanishes in the flames of the altar. The child Samson is dedicated to God "from his mother's womb." He is directed by the spirit, a Nazir "from birth to the day of his death" (Jgs 13:7). This role is also shared by Samuel in his birth story (1 Sm 2). In Matthew, the theme determines Nazareth as Jesus' home after his exile in Egypt: "He lived in a town called Nazareth, that the words of the prophets be fulfilled: 'he will be called a Nazarene'" (Mt 2:23).

Matthew ever builds on such biblical patterns and themes. Having identified Bethlehem as David's and therefore Jesus' birthplace (Mt 2:1), he brings him to Nazareth, by way of Samson and Samuel as Nazir, dedicated to God. This journey is also projected in the opening of one of the last of Isaiah's Immanuel songs: "There will grow a sprout from the stump of Jesse; a branch *(nezer)* will grow from its roots" (Is 11:1). Matthew is not collecting Old Testament prophecies that fit Jesus' life; nor is he finding easy proof texts to confirm the historical truth of his story. His story is an illustration of what he understands Isaiah's song to be about: a "new judgment," carried out with the spirit of wisdom, understanding and knowledge. It sings of an ideal king who judges the poor and the meek with righteousness and strikes down the violent and the unrighteous (Is 11:4–5 = Job 29:12–17). The center of the song of Jesse's root presents Isaiah's utopian vision, the reversal of destiny, the *shalom* of ancient Near Eastern royal inscriptions, centered on the motif of the king as shepherd:

> The wolf will lie down with the lamb and the leopard with the kid; the calf and the young lion and the fatling all together and a little child will lead them; the cow and the bear will feed and their young will lie together; the lion will eat straw like the ox. The suckling child will play at the hole of the cobra and the one weaned will put his hand on the viper's nest. (Is 11:6–8)

The figure of a historical person announcing the coming of the kingdom of God in his own generation hardly survives awareness of the author's involvement in an intertextual discourse. There the figures of John and Jesus reflect not events in the lives of individuals but other figures of the tradition, such as Moses, Elijah and Elisha. This Jesus revises the tales of Exodus, Deuteronomy, 1–2 Kings and Malachi, all eagerly read in the light of Isaiah. The gospels' plotlines hardly describe events, beliefs or even the self-understanding of their writers. Alone, they do not give us direct access to history. Citing and interpreting a prophecy of Elijah's return is a literary technique that may affect a given reader's expectations. It may even eventually influence the society to which a reader belongs, but it does not obviously reflect the expectations of the one who cites and interprets. The Elijah tradition of the gospels gives their readers access to the intellectual world of Judaism and remains within that world. The narrative roles John and Jesus play are long present in Jewish literary tradition. The composition of the gospels cannot be traced on the basis of the different dramatic roles John or Jesus play. Abraham in his stories similarly plays a new role in every story he enters. The leitmotif of Abraham wandering through the land and building altar after altar ties the many roles of Abraham together as one.[21] Jesus' role as a miracle worker and the themes related to miracle stories are hardly irreconcilable with other roles and themes. In fact, the teaching stories announce a transcendent judgment the miracle stories illustrate. This apocalyptic role of the kingdom's judge, changing the destiny of king and pauper, as of the righteous and unrighteous, is a figure, bringing the transcendent into the story. Miracle stories—especially those dealing with the production of food and a prophet's power over life and death—have their first function as illustrations of the living God's power to reverse human destiny and play the judge's role of blessing and cursing. Jesus, the healer and miracle worker, is not to be separated from more obviously apocalyptic themes any more than Jesus the teacher is. No author of the first century CE invented these roles. Nor did he invent the figures that bear them in his stories. One who wishes to separate and distinguish such roles historically needs to begin much earlier than the gospels. The fabric of the gospels was long in preparation. No author of merit—and Luke is an extraordinarily gifted storyteller—has written apart from a literary community and a common tradition.

CHAPTER 3

⬿

The Children and the Kingdom

The Reversal of Destiny and the Signs of the Kingdom

In presenting Jesus in the figure of a peasant philosopher, Crossan's understanding of the kingdom announced by Jesus brings all humanity under the judgment of divine rule. Instead of a Roman occupation, the kingdom Jesus preached is a rule by the oppressed: the poor, foreigners and especially children.[1] Satisfied merely with the conviction that Jesus thought and taught this, Crossan and the Jesus Seminar neglect its meaning. What is it about children, the poor or the foreigner that makes them ideal as signs of the kingdom? Why is it impossible to include the rich in the kingdom? Why cannot grown-ups be included with their children? Why not Jews along with Romans and Samaritans? Why not husbands with widows and the fatherless? To read the story as simply reflecting historical conflicts of first-century Palestine and what Jesus said in that context—especially when we know so little of such conflicts—distorts the texts far more than it clarifies.

Mark presents his miracle stories in tightly linked short chains of narrative. Two such chains are presented in succession between type scenes, presenting Jesus with power over the sea and the richness of divine blessing. The first is set between the tales of stilling the storm (Mk 4:35–41) and the feeding of the five thousand (Mk 6:33–44). The second comes between walking on the water (Mk 6:45–52) and feeding four thousand (Mk 8:1–10).

The integration of the miracle scenes into a single narrative is essential to understanding the function of this double chain. It takes its departure in chapter 4 at the close of a similar collection of parables on the kingdom (Mk 4:33). This had itself begun in a scene in which Jesus taught in parables, sitting in a boat on the sea (Mk 4:1–2). Alone with the twelve, whom he had just spoken of sending out to the people, he gives them a role that was first played by Isaiah, who had seen the kingdom of heaven (Mk 4:10), with Yahweh sitting on his throne. He is terrified. He has seen the King, Yahweh of the Armies, and must die; for he is "a man of unclean lips, living in the middle of a people with unclean lips." A seraph purifies his lips with a coal of fire and Isaiah's sins are forgiven (Is 6:1, 5–7). Since he is now a worthy messenger, Yahweh sends him:

> Go and say to this people: "Hear and hear but do not understand; see and see but do not perceive. Make the hearts of this people fat, their ears heavy; shut their eyes, lest they see with their eyes and hear with their ears and understand with their hearts and turn and be healed." (Is 6:9–10)

While the Isaiah story goes on to well-known themes such as exile, the surviving remnant and the dead stump becoming holy seed, Mark's revision of Isaiah goes in a different direction and expands on the contrasting motifs of the unclean and holy. He plays ironically with the theme of understanding. Like Isaiah, who saw his divine King, the disciples have "the secret of the kingdom of God." "For those outside, everything is in parables." They are Isaiah's generation with its unclean lips. They see and hear but are not allowed to perceive or understand "lest they repent and be forgiven." Isaiah's parable and riddle is what the disciples need to understand (Mk 4:11–13).

The text continues with more parables of the kingdom: the sower (Mk 4:14–20), the lamp (Mk 4:21–25), seed scattered (Mk 4:26–29) and the mustard seed (Mk 4:30–32). Everything is in parables, in riddles "according to the way they were able to hear it" (Mk 4:33). Mark returns to the theme of the disciples learning, contrasting with the people's relentless lack of understanding. "He did not speak with them without a parable, but privately, to his own disciples, he explained everything" (Mk 4:34). The double chain of miracles begins, reiterating the signs of the kingdom and its dominion over creation: from power over the sea to feeding thousands and then over again. The theme of the kingdom is guided gently with an expanding leitmotif of understanding and not understanding. It began with Jesus' needling tease of his disciples, to whom he had explained everything: "Why are you afraid; have you no faith?" (Mk 4:40). The first double chain closes with Jesus walking on water. Coming into the disciple's boat, he controls the winds (Mk 6:51). The author's ironic voice presents the disciples with their lack of understanding, played earlier by both Elijah's generation and Pharaoh of the Exodus: "And they were utterly astounded; for they had not understood about the loaves; their hearts were hardened" (Mk 6:52; cf. Ex 6:30–7, 3!). The chain closes as Mark returns to the theme of the disciples. Jesus joins them in the boat a third time. Only a single loaf of bread remains.

The purpose of Mark's reiteration is not to make Jesus a new Moses or a new Isaiah. Mark is not as interested in his figure of Jesus as in the disciples and their understanding. They bear the greater burden of the reiteration. Their lack of understanding and perception echoes the Bible's never-ending story of ignorance in the face of enlightenment, a theme that continues into the story of the transfiguration and beyond. Only rarely and fleetingly—as in Peter's confession that Jesus is the messiah (Mk 8:29)—does Mark allow the disciples to escape this dunce's role in the course of their education.

One must wonder whether enlightenment is not in fact reserved to the generation of Mark's readers. This dominating plea to understand the story as parable, which the metaphor of Isaiah's generation supports (Is 6:9–10), goes far beyond a simple stereotyped debate between the right and wrong, the wise and the simple. Mark draws on a well-established symbol system to further a debate within Judaism that seeks to critically define its piety, its ethics and its values. In considering the theme of understanding or not understanding the parables about the kingdom, we need to notice that those who are given eyes to see and ears to hear are a special kind of people. In the real world, they can be rejected or ignored: children, the poor, the sick and unclean. If they cannot be ignored, they stand on the periphery of piety's concerns: foreigners, strangers, even enemies. This is interesting, and we must ask why it is so.

At the heart of his chain of miracle stories, Mark presents a discourse about hygiene. It ranges from answering a complaint about the disciples' unwashed hands to a debate over the difference between ritual and moral uncleanness. Much as the book of Job pits Job's innocence against a caricature of piety voiced by his three friends, Mark's discussion pits a caricature of "the tradition of the elders" against the Torah's command "to honor your father and your mother" (Mk 7:1–23). In Mark's discourse on purity, the healing stories function as signs of the kingdom. Four variable but interactive associations are involved. A clean or unclean dichotomy is presented. The lack of purity of all Israel prevents it from becoming the holy people the covenant of Moses demands. One must separate the holy from the unholy, or, synonymously, the clean from the unclean (Lev 10:10; Ps 89:5–6; 1 Esd 8:70). The goal is to become the holy people true to the tradition (Dt 26:19; Is 62:2), that all humanity might return to its role as image of God, blessed and made holy at the creation (Gen 1:28; cf. 2:3). It is just such a utopian return and pious reversal that mark purity and holiness as signs of the kingdom. Obedience to the law finally becomes possible (Josh 24:19). The healing stories in Mark structure Jesus' miracle stories as parable[2] and turn on the theme of cleansing and purifying Israel. The essence of the distinction between clean and unclean is rooted in the theologically based taboo of mixing the sacred with the profane; the living with the dead; whatever is divine or transcendent with the mortal and ephemeral. The metaphor in biblical tradition involves whatever is in imbalance, mixed elements that do not go together, physical distortions such as the blind and the lame, as well as moral distortions such as disobedience or apostasy. The kingdom's positive reversals of destiny are repeatedly evoked by a miracle, turning the unclean to clean and the unholy to holy.

Four related tales present Jesus curing someone possessed of an "unclean spirit."[3] The first story is set on the Sabbath in the synagogue, and it opens the theme of Jesus teaching with authority. "Immediately," there in the synagogue, the unclean spirit recognizes Jesus as the "holy one of God," asking whether he has come to destroy them. In response, the "holy one" shows himself master over the unholy. Jesus silences the spirit and orders him out. A departing scream confirms the kingdom's authority over the unclean (Mk 1:23–28).

In the second tale, a madman—epitomizing the unclean, living among tombs with an unclean spirit—meets him. He screams day and night and hurts himself with stones, but no one can bind him—even with chains (Mk 5:1–20; Mt 8:28–34). Again, the immediacy of the spirit's recognition is stressed: "Seeing him from a distance, he ran and worshipped him" (Mk 5:6). The spirit begs not to be sent away from the area, but rather into a great herd of pigs—some two thousand of them, which then rush into the sea. The story closes on the people hearing, becoming afraid and asking the holy one to leave the area.[4]

The third tale offers a simpler version of Matthew's story of the Canaanite woman's daughter (Mt 15:20–28). In both Matthew and Mark, the story illustrates what makes a person clean or unclean (Mt 15:19; Mk 7:23). In Mark's tale, Jesus enters the region of Tyre and Sidon and a Greek woman "immediately" comes to him with her daughter. She has an unclean spirit needing to be driven out (Mk 7:24–30). Jesus refuses to help her. For Mark, it is the woman's answer as foreigner to Jesus' metaphor-loaded refusal that turns the story. It maintains a fine balance between the correctness of not throwing the children's bread to the dogs and the dog's own perspective of rights to fallen crumbs. The story is followed with the deaf hearing and the dumb speaking (Mk 7:32–37).

The fourth story of unclean spirits (Mk 9:14–29) is a variant on this episode. It is set in a discussion among Jesus, Peter and John about Elijah's role of reconciliation (Mk 9:9–12). When the three come to the disciples, a great debate finds crowds and scribes arguing about a man whose son has a dumb spirit the disciples cannot cure. Jesus' rebuke that the quarrelers belong to Isaiah's faithless generation fits the earlier discussion of Elijah's reconciliation well. The quarrel and the disciples' inability to overcome the impure spirit illustrate the absence of the kingdom. If the generations of Israel had been reconciled, the fate of the deaf and blind would have been overturned. When the boy is brought to Jesus, the spirit immediately recognizes him. When the boy's father asks for help "if he can," Jesus' response balances on the condition implied by the request: "All is possible to the one who believes." The father's faith responds with the same immediacy as the spirit's recognition. "I believe; help my unbelief." Having illustrated the power of faith over unclean spirits, Mark turns to the disciples' incapacity as healers. Such a spirit can only be driven out with prayer. Immediacy, recognition and Jesus' authority over the impure are the elements of contrasting balance between Jesus' purity and the spirits' uncleanness.

Still other purifying miracles draw on this same delicate balance of Jesus' role as nemesis to the spirits of uncleanness. A leper begs him: "If you will, you can make me clean." Jesus responds by accepting the condition of the man's request with exacting measure: "I will; be clean" (Mk 1:40–44). The leper is cured because Jesus has compassion and wills it. In the gospel theme of reconciliation, with stories of purifying Israel by driving out impure spirits and diseases and conditions understood as impure, Jesus has the role of reconciliation, as the stories illustrate the disobedience and revolt of priest and temple in a tradition of narrative rooted in the origin stories of the high priesthood of Aaron and Eli (Lev 10; Num 25; 1 Sm 2:27–36; 3:11–14; 1 Kgs 2:27, 35).[5]

This gentle rhetoric of balance continues as Jesus heals a woman's hemorrhage. An unclean person—someone who cannot be touched—touches Jesus' clothes (Mk 5:25–34). It is what draws from him the power that makes her well—a simple motif, celebrating faith, reiterated in the episode's narrative envelope about Jairus's daughter. The father's belief overmasters his fear of death, though the girl lies dead and hence is unclean. Jesus asserts that she sleeps and takes her by the hand as proof (Mk 5:21–43). This closure echoes the way Mark has Jesus cure Simon's mother of fever. He also takes her by the hand (Mk 1:29–31). In Matthew's version of this brief episode, the fever is used to epitomize Israel's suffering. In Isaiah's song, which Matthew cites, the story of Israel's history and suffering is reiterated by Yahweh's servant, who "took our suffering and bore our sickness" (Is 53:4). Matthew uses both the gospel story and its reference to Isaiah as allegory for Elijah's role of reconciliation through bearing Israel's sins (Mt 8:17; 1 Pet 2:24 = Is 53:5!).

The song of Isaiah, which Matthew cites, uses the metaphor of sickness and suffering as a punishment or discipline from God to educate Israel and bring a new generation to understanding. The motif of fever in our story seems to hold the entire discourse about suffering implicit. When Job, for example, argues that Yahweh's lack of compassion to his suffering ("his skin turned black and his body racked with fever") contradicts the tears Job himself had showed to the troubled, as it also contradicts the grief he suffered for the poor (Job 30:24–31), he does not yet understand that enlightenment comes through suffering sent to teach him humility (Job 33:14–18).

The role of miracle tales is to bring understanding, to make explicit that the kingdom of God reverses the fate of the poor. That is understanding. Mark's interest in the use of the story of Simon's mother is linked to the leitmotif of cleansing Israel. In the Pentateuch stories of the first generation wandering in the desert, fever—like leprosy—makes the people unclean, requiring them to be separated from Yahweh's holiness. The motif of fever is used to lay the first dark shadow of Israel's coming rejection, the "sudden terror" that will strike the entire nation:

> If you will not listen to me and will not obey all of these commandments, if you reject my statutes and if your soul abhors my ordinances, so that you not follow all of my commandments, but break my covenant, I will do the following to you: I will appoint over you sudden terror, consumption and fever that waste the eyes and cause life to pine away. (Lev 26:14–16)

The thematic principle of reciprocity that dominates the tradition requires that Yahweh reject them as they have rejected him. All metaphors evoke an uncleanness from which they cannot be cleaned:

> Yahweh will send curses, confusion and frustration on you, in all that you undertake to do, until you are destroyed and quickly perish on account of the evil of your doing, because you have forsaken me. Yahweh will make the pestilence cling to you until he has consumed you off the land which you are entering to take possession of it. Yahweh will smite you with consumption, with fever, inflammation and fiery heat, with drought and mildew and he will pursue you until you perish. . . . You will be a horror to all the kingdoms of the earth. (Dt 28:20–25)

The stories of healing the lame and blind in Mark (Mk 2:2–12; 10:46–52) are drawn from this same stream of tradition. For Leviticus, "the blind and the lame" are a collective trope for those who are not allowed to come close to Yahweh. Such cripples cannot be priests, come near the veil or approach the altar. They are unclean. They profane the sanctuary Yahweh makes holy (Lev 21:17–23). The Leviticus tradition of cultic purity marks a basic problem in the understanding of God, who—in accordance with his holiness—defines himself as the God who is "with Israel" (esp. Ex 3:12). His holiness requires that Israel become a "holy people." The coherence of the covenant theme in the narrative is taken up with this riddle of a holy God and an unholy people. It is clearly noted in the farewell speeches of both Moses and Joshua. One solution has been found in the opening chapters of Isaiah, where the prophet's "unclean lips," unable to bear the task of carrying Yahweh's holy word, are cleansed with fire from the altar (Is 6:5–7). In the center of Isaiah's book, a similar solution is found with the themes of redemption, ransoming and purifying. The fate of those rejected—the blind, the deaf, the lame and the dumb—is overturned and Israel's impurity is resolved with the analogous, transforming fire of suffering: the holy way to Zion, which becomes one of Isaiah's central metaphors for the kingdom of God (Is 35:1–10).

The "living parables" Mark develops in his miracle stories, with their ironic play on the disciples understanding and not understanding, use a technique whose template is found in the prophets. Isaiah's song of the vineyard is just such an allegorical parable:

> My beloved had a vineyard on a very fertile hill. He dug it and cleared it of stones, and he planted it with choice vines. He built a watchtower in the middle of it and hewed out a wine vat in it. He looked for it to yield grapes, but it brought wild grapes. And now, O inhabitants of Jerusalem, men of Judah, judge, I beg of you, between me and my vineyard. What more was there to do for my vineyard that I have not done. When I expected it to yield good grapes, why did it yield wild grapes? I will tell you now what I will do to my vineyard. I will remove its hedge and it will be devoured. I will break its wall down and it will be trampled. I will make it a wasteland. It will be neither pruned nor hoed, but briars and thistles will grow and I will command the clouds not to rain on it. The vineyard of Yahweh of the Armies is the house of Israel and the men of Judah are his pleasant plants. He looked for justice, but behold bloodshed; for righteousness, but look, a cry! (Is 5:1–7)

Israel and its remnant Jerusalem has become a desolate and deserted garden, evoking the ruined garden of the Genesis paradise, with these same "briars and thistles" (Gen 3:18). Jerusalem, rather than the garden of God's kingdom, has become the empty wasteland that existed before the creation, when there was not yet rain nor a faithful servant to till the soil (Gen 2:5; cf. Gen 1:2). The song of the vineyard opens a sixfold series of lamentations over Jerusalem (cf. Jer 2:21; Ez 19:10–14; Hos 10:1).

Isaiah uses the vineyard as a symbolic parable for Israel's history, as he does the description of his family life and the cue names of his children. They relate the blessings and curse that is the people's destiny. A more expansive counterpart to Isaiah's parable is found in the story of the children and wives of the prophet Hosea. Named and unnamed, hated and then loved, rejected and then accepted, they live out the story of Israel's relationship to Yahweh, with its destruction of Samaria and Jerusalem and their exile to the reversal of their fate in stories of return (Hos 1–3). The book of Job as a whole, the "suffering servant" songs in Isaiah (Is 42:1–4: 49:1–6; 50:4–11; 52:13–53:12) and the narratives of Ezra and Nehemiah play out such living parables on a grand scale and provide us with a template for the gospels. The gospel Elijah tradition, with its interpretive key in the prophecy of Malachi, assigns to Elijah the messianic role of preparing the way for the day of judgment, which inaugurates Yahweh's kingdom. He brings the people to repentance and forgiveness for their sins. He reconciles Samaria and Jerusalem. These are the generations marked by blindness and deafness both to the prophet's word and Moses' Torah. This tradition dominates large sections of the gospels. They constitute epitomizing examples of the Samaritan and Jewish literature that supported the indigenous intellectual tradition of first-century Palestine. Miracle stories of healing, cleansing and raising from the dead, stories of magic meals, with their various implicit and explicit references to judgment and repentance, as to curse and blessing, stories of calling and stories about the spirit and his prophets are all part of a narrative world that has provided essential events in the stories of the gospels.

THE KINGDOM AND THE CHILDREN SAYINGS

In the prologue of his book *The Historical Jesus,* John Crossan discusses the method he has used to determine that certain sayings were *ipsissima verba*: Jesus' own words.[6] Understandably, he makes no attempt to reconstruct exactly, word for word, what Jesus said. His inventory allows for the variations, for example, found in Matthew and Luke. The hypothesis of an oral tradition is critical to his argument, as it allows him to use what he calls a principle of "multiple attestation," as one of his most important criteria for distinguishing authentic sayings from other statements given to Jesus in the gospels. This principle attempts to eliminate sayings that could have been created by one of the sources.[7] "Authentic sayings" are attested by several independent sources.[8] Though the criteria for "multiple, independent attestation" appear arbitrary, they have a long tradition in New Testament scholarship. Crossan uses a single example to illustrate what he means by a clearly authentic saying. This is the "kingdom and children" saying.

> And they were bringing children to him, that he might touch them and the disciples rebuked them. But when Jesus saw it he was indignant and said to them, "Let the children come to me, do not hinder them; for to such belongs the kingdom of God. Truly I say to you, whoever does not receive the kingdom of God like a child shall not enter it." And he took them in his arms and blessed them, laying his hands upon them. (Mk 10:13–16; cf. Mt 19:13–15; Lk 18:15–17)[9]

He finds it attested in six different texts, four of which he judges independent (Thomas 22:1–2; Mk 10:13–16; Mt 18:3; Jn 3:1–10: actually Jn 3:3, 5). He dates the original of these sayings to 30–60 CE and argues that it either originated in Jesus' teachings or was attributed to him at a very early stage of the oral tradition. Because the saying also implies a perspective shared with other early, multiply attested sayings, it provides him with a parade example for authentic statements of Jesus.

The argument depends on the existence of an oral tradition linking Jesus' original teachings with Mark, Thomas and Q. Crossan's claims for an early dating expose considerable uncertainty. Several scholarly discussions are involved, stretching back over more than a century of debate. Among the most central of these claims are the following: (1) Paul's references to Jesus' life are earlier than the gospels and are used by them. (2) Mark is the earliest of the gospels and was used by Matthew, Luke and John. (3) Sayings common to Matthew and Luke, but not to Mark, were based on a written form of an oral tradition of sayings (such as Q). (4) The Gospel of Thomas reflects a similar collection of sayings and can be dated as early as the mid-first century CE. That none of these premises are conclusive or satisfactory for establishing the origins of either the gospel narratives or Jesus' sayings should make us cautious about using them in a cumulative argument. While the first three claims are necessary to Crossan's argument, *none should be used as if they were known facts.*

While the scenario of an expanding oral tradition originating in Jesus' teaching is necessary to the argument, it is not direct evidence of such a tradition. His arguments for both a written form of Q and an early date for Thomas, because of similarities with Q, not only begs the question but tendentiously argues that Q and Thomas offer independent witnesses. Much of what is unique in Thomas is demonstrably late, while what is judged early reflects the gospels. Little effort has been made to argue that in fact an oral tradition existed that collected Jesus' sayings.[10] However, whether or not one is inclined to allow Crossan's argument as likely, his parade example of an authentic saying of Jesus can be clearly falsified. It can be shown not to have originated in the teachings of Jesus.

Of the six occurrences of the trope Crossan calls "kingdom and children" sayings, four are classified as independent and two dependent. Only the authority of scholarly tradition of the primacy of Mark supports the judgment that the very close variations of the saying "Let the children come to me and do not hinder them; for to such belong the kingdom of heaven" (Mt 19:14) and "Let the children come to me and do not hinder them; for to such belong the kingdom of God" (Lk 18:16) are dependent on the similar saying in Mark: "Let the little children come to me; do not prevent them; for to such belongs the kingdom of God" (Mk 10:14). This saying, nearly identical in all three gospels, clearly offers a common trope, but the primacy of Mark's version, including the phrase "kingdom of God" he shares with Luke, does not stand on its own merits. The assumption that Mark is the source for the versions of Matthew and Luke is unprovable. Similarly, that the saying in Mark is the most likely original can be shown to be without merit.

Crossan also identifies the "children and the kingdom" saying in the Gospel of John within a discussion between Jesus and the teacher Nicodemus. Crossan considers this version of the saying as the latest of the variations on the saying, expanding on the theme of humility and innocence. The scene centers on the saying: "Truly, truly I tell you, unless one is born anew, he cannot see the kingdom of God" (Jn 3:3). This has been expanded with the motif of baptism with the spirit, the theme of the following episode (Jn 3:22–36): "Unless one is born of water and the spirit, he cannot come into God's kingdom" (Jn 3:5). While these sayings belong to any large spectrum of New Testament texts about the kingdom, and while they may well be related to the saying from the synoptic gospels, it is difficult to identify them with that saying or with the metaphor of children and humility that underlies them. The saying in John is driven by a theme that is important to John's gospel generally—new life and rebirth. These are thematic elements that cluster around resurrection more than humility. Through their motif of birth, they echo such well-known biblical motifs and variants as a remnant saved, a new covenant and a new Jerusalem, which we find, above all, in Isaiah and Jeremiah. That some sayings include similar elements, such as kingdom and children, reversal and rebirth, does not make them versions of a single saying. It certainly does not allow us to attribute their origin to an identical "original" saying.

The motif of the newborn as epitome of piety and humility, which we find in the synoptic gospels and echoed in the epistles (1 Pet 1:23; Eph 5:26), finds its roots, not in a reconstructed oral tradition nor in a historical teaching of Jesus, but in a broad stream of variations across a spectrum of texts in the Hebrew Bible (cf. Ps 8:3 and below). Crossan's decision to ignore the core of early Palestinian tradition as a potential source for his gospel sayings is responsible for his confusing the two different metaphors found in the gospels. The collected sayings in John 3:1–21 echo John's prologue and his discourse on the necessity to be "born anew." It also echoes a tradition from the prophets (Is 54:13; Jer 24:7; 31:33–34; Ez 11:17–21; 36:25–28; Zech 13:1). The line that Crossan draws to the "kingdom and children" trope from Matthew, Mark and Luke is not based on anything Jesus says. The plot order of John's gospel is responsible. John's saying about "rebirth" and "the cleansing of the spirit" occupies a comparable place in his story's progress as the "kingdom and children" saying does in Matthew's (Mt 21:15–16). It follows the story of the cleansing of the temple (Jn 2:13–17). Matthew has set his "children and kingdom" saying between the cleansing story and the cursing of the fig tree (Mt 21:12–14; 21:18–22). In Luke, the fig tree story is not presented as a story of Jesus at all, but rather comes in a parable and is interpreted much in line with Isaiah's parable of Yahweh and his vineyard (Lk 13:6–9; Is 5:1–7). In Mark, on the other hand, the cleansing episode (Mk 11:15–18) is set in the middle of two discussions on the fig tree (Mk 11:12–14, 19–26).

The narrative logic, implicit in the placement of the story within a gospel's plotline, becomes more visible when we compare it with some associations in the introduction to the Psalter and in the synopsis of poetry we find in the book of Jeremiah. The function of the fig tree episodes in the gospels is comparable to the separation of wheat from chaff in Matthew's parable of the kingdom (Mt 13:24–30) or John the Baptist's interpretation of Jesus' baptism with either spirit or fire, separating the good from the evil (Mt 3:11–12). Both illustrations have their roots in the "either-or" distinction between the contrasting paths of the righteous and godless in Psalm 1. The righteous bear fruit in the proper season (Jer 17:8: "They do not stop bearing fruit"), but the godless are blown away like chaff in the wind (Ps 1:3–4). They belong to themes of judgment. In Matthew, when Jesus comes out of the temple, he is hungry and goes to the fig tree to eat. But the fig tree has no fruit. Eternally judged by Jesus' curse, the fig tree shrivels (Mt 21:19). The story is followed by parables of vineyards, exploiting parallel themes.

The context of Mark's fig tree episode is structured within a three-day schema, where Jesus has the role of Bible illustrator. On the day after his triumphant entry into his kingdom in Jerusalem (Mk 11:1–11), Jesus sees a fig tree and finds it without fruit. Therefore, it is eternally cursed as in Matthew's gospel (Mk 11:12–14 = Mt 21:18–19). It is Jesus who has come out of season, as Mark makes the point that the righteous must be ready whenever the king comes—even out of season. This is a variation on the parables of the wedding of the king's son (Mt 22:1–14) and the ten bridesmaids (Mt 25:1–10). These stories bear a similar element of judgment as a sign of the kingdom.

Mark's curse out of season finds clarification in his second use of the fig tree motif. Jesus has returned to Jerusalem to cleanse the temple. Later he and his disciples pass by the tree—now shriveled. When Peter remarks on this wonder, Jesus interprets it in terms of discerning true faith and purity of heart (Mk 11:23–24). This second scene—with its interpretation—is echoed in Matthew as an independent parable built on the theme of preparing for the time when the son of man comes. Without warning, one will be taken and another left behind. The audience is cautioned to be ready to bear fruit at whatever time he comes (Mt 24:32–44).

In the Bible generally, such a theme is typically illustrated in Matthew's manner, as, for example, the stories of vineyards bearing or not bearing fruit. The song of Yahweh and his vineyard from Isaiah 5 is a particularly rich illustration of this type. In Jeremiah, the fig tree comes forward in a very polemical and supersessionist song, where kingdom themes of discerning, judging and separating dominate (Jer 24:1–10). With reference to Jerusalem's destruction by Nebuchadnezzar, Israel is compared to two baskets of figs placed outside the temple. One basket is full of good figs, the other of rotten and inedible fruit. The good is—like the original humanity of the creation story, given dominion over every fruit-bearing tree—"very good" (Gen 1:26–31). The bad, however, is "very, very bad" (Jer 24:2–3). The good fruit reflects those taken into exile, where Yahweh gives them a heart with understanding. In exile, they repent with a pure heart and return to the land. The rotten fruit represents those who remained in the land and those who had escaped to Egypt. A mixed metaphor draws on the fig tree itself, and not only its fruit. It will be "uprooted" by sword, famine and plague (Jer 29:16–20). A few chapters later, the metaphor of the fig tree expands to a discussion of the new covenant. He will give Israel a pure heart and make of them plants bearing their fruit faithfully (Jer 32:36–41; cf. Jer 8:13; Hos 9:10–14).

Crossan's distinction between dependent and independent variants of a common saying misleads. These sayings cannot be traced to a common oral tradition and similarity does not of itself imply dependence. Their function within the rhetorical structure of the gospels reflects a much more complicated and far-reaching intertextual discourse which shows that the gospel writers did not draw their sayings from a specific, narrowly defined oral tradition, stemming from a particular historical person. The gospels rather shared in a well-developed tradition of text interpretation, which is independent of any particular teacher or source. In considering Jewish traditions of *biography* formation, the succession of the three scenes in Mark 11 and Matthew 21 are built on three thematic elements, shared by both writers: the inauguration of the kingdom, the cleansing of the temple and discerning purity of heart. These scenes and the themes they illustrate find their origin among tropes belonging to ancient Near Eastern royal ideology. Access to this tradition comes most directly from prophetic literature and the David traditions of the Psalter, Samuel and Chronicles.

Crossan identifies the very earliest of his independent attestations of the "children and kingdom" trope in the Gospel of Thomas: "These infants being suckled are like those who enter the kingdom" (Thomas 22:1–2). Out of its context, it seems to be a close variant of the sayings from the canonical gospels. Unlike the New Testament sayings, however, this saying and its context within Thomas are not metaphorical but refer to real nursing babies. Themes of humility and innocence are not implied and the context in the Gospel of Thomas expands the quotation in a direction foreign to Jewish tradition, putting stress on a child's asexual character. As Crossan recognizes, Thomas argues that the kingdom is populated by celibate innocents. The disciples respond to Jesus by asking, "Shall we then, as children, enter the kingdom?" The Jesus of Thomas answers, "When you make the two one and the inside like the outside . . . and when you make the male and the female one, so that the male not be male nor the female female . . . then you will enter [the kingdom]" (Thomas 22:3–4).[11]

This celibacy saying has moved far from the children and kingdom saying of the canonical gospels. It has moved even further from biblical tradition as a whole and lies firmly within the well-known gnostic ideal of celibacy in Christian piety. It may well be a secondary interpretation of the children sayings, but it hardly reflects this tradition's "earliest form."

Crossan's parade example does not support his assertion of four independent attestations of a single original saying of Jesus. There are four *interrelated* sayings in the canonical gospels (Mt 18:3–4; 19:14; Mk 10:14; Lk 18:16) and a revision of this saying in Thomas 22:3–4. An independent text (Mk 3:3–5) deals with a related but distinct theme, and a seventh saying (Jn 3:3–5) is entirely unrelated. More to the point, Crossan leaves out a number of gospel episodes and sayings that, as we will see, center on the theme of the kingdom and the metaphor of children. Perhaps they have been ignored because they are not usually included in standard publications that list and compare gospel parallels.[12]

CLEANSING THE TEMPLE AND THE UNCLEAN

In Matthew, following Jesus' triumphal entry into Jerusalem riding on an ass with a foal, reiterating Zechariah's revision of Isaiah (Mt 21:2–5; Zech 9:9–11; cf. Is 62:10–12), the story of Jesus cleansing the temple is presented. The books of Kings give this royal task to the kings Asa, Jehoash, Hezekiah and Josiah. In Matthew's story, Jesus drives out those buying and selling in the temple and over-turns the tables of those changing money and the seats of those selling pigeons, quoting scripture at them: "My house shall be called a house of prayer, but you have made it into a den of robbers" (Mt 21:12–13). The logic of retribution, with which the scene functions so well, is particularly apparent in its revision of earlier sayings from Jeremiah and Isaiah. Jesus transforms the corrupt temple of Jeremiah: "Has this house, which is called by my name, become a den of robbers in your eyes?" into the ideal temple of Isaiah: "These I will bring to my holy mountain and make them joyful in my house of prayer" (Jer 7:8–15; cf. Is 56:7). The dominance of Isaiah's passage over Jeremiah's is not to be missed. Matthew recasts Isaiah 56. Isaiah's song called the one who keeps justice and does righteousness "blessed": "He who keeps the Sabbath and does not profane it." His examples of such a man are the "foreigner who has joined himself to Yahweh" and the "eunuch who keeps my Sabbaths." These he will "bring to my holy mountain and make them joyful in my house of prayer; their burnt offerings and their sacrifices will be accepted on my altar" (Is 56:1–6). Matthew's story of Jesus in the temple closes on a cryptic scene of healing the lame and the blind. They have come to Jesus (Mt 21:14), in obvious imitation of Isaiah's foreigner and eunuch, those whom Isaiah declared should be brought back into the temple. Their identification with the lame and blind opens Matthew's story to a much larger discourse about temple reforms in 1–2 Kings (see below, Chapter 9).

When Jesus heals the lame and blind in the temple, high priests and scribes witness the miracles together with children. As he leaves the temple, the children shout "Hosanna," reiterating the shouts from the crowds as he entered Jerusalem (Mt 21:9). The high priests and scribes do not join the celebration. They play the role of the opposition in a debate. They point out that the children have proclaimed him the son of David and become angry. Matthew sets the children who understand in contrast to the high priests and scribes of this generation who do not. Their authority underlines the kingdom's theme of the powers of this world transformed. The interacting motifs of healing the blind and lame, the anger of high priests and scribes, and the children's shouting recognition (Mt 21:16) demand discussion. It is not immediately obvious why our discerning children draw their conclusion from Matthew's sketch of the double scene of temple cleansing and healing. Nor is it obvious why the high priests and scribes find the children's recognition of Jesus as son of David objectionable. They do not seem angry at the cleansing of the temple but at "the wonders," at the healing of the lame and blind. This is what the children's shouts celebrate, as they recognize Jesus as the son of David. What is it the children understand and the high priests and learned scribes do not? This brief encounter with the children captures one aspect of a discourse about the proud and humble that confirms the reversal of fortune and the good news (Mk 1:1), which the saving king brings about when he enters his kingdom.

As in the announcement of Jesus' birth, where he is named Immanuel, Matthew is not merely collecting proof texts from Old Testament prophecy to build a claim about who Jesus is: son of David and representing divine presence. Matthew doesn't seem interested in that kind of argument. Those who examine the symbol system that underlies any particular literary work of the ancient world are mistaken if they limit the discussion to a single text or author, in this case, the text Matthew wrote. Every text speaks from and gives expression to a whole literary and intellectual world, through which what is written makes sense and captures its reader. Meanings far surpass what is intended by any individual author; and they surpass, as well, the reflection of the world in which a particular author writes. Narratives are responses to a multitude of possible meanings.

Matthew's complex metaphor has its roots in Psalm 8, to which Jesus explicitly refers: "From the mouths of babes and infants: strength" (Ps 8:3), presenting a challenge through the riddle, implicit in the contradiction of strength out of the weakness and helplessness of nursing infants. Matthew's reading of Psalm 8:3 connects the metaphor of children's voices with the kingdom and the temple and interprets them in a discourse on the proper form of prayer. The "strength" coming from the mouth of babes is defined as the ideal song of praise. It connects the themes of both the son of David and the salvation he evokes by making the divine name present. This the crowd told us already when Jesus entered Jerusalem (Mt 21:9). The children reiterate what the crowds announced.

Matthew is not the first to make this connection. He draws his interpretation from Isaiah (26:1–7) in a song that celebrates Jerusalem as Judah's surviving remnant in a poem Isaiah used to introduce the reader to his central story of the siege of Jerusalem by Sennacherib. This is set in the reign of another son of David, whose cue name, Hezekiah, can be translated "Yahweh's strength."[13] In Isaiah's song, Jerusalem is described as "our city of strength." It is not merely the city's but also Hezekiah's role in the story of the siege, when Jerusalem was as helpless as the child that Matthew evokes through his citation of Psalm 8. Hezekiah relied not on his own strength, nor on horses or the Egyptians, but on tears of prayer to Yahweh in the temple. The "strength" that came from his mouth represents the remnant of a righteous nation keeping faith. It is contrasted with the merely secure city, whose humiliation was threatened by an Assyrian army that was sent by God.

In this context of the remnant, Matthew sets his savior within Isaiah's great story of the siege of Jerusalem (Is 36–39). Assyria's king, Yahweh's Immanuel, is sent to punish Samaria and Jerusalem for their sins. Having destroyed Samaria and come to Jerusalem, however, he taunts its king, his city and its God. He appeals to the people on the walls "to choose a land—like the promised land—of grain and wine, of bread and vineyards" (Is 36:4–22). In contrast to Sennacherib's hubris, "mocking the living God" (Is 37:4), the city goes into mourning. The king—like the king of Nineveh in the story of Jonah—tears his clothing and puts on sackcloth. He sends his counselors to proclaim a day of judgment: "a day of distress, of rebuke and disgrace." He speaks of Jerusalem's future in a metaphor of stillborn children. "Children have come to the cervical canal, but there is no strength to bring them forth" (Is 37:2–3). Hezekiah has gone to the temple to pray in humility and tears, like a child, placing himself and Jerusalem in Yahweh's hands (Is 37:14–20).

In a doubling of this scene, Yahweh's answer to Sennacherib's mockery is matched by the people's rejection of the Assyrian general's attempt to seduce them into his patronage. Isaiah's figure of the "virgin daughter" of Zion, *true and faithful to her husband*, "rejects you, laughs at you with scorn, tosses her head at you" (Is 37:22). Yahweh mocks Sennacherib through his daughter's faithfulness, and his judgment against the Assyrians saves Jerusalem and its remnant. A scene worthy of an apocalypse brings Yahweh's angel in the night, echoing the Exodus story's angel of death, destroying 185,000 Assyrian soldiers before dawn (Is 37:22–38; Ex 12:29–30).

The story leaves an essential thread untied at its closure, that it might reach across the gaping emptiness of the exile's suffering between the portentous visit of Babylonians to view the temple treasure (Is 39) to the resonant song of reconciliation and return (Is 40:1–11). The thread is important, having held the motif of Jerusalem's remnant through four chapters. In the Hezekiah story the remnant survives, but the "child at the cervical opening" (Is 37:2) is still waiting to be born. It is in announcing the exile's closure, in the reversals of Israel's fate, that the potential of the child Shearyashub ("repentant remnant," Isa 7:3) finally matures and Immanuel can reject evil and turn toward the good:

> Prepare a way in the wilderness for our God, raise the valleys and lower the mountains; the hill country will become a valley and the Shefelah a plain. Yahweh's glory will be revealed. (Is 40:3–5)

Jerusalem's remnant, caught at the cervical opening, is reborn from the exile. A conquering king comes from the east with a sword that turns nations and kings to dust (Is 41:3; 45:1). The child is Israel, Yahweh's firstborn and suffering servant who has been educated in humility. The cycle of metaphor, first opened in Immanuel's birth, is fulfilled in the utopian vision of a new Israel. This child, like all humanity since the garden story, has learned through suffering to choose the good and reject the evil. Therefore, Yahweh can now say to his child: "You have I chosen and I have *not* rejected you; do not fear for I am with you" (Is 41:9–10).

THE HEART OF THE TORAH

The story of Jesus' entrance into Jerusalem is tied to the episode of the cleansing of the temple in a short chain of tales that create a larger story. The cleansing of Jerusalem joins an Old Testament debate over the heart of the Torah, which transforms the holy war goal of the purity of Israel and purity of Jerusalem into piety's goal of serving God with a pure heart. This debate is central to the purity of the new Jerusalem for those who return from exile, which Ezra 10 takes up with an ironic question regarding those who return from exile to create a new Jerusalem but do not serve God with a pure heart (see below, Chapter 8).

In Matthew's scene of Jesus' entrance into Jerusalem, Jesus takes up a holy war role. It is the role David plays in the Psalter. He is Yahweh's conquering hero, defeating the nations in uproar and epitomizing the righteous nation, fearing God (Ps 2:10–12). He is the one for whom Isaiah's "strong Jerusalem" opens its gates: "Open the doors that the righteous nation, keeping faith, might enter" (Is 26:2). The second scene in Matthew's story is set in the temple. The moneychangers are also given a holy war role. They will be the ones trampled underfoot by "the feet of the helpless and the steps of the weak," by those whom Jesus represents in his righteous anger.

> Those who live so high, he brings low; he humiliates the high-strutting town, brings it level with the ground and casts it into the dust; feet stomp it, the feet

of the helpless, the steps of the weak: you have leveled the path of the righteous and made it straight. (Is 26:5–7)

Matthew intensifies David's role as representative of the pious and righteous
who fear God and gives it to Jesus to play in the cleansing scene. Matthew's
thieves in his "temple-become-robber's den" are defeated by the messiah's
humility-become-strength, coming from the children's mouth. Matthew creates
a Hezekiah-like Jesus, come into his city of strength. Like the early Hezekiah of
2 Chronicles 29–31, Jesus reforms the temple. It is the Chronicles story, more
than any other, that marks Hezekiah as both David's son and pious king, reforming the cult and repairing the temple.

To explain this reference, we need to turn to the theme of David and his sons,
which Matthew also evokes. The motif of the lame and blind as played out in
the David stories begins in a cryptic episode in the story of David's siege of
Jerusalem (2 Sm 5:6–10). David has ruled as king in Hebron for seven years
when he and his men go up to Jerusalem to attack the Jebusites. The defenders
mock David: "Here you will not come in, for *the blind and the lame* will drive
you back." David responds in kind. Sending his men up a water shaft, he encourages them "to attack *the blind and the lame* hated by David's soul!" This remarkable exchange of bravado fills the story of David's siege of Jerusalem. It is
all the more remarkable as the lame and the blind are normally used as an epitome of the suffering who will be returned in a New Covenant utopia, in what
Jeremiah presents as his ideal of God's kingdom (Jer 31:8). With similar idealism, Job likens his own life to that of a just king. He had been "eyes to the blind
and feet to the lame, father to the poor" (Job 29:15). Yahweh himself is one who
"opens the eyes of the blind and lifts up the one bent low" (Ps 146:8). The "lame
and the blind," like widows and orphans, are hardly among those one expects a
good king to hate with the thoroughness of David's hatred. David's oath shocks
the reader, and it is obviously intended to shock (cf. 1 Chr 11:4–9). The riddle
is used by the author of 2 Samuel to explain the saying, "the lame and the blind
shall not come into the temple" (2 Sm 5:8). The key to the riddle is its anachronistic use as an etiology or origin story for the purity law in Leviticus, prevent-
ing the lame and the blind from offering sacrifice in the temple:

And Yahweh said to Moses, "Say to Aaron, None of your descendants throughout their generations who has a blemish may approach to offer the bread of his
God. For no one who has a blemish shall draw near, a man blind or lame, or
one who has a mutilated face or a limb too long, or a man who has an injured

foot or an injured hand, or a hunchback or a dwarf, or a man with a defect in his sight. . . . (Lev 21:16–20).

In its own context—apart from this editorial gloss—the motif of the lame and blind plays a haunting role throughout the David story in the books of Samuel. The Jebusites' challenge to David and his rude rejoinder draw on a tradition that is well rooted in ancient literature. A song of lament to the goddess Ishtar, for example, has many echoes in the Psalter's laments of David, surrounded and mocked by his enemies. The singer, addressing Ishtar, epitomizes the humiliation that his enemies heap upon him:

> How long, O my lady, shall my adversaries look on me; in lying and untruth plan evil against me? Shall my pursuers and those who exult over me rage against me? How long, O my Lady, shall the crippled and the weak seek me out? . . . The weak have become strong, but I am weak.[14]

Strengthening the weak, healing the lame, is a reversal that unlocks salvation's riddle. The Psalter gives voice to a similar trope and exposes the logic of such piety as David sings for help against those who seek his life (Ps 25:24–27; 40:13–18; 70:2–6): "I am helpless and poor; (*therefore*) Yahweh will take care of me," supporting humility as the epitome of piety. In turn, such pious motifs in hymns and prayers are given humorous illustration in tales such as the David and Saul story (1 Sm 18:12–29), where David plays the role of a poor man (1 Sm 18:23): the universal fairy-tale role of the young suitor, too poor to have hope of becoming the king's son-in-law (see below, Chapter 10). In the story of his siege and capture of Jerusalem, however, David had not yet reached chapter 15 of his story, where he learned the lesson of his weakness and humility's contrasting strength on his journey to the Mount of Olives. As in Matthew's gospel, the earlier stories of David build themes that later narratives expand and explain.

David's hatred of the lame and the blind finally finds its saving reversal. David, now king, has brought the Philistines and his enemies under his power. "David has won a name for himself" (2 Sm 8:13). He "reigned over all Israel and administered justice and equity to all his people" (2 Sm 8:15). The resistance to David's reign by the supporters of Saul's surviving son, Ishbosheth, was broken when Ishbosheth and Abner, his general (2 Sm 3:30–34, 12), were murdered.[15] David then marks his great peace by asking, "Is there still anyone left of the house of Saul, that I may show him love for Jonathan's sake?" (2 Sm 9:1) Saul's son, Jonathan, whom David had loved, had a son who was crippled, having been dropped by his nurse in terror of David's vengeance. The child's cue name is Mephibosheth ("from the mouth of shame"; 2 Sm 4:4). The Hebrew word for love *(chesed),* which David now shows the child, reflects the king's or God's personal favor and protection. It prepares the audience for David's beloved Jonathan's lame son, with his shaming role, that David had cursed and banned from Jerusalem. David's show of "love" for Mephibosheth, seeming to reverse the hatred he had sworn to the lame, barely disguises his need to control the only surviving threat to the legitimacy of his reign. David brings the crippled man into Jerusalem to eat regularly at the king's table (2 Sm 9:13). This compromised motif of mercy will eventually find its reversal in the shame of the echoing closure of the 2 Kings narrative, when Josiah's grandson, Jehoiachin—in history's progress, the youngest of the "sons of David"—is invited to be the daily guest at the table of another great patron, Babylon's king (2 Kgs 25:29–30). Saul's surviving heir and grandson, Mephibosheth—crippled in his feet—serves his title role with his "mouth of shame." Mephibosheth formally ends David's civil war by recognizing him as king (2 Sm 9;6) and he "lived in Jerusalem; for he always ate at the king's table, though he was lame in both his feet" (2 Sm 9:13). David's pretension to love the lame, whom he hated (2 Sm 5:8), inviting his competitor into Jerusalem to eat at his table, like one of his own sons, provides sufficient irony and opportunity for a later messianic reversal to support an Elijah-like role of reconciling the generations, represented here by both Saul and David and Israel and Judah.

Yet another story brings this cluster of thematic elements together into a coherent discourse. The story of the lost Torah, which was found when Josiah repaired the temple (2 Kgs 22–23), provides yet another interpretive key to the riddle of David's curse. Only Josiah's humility and tears holds Yahweh's anger from destroying Jerusalem during Josiah's lifetime. The repentant king and people had committed themselves with pure hearts to a new covenant. Josiah cleansed the temple of foreign gods, which were burned in the Kidron valley. The ashes were thrown on the graves of commoners to make them unclean (2 Kgs 23:1–8). In this story, the temple is cleansed of all that belongs to the cult of Baal and Asherah. The sole element brought *into* the temple is the festival of the Passover. No Passover had been celebrated since the time of the judges, and none had been held in the temple all the days of the kings of Israel or of Judah (2 Sm 23:22). The key is the verbal pun drawn on the Hebrew word for Passover *(pesach)* and that for the lame *(piseach)* whom David hated and banned from Jerusalem. Josiah, in imitation of David his father, reverses the curse of the lame and the blind by bringing the *pesach* into the temple. In Matthew's story, the lame (Hebrew *piseach*) come themselves into the temple to be cured by Jesus.

Once cured, what had been excluded from a holy people as unclean is now included and cleansed. The reversal of fate announces the kingdom, as the children recognize.

In Matthew's healing of the lame and the blind in the temple (Mt 21:14), the narrator addresses this theme from the David story. Matthew's temple has returned to its role of a house of prayer. In opening the next scene, Matthew's Jesus, like David, Josiah and Yahweh before him, continues the kingdom's chain of reversals. The curse on the lame and the blind is turned into blessing: their uncleanness into cleanness. He has tradition's role of the good king, creating a new Jerusalem and a new Israel. Like Job, he reverses his people's misfortune and cares for the blind and the lame at the gate (Job 29:15). Having once been cast out, they now return to their inheritance.

One of the central social and historical contexts of biblical stories, begging for further investigation, is the supersessionist conflict between the temples of Samaria and Jerusalem, implicit in our texts. Jeremiah's and Isaiah's retributive structures support a reader's expectation of saving reversal: a reconciliation of Samaria with Jerusalem and, most emphatically, a return of Samaria's much maligned cult to Jerusalem's Zion.[16] The chain of narrative discourse that I have traced from David's hatred of the lame and the blind closes with Jeremiah's Yahweh joining David and Josiah in inviting the lame and the blind. With them, they invite all of blind Isaac and lame Jacob's descendants into the temple. It is in this discourse that Matthew's simple story of cleansing and healing joins. It is this reversal of fate—bringing the lame and blind into the temple and healing them—that Matthew's caricature of high priests and scribes object to. They also object to the children's recognition of this reversal of fate. Matthew's reading understands David's curse of the lame and the blind as evoking a king's role, in which the lame and blind, like widows and orphans and children, play stereotypical roles of those who are to be saved in the kingdom. In this, he engages Psalm 68, where Matthew's role of the lame and the blind is played by widows and orphans, by the lonely and by prisoners and the helpless.

> Father of the orphan and defender of the widow is God in his holy temple. God gives the lonely a place to live; he frees the prisoner and gives them happiness. . . . You let the rain pour richly, O God, you cared for the thirsty land. You found a home for your people; in your goodness you cared for the helpless. (Ps 68:6–11)

In Luke's presentation of the beatitudes in Jesus' sermon on the plain, we find a similar play with this same tradition of the lame and blind, hated by David, and their restoration through Passover. Luke blesses the poor, the hungry and the weeping, reversing their destiny by finding an appropriate balance to their needs—possessing the kingdom, satiety and laughter, respectively. As his fourth sign of the kingdom, the lame are healed. Those who are hated and excluded will jump high with gladness (Lk 6:22). At first Luke's fourth reversal seems to lack the appropriate balance of the other three. Why do those who are hated and excluded jump for joy in the kingdom? In the larger context of the tradition the reversal becomes clear. Luke joins Isaiah and the Psalter (Is 29:18–20; 35:5–6; Ps 18:28–30). Luke's independent, creative use of a common tradition is supported by a variation of Matthew's story of the children shouting "Hosanna" and calling Jesus the "son of David" outside the temple. The story is set in the context of Jesus' entry into Jerusalem. A "multitude of disciples," play the children's role, and Pharisees play the debating high priests and scribes (Lk 19:37–40). The Pharisees tell Jesus to silence the disciples, and this marks his independence. Luke does not quote Psalm 3 as Matthew does but turns instead to the prophet Habbakuk (Hab 2:11): "The stones will shout" if the disciples are silenced. Otherwise, his story is fully comparable to the children's story of Matthew.

Immediately before the kingdom and children saying, which Crossan identifies in Luke, an implicit reference to the kingdom is made in the closure of the parable of the proud Pharisee and the humble tax collector, praying in the temple (Lk 18:16). The Pharisee prays in gratitude that he is not like other men. The tax collector asks God to show mercy to a sinner. The parable's proverb hardly poses a riddle: "One who exalts himself will be humbled, and one who humbles himself will be exalted" (Luke 18:9–14). It displays a quite common technique of moral sayings: citing its mate: "When men have humbled you and you say it is pride, then he will save the humble one" (Job 22:29). Luke creatively expands the Psalter's: "God is the judge: he puts one down and raises up another" (Ps 75:8), a phrase that closely echoes Hannah's: "Yahweh brings one down; he also exalts" (1 Sm 2:7). Luke's tax collector is a simple figure of the kingdom. A first-person lament in the Psalter complicates the parable immensely by combining it with the crippled of David's hatred. While the issues of discernment and true humility are maintained, the issues of debate bring the element of conflict into its interpretation.

As for me, when they were sick, my clothing was sackcloth. I afflicted my soul with fasting. I prayed with head down on my bosom, as though I grieved from my friend or my brother. I went about as one laments his mother, bowed down and in mourning. *At my stumbling, they gathered in glee. They gathered together against me, cripples whom I knew not slandered me without ceasing.* They impiously mocked me more and more, gnashing at me with their teeth. How long, O Yahweh, will you look on? Rescue me from their ravages, my life from the lions! (Ps 35:13–16)

The biblical discourse on humility is shared by other New Testament texts, such as the following proverb: "God opposes the proud, but shows mercy to the humble" (1 Pet 5:5–6). This catches well the message of Luke's parable. It can be read as a parallel of "To the scorner he is scornful, but to the humble he shows favor" (Prv 3:34) or as a revision of "You deliver the humble people, but bring down the proud" (Ps 18:28). The Proverbs version of the universal "pride, which comes before the fall" (Prv 18:12), might well have the best claim as Luke's source because it adds, with Luke, the contrasting "humility, which walks ahead of honor" (cf. Prv 29:23). One can multiply "sources" *ad libitum.* One could also create variations on one's own, as Luke in fact does, when he uses the proverb of his parable to interpret his "kingdom and children" saying (Lk 18:17). The authors of Luke and 1 Peter are part of a theological discussion, shared by the Epistle of James (Js 4:6) and other works of both Old and New Testaments (Prv 14:31–32; 17:5; 19:17; Job 22:7). In the intensely competitive literary world of proverbs and sayings, the close similarity of wording of one proverb to another hardly suggests borrowing so much as a common tradition.

While Luke used a "multitude of disciples" in a positive variation of the figures of Matthew's children, Matthew uses "scribes and Pharisees" to play a negative role representing all who are not children (Mt 23:1–12). He has Jesus present a sermon to "the crowds and his disciples" on the need for humility. This closes with a proverb: "He who exalts himself will be humbled and he who humbles himself will be exalted" (Mt 23:11). This begins a sevenfold diatribe, transforming the crowds and disciples of his story into the "children of Gehenna" (Mt 23:15; cf. Is 1:2). The diatribe includes six segments, each introduced with, "Woe to you scribes and Pharisees" (Mt 23:13, 15, 23, 25, 27, 29). The one exception expands this rhetoric and structures a threefold curse on the scribes and Pharisees. Offering us another messianic figure hating the lame and the blind, the scribes and Pharisees have become "blind guides" (Mt 23:16), "blind fools" (Mt 23:17) and "blind men" (Mt 23:19). Their false teaching is read out in a sevenfold indictment, each beginning with the phrase "if anyone swears" or "he who swears" (Mt 23:16–22). The diatribe empties into a lament over Jerusalem, while echoing Isaiah's curse on those who escape to Egypt.

The images of the lament over Jerusalem and the gathering of Jerusalem's children offer a reverse, negative echo of Isaiah's oracle. Clearly Matthew draws heavily on the book of Isaiah's closure. Yahweh finally allows Isaiah's "new Jerusalem" to be born and the people to be gathered with the comparable metaphor of a woman and her many suckling babes (Is 66:7–11). The children are "all those who love her . . . all those who mourn over her." It is their lament that needs to be reversed to replace tears with shouts of joy (Is 66:10–11). This final image of the kingdom, with children and chicks rejoicing, supports Matthew's contrasting parallel with Jerusalem and her "children of hell," misled by the scribes and Pharisees. The children of humility shout for joy as the king enters his kingdom.

The entire scene presents Jesus in the apocalyptic role of the kingdom's judge, who with curse and blessing prepares a new Jerusalem. This interpretation is locked by the final closure of his last address to the scribes and Pharisees. He points ahead to the coming kingdom: "You will not see me again, until you say 'Blessed is he who comes in the name of the Lord'" (Mt 23:39). This interpretive prophecy—of the scribes and Pharisees shouting the Psalter's praise (Ps 118:26)—reiterates the shouting of "the crowds and his followers" and the entire scene of Jesus' first entrance to Jerusalem (Mt 21:9). It also points ahead to a third reiteration in the story's future. For a reader of the gospel, this prediction is both fascinating and surprising. It closes the tightly structured, sevenfold, segmented monologue with thematic elements divided in groupings of three, six and seven segments. The whole is centered on a threefold curse of the blind guides and fools and set as a parallel to the closing lament over Jerusalem and its prophecy of reversal and reconciliation. The next time Jerusalem sees him, the blind led by the blind will all be like children, shouting with joy in the temple (Mt 21:15).[17]

It is Elijah's role that Matthew sets for Jesus. He must save Jerusalem from judgment (Mal 3:23–24). The riddle of the blind prepares the reader for such a reversal. The blind will see and the kingdom will come. The rest of Jesus' stay in Jerusalem takes the form of a discourse on the coming day when the earth is remade. Jesus sits down with his disciples on the Mount of Olives and tells them parables as signs (Mt 24:3–25, 46). Like Isaiah's, Matthew's Jerusalem is a figure for humanity. The narrative does not imply Jerusalem's destruction in 70 CE, nor does it refer to the disillusionment, suffering and persecution of the early church. It does not even point to Jesus' return to Jerusalem, where he is judged and executed. However we understand Matthew's historical overtones, all such "events" are put in the category of misleading signs in chapter 24. Matthew's goal is not historical interpretation but a reiterated, pedagogical goal he shares with the greater tradition.

In Matthew's scene at the temple, Jesus responds to the anger of the high priests and scribes and enters a theological debate (Mt 21:15–16). A text is presented for discussion: "Have you never read, 'out of the mouth of children and suckling babes: *perfect praise?*'" (Mt 21:15–17; Ps 8:3) In this illustration of the riddle in Psalm 8 and the related discourse, the theme of humility finds its abiding and dominating expression, appropriately linked to the motifs of both children and the kingdom. In this context, Crossan's concept of "authentic saying" is drained of meaning.

The complex metaphor in Psalm 8, "from the mouths of babes and infants, a strength"—whether sung by David while fleeing from Absalom as in the Psalter or as cited by Matthew—challenges the reader with its explicit riddle: the strength of a baby's crying. Matthew's reading connects the metaphor of children's voices with both the entry into Jerusalem and the cleansing of the temple. All three scenes are interpreted in regard to the proper form of prayer. The "strength" from the mouth of babes connects the son of David and the salvation he brings by making present the divine name (Mt 21:9). Matthew defines this as an ideal song of praise.

The story of Jesus' entrance into Jerusalem is centered in the episode of the cleansing of the temple and echoes another discourse on how Jerusalem can serve God with a pure heart. Jesus is assigned the role of David, the victorious king, by virtue of his tears of humility (2 Sm 15), for whom Jerusalem opens its gates (Is 26:2). Given this associative reading, one can recognize the role of the high priests and scribes as those who do not understand. Jesus' answer is one the wise of this world do not understand. It is clear that Matthew does not write of Jesus or high priests so much as about competing views of Jerusalem. He sets Isaiah's two Jerusalems in opposition to each other: the "secure city" played by the moneychangers against the "city of strength" belonging to Isaiah's righteous nation, which is illustrated by the victorious poor and needy trampling the secure under their feet.

Although Isaiah's metaphor does not exactly evoke the storming of the Bastille, it does draw its inspiration from the rhetoric of insurrection and war. It draws from both political philosophy and oppressed humanity's universal hope for justice, as do the songs of Hannah and Mary (1 Sm 2:1–10; Lk 1:46–55). The reader's identification with the story's figures is important. Matthew's children, announcing the king and his kingdom in the strength of their humility, are Isaiah's poor and needy. In the kingdom—in this utopian vision of Jerusalem—they are kings, with a new world under their feet. Depending on how much the whole of Psalm 8 is implied, Jesus does not play the role of humility himself but rather confirms the strength from the mouth of the humble children: "Hosanna to the son of David" (Mt 21:15), an echo of the crowd's cry when Jesus entered the city. They added "blessed is he who comes *in the name of the Lord*" (Mt 21:9). In Psalm 8, the child's voice also has its context in a hymn of praise to the name of Yahweh (Ps 8:2). For Matthew, Jesus "comes in Yahweh's name." The ideal song of praise is that recognition. From the protective strength of such praise, Jerusalem's salvation comes and the riddle finds its message.

There is an unquoted line of Psalm 8 that influences Matthew's interpretation. The metaphor of the child's voice, pregnant with a grown man's tears of humility, is given rhetorical echo:

> What is a man that you remember him; and the child of a man that you give him attention, made him a little less than God and crowned him with glory and honor, making him ruler over the work of your hands. (Ps 8:5–7)

These two metaphors find an unparalleled creativity in defining the patronage of Yahweh as Lord of creation (Ps. 8:2). They press a question about self-understanding. "What is a man?" This Palestinian counterpart of Plato's "Know yourself!" is closely linked to the ancient world's understanding of the world as a valley of tears. The voices of happy children in the Bible need to be tempered with tears of humility if they are to fully reflect the fate of humans. The wisdom of the innocent offers a critical illustration of the foolishness of sophistication. The reiterative praise of Yahweh's name in Psalm 8 (Ps 8:2, 10) sets the metaphor of the strength that comes from a child's mouth: a transforming answer to the rhetorical question of human nothingness. In the context of kings and Yahweh's messiah, such humility stills the uproar of creation's enemies and establishes the divine patron's peace on earth (Ps 8:3, 7; cf. Ps 2). "What is a man that you remember him, this child of Adam that you visit him" (Ps 8:5) offers a key for understanding the psalm. Implicitly it refers to the role of Adam's grandchild, Enosh, the first to call on Yahweh's name (Gen 4:26). Psalm 8 opens with its own imitation of Enosh: "Yahweh . . . how great is your name in all the world." The singer identifies the strength coming from every child's mouth as Yahweh's name. Calling on his name brings Yahweh to remember and care for his humanity.

That Yahweh always hears the cry of the child is a trope of biblical literature. He hears Ishmael's' cry in the desert (Gen 21:16–17) and Esau's tears before his father, Isaac (Gen 27:38–40). Salvation comes from the child's mouth. The dramatic climax of the Abraham story chain is reached when the child Isaac confronts his story's horror with his innocent question: "Father, where is the sacrifice?" (Gen 22:7). Abraham's answer, "God will provide," becomes a paradigm of faith in humanity's suffering and a testing ground for biblical narrative. One does well to continue in this stream of allusion through the tales of the patriarchs, noticing the scenes of Joseph's tears (Gen 45:2, 14–15) and the seventy days of Egyptian tears mourning for Joseph's father, balancing implied tears of seventy elders entering their exile in Egypt (Gen 50:3). There they suffer until a cry of the children brings Yahweh to remember them (Ex 2:23–24).

The Suffering Servant of Isaiah

The motif of the children calling on Yahweh's name can be traced through the wilderness story and the book of Judges to Isaiah's servant song, announcing the good news of universal redemption from exile (Is 48:20). In this one finds a key to the enigma of strength coming from the mouth of babes:

> Listen to me, O coastlands and hearken, you people from afar: Yahweh has called me from the womb; from the body of my mother he called my name. He made my mouth like a sharp sword; in the shadow of his hand he hid me; he made me [like] a polished arrow; in his quiver he hid me away. He said to me, "you are my servant, Israel in whom I will be glorified." (Is 49:1–3)

Israel plays the role of a new humanity. In his song, Isaiah speaks of God remembering him, as he returns to a theme much used in the seven songs of the kingdom of God in the introduction (Is 1–12). The motif of being called from his mother's womb, as Samson and Samuel were called from the wombs of their mothers (Jgs 13; 1 Sm 2) and as reused by Luke in his birth story of John (Lk 1:44), is at home in birth stories of a "son of God" (Jgs 13:5).[18] In the Babylonian creation story, Enuma Elish, such stories form a recognized genre: "Marduk was born in the house of Apsu; his father Ea created him; his mother Damkina gave birth to him; *his was the birth of a hero*."[19] In Isaiah's song, Israel speaks of the time before his birth (Is 49:1, 5–6), when he was called to be Yahweh's servant and "a light to the nations" and to speak as a prophet to the restored survivors of Israel (Is 49:6), much as Jeremiah had been called to be Yahweh's "prophet to the nations" (Jer 1:4–5).[20]

As Isaiah could not speak because he had unclean lips and had his lips purified with a burning coal, Jeremiah cannot speak because he is a child (Jer 1:6). He has his mouth touched and Yahweh's words are put into it. His power is to determine the destiny of nations. He has a messiah's authority of judgment: to shore up and to tear down, to destroy and to level, to build and to plant (Jer 1:10). Implicit in this sixfold recitation is the song for a poor man, sung by Hannah in Samuel's birth story, which evokes the strength of Yahweh as king (1 Sm 2:1–10).

In Isaiah's suffering servant songs, the newly born Israel will have Yahweh's spirit and "bring judgment to the nations" (Is 42:1; 49:1). This judgment is "true" (Is 42:3–4). For this truth, Yahweh called him at the creation to be the light of the world (Is 42:5–6). It is not a teaching that is understood by any man, one shouted in the streets. Nor is it a judgment that can be established by violent warfare; for there a bruised reed is broken (Is 42:3). To express the peacefulness of the Torah judgment that Israel brings to enlighten the world, Isaiah draws on the classic trope of royal ideology in a brief rendition of the song for a poor man. As in Jeremiah, the peace that victory brings gives people their breath to breathe (Is 42:5), "opening the eyes of the blind; rescuing prisoners from prison and from the dungeon of darkness" (Is 42:7).[21] The metaphorical circle of Israel as a bruised but unbroken reed is closed in the last of the songs as Isaiah raises the image of the exile-evoking, reed-pierced hands of a prisoner (Is 53:5).

The integration of Isaiah's servant songs with the remnant theology of his Hezekiah story ties the metaphors of creation and wisdom of the child in both Isaiah and Psalm 8. Israel as Yahweh's servant is set in contrast to the old Israel's "men without understanding" (Is 6:9). In identifying the suffering servant with Yahweh's children and evoking Israel's remnant, Isaiah brings together the same cluster of motifs we find in Psalm 8: "You ask me about my children, and you question me on the works of my hands" (Is 45:11). It links together—in reiterating identity—a messianic king with the "son of man, whom Yahweh cares for" (Ps 8:5), "rousing him in justice, leveling all roads and rebuilding my city" (Is 45:13). This stands parallel to the declaration in the previous song that "I will march before you and level the hills" (Is 45:2), and it dehistoricizes the reference to the Persian king Cyrus with a cryptic pun. "Thus says Yahweh to his messiah, to Cyrus, whose right hand I have grasped" (*hezaqti*: Is 45:1) identifies the conquering messiah, whose right hand Yahweh holds (Ps 16:8, 110:5; cf. Gen 48:13) with Hezekiah (*hizqiyahu*), the hero of Isaiah's central story (Is 36–39).[22]

In the great reversals of Isaiah's new Jerusalem, there will be no screams and tears as both graybeards and infants live out full lives (Is 65:19–20). Isaiah's Hosea-like Yahweh will never call Jerusalem "forsaken" nor her land "desert." Jerusalem's name will be "my delight." Her land will be called "the betrothed" (Is 62:4; cf. Hos 1–3). In such a wonderful and utopian world, Yahweh has the primary role of the Marduk child of Psalm 8:3. It is his mouth that is the mouth of Enosh, "issuing righteousness, a word invincible" (Is 45:22). In Isaiah's world of God's kingdom, it is only through Yahweh that one finds righteousness and strength and it is only in Yahweh that all the world's children are saved

(Is 45:22–24). At the very end of his book, Isaiah turns from his normal world of myth and legend and addresses his audience directly (Is 66:5–14). He speaks, like Matthew and Luke, of the beatitudes he has loaned them, and he speaks to those who are concerned about the word and are hated by their brothers. He speaks to those who are scorned because of Yahweh's name and mockingly challenged. In a few deft lines Isaiah speaks to these few who understand and discloses his riddles to them as he takes for himself the role of Yahweh's suffering servant (Is 66:5; cf. Lk 6:22–23; Mt 5:11). Jerusalem's rebirth when Zion goes into labor will be even easier than the births in the stories the midwives once told to Pharaoh, when he tried to murder Israel's babies in the Nile:

> Before she was in labor, she gave birth; before her pain came upon her, she was delivered of a son. Who has heard such a thing? Who has seen such things? Shall a land be born in one day? Shall a nation be brought forth in one moment? For as soon as Zion was in labor, she brought forth her sons. Shall I bring to the birth and not bring them forth? says Yahweh. Shall I who gives birth, shut the womb? says your God. (Is 66:7–9; cf. Ex 1:19)

The Child as Epitome of Humility and Piety

The discourse related to the sayings about the kingdom and children is subordinate to the dominant theme of humility. The metaphors Jesus uses to answer his disciples' question about the greatest in the kingdom of heaven demonstrates this (Mt 18:1–11). Matthew has Jesus call a little child to use in a living parable:

> If you do not change and be as a child, you will not come at all into the kingdom of heaven. The one who humbles himself, being as this little child, is the greatest in the kingdom of heaven. (Mt 18:3–4)

In the world of the Bible—where the greatest in heaven is and can only be God— the disciples' question is not very interesting or challenging. However, it allows our rabbi-inspired figure to give a display of rhetoric and to pen a more complicated discourse on humility and theology. In Jesus' answer, the classic role of the child as model of humility is expanded beyond the disciples' dunce-like question. It invites reflection on the divine. The obvious theological dogma, "God is great!" is left unsaid because the child with his humility has, nevertheless, a logical claim on being the greatest in the kingdom of heaven, where this world finds its reversal. Not the least gain is the association of humility with the divine, a challenging, though hardly unknown possibility in the greater tradition.

Children, humility and the image of God are brought together in an early Samaritan tale about a visit by Alexander the Great to Shechem. The great king demands that the Samaritans make an image of him and place it on top of Gerizim, the holy mountain. It must be done before Alexander returns from Egypt. The blasphemy demanded is unthinkable to the Samaritans—although Alexander's power over life and death was unsurpassed in their world. They fasted and prayed, hoping to survive their ordeal of choosing between God and Caesar. Alexander returned but found no monument or image of himself on the mountain. He angrily asked the high priest and the Samaritan leaders why they had disobeyed him. The high priest explained that unlike other nations, who make images and monuments incapable of either speaking or moving, the Samaritans made images of Alexander, which had a mind and could speak. The high priest assembled all parents of children born since Alexander's previous visit and told them to call their children. As soon as the children came, their parents called out: "Alexander!" Every child responded. The king, of course, was delighted and all lived happily ever after. This story's delightful reiteration of the "image of God" in Genesis subtly prepares the story's winning closure with all of God's images assembled—Alexander included—worshiping the one true God on Mount Gerizim.[23]

A similar rhetoric governs Matthew's presentation of the child in the image of divine humility and therefore the greatest in heaven. Matthew grows expansive and presents other parables on the same theme. Softly ironic, he exploits the childishly absurd disciples vying for God's place in heaven. In one way or another, they need to be like children if they wish to be great. All are interpretive illustrations of the creation story's metaphor of humanity created in the image of God. They often speak of "the kingdom" and frequently exploit apocalyptic metaphors, but they hardly imply historical expectations. The theme of judgment with its curse or blessing always refers to the transcendent and unapproachable. The language is mythological and is intended to instruct and enlighten. It projects the religious myth of ancient theater. Ever present is the chorus, providing the text with an interpretive matrix, chanting, with Isaiah, one or other song of Yahweh's servant, Jacob:

> Yahweh has given to me the tongue of those who are taught, that I might know how to sustain with a word him that is weary. Morning by morning, he wakens, he wakens my ear to hear as those taught. Yahweh has opened my ear and I was not rebellious; I did not turn back. (Is 50:4–5)

I am Yahweh; I have called you in righteousness; I have taken you by the hand and kept you; I have given you as a covenant to the people, a light to the nations, to open the eyes that are blind, to bring out the prisoners from the dungeon, from the prison those who sit in darkness. (Is 42:6–7)

It is a divine mercy and compassion that the text seeks, a model to imitate: to walk in the path of divine goodness, to imitate the God in whose image they are created. Matthew's first two parables hold the child as measure for one's place within the kingdom: for good or evil.

One who so accepts a child in my name, accepts me. However, one who brings one of these little ones to fall, would be far better off if a millstone were hung around his neck and he were drowned in the deep sea. (Mt 18:5–6)

Luke's variant of this proverb has the millstone, but it does not have the parallel verse on bringing the "little ones" to fall (Lk 7:1–2). Mark has Jesus ask his disciples what they "had discussed on the way" (Mk 9:33–37). They recount the central elements of Matthew's and Luke's tales about competing to be the greatest. Jesus, however, destroys the debate by springing the logical trap of their naïveté and reverses the competitiveness implicit in the debate forms of the story: "The first will be last." He takes a child in his arms as model and principle for imitation. Luke's and Matthew's versions are implicit in Mark's explanation of the logic of the *imitatio*. If one receives the child, one receives Jesus; and if one receives Jesus, one receives God (Mk 9:37). For Mark, the logic of imitation lies in the ancient role of the king as the image and representative of the divine.

While Mark links his small scene of instruction to his disciples in a chain of identifications, his example of a man who drives demons out is a close variant of Matthew's children shouting "Hosanna" at the temple. The man is not to be silenced (Mk 9:38–41; Mt 21:5). The parallelism supports the progression of Mark's themes. The demon hunter is an illustration of the child to be accepted. Similarly, Luke's and Mark's argument that the way one treats a child will be accounted as a treatment of Jesus, shows up in quite different forms in Matthew. The first time, it appears in a discourse between Jesus and the disciples (Mt 18:1–5). It also appears in a dialogue between Jesus and the mother of two of the disciples (Mt 20:20–28). Mark offers a conversation of Jesus with the disciples (Mk 9:33–37) and then reuses it in a story, which presents a double use of the theme. In the first, Jesus is questioned by the two disciples whose mother had spoken for them in Matthew (Mk 10:35–40). This is then used to create a tale of a jealous quarrel between these two and "the ten," allowing Mark to present an allegory of the twelve as the twelve sons of Jacob, representing all of Israel (Mk 10:41–45). Luke offers at least six significant variations on this theme. The first uses the motif of the disciples' quarrel to create a simple parable on "purity of heart" (Lk 9:46–48). Luke also has Jesus set the theme in a parable of a wedding feast in the second of three banquet stories. This too is a double story. The first part echoes the debate over what rank the disciples might be given in the kingdom. It reiterates advice in the book of Proverbs (Prv 25:6–7) to choose the lesser place of honor at a banquet (Lk 14:7–11) to avoid the humiliation of being asked to take a lesser seat, should one who is greater come. It also leaves the hope and honor of being asked to move to a higher place. Luke closes this anecdotal parable by citing the song of Hanna's allusion to the Job story, in order to mark the saving reversals of God's kingdom:

> (Yahweh) brings down and he exalts; he raises up the poor from the dust and lifts the needy from the ash heap to make them sit with princes and inherit a seat of honor. (1 Sam 2:7b–8b; cf. Lk 14:11)

Luke's second parable presents the theme of humility in the context of the kingdom and its reversals. Jesus advises his host to forget inviting friends and brothers, relatives and rich neighbors. They would invite him in return. With an elegant linguistic transference, Luke has Jesus advise inviting the poor and the crippled, the lame and the blind (Lk 14:12–14), all signs of the kingdom. Luke stays with the practical wisdom of Proverbs by having Jesus point out that though such guests have nothing to offer their host in return, he will be blessed with the resurrection of the righteous. The wish to be blessed is supported by Proverbs—where Luke took his inspiration—offering an epitome of the Torah: "He who is kind to the poor lends to Yahweh and he will repay him for his action" (Prv 19:17; cf. Dt 14:28–29).

Luke again takes up the question of who should be the greatest in the Last Supper scene. An anecdotal parable contrasts pride and humility. Jesus compares a king's power among the gentiles with the kingdom of God's reversal that the greatest among the disciples be as *the youngest*. This obviously echoes the patriarchal stories of Genesis, with their threefold variation on the inheritance of the younger brother: Isaac (Gen 21:11–12), Jacob (Gen 27) and Ephraim (Gen 48:17). Each reversal echoes God's will but not the father's. The Cinderella motif of David's choice as messiah, though the youngest with seven brothers (1 Sam 16:10–11), presents a variation that has roots in ancient Near Eastern stories about the divine choice of its kings (see below, Chapter 5). The pedagogical function of Luke's chain of parables is made explicit in the Last Supper story's closure. As Jesus, their leader, serves them, so must the leader in the kingdom be as one who serves (Lk 22:24–27). Luke's parables of humility remain within an interpretive context of messianic judgment, the kingdom and the new Israel. They draw on an imitative logic of succession:

> You are those who have continued with me in my trials and I assign to you a kingdom, as my father assigned to me, that you may eat and drink at my table in my kingdom and sit on thrones judging the twelve tribes of Israel. (Lk 22:28–30)

Luke offers a similar scene in the crucifixion story that again evokes a scene of judgment. Not the disciples but two criminals crucified with Jesus quarrel over their place in the kingdom (Lk 23:39–43). One plays the scorner: "Are you not the messiah? Save us and yourself." The other humbly asks to be remembered in the judgment. The role of scorner, played by one thief with his question of whether Jesus is the messiah, is the third reiteration of the scorner in Luke's crucifixion story. The first is played by the scoffing rulers who chant like a mob: "He saved others, let him save himself, if he is God's messiah, the chosen one" (Lk 23:35). The soldiers similarly mock Jesus: "If you are the king of the Jews, save yourself" (Lk 23:36–37). The mocking thief and his humble mate are part of this larger story. They bring the messiah and chosen one, the king of the Jews, into his kingdom. They illustrate not a saying but an entire discourse on pride and humility. Scorn's debate with humility creates a story of recognition whose accumulating weight is carried by the good thief's witness.

A unique illustration of piety in the Gospel of John displays the technique of using story as a pedagogical tool. Setting his story in the Last Supper narrative, John draws on a parallel pair of metaphors. The one who sits at the table is contrasted to the one who serves, creating a mirror reflection of master and disciple (Jn 13:3–20). Jesus' story becomes parable as he not only talks about but plays the role of the servant. As master, he washes his disciples' feet in a scene seeking imitation:

> You call me teacher and lord; and you are right for so I am. If I, then, your lord and teacher, have washed your feet, you also ought to wash one another's feet. For I have given you an example, that you also should do as I have done to you. Truly, truly, I say to you, a servant is not greater than his master; nor is he who is sent greater than he who has sent him. . . . Truly, truly, I say to you, he who receives anyone whom I send receives me; and he who receives me, receives him who sent me. (Jn 13:13–20)

In all, the synoptic gospels offer more than a dozen variations of stories, parables and proverbs on the theme of pride and humility. We could add further
minor variations on this theme, which could arguably be understood as independent elements in the context of the larger tradition. They are used to build
expanding commentary on the kingdom and the reversal of values, which belongs to it. Luke, for example, collects sayings on pride and humility within
three tales, condemning the behavior of the Pharisees, the lawyers and the Pharisees, and the scribes, respectively. The first two are given a debate form, while
the third comes in a cluster of sayings related to the themes of the kingdom. In
the first debate, he criticizes the Pharisees for hypocrisy. Recognition in the mar-
ketplace is paralleled with seeking higher places in the synagogue. This obvious
variation on the standard pride and humility proverb barely prepares the reader
for the rhetorically balanced but bitingly ironic commentary, likening the pos-
sessors of such pride in the kingdom of God to graves that men walk over without noticing:

Woe to you Pharisees! For you love the best seat in the synagogues and salutations in the marketplaces. Woe to you! For you are like graves which are not
seen, and men walk over them without knowing it. (Lk 11:43–44)

The second debate with the lawyers and Pharisees offers the parable, already
discussed, about places of honor at the banquet that Luke draws from Proverbs
(Lk 14:7–14). Those invited to the banquet in the kingdom are "the poor and
the crippled, the lame and the blind." Luke's final cluster of pride and humility
sayings is not set in a debate but is given as a warning against those who oppose
the virtues of the kingdom. Luke adds to these three pride-and-humility scenes
two others about the love of long clothes and prayers:

Beware of the scribes, who like to go about in long robes and love salutations
in the marketplaces and the best seats in the synagogues and the places of
honor at feasts, who devour widows' houses and for a pretense make long
prayers. They will receive the greater condemnation. (Lk 20:46–47)

The accusation of "devouring the houses of widows" breaks the rhetorical coherence of this cluster of sayings and draws it into the kingdom discourse.
Matthew places these phrases in a much larger group of sayings on the kingdom
and the judgment it brings, in the process of building his great diatribe against
the scribes and Pharisees (Mt 23, esp. 6, 14).

A substantial portion of Matthew's gospel collects and combines proverbs in meaningful clusters. One such discourse is presented as part of a series of Torah illustrations set appropriately within Matthew's Sermon on the Mount (Mt 5:43–48). Jesus plays Moses' role as teacher as Matthew offers his reader the largest collection of proverbs in the New Testament. They call forth imitation and support the admonition to be "perfect as the heavenly father is perfect" (Mt 5:48 = Lev 11:44). This sermon's criticism of loving those who love you parallels Luke's critique of inviting friends and relatives to the feast. Matthew uses the same method as Luke. As in the diatribe against the scribes and Pharisees, he links a number of sayings and collections of sayings thematically, thereby creating a narrative scene within his life of Jesus by the sheer weight of his material.[24] This technique is fundamental to the Psalter, plays a dominant role in the creation of the debates and figures of Job and his friends and structures the oracles in Isaiah.

An important aspect of the theme of the children in Matthew ties the identification between Jesus and his disciples to the union of the pious with God. The critical passage stands in a long discourse about calling the disciples, which consists of smaller, nearly self-sufficient short segments linked together around the motifs of disciples and following Jesus. One segment seems obviously inspired by the story of Elijah calling Elisha to follow him and become Yahweh's avenging messiah (1 Kgs 19:15–21). Matthew's allusion to the holy war in the Elijah–Elisha story is so strong as to make that story part of his context. Jesus' dislocated response to the disciples' implied thoughts of peace betray Matthew's reader's response to Elisha's request to be allowed to kiss his father and mother farewell before following Elijah:

> Elijah passed by him [Elisha] and cast his mantle over him. He left his oxen and ran after Elijah, saying: "Let me kiss my father and my mother and then I will follow you." (1 Kgs 19:19–20)

> Do you think I have come to bring peace on earth; I have not come to bring peace, but a sword. I have come to set a man against his father and a daughter against her mother and a daughter-in-law against her mother-in-law. A man's enemies will be those of his own family. He who loves father and mother because of me is not worthy of me and he who does not take his cross and follow me is not worthy of me. He who finds his life will lose it, and he who loses his life for my sake will find it. He who receives you receives me and he who receives me receives him who sent me. He who receives a prophet because he

is a prophet will receive a prophet's reward. He who receives a righteous man because he is a righteous man will receive a righteous man's reward. Whoever gives to one of these little ones even a cup of cold water because he is a disciple, truly I say to you he will not lose his reward. (Mt 10:32–42)

The immediate context of this segment of Jesus' talk evokes the rhetoric of apocalyptic judgment, distinguishing those the Father accepts and those he rejects. Matthew also links his chain of imitation and identification with the crucifixion narrative and closes the entire discussion of discipleship with the kingdom and children trope. This is an illustration and a commentary on Yahweh's promise to Abraham:

I will bless those who bless you and him who curses you, I will curse; and by you *all the families of the earth will bless themselves.* (Gen 12:3)

Matthew reads Genesis as parable and asks to be read as parable in return. His logic is a chain of imitation. The chain of identity and role transference is his instruction in piety. The identification of the children with the disciples is particularly important as it reflects the same pattern of transference and association one commonly meets in the Psalter, linking the themes of David and the messiah with the pious who sing the songs (see below, Chapter 10).

Matthew's parable on the judgment of the nations and the acceptance of the righteous into the kingdom of heaven links the trope of kingdom and children once again with the motif of disciples vying for right understanding (Mt 25:31–46). A mythic scene is evoked, with the "son of man" taking his seat on the throne of glory as judge of the world. Matthew draws on a motif from the scene of the priest Ezra's reading the law in Nehemiah. Ezra stands on a platform in the square with six of the elders on his right hand and six to the left and brings the Torah's judgment on the new Jerusalem (Neh 8:4). In the revision of Matthew's parable, the judge blesses the nations on his right and condemns those on his left, while using Ezekiel's distinction of sheep and goats (Ez 34:17). He recreates for his audience the same discourse on humility Isaiah gave in his version of Ezekiel's parable of the sheep and goats. As they had done to the least of their fellows in each of their lives, so had they treated the king. They had given him food to eat when he was hungry, drink when he was thirsty. They welcomed him when he was a stranger, clothed him when he was naked and visited him when he was sick or in prison. In his reiteration, Matthew simplifies the scene considerably, but he hardly goes beyond Ezekiel or Isaiah. Isaiah has Yahweh complain that his people seek him daily and delight to know his ways as if they were righteous and liked to be near their God:

> "Why have we fasted and you did not see it? Why have we humbled ourselves and you did not know it?" Behold in the day of your fast, you seek your own pleasure, and oppress all your workers. You fast only to quarrel and to fight. . . . Is such a fast as I choose a day for a man to humble himself? . . . Is not this the fasting that I choose: to untie the bonds of evil, to undo the bands of the yoke, to let the oppressed go free and to break every yoke? Is it not to share your bread with the hungry and bring the homeless poor into your house? When you see the naked, cover him and do not hide yourself from your own flesh. Then will your light break forth like the morning and your health will spring forth speedily. Your righteousness will go before you and the Glory of Yahweh will be your rearguard. Then you will call and Yahweh will answer; you will cry and he will say, "Here I am." (Is 58:3–9)

Isaiah's instruction to the Israelites that they can fulfill their wish to be near God in accordance to how they treat the oppressed is the instruction that Matthew puts in parable. Isaiah's parallelism between the way one treats others—whether epitomized as the oppressed, the stranger or the enemy—and one's relationship to God takes up the broad biblical discussion about the center of the Torah as love of neighbor (Lev 19:18; cf. Mk 12:31; cf. Lk 10:25–37).

The gospels generate chains of narratives and sayings in the process of composition. The author of Matthew's gospel, fulfilling his implicit role as teacher of *midrash*, is actively and systematically involved in rewriting earlier biblical tradition. This goal undermines the claim of a collection of oral sayings, such as Q, redundantly standing between the gospels and their biblical references. The common intellectual roots of the motifs of the child and the kingdom cannot be cut. One cannot isolate the figure of an apocalyptic prophet from the figures of miracle worker or healer, let alone teacher of Torah. In separating the sayings from their contexts in the gospels, Crossan and the Jesus Seminar have lost both. Moreover, these sayings hardly bear a meaning that can be exclusively tied to the early first century, potentially giving evidence of a historical Jesus. The sayings bear meaning within an intellectual tradition of written parable and discourse. This is the context in which they were written and in which they still can be read. The gospels have not been created by combining Mark's apocalyptically oriented version of events in Jesus' life with collections of oral sayings from a teacher. The narratives and their sayings are built in a common tradition of stories and sayings.

The Universal Quality of Children

In Matthew's story, the figure of the high priests and scribes plays a dramatically negative role. I doubt that Matthew tries to offer us a picture of scribes and the high priest of his own time and even less of any time in which he might think of placing Jesus. Matthew presents them in a role determined by the rhetoric of debate. They are Socrates' partners in discussion: those who do not understand. They are Isaiah's generation of blind and deaf. They are Malachi's priests who neither honor nor fear God (Mal 1:6). When we hear them objecting to the children calling Jesus son of David and savior, we should remember that their role is to misunderstand. They are shown with a righteous anger and the hubris of authority, for they play the haughty and proud that the humble may be seen all the more clearly. Matthew's debate between Jesus and the high priests does not center on conflicts a historical Jesus once may or may not have had with real Jewish leaders. Nor is their objection centered in Jesus' identity. It is rather the debate that is at issue: an interpretation of Jerusalem and the temple. Jerusalem is not to be the secure city that soldiers create but Isaiah's ideal city of strength. Isaiah's righteous nation of victorious poor and needy overturns all the secure of this world. The children recognize this.

Isaiah's ironic metaphor of the poor and needy trampling the secure of this world deals in a literary way with both political philosophy and a philosopher's hope for universal justice. It joins two metaphors. The first presents a utopian reversal of fortune, a sign of God's presence in this world, royal ideology's ultimate goal. This is typically illustrated in biblical literature with one or other rendition of the poor man's song, which I take up in the next chapter. The second metaphor also draws from the tradition of royal ideology and presents the role of the messiah as conqueror of nations in revolt against their divine patron, which I will take up in Chapters 5-6. In both Isaiah and Matthew, the kingdom is identified with the creation of a renewed Jerusalem. Both singer and hearer of the song are encouraged to imitate the role of the children. Identifying with it, they reverse their helplessness with strength. The role demands humility, to be like the poor and needy of Isaiah's strong city and to think of themselves as kings, with a new world under their feet:

> In that day, this song will be sung in the land of Judah. "We have a strong city; he sets up salvation as walls and bulwarks. Open the gates that the righteous nation which keeps faith may enter in. You keep him in perfect peace, whose mind is fixed on you, because he trusts in you . . ." (Is 26:1–3)

The tradition is wide-ranging. On the surface, it is a debate, presenting a critique of proud foolishness, illustrated by the human wisdom of the high priests and scribes, imitating Malachi's priests. Such wisdom is of course ignorance. The emphasis in Psalm 8 on the praise of Yahweh's name (Ps 8:2, 10) identifies it with the strength that comes from a child's mouth. It is the answer that stills the uproar of creation's enemies. With the proclamation of Yahweh's name, his rule on earth is inaugurated (Ps 8:3, 7). This is the kingdom of which the gospels speak.

In both Matthew and Luke, rhetorical techniques of reiteration, drawing on sayings, quotations, explicit and implicit references and allusions, involve a discourse that not only continues throughout the course of their gospels but also supports the creation of their narratives. In Luke's song of Mary (Lk 1:46–56), for example, the unborn child Jesus is given the same role other children have in the kingdom sayings. In singing, "he has toppled the mighty from their thrones; he has raised up the poor" (Lk 1:52), pregnant Mary echoes a verse from the song of Hannah, which had been used to set the great themes of the Saul and David story on their way (1 Sm 2:1–9). Like Mary, Hannah was visited by the spirit and she too sang her happy song's similar evocation of the kingdom's reversals: "Yahweh makes poor and he makes rich; he raises up and he brings down" (1 Sm 2:7). Luke's reuse of Hannah's song is not merely borrowed. It is adapted and fitted to its new context in the stories of John and Jesus. It illustrates and defines their heroic births, much as Hannah's song and Samuel's heroic birth functioned within the story of 1 Samuel. The reversal of this world's power and wealth are central elements in a clearly definable song type and theme. It can be found in every major ancient Near Eastern wisdom tradition and in nearly every ancient text tradition that gives voice to the ideology of kings and kingship. As it has been transmitted and reinterpreted within biblical tradition, this trope has played a decisive role in the development of the Jesus story. It goes far in defining his character, personality and mission.

CHAPTER 4

⁓⊗⁓

The Song for a Poor Man

POLITICAL PHILOSOPHY,
ETHICS AND ROYAL IDEOLOGY

The sayings identified by Mack and Crossan are characterized by very specific, reflective cadences. And it is true that the sources of the sayings are early. However, the particular presentation in the gospel stories is not the first time this or that message was given. The most telling objection to using such sayings for reconstructing a historical Jesus is that these sayings can be shown to have had their origins too early—far earlier than any possible historical Jesus. At the same time, there is no question but that they are to be associated with the figure of the great teacher. The sayings most favored by Crossan and Mack have a two-thousand-year history before the all too hypothetical oral tradition of Q and the tendentiously dated Gospel of Thomas. They go back at least to the Egyptian Sixth Dynasty in the third millennium BCE. There were many sages in the ancient world who shared the voice of the Jesus we find in the gospels and, while there may have been a cynic philosopher among them, the broad sweep of the tradition was hardly defined by that particular school. Whether the voice belongs to the figures of an Egyptian philosopher such as Amenemopet, a king of Israel like Solomon or the great prophet Moses, the specific figure who speaks such sayings within this remarkably coherent tradition is determined by the function of a particular text. Ancient literature swarms with the figures of wisdom: sages, prophets, priests and kings, each with their collected sayings reiterating one another. Separating the sayings of Jesus from the gospels, as the Jesus Seminar does, makes it impossible to identify them as sayings of Jesus, for their contexts in the gospel is their only claim to being the sayings of Jesus.

The Jesus of the gospels, who uses the sayings in his teaching, is well recognized as a mythic figure of theology, particularly in such roles as apocalyptic judge, son of God and messiah. This should not be ignored when we try to understand the sayings as belonging to Jesus. He is not a cynic philosopher, a Galilean peasant or even a charismatic preacher in the only texts we know him. He is the servant of God and the good shepherd. With John the Baptist, he is a refraction of Elijah. His presence announces the kingdom of God. This mythic figure of the gospels, however unhistorical, was not created by Mark or Matthew as was thought a century ago. Nor does such a figure imply a Christian perspective. Not just the sayings, but also the figures of Jesus we find in the gospels can be found prominently in ancient literature far earlier than the gospels. The saving figure of the universal king, victor over evil, transcendent judge, son of God, good shepherd and representative of the people is as old as the sayings given to him to speak. The myth of the messiah the gospels present has its roots in Egyptian and Babylonian royal ideology since the Bronze Age, from which we first find ancient kings announcing their utopian kingdoms in very gospel-like phrases. The miracle stories of the gospels illustrate the reversal of destiny of the poor or oppressed as signs of the kingdom. The sayings of Jesus, giving Jesus his personal generosity and tragic intensity, are rooted in a long tradition of literature centered on themes of the good king, a mediator between the divine and human realms of the ancient world. He is savior and shepherd of his people. He destroys evil; he creates good; and his reign is forever.

Crossan's wise peasant teacher and Schweitzer's apocalyptic prophet, or liberal theology's figure of Jesus as healer and miracle worker, are not different figures that can be separated from one another. Wisdom sayings, parables and miracles stories all illustrate the kingdom of God for the reader, as do also the more obvious themes evoking a new world or the day of judgment. Wisdom, prophecy and destiny reversing judgment cannot be separated as Mack would have them separated.[1] They are three aspects of the same system of symbols, defining the intellectual world implied in our narratives. Just as the miracle stories drew on the traditions of the tales of the prophets Elijah and Elisha, they also implied the theme of judgment. Similarly, what Crossan and Mack considered a philosophical tradition actually has its roots in a tradition of "signs of the kingdom"— marks of divine presence—expressed in reversals of fortune for the poor and the weak. That is, the cynic-like wandering philosopher of Jesus' sermons and the John-like prophet coming from the desert, calling the world to repentance, are but variant illustrations of a single cluster of literary themes.

Crossan and Mack—and with them the Jesus Seminar—have set these related themes in opposition to one another in an effort to present the figure of the philosopher as belonging to the earliest of Jesus' sayings. Among the sayings consistently viewed as reflecting an authentic saying of Jesus, belonging to a very early strata of Q, is the answer Jesus gives to John's disciples we discussed in the last chapter (Mack's QS 16: Mt 11:4–6; Lk 7:18–23). This is their paradigm text for the historical Jesus as cynic philosopher and teacher concerned with the poor:

> Go and tell John what you hear and see: the blind recover their sight, the lame walk, lepers are cleansed, the deaf hear, the dead are raised and the poor are given good news.[2]

This saying appears in several variations, though not always in texts of Q. One variant of this saying, for example, is found in Luke, where Jesus reads in the synagogue from the book of Isaiah:

> The spirit of the Lord is upon me, because he has anointed me to preach good news to the poor. He has sent me to proclaim release to the captives and recovering of sight to the blind, to set at liberty those who are oppressed, to proclaim the acceptable year of the Lord. (Lk 4:18–19)

The most likely source for this passage in Isaiah, however, announces a reversal of fortune for the oppressed in the kingdom in a context of reversing judgment:

> The spirit of the divine Yahweh is upon me. Yahweh has anointed me to bring good news to the poor; he has sent me to bind the brokenhearted, to proclaim freedom to prisoners, the opening of the prisons to those who are in chains. To proclaim Yahweh's year of grace and the day of vengeance of our God: to comfort all who mourn; to grant to those who mourn in Zion—to give them a garland instead of ashes, the oil of gladness instead of mourning, the mantle of praise instead of a faint spirit that they might be called oaks of righteousness, plantings of Yahweh that he might be glorified. They will build up the ancient ruins; they will raise up the former devastation; they will repair the ruined cities and the devastation of many generations. (Is 61:1–3)

The saying represented by Mack's QS 16 is not only found both in and outside of Q's oral tradition. It is far more deeply rooted in Jewish tradition than in cynic or Greek philosophy. Variations are found, as we will see, in more than two dozen passages of Isaiah. In an expansive format, it is recognizable in the eightfold blessings of the kingdom in Matthew's sermon on the mount, as well as in Luke's variation of these Beatitudes he sets in the plain, presenting reversals of destiny in the form of four blessings and four curses:

> Blessed are the poor in spirit; for theirs is the kingdom of heaven. Blessed are they who mourn; for they will be comforted. Blessed are the humble; for they will inherit the earth. Blessed are they who hunger and thirst for righteousness; for they will be satisfied. Blessed are the merciful; for they will obtain mercy. Blessed are the pure in heart; for they will see God. Blessed are the peace makers; for they will be called "sons of God." Blessed are they who are persecuted for righteousness' sake; for theirs is the kingdom of heaven. Blessed are you when men revile you and persecute you and utter all kinds of evil against you falsely on my account. Rejoice and be glad, for your reward is great in heaven; for so men persecuted the prophets before you. (Mt 5:3–12)

> Blessed are you poor, for yours is the kingdom of God. Blessed are you that hunger now, for you will be satisfied. Blessed are you who weep now, for you will laugh. Blessed are you when men hate you, and when they exclude you and revile you and cast out your name as evil on account of the son of man. Rejoice in that day and leap for joy, for behold your reward is great in heaven; for so their fathers did to the prophets. Woe to you who are rich; for you have received your consolation. Woe to you who are full now, for you will hunger. Woe to you that laugh now, for you will mourn and weep. Woe to you when all men speak well of you, for so their fathers did to the false prophets. (Lk 6:20–26)

This saying as an original saying of Jesus (QS 8 in Mack) and understood as certainly authentic by the Jesus Seminar, has been separated from any Isaiah-like apocalyptic context of judgment.[3] This is most apparent in regard to Luke's version, as only the four blessings (Lk 6:20–23a) are included as authentic, while the four curses (Lk 6:23b–26)—with their clear association with judgment sayings—are not thought to have the same authenticity, but are attributed to Luke. That this conclusion disrupts a classic form of wisdom poetry is ignored.

The similarities of the two texts of QS 8, the sermon on the mount and QS 16, the signs of the kingdom, are not coincidental. Jesus' answer to John's disciples (QS 16), discussed in Chapter 3, reflects a literary trope I call the song for a poor man (see Appendix 1). Within the Hebrew Bible, it forms a subtheme of the theology of the way, whereby the path of the righteous is distinguished from the way of the ungodly. It is closely related to the theme of blessing and curses, which is central to biblical symbols of divine judgment. The "song" is used to epitomize the reversal of fortune, expressing the victory or peace of God's kingdom. In biblical texts these three major themes become structural pillars of an expansive theology centered in Yahweh as king. They are, however, clearly distinguished in the literature of the ancient Near East, with the rhetoric of life's "path" of the collections of wise sayings. Curses and blessings have long been recognized to have their roots in ancient Hittite treaties and in a variety of royal inscriptions from Hammurapi to Esarhaddon.[4] They find their most famous biblical illustration in Moses' twelvefold curses and blessings of the covenant that are to be announced on Ebal and Gerizim when the tribes have entered the promised land (Dt 27:11–28:6, 8). The reversals of the poor man's song reflected in QS 8 and 16 are found in ancient Near Eastern texts from as early as the Sixth Dynasty and are used in the Bible primarily as a utopian epitome of the peace that comes when the world is placed under divine patronage. As variations of a clearly definable trope, they have an immediate bearing on the development of many of the sayings attributed to Jesus in the gospels. They are also fundamental to the production of other heroic figures in both the ancient Near East and the Bible.

The coherence and stability of this trope is long and substantial. In the song for a poor man, we have the ancient world's equivalent of Anderson's story "King John and the Bishop." Certainly one of the closest parallels to the Beatitudes comes from an Egyptian New Kingdom text dated to 1166 BCE, celebrating the accession of Ramses IV to the throne:

> O Happy Day! Heaven and earth are in joy. They who had fled have returned to their homes; they who were hidden live openly; they who were hungry are filled and happy; they who were thirsty are drunken; they who were naked are clothed in fine linen; they who were dirty are dressed in white; They who were in prison are set free; they who were chained rejoice; the troubled of the land have found peace. . . .
>
> The homes of the widows are open (again), so that they may let wanderers come in. Womenfolk rejoice and repeat their songs of jubilation . . . saying, "Male children are born (again) for good times, for he brings into being generation upon generation. You ruler, life, prosperity, health! You are for eternity!"[5]

This is not simply royal propaganda, exaggerating the political goals of Ramses' coming government. This song of the royal court, celebrating the justice that the inauguration brings by reversing the suffering of the poor man of Egypt, announces the good news of a savior ascending the throne of his kingdom. It illustrates a vision of utopia, which reflects the transcendent truth of his kingdom. With much of its function intact, it finds an echo throughout ancient literature. It captures the essence of the utopian vision of a world without war. Such royal propaganda implies and expresses a critical political philosophy in which justice and compassion take dominating roles. It is reiterated in the writings of the sages, in collections of law, in songs and hymns, in laments and in personal and individual prayers. In biblical literature, Hannah's song (1 Sm 2:4–9) sings these cadences to announce an end to Israel's suffering in the birth of her child, Samuel, who, like Ramses, is destined to be the savior of his people. The trope is also a constant of David's songs in the Psalter and it is Isaiah's most idyllic expression of the kingdom of God. A darker, contrasting shadow is found in the prophets' ubiquitous threats of a day of wrath and judgment against the proud and the rich, the men of power and violence.

In the New Testament, the song's proclamation of a happy day opens Mark's gospel and identifies his story as a living parable of the good news that defines the genre. It is reused within Luke's story of Jesus and John's births with considerable success in the songs of Mary and Zachariah. As in the story of Samuel's birth—and, for that matter, Marduk's in the Babylonian creation narrative ("born in the heart of Apsu: son of the sun god; indeed, sun of the gods")—the tale of a child's miraculous birth is given its classic function of inaugurating an eternal peace, which the saving acts of the hero, after he is grown and ready to take up the role he is divinely appointed to fulfill, bring into reality. Such expectations do not belong to a historical world—not even the Egypt of Ramses IV. They belong to a theological, ideal world, which meets everyman's needs. This song for a poor man is the centerpiece of the gospels' representation of Jesus' teaching and shapes the vision of their kingdom of God. In a sevenfold form, it opens the book of Isaiah and closes the book of Revelation (Is 1–12; Rev 21–22).

The Bible, whose earliest writings are in Hebrew and centered in Palestine, comes late to this idealistic and utopian tradition of justice. It interprets the mythology of the king from the perspective of one of the empire's subject peoples. Its goal goes beyond identifying Palestine's traditional deity, Yahweh, with the imperial and transcendent God of Heaven, projecting a universal justice. It also seeks to interpret Judaism's story of its past in terms of justice and judgment. Identifying with those who understand and seek to serve God with a pure heart, they submit themselves to the transformation of a world lost in ignorance into a lasting peace and happiness intended since the creation.

The worldview implicit in ancient Near Eastern and biblical texts is a view based on shared reflection. The Bible belongs to the ancient Near East in theme, in literary and mythic expression, in song and story—and historically. The Bible is not "against its environment" in either form or substance.[6] A common system of symbols is shared, which contrasts an ideal, divine transcendence and unity with transient humanity's fragmented experience. Such theology belongs to a world which—with profound pessimism—knew that men did not know the gods they wrote about.

Examples from Ancient Near Eastern Inscriptions

The accession hymn of Ramses IV (Appendix 1, no. 22) is remarkably lyrical and clearly expresses the social idealism that is the hallmark of this trope, as does a similar song written for the accession of Merneptah (no. 21). It announces the good news of the king coming into his kingdom, where, similarly, right conquers wrong and Egypt enters a time of peace and prosperity. As in other New Kingdom texts (nos. 19, 20), joy coming to the poor and oppressed expresses divine rule. In the Book of the Dead (no. 18) and in the sayings of Amenemopet (no. 23), the trope takes on a pedagogical function: instructing the reader and using religious motivation to support care and respect for the poor, the blind and the lame. An element of divine judgment enters the contrasting critique of the rich: "God prefers him who honors the poor to him who worships the wealthy." Giving bread to the hungry and caring for the thirsty and naked are supported as signs of a good and pious life (also no. 5).

Variations of the song for a poor man are found as early as the Sixth Dynasty in the middle of the third millennium BCE. Already at this early date, they help form a central template for autobiographical tales. They represent the good king or hero as role model for his people. Descriptions of feeding the hungry, clothing the naked (nos. 1, 2, 3, 6, 7) are already common, for example, "I gave water to the thirsty; I showed the way to him who strayed; I rescued him who had been robbed" (no. 7). This vision of the just life is also apparent in hymns and prayers that see generosity as a divine attribute. Care for the widow and orphan (no. 6), the humble and the distressed, are divine deeds (nos. 14, 15, 16). They are happy and blessed by the gods (no. 9). The texts reflect a recurrent theme that the gods take upon themselves the care of the poor, widows, fatherless and the imprisoned and ease or eliminate their suffering (no. 12). Amon-Re himself is described as "vizier of the poor." He judges the unjust with fire and saves the just (no. 15). He protects the humble and brings down the proud (nos. 16, 19, 20). The reversed fate of the rich and the poor marks divine intervention in the world (nos. 20, 21, 22). One does not put one's trust in the strong of this world (no. 17).

What is striking among these few early examples from Egyptian literature is that nearly the entire range of expression supporting this high ethical ideal is represented, with many of the same stereotypical patterns we find some thousand years later in biblical texts.

In the Semitic world of Mesopotamia and Syria, examples are found over a similar range of texts, defining justice. Themes of salvation and a world at peace, like themes of reversing the fate of the oppressed, are particularly strong among texts that celebrate kingship and military victory (nos. 27, 34, 35), but also in hymns and prayers to the gods as the true rulers of this world (nos. 30, 31). Principles of justice and right living are reflected in the wisdom sayings of philosophers (nos. 24, 26) as well as in addresses to the divine (nos. 28, 29).

With roots in royal propaganda, the song for a poor man supports a critical political philosophy in which justice and compassion are the primary evidence of divine rule, just government, prosperity and a state of peace. It is a frequent trope in the writings of philosophers; it is captured in collections of law; it is found in songs and laments and in personal and individual prayers. It finds its way onto victory steles and monumental inscriptions promoting the king and his reign. In these texts, a recurrent contrast between those who humbly seek guidance from the divine and those who look to the rich and powerful is striking (nos. 24, 39): "The son of a king is clad [in rags]; the son of the destitute and naked is dressed in [fine raiment]" (no. 24). It is for the gods, and kings who are servants of the divine, who feed the hungry and give drink to those who are thirsty; who care for the widow and the orphan, the weak and the prisoner (nos. 25, 28, 29, 30). These divine virtues are recognized as justice by the gods when they are performed by men (nos. 26, 27). The miraculous revival of the sick and sight given to the blind are a hallmark of divine presence: "At your command, O Ishtar, the blind man sees the light, the unhealthy one who sees your face, becomes healthy" (no. 31). Prayer to the gods to save those who suffer, including resurrection from the dead, forgiveness of sin and reconciliation are a fundamental part of this tradition and go far in defining concepts of salvation. "Where you look, one who is dead lives; one who is sick rises up" (no. 33; also nos. 31, 32, 36). This theme is used to present the king as reestablishing justice after a time of evil or suffering, often caused by the gods' anger (nos. 34, 35, 37, 38). Such transformation can be presented with metaphors of the king radically altering the earth. Mountains and valleys are reversed: "I cut through steep mountains, splitting rocks; opening passages, constructing a straight road for the transport of the cedars" (no. 35). In all such representations, the reversals of fortune mark the king's role as faithful servant of the gods. The primary purpose of such themes in ancient literature—with all their overtones of propaganda—is education. They set limits on human ambition. They civilize and make compassionate the violence that our authors found in the human heart.

EXAMPLES FROM THE HEBREW BIBLE

The text of the Hebrew Bible offers the richest and most comprehensive development of this tradition, as every section of the Bible has examples that could have been used. The examples from the ancient Near East are also paralleled in Greek, Roman and extrabiblical Jewish traditions, but are reflected here only through a few citations from the Dead Sea scrolls. There is no help for this, as a comprehensive presentation requires a study of its own.

In the Hebrew Bible's use of the song for a poor man, stereotypical representatives of the poor or outcast are often presented in set pairs; widows and orphans, the blind and the lame, the weak and oppressed are among the favorites shared with ancient Near Eastern texts. In the Bible's traditional literature, the direct court functions of political propaganda, dynastic promotion and celebration of military victory are absent. Instead, the use of this trope and its themes is almost always secondary, a function of education and piety. In this, the Bible's use of the trope continues the traits we find in wisdom literature and story. It transposes the functions of royal inscriptions into secondary forms. Given this important difference in function, the trope nevertheless maintains the central theological traits of the inscriptions. The reversals of salvation, changing the fate of both proud and humble, epitomize divine judgment, frequently in the absolute terms of an eternal peace. Such balance is not limited to grand apocalyptic visions but has many variations. In the reiteration of Ramses IV's announcement of his reign in Isaiah's announcement of the kingdom, the good news proclaims a year of grace, illustrated through reversals, each replacing a specific evil with a specific good:

> (Yahweh will) give a garland instead of ashes, the oil of gladness instead of mourning, the mantle of praise instead of a faint spirit that they might be called oaks of righteousness, plantings of Yahweh that he might be glorified. They will build up the ancient ruins; they will raise up the former devastation; they will repair the ruined cities and the devastation of many generations. (Is 61:2–3)

Nevertheless, even as such wonderful reversals of the fate of the oppressed create a rich imagery of salvation, Isaiah's "year of grace" is given by a Janus-faced

Yahweh who presents his dreadful face of terror on the "day of vengeance." Metaphors of salvation and blessing bear their implicit alternatives in messages of damnation and curse. The rhetoric is well captured in Jeremiah's great lament over Jerusalem: "Those who feasted on dainties perish in the streets. Those who were brought up in purple lie on ash heaps" (Lam 4:5). Hannah's song, which Luke rewrites in his birth stories of John and Jesus, includes a rich and excellent example of just such polarity:

> The bows of the mighty are broken, but the feeble gird on strength. Those who were full have hired themselves out for bread, but those who were hungry have ceased to hunger. The barren has born seven, but she who has many children is abandoned. Yahweh kills and brings to life; he brings down to She'ol and raises up (therefrom). He raises up the poor from the dust; he lifts the needy from the ash heap to make them sit with princes and inherit a seat of honor. For the pillars of the earth are Yahweh's. On them he has set the world. (1 Sm 2:4–8)

The tenfold balancing cadence of blessings and curses in this segment of Hannah's song is imposing. The mighty are balanced by the feeble, the full by the hungry, the barren by the mother of many, Yahweh killing is balanced by those he brings back to life and the poor and needy by princes at the banquet—the whole rounded off by a summary explanation of Yahweh's role at creation. It is just such balance which has structured Luke's sermon on the plain with four blessings and four curses (Lk 6:20–26).

The blessing of the poor, hungry, mournful and hated is contrasted to the curse of the rich, full, laughing and well spoken. The song holds its fourfold cadence as the fates of men are reversed and the whole summed up in a fourfold instruction, which replaces the hatred of the blessed with the command to love enemies, to do good for evil, to bless instead of curse and to pray on behalf of the abuser. The delicate reconciliation of opposites clearly marks Luke's variation as independent of Matthew's eightfold Beatitudes in his Sermon on the Mount (Mt 5:3–12). Harmonizing them in an impossible original (Mack's QS 8) ignores the complexity and depth of the tradition.

The logic of retribution reflects the ancient political structures of patronage. If Yahweh is acknowledged as God, his mercy and compassion follow in course. To those who are not his servants, however, all that remains is retribution. Even as Isaiah, in the closure of his book on the kingdom of God, gathers the nations to Zion in peace, that "all flesh might worship before me," the reciprocity of

Isaiah's metaphors—and the imperialism of their literary origins—force a relentless closure:

> Thus says the God Yahweh: Behold my servants will eat, but you will be hungry; behold my servants will drink, but you will be thirsty; behold my servants will rejoice, but you will be ashamed; behold my servants will sing with joy of heart, but you will cry with sorrow of heart and you will cry with anguish of spirit. (Is 65:13–14)

There is belonging and there is rejection; there is no middle way. It is the language of retribution that binds the rhetoric of the song for a poor man so tightly to the themes of judgment. Even when the issue is one of Torah illustration, strengthening Sabbath observance and love of the foreigner, the principle of doing to others as you would have them do to you is problematic. When it is captured under the darker shadows of metaphors of divine judgment, a need for compassion is immediate (Is 56:3–8; Is 58:6–11; cf. Lev 19:33–34; Dt 24:14–15, 17–22). Nowhere is this dark side of the Bible's understanding of salvation more striking than in Isaiah's last verse of his closing vision of a new earth and a new heaven, promising universal and lasting peace, while offering a "final solution" to those judged ungodly and connecting the tradition to the themes of holy war.

> As the new heavens and the new earth which I will make shall remain before me, says Yahweh, so shall your descendants and your name remain. From new moon to new moon, and from Sabbath to Sabbath, all flesh will come to worship before me says Yahweh. They will go forth and look at the dead bodies of the men that have rebelled against me; for their worm will not die; their fire will not be quenched and they will remain an abhorrence for all flesh. (Is 66:22–24)

The structure of a given example of the song for a poor man is useful for interpretation. Four- to twelvefold structures are common in ancient Near Eastern literature. The Babylonian theodicy, for example, structures its second tablet in a series of eight-line poems to present its suffering figure as an orphan.[7] Similarly, Psalm 119, the longest poem in the Bible, structures itself after the Hebrew alphabet, using its twenty-two letters to begin successively each of the eight verses of the poem's twenty-two stanzas. Such formalism is ubiquitous in ancient literature and is often used to steer commentary and create implicit riddle.

One variant of this formation balances positive signs and blessings with corresponding curses to illustrate the kingdom's victory over evil. Luke's efforts to sketch his story's bearing figure with the help of Isaiah, Elijah and Hannah, balancing citation with illustration, creates a reiterating chain whose brightest cluster is the presentation of his list of four blessings and four curses in Jesus' Sermon on the Plain. This expands with a fourfold instruction to love your enemy (Lk 6:20–36). The integrity of this text is without question, as it reiterates other efforts at building a figure on the basis of the song's profile. Among several of the biblical figures playing the same or a similar role, a striking parallel is found in the presentation of Job in the royal role of his life when God was with him:

> When the ear heard, it called me blessed and when the eye saw, it approved, because I delivered the poor who cried and the fatherless, who had none to help. The blessing of him who was about to die came over me and I caused the widow's heart to sing for joy. . . . I was eyes to the blind and feet to the lame. I was father to the poor and I searched out the cause of him whom I did not know. I broke the fangs of the evil one and made him drop the prey from his teeth. (Job 29:12–17)

Job offers an eightfold list of good deeds, echoing the song for a poor man (cf. Job 29:12; Is 6:9–10). The list is closed with a doubled negative deed, which interprets the list of good deeds in the proportions of myth as Job breaks the teeth of the great dragon. That such signs of the kingdom are truly blessed and take part in a divine justice is indicated by Psalm 146's parallel to Job, which presents Yahweh in the role of the good king, who—like Job—closes his song with his conquest over evil:

> [The God of Jacob], who executes justice for the oppressed, who gives food to the hungry. Yahweh sets prisoners free; Yahweh opens the eyes of the blind; Yahweh lifts up those who are bowed down [crippled?]. Yahweh loves the righteous; Yahweh watches over foreigners and upholds the widow and the fatherless, but the way of the wicked, he brings to ruin. (Ps 146:7–9)

In the beginning of the book of Job a similar eightfold role is given to Yahweh. A note of divine virtue attached to the care of the poor allows Job's own account of himself in chapter 29 to take on overtones of the miraculous and wonderful:

> As for me, I will seek God and to God will I commit my cause; who does great things unsearchable, marvelous, without number. He sends rain upon the

earth and water over the fields; He sets high those who are lowly; those who mourn are lifted to safety; he frustrates the devices of the crafty so their hands achieve no success; he takes the wise in their own cleverness and the schemes of the wily are brought to a quick end. They meet with darkness in the daytime and grope at noonday as in the night; but he saves the fatherless from their mouth and the needy from the strength of the mighty. The poor have hope and injustice shuts her mouth. (Job 5:8–16)

In the presentation of Yahweh as the just king, balanced themes of retribution are interpreted in the direction of reconciliation and atonement, rather than ruthless destruction. In this passage, injustice is described with metaphors of a beast of prey and the enemy warrior. The partially blind motif that Yahweh saves the "fatherless from their mouth" is explicitly mythical in the metaphor of another song, "I smashed the teeth of evil, ripped the prey from its mouth" (Job 29:17).

The poor and humble find protection and hope, while the proud are given correction through yet another eightfold song that follows:

Blessed is the man whom God reproves; therefore despise not the chastening of the Almighty. For he wounds, but he binds up; he strikes, but his hands heal; he will deliver you from six troubles; in seven, no evil will touch you. In famine, he will redeem you from death and in war from the power of the sword. You will be hid from the scourge of the tongue and will not fear destruction when it comes. In destruction and famine you will laugh and not fear the beasts of the earth. (Job 5:17–22)

This more positive pattern of discourse on the theme of judgment as it is developed in Job supports Matthew's presentation of his Sermon on the Mount. Like Job 29, Matthew offers a clearly cadenced eightfold list of positive signs of the kingdom. They are the Yahweh-imitating virtues of the pious man, which Jesus presents to the disciples on the mountain (Mt 5:3–10). After his list of the blessings of the kingdom, Matthew closes his instruction, with a fourfold interpretation of the disciples, who reflect the gladness of the kingdom through their victory over the evil that threatens the pious. Though scorned and persecuted, they are like the prophets of old: the salt of the earth and light of the world (Mt 5:11–16).

The stereotyped character of such lists allows them to be used to describe both justice and injustice. Job has the distinction, among biblical figures, of having his life's story structured by both. While the nostalgic reflections on his past life in

Job 29 presents his story in the pattern of the good king, his friend Eliphaz uses the reverse side of the description to cast the judgment that Job's life has been so evil that darkness and flood cover him:

> You have exacted pledges of your brothers for nothing and stripped the naked of their clothing. You have not given water to the weary to drink and you have withheld bread from the hungry. The man with power possessed the land; and the favored man dwelt in it. You have sent widows away empty and the arms of the fatherless were crushed. Therefore, snares are around you and sudden terror overwhelms you. Your light is darkened so that you cannot see, and a flood of water covers you. (Job 22:5–11)

The "song for a poor man" at times presents itself as a mantra, evoking blessing or curse and symbolizing God's presence or absence. It introduces an ethical logic of retribution. The pattern of retribution is paraphrased in Yahweh's declaration to Abraham that the nations will be judged by how they deal with Israel. The treatment of the poor and oppressed, foreigner and enemy, widow, fatherless, lame and blind: all figures of an endless identification of the stranger with oneself.

> When a foreigner lives with you in your land, you should do him no wrong. The foreigner who lives with you will be to you as the native among you and you will love him as yourself; for you were strangers in the land of Egypt. I am Yahweh, your God. (Lev 19:23–24)

Although the clustering of variations of the song for a poor man is related to themes of testing and judgment and illustrations reflecting the theology of the way, space hardly allows a full discussion of so many texts. Stories about lawgiving and figures of prophets rebuking king and people easily illustrate the trope of divine judgment. Collections of reflective proverbs or songs echoing the efforts of the pious in their practice of virtue also find easy expression in a metaphor of the path of life. Similarly, the cluster of motifs and figures belonging to the song for a poor man are attracted to the various themes, which deal with transcendent aspects of kingship. The songs that frame the books of Samuel and the songs of David in the Psalter betray just such close affinity between these three central tropes of the Hebrew Bible. They echo the ancient Near Eastern presentation of the good king and understanding of the king as representing divine judgment and rule. The myth of God's kingdom dominates and forms the central theme of the book of Isaiah. Matthew's use of Isaiah imitates far more than it exploits prophecies about future salvation.

Isaiah develops his book, like the five books of the Psalter and the fivefold structure of the book of Job, on the kingdom in five movements, each of which is presented, like the introduction, in a sevenfold structure.[8] Isaiah's richly varied use of the song for a poor man, evoking the kingdom, dominates. He uses contrasting metaphors to evoke more than the literal meaning of his words allows. For example, he brings together the death-like barrenness of a desert's aridity and the life-giving fertility of spring rain to create a transcendent metaphor for the reversals that the kingdom determines (Is 35). He joins this life-affirming imagery to an eightfold song for a poor man. This double metaphor of judgment is intensified by its context in piety's theology of the way. With this, he supports his pedagogical purpose, as the pious in their self-discipline and dedication to the temple become one with Isaiah's exiles of Israel past, returning to Zion's utopia:

> The wilderness and the dry land will be glad. The desert will rejoice and blossom; like the crocus, it will blossom abundantly and rejoice with joy and singing. The glory of Lebanon will be given to it, the majesty of Carmel and Sharon. They will see the glory of Yahweh, the majesty of our God: Strengthen the hands of the weak; firm the knees of the feeble. Say to those that have a fearful heart, "be strong; do not be afraid." Behold, your God will come with vengeance; with a divine retribution he will come to save you. Then the eyes of the blind will be opened and the ears of the deaf unstopped. The lame man will leap like a hart and the tongue of the dumb man will sing; for waters will come forth in the wilderness and rivers in the desert. The burning sand will become a pond and the thirsty ground springs of water. The haunt of jackals will become a marshland. The grass will become reeds and rushes.[9] And a highway will be there and it will be called The Holy Way; the unclean will not pass over it, and fools will not err therein. No lion will be there; nor will any ravenous beast come upon it. They will not be found there, but the redeemed will walk there. The ransomed of Yahweh will return and come to Zion with singing; everlasting joy will be upon their heads; and they will obtain joy and gladness and sorrow and sighing will fly away. (Is 35:1–10)

The kingdom's reversal of the destiny of the suffering and vulnerable provides Isaiah with ready symbols of salvation. The same motifs are given the form of a moral sermon on fasting and Sabbath observance, as Isaiah answers the ever implicit question of his parable: how can we understand God's way? This song offers both template and theme to Matthew's figure of Jesus as demanding conversion to the values of the kingdom. The figures of the poor man—the oppressed, the hungry and the naked—are the measure of one's relationship to God. They are set within the context of the path of righteousness, piety's epitome of the Torah.

> Is not this the fasting that I choose: to untie the bonds of evil, to undo the bands of the yoke, to let the oppressed go free and to break every yoke? Is it not to share your bread with the hungry and bring the homeless poor into your house? When you see the naked, cover him and do not hide yourself from your own flesh, then will your light break forth like the morning and your health will spring forth speedily. Your righteousness will go before you and the Glory of Yahweh will be your rearguard. Then you will call and Yahweh will answer; you will cry and he will say, "Here I am." If you take away from your midst the yoke, the pointing of the finger and speaking wickedness, if you pour yourself out for the hungry and satisfy the desire of the afflicted, then will your light rise in the darkness and your gloom be as noonday. And Yahweh will guide you continually, and satisfy your desire with good things, and make your bones strong. You will be like a watered garden, like a spring of water, whose waters fail not. (Is 58:6–11; cf. Mt 4:16–17, 6:16–21, 25:31–46)

The pious morality encouraged by the understanding of the care for the poor as measure of one's love of God is a theme Isaiah shares with Deuteronomy's epitome of the Ten Commandments (Dt 6:5). The motif of compassion, which in both Matthew and Luke attracts citation, is present in more than thirty variations in Isaiah. His concept of the kingdom is not merely positive. It is never far from motifs of divine judgment and a vision of the kingdom as a world transformed. For example, the motif of the pious becoming themselves the light of the dawn in their care for the poor takes on apocalyptic overtones, as this light-bringing blessing shows its darker side.

The fate of those who have abandoned Yahweh and are destined for the sword reflects a fourfold reversal: they will become hungry, thirsty, sad and sorrowful. With measured reciprocity, those who are his faithful servants will eat and drink, rejoice and sing for joy. These contrasting destinies are confirmed with the summary curse capping and dominating the whole: "you will cry for the anguish of spirit." Isaiah's closing song of a new heaven and a new earth begins with a similarly structured reversal of the world as we know it:

> No more will there be an infant that lives but a few days, or an old man who does not fill out his days; for the child will die a hundred years old and the sinner of a hundred years old will be cursed. . . . The wolf and the lamb will graze

together; the lion will eat straw like the ox; while the snake's food is dust. (Is 65:19–20, 25)

In spite of its pietistic lapse cursing the sinner, this fourfold resolution of this world's oppositions creates a metaphor of eternal peace and a utopian end to violence. The maintenance of the snake's destiny with death's food, with its implicit evocation of the garden story, caps an understanding of paradise regained.

The integration of judgment themes with reversals characteristic of the song for a poor man is clearest in the opening songs of Isaiah's sevenfold curses against the nations. A taunt song likens the king of Babylon's fall to the myth of Lucifer, who in pride climbed to heaven, only to be cast down to the underworld (Is 14:4–21). Isaiah's song of the king of Babylon's fall is set *on the day Yahweh gives Israel rest from its sorrow.* On this day of return to creation's Sabbath, peace comes through Babylon's destruction. Its end is likened to the closing of the morning star's light: "How the oppressor has ceased, the golden city ended."

In this great apocalyptic vision, emptying earth and turning all upside down, a parallel song is sung. On that day, Yahweh will also punish in heaven as he has punished the kings of the earth (Is 24:21). This mythic context for a judgment of the gods is captured in the Psalter. The legend of Lucifer and his fall from heaven is echoed. Yahweh enters the divine assembly and condemns the gods for siding with the wicked. They are unjust to a sixfold list of the oppressed: "the weak and the fatherless . . . the afflicted and the destitute . . . the poor and the needy" (Ps 82:3–4): "I say you are gods, sons of the Most High, all of you. Nevertheless, you will die like men and fall like any prince" (Ps 82:7). The logic of identification of figures follows a pattern that is parallel to the origin story of the "fallen ones" (1 Enoch 6:6, 7:1, 9:9, 10:9; cf. Ez 32:27; Gen 6:1–4), who play the role of this world's terror in the holy war tradition (Num 14). The reversal of fortune exemplified in Lucifer's fall, the fall of the proud, is given a contrasting rise of the humble in three songs, interpreting the story of David. The first is found in the closure of the song of Hannah, already cited, which is sung in the temple to celebrate the heroic birth of Samuel (1 Sm 2:4–10).

Hannah's song finds a structural mate in the Song of the Bow set at the center of the narrative of 1–2 Samuel (2 Sm 1:17–27), David's searing lament, sung at the death of Saul and Jonathan. The Lucifer theme forms the song's leitmotif: "How the Mighty have fallen!" It marks the punning reversal of fate that has sent Saul (*Sha'ul*) down to the realm of the dead (*She'ol*). Isaiah has concentrated on the solar element of the morning star in creating his leitmotif in the songs of the kingdom that he might appeal to his audience to walk in Yahweh's light. The author of 1–2 Samuel organizes the metaphor so that the fall of Saul will lead to the rise of David. This reversal of Israel's fate, bringing Israel back to Yahweh, is marked by the reiterating terror of the fall of the proud. Men will be humbled, but Yahweh alone exalted (Is 2:9, 11, 17). In Isaiah's second song of the kingdom, a similar terror has overtaken Jerusalem's mighty. They met Lucifer's fate as the mouth of She'ol opened to swallow them (Is 5:15–16).

Judgment of the proud and arrogant comes also in the third song, which closes David's story. David sings a victory song after he has been saved from all his enemies. Both Israel's and David's fortunes have been reversed: "You delivered a humble people, but you look on the proud to bring them down" (2 Sm 22:28 = Ps 18:28). In the immediately following song, billed as "David's last words," an oracle presents a divine decree. David is "raised up" in fallen Lucifer's stead:

> The God of Israel has spoken, the Rock of Israel has said to me: When one rules justly over men, ruling in the fear of God, he *dawns on them like the morning light.* (2 Sm 23:3–4; cf. Jgs 5:31)

This picture of David as the good king, ruling in righteousness and interpreted mythically as the dawn's new light, presents the messiah as taking up fallen Lucifer's heavenly role and presenting Daniel's figures of the wise as stars in the firmament within Prince Michael's final deliverance:

> Many of those who sleep in the dust of the earth will awake, some to everlasting life and some to shame and everlasting contempt. Those who are wise shall shine like the brightness of the firmament; and those who turn away to righteousness, like the stars for ever and ever. (Dan 12:2–3)

In Isaiah's seventh song of the kingdom, three of the more important aspects of the song for a poor man are brought together to create the figure of the saving king. He is the philosopher king, judging in righteousness rather than appearances. His is a merciful judgment of the poor and meek, but he is also an avenging warrior against the wicked. The kingdom that his holy war's victory over evil inaugurates is utopian: a miraculous, world-transforming end to all violence. This world will be led not by the fearsome warrior but by the epitome of helplessness, a little child:

> His delight will be in the fear of Yahweh; he will not judge by what his eyes see or decide by what his ears hear; but with righteousness he will judge the poor and decide with equity for the meek of the earth. He will smite the earth with the rod of his mouth and with the breath of his lips he will slay the

wicked. Righteousness will be the belt at his waist; and faithfulness the truss of his loins. The wolf will live with the lamb and the leopard will lie down with the kid and the calf and the lion and the fatling together and a little child will lead them. The cow and the bear will feed and their young will lie down together; the young lion will eat straw with the ox. The nursing child will play at the hole of the cobra and the weaned will put his hand on the viper's nest. They will not harm or destroy on my holy mountain; for the earth will be full of the knowledge of Yahweh as the waters cover the sea. (Is 11:3–9)

The motifs clustering around the song for a poor man find frequent illustration in biblical story. The philosophical theme of the poverty of human existence is used effectively in the presentation of Job's suffering as nakedness. In his reaction to the loss of all his wealth, Job is a man of true humility:

Naked I came from my mother's womb and naked shall I return. Yahweh gave and Yahweh has taken away; blessed be Yahweh's name. (Job 1:21)

Solomon presents this same trope about wisdom's beginning as evidence of life's futility and the need for humility:

As he came from his mother's womb, he will go again, naked as he came, and he will take nothing for his toil, which he might carry away in his hand. This is also a grievous evil: just as he came so shall he go, and what gain has he that he toiled for the wind. (Eccl 5:14–15, 6:2–3)

In the Psalter, the motif of one's death is offered as a variant for the fragility of human nakedness. It is used in two different ways. First it stresses the equality all men have in the grave. It also provides a reason for not fearing the rich man:

You will see that even the wise die; the stupid and the foolish alike must perish and leave their wealth to others. Their graves are their homes for ever; their dwelling place to all generations, though they once called lands their own. . . . Do not be afraid if one becomes rich; if the glory of his house increases. When he dies, he will carry nothing away, his glory will not follow him down. (Ps 49:11–12, 17–18)

Although Solomon takes this phrase even further in his effort to doubt his own wisdom (Eccl 2:16–17), the great narratives of David and his sons illustrate this timeless truth about the poor man as a building block in the larger story's plotline.

David begins his career among the great ones as a poor man. His is the classic poor man's role of the fairy tale, in which the penniless hero marries the king's daughter. First, he must prove a worthiness equal to his heroic role. A hundred Philistine foreskins is the price for David's bride. When our Hebrew Jason sets out on his quest with his Argonauts, he returns—a true hero—with a double portion of foreskins. The Bible's greater story is not only matching David's prowess to other heroes of ancient literature but also using David as a model of piety and stressing his poor man's essence (1 Sm 18:23). This allows him to lock his story prophetically to the closure of this long chain of narrative, when all of Jerusalem is carried into exile and only *the poor remain* (2 Kgs 24:14, 25:12). Like Job's life in his nakedness, the story of David's house begins and ends in its poverty by illustrating the saying that begins and ends this collection of Solomon's sayings: "Endless emptiness; all is emptiness" (Eccl 1:2, 12:8).

The vanity of the story of David and his sons—Israel's great kings—illustrating the poverty of humanity's strength is a theme that finds its center in the story of the parable of a rich man and a poor man. The story is told by the prophet Nathan and forms an interpretive centerpiece of the story of David's fall, itself a parable. Three variations of a single tale are used to prepare the audience for a judgment against David, which ultimately will return his sons to the role of the poor man and to the path of the righteous. The story of David's fall begins on the day he is not with his heroes fighting Yahweh's wars but stays home instead. Wandering the roof of his house, he sees the beautiful Bathsheba. She is the wife of David's faithful servant, the foreigner Uriah. She is bathing on a roof nearby and David falls deeply in love. In the course of the affair, Bathsheba becomes pregnant. Unable to hide his adultery, David arranges for his servant's murder by having him placed at risk in battle (2 Sm 11). With the deed done and hidden by David's marriage to Bathsheba, Yahweh sends his prophet Nathan with his parable. The rich man will have a feast. Though he had huge herds himself, he steals a beloved lamb, the singular possession of a poor man. David, unaware of Yahweh's engagement in retelling tales, does not recognize himself in Nathan's story and becomes angry. "That man is the son of death," he declares in his righteous judgment. Having condemned himself with his own words, David's son dies in his stead. From that time on, it is prophesied, the sword will never leave David's house (2 Sm 12:1–15).

The rest of the story of David and his sons is taken by the ravages of this sword (see below, Chapters 9–10). Toward the center of the chain of narrative, at the height of King Ahab's reign over Israel, Nathan's parable is revised to bring yet another rich man to face his poverty. Like Uriah's roof, Naboth's vineyard lies beside the palace of the rich man, Ahab, who wants the poor man's only possession for his kitchen garden. Naboth, however, though poor, is rich in piety. Like Uriah, who would not rest from his duty to sleep with his wife, Naboth will not sell his vineyard, the inheritance of his fathers, the sale of which is forbidden by the Torah (Lev 25:23–24). With his story's main plot centering on how Ahab gives the entirety of Yahweh's inheritance to Baal and Asherah (Dt 32:8), Naboth's argument is persuasive to the Torah-wise reader. Ahab is angry that Naboth—unlike Esau (Gen 25:29–34)—refuses to sell his inheritance. His wife Jezebel shows him how a king should act by writing letters to the elders of the town. She demands that Naboth be charged with cursing God and the king and that he be stoned. And so they do and Naboth dies. When Ahab goes to take possession of the vineyard, however, the prophet Elijah curses him with a comparable fate. Where the dogs lick up Naboth's blood, they will lick up Ahab's (1 Kgs 21).

Close to these parables of the rich man and the poor man are two songs on the theme of learning humility. Much as the people of Libya gossip over Merneptah's victory, nations gossip over Yahweh's miracles: "filling our mouths with laughter."[10] The song delightfully illustrates how the gods make names for themselves: "Yahweh has done great things for us and we are glad" (Ps 126:3). This brief, simple song celebrating the miracle of the harvest combines a metaphor of a desert wadi suddenly flowing with God-given water with a proverb to capture both the surprise and joy of the miracle:

> When Yahweh turned Zion's destiny, we were as in a dream. Our mouth was filled with laughter and our tongue with shouts of joy. They gossiped among the nations: "Yahweh has done great things for them." Yahweh has done great things for us and we are glad. Turn our destiny Yahweh, like rivers in the desert. May those who sow in tears reap with shouts of joy. He who goes forth weeping, bearing the seed for sowing, will come home with shouts of joy, bringing his sheaves with him. (Ps 126)

The psalm also provides a response to another song, where a righteous generation identifies with the poor and takes Yahweh as its refuge (Ps 14:5–7). The technique of interpretation is identical to what we find in the sayings and parables about the harvest of the kingdom in Mark 4. This is the harvest to which the parable of the sower refers.

While Psalm 126 takes up mythic themes of agriculture and moves from the tears of humility to rejoicing over the harvest, Psalm 113 approaches the theme of the kingdom directly and theologically. Its joyful questions answer the opening question about the image of God.

Who is like Yahweh, our God, seated on high, who looks far down upon the heavens and the earth? He raises the poor from the dust and lifts the needy from the ash heap to make them sit with princes, with the princes of his people. He gives the barren woman a home, making her the joyous mother of children. (Ps 113:5–9)

Apart from the many possible allusions to stories like Sarah, Rachel, Tamar, Ruth and Hannah, illustrating the way the barren become joyful mothers, and apart from this psalm's echoes through the book of Job, the question posed is, Who is like Yahweh seated on high? Who can look down on the heavens and the earth? The question is usually understood as if it were rhetorical, with an implied, pious "no one." However, such a narrow reading ignores the possibilities of those he raises from the dust to sit with princes. The question finds an answer in the role Isaiah gives to the figure of Israel as Yahweh's suffering servant (Is 57:14–21). This answer fits the whole of Psalm 113's theme. As in the psalm, Isaiah uses literal language about Yahweh as the "High and Lofty One." He not only lives in the high and holy place, he is the great one who lives with the humble and contrite, with his wounded Israel, whom he has healed. Similarly, *castrati* and strangers are acceptable to Yahweh because they exemplify Israel's suffering. It is only a short metaphorical step to turn to Isaiah's acceptance of *castrati* and strangers for a revision of the laws about the Sabbath and the unclean. For Isaiah, such revision is a process of education in humility. Gathered on the heights of Yahweh's holy mountain are Israel's outcasts:

Let not the foreigner who has joined himself to Yahweh say, "Yahweh will surely separate me from his people." Let not the eunuch say, "Behold, I am a dry tree." For thus says Yahweh: "To the eunuchs who keep my Sabbaths, who choose the things that please me and hold fast my covenant, I will give in my house and within my walls a monument and a name better than sons and daughters. I will give them an everlasting name, which will not be cut off. The foreigners who join themselves to Yahweh, to minister him, to love the name of Yahweh, to be his servants, everyone who keeps the Sabbath and does not profane it and holds fast my covenant, these I will bring to my holy mountain and make them joyful in my house of prayer. Their burnt offerings and their sacrifices will be accepted on my altar; for my house will be called a house of prayer for all peoples." Thus says the God Yahweh, who gathers the outcasts of Israel, "I will gather yet others to him besides his gathered ones." (Is 56:3–8)

The rhetoric of holy war, with its negative judgments or curses on proud and haughty nations in uproar (Ps 2:1–3), typically takes on a moralizing role in the Psalter. Psalm 10, for example, sets the "wicked in their pride" in the role of nations in uproar. Denying that God exists, they pursue the poor, murder the innocent and capture the helpless in nets. The prayer calls on God to remember the humble. The "helper of the fatherless" is called on to "break the arm of the wicked and evil man," that is, their upraised arm in battle. That they be totally uprooted (Ps 10:15); that "the nations perish" is the wish of the humble. This causes ears to hear with understanding. The judgment of the fatherless and oppressed is to remove all who terrify the innocent (Ps 10:18).

The rhetoric of divine judgment in the moralizing interpretation of holy war often makes use of the stereotyped figures in the song of a poor man. The retributive logic of such judgment is well expressed by David's curse on his adversaries in the Psalter (Ps 109).

They have repaid me evil for good and hatred for my love, saying: "Set an evil man over him and a prosecutor *[satan]* to stand at his right hand; When he is judged, let him be condemned and let his prayer be turned into sin. Let his days be few and let another take his possessions. Let his children be fatherless and his wife a widow. Let his children be vagabonds and beg; let them seek their bread also from desolate places. Let the creator seize everything he has and let foreigners spoil his labor. Let there be none to extend kindness to him; nor let there be any to favor his fatherless children. Let his posterity be cut off and in the generation following, let their name be blotted out. May the iniquity of his fathers be remembered by Yahweh and let not the sin of his mother be blotted out. Let them be before Yahweh continually that he may cut off the memory of them from the earth. He did not remember to show kindness, but he pursued the poor and needy man and the broken-hearted to their death. He loved cursing and it came to him; and he hated blessing and it was far from him." (Ps 109:5–17)

This curse is likened to "clothing, which will seep into his body like water and into his bones like oil" (Ps 109:18–19). David is placed in Job's role of defendant. He is confronted by his accuser (Hebrew *satan*; cf. Job 1:6). David calls on Yahweh to condemn the accuser: because I am "poor and needy and my heart is wounded" (Ps 109:22). Like Job, David takes up the role of the innocent sufferer. With Job, he argues against the claim that suffering is a punishment for sin (Job 19). David suffers persecution as Yahweh's faithful servant (Ps 109:23–25).

He awaits judgment—the reversal of the fortunes of the just and unjust, the rich and the poor (Ps 109:29). The song also constructs an illustrating myth as David calls for Satan's fall to echo the fall of Isaiah's Lucifer. As the nations are to be judged according to the way they treat Abraham's descendants (Gen 27:29), one is judged in this psalm by how one treats the poor and the oppressed.

From such identification, it is but a short step to the path of mysticism, expressed in the theme from the Torah of purifying the soul through "suffering for God's sake" (Cf. Mt 5:11–12; Lk 6:22–23). Here too David—confessing his sin—competes for Job's role:

> For your sake, I have born insult; confusion has covered my face. I am become a stranger to my brothers and a foreigner to my mother's children . . . the taunts of those who taunt me have fallen on me. When I wept and purified my soul with fasting, that became a reproach to me. I made sackcloth also my clothing and I became a proverb to them. They who sit in the gate gossip about me; I have become the song of drunkards. (Ps 69:8–13)

David asks his suffering to be reversed by his redeemer, who will set him free from his enemies (Ps 69:16–17). The images of David's suffering, which fed Matthew's story of Jesus' passion (cf. Ps 69:22; Mt 27:34, 48), clearly identify David with the oppressed of the song for a poor man. He himself is with "the righteous." Afflicted and in pain, he belongs to the humble, to the poor and the prisoners whom Yahweh hears (Ps 69:29–37).

EXAMPLES FROM THE DEAD SEA SCROLLS

The Dead Sea scrolls use the metaphors of the song for a poor man quite concretely in interpreting their or their community's own world. Such transference is most obvious in the scrolls that interpret and comment on biblical texts. A practical dualism dominates the Qumran commentary. We are presented with the wicked or ruthless who grind their teeth and plot to destroy, who discharge their bows and murder. They will be laughed at and cursed and are presented as opposed to the poor and the just, who will be rescued. They inherit the earth and delight in God's holy mountain. The commentary goes beyond a simple reiteration of biblical metaphors in condemning "the wicked of Ephraim and Manasseh" who attempt to lay hands on "the priest and the members of his council." The "poor" become the "community of" or "congregation of the poor" (nos. 42, 43, 44–46: 4Q171; cf. Ps 37:11–15, 21–22).[11] While the biblical psalm often implicitly identifies the singer with the mystical conflicts of the pious, the songs from the Dead Sea scrolls are quite explicit in their identification: "the powerful wicked . . . harass . . . the whole day they crush my soul, but you, O God have calmed my soul and have freed the soul of the poor . . . from the power of the lions" (no. 49: 1Q Hodayot, xiii, 12–20).[12]

Yet other songs in the scrolls use the assured promise of signs of the kingdom as a teaching model in a stream of tradition that includes Isaiah and the gospels. For example, the metaphor of the poor raised up and sitting among nobles is used in one text to justify the argument that, therefore, one "should always seek his will," work "in discipline" and "refine your heart and . . . thoughts" (no. 51: 4Q413, frag 2, iii).[13] Such interpretations understand the biblical passages to address the world of the interpreter and to present a guide for life. One sermon combines the projection of a royal messiah with a description of "judgment with mercy" for the devout. Freeing prisoners, giving sight to the blind and straightening the crippled are the signs of his kingdom. Coming in judgment, he will do good deeds and perform a sixfold cluster of miracles. These include healing the wounded, bringing the dead to life and proclaiming good news to the meek (no. 52: 4Q521, frag 2, ii).[14]

While such texts clearly imply the process of story creation in the service of piety and preaching, their efforts to apply what is implicit in the motifs as instructions does not allow us to interpret them too freely. While references to the theme and metaphors of the song for a poor man are infrequent, they are still sufficient to place the Qumran texts solidly within the related traditions of the Hebrew Bible.[15] Bringing down the arrogant and raising up the poor as marks of salvation are clear reiterations of this well-worn template (no. 48: 4Q88, col ix; no. 50: 4Q427, frag 7 ii).[16] One of these texts, using blessing formulas as a leitmotif, shows a literarily ambitious and creative use of form. It begins with fourfold blessings for proper behavior, each balanced with a corresponding rejection of the appropriate bad behavior: "Blessed is the one who speaks the truth with a pure heart and does not slander with his tongue," and so on.

While fragments of the Isaiah commentary allude cryptically to the destruction of a tyrant and a struggle that threatens the innocent (no. 41: 4Q163, frag 18–19),[17] the War Scroll presents the struggle against the nations of biblical tradition as a historicized apocalyptic battle and judgment, which seems both sectarian and central to the piety implied by the text. Echoing Isaiah's imagery of the gathering of Jerusalem's remnant, the author of the War Scroll gathers "the nations for destruction, without remnant." As these nations are brought low, the theme of judgment requires reciprocity: the good are to be lifted up. The figures of the song for a poor man fill out the composition. They are the remnant of

God's people and therefore acquire a self-identifying "we" from the author. The comic and mock character of this army marks it as wisdom literature. It is neither prophecy nor a projection of any expected future. The author and his audience identify with those who fight all that is evil in this world. They array themselves in battle as God's army and can be identified by their lack of fitness for service in a human army. They have the strength coming from the mouth of babes (Ps 8:3) and are identified through a sixfold list drawn from Isaiah and the Psalter: the dumb, who will sing about God's miracles; hands of the frail, trained in war; shaking knees, strengthened to stand; broken backs strapped with a warrior's belt and—the textually uncertain—hardened hearts, who have become the poor in spirit. All of these "perfect ones of Israel" will wage holy war to destroy the wicked nations, whose heroes will not be left standing. These metaphors are richly pregnant and belong to the biblical tradition of holy war, which the author is at pains to lay at rest (no. 40: 1QM, frag 8–10, col i).[18]

EXAMPLES FROM THE NEW TESTAMENT

The widely accepted argument that the sayings of Jesus can be sharply separated and distinguished from stories and sayings presenting Jesus as an apocalyptic prophet is clearly wrong. The philosophical tradition of wisdom literature has direct connections to the royal ideology of blessings and curses. They form a central metaphor in the myth of judgment and the vision of the kingdom's utopian peace. The Beatitudes of Matthew's Sermon on the Mount—which has its variant in Luke's Sermon on the Plain—are judged by the Jesus Seminar as certainly authentic sayings and are pivotal for the reconstruction of biographies of a historical Jesus as Galilean peasant, revolutionary or cynic philosopher (Mt 5:3–12; Lk 6:20–27). We have seen, however, that Matthew and Luke's variations of this trope, within the biblical and ancient Near Eastern genre of curses and blessings, reflect independent forms of such sayings, associated with judgment's reversal of fortune. Luke's Beatitudes, although viewed as less authentic than Matthew's, draw on a related strain of the same stream of tradition and present Jesus with the role of judge in the kingdom. Rather than cynic philosophy, the preference for the poor and oppressed in this tradition is fully in harmony with the tradition's utopian visions of a messianic kingdom and judgment. Moreover, Matthew and Luke's reuse of the list of signs of the kingdom in the John the Baptist story (Mt 11:2–6; Lk 7:18–23) is not based in an oral tradition traceable to Jesus' preaching. They draw on a written tradition

that can be traced to stories, songs and proverbs from as early as the third millennium BCE and whose themes are explicitly and implicitly central to both Jewish and Samaritan biblical tradition.

It is already clear that the examination has falsified the thesis of the Jesus Seminar. The teaching of Jesus cannot be reconstructed from the hypothetical Q
source for Matthew and Luke's gospel and the fourth-century Gospel of Thomas.
The sayings we have looked at are not atypical of the sayings Jesus is given to
speak in the gospels. They belong not to oral tradition, but to a large and important cluster of ancient wisdom sayings and have been used by both the gospel
writers and the Jesus Seminar to create their figures of Jesus. This argument is
explicit in the gospels themselves. Jesus' life is an illustration of the ideals of the
biblical tradition. Among the sayings closest to the signs saying is the list of miracles Jesus quotes from Isaiah in the synagogue of Nazareth:

> The spirit of the Lord is upon me because he has anointed me to preach good
> news to the poor. He has sent me to proclaim release to the captives and re-
> covering of sight to the blind, to set at liberty those who are oppressed, to pro-
> claim the acceptable year of the Lord. (Lk 4:18–19)

One must ask how this passage is different from the signs of the kingdom in
Luke 7. Can one passage be understood as a "certainly authentic saying of Jesus,"
while the other belongs neither to Q nor to Thomas? Luke's dependence on Isaiah is not greater in his synagogue story, simply because the audience is told that
he quotes from Isaiah. Even as this story's motif of public reading calls for the
explicit reference to the Hebrew Bible, the text Jesus is given to read offers a reiterating variation, quite in line with the citation in Luke 7:

> The spirit of the lord God is upon me, because the Lord has anointed me to
> announce good tidings to the meek. He has sent me to bind up the broken
> hearted, to proclaim liberty to the captives and the opening of the prison to
> them that are bound; to proclaim a year of acceptance of the Lord. (Is 61:1–2)

The differences between these passages in Luke and Isaiah have nothing to do
with translation from Hebrew to Aramaic or Greek. Such variation belongs to a
tradition of secondary texts, which interprets through reiteration and revision.
Whether the sayings are presented by Matthew or Luke, grounds for judging one
New Testament saying as more "authentic" than another are absent. Whether the
gospel puts forward a reading of Isaiah in the synagogue, a thematic element in

a story fulfilling prophecy or a saying of Jesus identifying the signs of the kingdom, we are dealing with related reiterations of Isaiah. They present the Jesus story as a living parable of Isaiah's kingdom of God.

Perhaps our best examples, showing Luke's independence from a hypothetical oral sayings tradition shared by Matthew, can be found in the songs used in his birth of a hero story (Lk 1:46–55, 76, 79). It has been long recognized that Luke's creative development of the theme of the kingdom in this story is due to his use of the song of Hannah, one of the clearest examples of the song for a poor man in the Bible (1 Sm 2:1–10). The motifs Luke's birth story shares with Matthew's are not important elements, reflecting his story's orientation or function. The songs themselves, the birth stories, and the whole of Luke's gospel are centered on themes that the songs introduce. The common ground of Luke's and Matthew's gospels is not adequately accounted for by their use of close variant sayings. Nor is the common denominator of these gospels reflective of events and teachings of an individual's life, reaching the writers by way of oral tradition. Rather, such shared elements are well explained by the similar themes of the gospels in which they are found. The gospels and the literary world they reflect expand a tradition of theological discourse and debate. This is far older and culturally far more deeply rooted than any particular figure or setting that might be used for illustration.

Apart from the Beatitudes and the signs of the kingdom saying, Luke's variations on the song for a poor man are not usually attributed to Q, though all share both central themes and literary origins with similar sayings in both Matthew and Mark. Similarly, Matthew's reiterations of the song for a poor man also are independent of Q, yet share both sayings and stories with Luke and Mark. Q, with or without the Gospel of Thomas, is an artificial and questionable construct, entirely dependent on a studied neglect of written sources ready at hand. The gospel narratives demonstrably build their figures of both John and Jesus through varied reiterations of earlier biblical and ancient Near Eastern literature. Their common denominator is the tradition they consciously seek to epitomize. The mechanically simplistic question of whether Matthew and Luke have used each other or not is not very useful in answering the question of what the gospel writers do with the literary and intellectual traditions of Palestine and the Near East that they inherit and share. Questions about the origin and meaning of the traditions reiterated in the gospels lead us directly to Jewish and Samaritan texts and traditions. These are far older than any particular historical figure of the gospels.

The process of biographical story creation is complex. It is especially difficult to determine whether we are in fact dealing with the story of a particular man's life and a biography illustrating values we hold because of him. We may be dealing with a narrative figure whose function is to illustrate universal or eternal values. The difference between the two rests on our ability to separate the bearing figure of a narrative from its message. Biblical scholarship's historical criticism, related to the "quest" for the historical Jesus, has been caught by its insistence on such a separation by opposing the Christ of the gospels to a historical Jesus. To some extent, the members of the Jesus Seminar have softened this dichotomy between the Christ of faith and the Jesus of history they have proposed. They have used a selection of favorite motifs and stories central to the figure of the gospels and projected their implied figure as historical. They have not, however, succeeded in escaping the dichotomy so much as they have compromised their historical figure.

PART TWO

The Royal Ideology

CHAPTER 5

⚜

The Myth of the Good King

CREATING FIGURES OF PARABLE

This part of the book addresses three roles a king is given in ancient literature: the role of the ideal king, the king at war as protector and savior of his people and finally the myth of the dying and rising god. The first of these roles, as the ethical ideal of political philosophy, presents the figure of the king as an example for admiration and imitation. Biblical story often sets its figures speaking or singing. What they say can involve either a single example or a substantial collection of traditional sayings or songs. Debates can be presented, as well as collections of cultic regulations, laws or oracles of various kinds. The story with its figure and his or her identifying role provides a context for such complex presentations. Some themes are transformed by being given to one character rather than another in a story. Stories and sayings are often linked together to build substantial chains of narrative. In some cases—as in the stories of Abraham and Jacob—the life of a heroic figure is created as example tale in the form of a biography, beginning in the figure's call or birth and closing in a story of his or her death and burial.[1] While the figures of David in the Psalter and Jesus in the gospels are among the more complicated, there are many figures in the Bible whose ethical character has been formed by the song for a poor man.

The origins of any particular saying or song are difficult to identify with any particular figure or narrative context. Attributions are often trivial or obvious, as in the attribution of proverbs to Solomon (Prv 1:1), oracles to the prophet Isaiah (Is 19:1a) and songs to Moses (Ex 15:1, 13–17; Dt 31:30) or David (2 Sm 22:1;

Ps 51:1).[2] The most central figures of biblical story rarely speak with a single mind, any more than an Abraham, a Moses or a David is given a single life to live.[3] It is increasingly difficult to accept the assumption of oral tradition in antiquity as transmitting the figure or speech of any historical person. At times, the same statements are used with different characters. This can be a very effective technique in bringing two widely separated texts into a discussion on common themes. For example, the question Yahweh asks Cain, angry over his unaccepted offering, "Why are you angry?" (Gen 4:6), takes on added significance when it is read with Yahweh's similar question to Jonah's anger and wish for death over Nineveh's conversion, "Are you right to be angry?" (Jon 4:4), or the reiteration of question, anger and death wish in a living parable, when Jonah loses his shade tree (Jon 4:9–11). While the Cain and Jonah stories lend themselves well to reading as parables on related themes, the themes take on greater depth when other texts are evoked. How is such a wish for death heard when the prophetic figure expressing it is an Elijah, afraid for his life because enemies wish to kill him (1 Kgs 19:4)? How is Yahweh heard by the reader, when the undermining challenge to such anger and wish for death is made by friends to a Job on suicide's edge (Job 5:2–7)?

The setting and choice of speaker to whom sayings and songs are given are not always stereotyped. They frequently reflect a collector's strategy in their present biblical context. Stereotyped reiterations, moreover, can vary greatly in the size of the element reused. Genesis presents a twelvefold list of nations for the genealogy of Canaan (Gen 10:15–18). However, when the list is reused or epitomized in Yahweh's holy war against the nations of Canaan, a widely varying six- or sevenfold list is offered as epitome (Ex 23:23). In yet further variations on the holy war theme, new versions of this list are offered, sometimes departing considerably from the genealogy while maintaining their common epitome of the displaced foreigner marked for destruction (from Dt 7:1 to Ezra 9:1; below Chapter 8). Reiterations may be verbatim or nearly verbatim (Gen 1:27, 5:1b–2) and may involve a wide range of motif and theme (Ps 1:3; Jer 17:8). Well-known scenes can be rewritten in new contexts or with new characters. A pregnant and mistreated Hagar runs away to be visited by God in the desert (Gen 16), only to be sent away a second time with her grown child by a "still" jealous Sarah (Gen 21). Similarly, Abraham and Isaac present their wives as their sisters while visiting a foreign king, Egypt's pharaoh or Gerar's Abimelek. (Gen 12:10–20, Gen 20, 26:1–11).[4] Such reiteration of motif, plot and theme, both in prose and poetry, are often marked with substantial nuance and implicit discourse between the variants. Psalm 8, for instance, can sing, "What is a human being that you remember him?" expanding the question rhetorically with pious wonder at the creation (Ps 8:5–6). Job, however, throws the same question out to a God who won't let him alone and turns the question into a lament (Job 7:17–19)! While the range of new meaning that different contexts and figures contribute is broad, the freedom of this continuous blending of tradition is such that an identical phrase—when clustered with other similarly traditional and stereotypical segments of speech—can serve irreconcilable functions. That the thematic element reiterated often maintains its defining significance in spite of its context suggests that we are dealing with a biblical discourse—an implicit conversation among authors. Such discourse encourages the development of clusters of elements, which—like the song for a poor man—bear significance beyond any particular figure or story in which the cluster appears.

The implications of such techniques might be clearer with the help of three examples.

David's Transformation

The last stanza of a song David sings both in the Psalter and at the close of the chain narrative of his trials describes a utopian peace:

> You delivered me from the struggles of my people and kept me to be the head of many nations. A people whom I never knew shall serve me; foreigners will submit to me. They will hear and obey me. Strangers will lose heart; come staggering from their hidden holes: "Yahweh Lives!" Blessed be my rock and exalted my God, the rock of my salvation. God has given me vengeance. He has brought the nations down under me and raised me up above my enemies. You delivered me from the men of violence. Therefore I give thanks to you, Yahweh, among the nations and sing praises to your name. (2 Sm 22:44–50; Ps 18:44–50)

This passage is all the more striking as it stands in sharp contrast to the murderous holy war rhetoric of the previous lines (2 Sm 22:38–43). David's enemies have been pursued relentlessly and crushed ruthlessly. Unable to rise, they call to Yahweh for help, but he does not answer. They are not worth answering, accounted less than the dust of the ungodly blown away by the wind at the threshing floor (Ps 1). They are likened to offal in the street. The immediate transition to the song's final stanza quoted here abandons the sectarian dualism of piety in Psalm 1 and takes up a more universal theme from Psalm 2. The kings of the world, in uproar against Yahweh and his messiah (Ps 2:1–2), are addressed by the messiah's wise advice that they serve Yahweh in fear (Ps 2:10–11). These enemies of David—utterly defeated and destroyed—accept the advice of the messiah of Psalm 2! They crawl out of their holes and cry out their allegiance, "Yahweh lives!" (2 Sm 22:47). Having been shocked by the theological implications of the defeated enemy's unanswered call to Yahweh for help in the previous stanza, the reader finds the ground under the song's rhetoric shifting in the closing lines. David is no longer threatened. He has become the victorious ruler of nations and foreigners. No longer in uproar, they are no longer his enemies, to be pursued and killed. They now serve him, submitting to his rule with every good client's humility. The panic-filled trembling of their surrender is transformed into the Psalter's mystical trembling of the "fear of God," wisdom's beginning. A remarkable scene of transformation from death to resurrection is rendered. Enemies are reconciled and foreigners become loyal subjects in God's kingdom.

This resurrection theme of the defeated nations submitting themselves to David, closing the David story, is less plot oriented than its placement at the end of the king's life might lead us to expect. When David sings his song, the uproar of the nations is over. His song announces a peace. It is "the song which David sang when Yahweh had saved him from all of his enemies and from the hand of Saul" (2 Sm 22:1). As set out already in the promises to Abraham (Gen 22:17–18), the nations of the world will submit to this utopia of David's Jerusalem. David's song transforms Jerusalem from the city of the failed, cursed and impotent old king of 2 Samuel's narrative by interpreting it as Isaiah's Zion. The young shepherd boy, anointed to replace the failed Saul and grown up to be the equal to both Saul and his failure, has become no less than the messianic figure of the Psalter: son of God, Yahweh's chosen warrior, a king who rules over strangers and foreigners in the kingdom of God (Ps 2). This remarkable closure for the story of David's life in a collage of song and story transforms the dominant thematic elements of David's story of failure. It turns uproar into submission, foreigners into clients, enemies into servants and death into life.

The Greatest of the Sons of Qedem

The radical transformation of David's life offers a convenient analogy to the Bible's brief sketch of a life of Job, which presents this great philosophical figure, who struggles with God over righteousness, as a figure of parable, mirroring Israel's own story of suffering and struggle (cf. Gen 32:23–33; Is 49:1–6). In a scene echoing Israel in exile, Job looks nostalgically back at the life he had when God was with him (Job 29). In this "biographical" sketch of twenty-five verses,

Job plays a number of roles that mark him as the ideal servant of the kingdom. In the presentation of this figure, elements belonging to the song for a poor man dominate. Job, the foreigner, is treated as his cue name demands. Job ("enemy") is rejected by God, his friends and his family. He is, however, the model of righteousness (Ez 14:14, 20), caring for the stranger, the widow and the orphan. These roles, which illustrate this figure of Job as a person, form a cluster of thematic elements belonging to royal ideology. They are typically used to present the figure of a good king. Each element is reflected in the lives of a wide spectrum of biblical heroes.

The story in which the great songs of Job with their atmosphere of trial and debate are sung is a story of a bet between Yahweh and Satan ("prosecutor"). Their wager asks whether Job is *truly* Yahweh's faithful servant or whether he has been faithful because it provided him with the good life. The bet, in all its simplicity, centers on Job's purity of heart. The trial of Job is an illustration of the Torah epitome to love God "with your whole heart, your whole soul and with all your strength" (Dt 6:5; cf. Dt 10:12; Josh 22:5; Mic 6:8; Mt 22:37). Satan, playing the role of prosecutor, sketches a plan for Job's life that will test his true heart. Remove all of God's support from Job. Will he bless God or will he curse him? Yahweh agrees to the plan, with one condition: that Job's life (God's own divine breath in Job) not be touched. The debates begin with Job sitting in ashes, scraping his running sores with a potsherd (Job 2:8). The delicacy of a wordplay on "blessing" *(brkh)* will mark the bet as won or lost. While the word normally means "blessing" *(brkh),* Satan and Job's wife use a euphemism that can turn it to a curse *(brkh*: Job 1:11; 2:5, 9; Is 8:21; Ex 22:27; Jgs 9:27). The distinction is precisely in the heart of the speaker.

By chapter 29, the happy days of Yahweh's blessing are long gone. The nostalgic song stands in striking contrast to Job's present situation. He sings of a time, long past, when God "watched over him" and was his "keeper" (Job 29:2), a role Yahweh accepted in the story of Cain, Job's ancestor in the land of Qedem (cf. Gen 4:16; Job 1:3). Job sings of his life "in the old days, when Yahweh had let the divine lamp light up his life" (Job 29:2–3). He describes himself as having been "like a king" (Job 29:25). The scene evoked is of the good king sitting among his soldiers and comforting them in their losses. Not his warrior status but the royal compassion he shows to his soldiers is stressed. The figure has many elements in common with the classic form of the "testimony of a good king" of ancient Near Eastern royal inscriptions. The common patterns are so striking that one must ask whether Satan's wager directly evokes the integrity of this figure: a spotlight cast on the purity of heart of ancient wisdom's foundation. This small biographical sketch provides a parable of the ideal kingdom. In his conversation with Yahweh, Satan speaks of having wandered "back and forth and up and down through the world" (Job 1:7, 2:2). The language of his search echoes an instruction that sent Jeremiah searching Jerusalem's streets to find just such a man as Job, "one who does justice and seeks truth" (Jer 5:1).

Referring to Satan's task, Yahweh speaks of Job in the role that the ancient world presents the king: "Have you seen my servant?" The righteousness of the king in his role as faithful servant of the divine is measured by his commitment to justice, by his fear of God and by his turning away from evil (Job 2:3).[5] In Job's relentless effort to bring God to trial, however, he is one of the princes in uproar of Psalm 2. The role is forced on him by the trial of his integrity and supports an ironic function. Like the young David hunted by King Saul (1 Sm 26:19), Job has been thrust out of Yahweh's service by his "opponent." His integrity is preserved during this uproar as he listens to the counsel of the Psalter's messiah. Job's kiss is ever clean and his fear of God unshaken (Ps 2:11–12). Though the plot proposes to test Job's integrity, the debates with his three friends rarely touch the issue. They rather give an occasion for his suffering and win the audience to his side. The theme of Job's loyalty and the bet itself are dispatched before the debates begin.

Although the book's ambitions are large, the question of whether he will "curse God and die," as his wife reasonably suggests (Job 2:10) and as Satan had predicted (Job 2:5b), is never separated from its alternative: that he will bless God and live. The question of whether to bless or curse God is a single question that is answered in the Janus-faced equivocation of *brkh*'s syntax. Overtones of judgment dominate. Job's answer to his wife's outburst is tradition laden. Like Eve in the garden story, striving to know both good and evil, Job's wife will have her husband know both curse and blessing. Like his ancestor Cain, with sin crouching at his door, Job is tempted to turn against the good (Gen 4:7). Job's answer returns discernment of good and evil, blessing and curse, to God, to whom alone such judgment belongs. For Job, mankind's role is to accept whatever the divine *brkh* offers. "If we accept the good from God, we must also accept the evil" (Job 2:10).

The role of Job as foreigner gives opportunity for an Arabic-laden rhetoric, which contrasts brilliantly with a lucid classical Hebrew. It presents its Jewish audience with an identity-creating epitome of the Torah as love of the stranger (Lev 19:10, 18, 34; Dt 10:18–19). Job fills the role of the foreigner for whom Solomon prays: one who comes from a far country, a model of piety in all that he does (1 Kgs 8:41–43). Like Satan, his "opponent," Job's cue name ("the enemy," "one attacked") determines his role in the story. He is presented as a foreign king, the enemy implied by his name. As foreign enemy, he shares a role with the king of Nineveh in the story of the prophet Jonah; Job responds to Yahweh's *brkh* by imitating this king whose city had been cursed. Job stands up, takes off his robe, shaves his head, falls to the ground and sits in ashes (Job 1:20, 2:8). Nineveh's king "arose from his throne, removed his robe, covered himself in sackcloth and sat in ashes" (Jon 3:6). Job is "the greatest among all of the sons of Qedem" (Job 1:3). This not only links his story to Cain's, which has Yahweh play the good Samaritan as Cain's "keeper." It also clothes Job with a royalty that rivals Nineveh's in both grandeur and enmity to Israel. He is Qedem's king of Babylon (Gen 11:2). The long debates among the story's sons of Qedem are foreign: in language, with Arabic nuance; in metaphor, with rich desert imagery and in its relentless critique of a stereotyped Jewish piety. All support a dominating motif of alienation. Not only Job but his book is the stranger among the books of the Hebrew Bible and, at the same time, an enemy in uproar against the tradition (Lev 19:34; Ps 2:1).

In developing Job's role as the faithful servant to whom Yahweh is unfaithful, the story also offers a reverse echo of David's treatment of Uriah (cf. 2 Sm 12:8–10, 22:51). Yahweh's singular restriction on Satan's power over Job allows Job to be dead Uriah's protesting voice against David. Yahweh's treatment of Job as an enemy parallels Saul's sin against David, his faithful servant (1 Sm 26:21), and may also lie behind the role of the messiah in Psalm 89, where it is the son of David who, Job-like, begs relief from Yahweh's wrath—a cry unanswered from a faithful servant abandoned by his God (Ps 89:39–52). Such parallels in the story roles of David's tradition draws support in Job's nostalgic return to his past. A small echo of the magic oil through which the messiah becomes the "anointed one" might be glimpsed in the idyllic picture Job draws: "when my steps were washed with milk and the rock poured out for me streams of oil" (Job 29:6). Linguistic ties of feet to step allow Job's description to be linked with the patriarch Asher. As the darling child among his brothers, his are oil-dipped feet (Dt 33:24). They find their counterpart in Job's milk-washed step (Job 29:6a) and evoke a paralleling luxury of "the rock," pouring out for Job "streams of olive oil" (Job 29:6b). This verse surpasses even the Israel-embracing Jeshurun in a song that also looks back to former times. Jeshurun's former land's oil-bearing flint is likened to a faithful God, Israel's rock of salvation (Dt 32:1–14). The magic wonder of Job and the oil of blessing in Deuteronomy are also used in the story of Elijah's magic oil jug. Expectations are evoked of a Moses-like rock, pouring out rivers of oil (cf. Job 29:6b; Dt 32:13; 1 Kgs 17:16). Job's paths are anointed. The issue is not restricted to clever rhetoric. The lyrical play of Job's feet washed in milk, paralleled by the blessed fertility of oil-bearing rock, reflects a more complex symbol system that will be examined more closely in the following chapters. The desert context of Israel's testing (Dt 32:10–14) and the famine-creating drought of Elijah's story support an understanding of the trials of Job, the desert king become innocent sufferer. It is a variation on Israel's own story.

Job remembers the honor once shown him at the city gate:

> When I went out to the gate of the city, when I prepared my seat at the square, the young men saw me and withdrew and the aged rose and stood. Princes refrained from talking and laid their hand on their mouth. The voice of the nobles was hushed and their tongue cleaved to the roof of their mouth. (Job 29:7–11)

Young and old gave place; princes and rulers were silent, as Job spoke in his role as judge at the city gate. When his city's great men lay their hands on their mouths in respect to their king (Job 29:9), their humility gives Job the recognition and respect Job himself, finally humbled, will offer to Yahweh at the story's closure. It is with fulsome irony that Job, "having spoken once" (sic), humbly lays his hand over his mouth in respect to his divine patron (Job 40:1–5). The king's role is to be God for his people, as Moses was for Aaron (Ex 4:16) and the king of Psalm 2 and 110 for all the world's princes. Even as Solomon, whose wisdom was greater than the sons of Qedem, Job's philosopher's role before his people at the gate bears echoes of a divine wisdom (1 Kgs 3:28; 4:29–34). The idyllic picture of Job as philosopher king and judge of his people stands opposite Isaiah and his generation in Israel. Job's people see and hear with understanding, whereas Isaiah's Israel had ears kept heavy and eyes closed by Yahweh's prophet (Job 29:11; Is 6:9–10). The intensity of this contrast between Isaiah's Israel and Job's role as a foreign Solomon is so great that one must ask whether it is the stranger Job that the Solomon of Ecclesiastes refers to with envy:

> There is an evil which I have seen under the sun and it lies heavy upon men: a man to whom God gives wealth, possessions and honor, so that he lacks nothing of all that he desires. Yet, God does not give him power to enjoy them. Rather, a stranger enjoys them . . . (Eccl 6:1–2)

When Job's enlightened princes finally give voice to their hushed respect, they call him "blessed" (Job 29:10–11), as Elizabeth calls Mary (Lk 1:42). Mary responds to this greeting by singing Hannah's song, celebrating the reversals of destiny that mark the good news to the poor and inaugurate the kingdom (Lk 1:46–56; 1 Sm 2:1–10). So too Job replies to his princes with a similar eightfold version of the song for a poor man:

I delivered the poor who cried and the fatherless who had none to help. The blessing of him who was about to die came over me and I caused the widow's heart to sing for joy. . . . I was eyes to the blind and feet to the lame. I was father to the poor and I searched out the cause of him whom I did not know. (Job 29:12–13, 15–16)

The good king, inaugurating the kingdom of God's *shalom,* announces his good news: "the day of joy" to end war (cf. Num 10:9–10; Is 40:9). Job's victory was won on "the day of need" for the helpless. He protected the poor, the orphan, the crippled and the widow; the blind, the lame, the helpless and the stranger. When this eightfold list closes with the stranger, it evokes the closing stanza of David's song of peace, when Yahweh saved him from all his enemies:

I will praise you, O Yahweh among the nations and sing praises to your name.
He has given his king great victories and shows steadfast love to his messiah,
to David and his descendants forever. (2 Sm 22:49–50)

This movement from war to peace transforms David into a universal king, even over foreigners he does not know, essential in giving David's story its universal character (2 Sm 22:44–46). Job's story uses this holy war rhetoric, however, with themes of social justice. In his care for the poor, he reflects the ideal, victorious prince of peace. In the center of Job's eightfold list of the oppressed for whom he has been savior, arbitrating the song's center in terms of judgment, is the self-description: "righteousness clothed me as a judge's cap" (Job 29:14). To be clothed in righteousness is the ideal of the priest in the Psalter. It brings joy to the pious (Ps 132:9). A variant is quoted by Solomon at prayer: "Let your priests, God Yahweh, be clothed with salvation, and may your saints rejoice" (2 Chr 6:41–42).

Job's role is also cosmic and mythological. While Job at the gate is dressed like Solomon at prayer, causing the pious to rejoice, he is also the conquering king in holy war (Job 29:17). This violent closure to our eightfold list of royal piety marks the trope with its apocalyptic essence. It gives the transcendent meaning of Job's good deeds: "I broke the fangs of evil; I ripped its prey from between its teeth." Job has a mythic, messianic role. By conquering evil, he creates a kingdom of peace in which care for the poor, the widow and the stranger reigns. This important verse evokes an ancient Near Eastern version of the myth of St. George and the Dragon, echoing, as we will see, Marduk's defeat of Tiamat in the Babylonian creation story. The Psalter uses a comparable metaphor. There, Yahweh is called to rise and strike David's enemies on the cheek, breaking the teeth of the wicked (Ps 3:8). In another song, the snake-like fangs of the ungodly are joined with literal jaws of a lion: "O God, break the teeth in their mouths, tear out the fangs of the young lions" (Ps 58:7), forcing the monsters to vomit their booty.

The metaphor recasts the ancient Egyptian myth of the sun god's victory over the Apophis dragon. Although dislocation of the evil one's fangs may be a biblical gloss, the specific motif of ripping the prey from between the dragon's teeth can be traced to the tale of Seth's conquest of the dragon of the west. This Apophis dragon is a legendary representative of pharaoh's enemies. As in the Bible's revision of the myth, the Egyptian conquest over evil is closely linked to the song for a poor man and is presented with a pedagogical rhetoric: slogans encouraging the care and protection of the oppressed.[6] The evil one is stereotyped as a dragon that attacks the sun barge and threatens to prevent the sun from beginning the new day. This perhaps has evoked the motifs of life and rebirth in Job 29. Two well-known texts support this suggestion. "A Hymn to Amon-Re"[7] builds directly on the Seth-Apophis myth. The Eye of Amon-Re defeats the rebels by sending a spear to pierce the evil dragon and to "make the fiend disgorge what he has swallowed" (line iv.1). The conquest over the dragon leads immediately to a song of praise with an Egyptian variation of the song for a poor man:

Who extends his arms to him he loves, while his enemy is consumed by a flame. It is his Eye that overthrows the rebel and sends its spear into him that sucks up Nun and makes the fiend disgorge what he has swallowed. Hail to you, O Re, lord of truth, whose shrine is hidden, the Lord of the Gods, . . . who hears the prayer of him who is in captivity. Gracious of heart in the face of an appeal to him, saving the fearful from the terrible of heart, judging the weak and the injured. . . . When he comes, the people live. He who gives scope to every eye that may be made in Nun, whose loveliness has created the light. In whose beauty the gods rejoice; their hearts live when they see him. (no. 8: Papyrus Bulaq 17, stanza 4)

The theme is reiterated in a later stanza, in which the crew of the sun barge rejoices as the sun continues its course unhindered:

The crew is in joy when they see the overthrow of the rebel, his body licked up by the knife. Fire has devoured him; his soul is more consumed than his body. That dragon: his power of motion is taken away; the gods are in joy; the crew of Re is in satisfaction; Heliopolis is in joy; for the enemies of Atum are overthrown (stanza ix–x).[8]

The reuse of these themes in the Merneptah stele, which is dominated by the tropes of the song for a poor man, attaches the myth of the defeat of the dragon to the victory over all of pharaoh's enemies—echoed in David's song (2 Sm 22:1). Furthermore, it draws on the specific thematic element of Job's evil one, forced to give up its prey from between its teeth. It places that motif in a similar logic of retribution and compares the monster to a crocodile:

> Ptah said about the enemy of Rebu: gather together all his crimes and return them on his (own) head. Give them into the hand of Merneptah-hotep-hiv-Maat, that he may make him disgorge what he has swallowed like a crocodile.[9]

Job's violent victory over the dragon, accomplished through his eightfold compassion for the poor and the oppressed, offers the reader of his book an early glimpse of Leviathan, Yahweh's pet, who is later described as a fire-breathing crocodile spreading terror even among the gods (Job 40:25–41:36). Leviathan's description as "king over all the children of pride" sets this great crocodile in the role of Job's opposite, illustrating the song of the poor man's inexorable opposition between the pride of evil and the humility of the saviour. Humility conquers pride; even terror itself.

The saying "my roots spread out to the waters, with the dew all night on my branches" (Job 29:19) expands on the previous verse in which Job speaks of his expectations of a long, secure life. This offers an image of Job as a righteous tree on the day of judgment (Ps 1:3; Jer 17:6–8; Job 14:7–9). He not only represents the pious in his care for the poor; he is the righteous man bringing eternal life. Similarly, Job's expectation that his "bow" would be ever new in his hand is a phallic metaphor of a king's virility and potency, which in Egyptian hymns and the Psalter possesses an eternal endurance (Job 29:20). This figure of Job and his potency can be contrasted both to Ichabod and as Saul's shame (2 Sm 1:19–27) to David's final impotence (1 Kgs 1:1–4).

Job closes his reflections on his former life by returning to his opening metaphor in order to define his figure as a Cain, transformed by righteousness. As God once watched over him, he too was a watcher for his people, the good shepherd of Psalm 23, choosing their path for them (Job 29:25; cf. 29:2). Again Job's story becomes parable. Similarly, Psalm 78 explicitly presents itself as a parable to embody Israel's story. Through this story, the reader—like the reader of Isaiah—might learn from the story told. The list of reversals of fate in Job 29 mark him as the good king and orient his story toward *imitatio*. This literary strategy is well represented. Like Psalm 78, Job's story reflects mankind's journey. When Yahweh sleeps as in the Psalter (Ps 78:65) or rests as on the Sabbath after creation (Gen 2:2–3), or, as in Job's case, ceases to watch over him (Job 29:2), a Cain-like human fails. The test of Job, set by Yahweh and Satan for Qedem's king, is the role David is chosen for (Ps 78:70). He is the shepherd king. It is his royal task to watch his flock with the integrity of his heart (Ps 78:72). This role is expressed in his opening considerations of the time "when God's candle shone on my head; when, with his light, I walked in darkness": "you will light my candle" (Job 29:3; 2 Sm 22:29). Job, receiving his light from God, becomes his people's light, mediating the divine (Job 29:3, 24–25). The metaphor parallels the role of Adam, passing on the "image of God" to his son (Gen 5:3). Job passes the divine light to his people that the light of his face—like the face of Moses—might shine in their darkness (Job 29:24–25; Ex 34:29–35). This interesting double reflection on divine revelation and humanity as God's image (Gen 1:26, 5:1, 9:2) is expanded in the metaphor of Elihu's fresh new wine, interpreting Job's self-description: "I put on righteousness and it clothed me" (Job 29:14). Elihu comments on Job's nostalgic reflections on his former life and particularly on Job's understanding that the spirit of God gave him his life (Job 33:4). Elihu reminds Job that if God had withdrawn this life from the world, all would die (Job 34:14–15). So too, Elihu argues, it is with righteousness. He knows that God is righteous because his servant Job is; all righteousness, like life, comes from God (Job 35:5–8). In this argument, Job becomes piety's legitimation. True to the function of the king as God's reflection on earth, all arguments of human value have their corresponding reality in the divine.

Job as a figure of parable epitomizes the values the tradition presents to the pious for *imitatio*. Job's reiteration of the Abraham story—another tale of Yahweh testing his faithful servant—can be recognized in the structural relationships of the envelope story of the death and resurrection of Job's family (Job 1–2, 42) to the book's presentation of Job's test through suffering. The story of the good king and the test of his virtue has its universal goal in all mankind's enlightenment (Job 33:23–30, 34:21–30, 36:16–21, 37:21–23a). Job, as a biblical figure for *imitatio,* echoing the story of the children of Israel in Sinai's wilderness, also echoes Isaiah's presentation of Jacob as Yahweh's suffering servant (Is 40–55), itself a refraction of the story of Israel's test through an exile's desert.

Noah as Piety's Ideal

Similar to the figure of Job at the city gate is that of Noah at the opening of the flood story. He is presented as piety's ideal. In contrast to the *adam* (mankind), whose wickedness was great and whose heart so evil that Yahweh regretted having made him (Gen 6:5–7), "Noah found favor in Yahweh's eyes" (Gen 6:8). A threefold description presents his life for imitation. Three close synonyms describe him: "a righteous man, pious in his generation; Noah walked with God" (Gen 6:9). To "find favor in Yahweh's eyes" is Abraham's wish when Yahweh visits him at the oak of Mamre (Gen 18:3). Such favor is a king's grace to those under his protection. The description of Noah as a righteous man fits well the Psalter's metaphor for piety of "walking in the path of righteousness" (Ps 1:6). A righteous man is without guilt. He does not harm the poor, the innocent or the stranger (Ex 23:6–9). In contrast to Noah in the story is the *adam* (mankind), whom Yahweh made in his image (Gen 1:26) and now wishes to destroy with a flood. Noah's story is one of three tales that deal with a contrast between a single righteous man and an evil society. Abraham, in the thematically similar story of Sodom's destruction, is a man like Noah. He is "chosen that he may charge his children and his household to keep to the way of Yahweh by doing righteousness and justice" (Gen 18:19). The third story contrasting a righteous man with an evil society is presented in Jeremiah, who engages thematic elements of both Noah's and Abraham's stories. It too is set in a scene of divine judgment that threatens to return the world to the empty chaos before creation (Jer 4:23–26). Jeremiah's Jerusalem is "skilled in evil, but does not know what it is to do good" (Jer 4:22). As in the Noah story, a single just man is given the role of savior. But when Jeremiah is told to run "to and fro through the streets of Jerusalem . . . to search its squares . . . and find a man who does justice and seeks truth" (Jer 5:1–6), no one is found.

The second element supporting the figure of Noah as pious, drawing on the Psalter's motif of integrity, is "perfect and without fault." These elements are particularly important in the cult of sacrifice with which the flood story closes. The integrity of the lamb offered is metaphorically likened to the purity of heart of the pious, whose way is contrasted with "the way of mankind" (Ps 101:2, 6; 119:1–2). That Noah "walked with God," with its close variant "to walk before God," is a typical epitome for piety. Enoch "walked with god" and, after living on earth a perfect 365 years, is taken up to heaven like Elijah (Gen 5:24; cf. 2 Kgs 2:11). Abraham was instructed to "walk before God and be perfect" (Gen 17:1). He "walked before the face of God," who supported him in all he did (Gen 24:40).

Noah's role as disaster survivor supports the reader's identification with those who have survived exile, with new beginnings. Noah as survivor has variants in the metaphors of both Isaiah's remnant and Jeremiah's new covenant. Noah as figure of piety and as a new Adam is presented in an envelope structure for a version of the flood story drawn from the myths of Atrahasis and Gilgamesh.

The biblical version rewrites and reinterprets these earlier myths. The figure of Noah, however, comes from neither but has its roots in ancient Near Eastern royal ideology.

THE TESTIMONY OF THE GOOD KING IN
MONUMENTAL INSCRIPTIONS

Already in 1973 the Italian scholar Mario Liverani warned against distorting historical judgment by reading ancient inscriptions while ignoring their literary patterns. This is especially important in evaluating monumental inscriptions with biographical or autobiographical narratives, centered on the exploits of a king, his piety and valor and the quality of his rule.[10] In an analysis of some twenty monumental steles of kings—from ancient Mesopotamia, Anatolia, Syria and Egypt, I have been able to identify a stock cluster of elements used to describe the ideal life of the king. These texts are written on the occasion of the dedication of a temple, the end of a war or as memorials to the previous king and his reign. Three times their number could easily have been found, especially if one drew from victory hymns, campaign texts and building inscriptions. As these texts share considerable common ground in their use of metaphor, dramatic expression and social language, a comparison of the successive elements shows that this entire genre of literature presents a stereotypical figure rooted in piety and tradition.[11] In describing the elements and patterns of royal biographies and the way they relate to the creation of biblical narrative, the most striking characteristics are found in plotline. Six examples reflect the range of these stories and their many echoes in the Bible.

Esarhaddon (Text no. 4, Appendix 2).   After introducing himself as king of the universe and servant of Marduk, Esarhaddon describes how suffering and rebellion had preceded his reign. The gods were angry and planned evil against the kingdom. They sent a great flood against Babylon, and the people's destiny was determined that they be sent into exile and enslaved for seventy years. Merciful Marduk, however, repented and transformed the city's fate by returning the people from their exile in the eleventh year. Esarhaddon was chosen above his older brothers and, though reluctant in his humility to take up his great office, he was encouraged by the signs from heaven to rebuild the city and restore its temple. This story is echoed in many biblical narratives, and its plotline develops in well recognized patterns. The evil of the former king, rebellion against the gods, divine anger, planning destruction by flood—even the choosing of Esarhaddon—

find reiteration in Noah's story of the great flood in Genesis 6. The exile of the people, their enslavement for seventy years, the reversal of their fortune, the election of a savior and the divine command to restore and to rebuild the city and the temple all find descendants in the biblical story of exile and return as they are presented in Isaiah, Jeremiah, Ezra and Nehemiah. Singular elements such as Esarhaddon's reluctance and humility, that he is called to kingship before his older brothers and the echoes of the song for a poor man are clearly reiterated in the stories of the reluctant Moses (Ex 4:10–16) and Isaiah (Is 6:5–7) and in the story of David, chosen by Yahweh though the youngest of seven brothers (1 Sm 16:1–13). Esarhaddon's title, King of the Universe, which he shares with all his royal predecessors, is also Yahweh's title in the Bible, well reflected in Zechariah's utopian prophecy that "Yahweh will be king over all the world" (Zech 14:9). "Servant of God" is a ubiquitous description of Moses, Job, David and especially Israel (Num 12:7; Ps 31:17; Is 49:3). Esarhaddon's prayer that his seed be an eternal seed finds precise reiteration in the "holy seed" of Isaiah's Immanuel theme (Is 6:13) and in the eternal seed of the House of David (Ps 89:5). That the Assyrian king presents himself as "the plant of life" for his people is a delightful reiteration of Gilgamesh's "plant that makes one young again." It is comparable to the description of pharaoh as the "fountain of life" for his subjects—both obvious forerunners of the medieval "fountain of youth." In the biblical tradition, this widely used motif first presents itself in the tree of life of the paradise story. The role of return to paradise and the tree of life is given to the stream flowing from the temple in Ezekiel's eschatological vision (Ez 47; cf. Ps 36:10). This is reused in the book of Revelation to close with a return to paradise (Rev 22:14). A related motif is found in the king's prayer for the blessing of a long life and fertility. This finds ubiquitous resonance in the Bible (e.g., Ex 20:12; Gen 17:6). Like Esarhaddon, David rules in righteousness (2 Sm 8:15) and walks in the path of light (Ps 27:1, 112:4, 119:105).

Sargon of Akkad (Text no. 1). In the story of Sargon, the king is given the birth of a hero. Its pattern of the child whose life is threatened but is rescued and raised in obscurity is well-known from the Greek Oedipus legend, and also finds a Mosaic reiteration. The child Moses is similarly born secretly, placed in a basket of reeds and later "drawn from the water" (Ex 2:1–10). Sargon is raised by a poor man—directly paralleled by Oedipus's shepherds. In the Bible, this element is given an ironic reversal as the very daughter of the one who would kill Moses, saves him. The motif of miraculous—even virginal—conception by Sargon's priestess-mother rests in the status of the mother. It finds its biblical occasion in the prophet Isaiah, who impregnates his prophetess that she might give birth to the coming terror that will overwhelm Israel (Is 8:1–3). Matthew and Luke's virgin Mary is a more distant variant that plays on a motif of divine insemination. That motif is more obvious in the story of Samson's birth (Jgs 13). Sargon's role as Ishtar's lover has echoes in the Gilgamesh story but is absent from the Bible, except perhaps as played by Adam as Eve's consort, "the mother of all living" (Gen 3:20), a title also given to Ishtar. His role as her father's gardener is a royal role that Adam is given in the paradise story (Gen 2:5, 8). Sargon's conquering mountains and valleys, with its variant in the king's conquest of Dilmun's desert and Kazallu's mountains, answers to the theme of the conquering hero, a motif also present in Nebuchadnezzar's story (no. 6). It is famously reiterated in Isaiah to prepare the path for Israel's return to Jerusalem (Is 40:3–5). In turn, Isaiah is cited and reinterpreted by Luke for use as a metaphor for the path of the savior inaugurating the kingdom (esp. Lk 3:5–6). Finally, the presentation of Sargon's life as a role model for his successors clearly sets the primary function of ancient biographical narratives in instruction.

Idrimi (Text no. 13). The pattern of Idrimi's story has long been seen as a forerunner of the story of David's rise to the throne.[12] Idrimi's flight to the desert, his life among the Hapiru and his role as chief of Ammiya, where he lives among the Hapiru for seven years, is paralleled by David's flight (1 Sm 19:9–20:42), his life with the Philistines (1 Sm 27) and his chieftainship in Hebron for seven years (2 Sm 2:1–7, 5:5). Like both Esarhaddon and David, Idrimi rises to power, though the youngest among his brothers. Like David in the Goliath story and Elihu with his intellectual's new wine in Job (1 Sm 17; Jb 32:6–14), Idrimi has thoughts no one else thinks. The double story of Saul threatening his servant David's life (1 Sm 24, 26) has its counterpart in Barratarma's hostility toward his servant Idrimi. When David finally becomes king and enemies rise up against him on all sides (2 Sm 5–10), he takes a role comparable to Idrimi's before him. Idrimi's goal of bringing an end to war is echoed by the biblical story's evoking the eternal peace of the kingdom to Solomon. Finally, like Idrimi, David builds his house and restores the cult of the ancestors, the ark of Yahweh, to Israel.

Ashurbanipal II (Text no. 3). The story of Ashurbanipal is also idealized and filled with hyperbole. He is perhaps to be compared with the story of the young Solomon (1 Kgs 2:12–10:13). He is high priest, beloved of the gods and king of the world. He is a hero, a servant of god without peer, shepherd of all and ruler over all nations. Fearless himself, he holds as his own the divine attribute of terror. He is the "irresistible flood." Like Solomon before his fall, he rules in wisdom and knowledge. However, unlike Solomon in his pride, who creates a divided house, Ashurbanipal is servant in his "garden of happiness" and rules a paradise with forty kinds of trees. He reforms the cult, builds temples and restores towns. He is the beloved of the gods (cf. 2 Sm 12:24–25).

Nebuchadnezzar II (Text no. 6). This very short inscription tells its story quickly with a large cluster of stereotyped elements. Nebuchadnezzar is servant of Marduk, a wise and successful ruler. The story's plot develops dramatically when the king, like Solomon, wants his timber from Lebanon but cannot have it. Three evils are presented: foreigners, robbers and a people scattered over the face of the earth. Like Isaiah's Cyrus, Nebuchadnezzar accepts his role as Lebanon's savior and brings Lebanon's exiles back to their homes (cf. Is 44:28–45:1). Nebuchadnezzar is the eternal king of Babylon and, like David, prays that his dynasty be forever.

Mesha (Text no. 21). Mesha's narrative shares the same ideal picture of kingship and the same story pattern, though it is considerably longer and more complicated. A number of interesting motifs support the plot. David-like, he uses two hundred soldiers to fight his holy war and brings peace to one hundred towns. Again like David in the title of Psalm 18, Mesha is saved by his god, Chemosh, from all of his enemies. Moab suffered because Chemosh, like Yahweh, was angry at his people and abandoned his land. Defeat comes because Chemosh fights on the side of the enemy, as Yahweh did on the side of Assyria and Babylon. Mesha speaks of the sacred ban and dedicates the enemy and his property as sacrifices to Chemosh. The land is cleansed of both foreigners and foreign gods, as in the biblical holy war tradition. The purification of the cult places and the removal of elements of Yahweh, being led in war by Chemosh, marching through the night and attacking at dawn, like Merneptah led by the sun god Re, brings victory at high noon.[13] These are all stereotypical thematic elements of holy war stories in the Bible and throughout the ancient Near East. Similarly, the projection of a peace in which Chemosh returns to his people and land, every person has his own cistern, ruins are restored, towns and roads built and the whole of Diban subjugated to the king are all classical elements, marking peace and prosperity.

All of the inscriptions analyzed reflect comparable parallels in biblical narrative.[14] Certain elements are important for plot development. Hard and evil times before the king's reign establish an expectation that his saving reign will reverse the fate of the people, much as attacking enemies eager to murder in every heroic story leads to expectations of victory and judgment. Such former divine anger opens the role of the hero as chosen one, the reformer and restorer of proper worship. The most immediate surprise in the analysis of these narratives is how little the stories depart from a broad tradition and symbol system of royal ideology, which is common to most of the ancient world. Particular motifs and metaphors, as well as the progression and pattern of plotlines, are thoroughly stereotyped. We should consider an interactive scribal tradition, creating a genre or story type. An implicit template, presupposed by the story, is most marked in short, simple inscriptions like Sargon's, where the story of the king's life holds to a few coherent themes. The Syrian Zakkur narrative, for example (no. 17), holds itself almost entirely to themes of piety and creates a model of the good king. He is brought up and chosen by the God of Heaven to be king. Like the messiah of Psalm 2, he fights against generic nations in uproar. Also like David of the Psalter, he is a model for piety and patience and assured that Baal will save him. Like all great kings since the story of Gilgamesh, he builds his city and its walls and shrines to his god.

THEMATIC FUNCTIONS IN THE STORY OF THE GOOD KING

The associations between Near Eastern texts and traditions stretch well beyond similar motifs sharing a similar purpose. The clustering of elements and patterns, and the techniques for setting different themes together to build greater stories, help us identify specific motifs and themes as belonging to a common ideology and sharing a common symbol system.[15] In identifying the large cluster of different motifs in what I have called the song for a poor man, the recognition of such stereotypical elements gives the reader access to the literary and intellectual world implicit in the text. This is also true in the clustering of thematic elements in the Elijah tradition or around the figure of the child or the motif of tears in biblical texts. The order of presentation and the hint of specific nuance in such clustering allows us to identify and define specific patterns, both expressed and implied.[16] The purpose of the analysis of the testimonies of the good king is to see how the texts work in this early genre of biography. These texts also share many metaphors, dramatic expressions and social language with Egyptian literature.[17] Found in both story and song, their common ground is located in their understanding of the role of the king.

With one exception, each of the twelve functions presented below is found in the majority of the inscriptions under consideration. The exception is the announcement of the "good news," an often dramatic or miraculous element, creating astonishment or evidence that the gods are with the king. The function is well integrated in the nine inscriptions in which it appears (nos. 1, 4–8, 10, 13, 21). All of the other functions are found in at least fifteen of the twenty-one inscriptions. Two functions (dedication and declaration of patronage) appear in every inscription. Given the close relationship of such functions to the form of the texts considered, this could be expected. Similarly, two functions (legitimation and expression of piety) occur in all but a single text. The consistent clustering of these four functions helps identify the genre of the text. Four inscriptions use all twelve (nos. 1, 6, 7, 8), five use all but one (nos. 4, 10, 15, 18, 21) and six all but two functions (nos. 2, 3, 5, 9, 13, 19). Those which reflect the fewest functions (no. 11 with six; nos. 12, 14, 20, with seven functions), are among the very shortest and are relatively weak in narrative engagement, though they share the genre-defining cluster of themes of dedication, patronage, legitimation and piety.

The Dedication of the Memorial

Some of our stories serve as memorials to the king, while others are dedications of a cult place. Thirteen of the twenty-one inscriptions are presented in autobiographical form, where the king plays the role of author as well as subject. Eight present the story of the king in the third person. The Idrimi stele (no. 13), which is engraved on a statue of the king, presents its first-person form by locating the closing lines in a cartoon balloon coming out of the king's mouth. In spite of the autobiographical form, some of these inscriptions are likely posthumous.

The Legitimation of the King

The rhetoric of legitimation usually identifies the king as son or as son and grandson of the former king or kings (no. 21). Some of the stories use the occasion to argue for an enhanced legitimacy. Azatiwada (no. 15) argues that his patron is Awariku, the great king of the Danunians. Similarly, Bar-Rakib (no. 20) refers to his father, king of Sam'al, as the client of the great Assyrian king, Tiglath-Pileser. Yet others turn to the gods to enhance their claims. Cyrus (no.

8) refers to his father and grandfather as ones "whom the gods loved," thereby tying his legitimacy to a divine patron. Similarly, Idrimi (no. 13) refers to his overlord, the Hurrian king Barratarna, as his family's traditional patron, and he also identifies himself as "son of Ilimilimma, servant of Adad, Hepat and Ishtar." While Esarhaddon (no. 4) uses the grandeur of his royal titles to support legitimacy, Sargon offers a miraculous birth as the son of a (virgin) priestess and an unknown father. In the Bible, claims for legitimacy are most obvious in the presentation of Proverbs as "the proverbs of Solomon, son of David, king of Israel" (Prv 1:1) or of Ecclesiastes as "the words of the speaker, the son of David, king in Jerusalem" (Eccl 1:1). Some authors present their work with a rhetoric closer to Zakkur's, who argues for a divine legitimacy, much as in Hosea, "The word of Yahweh, which came to Hosea, son of Beeri, during the reigns of Uzziah" (Hos 1:1), and Zephanaiah, "This is the word of Yahweh, which came to Zephanaiah, son of Cushi, son of Gedaliah, son of Amariah, son of Hezekiah" (Zeph 1:1).

Divine Patronage

This function is usually fulfilled by a declaration that the patron deity or the gods choose the king, stand by him, lead him in battle, listen to his prayers, entrust him with the kingdom, turn the hearts of the people to the king or—as in the Pannamuwa inscription (no. 19)—save him from past destruction. The king declares himself to be the client, servant or worshiper of the divine. He gives tribute to the gods or calls on them to carry out his curse.

In integrating this function in a dramatic narrative, the rhetoric varies from the formal cadences of official statements about loyalty to the king's divine patron to a rhetoric common to folktales. Yahdun-Lim (no. 2) declares that Shamash is the patron of Mari, but Ashurbanipal II (no. 3) makes the relationship more intimate, declaring himself the favorite of the gods. Sargon's inscription (no. 1) draws entirely on folktale. The function is implicit in his heroic birth and in his claim to be Ishtar's lover and her father's gardener. Similarly, Zakkur (no. 17) claims that Baal Shamem raised him. In the Bible, Samuel is raised in the temple and Israel, in Isaiah, grows up and is educated by his father, Yahweh.

Theologically rich and variable, the Mesha inscription (no. 21) makes divine patronage the central dramatic element of the king's life story. As in David's song of gratitude to Yahweh "after Yahweh had saved him from all of his enemies (and from Saul)" (2 Sm 22:1), the god Chemosh "protected (Mesha) from all his enemies." His story illustrates this through a narrative of retribution and reversal in Mesha's war with Israel. Like Yahweh in biblical narrative, Chemosh "dwells in the land." The theme breaks off when Chemosh finally returns to the town of Horonaim. The opposition between Israel's Omri and his son and the divine Chemosh is pedagogical. Although Omri was the servant of Chemosh and the tool of his anger against Moab, he and his son—like Isaiah's Sennacherib—are proud (Is 37:21–29). They act with hubris in oppressing Moab. They *dwell in* Madeba in the place of Chemosh. Moab's former evil is doubly reversed. Israel "perishes forever" and its presence in Moab is replaced by Chemosh, who once again *dwells* in the land.

Assertions of divine patronage over Israel and Jerusalem dominate biblical literature as thoroughly as they do Mesha's story. It is the first premise of ancient royal ideology that the gods represent true kingship and are the source of all just rule. The Psalter reiterates the voice of Mesha and Merneptah. The names of godless nations are eternally erased: their cities turned into deserts and their memory lost. In their stead, Yahweh is enthroned forever (Ps 9:6–8).

Declaration of the King's Virtue

This declaration is in all of our texts and is offered with rich variation. Sargon's (no. 1) self-presentation as Ishtar's lover and her father's gardener is the most ambitious. More typical is Yahdun-Lim's (no. 2) fulfillment of more standard royal duties. He is a digger of canals, builder and provider for his people. Seven of the kings assume the role of the wise, just and righteous ruler who brings peace to his land. Two are teachers. Others describe themselves "like family" to the people, or they are too humble and hesitant to seek power for themselves. Nabonidus (no. 6) is innocent of all harm to Babylon and goes into mourning when the gods depart. Idrimi (no. 13), like the biblical Joseph, has a priest or wise man's ability to know the future. Others—like many biblical kings—listen to prophets and diviners. Some have future-revealing dreams and some pray. Suppiluliuma (no. 10) describes his piety ("fear of God") even toward enemy gods. Obedience, truth, generosity and humility are the virtues of a good king. Mesha's role as dutiful client is implicit. He is ever the humble servant of Chemosh. His piety is explicit only in the dedication of captives in sacrifice to Chemosh. The contrasting biblical story of Saul, who refuses to dedicate Agag to Yahweh in 1 Samuel 15, shares the same value of the king's humble role as servant of the divine. Saul's lack of piety in the biblical story is the effective cause of his fall from grace. In hubris, Saul acts as if he himself were king. The Mesha story is cast in the inscription as an example story, with Mesha as ideal servant of the only true king, Chemosh.[18]

Past Suffering

While functions of patronage and piety provide both context and tone to these narratives, the theme of suffering opens their plot. In Yehawmilk's cry to his goddess for help (no. 16) and in the claim that he eliminated war and slander (no. 18), the former suffering in war and slander is only implied. Like Moses in his basket on the Nile, the baby Sargon (no. 1), in danger of his life, is cast adrift in a basket of rushes. Rebellion and conspiracy are found in several texts and create dominant plotlines in the stories of both Mursili II (no. 10) and Mesha (no. 21). Suffering illustrates the evil to be overcome by the good king. It lies close to the theme of divine patronage. As in the Bible, gods are responsible for human fate. Esarhaddon (no. 4) must deal with angry gods who flood Babylon and send its people into slavery. Perhaps in contrasting parallel, Yahweh sends a flood against the Egyptians and frees Israel from slavery (Ex 14–15). In Nabonidus's tale (no. 6), Mandeans plundered temples and cult places, bringing the king into mourning for the loss of the gods. Similarly—and ironically—Cyrus (no. 8) deals with the godlessness of Nabonidus by bringing Babylon's gods back from exile. Xerxes (no. 9)—like Hezekiah and Josiah—destroys the cult places of evil gods. Three stories draw out the dramatic potential of this theme. Idrimi (no. 13) is the youth with new thoughts, while Nabonidus (no. 7) is alone in the world. Both must flee to the desert—with David—to save his life. One is gone for seven years and the other for ten. Returning, Oedipus-like, they do not seek greatness but have it thrust on them. Similarly, when Pannamuwa's (no. 19) father and seventy brothers are killed, he must escape in a chariot. His homeland becomes his desert at the hands of the usurper. All three kings appropriately find their refuge in the gods (Ps 2:12). Also like David, all make friends and win the love of the people. After many struggles, they come to the throne, a fate destined for them by the gods. Like Mesha, Esarhaddon's story is marked by the suffering of his people. Like the people of Jerusalem, they have been cursed by their god with a Jeremiad sentence of seventy years' desolation (cf. Jer 25:11–12, 29:10). In Mesha's story, this motif is provided by his own thirty-year struggle to liberate Moab following Israelite oppression of his land for forty years under Omri and his son, allowed because Chemosh was angry with Moab. The hubris of Omri and his son challenges the role of Chemosh as king and provides Mesha with his savior's role.

Divine Involvement

The gods affect the world directly in only some of the inscriptions. Many stories are quite satisfied with a passive god functioning as the king's patron. Shamash listens to Yahdun-Lim (no. 2) and Asshur entrusts power to Esarhaddon (no. 4). But he actively chooses Ashurbanipal II (no. 3) to be king, announces his reign and even gives him instructions for hunting. In some stories, the gods also play essential roles and initiate the story's plot. They ask Nebuchadnezzar II (no. 5) for timber from the Lebanon. They deliver Panamuwa (no. 19) from the destruction of his father's house. They destroyed Babylon in the past (no. 6). They withdraw from the city and leave the temples empty and the people like living dead. Marduk orders the Persian Cyrus to attack Babylon and, in the same inscription, his mercy has the people welcome Cyrus without resistance (no. 8). In Cyrus's story, only a godless Nabonidus suffers defeat. In Nabonidus's own stories (nos. 6, 7), the gods—like Yahweh in Exodus and Kings—control all action. They call Nabonidus to kingship. They choose him to rebuild the temple. They give him lands to rule. They turn the land into a desert. They watch as shepherds over him. They cause his enemies to become his friends and break weapons raised against them. They cause his people to love him and they appoint the day for an end of suffering and exile. Less dramatically, Hadad protects Pannamuwa (no. 18) and grants everything he asks. The gods are with him in his victory. In other stories, the gods put down rebellion (no. 9) and—as in Exodus and Joshua—march in front of the king's army (no. 10). They cause the enemy to die in heaps and to fear the king. One common narrative pattern (cf. nos. 10, 15, 17) begins on the theme of past suffering. The gods reverse this in response to the king's humble prayer. This same pattern dominates the Hezekiah story and the songs of David in the Psalter.[19] In Mesha's story (no. 21), Chemosh is responsible for all that happens in Moab. The stele is made and dedicated to Chemosh because he "delivered the king from all his enemies." The narrative is a history of salvation: a story of the acts of Chemosh in Mesha's life. Beginning in the distant past, in the time when Chemosh was angry and absent, Moab's god told Mesha to take Nebo from Israel. He drives Israel before Mesha at Jahaz; he sends him in turn against Horonaim, takes the city and lives there. The role of Chemosh in this story is less miraculous and dramatic than the role Yahweh plays at Jericho, Ai and Gibeon (Josh 6–10). Nevertheless, it closely resembles the lesser stories of Joshua's conquest of Judah (esp. Josh 10:28–43).

Victory

Victory is usually over a cosmic or transcendent evil. It supports the king's role as servant of the gods in their struggle against evil. Azatiwada (no. 15) establishes peace with every king and makes evil men subject to his power. Panamuwa (no. 18) simply eliminates "war and slander," while Idrimi, like Isaiah's Yahweh, makes an end to warfare. In the Mesha stele (no. 21), theological language describes victory and Israel's destruction. This former weapon of Chemosh's wrath—is no more. In contrast, Chemosh's return is forever. Omri's former patronage is replaced by the grace of Chemosh's rule. The story goes on to describe transcendent victory over Yahweh with specific battles as examples. Mesha captures three towns: Ataroth, Nebo and Jahaz. These are the proud representatives of the all-inclusive one hundred towns of Diban. Chemosh sends his king on a further campaign against Horonaim when the text breaks off. With similar rhetoric, Joshua takes Makkeda, Libna and Lachish, before going on to Eglon, Hebron and Debir to end in a paraphrasing summation (Josh 10:28–43). Yahweh's relation to the land of Canaan parallels that of Chemosh to Moab. The theological perspective of Mesha's story can also be related to how David forced Philistia, Moab, Aram and Hamat into becoming his clients: "Yahweh gave David victory, everywhere that he engaged the enemy" (2 Sm 8:14; cf. 22:1).

The Reversal of Destinies

Within the ideology of royal inscriptions, elements of reversal illustrate the king's ability to reestablish creation as God intended. The function of this element is paired with past suffering: out of suffering comes salvation. The ability to reverse the destiny of the oppressed defines the king's power to mark the world with his will. While many short inscriptions lack this element, all of the larger, more expansive inscriptions emphasize it. The mythic qualities of this element are fundamental and frequently presented in fixed patterns. A new creation and new beginnings are expressed, as when Pannamuwa restores his land's fertility (no. 18; cf. Jer 31:12). In biblical narrative, the discourse on the heart of the Torah surrounds the many variations on the song for a poor man. Several Syrian inscriptions express the king's ability to bring divine love and care to his clients (nos. 14, 15, 19). In Esarhaddon's story (no. 4), such divine mercy is shown in the return of the gods to their temples and the resettlement of ruins (also nos. 3, 6, 7). Idrimi (no. 13) cares for the oppressed by settling nomads, improving housing and reestablishing the cult of his ancestors.

Balance and reciprocity frequently mark the reversals. Specific reversals are chosen to fit their story. The unsubmissive submit; the enslaved are freed (nos. 3, 4). Insecurity is transformed into security (no. 15). Geography is transformed as a divine highway is cut through the wilderness. Valleys are raised and mountains are leveled (nos. 1, 4, 5; cf. Is 40:3–5). The world is transformed socially when Azatiwada humbles the strong western lands to resettle them in the east (no. 15). Xerxes gives the motif a universal turn by simply making all that was bad good (no. 9). Cyrus stresses the transcendent quality of his role as savior (no. 8). He not only reverses the suffering of his people but raises the dead from their graves.

Establishing a Name

Fully half of the inscriptions explicitly express the purpose of "creating a name" for the king—a motif that the tower of Babel story marks as human pride to be humbled (Gen 11:1–9). The king's achievements and renown form an element in Assyrian royal inscriptions, with each king surpassing his predecessor in his virtuous deeds.[20] In the spirit of imitation, Sargon (no. 1) calls on his successors to do as he has done. In the Bible, this trope of imitation helps structure 2 Kings, where kings follow in the way of David or in the evil path of Jeroboam. A few kings speak of great deeds, like the building of zoological gardens (no. 2). Others, like Cyrus (no. 8), speak of the recognition nations or great kings give them (nos. 19, 20). Most use the role of hero—or the motif of youngest son, implying heroic stature—to enhance their personal ties to the heroic and the divine. Sargon uses his birth to hint at greatness (no. 1). He also speaks of his father as unknown, much as Nabonidus (no. 7) claims to be an "only son, one alone in the world." Both are in the tradition of the well-known self-description of Nabopolassar as "son of a nobody," one who has founded his own dynasty. Ashurbanipal (no. 3) painted murals recounting his heroic deeds.[21] Most kings, like Noah, Abraham, Moses and David, were chosen by the gods for greatness. Cyrus, like Abraham, is the "friend" of his god (no. 8). Idrimi's special thoughts are linked to the divine Adad, the reader of men's hearts, who turns to him, much as Yahweh turned to Abraham (Gen 18:17). A transcendental quality is also implied by Nebuchadnezzar II's (no. 5) claim to be "eternal king" and by his role as savior of his people. Similar divine qualities may be implied by the fear Suppiluliuma's enemies have of him (no. 10).[22] Azatiwada (no. 15) is "blessed" and a righteous king.

Building

The building and repairing of temples belongs to the end of war. These activities mark the prosperity and peace when God is in his heaven and all is right in this world. It is part of every king's glory. The roots of this theme are as deep as those of the Gilgamesh story, where the author, addressing his audience directly, speaks of the walls of Uruk that Gilgamesh built. He speaks of the temple of Eanna and of the adventures once engraved on a stele. The narrator invites us to see the fine burned brickwork and to remember Gilgamesh's great deeds.[23] At the end of the adventure that Gilgamesh's memorial stele invited the author to tell, Gilgamesh takes his own boatman to admire this same fine brickwork.[24] Yahdun-Lim's story (no. 2) closes with an account of repairs of the banks of the Euphrates and the building of a temple to Shamash. Asshurbanipal II (no. 3) erects temples and establishes festivals, while Esarhaddon (no. 4) rebuilds the walls of Babylon and restores Esagila. The first inscription of Nabonidus (no. 6) closes with a description of various building projects, including rebuilding Babylon's temple. His second inscription (no. 7) opens with a dream of being chosen to rebuild the temple in Harran. It closes with the temple completed. Azatiwada (no. 15) builds the city of Azatiwadaya and establishes offerings to Baal. Similarly, Zakkur (no. 17) rebuilds the city of Hazrach and its defenses and constructs shrines, while Yehawmilk (no. 16) more modestly builds an altar to Baal. Pannamuwa, (no. 18) builds "towns and villages" and makes offerings to the gods. Bar-Rakib (no. 20) ignores the religious function of such building and builds his own palace, as David did (2 Sm 5:11). Solomon, after spending seven years building Yahweh's house, takes fourteen to make his own even grander (compare 1 Kgs 6:15–22 with 1 Kgs 7:1–12). The Mesha stele (no. 21), like the Nabonidus texts, is set up to dedicate a sanctuary in Karchoh. In the story, Mesha builds Baal Meon and Kiriathaim. He reforms the cult and, destroying objects belonging to Yahweh, restores the cult to Moab's god. When he takes Jahaz, he builds Karchoh, Aroer and a road in the Arnon. He rebuilds Beth Bamoth and Bezer. The story's plotline links the theme of building to victory in war, much as the story of David's building projects is linked to his conquest of Jerusalem (2 Sm 5:9). Solomon's construction of the Jerusalem temple (1 Kgs 5:15–7:51) is even better associated with the theme of construction as piety.

Announcing Good News

This limited thematic element marks events as part of the divine plan. It is usually subordinate to the theme of a transcendent or utopian peace, though it also has independent qualities. It shows itself in special signs from the gods, often identified through numbers, marking the story's subordination to a destiny determined by divine curse or blessing. In Esarhaddon's narrative (no. 4), variations of this element create the reversal of fate from divine punishment to mercy. It is a guiding principle for Esarhaddon's reign. In a close parallel, already mentioned, Yahweh appoints seventy years for Israel's exile (Jer 25:11), expanding the curse of Israel to include destruction of the whole world by the sword.[25] Like Jeremiah and the book of Kings, Esarhaddon speaks of divine anger and, as in Genesis, he speaks of the evil of god's plan. Marduk, like Yahweh (Gen 8:21–22), regrets his plan to destroy Babylon and is merciful, reversing the city's fate and ending an implicit ten years of desolation by inaugurating a restoration in the eleventh year as he calls the story's hero to the throne of Assyria.[26] The key to divine destiny is in the numbers.[27] When Esarhaddon hesitates, favorable signs encourage him in his role as savior. The time of destiny can also be a movement of the plot. Nabonidus (no. 7) refers to the end of his ten years of wandering in the wilderness as occurring on *the appointed day*, marked by divine Sin's graciousness.[28] In the fullness of time, fate turns and Nabonidus prepares Babylon's restoration.

Other texts describe a final period, the ultimate goal of the king's rule, as divinely intended blessing. Nebuchadnezzar prepares a time of peace (no. 5). Promises of eternal or enduring rule are common (nos. 5, 6). They show that the powers of evil have been decisively defeated. This theme's eschatological potential is suggested by Cyrus (no. 8). Joy and shining faces from the whole land meet the good news of Marduk speaking Cyrus's name (Is 45:1–13). As in the Hebrew Bible, Cyrus brings life back to a land that had been dead, marking a resurrection theology that also plays a large role in the Bible's myth of exile.[29]

Peace at Last

The thematic element of *shalom* represents a utopian, comprehensive and usually transcendent state of peace. This is the goal of every king's reign.

Asshurbanipal's declaration (no. 3) that he has conquered all the lands from the Tigris to the Lebanon and from the Subnat to Urartu illustrates a utopian *shalom*. Like the biblical Solomon, who "ruled over all the kingdoms from the Euphrates to the land of the Philistines: all the way to the border of Egypt" (1 Kgs 5:1), Asshurbanipal has a kingdom that reaches to the borders of chaos. He has Solomon's wisdom; he builds his palace and paradise garden; he hunts and he tames the wild.

The theme of peace, as we have seen, can be expressed through other functions. Yahdun-Lim (no. 2) marks transcendence and permanence by expanding his realm to the mountains, uniting the region and setting an eternal tribute. Esarhaddon's story (no. 4) is also marked by a transcendent peace. His house, Babylon and the temple will endure forever and he will rule until he is old; he describes himself as "the plant of life" for his people. This function given Esarhaddon echoes the role Ezekiel is given in his utopian vision, in which Yahweh leads his prophet to the temple's life-creating spring and the trees of life, which shade a transformed Dead Sea (Ez 47:1–12). In the New Testament revision of this scene, as the tree of life takes over the temple's role as the goal of the kingdom of God, a messianic lamb carries out Esarhaddon's role (Rev 22:1–5). Esarhaddon, whose legends were among the most famous in antiquity, is the righteous man of the Psalter: a tree whose leaves do not wither (Ps 1:3). He is a plant of life for his people. Like the young Solomon, he creates a rule of justice that is eternal (1 Kgs 3:16–28, 5:7–12).

An eternal throne and an enduring dynasty mark *shalom* in the story of Nebuchadnezzar (no. 5) and the first of Nabonidus' stories (no. 6). While Nebuchadnezzar stresses the happiness and peacefulness of his reign and Kalamuwa (no. 14) his compassion and the people's love for him, Nabonidus concentrates on his power and will to rule. Like David's Yahweh, Marduk will give Nabonidus everything he desires. Marduk hears him (cf. Ps 1:3; 18:6). Nabonidus shares David's selflessness, praying for a long rule if Marduk wishes it (cf. 2 Sm 15:25–26, 22:7, 23:5). His second story (no. 7) centers on the theme of temple restoration. As with David, the gods give Nabonidus victory over all his enemies (cf. 2 Sm 7:9, 22:1). The transcendence of his victory is marked by breaking the weapons of eternal enemies (cf. 1 Sm 2:4; 2 Sm 22:22). All the kings of the world send messages of friendship, as they do to Solomon (cf. 1 Kgs 10:1, 24). The gods return to their temples at the appointed time. Like Abraham after he defeats the kings of the north, Nabonidus rewards his men generously but returns home himself unchanged (Gen 14:21–24). The Idrimi story (no. 13) not only has the king rule Alalakh for a consummate thirty years but puts an end to war (cf. no. 18; Is 11:1–9). Azatiwada (no. 15) destroys all evil, turns evil men into subjects and humbles the strong. The reversals of fortune marking the king's success and the divine blessing of his reign blend smoothly with elements of resurrection expressing *shalom*. Thus Azatiwada (no. 15) and Panamuwa (no. 19) both give life to their people and Cyrus (no. 8) raises Sumer and Akkad from the dead, reflecting the absence of the gods. Conquering Babylon without a battle (cf. Is 9:5; Mic 5:4), Cyrus presents himself as king of the world, one whom the gods love (Ps 2:8, 89:28): a just king, forbidding both terror and slave gangs. Similarly, Suppiluliuma conquers without a battle as an outnumbered enemy sues for peace (no. 10) and all fear Suppiluliuma. His prisoners, beyond counting, rush to make peace (cf. Josh 9:1–15). For Yehawmilk (no. 16), peace is a gift of the goddess Baalat. While almost all of our texts emphasize themes of prosperity, the stories of Panamuwa (no. 19) and Bar-Rakib (no. 20)—with their reorganization of government, wealth and wisdom—most closely parallel the peace and prosperity of Solomon's reign (1 Kgs 4–5).

Thematic elements reflecting the utopian goal of peace abound in the Bible. The kingdom, the presence of god, a new creation, visions of a transcendent messiah and other metaphors reflecting the birth of the new Jerusalem, the eternal reign of David, the splendor of Solomon's reign or the building or rebuilding of the temple share this theme. Plot-oriented, ironic glimpses of lost utopias also offer important echoes of this function in biblical narrative.

THE HISTORICITY OF ANCIENT BIOGRAPHY

Although these testimonies, often lacking confirmation, do not provide significant sources for the history of events, they do help us with a history of ancient literature and some of its central themes. Their close ties to biblical literature have a richness that is here only suggested. Of far greater importance than the few shards of historical information these monumental texts provide is the access they give to a literary and intellectual inheritance. They illustrate literary techniques, patterns and elements closely shared by biblical tradition. The story of Adad-Guppi, mother of Nabonidus, for example, uses a rich metaphorical language of piety that is commonplace in the Psalter.[30] Walking in the path of righteousness, Adad-Guppi prayed day and night to the god Sin (cf. Ps 22:3). She worshiped the gods whether in heaven or on earth (cf. Ps 89:53). To appease them, she dressed in torn sackcloth, like the king of Nineveh in Jonah's story (Jon 3:5). She praised the gods (cf. Ps 22:26–27) and served them food for ninety-five years (cf. Gen 17:17). Such motifs reflect a shared religious world and should inform our reading of both biblical and ancient Near Eastern texts.[31]

Both Esarhaddon and Mesha's stories share techniques in the building of chain narratives. They help us understand how 2 Kings was put together as a coherent story. For example, after referring to the total destruction of Israel, Mesha recounts his victories in a series of example stories. He takes Baal-Meon and Kiriathaim. This gives way to a more complex story of the conquest of Ataroth, a town built by the king of Israel. It is followed by the conquest of Nebo at Chemosh's instruction. The story of Israel's humiliation continues with the taking of Jahaz, which Israel's king also built. These references to Israel's towns allow the story to shift to Mesha's building projects. Peace is celebrated as the king rules one hundred towns, with an equal number of stories to be imagined.

A Hittite story about Telepinu develops a similar chain of narrative.[32] Because of its high moral character, it has even greater similarities to the narratives of Samuel and Kings. The story begins in the voice of Telepinu and is set in the past. In recounting the reigns of his seven predecessors, he shows that the succession to the throne is determined by a reiterated pattern of murder and intrigue in the court and royal family. Telepinu survives his Shakespearean bloodbath and declares peace. He offers an instructive proverb on love of one's enemy: "They did evil to me but I will not do evil to them." The final segment of this story chain uses a parable to illustrate this proverb. A great conspiracy is made against Telipinu, through which his father and brothers are killed. The conspirators are tried and sentenced to death. Telepinu, however, reverses the destiny of the murderers. Foreshadowing the Old Testament prophets (Is 2:4; Mic 4:3; cf. Jl 3:10), Telepinu frees the prisoners by taking their weapons and replacing them with a farm yoke.

Faced with a curse because of the blood spilled in the royal family—explained by prophets as equal to the bloodshed in Hattusa—Telepinu issues a decree based on ethical principle. He bans collective punishment forever and limits blood guilt for a murder to the guilty man. The murderer will pay with his own head, but not his house and children. Telepinu's solution is the same as Ezekiel's to the problem of collective guilt and is reiterated in the closure of the David story on the theme of reconciliation (see below, Chapter 10). As in Jeremiah's new covenant (Jer 31:29–30), Ezekiel presents a new morality that puts an end to blood guilt and revenge (Ez 18). No longer will sons pay for the sins of their fathers. The sinner who repents will preserve his life. The proverb that Deuteronomy presents as divine law established in the wilderness is illustrated by both Jeremiah and Ezekiel in a final transformation made necessary by the suffering of Jerusalem's exile. They reflect the particular plotline, motive and perspective shared by the Hittite story, namely, to end the chain of royal assassination. In the story of King Amaziah of Jerusalem, the book of Kings illustrates and cites this proverb in a clear reiteration of the Telepinu story. Amaziah responds to the assassination of his father by ending regicide in the kingdom (2 Kgs 12:20–22), closing a long discourse on revenge that began in the story of Cain (Gen 4):

> As soon as the royal power was firmly in his (Amaziah's) hand, he killed his servants who had killed the king his father. But he did not put to death the children of the murderers, as it is written in the law of Moses where Yahweh commanded: "The fathers will not be put to death for the children, or the children be put to death for the fathers; but every man shall die for his own sin." (2 Kgs 14:5–7; citing Dt 24:16)

Our review of royal biography shows that the narrative techniques, motifs and themes of biblical story were solidly in place long before any biblical narratives were written. The virtues of humility, social justice and integrity are all marks of a piety oriented toward an ideal kingdom. What is yet lacking is to show how the great themes of ancient Near Eastern idealism are integrated and transformed in an expanding and creative development. Three themes with roots in ancient myth will be taken up in the following chapters: (1) the role of the king as son of god and divine warrior, maintaining creation's dominance over chaos; (2) the interrelationship of renewal and resurrection to illustrate a pedagogy that centers on the role of the king in providing fertility and life and (3) the role of the king as sufferer, transforming a world of violence. Integrated in the world of ancient Near Eastern story and song, these elements create a discourse about the transcendent that is centered in justice, eternal life and peace. They are epitomized in the figure of an apocalyptic judge and a world-transforming savior-king.

CHAPTER 6

⟡

The Myth of the
Conquering Holy Warrior

THE COHERENCE OF BIBLICAL NARRATIVE

Understanding why a particular story is told is crucial in defining what is essential in early Jewish self-identification. The previous chapter identified a number of basic elements that are dominant in this identity. Given the secondary nature of our traditions, the meaning-bearing capacity of our texts always exceeds the intentions of the biblical authors and the culture they represented. When one considers the implications of the reuse of tradition—and indeed every act of authorship involves such—one needs to consider that, as writers, we write what we do not entirely intend: our souls are not entirely our own. The identity creation involved in tradition building is not easily controlled but is dependent on the tradition it reinterprets and reuses. The present chapter looks at the implicit associations of some of the central biblical motifs that originated in ancient Near Eastern myth. The motif of violence associated with creation stories is closely linked to the pedagogical function of the motif of the wrath of God. It is always a divine anger that promotes understanding. In the Genesis creation story (Gen 1:1–2:3), however, motifs of divine anger and destruction are absent, at best distantly implied through implicit reference. They enter the narrative in the garden story (Gen 2:4–3:24) and in the chain of stories that follow, especially the flood narrative.

The central themes and motifs common to the traditions of the ancient Near East underwent periods of popularity and decline. Earlier literature was revisited in antiquarian enthusiasms of renaissance. The reign of Nabonidus over Babylon (559–539 BCE), for example, ushered in such a renaissance drawn to Old Babylonian and Sumerian themes and traditions, in many ways comparable to the Assyrian period renaissance during the reign of Asshurbanipal (668–627 BCE). The Hellenistic stories and legends of Sennacherib and Esarhaddon—like those of Alexander—remained at the center of literary focus centuries after these kings had disappeared from history's stage. Egypt also had its renaissance movements, in which Eighteenth Dynasty and Amarna period texts played a major role. The libraries of the ancient world—and especially Alexandria's—were the products of such thinking. Their influence in literary production undermined both the chronology and the geographical borders of ancient literature. The common associations of international literature are already dominant by the Assyrian period.[1] Understanding the reuse of traditions involves examining how the text interprets the tradition, motif and intellectual world that is reused. The new, seemingly independent context has at best a fragile integrity. Not only is a common chronology not implied in the sharing of traditions, but a shared understanding and function can hardly be assumed. What is reused has the capability of transcending any single author's use of the tradition.

The Bible tells a story of two worlds, illustrating a recurrent struggle. One is the world of a transcendent heaven that determines human fate and the other a transient world of men that resists understanding. While its goal is enlightenment, this central opposition expresses tragic and irreconcilable differences between the divine and the human. The events of old Israel and its tragic fate belong to the transient world of mankind. This stands in illustrative contrast to an ultimately unknowable and transcendent world of truth and wisdom. The narratives that have come to us in the first five books of the Bible—stories of creation, origins and divine guidance—play a major role in creating this mythic construct. Basic and indispensable to the Bible's story of old Israel is the starting point at the creation in Genesis, a point of departure whose Greek analogies have been long recognized.[2] Genesis, even more than Chronicles, begins at the beginning, as its name implies and its first word emphatically states. From there, biblical narrative continues in a thematically associated succession of stories centered on the life or reign of successive heroes, prophets, saviors and kings through twelve books. They find closure at the end of the book of 2 Kings in a brief scene of the humiliated last scion of Israel and Israel's forty kings receiving his daily ration of Babylonian hospitality "all the days of his life."

The story was not written at any one time, nor by any single author. Neither the story nor its composition is continuous in its plot. One finds a chain of ancestors and heroes lightly linked in succession. What binds them most closely is an ideological and thematic coherence, which has allowed an extended chain of narrative to be received as an interrelated whole, involved in a recurrent internal discourse. While the stories move progressively through both story and time from beginning to end, the implied voice of the narrative chain, which allows us to read the narrative as a whole, stands at once at the creation and at the fall of Jerusalem. This voice is both implicitly anachronistic and interpretive: ever telling a story about Israel past: the whole story from beginning to end.

The books of the prophets, such as Isaiah, Jeremiah and Jonah, offer commentary and interpretation to the Bible's story of Old Israel. Their perspective within the present canon has been determined by such self-identifying metaphors as Jeremiah and Ezekiel's new covenant and the stories of restoration in Ezra and Nehemiah. Such has become the narrative point of departure for the Bible's flight into the past.³ The stories and themes we confront in the very opening of this tradition in Genesis center in a self-identifying illustration of testing and struggle, from Eve's tree in the center of the garden and Abraham's sacrifice on Mount Moriah (Gen 22) to Jacob's struggle with his night demon (Gen 32:24–30). Both the creation of the world and the creation of Israel arise from a single transcendent struggle: a never-ending story.⁴

Genesis begins with creation. But where does creation begin? Was there anything before creation? Does creation begin in the beginning or not? Within linear time as opposed to infinity, it does so by necessity; one begins with Aristotle's prime mover. Creation is of its essence ex nihilo. I have no intention of opposing the logic of such a worldview. However, our question does not in fact relate to the world's existence, whether or not we assume for it a beginning, and its logic is a narrative one. Traditions of the ancient world do not begin their creation stories simply with nothing. The well-known Babylonian creation story Enuma Elish begins in the world of the gods, in a mythological battle between Marduk and Tiamat.⁵ The creation of the world has much to do with the division and mingling of sweet and salt waters. It is created most immediately when Tiamat's corpse is split in battle by the four divine winds of Marduk. This story has left indelible traces on biblical myth, particularly in the story's opening opposition, which describes earth as formless and empty like a desert, while the divine spirit moves over the waters of the deep on the other: the world as nothingness and the divine as the source of life and creation.

Greek traditions generally imply a story model of creation, a model we first find in an Egyptian prayer to Atum already in the Pyramid Texts of the Sixth

Dynasty.[6] According to this Egyptian version, creation begins in Heliopolis, with the descendants of the children of the god Atum. It uses a metaphor that is echoed centuries later in the story of the biblical God creating Adam in his image, who in turn passes it on to his son Seth (Gen 5:2–3). The Egyptian myth includes four representations of Atum from the first two generations of his children: Shu, the god of air, with his spouse Tefnut, the goddess of water, and Geb, the god of earth, with his spouse Nut, the goddess of heaven. The four paired elements called on by God in Genesis 1, with which creation begins—light separating from the darkness with which it was mingled and the seas from the earth they had covered—provide a close variation.[7]

Nevertheless, one can also say that nothing stands before the creation in Genesis. "In the beginning [or simply, "First"], God created the heavens and the earth and the earth was deserted and empty." Not the heavens, but earth is where nothingness is found. This is an obvious variation on the Greek concept of chaos as a void that creation orders. In the place of chaos, form is given to undifferentiated matter. Creation structures chaos, just as surely as transcendent forms hold all reality in existence against the nothingness of the void. It is important to recognize that creation, in such a worldview, is not an event of the past but a narrative expressing an ideal: the world divinely intended. There are many echoes of this perspective in the Bible. For example, the waters from the deep return to destroy life in the flood story (Gen 7:10–11). The earth is held in creation and the waters of chaos kept under control by Yahweh in the Psalter (Ps 46:3–6; 65:7–8; 89:10; 93:1, 4; 96:10). The theme of an ongoing need for creation that is implicit in a creation-out-of-chaos ideology is basic to biblical theology. The Bible's "mighty acts of God" are creative acts throughout the tradition. Yahweh's victory over the sea in the Moses narrative (Ex 15:10) reiterates the divine spirit blowing over the deep. It is a creative wind that blows over the waters. As Egypt is destroyed, Yahweh creates Israel as a people.

Such mythic revision implicit in biblical narrative also has pedagogical purpose. Within the large world of literary allusions, creating discourse in the Bible, the theme of Yahweh's victory over the sea crosses another dominant motif of biblical poetry. It is captured by the question, What is a man? Once asked, a huge spectrum of answers is provoked. Hosea uses it in an implicit echo of the victory over the sea story: humanity can be "removed like foam on the surface of the water." The illustration implicitly confirming his assertion is, of course, the story of Exodus 15. "When Yahweh's wind blows, [people] wither like grass" (Is 40:6–7). Men come and go as quickly as grass or flowers in the field (Job 14:2; Ps 103:15–16). The Exodus account of Egypt's destruction and Israel's creation offers story illustration for the philosopher's "way of all flesh." Men are a "puff of wind" (Ps 39:12; 62:10; 103:16; 144:3–4). People are but shadows that cannot survive (Job 8:9: 14:2), empty thoughts (Ps 94:11), created for nothingness (Ps 89:48; Gen 3:19).

The lyric beauty of Elihu's song in Job, where the young man takes on Adam's role, well illustrates the theological centrality of this theme. Humanity stands between a creative spirit and the earth's nothingness.

> The spirit of God formed me; the breath of Shaddai gave me life. . . . You and I are the same before God. I too was nipped from clay. Do not be overwhelmed by fear of me. (Job 33:4–7)

While the celebration of life is among the highest values of biblical tradition, one should not miss the darker motif supporting the Enlightenment principle that all are created equal; for all are made of clay. Even more striking in Job's excursion into Genesis creation theology is the reference to a potential fear Elihu is at pains to remove. It refers to the "fear and terror": the taste for blood and violence that humanity brings to the world after the flood (Gen 9:2).

CREATION AND DESTRUCTION

Despite the recurrent creative, life-giving spirit playing in the Bible's texts, it is often the darker motif of destruction that brings out the reiterative quality of biblical narrative. The creative spirit is inseparably paired with a motif of destruction and war. The spirit of God creates armies: "By the word of Yahweh the heavens were made, by the breath of his mouth, all their armies" (Ps 33:6). The myth-creating cluster of the motifs of God's spirit and destruction is commonplace in biblical stories (e.g., Jgs 14–16), viewing the spirit of God as dangerous. Job offers an argument to affirm this in presenting Yahweh's spirit in the metaphor of the roaring lion's breath: "By the breath of God they die; by the wind of his rage they are consumed" (Job 4:9). Isaiah too speaks of the creative spirit's destructive power, evoking the story of the destruction of Sodom: "The spirit of Yahweh is as a stream of brimstone. It sifts the nations with a sieve of destruction" (Is 30:28, 33; cf. Gen 19).

However playful its alliteration and however much its doubling may be derived from Egypt's divine couples sharing in the creation, the biblical *tohu wa-bohu* bears many nuances well beyond its translation of "formlessness and emptiness." The cosmic need for continuous creation to hold chaos in check suggests as much. *Tohu wa-bohu* in its nothingness—like the spirit in its fullness—

is before creation and anticipates it. The theme of the return to chaos is a central leitmotif in the Pentateuch. As soon as we move from the creation, we are already dealing with paired motifs of creation and destruction, with a God who is ever occupied with regret over what he has made. The most devastating destructive story, in which the whole world is at risk, is of course the story of the great flood, in which the waters of chaos bear overtones of destructive evil (Gen 6–9). In the following tower of Babel story, however, the metaphor of destruction returns to its mitigated pattern of banishment and exile. The theme is first used at the close of the garden story and ever bears overtones of the coming deportations with it. Adam and Eve were banished from the garden, with the way back to the tree of life blocked by cherubim and a magical, invincible sword (Gen 3:24). Similarly, Cain is driven from the land to become a fugitive and a wanderer. So in the Babel story, the people are scattered and spread over the face of the earth, much as, at the close of the greater narrative, old Israel is once again driven from the temple's garden and from Jerusalem and scattered among the nations. This variant of the garden story's closure is reiterated throughout the books of Kings and Isaiah. As in the Genesis story, Isaiah's city of emptiness is not a historical city, but the universal city of humanity that is destroyed and its population scattered over the face of the earth. The cosmic element of a return to the creation story's empty and formless chaos is evident already from the song's opening line: "Yahweh ravages the earth and makes it a desert; he spreads the people across its surface." The people of this city are those who "broke the covenant with eternity." In response, Yahweh crushes the "city of emptiness" (Is 24:10). The logic of retribution dominates the story's morality: "Because of our city's emptiness, Yahweh has decided to make its center a desert" (Is 24:12).

The dry variation of the Genesis flood—in which Yahweh makes a city a desert—is Yahweh's preferred choice of "evil." The trope has its best-known example in the tale of Sodom's destruction, which turns a city with its rich and beautiful valley (Gen 13:19) into a "city of emptiness" and a valley of salt. Those who are not accepted by Yahweh stand opposed to creation. They belong to the wilderness of a godless void. For Malachi, Edom plays the role of the "city of emptiness." Edom is marked for eternal hatred:

> Esau is the brother of Jacob . . . yet I love Jacob and hate Esau; I have made his mountains into a desert, his inheritance into a wasteland . . . [Edom] will be called "the land of the godless" and its people "they whom Yahweh hates with an eternal hatred." (Mal 1:2–4)

This theme with its open scorn of desert peoples does not imply a chauvinistic or nationalistic hatred so much as it reflects a radical strain within a universal form of theology. Its ever implicit counterpart, after all, is the figure of the east as source of wisdom and understanding, where Jobs are the foreigners to be loved and respected (Lev 19:34). In their story roles, Ammon, Moab and Edom play the godless. It is a shared function. They epitomize humanity as such: not the non-Israelite, historical world of Palestine but the myth-oriented "nations" of the Psalter in many variants (Ps 2:1). They are condemned to play the role of an eternal wilderness. They stand opposite God's creation.

In an important variation of the dualistic motif of the "city of emptiness" (Jer 25:9–11), Jerusalem plays the victim of divine wrath. Yahweh calls his servant Nebuchadnezzar, the king of Babylon, to turn the whole land to ruin, to empty it and make of Jerusalem an "eternal desert." However much this poem might draw an allusion we are used to thinking of as history, Jerusalem's wasteland is the world Yahweh regrets making. The whole world suffers the emptying of creation and becomes the empty land we see in the opening chapters of Nehemiah and Lamentations. As in the flood story, it is the world of creation, which is reversed and turned into desert and the empty chaos from which it came. In a variation on this, Jeremiah presents Yahweh as regretting his creation. Evoking the image of the woman who ate of the "tree of knowledge of good and evil," Yahweh complains of old Israel: "My people . . . do not know me. . . . They are clever at doing evil, but have no understanding of what it is to do good" (Jer 4:22). Jeremiah renders Yahweh and the earth's curses against Adam and Cain in Genesis 3–4 complete (Jer 4:23–26). The earth is an *empty desert*, without creation. "I looked at the earth and behold, it was formless and empty, and at the heavens: the light was gone!" The vision ends in a reiteration of the universal destruction of the nations we saw in Jeremiah 25: "There was no mankind . . . all its cities were laid waste" (Jer 4:25–26). Notwithstanding the totality of the destruction promised, and already at the crescendo of Yahweh's damning judgment, hope intrudes into the text: "The whole I will not lay waste . . . suffering, but not totally . . . even on that day I will not wholly destroy . . . but they will "glean a remnant of Israel" (Jer 4:27; 5:10, 18; 6:9). A time of testing is projected: they will "go to a land of strangers" (Jer 5:19); the children of Jerusalem "have eyes which did not see and ears which did not hear" (Jer 5:21); "Yahweh will make it into a desert and an empty land" (Jer 6:8). Yahweh instructs them to "seek out the paths of *'olam* and walk in the good way." The rejection of this way leads to the threat of trial and pain "as of a woman in labor" (Jer 6:24). The "way of goodness" plays a central role in this expanding cluster of motifs. The motif of an only son also enters. For the time, mourning is required (Jer 6:26). Jerusalem is to be tried by fire, while the rejection of the "silver slag" of old Jerusalem (Jer 6:30) creates an expectation of a more purified and more acceptable future. These metaphors identify the figure of Jerusalem as a woman in labor and as a desert. They link such suffering to images of war and destruction, to emptying the land, of mourning the loss of Jerusalem's firstborn, of the fire of testing and refining silver. All metaphors center in a pedagogical plea to follow the path of goodness. They give place to a sermon that promises entrance to the temple. Hope is for those who change their path that "they might live forever in this place, in the land that once long ago had been given to their ancestors" (Jer 7:7).

Balance and appropriateness require the logic that since mankind is made in the image of God, humanity becomes what it mirrors. Accordingly, the worship of empty or false gods implies a rejection of creation. The primeval nothingness from which humanity came competes with the creative fullness of its destiny. The complex discourse, surrounding the wordplay of chaos as *tohu wa-bohu* ("formless and empty") is used in many reiterating variations throughout the tradition.[8] It is the essence of the first commandment given to Moses at Sinai. "You must not have other gods before me" (Ex 20:3) becomes a moral sermon for the reader of Genesis. Similarly, the cluster of motifs surrounding the theme of Jerusalem's emptiness is not based on a historical description of the past, either real or imagined. The implicit premise that becoming the people of God is a struggle against creation's chaos is hinted at in a small story about the prophet Samuel. In his instruction to the people, the metaphor of cosmic emptiness is identified with the emptiness of the gods. "Serve Yahweh with your whole heart. Do not seek after emptiness . . . because they who do are emptied" (1 Sm 12:20–21). A close companion to Samuel's statement is cited in Jeremiah, where those who "worship emptiness return to emptiness" (Jer 2:5). The emptiness and nothingness of those who worship such gods is illustrated by the story of the Assyrian conquest of Samaria and the deportation of the Israelites in 2 Kings. For following such empty gods, Israel itself is emptied, as Kings demonstrates the emptiness and nothingness of the people who follow such gods: "Going after false idols, they became false and they followed the nations that were round about them" (2 Kgs 17:15–18).[9]

Isaiah's scornful rejection of godless idols bears the full weight of the creation story (Is 44:9): "Those who make images of the gods, are (themselves) nothing; what they love does not succeed" (cf. Ps 1:4, 6). Isaiah sets his struggle against false gods and the "godless" made in their image with a desert metaphor:

If the helpless and the poor look for water and there is none, and their tongues dry out in thirst, I Yahweh will answer them, I, the God of Israel, will not abandon them. I will let a river flow over the naked land, I will make springs open in the valleys; I will make the desert into an oasis, the dry land into a fountainhead." (Is 41:17–18; cf. Ps 107:33, 35)

Playing on the theme of Yahweh's creation, turning the desert into fertile land and the fertile land into desert, Job uses the ancient Egyptian theme of turning "nations in uproar" into a desert to demonstrate Yahweh's power. Yahweh, like Amon-Re, "makes nations great or he lays them waste" (Job 12:23). Examples of this lie ready at hand throughout the tradition (1 Sm 2:1–10; Ps 107). The one that marks the eternal character of the reiteration of creation's struggle, in both cosmic and personal terms, is found in the closing address of Psalm 89. David uses the voice of Israel being tested to sing his lament:

Will you hide yourself forever? Remember how short my time is . . . remember the nothingness with which you created all the children of Adam . . . (Ps 89:47–48)

The moral emptiness and hopelessness threatening in the closure of Psalm 89 finds a rejoinder in Isaiah, within a long moral diatribe against Israel's sin, which has separated the nation from its God: "Truth stumbles in the streets and righteousness has no entrance; the place of truth stands empty" (Is 59:14–15). In such despair, Isaiah introduces his reversal to illustrate a new creation. Where "no man was to be seen" (Is 59:16), a redeemer is announced, identifiable with Yahweh's name and glory. He stands against the flood of affliction, which Yahweh's creative spirit blows away (Is 59:19–20). His glory reiterates creation's light and disperses the darkness that covers the earth. God rejects the past of old Israel. With equal freedom, a new Israel is created, drawn to the light (Is 60:1–4).

THE HUMILITY OF THE KING

The Bible shares the theme of creation with many ancient Near Eastern traditions, especially as it is associated with motifs of violence and destruction. Nowhere is this more clear than in the Babylonian creation story, the *Enuma Elish*. The creation of humanity and Marduk's transformation into god of the universe follows his conquest over the primeval sweet and salt waters represented by the divine Kingu and Tiamat.[10] The story has long been profitably compared to the creation narrative of Genesis and might well serve as a template to help us understand the particular association of the motifs of creation and destruction. Like the Genesis creation story, the Enuma Elish is a secondary tradition. It underwent a considerable history of interpretation long before the text, as we know it, was written. During the first millennium BCE, it was used for a dramatic reading during the Akitu festival celebrating the Babylonian new year. This festival centered on the reinvigoration of the monarchy. The text of the story, as it has come to us since early in the second millennium BCE, shares an intellectual and mythological world with a considerable range of ancient literature. In the context of the ritual instructions for the Akitu festival establishing Marduk as king, the creation story's close ties to kingship become apparent.[11] The high priest prays to Marduk and to "my lady." The text is reiterated in the biblical understanding of Yahweh as Israel's king, who has given David, his messiah, kingship insofar as David fears God. Marduk is "lord of the great gods." He measures the sea and determines destiny. He is ruler and source of light for his city.

The priest's prayer to "my lady" gives her the role of savior in a song for a poor man by describing the goddess as one who impoverishes the rich and enriches the poor. She destroys the enemy and those who do not fear her. She frees the prisoner and takes the downtrodden by the hand. She is asked by the priest to secure the destiny of the king who fears her and, in doing so, to give life to Babylon's citizens, who stand under her protection. Emphasis is laid on motifs of divine mercy and humble rule, divine fertility, the conquest over the sea, the divine role as light of the world overcoming darkness and the creative names of the goddess. Introducing this ceremony and leading the king into the temple Esangil, the high priest first removes the king's scepter, ring and mace—the marks of his office. He takes the royal crown from the king and lays it on a chair before Marduk. He goes back to the king and, striking him on the cheek, leads him before Marduk. Pulling him by the ear, he makes the king kneel on the floor. The king recites a prayer of humility, declaring his innocence of crime and his constant commitment to good government, including not hitting or humiliating his ministers (cf. Ps 65:4: 89:2–9). When the prayer is completed, the priest tells him, "Do not fear . . . the Lord has heard your prayer." He will establish the king's rule "forever; he will scatter the king's enemies; destroy those who hate him" (cf. Ps 89:23–24, 29–30). The priest restores the king's role and returns the scepter, ring and mace. He gives the king his crown and slaps his face once again. The text comments on itself: "When the king is struck, if his tears flow, the Lord will be merciful" (cf. Ps 89:28–37).

If, however, his tears do not flow, the Lord will be angry with him. His enemy will attack and bring him down" (cf. Ps 89:38–45). While the remainder of our text is missing, it is clear that a central function of the festival is to reestablish the king's rule in humility. The new year brings a new creation. The kingdom is held in existence in the context of a divinely given eternal covenant with a king, who is himself capable of repentance and mercy. Implicit in this and other ancient Near Eastern literature is the understanding that compassion expresses the divine. The corresponding human virtue is humility, a virtue required of kings and sons of god, guarding them against hubris. In Egyptian creation ideology, we find an instructive variant of our king's tears in the common etiology for the word for "men" *(romet)*, who were created from the "tears" *(remet)* of Re. Much as Genesis finds humanity's essence sealed in its likeness to the divine, Egyptian tradition finds human destiny in its tearful share in the creator, expressing its essence.[12]

Just as the violence of the priest's blow leads to a king's tears, so violence or the threat of destruction leads to divine repentance. It is a humbling, divine horror that the gods learn from the violence they themselves unleash, that they might regret the evil they do. In the opening of the biblical flood story, Yahweh sees humanity's evil increasing over the earth (Gen 6:5a) and takes up the role played by the king in the Akitu festival. Seeing that the human heart was corrupt, constantly committed to evil (Gen 6:5b), Yahweh suffers. He repents having made humanity on earth. It has "cut him to the quick" (Gen 6:6). The humbling of Yahweh is so pronounced in this verse that it leads to a reversal of creation and to the "removal of the human I have made from the earth's surface." Humanity had been created to rule over the fish of the sea, the beast and the bird of the air and over all the earth and the snake creeping on the ground (Gen 1:26). However, as in the Akitu festival so also in Genesis: if a king shows himself incapable of humility, both the king and his kingdom are to be destroyed. The whole is removed "from humanity to the beast, snake and bird of the air." The forces of the deep are loosed and creation is undone. At the close of the flood story, Yahweh once more repents of the evil he has done in sending the flood, a regret that is gently suggested by his nostalgic reaction to the sweet smell of Noah's sacrifice (Gen 8:21) in a well-known echo of the Babylonian flood story of Atrahasis, whose tale of a flood offers a close parallel to Genesis, still well-known in the Hellenistic period.[13]

Isaiah's threefold reiteration of Hezekiah's tears should not go unnoticed. In the first scene, Hezekiah hears Assyrian Rabshakeh mock the king's reliance on Yahweh to deliver Jerusalem from the siege by the Assyrian army (Is 36:13–20). He goes into the temple, mourning, tearing his clothes and covering himself with sackcloth, instructing his servants to lift up their voices in prayer for the remnant of Jerusalem that is left (Is 37:1–4).

In the second scene, the king of Assyria sends a message to Hezekiah and the king takes the letter to the temple. He spreads open the letter for Yahweh to read and prays that Yahweh will deliver Jerusalem. Because of Hezekiah's humble prayer, Yahweh answers the Assyrian's pride and arrogance through his prophecy that the Assyrians will not enter the city (Is 37:8–35). That night, the angel of Yahweh destroys 185,000 soldiers of the Assyrian army and it withdraws; the king returns to Nineveh and is killed by his own son in the temple as he worships Nishroch, his god (Is 37:36–38).

In the third scene, Yahweh answers Hezekiah in his anger and tells him he will die. Hezekiah responds in prayer. He asks Yahweh "to remember that he has walked before God in truth and with a pure heart and Hezekiah wept greatly" (Is 38:2–3; cf. Ps 34:1, 12, 16, 18). In his tears, he illustrates and echoes humility, expressive of purity of heart (Ps 15:2; 17:3; 24:4; 27:8; 37:31; 51:12; 84:6; 86:11; 119:10; 138:1). Yahweh responds to Hezekiah's tears with renewal and rebirth for his kingship: "I have heard your prayer; I have seen your tears. Behold, I will add fifteen years to your life" (Is 38:5). Yahweh hears his prayer and sees his tears. Therefore, he reverses his fate and rolls time backward.

The thematic element of the king's repentant tears of humility leading to renewal is used in Chronicles in the story of Rehoboam (2 Chr 12:1–16).[14] As soon as his rule is confirmed, he "abandons Yahweh's law" (2 Chr 12:1b). The story illustrates the appropriate proverb: "Do not abandon my Torah; keep my commandments and live; keep my Torah . . . " (Prv 7:2). Rehoboam's betrayal will cost him his life. Punishment comes with balanced retribution. As Rehoboam abandons Yahweh's Torah, so he will be abandoned into Shishak's hands (2 Chr 12:5). Again, the Akitu festival—with its test of a king's humility—holds as a template for the Bible's stories of humble kings, contrasting strongly to the stiff-necked people of Israel in 1–2 Kings, who are rejected because they will not humble themselves (2 Kgs 17:13–20). Facing death, Rehoboam repents, "humbling himself." When Yahweh sees his tears, the king is allowed to take up his rule once again:

> The princes of Israel and the king have humbled themselves. . . . They have humbled themselves and therefore I will not destroy them . . . my anger will not be poured out over Jerusalem by Shishak's hand. (2 Chr 12:7)

The economy of biblical theology often requires Yahweh to play two roles in his story that are usually given to different divine figures in the richer world of gods in other ancient Near Eastern texts. He becomes both destroyer and savior. He blesses and he curses and he does both good and evil. In a thematically related Egyptian doublet tale of the destruction and salvation of mankind, one finds a comparable dissonance of roles assigned to transcendent Re, the father of the gods.[15] As the first episode opens, Re appoints Hathor as destroyer of mankind. The sun god, Re, gives expression to the wrath of the gods, while Hathor plays the role of Sekhmet ("the destroyer"). In the second tale of the doublet, Re plays a role of savior, expressing compassion and fear of Hathor, and turns to oppose his colleague. He mixes red ochre with beer to deceive her into thinking of it as blood fit for a god to drink. He disarms Hathor's fury by giving her the sleep the gods had sought. In the biblical story, the motif of Yahweh learning compassion introduces a variant on the rainbow as Ishtar's necklace from the Gilgamesh Epic. Yahweh places a warrior god's bow in the sky to remind him of the lesson he has been taught on the nature of mankind. The bow is a symbol predictive of a future in holy war. It does not lead to a restoration of the kingdom or to the reestablishment of human authority (Gen 1:26–28). Nor does it bring the peace from destruction that Genesis 5:28 intimated and Yahweh's wrath sought that he might once again find a Sabbath day's rest (Gen 2:3; cf. 8:22; Chapter 8, below).

In the Enuma Elish, Apsu's expressed wish to destroy mankind is in search of a comparable rest: "I will destroy them and put an end to their uproar. Let peace be reestablished that we might have rest." His wish is disputed among the gods as Tiamat introduces the element of divine repentance, setting in motion a reiterative delay in the story's plot. She argues against Apsu's violence: "Shall we wipe out our descendants? Even though they bear themselves terribly, let us accept this with patience." Apsu's threatened wrath strikes such fear among the gods that they are paralyzed. The ensuing silence puts Apsu to sleep. Ea plays the role of priest in the Akitu festival and, miming its ritual, removes all of the symbols of royal office from Apsu, kills him and puts the royal adviser Mummu in chains. He builds a temple over Apsu and lives there with his bride, Damkina. A child is born to them "in the heart of Apsu." This savior is described as the son of the sun god, indeed, "the sun of the gods."

In a plot-oriented context, threatened violence followed by divine repentance finds a double reiteration in the Moses–Yahweh debates of the wilderness narrative of the golden calf. When the people "rise up to play" (Ex 32:6), Yahweh's wrath threatens to destroy them (Ex 32:10). Moses objects and asks Yahweh to repent of the evil he wishes against his people (Ex 32:12). Yahweh's repentance leads to a doubling of the scene. In the second scene, as Moses brings the tables of testimony down the mountain, "Joshua hears the noise of the people as they shouted." Now it is Moses' turn to be angry, while Yahweh reserves his wrath for another occasion (Ex 32:34). While this threat from "the noise of the people" ultimately resolves itself in the destruction of the entire wilderness generation, the expectation of future conflict and future wrath caused by the children of Israel's murmurings forms a leitmotif of the story's plot (Ex 23:20–21; 32:34; 33:3; cf. Ps 65:8–9; Is 17:12–14).

Other related stories play on these same motifs of destruction, noise and rebellion with the enthronement of the king. Psalm 89, for example, reiterates Psalm 65's conquest over the roaring sea in a creation ideology that echoes Marduk's destruction of Tiamat. It presents Yahweh as "ruling the raging of the sea" and stomping down the mythic Rahab like carrion and scattering his enemies (Ps 89:9–10; Ps 65:8a–b). The first half of this complex psalm begins with expressions of piety (Ps 89:1–2). It presents recurrent allusions to the enthronement or confirmation of Yahweh's son in his messianic reign (Ps 89:3b–5:20–25, 27–30). Expanding with creation metaphors, it presents Yahweh as king over both heaven and earth (Ps 89:6–9, 12–19), drawing motifs from the battle against the sea (89:10–11, 26). From the center of the psalm, however, the song turns to a debate over Yahweh's betrayal of his messiah (Ps 89:31). It is here the clearest motifs of rebellion as noise and angry scorn are found (Ps 89:39, 40, 42–43, 46). At the very close of the psalm (Ps 89:51–52), the scorn and ridicule of the nations and enemies is emphasized. Much in the spirit of Job's role, the song presents its king as an allegory for Jerusalem's history and lends its voice to question Job's silent deity: "How long will you hide yourself?" (Ps 89:47).

THE SON OF GOD AND A NEW CREATION

The link between the biblical narrative of creation and the Enuma Elish is clearly marked in the theme of the conquest and binding of the sea as a force of emptiness and evil. In Genesis 1:2 the "divine wind" or "spirit of God" hovering over the surface of the waters," set in opposition to the "darkness on the face of the deep," has long been recognized as reflecting the winds that Marduk uses as weapons to split Tiamat's carcass and establish the order of creation in the Enuma Elish. Similar variations can be found in many texts, giving storm and wind the creative power of the divine, especially those that understand an expression of humility as the appropriate human role (Job 38; Job 39:37–38). The opposition between the divine spirit and darkness is paralleled by the metaphor of divine patronage of "binding" or "loosing" typically linked to kingship (Ps 89:26). This recurrent pair of motifs is found in the Egyptian text, "The

Repulsing of the Dragon."[16] In Assyrian and other Mesopotamian royal inscriptions, the motif pair is used to celebrate military victories over historical enemies. Enemy kings are bound in chains. A king is placed under the Assyrian yoke. The imperial ruler uses enemies as a footrest and has them prostrate themselves before him as slaves. The Assyrian king has the power of binding and loosing nations under his patronage.[17] In the chronologically and culturally more coherent biblical tradition, we find an equally wide range of texts echoing the binding of Mummu in the Enuma Elish: from the mythic setting of borders to an unruly sea in Job 38 and Psalm 104, to the binding and loosing of the chains of enemies generally. Jeremiah offers the interesting choice between being bound by the chains of Yahweh's patronage or by the chains of death (Jer 5:4–6).

The divine hero of the Enuma Elish, the victor over Tiamat's chaos, is not present when the lesser gods create their uproar and keep Apsu from his sleep. Marduk is not born until after Apsu is murdered and the temple is built over his body.

Marduk is born in the house of Apsu; his father Ea created him; his mother Damkina gave birth to him; his was the birth of a hero.[18]

A brief tale of the child Marduk laughing and playing with his toys, the winds from the four corners of the earth, and especially of his happy noise keeping the gods from sleeping, doubles the plotline of sleeplessness and opens the narrative to a new cycle of noise and violence. Marduk plays but the gods demand rest. In the ensuing battle, Marduk crushes Tiamat's rebellion and takes up the reins of a renewed kingship. He creates a *new order* and control over the waters of chaos. The festival for the king centers in the theme of new birth and resurrection: a renewal of his government.

Neither the books of Samuel nor Chronicles give David a birth story, let alone the "birth of a hero" like Samson's or Moses'. The David story, however, does begin with a classical "birth of a savior" story in the tale of Hannah in 1 Samuel 1–2. This story type is often used for the birth of kings in the ancient world of stories, from Gilgamesh and Idrimi to Oedipus and from Cyrus to the gospel tales of John and Jesus.[19] In the pattern of Idrimi's tale, the story of choosing David as messiah builds on youngest son and Cinderella motifs to evoke expectations that he is truly chosen by God (1 Sm 16:4–13).[20] With a similar function, the stories of Sargon and Pannamuwa present a motif of threat to the life of the king as child, which plays so prominently in the stories of Joseph, Moses and Jesus. Certainly the story of the child Cyrus, raised by Mithridates the herdsman, who had been ordered by the king to kill the child, is—like the Greek legend of Oedipus—a clear ancestor of the European fairy-tale motif of danger to the child, which occurs in various stories, from Hansel and Gretel and Sleeping

Beauty to Snow White.[21] An alternative to a birth story for David is found in the closing scene of the book of Ruth, when Ruth, David's great-grandmother, gives birth to the child Obed (Ruth 4:16–22). Primary emphasis is placed on the divine grace of the child, reversing the hopeless future of the bereft Naomi. The motif of the barren giving birth is a central element in the "birth of a hero" stories of Isaac (Gen 18; 21), Joseph (Gen 30:22–24), Samson (1 Sm 1–2), Samuel (1 Sm 2:1–10) and John (Lk 1–2).

David acquires the Enuma Elish birth of a hero story in Psalm 2, which introduces the theme of Yahweh's messiah. This presentation of the birth of the messiah has two important variations. In Psalm 89, David is chosen as Yahweh's servant (Ps 89:4–5) and is given attributes of the good king. He is a Marduk-like warrior (Ps 89:20). Yahweh supports him and, in Yahweh's name, his fertility-bringing horn is raised (Ps 89:18, 25). He is given power over the sea and rules the waves (Ps 89:26). He is humble and fulfills the ideal of piety by seeking refuge in Yahweh (cf. Ps 2:12). Acknowledging Yahweh as his father, he becomes his firstborn (Ps 89:27–29). The royal titles of "servant" "chosen one" and "firstborn," as the virtue of humility and acknowledgment of his patron deity as "father," are central elements illustrated in the story of David in 1–2 Samuel.[22] The metaphor of Yahweh giving birth is presented in a decree of Yahweh in Psalm 2, as he responds to the nations in uproar:

> He will speak to them in his wrath and terrify them in his fury, saying: I have established my king on Zion, my holy hill. I [Yahweh's messiah] announce Yahweh's decree. He said to me, you are my son. Today, I bore you. Ask of me and I will make the nations your inheritance and the ends of the earth your possession. (Ps 2:5–8)

The messiah's formal announcement of Yahweh's decree echoes two Egyptian hymns from the New Kingdom. Both announce the good news of Pharaoh's accession to the throne. Of Merneptah, it is sung: "Be glad of heart, the entire land. The good times are come!" and of Ramses IV: "O Happy Day! Heaven and earth are in joy"! Both go on, appropriately, with variations on a song for a poor man, presenting the blessings of the kingdom. Already with its opening motif, Psalm 2 clearly evokes the messiah's accession to the throne.

A parallel scene to the establishment of Yahweh's king on Zion, the hill of Jerusalem where Yahweh has his temple, as well as the most striking announcement that Yahweh has given birth to the king on this day, presents itself in the Babylonian creation story. Marduk is son of god, born to Ea and his wife Damkina on Apsu's holy hill, where Ea built his temple. Of course, there is a strong difference between Ea's wife Damkina giving birth to Marduk and a male deity like Yahweh doing so. It should be clearly recognized that the Hebrew verb *(yelidtika)* is to be read unequivocally: "I have given birth to you" and not "I have begotten you" as it is often translated in English versions of the Bible. There is a prophecy from ancient Mari (eighteenth century BCE), which speaks of the god Adad in a similar context of "rearing" (giving birth?) and bringing a king to the throne, which helps understand the enigmatic lines of Psalm 2 and 110:

> Am I not Adad, lord of Kallassu, who reared him between my loins and restored him to the throne of his father's house? After I restored him to the throne of his father's house, I have again given him a residence.[23]

An even more striking and unequivocal confirmation comes from the Egyptian festival of Heb-sed, celebrated to renew the pharaoh's strength and vitality in his role as son of Re. Unlike the annual Akitu festival, Heb-sed was a jubilee celebration of renewal. It is usually identified with the thirtieth year of a Pharaoh's reign. Historically, it was celebrated at various intervals and, like the Akitu festival, was dedicated to the renewal of the king and his potency. It has origins going back to the Old Kingdom. On a small limestone relief at the Fitzwilliam Museum in Cambridge, Pharaoh Akhenaton is sketched in his jubilee cloak, worshiping the sun.[24] This fourteenth-century BCE drawing is a diptych: a picture story in two scenes, read from left to right. In the first, the king is presented with his hands raised in an attitude of prayer pointing toward the sun, whose rays dramatically surround him. Offerings are laid out on a table and the king carries a ceremonial whip, his sign of office, over his right shoulder. In the second scene, which presents the outcome of the king's prayer and the purpose of the festival, Akhenaton walks upright in procession with his body bathed in the rays of the sun. He bears the classic *ankh* and *was* signs, representing life and governance. He is flanked by two priests bowing low in his presence, one bearing sandals and the other a papyrus role. What is most striking is that the drawing centers on the person of the Pharaoh in an advanced stage of pregnancy! He is received by his priests as an object of worship and celebration. The festival celebrates the rebirth and renewal of his reign.

A similar interpretation is given to the earlier festival of Akhenaton's father. In a pair of torsos carved from basalt in full relief, Amenhotep III is presented "with his abdomen distended like that of a pregnant woman." An explanatory text clarifies the figure's underlying theology: "The king can create himself by himself."[25]

Universal Hymns

The presentation of Akhenaton, reborn by the rays of the sun, echoes the description of Marduk as "the son of the sun god; indeed, himself, the sun of the gods." Even so, Akhenaton's relationship to the sun god is much closer to Yahweh giving birth to the king in Psalm 2: "You are my son; today I have borne you" (Ps 2:7). The famous Egyptian Hymn to the Sun God was a central text that historically reoriented the Egyptian kingdom in its new context of empire.[26] Following the much older literary trope of collecting proverbs in the form of instruction to his son and successor, as in the book of Proverbs, the Hymn to the Sun God is sung by Akhenaton himself.[27] In the same way, the Psalter gives most of its messianic and royal songs David's voice. The Egyptian hymn identifies the rays of the sun as an army of divine forces fighting against those who resist pharaoh, the sun god's beloved son. The dawn driving away darkness illustrates divine support for imperial rule (lines 2–4). The song is universal and involves the whole of creation. The sun rules the Egyptian empire in Syria and Nubia. It controls the destiny of all and brings the Nile to foreigners that they might live (lines 7–10). Its rule over the world is the source of all fertility, of the breath of life itself (lines 5–6). In the closing stanza, the song paraphrases a story, placing the maintenance of creation in Pharaoh's hands. Akhenaton, as divine son "holding the sun in his heart," is the sole source of knowledge and strength—sole mediator between the divine and humanity. He holds power over life and death:

> At your dawn, they live; in your setting, they die [cf. 1 Sm 2:6].... Since you created the earth, you bring them to life for your son who (himself) came forth from your body of fire, ... Akhenaton, living and youthful, forever and ever.[28]

The song offers a revealing parallel to the renewal of the king and his reign. It also gives us a written version of Akhenaton's diptych of the Heb-sed festival, which celebrates his renewed fertility. In the hymn, the sun's rays form the "body of fire," which gives birth to his son the king. In the relief, solar flames mark both fertility and grace, as the king himself prepares to give birth. In the more distant biblical variation of this motif in Psalm 2, a heavenly Yahweh gives birth to his son, the king, and enthrones him on his sacred mountain. The rising of the kings of the earth against Yahweh and his messiah (Ps 2:1) are paralleled by the lions rising in the darkness against Akhenaton's sun. Both the messiah and Akhenaton hold them imprisoned and bound in chains. The messiah—like Akhenaton—is a divine mediator who determines destiny. He rules as emperor over all nations of the world.

Biblical echoes of this tradition are not limited to motifs of childbirth, designations of the king as son of God or the representation of the king as mediator between heaven and earth. Elements of holy war and new creation also create close associations between the Egyptian hymn and the Bible—especially with the creation hymn, Psalm 104.[29] This great hymn is a universal song, dedicated to the divine Yahweh as sun. In discussing these hymns, the Babylonian creation story, Enuma Elish, serves as a template for our comparison. The Nile's mythic underground streams may be borrowed to advance a hypothesis of an interrelated literary stream of antiquity, watering many intellectual worlds, artificially separated by language, geography and time. But the Bible shares more than the use of metaphors with the world of ancient myth. The Bible's implicit understanding of the divine marks common ground between its perception of God, who rules over the whole of creation through his messiah, and the universal metaphors of the more pluralistic world expressed in Egyptian or Assyrian texts of empire.

The rhetoric of Akhenaton's hymn is used to identify Yahweh with the sun (Ps 104:2). The cosmic geographic metaphor of a universal Nile flowing through the underworld finds its life-giving reversal in rising to the heavens to provide rain for fields and towns in distant foreign countries of Asia. While the theological reversal of death to life-giving resurrection is typically presented in biblical literature with Dionysian metaphors (see below, Chapter 7), the Egyptian metaphor finds its echo in the Bible in the creation story's separation of the waters above and below the firmament of the sky (Gen 1:6–7). It might be argued that the universal metaphor of the Nile going underground to rise once again in Asia is a close functional variant of the waters in the center of the garden in Eden, which become four rivers watering the four corners of the world (Gen 2:10–14). In the biblical hymn to the sun, springs arise in rivers flowing between mountains to provide drink and food for animals, birds and man (Ps 104:10–14). Such life-bringing water has its parallel in the Egyptian motif of life coming from the rising of the sun, creating fertility in women and men, maintaining and nursing a child in the womb of his mother (cf. Gen 4:1) and in the strikingly beautiful springtime motif of the sun creating breath to sustain us all.

The Egyptian hymn's resurrection motif of the land in darkness, likened to death, transformed by the sun's light, can be compared to the Bible's contrast between the "darkness over the deep" and the "divine spirit moving over the waters," leading to the creation of light (Gen 1:2). The control of the world through light and darkness—while only intimated in Genesis's naming and ordering of night and day and in lights placed in the firmament to distinguish, rule and create the cultic calendar—is directly illustrated in Psalm 104 and includes the Egyptian hymn's submotif of a lion coming out to hunt its prey:

You make darkness and it is night, when all the beasts of the forest creep forth. The young lions roar for their prey, seeking their food from God. When the sun rises, they get them away and lie down in their dens. Man goes forth to his work and to his labor until evening. O Yahweh, how manifold are your works. In wisdom have you made them all. (Ps 104:20–24; cf. Prv 8:22–36; cf. also Job 38:4–12)

Psalm 104 also uses imagery central to the Enuma Elish, whose scenario of violence and struggle contrasts harshly with the gentle, positive motifs of life-giving water. Great emphasis is placed on Yahweh as ruler with control over the sea. Like Tiamat running from Marduk's four storm winds, the sea flees from Yahweh's thunder. Yahweh controls the deep (Ps 104:6), a motif that is echoed in the flood story, where the sea obeys Yahweh's command to cover the mountains with destruction, carrying out Yahweh's curse of the earth, as well as to recede and uncover the mountains. Yahweh binds the sea, determines its destiny and gives life to creation. He sets boundaries on the sea that it not cover the earth (Ps 104:6–9; cf. Job 39:9–28; Prv 8:29; Jer 5:22). The Bible's hymn to the sun has a creation that functions; it is effective. It has a tamed sea of Yahweh's creation (Ps 104:10–28). Echoing Genesis, this psalm offers a variation of the motif central to the Enuma Elish and the Egyptian hymn—the king's control over destiny: "You take away your breath and they return to dust. You send your spirit and you renew the surface of the earth" (Ps 104:29–30; cf. Ps 90:3). This verse, with its death and resurrection metaphor, precisely expresses the theme of the king's humble dependence on his divine patron. God takes away his breath and he returns to the dust from which he was formed (Gen 3:19). Just so, this same God gives his spirit to renew that life (Gen 2:7). The motif of death's dust, contrasting with a renewed earth, translates the renewal liturgies of ancient Near Eastern kingship into a theological plea for a renewed Jerusalem as utopian kingdom. Psalm 104 does not merely reflect a borrowed cultural artifact from Egypt. It is an essential part of a tradition held in common with the Egyptian intellectual world (cf. Is 57:15; 65:17; Jer 4:11–17, 23–26; 31:31; Ez 36:26).

Echoing the themes of the Hymn to the Sun God and the wall plaque featuring Akhenaton pregnant with the renewal of his reign is an inscription on the walls of the great temple at Karnak. Thutmosis himself addresses the reader: "I am his [Amon's] son, who *came forth out of him* . . . "[30] The name "Thutmosis" can be translated with similar overtones of divine parentage: "[the divine] Thoth has given birth."[31] At Luxor, a later but still imperial text presents the divine Amon speaking of the "son of my body, my beloved Ramses (II) . . . whom I brought up from the womb . . . whom I have begotten in the fashion of my own limbs."[32] An oracle from the temple in Memphis also says of Ramses: "You are my son, the heir who was born of my limbs."[33]

In an Eighteenth Dynasty hymn, Thutmosis III (c. 1490–1436 BCE) is identified as the son of God. He is "begotten by Amon-Re."[34] In a first-person address to this famous king, the supreme god ascribes him with many of the characteristics that later appear in Psalm 2 and in the Psalter's presentation of David. From a typological perspective, the cluster of motifs describing the king in Thutmosis' hymn presents us with the first messiah. Thutmosis is his father's "avenger," much as the messiah of Psalm 2 will crush those who plot against Yahweh, his father (Ps 2:9). Because of Re, Thutmosis conquers and is feared by foreign countries. His reign reaches "as far as the four supports of heaven." Similarly, the messiah destroys the nations (Ps 2:8–9), advises them to serve Yahweh in fear (Ps 2:10) and is given the ends of the earth as his possession (Ps 2:8). Yahweh, like Re, "binds" foreign countries to his patronage (Ps 2:3), causes the king's enemies to "fall beneath his sandals" (Ps 110:1) and crushes rebels (Ps 2:9). Yahweh gives the king the world for his dominion (Ps 2:8) and stills the roaring of the sea. His Nile-like "river of God" waters and enriches the earth's outer corners (Ps 65:8–10). Re's heart is glad when Thutmosis enters the temple, while Yahweh brings a happy David there (Ps 23:5–6; cf. Ps 84:1–4). For both, entrance into the temple gives the king life (Ps 21:5). Like the messiah on Zion, Thutmosis is enthroned in Re's dwelling place (Ps 2:6). Both Re and Yahweh protect their kings (Ps 89:21–23) and call them (as Amon-Re calls Akhenaton) "my son, my beloved [Ps 2:7; Ps 89:28] . . . *whom I begot in the divine body*" (Ps 2:7). As in Yahweh's promise to David through the prophet Nathan (2 Sm 7:16), "Your throne will be established forever," the hymn of Thutmosis closes with Re's eternal promise to his king: "I have established you on the throne of Horus for millions of years" (cf. Ps 61:7–8; Ps 89:5).

THE VIRTUE OF SUFFERING

Central to the ideology of the hymns of the Egyptian empire is the king's support for the downtrodden. While such support usually finds expression in forms of the song for a poor man, this well-defined theme is also expressed in many first-person laments centered on suffering innocence: songs that seek relief from the king as personal savior.[35] This Job-like theme is a classic marker of royal ideology and is commonly associated with the role of the king as shepherd or savior of his people. It is even more common in Mesopotamian literature.[36] The intimate connection of personal piety to royal propaganda and creation mythology is most clear in imperial literature, as in the Neo-Babylonian Prayer of Lamentation to Ishtar. The apocalyptic reversals typical of the song for a poor man are combined with the figure of the innocent sufferer:

> O Deity of men, goddess of women, whose designs no one can conceive, where you look, one who is dead lives; one who is sick, rises up; the erring one who sees your face does right [line 39; cf. Job 42:5–6]. I have cried to you, suffering, wearied and distressed, as your servant. See me, O My Lady, accept my prayers; faithfully look upon me and hear my supplication; promise my forgiveness and let your spirit be appeased. Pity my wretched body, full of confusion and trouble. Pity my sickened heart, full of tears and suffering. Pity my wretched intestines, (full of) confusion and trouble. Pity my wretched house, mourning bitterly. Pity my feelings, satiated with tears and suffering.[37]

The clustering of motifs in this hymn is brilliant. The voice of lament joins with a cry of impatience, combining motifs of suffering with war and the threat of enemies:

> How long, O My Lady, will my enemies stare at me and in lying and untruth plan evil against me? Will my pursuers and those who exult over me rage against me? How long will the crippled and the weak seek me out [sic! cf. 2 Sm 5:6–8]; one has made for me long sackcloth. (cf. Ps 2; 22)

The cry of impatience ends with an ironic play on the song for a poor man: "The weak have become strong, but I am weak!"

> Silent is my chapel; silent is my holy place . . . for my god [has] his face turned to the sanctuary of another; my family is scattered; my roof is broken up. (Cf. Ps 89:47–48; Job 1:13–19)[38]

The singer closes his lament with abasement and repentance that the divine rage, which has been turned against him, might be changed to mercy. He prays that his enemies be trampled like the ground. In a metaphor that has evoked images of subdued enemies ever since the Narmer palette, he pleads that his foes be forced to crouch under him (cf. Ps 2:12a; 110:1d). The text closes, in spite of divine silence, in praise of his god (cf. Ps 89:53).

While the figure of the innocent sufferer, like the song for a poor man, is found throughout Job, the Psalter and Isaiah, it plays a key role in songs about the king. In Psalm 89 especially the distinctive figure of Yahweh's suffering servant is integrated as an ideal figure of piety. In the final stanza of this song, strong cadences of lament dominate with pathos, which holds until the close of the psalm (Ps 89:39–52). "You have rejected . . . your *messiah* . . . you have taken the staff from his hand and overturned his throne to the ground" (Ps 89:38, 44). The removal of the king's symbols of office in the Akitu festival, teaching humility, is never distant. The messiah must be humbled if he is to rule.

The biblical lament in Psalm 22 evokes the image of suffering with greater pathos: "My God, my God, why have you abandoned me?" (Ps 22:2; cf. Ps 28; Ps 142:1, 6–7; Ps 143:7). The next verse, "I cry in the daytime but you do not hear; in the night, but I find no rest" (Ps 22:3), has a singer who finds identity with him who "praises Yahweh day and night" (Ps 61:9) and raises the contradiction of his plight with the reassuring beatitude in Psalm 1 for the man who similarly "commits himself to Yahweh's Torah" (Ps 1:2). The lament's silent God opposes the figure of Yahweh who does hear prayers (Ps 65:2). While in Psalm 2 Yahweh laughs scornfully at the enemies of the messiah (Ps 2:4; cf. Is 49:7; Ps 8:7), Yahweh has abandoned his suffering servant (cf. Ps 35:22; 38:22) whose lightly disguised Samaritan enemies are likened to ferocious beasts, lions with gaping jaws (Ps 22:13–14; cf. Am 1:4; Job 16:9–10). The Psalter's lament finds its center in an expression of humility. David—like Job and like Babylon's king at the festival—humbles himself. He is "a worm, not a man: the subject of ridicule . . . and scorn" (Ps 22:7–8; cf. Job 42:6). The rest of the song continues the theme of suffering. Having once learned humility, David sings with confidence of his innocence and identifies himself as piety's ideal. Like John (Lk 1:41), he recognizes his God from his mother's womb (Ps 22:11).

MERNEPTAH AND THE CREATION OF PEACE

The famous victory stele of Merneptah celebrating victory over the Libyans does not function as a record of victory.[39] The "Israel stele" serves, rather, the larger function of celebrating the transcendent greatness of the Pharaoh by recalling this example of his power. The text has mythic qualities. Evoking the dream described on the Great Karnak Inscription, of the statue of Ptah giving Merneptah a magic sword "banishing all fear"[40] and illustrating the scene of the Cairo column showing a deity giving him a sword to destroy the chiefs of Libya,[41] the Israel stele uses this magic sword as a sign of the king's role as god's son, sitting on the throne of Shu.[42] The opening of the song underlines the dramatic and propagandistic rather than the historical character of the inscription. Desolate Rebu are set in contrast to secure and rejoicing Egyptians. The mythical quality of the presentation is also intimated in the opposition between the Libyan chief and pharaoh. The Libyan created an uproar and therefore is the object of the king's just anger. His rebellion against his Egyptian patron and overlord has removed him from the king's grace. His fate is that of a barren desert and his humiliation complete. Fleeing in darkness, without a feather to cover his head, his women are taken from him while he looks on. The Libyan prince is godless, the attacker of "every god who is in Memphis." As a consequence, the gods have found him guilty and Memphis is returned to the protection of their own son.[43]

In this mythic depiction of the past, Merneptah mediates divine grace. He is savior of the people and guardian of peace. He controls destiny and reverses the suffering and ill fortune of his people. He opens gates that were closed and gives breath to those who had been smothered. He reestablishes justice as the sign of a peace that heralds his coming in a manner remarkably close to the song that was sung at his accession to the throne.[44] He offers a version of the song of a poor man: opening what was closed, setting free those who were bound, letting princes recover their wealth and the poor reenter their cities.[45]

The inscription presents pharaoh in the figure of divine savior, explicit in a petition of the gods of Heliopolis in the central movement of the hymn.[46] In line with the central themes of the Heb-sed festival, the hymn celebrates the renewed rule of the king: "Give him duration like Re." Merneptah's future is universal and imperial. The seat of his strength is Egypt, but he is the savior and patron of the oppressed of all lands. As in Akhenaton's hymn to the sun god, all find their breath from Merneptah.[47]

> The countries of Syria and Nubia, and in the land of Egypt; you set every man in his place; you supply his necessities. . . . You make a Nile in the underworld; you bring it forth . . . to maintain the people (of Egypt) . . . the lord of every land, rising for them. . . . All distant foreign countries, you make their life; for you have set a Nile in heaven, that it may descend for them and make waves upon the mountains . . . to water their fields in their towns.[48]

The thematic element of peace for all men, with the idyllic picture of pharaoh as universal patron of Egyptians and foreigners alike, dominates the third and final part of the song. This closing act begins with a classic proclamation of good news that belongs to the utopian theme of the kingdom, finally brought in balance with the order of creation. "Great joy has come to Egypt!" This is the same good news announcing a new day for Egypt that accompanied Merneptah to the throne with shouts of, "Be glad, the entire land! Good times have come."[49] This declaration finds a more cosmic parallel in the announcement of the accession of Merneptah's successor, Ramses IV: "Oh Happy Day. Heaven and Earth are in joy, for you are the great lord of Egypt."[50]

In the Israel stele, peace is celebrated through happy gossip praising the king. There is no fear. All are happy and calm. Re has returned to the land. The song reiterates the patterns of Akhenaton's hymn to the sun god. God's gift of peace—like the Nile—comes first to Egypt and then to the "foreign peoples and the beasts of every desert." The Pharaoh is "the lord of every land . . . for all distant countries he creates life."[51] The hymn closes with a ten-line song celebrating *shalom* among the "nine bows":

> The kings lie prostrate, saying *shalom!* Not one raises his head among the Nine Bows. A desert is Libya; Hatti is scorched.[52] Plundered is Gazza, with every evil; carried off is Askalon; bound is Gezer; Yenoam is as one not existing. Israel is laid waste, his seed is no more; Hurru has become a widow for Egypt. All lands are united, they are in peace; everyone that was in uproar is bound by King Merneptah; they are given life like Re, forever.[53]

This closing stanza is not part of an inscription giving an account of conquest. The stanza begins and closes on the theme of *shalom*. It is a mistake to read this metaphor of prostrate princes as implying a degradation of the king's enemies, their blessing of peace implicitly undermined by an authorial mockery of their humiliation. Prostration before the king is the normal position of the client before his patron, the servant before his king. Such humility is the greatest virtue of every client: even Merneptah's before Amon-Re. The nine bows ideally and symbolically represent all foreign lands as clients of the king.

The figure of Merneptah as patron over the nine bows with princes prostrate before him, not a single one raising his head, is echoed in the figure of the messiah in Psalm 2. "The nations in uproar," plotting to break the chains that bind them to Yahweh, play the role of the nine bows in Egyptian mythology. David is given the ends of the earth for his possession and foreign rulers are admonished by him—as by Seti I—to be wise and serve Yahweh with fear and trembling. And what is the message of our text? For Merneptah's nine bows as for David's nations in uproar, the ultimate message is the same: "Blessed are all who take refuge in him."[54] The opening lines of Merneptah's closing song speak of peace. No one rebels; all are bound and say *shalom*.

The positive nature of the nine bows motif is clear in the Hymn to Amon of Amenhotep III. He is presented as having been raised by the "mistress of the nine bows to be the sole lord of the people." The four traditional corners of the world—the South (Kush-Nubia), North (Retenu-Palestine-Syria), West (Tehenu-Libya) and East (Punt-Arabia)—all crave peace. It is the king's role to give it to them. The Asiatics "present themselves with their children, that you might give them the breath of life."[55]

One of the lines of the stele's last song reads, "Israel is no more" and "Hurru has become a widow for Egypt." Hurru—a regional name from the Eighteenth Dynasty—designated Palestine and Coele-Syria and personifies the land and its fertility.[56] Her widowhood allows Egypt to assume the guardianship of the land. Similarly, Ramses II is given the epithet "husband of Egypt."[57] Israel is best understood as an eponym personifying the father of the people of Hurru, including the towns of Ashqelon, Gezer and Yeno'am: Israel's seed turned into deserts. Pharaoh's role as new husband of the widowed land, Hurru, engages an essential metaphor of patronage. It is similar to Yahweh's role in Hosea and Ezekiel as *ba'al* (husband) of Jerusalem and Samaria. Jeremiah gives such a role to Assyrian and Babylonian kings.[58] The role of Israel as personifying the people of Palestine and—in the Merneptah stele—as *late* husband of Hurru—does not imply any particular ethnic group within Palestine, but rather functions as a narrative figure for all of Palestine, particularly where Merneptah had his interests—the lowland region from Gaza to Yeno'am.

The listing of Israel, "whose seed is no more," and the widow Hurru as a pair introduces the theme of fertility as well as the metaphor of matrimony. The text associates the emasculation of Israel and the role of Hurru's widow with the desert images of Hurru's towns. A single song of promise is created, celebrating Egyptian patronage over its clients in Palestine. The purpose of the motifs of destruction, desert and impotence that dominate this song mark the difference between the presence and absence of pharaoh's grace. It is he who determines destiny, who curses and blesses. He holds creation fast. He destroys and gives the breath of life. He makes barren and he fills the land with fertility. Apart from divine pharaoh's patronage, all is a ruin, a desert and a wasteland. This is a language of transcendent *status*. Apart from the king—as apart from Yahweh—there exists only the cosmic desert of nothingness. Bound to him is peace and life.

‹♖›

CHAPTER 7

The Myth of the
Dying and Rising God

The figure of the messiah in Psalm 2 and the Psalter takes up the role of Yahweh's divine warrior to bring the nations in uproar to submit to Yahweh's imperial patronage through holy war. However, the narrative traditions move in a different direction. Beginning in the leitmotif of the curse of the land from which mankind was created, Genesis projects an ideal figure of a new mankind to replace violence and corruption—which had led Yahweh to reject his creation in the story of the great flood—and to bring an end to war and bloodshed. This biblical chain narrative of new beginnings—both for the land and for the humanity created from it—draws heavily on the patterns of ancient Near Eastern myths of seed and harvest and the annual cycle of the seasons. Such myths of the death and rebirth of the god of fertility, using metaphors of drought and the spring rains, were centred in the important harvest festival of the new wine. In the biblical story, this mythic theme is integrated with the metaphor of covenant through which Israel was bound to its God with ties of loyalty and obedience to create an army of salvation, giving the pious of Judea the task of imitating the Psalter's role of the messiah. Each generation's reiterated failure, however, in both loyalty and obedience, allows the narrative to develop a never-ending chain of stories marked by death and rebirth. The New Testament gospel stories, reusing the concept of a new covenant from the Hebrew Bible, pursue this hope of a new humanity in its effort to create a generation of understanding. The narrative development of the old covenant theme ties the tragic figure of David inexorably to the theme of holy war and to the story of old Israel's destruction by Yahweh. It forms the central issue of the closing section of this book. The story of Jesus cannot be understood apart from the metaphor of covenant within the Bible's story of never-ending failure. The gospel's presentation of Jesus' death and resurrection has its most immediate roots in the biblical revision of ancient Near Eastern myths of resurrection. A single scene in Matthew's Last Supper story opens this theme.

The Blood of the Covenant

In describing Jesus' last meal, the gospels have him refer to the wine he gives his disciples to drink as "the blood of the covenant" (Mt 26:17–29; Mk 14:12–25; Lk 22:7–23). He tells the disciples that he will not drink this wine again and speaks of a "new wine" of the future, which he will share with his disciples in his "father's kingdom."

> Now as they were eating, Jesus took bread, blessed and broke it. He gave it to the disciples and said, "Take, eat. This is my body." And he took a cup, and when he had given thanks, he gave it to them, saying, "Drink of it all of you, for this is my blood of the [new] covenant, which is poured out for many for the forgiveness of sins. I tell you I will not drink again of this fruit of the vine until that day when I drink it new with you in my father's kingdom." (Mt 26:26–29)

Matthew's Last Supper scene is borne by three thematic elements, all well-known from earlier biblical literature: the metaphors of my father's kingdom, of new wine and of the blood of the covenant.

Like the "kingdom of God," the metaphor of my father's kingdom is not apocalyptic in the sense that it implies expectations of the end of the world as Schweitzer thought. It is rather a utopian and idealistic metaphor for a world of justice. In ancient Near Eastern and biblical literature, it is related to the figure of the savior-king who, by reestablishing divine rule, returns creation to the original order. Matthew draws on Isaiah for his use of the metaphor in his vision of Jerusalem at peace, saved from foreign occupation by divine terror: a city in which Yahweh is the judge, ruler and king (Is 33:20–22). Jesus is the bearer of Isaiah's "good news," the proclamation with which Mark opens his gospel (Mk 1:1). A savior is epitomized with a single metaphor in both the Hebrew Bible and the New Testament. He reiterates the songs of Thutmosis III and Ramses IV. He is the king, bringing an end to all war:

> How beautiful over the mountains are the feet of him who brings good news, who announces peace and proclaims salvation. He says to Zion: your God is king. Listen! Your watchmen lift up their voice; together they sing for joy. For eye to eye they see the return of Yahweh to Zion. Break out together in singing, wastelands of Jerusalem; for Yahweh has comforted his people, redeemed Jerusalem. Yahweh has exposed his holy arm before the eyes of all nations. All the ends of the earth will see the salvation of our God. (Is 52:7–10)

The metaphor of "new wine" draws on the biblical tradition of royal ideology from a different direction. The long speech of Elihu in Job captures the intellectual intoxication of new wine. It transforms lack of understanding into insight and truth. Job's debate with his three friends has run aground. They repeat but old truths of tradition, without insight into the transcendent God with whom Job must deal. Job, on the other hand, is so taken up with his own innocence, that he claims as his own a righteousness that God has given him. Elihu presents his long commentator's speech with an author's voice, designed to bear Job through his transformation through suffering to understanding and humility (Job 32–37). Elihu speaks truth to the old men quarreling over old wine and old ideas. A young man has held himself silent before his elders, but now Elihu's new wine (Job 32:19), coming from a divine spirit, overwhelms him:

> I am young and you are old; therefore, I was timid and afraid to give you part in my knowledge. I said, "Days should speak and the multitude of years should teach wisdom." However, it is the spirit in man, the breath of the Almighty which gives understanding. The old are not always wise; nor is it age that understands judgment. Therefore I said, "Listen to me, now you will share in my knowledge." Behold, I waited for your words; I gave ear to your reasons, while you looked for what to say. I listened to you, but there was none of you that confuted Job or gave answer to his words. Do not say, "We have found wisdom." It is God who will put him [i.e., Job] down, not a man. His words were not directed to me and I will not answer him as you have done. . . . I am full of words; the spirit within me holds me back. Look, my heart is like wine, which has no vent, like new wine in sacks ready to burst. I will speak that I might find relief; I will open my lips and answer. . . . My words declare the uprightness of my heart; what my lips know, they speak clean. The spirit of God has made me and the breath of the Almighty gives me life. (Job 32:6–33:4)

In Matthew's scene, the wine of the Last Supper reflects the blood of the covenant, to be transformed through Jesus' suffering into the new wine of the kingdom. Matthew draws on Elihu's evocation of suffering as a transforming righteousness and truth, itself as divine as the breath of life in us is from God. The synoptic gospels reuse Elihu's metaphor of old and young wine in the form of proverbs (Mt 9:17; Mk 2:22; Lk 5:37–39). In John's gospel they are transformed to story, where we find Job's metaphor implicit in the well-known story of the wedding feast at Cana. The old wine had been used up (Jn 2:1–11). The new wine—which Jesus creates—is called good (cf. Gen 1:4, etc.). Like the wine of Matthew's Last Supper, it is a sign of the "time to come." Also like the understanding of that wine as Jesus' blood, John links his story of the miracle at Cana to a variant of the story of the cleansing of the temple. Just so, the temple is evoked as metaphor for Jesus' own body, to be remembered as a riddle of resurrection:

> When he was raised from the dead, his disciples remembered he had said this and they believed the scripture and the word which Jesus had spoken. (Jn 2:13–25)

Matthew's metaphor of the "covenant of blood" refers to the stories of Moses in Egypt and at Mount Sinai, a story in which Israel is created as Yahweh's people through a pact, or covenant, which they enter into with their divine patron. The scene at Sinai closes an expansion on the Ten Commandments (Ex 20:1–17). It brings together a miscellany of social, religious and cultic traditions into what the narrative refers to as the "book of the covenant" (Ex 20:22–23, 19). The story presents these instructions and commands as "ordinances," which are presented to Israel to test them: "That the fear of him may be before your eyes, so that you not sin." Yahweh enters into the covenant of blood with his people at the opening of the story of holy war's failure:

> Moses came and told the people all the words of Yahweh and all the ordinances; and all the people answered with one voice and said, "All the words that Yahweh has spoken we will do." Moses wrote all the words of Yahweh. He rose early in the morning and built an altar at the foot of the mountain, with twelve pillars, according to the twelve tribes of Israel. He sent young men of the people of Israel, who offered burnt offerings and sacrificed peace offerings of oxen to Yahweh. Moses took half of the blood and put it in basins and half of the blood he threw against the altar. Then he took the book of the covenant and read it in the hearing of all the people. They said: "All that Yahweh has

spoken we will do and we will be obedient." Moses took the blood and threw it upon the people, saying: "Behold, the blood of the covenant, which Yahweh has made with you in accordance to all these words." (Ex 24:3–8; var.: Josh 24:14–28)

With considerable dramatic impact, the covenant scene constructs a harmony from different cultic scenarios. Fundamental is the description of the burnt and peace offerings to bring reconciliation, which are drawn from Leviticus 1 and 3. The odor of both—like Noah's peace offering—is sweet (Lev 1:17; 3:5, 16; cf. Gen 8:21). In both descriptions of sacrifice in Leviticus, *blood* is thrown on and around the altar. The Exodus story of the covenant includes a motif from the ritual of purification, in which ashes from the sacrifice are dissolved in water and then sprinkled directly on the people to purify them (Num 19:16–19). The reuse of the purification ritual's sprinkling in the Exodus story (Ex 24:5–8, where blood is sprinkled on the people) suggests that the story of the covenant identifies the blood of the sacrifice with the life of the people. This, we will see, harmonizes well with the understanding of covenant in the Noah and Abraham stories.

Echoes in Matthew's story of an older text from Jeremiah (Jer 31:31–34) have long been recognized.[1] Yahweh speaks of a "new covenant" (i.e., "new testament"), one in which the divine law is written on the hearts of "Israel and Judah's house." It is a covenant in which all sin is forgiven because all "know Yahweh." Matthew's use of the Last Supper scene to introduce the following narrative of suffering and death allows us to recognize the reference to the "blood of the covenant" as a *plot-related citation* from Zechariah. This citation encourages a theological interpretation of the story of Jesus' passion. Jesus' passage through suffering and death to resurrection reiterates the story of Israel's exile and return:

Because of the blood of my covenant with you, I have freed prisoners from the dry pit. Return to your stronghold, prisoners of hope; today I declare that I will restore to you double. (Zech 9:11–12)

Zechariah's reference to the covenant is a citation from Isaiah's proclamation of the "good news to the poor," announcing the reversals that Yahweh's year of grace brings:

The spirit of the God Yahweh is upon me. Yahweh has anointed me to bring good news to the poor; he has sent me to bind the brokenhearted, to proclaim freedom to prisoners, and the opening of the prisons to those who are in chains. To proclaim Yahweh's year of grace and the day of vengeance of our God: to comfort all who mourn; to grant to those who mourn in Zion—to give them a garland instead of ashes, the oil of gladness instead of mourning, the mantle of praise instead of a faint spirit that they might be called oaks of righteousness, plantings of Yahweh that he might be glorified. They will build up the ancient ruins; they will repair the former devastation; they will repair the ruined cities and the devastation of many generations . . . instead of your shame, you will have a double portion; instead of dishonor, you shall rejoice in your lot. Therefore, in your land you will possess a double portion; yours will be everlasting joy. (Is 61:1–7)

On the level of Matthew's plot, the citation from Zechariah allows the Last Supper scene to lay the ground for the resurrection story (Gen 37:24; Jer 38:6). The reversal of the sufferer's fate that Zechariah prophesies is a sign of the kingdom and already marks the suffering and death of Jesus with a promise of victory over death.

Matthew clearly intends his allusions to bear meaning for his story as Zechariah celebrates reconciliation and the end of war:

Rejoice, daughter of Zion, shout aloud, O daughter of Jerusalem. Lo, your king comes to you. Triumphant and victorious is he, humble and riding on an ass. I will cut off the chariot from Ephraim and the war horse from Jerusalem and the battle bow will be cut off; he will command peace to the nations. His dominion will be from sea to sea and from the river to the ends of the earth. (Zech 9:9–10)

Matthew gives Jesus this hero's role in the scene of his entry into Jerusalem (Mt 21:1–11; Mk 11:1–11; Lk 19:28–40). This illustration from Zechariah also draws on close variants in Isaiah. An even more expansive version of the innocent and righteous sufferer is found in Isaiah's figure of Israel as Yahweh's servant and firstborn: one, who bears the sins of many (Is 53:4–12). As in Zechariah, Isaiah's use of Israel as Yahweh's suffering servant presents an atoning figure, an alternative to a returning Elijah, who is to reconcile the generations and prevent Yahweh from coming in judgment. In Isaiah, the people, as suffering servant, take on the role of conquering king. They enter the gates of the kingdom, clearing the stones and making a highway for those who have been transformed into Yahweh's holy people. Purified through suffering, Isaiah's Israel finally fulfills Deuteronomy's impossible hope of a "holy people" for a holy God (Dt 7:6). It is

Isaiah's people whom Jesus personifies in Matthew's theology. It is this figure his character imitates in the scenario drawn from Zechariah:

> Go through, go through the gates; prepare the way for the people. Build up, build up the highway; clear it of stones. Lift up the standard for the people. Behold, Yahweh has proclaimed to the end of the world. Say to the daughter of Zion: "Behold, your salvation comes; behold, his reward is with him and his wages before him. They shall call them 'the holy people; the redeemed of Yahweh.'" (Is 62:10–12)

For Matthew, the metaphors of the good king announcing the good news of the kingdom, of Elijah turning back Yahweh's curse, of Zechariah's king and of Isaiah's suffering Israel atoning for all humanity's sin, are all useful in defining Jewish piety. It is this ideal that Matthew's figure of Jesus offers the audience.

A similar theology accompanies the alternative covenant tradition of the Passover, which the Exodus origin story features in a sacrifice at night. In this story of the first Passover, the doorposts of the Israelites are sprinkled with the blood of the lamb rather than the Israelites themselves or their firstborn. The firstborn of the Egyptians is sacrificed instead. The "destroyer," with a king's power over both life and death, "passes over" the houses of the Israelites. Judgment is delayed (Ex 12:21–27) as the story holds fast to the principle that the firstborn belongs to Yahweh.[2]

In Matthew's rendering, Jesus is put in the role of the animal sacrificed. Those sprinkled with its blood are the guilty to be reconciled. By pacifying the divine, the people find reconciliation and forgiveness for their sins, precisely as in the song of the "new covenant" of Jeremiah and precisely as understood in the "covenant of blood" narrative of Exodus 24. It also reiterates the role of reconciliation, which the returning Elijah engages: to prevent Yahweh from again cursing the land.

The story of Moses is also taken up in Matthew's use of the blood of the covenant theme in his Last Supper story. In the Exodus tale, the sprinkling of the "blood of the covenant" onto the people leads immediately into the extraordinary scene of a sacred meal that the seventy elders share with the God of Israel. Having climbed the mountain, the seventy stand on a pavement of sapphire, "as clear as heaven itself." In this scene of mystic rapture, the people "saw God, ate and drank" (Ex 24:9–11). When Jesus and his twelve disciples of the new covenant evoke this scene in their last supper together, it is such heavenly fulfillment and rapture that Jesus alludes to when he gives the disciples wine to drink.

But he will not again share this until he drinks "a new wine with them in his father's kingdom" (Mt 26:29; also Lk 22:18–19, 28–30). The gospel scene also draws on Isaiah's reading of Exodus:

> Yahweh empties the earth, makes it a wasteland, turning it upside down. . . . A curse has devoured the earth and its inhabitants . . . because they have broken the eternal covenant. . . . Only a few remain while a new wine mourns as the vine wilts. They will not drink wine with song. . . . In the streets, one hears complaints about the wine; for all joy is gone. (Is 24:1–11)

In restructuring Isaiah's day of wrath, Matthew will not have his Jesus drink a wine of gladness. He prepares to drink "the cup of his suffering." Jesus holds his new wine in mourning and cannot drink it in gladness and song (Mt 26:39, 42). The old wine of the covenant's blood is drunk in preparation for Jesus' death and burial. There is no wine in the grave, as the disciples must await the resurrection of a new spring, bringing the new year's wine. Isaiah's song of Yahweh entering his kingdom (Is 24) offers a useful key to understanding both Matthew's narrative of the Last Supper and the Exodus story of the elders sitting on heaven's sapphire floor, eating and drinking with God. Isaiah's song bears overtones of the exile. Israel's captive prisoners are gathered. "Divine terror, the pit and the trap" have fallen over the inhabitants of the earth (Is 24:17). Jerusalem's destruction is projected in a scene of the earth, sun and moon returning to chaos before creation (Is 24:3; cf. Jer 4:23). This metaphor of cosmic destruction closes with a utopian hope of future reversal. The punishment in the pit is transformed as Exodus' scene of the elders is rewritten: "Yahweh of the armies will rule and before his elders, (the rapture of) his glory (Is 24:22–23)." Much as a day of suffering is marked by a lack of wine and an end to singing (Is 24:7–9, 11), the heavenly feast transforms the day of suffering as the transcendent king enters his kingdom:

> On this mountain, the Lord of hosts will make a feast for all peoples: a great feast with rich meats and old wines. . . . The veil that is cast over the nations will be destroyed; he will swallow death forever and the God Yahweh will wipe tears away from everyone's face. He will take away the reproach of his people from the whole earth. (Is 25:6–8)

By having Jesus point ahead to meeting the disciples once again in his father's kingdom, there to drink the new wine, the gospel writers identify Jesus' impending suffering ("his covenant of blood") with both Israel's new covenant and their suffering in exile. Similarly, the future evoked—drinking a new wine with God in his kingdom—is Isaiah's ecstatic future, overcoming death. That the reader's attention is focused on this future of eating and drinking with God is important. How the Passion story is to be read is at stake. The suffering figure of Jesus plays the Pentateuch's lost generation. The disciples are with Moses and the elders on Mount Sinai. In their heavenly feast, death is overcome through the rapture the story evokes. As in Jeremiah and Isaiah, so in the gospels, the goal is understanding: a glimpse of the transcendent that resolves human suffering (Jer 31:34; Is 25:9; Mt 26:29). The indirection of reiterative narrative and song allows us to read a story about Jesus and his disciples sharing a cup of wine the night before his death through multiple evocations of figures of suffering. Isaiah's Jerusalem, the elders of the wilderness and the innocent, righteous one of Israel all contribute to the story's overtones. Like the figure of the prophetic shepherd from Zechariah, "struck down, scattering the flock" to whom Matthew turns as he has Jesus go up to the Mount of Olives (Mt 26:31; Zech 13:7), all of these figures stand within a universal pedagogy of wisdom through suffering.

DIONYSUS, BAAL AND TAMMUZ

The passion narrative reiterates the myth of Dionysus, with its many motifs of wine and fertility borne by a dying and rising divine figure. Similar Roman traditions and festivals of Bacchus place a greater emphasis on the seasonal cycle of cereals. In the more complex Hellenistic world, however, where festivals of Dionysus are among the most popular in antiquity, this divine–human figure plays different roles. Among many variations, the most popular themes are the drinking of wine as blood, the dying and rising of one who is half god and half man, the transformation of tears of mourning into gladness and singing, suffering transformed into the intoxication of new wine, the ecstatic meal, the fertility of spring and a new creation. Such themes are abundantly present in biblical literature and reflect similar patterns and purpose. Some we have already seen. The figure of a god-man who is destroyed, who relinquishes his life and who is born again is as fundamental to the mythic reflection of the natural cycle of grain agriculture as it is central to the theme of resurrection. Freely overcoming death through suffering marks the self-sacrifice of the hero, leading to expressions of joy through wine and food. This theme is basic to the figure with which Plutarch describes his Dionysus. He is a symbol for the divine, the everlasting quality of life. The ebb and flow of Dionysus' life force is an inevitable reflection of antiquity's struggle between famine and fertility. This figure of Dionysus has as much in common with the gospel figure of Jesus as it has with Isaiah's Israel. This figure is exploited eagerly in the wide range of songs and stories of the savior-king and is echoed throughout the Bible's rich contrasting repertoire of metaphors for fertility and barrenness.

Even so, differences in the Bible's use of these themes and their expression in the late Hellenistic festivals and mystery cults of Dionysus are quite striking. The festivals as such, including public drunkenness and a wide range of public sexual celebration, hardly dominated the religious festivals of Palestine's Samaritans and Jews. Nor did they dominate the traditions collected in biblical literature. The frequent use of themes related to the sexual potency of the king, of erotic songs celebrating Jerusalem's love for its God as her bridegroom and the many erotic and even pornographic metaphors of prophetic poetry, though, hardly mark this tradition as antagonistic to a religiously oriented sexual expression. It reflects, however, a more ascetic form of piety than was typical of Dionysian orgy.

Dionysian stories drew on a wide range of interrelated figures, themes and tale types, long at home in the ancient Near Eastern and Mediterranean worlds. In Matthew's story, Jesus prepares and introduces his companions into the community of his death by evoking a symbolic drinking of his blood interpreted as a ritual of binding the faithful to the divine. Though clearly reflecting the Dionysian tradition, it is the product of a more complex synthesis of cultures in Palestine, with roots stretching long before the Greco-Roman period. In language and geography, this tradition reflected in the Dionysus myth has a breadth far exceeding the world of Greek literature. While the figure of Dionysus, in particular, may well go back to the Mycenaean period in the Late Bronze Age, his underlying themes of life and fertility, of life's victory over death, of the spring wine, and so on, all so central to the Dionysian myth of resurrection, are also major themes of ancient mythology in cultures ranging from ancient Ur and Babylon to Thebes. The myth is as old as stories come in the ancient Near East.[3]

For example, close to the Hebrew language of biblical tradition is the millennium earlier Ugaritic poem of Baal from the ancient coastal city of Ugarit in the fourteenth and thirteenth centuries BCE. Almost every element of the story of Baal's battle with Mot finds a reiteration somewhere in the Bible and almost all of the elements in the myth of Dionysus echo this story. It is a tale of a divine king, whose death and resurrection celebrate life's victory over death.[4] Like Yahweh, Baal ("lord," "ruler," "husband") is a storm and warrior god. Closing a story in which Baal takes possession of his house is a rich echo of the story of the child Marduk, playing with the four winds. Baal has a window made for his new house. Through this window in the clouds, he shouts and makes thunder. The terrifying noise causes the earth to tremble and the mountains to shake with fear. His enemies cling desperately to the trees and slopes of the mountains. Deeply impressed by what his noise and terror can do, Baal declares himself the sole king of the kingdom. He alone will rule and none other.

The hubris of his ambitions quickly and inevitably lead him into a contest with the god Mot ("Death"). Angry that Baal will not invite him and his kin to eat or drink wine with him, Mot swears that he will pierce Baal. He sends Baal—who is also the god of life and fertility—his own proud message. Although ruler Baal may have his house of silver and his palace of gold, Mot controls the throat of the desert and the mouth of the sea. With such a throat and with such a mouth, he can swallow all the living. He reminds Baal that even he, the god of life, must descend the throat of death (cf. Job 40:25–41:26).

In humble response, Baal—the greatest of heroes—acknowledges that he is ever Mot's servant. Mot, meanwhile, happily plots to bring Baal into the realm of death, when he comes down to Mot for a feast, celebrating the completion of Baal's temple. When the gods have eaten and drunk the wine's blood, he will plant Baal in his grave and the gods will know that he is dead. When Mot invites Baal to climb down to "freedom's house," Baal obeys. Before his death, however, "in a field near death's shore," Baal makes love to a cow, which conceives and bears him a son.

Messengers bring news to the gods of Baal's death in the field near death's shore. The god El descends from his throne and sits in the dust on the ground, evoking the sorrow of Job. Shaking dust onto his head, he tears his clothes in two pieces and scrapes his skin with a stone (cf. Job 1:20; 2:8). With two chips of flint as a razor, he cuts his face. Three times he "furrows" his arm, his breast and his back like a valley, as he calls out, "Baal is dead!" Just so, sings the song. The children of Dagan ("grain" = Baal) join and identify themselves in El's mourning: "In Baal's footstep, I too will go down into the ground." The goddess Anat searches for her brother and finds his body on the shores of death. She too goes into mourning and will bury him among the gods of the underworld. She too tears her clothes in two pieces and scrapes her skin with a stone. With two chips of flint as a razor, she cuts her face. Three times she "furrows" her arm, her breast and her back like a valley. She too calls out, "Baal is dead!" She carries him on her shoulder and buries him in the ground. After making a sacrifice for the dead, she rejoins El. Full of love for her brother, Anat demands that Mot return Baal from the realm of the dead. Mot refuses. He has swallowed Baal like a lamb. Anat searches longingly for her brother and attacks Mot. She splits him with a sickle, winnows him, grinds him up and burns him. She grinds him on a mill and sows his flesh in the field, which the birds eat.

After a gap in the text of some lines, the narrative continues with a threefold evocation of Baal's revival. This begins with Anat's prophecy: Baal has gone into the earth. Yet if Baal the strong is alive, El the merciful will have a dream and a vision that the heavens will rain with oil and the rivers run with honey (cf. Ex 3:8; Ez 32:14; Jl 4:23). In the story's doubling fulfillment of this prophecy, El has his dream and vision and laughs with joy: Baal the strong lives (cf. Ps 18:46)! He calls to Anat to tell the goddess of the sun, Shapshu. "The furrows of the field are dried up. The plowed furrows will grieve for Baal (cf. Job 31:38). Where is Baal?" Anat takes herself to Shapshu and asks after her brother. Shapshu answers that she has seen the curse. Anat gives strength to Baal, who, now rising from the dead, attacks Mot and returns to his throne to resume his rule over the earth. The conflict with Mot continues for seven years (Gen 41:1–4). A duel of giants—echoing the tale of Gilgamesh wrestling with Enkidu—ends in a mutual affirmation of strength (cf. Gen 32:24–29). Mot, with fear and terror, accepts his destiny in the cycles of sowing and harvest. Baal returns to his throne, and the story closes with an offering of reconciliation: bread and wine to the goddess Shapshu.

The songs and images that created this tradition find striking and detailed echoes in the Bible, especially in ubiquitous shifting metaphors of the barren desert, standing in contrast to the promised land, its rivers flowing with milk and honey. It is also present in resurrection images of the springtime desert coming to bloom, a dead stump sprouting a new spire and the barren woman giving birth. Less specific parallels support the plots of biblical narrative from Genesis to Revelation. The story of Job, sending the virtuous man into mourning for the family taken from him in a single day, echoes El's reaction to the news of Baal's death.

The story of Elijah on Mount Carmel (1 Kgs 18), discussed earlier, offers the most direct narrative parallel to ancient Ugarit's epic of a millennium earlier. As in the epic, drought threatens all life in the land and evokes the question of who is the living God. King Ahab and the prophet Obadiah go in different directions to search all the springs and brooks for grass to keep their cattle alive. Elijah sends Obadiah to the king with a challenge—"as Yahweh of the armies lives"— to meet him in a duel with the prophets of Baal and Asherah. When they set their offerings on their altar and call on Baal to set fire to it—"the god who answers with fire, he is God" (1 Kgs 18:24)—Baal does not answer; "no voice was heard." No terror was created and no fertile rain came. The prophets of Baal shout louder and the story of 1 Kings reiterates the fertility ritual of cutting furrows in the body, so fertilizing blood flows. With their blood, Baal's suppliants try to prepare their bodies for the hoped-for rains. It is from blood that the new wines come. With the sun at its height, the prophets dance in their ecstasy. Yet

Baal's voice is not there; there is no answer, not a sound. Elijah has nothing but scorn for the prophets of Baal and Asherah's ritual of mourning. He rebuilds Moses' altar with twelve stones, representing the twelve tribes of Israel (cf. Ex 24:4). He calls to Yahweh, who does answer, proving that he is the living God.

While the Pentateuch explicitly forbids the ritual of shaving the face and furrowing the body with cuts of mourning for the god of fertility (Lev 19:27–28; Dt 14:1), references to this custom in the prophets (Jer 16:6; 41:5; 47:5; 48:37; Ez 7:18) clearly show that the tradition was well-known. Less competitive forms of mourning, also expressing a hope in resurrection—whether rooted in personal losses of family or in disasters of drought and famine—are well illustrated in the metaphor of the exile as a famine before the "day of Yahweh":

> Hear this you old men. . . . Has such a thing happened in your days or in the days of your fathers? . . . what the cutting locust left . . . what the swarming locust . . . the hopping locust . . . the destroying locust has eaten. Awake drunkards and weep. Wail, all you drunkards of wine because of the sweet wine. It is cut off from your mouth. . . . Lament like a virgin girded with sackcloth for the bridegroom of her youth. The cereal offering and the drink offering are cut off from the house of Yahweh. . . . Gird on sackcloth and lament, O priests. . . . Sanctify a fast, call a solemn assembly . . . and cry to Yahweh. . . . The day of Yahweh is great and very terrible. Who can endure it? (Jl 1:1–2:11)

Following this opening lament, Joel translates the ritual of mourning and loss to a sermon about piety and hope. He closes this sermon, transforming the metaphors of past suffering with hope for an ideal future in which Israel and its God become one:

> Return to me with all your heart, with fasting and weeping and with mourning. Tear your hearts and not your garments. Return to Yahweh your God, for he is gracious and merciful, slow to anger and abounding in steadfast love. He repents of [this] evil. . . . Yahweh was jealous for his land and had pity on his people. Yahweh answered and said to his people, "Behold, I am sending you grain, wine and oil.". . . Fear not, O land, be glad and rejoice; for Yahweh has done great things. Fear not you beasts of the field; for the pastures of the wilderness are green. The tree bears its fruit. The fig tree and the vine give their full yield. Be glad, sons of Zion, and rejoice in Yahweh your God. He has given the early rain for your vindication. He has poured out abundant rain, the early and the latter rain, as before. The threshing floors will be full of grain. The vats will overflow with wine and oil. (Jl 2:12–27)

In Isaiah's song of the vineyard (Is 5) and, above all, in the Song of Songs, the figure of Jerusalem as Yahweh's bride is described with similar images. She is Yahweh's garden and he is the lover in the garden, taking his bride. Again and again, the central myth of the Bible is fertility.[5] The central metaphor is the figure of Yahweh in the role of Ugarit's Baal, the living God. In the center of his book, Isaiah returns to his metaphor of Jerusalem as Yahweh's vineyard near the close of a collection of poems that scholars often refer to as Isaiah's apocalypse (Is 24:1–28:22) because of its utopian rhetoric and theme of Yahweh's kingdom. When Yahweh has slain the fleeing dragon Leviathan with his strong sword, he will sing a new song of a pleasant vineyard. In that ideal garden he is the keeper and Jacob and Israel the vines. They will take root and blossom, "filling the whole earth with fruit" (Is 27:2–6). This happy prophecy of a new Israel caps a series of contrasting poems of sorrow and gladness (Is 24:1–13; 25:6–8). The collection of songs closes in a diatribe against "the drunkards of Ephraim."

> They reel with wine and stagger with strong drink. The priest and the prophet reel with strong drink. They err in vision; they stumble in giving judgment. All the tables are full of vomit; no place lacks its filth. (Is 28:7–8)

Turning to the rulers of Jerusalem, he accuses them of making a covenant with death (Hebrew *mot*) and with the world of the dead (Is 28:14–15). He will sit in judgment of their blindness and ignorance. A new cornerstone is to be laid for Zion, a sure foundation. The covenant they have made will not stand.

The larger cluster of themes in biblical narratives, the Baal epic and the myth of Dionysus have roots in the ancient Mesopotamian traditions attached to the Sumerian goddess Inanna and the Babylonian Ishtar with their lovers and husbands, Dumuzi and Tammuz. The myth is referred to already in the Gilgamesh Epic and finds many variations.[6] Some of the most stable elements in the myth involve themes of a human who becomes divine in a process involving death and resurrection. The central figure descends into the realm of the dead for three days before awakening to a new life. Tragic themes are evoked in the figure of the innocent beloved who is abandoned to suffering and death. Mourning and humble tears, evoked by the descent of Inanna and Dumuzi into the realm of the dead, awake fertility and renewed life. The resurrection of the dead from the grave imitates the resurrection of the goddess and her lover. A ritual performance of the death of the gods, followed by the priest's tears for them, reflects not only the annual agricultural cycles of the seasons but also recurrent threats of drought and famine. Salvation in this tradition is quickly identified with relief from famine and the spring rains. References to the harvest and the drinking of date wine and beer at the festival are combined with expressions of erotic pleasure. They often create lyric expressions of the passionate love and union of the human and the divine. The function of the myth represents and evokes feelings of wonder over birth and new life as well as of suffering over sickness and the loss death brings.

Central to this tradition is the festival of tears, evoking rain and a new creation. It also involves the motifs of repentance and humility that occupy such a central place in biblical tradition. Sexual imagery in the poems is drawn on a grand scale. The whole world's fertility: water, bread and all that is good flow from Inanna's breasts. She—like Ishtar and Eve—is the mother of all living (Gen 3:20). Queen Inanna "exalts" King Dumuzi, who is "the beautiful one" and "the beloved," she sings the lovely erotic song of her vulva: the "boat of heaven." Her "new crescent" (the symbol of divine love) is the "fallow land" and the "wet ground." Such explicit rhetoric has its male counterpart. Dumuzi is upraised. His is the "high-standing cedar," the "grain-stalk." He is a wild bull of a man called to divinity. As divine king, this farmer figure becomes Inanna's husband, who "plows the vulva" of the fallow land. He "makes her milk flow." Dumuzi and Inanna's palace is the "house of life." Its stores give "long life."[7] In countless love songs, Dumuzi's pubic hair is likened to spring lettuce. He is "the honey-man," Inanna's "well-stocked garden," her "high-standing grain" and her "tree" bringing its apples to the top.[8] Such rich eroticism ensures the myth's engagement throughout antiquity.

Metaphors of Resurrection and Eternal Life

Fundamental to both the Dionysus myth and the earlier legends and traditions of Baal and Tammuz is the seasonal rhythm of agriculture that looks forward to the spring's resurrection. The journey into the underworld, the world of the dead, with its metaphors of mourning and transforming tears becoming rain is a myth-creating pattern. The grain's resurrection following the rain in the springtime epitomizes this universal cycle of nature and supports new year festivals of new wine with wide-ranging metaphors celebrating spring's new life. At the heart of the biblical fertility religion, as at the heart of the commentaries on it as we find in the gospels, is the metaphor of resurrection.

One of the variations to Matthew's Last Supper scene, in the Gospel of Luke, integrates the metaphor of the blood of the covenant with the theme of new wine, allowing for an intimate introduction to Jesus' coming suffering. Luke has

Jesus speak of the cup, poured out, as a "new covenant in my blood" (Lk 22:20). In doing so, he draws his readers into a central discourse of the prophets on Israel's covenant with Yahweh. This discourse ties the reversals of fortune of the song for a poor man to resurrection motifs and to metaphors of new beginnings.

"The heavens are Yahweh's, but the earth he has given to the sons of men" is a famous line of the Psalter (Ps 115:16). It represents the understanding of the world Isaiah is out to change. In this psalm, the world ruled by the "sons of Adam" is contrasted to *'olam*, a *Narnia*-like metaphor for the transcendent world of the divine, governed by God. The Bible's entrance to the transcendent realm—its wardrobe—is the temple. When the psalmist in Psalm 24, on the other hand, sings of the earth as Yahweh's possession, his perspective understands the world as having its foundations in the temple, the temple as resting on God's holy mountain and the pure of heart as those able to stand in it. Enlightenment and rapture come at the opening of the gates of *'olam,* as Yahweh, the King of Glory, enters the temple. In Exodus, Moses, speaking to Yahweh, describes the mountain of God as the pathway to *'olam*:

> You will bring [your people] and plant them on your mountain: that place, Yahweh, which you have made your home: the temple, O Yahweh, which your own hands have built. (Ex 15:17)

The temple as the mountain of God is the transcendent realm. It is built by Yahweh's hands. It is not Solomon's temple, built by human hands—a temple Yahweh rejected and sent Nebuchadnezzar to destroy (2 Kgs 25). The transcendent was not found in the earthly temple of Jerusalem past. Rather, the transcendent is Zion's holy mountain (Is 31:4), the garden of the beloved in the Song of Songs (Song 6:2), Eden's garden on the edge of Qedem (Gen 2:8). There one finds the way back to the tree of life (Gen 3:24; Ez 47:12; Rev 22:14). It is a temple belonging to a New Jerusalem (Ez 40:5–43:12).

Closely linked to this vision of the temple is the classic contrast between the desert's barrenness and the land's fertility. This opposition echoes the formlessness and emptiness of the world before creation with the spirit of God moving over the waters. In this cluster of motif and metaphor, the wilderness wandering and the exilic wasteland are times of suffering, turning Israel's cry of complaint to the reader's humble tears of understanding. There is ever a survivor with whom the audience might identify. From Noah (Gen 6:8) to Lot (Gen 19:20–21), as from Caleb of the wilderness (Num 13:30; 14:24; var. Num 14:5–6, 30) to Isaiah's servant, Jacob, whom Yahweh had chosen (Is 41:8), a remnant survives disaster and the world is renewed. Isaiah's dead stump lives.

This motif of David's lost dynasty springing into the renewed life of Jerusalem's return from exile takes part in the larger discourse of the Psalter's metaphor of the tree of life. It is biblical pietism's metaphor for the life of the soul, which introduces the Psalter:

> He who loves Yahweh's Torah and meditates on it day and night is like a tree, planted by the edge of the canal. It yields its fruit in its season. Its leaf does not wither. In all that he does, he prospers. (Ps 1:2–3)

The pious are contrasted to "the wicked," who are blown away by the spirit, like chaff by the wind. This parabolic metaphor reaches across the tradition to oppose another psalm's pathetic image of exiles weeping on the banks of another stream in Babylon. Their lyres are hung on willows—surely weeping. They do not sing a lyrical love song for the Torah, but echo songs of Zion with the sound of their tormentors' mockery (Ps 137:1–6). Such intertextual commentary marks the Psalter and its introduction in Psalms 1 and 2 and closure in Psalms 149 and 150, with the voice of the new Zion. A spectrum of motif and metaphor shared by these two contrasting passages illustrates the richness of the Psalter's syntax.

The motif of the tree whose leaves never wither gives implicit expression to the goal and purpose of the Psalter as a whole: to praise God, express joy and happiness, find serenity and peace. Psalm 1 opens the first of five thematically clustered books of songs. Together, they form a Torah of praise, not only echoing the five books of the Torah but also closing the Psalter with its own five songs, each beginning and closing with the words "Praise Yahweh" (Ps 146–150). The Psalter illustrates the way or path of the pious—the way of Yahweh, of righteousness, and so on—through a life centered in loving the Torah. The pious are opposed to those unhappy souls, who are given roles of restless hopelessness, traveling the path of the wicked and godless in all its many deformations.

The figure of the pious as the tree of life can also stand alone, illustrating the joys of piety. To love the Torah is to be the beautiful branch whose fruit is the survivors of Israel. This lone remnant of Jerusalem will be called holy, dedicated "to life" (Is 4:1–3). The ubiquitous metaphor of Psalm 1 is reiterated in Joshua's instructions to the people after the death of Moses. The generation of the wilderness has been tragically lost and a new generation prepares to cross the Jordan. "Love the Torah day and night . . . that you be blessed in all that you do; and that your paths be blessed." To love the Torah is to have God with them on their journey (Josh 1:8–9). A similar theme returns to the motif of the well-planted tree, "The righteous grows like a palm tree: as great as the cedar of Lebanon. He is planted in Yahweh's temple" (Ps 92:13–15). Like Abraham, with Sarah, who bears him Isaac in his old age (Gen 21:7), the psalm's righteous "bear fruit in old age: ever full of sap and green to show that Yahweh is righteous." Similar sentiments allow David to serve as an eternal epitome for the pious as he too links the motif of the tree of life to the temple: "I am like the green olive tree in the house of God. I trust in his steadfast love, 'olam and forever" (Ps 52:10). The transcendent is intrinsic to this metaphor, as is clear in a variant describing the unrighteous "like plants, which bloom but die for ever," while Yahweh is "enthroned le-'olam" (Ps 92:8–9).

The astonishingly wide range of metaphor born by the motif of the tree of life is shown in a remarkable passage on the theme of hope. The tree of life, ever bearing its fruit, is a central question in Job and may provide us with the matrix for this metaphor:

> For a tree, there is hope. If it is felled, it will sprout again. It never stops setting fresh sprouts. Even if the roots are old and the stump dies in the ground, it will grow again. As soon as it smells water, it will set a sprout like a new planted tree. (Job 14:7–9)[9]

Job sets his metaphor of hope to provoke a contrast with human hopelessness: "If a man dies, it is over for him. A man breathes his last and is gone" (Job 14:10). Job's complaint echoes the alewife's taunting reply to Gilgamesh, mocking his relentless search for eternal life. Like Gilgamesh, Job is a man. The confrontation sharpens. There is hope for a tree; but for a man? Does he die forever? With Baal and Dumuzi, Job would hide in the realm of the dead until God's wrath has passed (Job 14:13). Hope rises and the question is posed: "Can one who is dead live again?" (Job 14:14). Having asked, Job places himself in the role of Hosea's Ephraim and Manasseh: mocking the shallow hope of piety, which places human fate at the mercy of Yahweh's spring rain:

> Come, let us return to Yahweh. He has torn us that he may heal us; he has stricken us and he will bind us up. After two days, he will revive us. On the third day, he will raise us up that we may live before him. . . . He will come to us as the showers, as the spring rains that water the earth. (Hos 6:1–3; cf. Job 14:15; Jon 1:17)

The motif of resurrection in Hosea, as in Job, inspires hope and overcomes death through forgiveness. Both sit on the critical side of biblical discourse, their doubts ever undermining the song's confidence.

In Ezekiel, an oracle explains that Israel was destroyed because of Yahweh's anger at their offerings to idols. In punishment, they were spread among the nations. Now for his own sake Yahweh will bring them back to the land. This return from exile is expressed through a series of reversals of Israel's fate. Creation is reestablished as new beginnings return Israel to Yahweh's original plan. Israel will be an Elihu ("He/This is my God"; cf. "I am the God who is": Ex 3:14). Israel will possess a new heart and a new spirit (Job 32:18–19). Their hearts of stone will be turned to hearts of flesh. Their new spirit will lead them finally to walk in his laws and obey his commandments. They will again live in the land and now they will truly be his people—and he their God. It is a song of new beginnings. The suffering and tears of exile have made the grain grow and have brought an end to famine. Spring is breaking. The cities will be reinhabited and ruins rebuilt. The empty land will become the Garden of Eden (Ez 36:16–36).

In a dramatic illustration of victory over death, Israel's exile is likened to a valley filled with dry bones. Israel's new spirit gives life and raises the dead. The theme is set with a close variant to Job's question. Yahweh asks his prophet, "Son of man, can such bones live again?" Ezekiel, responding, speaks with the humble voice of piety: "Only you can know" (Ez 37:3). This good student's response is followed with a wonderfully hilarious scene of the dead bones dancing with a new life as Yahweh orders Ezekiel to prophesy:

> O dry bones, hear the word of Yahweh. Thus says the God Yahweh to these bones, "Behold I will cause spirit to enter you and you will live. I will lay sinews on you and will cause flesh to come upon you and cover you with skin and put spirit in you and you will live and know that I am Yahweh." So I prophesied as I was commanded. As I prophesied, there was a noise and, behold, a rattling. The bones came together, bone to its bone. As I looked, there were sinews on them and flesh had come upon them and skin had covered them, but there was no spirit in them. Then he said to me, "Prophesy to the spirit. Prophesy, son of man, and say to the spirit: thus says the God Yahweh: Come from the four winds, spirit. Breathe upon these dead that they may live." So I prophesied as he commanded. The spirit came into them and they lived. They stood on their feet: an exceedingly great army! (Ez 37:4–10)

This parable is followed by Yahweh's authoritative commentary:

> These bones are the whole house of Israel. Look, they say, "Our bones are dried up and our hope is lost. We are entirely cut off." Therefore prophesy and say to them, "Thus says the God Yahweh: I will open your graves and raise you

from your graves, my people. I will put my spirit within you and you will live and I will place you in your own land. Then you will know that I, Yahweh, have spoken and have done it." (Ez 37:11–14)

In Jeremiah, the Psalter's "new earth" and Ezekiel's "new heart" and "new spirit" are used to transform the metaphor of covenant. The days are coming when Yahweh will make a new covenant, a new testament. This new covenant contrasts with the one Yahweh made with Noah, with Abraham and with Moses at Sinai, the covenant Israel had broken (Jer 31:31–32). Central to Jeremiah's argument is that his new covenant transforms the laws of Moses given to test them. The new Torah is internalized: written on their hearts. Rather than the angel of the wilderness journey: one who would not forgive their sin, sent to lead them in a holy war against the nations to test them and to judge them (Ex 23:20–33), Yahweh now chooses to forget the past (Jer 31:31–34). Transforming the conditions and permanency of his covenant with Noah (Gen 8:28), Jeremiah prophesies:

Thus says Yahweh, who gives the sun for light by day and the fixed order of the moon and the stars for light by night, who stirs up the sea so that its waves roar—Yahweh of the armies is his name. "If this fixed order departs from before me," says Yahweh, "then will cease also the descendants of Israel from being a nation before me for ever." Thus says Yahweh, "If the heavens above can be measured and the foundations of the earth below can be explored, then I will cast all the descendants of Israel for all that they have done," says Yahweh. "Behold the days are coming," says Yahweh, when the city will be rebuilt for Yahweh. . . . The whole valley of the dead bodies and the ashes and all the fields as far as the brook Kidron, to the corner of the Horse Gate to the east will be sacred to Yahweh. It will not be uprooted or overthrown again forever. (Jer 31:35–39)

This new covenant, promising Jerusalem's renewal, transforms Old Jerusalem's valley of death, Gehenna. His vision is of a new covenant of the heart, in which sin is forgotten. The opening oath, in which Yahweh regrets destroying Jerusalem, promises to hold this new covenant in existence as surely as he upholds his creation. This transforms the promise in Genesis, in which Yahweh—also regretting the evil of his flood—swore "in his heart" in his first covenant to uphold the eightfold cadence of nature's rhythm:

I will never again curse the ground because of man; for the imagination of man's heart is evil from his youth. Neither will I ever again destroy every living creature as I have done. While the earth remains, seedtime and harvest, cold and heat, summer and winter, day and night will not cease. (Gen 8:20–22)

The miming reiteration of Genesis underlines Jeremiah's vision of a covenant's transformation as Ezekiel's valley is turned into a city of life. As Jeremiah returns to the theme of a new covenant in the following chapter, the language of his metaphor fits the language of the Psalter and the schoolmen. His narrative world of divine wrath is transformed. With reference to Jerusalem's destruction at the hands of Nebuchadnezzar, the great epitome of divine terror—sword, famine and pestilence, all the great evil Yahweh did against his people—finds its transformation through Jeremiah's new covenant. The fear of God is internalized in the hearts of the pious (Jer 32:36–41).

These stories are about justice and they are about judgment. They illustrate the day of wrath. This is not about an apocalypse of the future or any expectations of an end to the world. It is a parable about new beginnings and a future marked by life. It is a narrator's effort to move away from a god of justice, who would give no hope to humanity, to a God of Jonah's divine compassion and mercy. Jonah holds the clue. Even with his would-be prophet of doom eager to bring terror to great Nineveh, Yahweh was "merciful and slow to anger." He determined that Nineveh would be saved. *Therefore* he found fertile tears of repentance, ears and eyes of understanding and insight in that great city's king and people and in all their livestock (Jon 3:5–10; 4:2; cf. Gen 50:20-21). This is what Isaiah and Deuteronomy seek for their audience.

Isaiah's first message through his prophet, sealing old Jerusalem's fate and destiny, closes by offering these three stories their counterpoint. Israel's final destiny is transformed through a brilliant reworking of the tree of life metaphor: "If there be a tenth left, that too will be uprooted. It will be burned again as when a terebinth or an oak is felled and a stump remains." Then—most simply—Isaiah adds the resurrection motif: a fated world is made new: "That stump is holy seed" (Is 6:13). Interpretation of Isaiah—as of the gospels—must follow the pattern of its reiteration. One of the most important themes in Isaiah uses contrasting metaphors of the forests of Lebanon with its great cedars to represent Assyria in contrast to the dead stump of David's house, playing Jerusalem (Is 10:12–11:9). The dominant story line deals with the Assyrians and their arrogance, and prefigures their fate in the Hezekiah story (Is 36–39; above, Chapter 3). They were tools in Yahweh's hand, the ax, the saw and the rod, sent to punish Jerusalem and Samaria. In arrogance, however, they thought their own power wielded the tools. Pride comes before the fall. With an echo of the burning bush (Ex 3:2), Yahweh's glory kindles a burn-ing—the "light of Israel." The light becomes a fire and Yahweh's "Holy One" a flame that burns and devours Assyria's thorns and thistles in a single day, as Yahweh destroys the corresponding "glory" of Assyria's forest and fruitful land. The remnant is "so few that even a child could count them" (Is 10:16–18). The message of the parable, echoing Yahweh's victory—in a single night—over the Assyrian army in the Hezekiah story, is explicit: Israel's remnant will learn to trust in Yahweh (Is 10:20; Ps 2:12).

Isaiah sketches his vision of Yahweh's wrath turning away from Jerusalem and against Assyria in retribution: "Destruction is decreed: overflowing with righ-teousness" (Is 10:22). It is the affirmation that is fundamental to the theology, not the history, of the affair. The decree, overflowing with righteousness, leads the poet from the felling of Lebanon's great cedars to the dead stump of David's dynasty. Resurrection motifs transform this tree of death into a sprouting shoot and a branch growing from its roots (Is 11:1), as Jerusalem turns and seeks Yahweh. The shoot and the branch are personified in the song's expansion with the closing birth of the Immanuel child, whose name shall be "Wonderful," "Counselor," "Mighty God," "Everlasting Father" and "Prince of Peace (Is 9:2–7). The reiteration of this child in the metaphor of the dead stump's new life presents the figure of the divine king reborn in humility as piety's ideal, whose eightfold gifts of the spirit return us to paradise:

> The spirit of Yahweh will rest on him, the spirit of wisdom and understand-ing, the spirit of counsel and might; the spirit of knowledge and the fear of Yahweh, and he will delight in the fear of Yahweh. (Is 11:2–3)

The savior-king, as piety's ideal, bears the signs of all figures of salvation in Israel's story. Unlike the lost generation, he does not judge by what he sees and hears, but with righteousness. He judges the meek and the poor of the earth (Is 11:4–6). With the figure of his king anchored, and with the justice of mercy reestablished, Isaiah turns to a vision of paradise as the goal of his work: a dou-ble eightfold cluster presents signs of the kingdom:

> The wolf will dwell with the lamb; the leopard will lie down with the kid and the calf and the lion and the fatling together and a little child will lead them. The cow and the bear will feed; their young lie down together. The lion will eat straw like the ox. The suckling child will play over the hole of the asp and the weaned child will put his hand on the adders' den. (Is 11:6–8)

In this vision, violence is removed from Yahweh's holy mountain and the earth returns to creation's peace, full of understanding. Implicit in the resurrection themes of the prophets is that just as Israel was a failed people and Jerusalem no city of God, creation is a failed creation. It must begin anew. God cannot rest. In the closing arias of his work, Isaiah returns to this song, using the language of forgetting the past and of new creation. His vision transforms his world into a "new heaven" and a "new earth," without suffering and tears:

I create new heavens and a new earth; the former things will not be remembered or come into mind. Be glad and rejoice forever in what I create. For I create a Jerusalem of rejoicing and her people (a people) of joy. . . . No more will be heard the sound of weeping and the cry of distress. (Is 65:17–19)

In the closing lines of this song, as in Yahweh's oath in Jeremiah's new covenant, revising Yahweh's promise to Noah, Isaiah turns to Genesis to reverse the terror that has reigned since the flood (cf. Gen 9:2). Isaiah explicitly paraphrases his own song of the tree:

Like the days of the tree will the days of my people be; my chosen will long enjoy the work of their hands. They will not labor in vain, or bear children for terror for they will be the children of the blessed of Yahweh's and their children with them. Before they call, I will answer; while they are yet speaking, I will hear. The wolf and the lamb will feed together; the lion will eat straw like the ox and dust will be the serpent's food. They will neither hurt nor destroy in all my holy mountain. (Is 65:22–25; cf. 11:6–9)

In his final chapter, Isaiah deals with the terror under which children have been born since Noah. A transformed remnant of Israel is his solution—a humanity that has finally learned what it had not understood in the paradise story. His new heaven and new world—with its lion eating straw and its snake satisfied with its dust—is no longer divided between the transcendent realm of heaven and the ephemeral world of human terror. Yahweh's rule over the world is linked to the "prince of peace," Isaiah's Immanuel child (Is 9:6–7). Filled with Yahweh's spirit, humanity belongs to the "humble and contrite in spirit, who trembles at my word" (Is 66:1–2).

PART THREE

The Never-Ending Story

CHAPTER 8

Holy War

In the literature of the ancient Near East, all war is "holy war." As in the myth of the good king—so clearly illustrated in the Mesha stele (Appendix 2, no. 21)—the first task of the king is to follow his god in holy war. The central plotline of the Saul and David narrative in the books of Samuel center on themes of holy war (e.g., 1 Sm 15; 2 Sm 8). In the Psalter, the figure of the messiah is ever Yahweh's holy warrior (e.g., Ps 2; 18; 20). And in the New Testament, not only is the figure of Jesus given heavily weighted mythical titles of the king at war, such as savior, messiah and son of God, but the construction of his story is centered on the kingdom of God and its judgment as holy war's goal. The New Testament appropriately closes with references to the final battle between the forces of good and evil to be determined when the "seventh bowl of the wrath of God" is poured out in holy war at Armageddon (Rev 16:1–20). No literature is more taken up with holy war and a god of armies than is the Bible, and no figure is more central to holy war than the figure of the messiah as expressed in the stories of Jesus, David and Hezekiah. The messianic role of the king in the biblical theme of holy war has its ultimate roots in ancient Near Eastern mythology. It reiterates the myth of Marduk, in which the divine king creates the world through his victory over the chaos dragon, Tiamat. Echoing New Kingdom Egyptian victory hymns and Assyrian and Babylonian praise of the king as servant of Assur and Marduk, the wars of the messiah have their goal in bringing the whole world under divine patronage, to recover the creation God intended. It also draws heavily on the ideal role of the good king, led into battle by his god and destroying the enemy at the command of the divine, ever furthering a utopian and eternal kingdom under divine patronage. It is centered in the royal myth of the dying and rising god, ensuring the seasonal cycle of fertility and life's victory over death.

The Hebrew Bible takes up these three themes by casting a cyclical narrative of creation and destruction, blessing and curse. Israel is given the goal of a new humanity to replace the foreigners, represented by the peoples of Canaan. A re-iterative theme of covenant, mirroring the ancient social and political structure of the patron and his client and demanding personal loyalty and obedience, develops the tragic story of old Israel's fall, closing in the destruction of Samaria by Shalmanezer and Jerusalem by Nebuchadnezzar at Yahweh's command. This narrative chain is cast as a never-ending story of human failure, in which the figure of the messiah is recurrently presented, as in the Psalter, as a model for personal piety: an ideal figure for a reader's imitation.

CREATED IN THE IMAGE OF GOD

In the story of creation (Gen 1:1–2:3), the world is formed in the structure of the seven days of the week. The creator names and orders the earth, the sea and the sky from an original chaos. The creation ends on the sixth day and God rests on the seventh. The story proposes an idyllic creation. Light is made with a word, separated from darkness and ordered as day and night. Waters are parted above and below a shield-hammered sky. The sea is set in its place and the earth commanded to green. Lights are placed in the sky: the sun and moon to control day and night, and the stars to provide omens and mark the seasons. As God sets out on his week's work, he sees what he does and calls it "good" before going on to the next day and its task. A quiet cadence enters the story. God's seven acts of wonder and goodness are crowned on the sixth day with a final deed to complete the well-structured order of this new world. In six short verses, with an uncertain and vulnerable mixture of singulars and plurals, the plan is sketched whereby God will achieve his Sabbath rest:

> "Let us make humanity in our image, after our likeness that they will rule over the fish of the sea, the birds of the air, the cattle and all the earth and over every crawling thing that crawls on the ground." So God made mankind in his own image; in the image of God, he created them: male and female he created them. God blessed them and said to them, "Be fruitful, multiply, fill the earth and set it under you. Have dominion over the fish of the sea, the birds of the air and every living thing, which moves on the earth." God said, "I have given

you every herb-bearing seed on the face of the whole earth and every tree with fruit, yielding seed. It will be food for you. To every beast of the earth, every bird of the air and to everything which crawls on the earth in which there is life, I have given every green plant for food." And so it was. God saw what he had made and it was very good. There was evening and morning: a sixth day. (Gen 1:26–31)

That people and gods create each other in their own image is not an idea new to Feuerbach.[1] It is a theme central to biblical narrative. It is a trope of ancient Near Eastern literature, implicit already in the early Egyptian mythic play on the essence of men *(romet)* and the tears *(remet)* of the sun god Re, from which mankind was created.[2] It is reflected in Assyrian presentations of the king in battle, miming a transcendent Assur in his war chariot. The motif of the likeness of humans and gods can be both commonplace and ironic in the literature of the ancient world. It is evoked through the sculpture and casting of images of gods and goddesses in the form of men and women. It is central to both political theory and ethics. A divine world offers the potential of an ideal and utopian order as critique to the world actually known. The rule of law and wisdom finds epitome in the formulation of codes governing the good life. They are presented as the words and commands of God given through his spokesman—whether Ur-Nammu and Hammurapi or Moses on Mount Sinai. Their ever explicit purpose is to establish equity and banish evil, violence and strife.[3] Throughout ancient literature, the ideal role of the king as humble ruler, protector and representative of the people is used to criticize and challenge abuses in government with the integrity and values cherished in antiquity. The metaphor of the transcendent, which gives the divine so dominant a role in this literature, has as its primary function the measure of humanity. The gods of the real world, apart from the scribes who write of them, the prophets who provide them with voices and the priests who serve them, are almost always silent. "Who creates whom" is hardly a modern question. It was, in fact, a much discussed topic in ancient Greek literature. The Bible shows its greatest integrity when such critical self-understanding rises to the surface of its text. It is, however, at its weakest and most dangerous when it seductively creates and defines its God in its author's image.

The creation of mankind "in the image and likeness of God" in the opening chapter of Genesis opens a chain of stories, which sets the Pentateuch's critique of humanity and the institution of kingship on its long journey. In this first of three presentations, the Platonic idealism implicit to the story's irony of a God-miming humanity has God create mankind in his image that they might rule the world, while he rests in his heaven (Gen 1:26–28; cf. Ps 115:16). Having made his king male and female, he blesses them with fertility and gives them plants for food: both for them and for all the animals. He is a proud father, this God who made people "in his own image: just like him." The story's echo of the Narcissus myth allows one to predict the coming tragedy.[4] Certainly the reader must engage some skepticism about this doting father's declaration that what he had made last was "very good"!

Similarly, the reuse of Isaiah's utopian vegetarianism to describe humanity's rule over the world without violence (Gen 1:29–30; cf. Is 11:6–8) asserts an order that is not just fragile, but a clear opening to the greater story's coming plotline. The followers of the cult of Orpheus in the Hellenistic world, for example, like the Pythagoreans, were vegetarians. Their refusal to eat the flesh of animals was not merely based in beliefs of the soul's immortality. They were also intent on rejecting state cults of animal sacrifice, in which people ate delicate meat while gods ate bones, much as the Pentateuch gives its deity fat and entrails for his meals. When God, having finally created humanity in the role of a king to rule the world he made, stops his work to hold his Sabbath (Gen 2:1–3), the reader's unease and foreboding must turn to alarm, if God rests in his heaven and the world is left to his God-like deputy. The narrative line turns first to the paradise narrative, with its short-lived, idyllic theme of fertility, of fertility's blessings and of the alienating knowledge of mortals made in the image of immortals.

With this epitomizing portrayal of humanity, the creation story opens a long chain of narrative that pits God and men against each other in a contest for supremacy. The creator God had not considered that his humanity might want to be like him and independently determine what was good and what evil. The story of Yahweh's garden—set at the creation—offers a paradigmatic tale of paradise lost (Gen 2:4–3:24). The parable begins with the potter-deity Yahweh forming a human being (adam) from the ground (adamah). Adding his own breath, he makes it "a living soul" (Gen 2:7). He plants a garden with beautiful trees and trees with all that is good to eat. This figure of humanity is set in the garden to be its "servant," its "keeper" (Gen 2:15). He is given two mythic roles of the good king, found in the legend of Sargon: consort of the mother of all living and the gardener of Ishtar's father (Appendix 2, no. 1). This figure of the good king now joins the creation story's "every tree with seed in its fruit" and "every green plant," which had been given him as food (Gen 1:29–30) in the perfect creation, which God had seen was "very good" (Gen 1:31). The scene set, our hero, "humanity," is put to a test designed for failure, as singular exceptions and forbidden trees are presented to this figure of an innocent mankind to discern. Knowing neither good nor evil, all may be eaten freely from any of the trees. Only a single thing must not be eaten, for it will bring death: the fruit of the tree of knowledge of good and evil, "for in the day you eat of it you shall die the death" (an emphatic doubling of the verb *mot* "to die"; *mot tamut*: Gen 2:17).

The test is delayed and a new story line adds complexity as Yahweh recognizes that it is not good for a human being to be alone. He sets out to create a companion: one like the person he had made as his gardener. In an interesting expansion of the "image of God" theme, Yahweh forms further creatures from the ground as he had the first. When each living creature is brought in turn to the person by Yahweh to learn what he would call them, the person names all the animals. None, however, is judged quite like him. Having failed in his first attempt, Yahweh then turns to a gardener's method of reproducing. He takes a part of the person—a rib—and makes it into a woman. A song Adam sings tells the reader of Yahweh's success. Its gentle eroticism removes all loneliness from the scene:

Finally at last! Bone of my bones; flesh of my flesh; she shall be called "woman" [*'ishah*], because she has been taken out of man [*'ish*]. Therefore, a man leaves his father and his mother and cleaves to his wife and they become one flesh. (Gen 2:23–24)

Rhetorically connecting already with the following scene's play on innocence and naïveté, the reader is told that the man and his wife were naked but not ashamed (Gen 2:24). The story returns to Yahweh's test. A snake is described with a pun on the word "naked" (*'arum*): He is the most clever (*'arummim*) of all the beasts of the field. Knowledgeable and, therefore, far from innocent, he takes up his role as tempter. From the start his speech suggests entrapment: "Did God say, you shall not eat of any tree in the garden?" (Gen 3:1) When the woman corrects him, eager to present the command Yahweh had given, she wraps her answer with the naive awe of her willing obedience: "Not even touch it, lest you die." The clever snake is now ready to support a separation of the story's levels of understanding. The snake speaks to her with the perspective of her mortality already implicit. Distinguishing immediate danger from death's finality, he encourages her to seek divinity, like Faust setting knowledge higher than life itself:

You will not die the death. For God well knows that when you eat of it your eyes will be opened and you will be like God, knowing good and evil. (Gen 3:4–5)

The woman's response is presented with a mix of rebellion and hubris. Made in God's image, she will—like God—see for herself what is good. "She saw that the tree was good for food, a delight for the eyes and to be desired to make one wise," she took it and she and her husband ate it. She will be a king, determining what is good and what evil. Or, alternatively, having known only good, she will now know evil as well.

In closing his scene, the narrator addresses the reader directly with the story's irony: "The eyes of both were opened and they knew that they were naked (*'arum*)." So much for the cleverness (*'arummim*) their listening to the snake gave them! The irony continues. Immediately, they hide what they have learned by making aprons from the garden's fig leaves. Job had used this same knowledge— "Naked I came from my mother's womb and naked will I return"—as the epitome of wisdom (Job 1:21). The following, very brief scene offers interpretive commentary. Yahweh is taking a walk in the garden "in the spirit of the day," a phrase, which, while fully understandable as referring to the afternoon breeze, has overtones of an opportunity to be seized or lost. The man and his wife hide from him. When Yahweh calls to him, the man explains that when he heard Yahweh's sound, he was afraid for his nakedness and hid. Without the fear of God—wisdom's beginning in Proverbs and the Psalter—they—unlike Job—are afraid of their own nakedness. The reader is left to wonder, with Isaiah, whether they—who once knew only the good—will ever learn to distinguish good from evil. The story never leaves its play on understanding. Yahweh tries to put the question at the center of his test: "Did you eat of the tree which I commanded you not to eat?" Instead of answering, the man betrays the one made in *his* image: "The woman whom you gave to be with me." She in turn passes guilt to the snake: "The serpent beguiled me" (Gen 3:11–13). Just so, the curses fall with retribution's justice, giving them a knowledge of evil. The snake, who had seduced the woman to eat the fruit of death, will now eat dust (the image of humanity's mortality), as mankind and the snake become eternal enemies. The woman's descendants "will crush its head" and the snake's descendants "will strike his heel" (Gen 3:15), a reference to the similarly "clever" Jacob, whose hand grabs his brother's "heel" to steal his right as elder even from his mother's womb (Gen 25:26). Less immediately, it refers to insulting enemies who strike at the footsteps of the messiah (Ps 89:52).

In Yahweh's curse of the woman, the blessing of fertility and the equality she had with her husband are replaced by a metaphor of trial and suffering, an end to the cooperative unity of Yahweh's kingdom. The woman is destined to be torn between the desire to be one with her husband and the pain of giving birth. The ideal of paradise is reversed. No longer are the two as one, but are alienated by both pain and desire. Their relationship turns on the potential of the king as tyrant. Turning to the man, Yahweh curses the ground. Desert plants will grow. Hard work is his destiny until in death he returns to the earth. Having built a scene of pain, alienation, barrenness and death, the story closes on motifs of contradiction as Adam names his wife "Eve" (*hawah:* in Akkadian "mother"), "for she became the mother of all the living" (Gen 3:20). It is the epithet of the fertility goddess, celebrating life—a title borne by the Akkadian goddesses Mami and Ishtar, by Inanna and Ugarit's Asherah.[5] Still in his farmer's role of slave to a now cursed ground, Adam is sent from the garden "to serve the ground which he took from there" (3:23b), binding the garden story to the parallel narrative of Cain and Abel that follows. The cherubim block their way to the tree of life to confirm their mortality, providing the impossible thought of immortality. The story closes in disharmony and foreboding as the first human beings leave the garden for their future, a path that takes them away from the tree of life. Humanity, having been placed in the garden of paradise to serve it and watch over it (Gen 2:15), as Israel in the future is given its land flowing with milk and honey, is now banished and sent into exile (Gen 3:23–24). Ezekiel speaks of them as being—like Lucifer and the fallen ones—cast from the mountain of God, driven out by the guardian cherub (Ez 28:16; cf. Gen 6:1–4).

The Cain and Abel story offers another perspective of mankind. Adam "knew his wife" and she conceived and bore a son, whom she named Cain (*Qain* "creature"); "because I have made (*qaniti)* a man with Yahweh" (Gen 4:1; cf. 21:1–2). Cain, the creature, is a figure for everyman, as Adam (human) was in his story. Cain's story is a mirror for all God's creatures. A brother is born, whose cue name, Abel (*hebel* "emptiness," "vanity," "a mist"), similarly, speaks of a role for everyman. His life story is to be available to die (cf. Eccl 1:1). While Abel is a shepherd, Cain, like his father, Adam, is the "servant of the ground," and it is in this role that the story's plot engages its reader.

The story's surface is quickly taken up in a discourse on sacrifice and purity of heart: about whether one should live with uprightness or try to influence God's behavior through sacrifice, subtly making demands on the receiver of a gift—a good theological issue at any time.[6] However, we should not ignore the story's overtones. Yahweh accepts Abel's piety and rejects Cain's. Cain, the first of all the living to whom Eve has given birth, takes the produce of the ground Yahweh has cursed (Gen 3:23)—and offers it. The younger son, however, sacrifices the firstborn of his flock, evoking a promising future in which the sacrifice of the firstborn marks the firstborn of Israel as belonging to Yahweh (Ex 13:1–16; cf. Ex 34:19). While Abel assumes the role of the future Israel—heir to the promised land, a blessed land flowing with milk and honey, Cain, the servant of a land cursed by Yahweh, holds Canaan's future implicit. Like Adam his father—and Ishmael and Esau of the future—Canaan will be banished from the land, much as is Cain's fate in this story. Yahweh's preferring Abel's sacrifice over Cain's sets the direction of a story line of younger brothers superseding the firstborn, which has its dramatic center and turning point when the displaced Esau plots to murder his brother (Gen 27:41).[7] The story closes as firstborn Esau, like Cain and Ishmael before him, must find his home in the wilderness (cf. Gen 27:28; 27:39).

"If you do the good, you can hold your head high" (Gen 4:7). But what if you do evil? Has this son of Adam learned to distinguish good from evil? Cain chooses evil in great measure and kills his brother Abel. A new scene and a new discourse open. Yahweh asks Cain where his brother is, and Cain opens the story's center with a counterquestion. Evoking echoes of Adam's double role as servant and keeper of the garden, Cain, the keeper of the ground, asks, "Am I my brother's keeper?" (Gen 4:9). Reversing the earth's grateful acceptance of Baal's fertile blood, the cursed wilderness earth of Adam and Cain swallows the blood Cain has spilled and cannot accept it. The voice of his brother's blood cries to Yahweh from the underground. The once cursed earth now curses Cain, making him "a restless wanderer driven from the earth's surface" (Gen 4:12, 14). With a fugitive's fate, helpless before any who might find him to kill him, Cain, the murderer, finds his punishment too hard. He is the wicked man of Eliphaz's parable presented as answer to Job's anger with God. He

> writhes in pain all his days, through all the years that are laid up for the ruthless. Terrifying sounds are in his ears; in prosperity the destroyer will come upon him. He does not believe he will return from darkness, and he is destined for the sword. He wanders abroad for bread, saying, "Where is it?" He knows that a day of darkness is at hand; distress and anguish terrify him. They prevail against him, like a king prepared for battle. Because he has stretched forth his hand against God and bids defiance to the Almighty. (Job 15:20–25)

Cain, in his terror, cries to Yahweh for mercy, and his tears of repentance are answered. Swearing sevenfold vengeance on any who would take his life, Yahweh accepts the role of a brother's "keeper" that Cain refused. He watches over even the murderer. Like Isaiah's redeemer, he marks Cain in Abel's stead as one who belongs to Yahweh (Gen 4:15; cf. Is 44:5). Cain goes to live in the land of Nod ("aimlessness," "homelessness"). Yahweh takes the role of "avenger of blood," one who does not forget the cry of the afflicted (Ps 9:13; Gen 9:5).[8] Closing an origin story of the nomads, Cain's descendant Lamech, however, competes with

Yahweh. He, Lamech, will be avenged seventy-seven times, an oath that prepares for the day to come when Yahweh regrets his creation.

THE GROWTH OF A THEME

The Adam and Cain stories are joined to a variant origin story, which marks the transition between the account of creation and the story of the flood through a genealogical history from Adam to Noah. Abel is replaced by a new son, Seth, that the genealogical succession—and the legitimacy of Adam's reign—might proceed through the younger son (Gen 4:25; 5:3). In the genealogy that follows, the motif of humanity in God's image uses a succession from father to son, from Adam to Seth and continuously as the "image" is passed to all. In presenting this motif within a genealogy, Genesis adds legitimation to humanity's rule over the earth. As "son of God," a king rules his world in dynastic succession.[9] The larger narrative's as yet unresolved problem of mankind's alienation from the ground from which he was taken finds its final reconciliation in the birth of Noah, with his ironic cue name, "to rest." "Out of the ground Yahweh has cursed, this one shall bring us relief from work and from the toil of our hands" (Gen 5:29)! The flood story's resolution of the curse of the ground is subsumed under the motifs of rest and Sabbath, which closed the creation story (Gen 2:1–3). In the flood story, they are essential elements of the discourse on holy war.

The hero of the flood is presented in the figure of a righteous man, pious in his generation, one who, like Enoch, walked with God (Gen 6:8–10). As we saw in Chapter 5, this figure, along with Job and Abraham, is drawn in the ancient Near Eastern tradition of the good king. He is the son of Adam and his legitimate successor, ruler over the unhappy world Yahweh has taken in mind to destroy. In presenting Yahweh's case for destroying all creation with the flood, Genesis draws on this figure of Noah as ideal king to set him in opposition to a brief enigmatic sketch of figures of corruption. These lead Yahweh to conclude that every imagination and thought of the human heart was evil all the time (Gen 6:5). The "sons of God" see that women are beautiful and take them as wives (Gen 6:1–3). Genesis immediately interprets these as the *nephilim* ("fallen ones") and relates them to the origins of giants and heroes, which play roles in the stories of Jacob, Joshua and the twelve spies sent to report on a land of giants (Num 13–14), David's duel with Goliath (1 Sm 17) and others (2 Sm 21:16–22). The *nephilim* have a considerable mythology,[10] centered in the myth of Lucifer ("the morning star") and the fallen angels, who rebelled against serving God in heaven. God judged the *nephilim* for their mistreatment of the weak and the fatherless: "You are gods, sons of the Most High, all of you. Nevertheless, you will die like men and fall like any prince" (Ps 82:6–7). Likening the king of Babylon to Lucifer in his great taunt song, Isaiah presents perhaps the clearest biblical version of the myth:

> How are you fallen from heaven, O bright star, son of the morning; how are you cut down to the ground, you who ruled over nations. You said in your heart, "I will ascend to heaven. I will raise my throne above the stars of God. . . . I will ascend above the heights of the clouds. I will be like the Most High!" Yet you will be brought down to She'ol, to the depths of the pit. (Is 14:12–15)

In a reversal, David's "last song" presents the just king as a new Morning Star:

> When one rules justly over men, ruling in the fear of God, he dawns on them like the morning light, like the sun shining on a cloudless morning, like rain that makes grass sprout from the earth. (2 Sm 23:3–4)

In Genesis the contrast between the fallen ones and the perverted kingship of men to Noah as the good king is strongly supported in the version of the flood story found in the early Jewish pseudepigraphical book of 1 Enoch. The parallelism between the figures of Enoch and Noah and the emphasis in 1 Enoch on the giants' drinking human blood as the great crime that unleashes divine wrath are basic to the Genesis presentation:

> They and their chiefs took for themselves women from all they chose. They began to go into them, to be defiled by them, and to teach them sorcery, incantations and the cutting of roots and to explain herbs. They became pregnant by them and they gave birth to giants, some 3,000 cubits tall. . . . The giants plotted to kill the men and to consume them. They began to sin and to (act) . . . against all the birds and animals of the earth and in the sky and the fish of the sea, and to consume the flesh of one another and drink the blood. Then the earth denounced the wicked for all that had been done on it. (1 Enoch 7:1–6)[11]

While both Joshua and David know a giant's penchant for eating human flesh and drinking blood, it is the earth in the Cain story that spreads its mouth wide to swallow Abel's blood, betraying the clear signature of the chthonic deity Mot, from the myth of the Ugaritic Baal. In resolving the curse of the land, a logic of reciprocity develops a chain. It moves the story from the blessing of the land in the creation story to Yahweh's curse in the garden story, the land's curse of its own child and servant to mankind's reconciliation with the earth from which it came. This template, moving from fertility to barrenness and from life to death structures a time of testing, the course of which brings or delays devastation and judgment. A surviving remnant begins the cycle anew with the blessings of a new generation. The pattern contrasts a figure of the righteous individual—Noah and Joshua—with the rejected past generations from the sons of God to the *nephilim* (Gen 5:1–6:4) and the lost generation of the wilderness (Dt 8; 9:7–29; Num 14). A cycle of blessing, testing, punishment and new beginnings forms the accumulating chain of the Pentateuch narrative. It pits the heroic individual of integrity against either a generation defined by ignorance and fear or the great men of this world, defined by violence, greed and apostasy.

The template also marks single tales and individual heroes from the story of Sodom's destruction (Gen 13:10–13; 18:16–19:38) to the book of Job. This role of the singular, righteous man holds the reconciling savior's role, which the mythical Elijah is given by Malachi: to prevent Yahweh from cursing the land once again (Mal 3:24). The Bible's story of Noah and the flood—a Hebrew revision of a well-known Mesopotamian story from the legends of Ziusudra, Atrahasis and Utnapishtim—is a tale of divine judgment.[12] It comes at the appointed time, a day of wrath, as the gods regret their creation and give the earth into the hands of chaos. Eve's role as "mother of all living" is undone as Yahweh blots out "all the living" (Gen 7:4).

In the many biblical revisions and commentaries on ancient Near Eastern fertility myths, two figures of Genesis rival Jonah through a visit to the underworld: Lot and Noah. In the story of Sodom's destruction, with its close ties to the flood, Lot's escape from Sodom reiterates one of the Greek myths of Orpheus, known from the fifth century BCE. Orpheus is best known as the great singer and poet and finds his biblical counterpart in David. In the Orpheus myth, as we know it from Aeschylus, the hero uses his seductive music to win great concessions from the gods. Offering variations on Gilgamesh's hope to bring his beloved Enkidu back from the realm of the dead and his later journey across the waters of death in search of his own immortality, Orpheus is given permission to travel through the valley of death to reclaim his wife, the nymph Euridice. There is one condition. When he leaves the land of the dead, he must not look back to see if Euridice is following him. His longing for his beloved wife, however, is so great that he looks back in his anxiety and loses her forever. In Lot's story, a dominating element is belief and obedience to the angels. His sons-in-law do not believe that Yahweh plans to destroy the city and pay for that disbelief with their lives. In the dawn—when gods march to war with the rising sun—Lot himself hesitates to flee before the coming destruction. The angels, however, reflect Yahweh's compassion. They take the good man from the city by the hand. They order Lot, his wife and his daughters, "Flee for your life; *do not look back or stop anywhere in the valley*" (Gen 19:17). Curiosity, however, is too great for Lot's Pandora-like wife! She looks back to view the destruction and turns into one of the pillars of salt that mark the shores of the Dead Sea even today. The Lot story also uses motifs of wine and the renewal of life. Having survived the destruction of the cities of the valley and all their men, Lot's daughters, hiding in a cave, make their aging father drunk with wine. On successive nights the two girls become pregnant and give birth to sons and a new beginning (Gen 19:30–38).

A threefold narrative about kingship, blood and covenant, beginning in a blessing and ending in a curse, closes the narrative of the flood story. It draws on motifs from the creation and projects a chain of covenant stories forward to Moses' covenant of blood on Sinai. After the waters of the flood have receded, Noah leaves the ark to build an altar and offer a pure sacrifice as a gift to Yahweh (Gen 8:20). Like Abel's, his offering seeks acceptance and reconciliation (cf. Lev 1:3–4; 2 Sm 24:18–25). And like Abel's, his offering is accepted by Yahweh, who "smells its pleasing odor." The reconciliation of the generations is successful as Yahweh pledges never again to "curse the ground because of man" (Gen 8:21). He pledges instead with an eightfold oath to maintain the world in existence. Never again will he destroy "all living" as he had in the flood. In this song, Yahweh reverses the creation story's Sabbath:

> For all the days of the earth, sowing and harvest, cold and heat, summer and winter, day and night, they will not rest. (Gen 8:22)[13]

Beginning with Yahweh's promise, the Genesis narrative also rewrites the closure of the Mesopotamian narrative, where the gods are sketched with irony and even scorn, cowering with fear and regret of what they had done to their own children:

> The gods were frightened by the deluge, and, shrinking back, they ascended to the heaven of Anu. The gods cowered like dogs, crouched against the outer wall. Ishtar cried out like a woman in labour. The sweet-voiced mistress of the [gods] moans aloud: "The days of old are turned to clay, because I spoke evil in the assembly of the gods. How could I speak evil in the assembly of the gods, ordering war for the destruction of my people, when it is I, myself, who gave birth to my people, like the spawn of the fish who fill the sea. The gods,

all humbled, sit and weep with her, their lips drawn tight . . . one and all. Six days and six nights blew the flood wind, as the south-storm swept the land. . . . I [Utnapishtim] offered a sacrifice. I poured out a libation on the top of the mountain. . . . The gods smelled the savour; the gods smelled the sweet savour; the gods crowded like flies around the sacrifice. When at length as the great goddess arrived, she lifted up the great jewels, which Anu had fashioned to her liking: "Ye gods, here, as surely as this lapis, upon my neck I will not forget, I will be mindful of these days: forgetting them never! (Tablet XI.113–127, 155–165)[14]

Yahweh returns to his creation. No longer is the earth left alone in a world, where "the heavens belong to Yahweh and the earth given over to the sons of man" (Ps 115:16). Yahweh abandons his Sabbath rest and takes up an active role in the world, accepting the burden of kingship himself (cf. Gen 1:26–2:3; 8:22). Noah is given the role of the risen Baal. Having survived the waters of death, he rises from the ark as a new Adam, a figure representing new beginnings and the story's future. This rewriting of the scene of divine regret for bringing the flood, allows the author to press Yahweh to abandon his rest as he recasts his story within a theology of kingship. His solution lies within the ancient understanding of the divine as true patron and king, while the human king, shepherd and representative of the people, is personally bound to the one great king of the universe with a client's oaths of service and obedience.[15]

In the second scene, Yahweh's plan for the new world is cast as a pact or covenant with Noah. It begins with the words of the blessing given at the creation: "Be fruitful and multiply and fill the earth" (cf. Gen 1:28; 9:1). But he will also make a new beginning. In contrast to the ideal of creation offered in Genesis 1—where humanity was to rule the world like good kings in God's image, while God sought his retirement in a Sabbath day's rest, which all the gods of the flood myth demand—the covenant's blessing of fertility presents its reader with a new humanity. This humanity is no longer the old Adam and Cain, with their "plants of the field and bread to eat," however sweaty his brow (Gen 3:18–19). This Adam neither opposes nor avoids eating and sacrificing animals. Rather he eats meat in the image of Yahweh, the recipient of both Abel's and Noah's sacrifice. He likes the sweet aroma of a roast lamb. This new Adam of Noah's covenant is far from the cults of Genesis 1's vegetarianism. In a speech set between reiterated blessings, the essence of a tragic new Adam is sketched (Gen 9:1; 9:7). Having promised never again to curse the ground because of the evil in men's heart (Gen 9:22), Yahweh decides to fill it to overflowing with the image of divine dread:

The Fear and the Terror of you will be upon all the living of the earth and on every bird of the air, on everything that creeps on the ground and all the fish of the sea. Into your hand they are delivered. Everything which moves, which has life, will be food for you. Just as I gave you the green plants, I [now] give you everything. But meat with its life, its blood: you must not eat.

For your lifeblood I will require a reckoning. From the hand of all living—from a man and his brother—for the life of a person, I will make a claim.[16] Whoever sheds the blood of man, by man will his blood be shed because God made man in his own image. (Gen 9:2–6)

Once again—as in the opening of the garden story—humanity is given permission to eat everything, with a single exception: "Meat with its life, its blood in it, you must not eat." This critical variant of an Orphic and Pythagorean abhorrence for blood sacrifice finds continuity and expansion in Leviticus, in which Aaron, the high priest, takes the blood of a bull that has been sacrificed and smears it with his finger on the horns of the altar for purification. He then pours the blood out at the base of the altar as an atonement for the animal killed (Lev 8:15). The declaration that the person eating blood will be "cut off from the people" marks such an action as a breech of the "covenant of blood."

If any man of the house of Israel or any stranger, living among them, eats blood, I will set my face against that person and cut him off from his people. The life of the flesh is in the blood and I have given it for you upon the altar to make atonement for your souls; for it is the blood that makes atonement, by reason of the life. (Lev 17:10–11)

While the parallel to the garden story's test implied in the ban on blood encourages doubt that this renewed creation can be more successful than the first, other reiterations suggest that the scene actively forebodes disaster. While the creation story presented mankind as king and patron over the world and all that lives on it (Gen 1:28), this new Adam is given the role of predator and hunter, a king bringing terror, one who swallows all the living. That he must not drink blood is his test. As it bears life, blood belongs to Yahweh, who will hold this new Adam accountable. The image of God is revised and redefined as "fear" and "terror" (Gen 9:2), threatening metaphors of holy war.

In terms of story plot, the presentation of humanity in the image of Yahweh's "fear" and "terror" lays the foundation for a more active role in creation for Yahweh. His placing of his bow in the sky is a variation of the necklace that Ishtar places in the heavens as a similar reminder of the flood's devastation.

Yahweh's bow has a Janus-faced reflection. Not only does it close the terror of the flood with the necklace-like brilliance of a rainbow, it is also a sign of the covenant and a warning for the future: a warrior's bow, which Yahweh will use instead of a flood. It is to be carried in holy war to punish mankind. Genesis draws on the myths of the Greek god *Ares* with his bow.[17] With his cue name signifying "war" and "destruction," he was, in Zeus' opinion, "the most odious of all the gods of Olympus." He had two sons: Deimos ("Fear") and Foibos ("Terror"). With their help, Ares enjoyed himself by destroying cities and drinking the blood of the dying. Sophocles identified him with the plague (*Oedipus Rex*, line 190), reechoed in the Bible's use of a threefold "terror, leprosy and fever," used to put out the light of those who break Yahweh's law (Lev 26:16) and the parallel "sword" and "plague," which punish those who break the covenant (Lev 26:25).

Having set the conditions of his covenant with Noah, Yahweh promises never again to cut off "all flesh" with the flood's waters (Gen 9:11). In the future—metaphors belonging to the storm god, Baal, are used—when he brings clouds over the earth and sees his bow, he will remember his covenant (Gen 9:12–17). As the covenant with Noah opens Genesis to the story of war, the second condition of Yahweh's pact—regarding blood guilt—becomes critical if his plan is to succeed. Yahweh will hold a monopoly on war and retribution, much as he holds a monopoly on kingship. The issue of blood guilt provides the key to understanding how holy war is Yahweh's tool to overcome the corruption in the human heart. "Yahweh will require a reckoning for our souls; it is the blood which makes atonement." This introduction to the image of Yahweh in the "fear and terror" that mankind brings into the world is ambitious. The reciprocity of its point of departure suggests that the theme of holy war begins as a pacifist project. As no man can pursue war without spilling blood, Yahweh's monopoly on holy war as war's only legitimacy should make pacifists of men. The reader, however, must again worry that Yahweh has forgotten that mankind is created in *his* image.

In the final scene of the flood story, a Dionysian Noah, reborn from the waters of death (cf. Ps 23:2, 5), plants a vineyard and becomes the first to drink the new wine and sleep in drunkenness (Gen 9:20–21). The scene ends with a reiteration of the paradise story's motif of shame (Gen 3:10–11) and, much like the paradise and Cain stories, with a destiny determining curse. This curse of the future Canaan sets the Pentateuch's holy war chain of narrative in motion (Gen 9:24–27). Themes already begun expand and their discourse is carried further as the story moves from its figures of humanity opposed to the divine to figures of geo-ethnicity, such as Canaan and Israel, standing in mirrored opposition to each other, a structure that informs the narrative from Genesis 10 to the close of 2 Kings. The garden story's fate-determining curse of the land is a curse closely linked to the curse of Cain by the land. While the garden and Cain stories are full of images of desert and drought, resolution to the curse allows the land to be blessed with fertility. Barren land is transformed to fertile vineyard.

ALL THE ARMIES OF YAHWEH

The figure of Noah and the story of his pact with God find reiteration in the stories of Abraham. Like Noah and Job, Abraham was a righteous man, pious in his generation. He walked with God (cf. Gen 6:9). He is also the second of three figures, Noah, Abraham and Moses, who make covenants with Yahweh and introduce the theme of holy war in the Pentateuch. Taking its departure from the story of the tower of Babel, where all mankind was scattered over the face of the earth, the story has Abraham play the role of the exception in whom Yahweh found favor:

> Leave your country, your kindred and your father's house to a land that I will show you. I will make you a great nation, bless you and make your name great. You will be a blessing. I will bless them that bless you and curse them that curse you. In you all the families of the earth will be blessed. (Gen 12:1–3)

Abraham's call sets the agenda for the rest of Genesis' narrative, which moves toward the seventy sons of Jacob entering Egypt to become the seventy elders of a great nation (Gen 46:1–15). The presentation of Abraham as a figure for the judgment of the whole world establishes a leitmotif of holy war. It begins a chain connecting the legends of Abraham with those of Isaac and Jacob, transmitting Abraham's role to the people Israel (Gen 12:3, 7; 13:15; 15:5, 18; 17:8, 19; 18:18; 22:18; 24:7; 26:3–4; 28:14). Abraham wanders through his narrative chain from story to story, building altars and speaking with God. The chain of narrative centers on the themes of covenant and holy war.[18] In a vision, Yahweh tells Abraham to take a three-year-old cow, she-goat and ram, together with a turtle dove and a young pigeon. Abraham cuts them in two and lays them on the ground over against each other, guarding them against birds of prey. At sunset, a dreadful darkness covers him as he sleeps. The scene is allegory and echoes the ritual of covenant making in Jeremiah. The animal split in two stands as a symbol of the punishment that will be visited on one who breaks this pact with God (Jer 35:17–19). The choice of animals supports the allegory. The cow is an offering for blood guilt (Dt 21:1–9). The goat signifies strength (Jgs 13:19–23) and is the offering for the Passover (2 Chr 35:7; cf. 1 Kgs 20:26–30). The ram signifies the leader, the general, the "powerful of the land" and symbolizes the king in his hubris who is humbled (Ez 17:1–21). The dove, on the other hand, represents the life of the helpless, which should not be given over to beasts of prey: the great powers of this world (Ps 74:19). Abraham's task is to remember the covenant and keep the land from dread (Ps 74:20). The fifth, the young pigeon, is a figure of the children of God the covenant creates, to be carried on eagle's wings and freed from their slavery in Egypt (Ex 19:3–6). Yahweh plays the eagle for a faithful Israel, protecting Israel and taking them up on his wings and feeding them in the wilderness (Dt 32:10–19), lest their corpses be the food of wild birds and animals (Jer 19:1–9; 34:18–22; cf. Jer 7:30–34).

A second vision comes to Abraham as the sun sets. A smoking oven and a flaming torch pass between the pieces. It is a prophecy to be illustrated by Sodom's day of judgment, when the smoke of the land goes up "like the smoke from an oven" (Gen 19:28). This oven, in which silver and gold are refined, marks the coming trials through which Israel is to be purified through its suffering in the land of Egypt (Ex 19:18) and, in a more distant future, is identified with Zion and the suffering of Jerusalem (Is 31:5–9). Malachi draws on this metaphor for a final judgment, in which the furnace burns the chaff of evildoers and separates them from the righteous (Mal 3:18–19). The oven and its fire is the weapon of the king in holy war, expressing divine wrath (Ps 21:10).

The central story of this chain about Abraham presents an origin story for the language of "cutting a covenant" (Gen 17:2–14). In this scene, not animals cut for the sake of wordplay but the cutting of the foreskin of the penis carries the metaphorical burden. A double etiology is cast. The pact is not only between Abraham and Yahweh, it is eternal: between Yahweh and Abraham's "seed"—forever. Therefore, the foreskin is cut because of the seed coming from the penis. The symbolism is also supported by the promise of the covenant offering Abraham the fertility of many peoples.

> A boy of eight days will be circumcised among you—every male, throughout the generations. A child born in the house or one bought, also every male child who is not of your seed. A child of the house or one bought with your money will be circumcised. My covenant will be in your flesh, for an eternal pact. A "foreskin-man," who has not had the flesh of his foreskin circumcised, that man shall be exterminated from the people; he has broken my covenant. (Gen 17:12–14)

This remarkable passage explains the custom of circumcision as the sign of the covenant, cut into the flesh of the entire people bound by it. Much as the sign of the covenant in the Noah story, Yahweh's bow, this sign too is tied to war. The covenant is a "covenant of blood." The reference to a "foreskin-man" obviously engages a coarse term of abuse (Jgs 14:3; 15:18; 1 Sm 14:6; 17:26, 36). Such a man, not bound to his god, is without honor; he is to be excluded from the people to die in ignominy (Ez 28:9–11; 31:32). Similarly Pharaoh and the Egyptians, Assyrians, Elamites and Edomites are all cursed by Yahweh to die as "foreskin-men." All the kings of the north are cursed and condemned to such a dishonorable fate. Yahweh topples them from their proud heights. He sends them into the underworld, the realm of the dead, their soldiers calling to them from the grave (Ez 31–32). In transferring this language to the destruction of Samaria and Jerusalem, Jeremiah draws the same metaphor to speak of the destruction of foreigners. While all the nations are "foreskin-men," the Israelites are "foreskin-men of the heart" (Jer 9:24–25). In Lamentations, the author sketches a picture of the death of a "foreskin-man" in battle, with a light overtone of the story of the fallen angels:

> How Yahweh in his anger has set the daughter of Zion under a cloud. He has cast the splendour of Israel down from heaven to the earth. He has not remembered his footstool in his anger. Yahweh has destroyed without mercy all the habitations of Jacob; in his wrath he has broken down the strongholds of the daughters of Judah; he has brought to the ground in dishonour the kingdom and its rulers. In glowing anger, he has chopped off every horn in Israel. (Lam 2:1–3)

The language of covenant draws on the patronage relationship between the king and his God. In Abraham's story, the motif of circumcision as sign of that covenant is a sign of submission to the God to whom one belongs. The exclusivity of this sign to the men of Israel is not simply an aspect of national identity. It is also related to the nature of the covenant, which makes all Israelite men soldiers in Yahweh's army. The metaphor-creating symbolic function of circumcision is not rooted in any historical need of a small nation to defend itself, but rather in the theological understanding of piety as an army of salvation, requiring hearts to be circumcised. The historical roots of the metaphor lie much further back in history, to the understanding of soldiers at war, as expressed in texts as early as the Eighteenth and Nineteenth Dynasties.[19] Conquered lands are often described in inscriptions with the metaphor: "Their seed is no more." It expresses not only total destruction but also a transference of the land's patronage to pharaoh, who now is responsible for his new land's fertility and future. The element of seed and the fertility it brings reflects a divine gift, expressed in offspring and a man's future. In Egyptian texts, the phrase "his seed is no more" is connected to the military practice of accounting for enemies killed in battle. The circumcised soldier belongs to a god: his seed is under the protection of a divine patron. Rather than offend a god, the one who killed the dead soldier cuts off his hand, and an accounting is made. In contrast, uncircumcised soldiers, "foreskin-men," have no god and, therefore, no protection. Their penises are cut, their fertility captured and they die ignominiously, their souls committed to death. Implicitly, those who are circumcised are protected from the underworld's darkness. In one inscription, the seed of the king is preserved in heaven. Similarly, the phallic metaphor of "raising the horn of the king" is a sign of holy war's victory. It promises life-giving fertility, much as the loss of tension in a hero's bow or the sinking of his horn or, as in Egyptian inscriptions, cutting it off, epitomizes the loss of potency and becomes a sign of disgrace (cf. Job 29:20; 2 Sm 1:17–27).

Abraham's covenant story presents the foundation for the holy war narrative of the Bible, which dominates the plotline from the story of Israel's exodus from Egypt to the end of 1 Kings. The seed of Abraham, the children of Israel, bound to their God through circumcision, become the conquering army of Yahweh against the nations of Canaan (Gen 15:13; Ex 12:41). As Abraham's covenant of blood is reiterated in the stories of Moses (Ex 20–23) and Joshua (Josh 24) to David (2 Sm 7), the theme of holy war comes to determine the fate of David and his sons and does not rest until Yahweh sends Nebuchadnezzar to destroy Jerusalem (2 Kgs 24–25). Even there, it does not end but is taken up again in the new Jerusalem tales of Nehemiah and Ezra, where it takes the form of ironic parable for yet another generation.

Ezra and the Cleansing of Jerusalem

Abraham as stranger and wanderer in the land of Canaan (Gen 12:1; 23:4) marks the self-identity of the pious reader of the stories of old Israel. As "children of Israel," they imitate Abraham and strive to wander in whatever path Yahweh might show them (Gen 12:4). In the narratives of covenant and holy war, this identity is ironically mirrored in the identity of the enemy, dwelling in the land. Israel, too, is to be set under Yahweh's ban and sent into exile. In these stories about the rebuilding of Jerusalem, the Torah's demand for holy war against the peoples of Canaan finds its paradox in the Torah's epitome to love the stranger and care for the foreigner who lives in the land (Lev 19:18, 34).

Rarely is the identification with the foreigner more unequivocally illustrated than in David's deathbed scene in 1 Chronicles, in which he humbly acknowledges Yahweh as his true king and patron. In this scene, David speaks for all Jews. He is a "passing guest and stranger like all my fathers" (Ps 39:13).

> It is from you [Yahweh] that all things come, and what we give to you, comes from your hand. For you, are we foreigners and immigrants like all of our fathers. Our days on earth are like shadows; there is no hope. (1 Chr 29:14–15)

This self-identification of the reader with the enemy and object of holy war is centered on the epitome of the Torah, so closely linked to the story of Abraham's descendants as foreigners in the land of Egypt:

> When a foreigner lives with you in your land, you must not do him harm. The foreigner who lives with you will be to you as the native among you and you will love him as yourself; for you were foreigners in the land of Egypt. (Lev 19:33–34)

In Deuteronomy's version of the law, this self-definition as foreigner is consistent and unrelieved. The logic is explained in the course of Moses' long farewell speech, which interprets the laws given on Horeb (cf. Dt 5:6–21; Ex 20:2–17). Moses interprets the Torah in light of Israel's future and offers an epitome of the Ten Commandments. He expands the first commandment with absolute demands of purity of heart: "You must love your God with all your heart, all your soul and with all your might" (Dt 6:5).[20] The commentary of Moses' farewell speech expands the Golden Rule, not with the love of neighbor, stranger and enemy, but with a curse of the nations of Canaan (Cf. Gen 9:25; 10:15–18). Seven of Canaan's sons are listed, all described as nations greater and mightier than Israel, whom Yahweh will wipe out in holy war. They must be utterly destroyed (Dt 7:1–5). Moses explains that such holy war is to "cleanse" the land; for Israel is not like other nations. It must be a perfect and holy people for a perfect and holy God. This bold revision of Exodus (cf. Dt 7:6–11; Ex 19:5–6) has considerable ambition. It sets Deuteronomy a task wrapped in paradox. One involves a philosophically troubled goal: the "perfect and holy people" of Exodus are to be created out of the world's most unpromising nation. The law of retribution demands that Janus's other face be the face of holy war, set to destroy the sons of twice-cursed Canaan: the strangers dwelling in the land of Israel. Deuteronomy will unite these opposites that the command to love one's neighbor be established all the more by the love of the enemy. The more hate-filled the language, the more intriguing is the riddle of waging holy war against oneself.

Moses offers the key to his provocative riddle without delay. Immediately following this contrast of the love of God to the seductive idolatry of the nations, he offers instruction in obedience to the Torah. He reminds his audience of how Yahweh had guided them through their adventures during forty years in the wilderness, with the purpose of humbling them and testing them (Dt 8:1–6). They had become hungry and he fed them with manna that he might teach them that "man does not live by bread alone, but rather from what comes from Yahweh's mouth." His care for them was so great that he kept their clothes from wearing out and their feet from swelling. His discipline was that of a father for his son. The wilderness wandering was Israel's education in humility. Through two chapters of instruction of how Israel is to walk in Yahweh's path and fear him (Dt 8:6), holy war, with its paradox of a foreigner's identity, is never far from the text. Out of Yahweh's love, Israel is chosen as his firstborn. Nevertheless, this great, mighty and terrible God executes justice for the fatherless and the widow. He loves the stranger and gives him food and clothing (Dt 10:12–18). How do you love God with a pure heart and fear him? The answer: "Love the stranger; for you were strangers in the land of Egypt." This defines the "fear of Yahweh" in the story (Dt 10:19–20). Although Moses refers again to the theme of holy war against the peoples of Canaan, the command to love the foreigner receives a sevenfold reiteration. Israel is a holy people, and it will be judged by its care for the stranger, the father and the widow (Dt 14:28–29; 16:11, 14; 24:17–18; 26:12). This is Judaism's self-identifying confession and paradox:

> A wandering Aramean was my father and he went down into Egypt and was a foreigner there, few in number. He became a mighty nation, great and populous, but the Egyptians treated us harshly, afflicted us and laid on us hard bondage. We cried to Yahweh the God of our fathers, and Yahweh heard our voice, saw our affliction, toil and oppression. Yahweh brought us out of Egypt with a mighty hand and an outstretched arm, with great terror, signs and wonder. He brought us into this land, a land flowing with milk and honey. (Dt 26:5–9)

Moses' farewell speech sets Israel and its entrance into the promised land in a fate-determining test. They will receive blessings from Mount Gerizim if they obey and a curse from Mount Ebal if they do not. On the day they enter the land and become Yahweh's people, six of the tribes will go up on Mount Gerizim and six will climb Mount Ebal. The Levites will call out with a loud voice twelve curses (Dt 27:1–26). These curse those who do not do justice to the stranger, widow or fatherless. Moses closes his address with an alternative paired list of blessings and curses (Dt 28:1–19), predicting Israel's failure of the test. They will return to their role of strangers in the land of Egypt.

The figure of the messiah as prince of peace (Is 9:6), epitomized in just such reversals of the fate of the oppressed and playing such a central role in the portrayal of David in the Psalter and of Jesus in the gospels, is central to this literary revision of the ancient Near Eastern traditions of holy war within its myth of the good king. Divine rule is reestablished in the world, and the oppression and violence of kings is transformed in a utopian vision of peace, in which the poor and the oppressed play the role of a new humanity in which war is no more (2 Sm 1:17). The theme of holy war, however, is not resolved and casts Israel into a never-ending story, with cycles of creation and destruction, ever returning to a new beginning and to a new failure. By Yahweh's will, Israel has been chosen by the covenant theme to represent—as Noah does after the flood—a new Adam for the Bible's story and to displace the nations of Chaos. Israel's disobedience to its covenant with God turns this curse against Israel itself. First Samaria and then Jerusalem fall under Yahweh's ban and are dedicated to destruction.

This failure of old Israel is succeeded by a production of narrative, identifying those who returned from exile, repentant and wiser for having learned from the past. They attempt to establish a new Jerusalem or a new Israel centered on purity of heart. These narratives—Ezra, Nehemiah, 1 Esdras, the Damascus Covenant, 1–2 Maccabees and the gospels—open and continue a never-ending cycle of story.

The Bible engages many voices to explore the theme of holy war: voices of nationalism, xenophobia and racism, voices raised against strangers and neighbors and brothers and voices rejecting both war and violence. Holy war—for all its realism and for all the hatred engaged by its most prominent figures and heroes—comes to us in the Bible not as a fact of history but as a discourse in literature. It forms not policy but philosophy.[21] The curse of Canaan and the difficult and violent holy war theme it begins is a theme perhaps best entered through the backdoor with the help of stories that continue Israel's narrative after retribution has destroyed old Israel—stories of the return from exile and the building of a new Jerusalem. The plan of holy war, which Yahweh's threefold covenant with Noah, Abraham and Moses had set out to accomplish, ended in failure. The Canaanites were not driven out (Gen 10:15–19) but remained in the land. Instead, Israel itself fell under holy war's ban and was driven from the land. From Jerusalem's ashes, a phoenix rises as Cyrus fulfills Jeremiah's prophecy and sends the survivors of the houses of Judah and Benjamin with gifts of gold and silver to rebuild Yahweh's temple (Ezra 1:1–6; cf. Ex 12:35–36).

This theme provides us with the saddest scene in all of biblical literature, which closes the book of Ezra. The sadness cannot be shaken even as it undermines the reader's expectations. The story of Jerusalem's cleansing in the book of Ezra begins when Ezra, the priest, the scribe of the law of the God of heaven, is sent by the Persian emperor, Artaxerxes, as his emissary to Jerusalem. In a first-person narrative, Ezra tells of arriving in Jerusalem with his entourage. Officials come to him to report that the people of Israel, the priests and the Levites had never in fact separated from the Canaanites and the peoples of the land but had intermarried with them. "The holy race has mixed itself with the peoples of the land" (Ezra 9:2). Ezra tells his readers: "I tore my clothes and my cloak; I pulled the hair from my head and sat there appalled." He confesses his shame in a prayer. Ezra speaks of Jerusalem's guilt for abandoning God's commandments "from the days of our fathers to this day" (Ezra 9:7). What Ezra cites, however, as the law Jerusalem had abandoned and as the ground for their guilt is a highly tendentious collation of several passages from the Torah, giving instructions for the conquest of Canaan under Joshua:

> The land which you are entering, to take possession of, is a land unclean with the pollutions of the peoples of the lands, with their abominations which have filled it from end to end with their uncleanness. Therefore give not your daughters to their sons, and never seek their peace or prosperity, that you may be strong and eat the good of the land, and *leave it for an inheritance to your children forever.* (Ezra 9:11–12; cf. Ex 34:11–16; Lev 18:24–30; Dt 7:2–4)

After he closes his prayer, the narrative shifts from Ezra's voice to the third person. The author's dramatic gloss on Ezra's wish for purity touches directly his prayer of shame and guilt over "pollution by the peoples of the land" (Ezra 9:11) that a faithless remnant continues.

Commissioned by Artaxerxes to rule Judah and Jerusalem in accord with God's law, Ezra marks Israel's wives "foreign" *(nakriyyot)*, descendants of the people Joshua and his generation had not driven out. Creating a pun with the verb "to cut, to cut off" *(nikrat)*, Ezra has the people "cut a covenant" and thus cut the women off with rhetorical effectiveness. The punning, excluding their wives from the new Israel, seems as harsh as it is tendentious (cf. Gen 17:14). The rhetoric invites debate: Does the law require obedience or compassion? The book of Jonah, of course, had opened that debate with another story, supporting compassion even for the hated foreigners of Assyria's great Nineveh. The Torah not only supports and protects the rights of strangers and foreigners in Israel (esp. Dt 10:19; 14:19, 29; Lev 19:18, 34), such laws for the foreigner and stranger are commonly used to epitomize the essence of the Torah. The book of Ezra's xenophobic priest evokes a debate we have seen already about purity, the identity of the foreigner and the children of Jerusalem's future.

In the book's final, dramatic scene, Ezra's tears purify Jerusalem. The people—crying with their reformer—make their new covenant in an effort to reach a goal that Yahweh with the same means had failed to reach through centuries of war. By their oath, the people banish all their foreign wives and children, as Ezra and the righteous ("those that had trembled before God") demand. After three days, they complain of the unreasonableness of Ezra's decree—that they cleanse the nation immediately. Their complaint closes the story on Ezra's "success" in discord and utter sadness. The task of banishing their wives and children is too much in such a short time, *while standing in the rain* (Ezra 10:13). The reader needs to ask, Does their righteousness tremble before God or before his rain? The literary intrusion of rain is as disruptive as it is unsettling to the plot. Shaking from the awful demands of their pact, as from the rain's coldness marking God's presence in the scene, the people complain with a loud voice. However, their cry goes unanswered; nor does the rain stop.

Rain in the Bible comes through God's command. As both theodicy and irony are important aspects of our narrative's rhetoric, the note of discord that the cold winter rain stresses is supported by the inappropriateness of the motif in its context. The rain is a portent, reflecting impending danger or judgment. It bears the marks of covenant and war (Ez 1:28). Ezra's rain is a cold winter rain that causes the people to shiver. It is the rain that falls when brother fights against brother: a rain to make men shake (Ez 38:21–22). The misery of Ezra's closing scene is unmitigated misery. After a long delay, created as much by the list of those who had married foreign wives as by the people's delay in obedience, the book closes with sadness intact. The people's new covenant cuts *them* from their loved ones forever (Ezra 10:44).

Ezra's motif of the people murmuring against their priest, Jerusalem's leader (Ezra 10:12), echoes the Exodus tale of the murmuring against Moses in the wilderness. They resist Ezra's demand for unflinching obedience with complaint and delay. In its reiteration of the Moses story, however, Ezra's role as a new Moses has lost both its humor and its persuasiveness. The reader has been educated in the Bible's long story of Israel's fall from grace, and that completed journey now provides him Ezra's scene before Jerusalem's walls. Rather than closing with 1 Esdras on joy for a purified Jerusalem, the author chooses to have his readers watch the slowly disappearing figures of wives and children in the rain.

The effort to replace a failed covenant of the past with a new one creates out of wives and children, a new exile of widows and orphans, directly contradicting the greater tradition's concept of justice:

> Justice is created for the oppressed; bread is given to the hungry; prisoners are freed; the blind see; the crooked are made straight; the righteous are loved; *foreigners are protected and widows and orphans supported*, but the way of the godless is twisted. (Ps 146:7–9)

This tradition links the fate of foreigners with widows and orphans (Ps 94:6; Zech 7:10) and prophesies that the mistreatment of widows and orphans will provoke Yahweh to make widows and orphans of Israel's own wives and children (Ex 22:20–23): the very fate to which Ezra's author directs his story. A reader's implicit expectations change a formal closure into never-ending story. Hardly a new Israel, Ezra's Jerusalem fails its test of righteousness. Having begun his narrative with an explicit fulfillment of Jeremiah's prophecy of return (Ezra 1:1; Jer 25:11; 29:10), the author closes by fulfilling that same prophet's vision of Jerusalem as a moral wilderness, where not a single righteous man can be found (Jer 5:1–6).

The debate provoked by the book of Ezra is about the Torah. The priest Ezra's understanding of the law is not obvious but problematic. The description of his great learning identifies him as the target, not the voice of the author. His wisdom is the proverbial foolishness of the learned man. Contrary to his demand that the law be obeyed and wives and children sent away, the Torah supports and protects the rights of foreigners in Israel (Dt 10:19; 14:19, 29; Lev 19:18, 34).

Rather than a story of piety and promising new beginnings, the book of Ezra presents hubris and tragedy, another downward cycle in the never-ending story of the lost generation. The author has tears for the people of Jerusalem and their Persian-appointed Ezra who—after delays and fears—finally completes the project decreed by the inspired Cyrus at the book's opening. This decree introduced the fulfillment of a prophecy by Jeremiah (Jer 29:10–14). Israel's exile is over, and God will bring the people back to Jerusalem:

> When you call to me and submit yourselves to me, I will hear you. You will search for me and find me, *if you seek me with all your heart.* (Jer 29:12–13)

Whether the prophecy has come true is the author's undermining question. The book of Ezra is not a chapter in a triumphant "salvation history," recounting acts of God.[22] It is rather a piece of sharp, critical discourse. In the scene of Ezra and the people's prayer, the condition for Yahweh's hearing is classic to biblical theology. "If you seek me with all your heart," is the key to the whole of the author's subtext. It functions as leitmotif to his interrogation. Do we find the purity of heart demanded by Yahweh when we face the sadness of the narrative's closure? In this scene, the fulfillment of Abraham's covenant—the blessing of children—leaves the city.

The irony that casts such a parable as we find in the story of Ezra marks the Bible's revision of the ancient Near Eastern theme of holy war as a test of whether one can love both God and one's neighbor with a pure heart, a paradox whose only abiding solution is the love of the other—the enemy—as oneself. Banishing the foreigner from the New Jerusalem reenters the Bible's never-ending story. This paradox is the literary context of all the Bible's stories of holy war, which set their goal in a vision of *shalom* and in the end of all war. Noah's new humanity began its journey in the "fear and terror" of the covenant, in a violence whose utopian solution is the return to the creation God originally intended. The role of the messiah in holy war has its goal in Isaiah's prince of peace (Is 9:6), transforming the rebellion of the nations in uproar against the patronage of Yahweh and his messiah (Ps 2:2) by addressing the theme of Israel's own rebellion and opposition to Yahweh's plan.

PATRONAGE AND THE MAINTENANCE OF CREATION

The theme of the king's covenant with his divine patron is expressed through personal motifs such as loyalty and grace. Holy war, the offering of the enemy in human sacrifice and the deportation, displacement and destruction of populations—all well-known aspects of ancient Near Eastern texts—provide the means for reestablishing divine rule over the world.[23] In developing the leitmotif of the covenant between Israel and Yahweh, the Bible has adopted the mythology of this universal, even imperial worldview in its theology. At the same time, its perspective is ever that of a subject people. Without in any way wishing to be systematic or complete, I would like to discuss a central cluster of elements in the theme of holy war, reflecting the ancient political system of patronage, in order to sketch the ideological association of holy war with the theme of eternal peace.

One of the simplest and best known expressions of God as patron and the king as servant is the carving on the Hammurapi stele. The god Shamash hands the king his laws. In the prologue, Hammurapi describes himself as having been called by the gods from the beginning of creation to promote the people's welfare, to make justice prevail, to destroy the evil and wicked and to light up the land as the sun.[24] He is the shepherd Enlil appointed and he is responsible for his people's prosperity. That the king is divinely chosen is fundamental to the understanding of the messiah. The first function of the king under divine patronage is to represent God on earth. This maintains the understanding of the divine as transcendent and universal.[25] In New Kingdom Egyptian hymns, the Pharaoh, as son of the sun God, carries out his role as divine warrior. As son of God, he rules over Egypt and through war he brings the presence and direct rule of the gods to the world. In the Pentateuch, such a role belongs to Yahweh as God's name and presence in Israel.[26] Like the Assyrian God Assur, Yahweh alone is true king. The particular role of Yahweh's son and divine warrior-king or "messiah" is to enforce the rule of the divine patron through war. The king fulfills a threefold function: *government, fertility and creation.* As ruler, he is the shepherd, watching over his people; through his potency, he produces abundance in the land and as conqueror, he maintains the world in the order of God's creation.[27] In Isaiah, Yahweh plays this kingly role of demonstrating his "glory" and presence on earth (Is 40:3–4; 41:15; 45:2).

As in the Mesha stele, the king is defined first as warrior in the divine struggle against chaos. Victory in battle always has cosmic overtones and significance. A utopian, lasting peace is established. In Merneptah's eightfold description of his victory over Lybia, an idyllic calm comes over the land; fear disappears; fortresses are ignored and people sleep outside at night; cattle no longer need shepherds and everyone comes and goes with singing. Not a single enemy is left; the whole world falls under the king's patronage.[28] For Thutmosis III's victory song, the whole world is at peace: the great ones of Djahi' in the south, the Asiatics of Retenu in the north, God's land in the east, the western lands and the islands of the great green sea. "The great ones, all foreign lands" are bound under the king's patronage.[29] Like David, his rule is eternal: his throne is "for a million years" and his house "the work of eternity." Blessing flows from him, as from Abraham, to all the world's nations. He leads the living for eternity.[30] Grace and mercy are also universal and, in fulfillment of the Golden Rule, includes the enemies of tradition. As in the Bible, the goal of war is to "bind" and "chain" the enemy, bringing him to "submit" to his proper role as client of the divine. The extension of imperial patronage frees and brings peace to a new subject of the gods. The deportation of the rebellious and the granting of new land to the submissive are also typical aspects of the divine patron's control over destiny.[31]

The Yahweh of the prophet Jeremiah makes a cosmic desert out of a faithless Jerusalem (Jer 5:1–17), sending wolves and bears to ravage an empty city. Similarly Merneptah in the Israel stele turns the land of Tehenu (Palestine) into a desert and the town of Yenoam into a wilderness. The Pharaoh also gives fertility to the land. Like Yahweh in the garden story, creating the first human being (Gen 2:7), Merneptah breathes into the nostrils of his new people (so also Is 42:5). His patronage is life and it is death. It is famine and prosperity, desert emptiness and boundless fertility.[32] Such a double-edged sword of blessings and curses, of conquest and the ensuing patronage that follows, has its clearest expression in the blessings and curses of vassal treaties.[33]

In Egyptian New Kingdom texts, the stereotypical "nine bows"—an implied list of foreign nations encompassing the world outside Egypt—define pharaoh as universal patron. In inscriptions of both Merneptah and Haremheb, Egypt's patronage over the nine bows is used as a symbol for world peace.[34] In the Babylonian creation story, Marduk's struggle against Tiamat and her eleven monsters can be understood as a variation of the same forces of chaos represented by the stereotypical rebellious twelve kings of Hatti in Assyrian campaign inscriptions.[35] Such a list of nations in uproar—understood as identifying peoples dedicated to destruction—is central to the theme of holy war in the Bible. Israel's failure at holy war in the stories of the Pentateuch and Joshua follows principles of retribution and brings Yahweh's wrath against his own people.

A comparable understanding of holy war is found in the Mesha stele. This inscription understands Moab's god Chemosh as the king's refuge and the cause of victory over his enemies. The earlier subjugation of Moab by Israel is seen by Mesha as divine punishment. In his anger, Chemosh abandoned his land and destroyed it by using Israel as his tool to punish Moab. Relenting, the god Chemosh returns to his land in the reign of Mesha. In capturing Israel's town of Ataroth, Mesha kills the entire population that Chemosh might be intoxicated by their blood. This new wine is poured out as an offering, while its chieftain Arel is presented as an offering to Chemosh in Kerioth (a temple?). Mesha also captured Nebo, killing everyone: "7,000 men, boys, women, girls and maid servants." He "dedicated them to destruction for (the god) Ashtar-Chemosh." Throughout this short narrative, it is always the divine patron, Chemosh, who counsels Mesha before battle, fights for Mesha, wins his battles and drives the enemy before him. Chemosh's holy wars close in a transcendent peace. A hundred towns are added to Mesha's land because his god, Chemosh, "lived there in his time."

The Bible's holy war lies in a continuum of literary and mythic metaphor, based in the social structure of patronage. In the following brief survey, I limit myself to elements that seem to inform Ezra's parable. Throughout the Bible, the formulaic list of nations that Ezra identifies as "the people of the land" (Ezra 9:1) is used to epitomize nations in uproar against Yahweh's patronage. The themes of obedience, patronage and holy war dominate many of the wilderness narratives. Already in Yahweh's first appearance to Moses from the burning bush on the mountain of God (Ex 3), the narrative structure is set. Having heard the cry of his people, Yahweh calls Moses to free his people and bring them to the land of the "Canaanites, Hittites, Amorites, Perizzites, Hivites and Jebusites," to a land flowing with milk and honey (Ex 3:7–10). Yahweh describes himself as Israel's patron—the God who will be with them (Ex 3:12). This small theological element, identifying Yahweh as the God Israel knew, expands an ironic leitmotif of the story of Israel as God's chosen people, beginning in blessing and promise and ending in curse. In response to its suffering, Yahweh chooses Israel as his people; "he will be with them." He will free them from their enslavement in the land of Egypt and give them a land of boundless fertility: the land of the six nations of Canaan (Ex 3:17). The price of this patronage is always marked by the logic of retribution. As Yahweh killed the firstborn of the Egyptians to effect Israel's rescue, the firstborn of Israel now belongs to Yahweh (Ex 13:15). The feast of Passover and leavened bread are to remind them (Ex 13:1–16). While the narrative serves as an origin story for both animal sacrifice (Lev 27:26–27) and the role of the Levites in the temple (Num 3:13), it prepares the reader for the story of punishment of a later, less faithful Israel. Jeremiah similarly uses the suffering of a first birth to prophesy the destruction of Samaria and Jerusalem and their subsequent deportation (Jer 4:31). In Kings, the neglect of Passover becomes the mark of Israel's neglect of its God (2 Kgs 23:21–23). With even greater force, Jeremiah uses the Exodus story directly to explain why the Babylonians lay siege to Jerusalem. Yahweh, he argues, freed Israel from Egypt with a strong hand and great terror. Yahweh gave them a land flowing with milk and honey and they took it. Yet they never listened to him or followed the Torah. Therefore disaster befell them (Jer 32:21–25). Jeremiah describes how the justice of this God works:

> He is the great God, the warrior. Yahweh of the armies is his name. Large in purpose and great in what he does, whose eyes observe all the ways of men, that he might pay each according to his way, according to the fruits of his actions. (Jer 32:19)

The principle of retribution—that God will deal with Israel as they themselves deal—sets the logic of the story. Its message is to the reader: "Punishment fits the crime" or "evil turns back upon itself." Ezra did not understand this message of the Torah, though his author did.

The specific misunderstanding of Torah that the book of Ezra centers on can be seen in the story of Yahweh's promise to send an angel to guide Moses and the Israelites in the future. If Israel defies this messenger, he will not forgive it. After he destroys the nations of Canaan, Israel must not worship their gods. If they worship Yahweh, however, all the land's blessings will be theirs (Ex 23:20–26; 34:10–16). A reiteration of this scene (Ex 33:1–3) has Yahweh send his angel because if he himself were present, his impatience would cause him to annihilate his people immediately. An implied prophecy is obvious to any who know the story's closure.

The angel becomes Yahweh's "terror," "a swarm" and a "plague" that Yahweh will send to drive the Hivites, Canaanites and Hittites from the land. He commands them not to make a covenant with these nations or with their gods. Nor must they allow them to remain in the land (Ex 23:27–33). This story chain in which the angel leads Israel finds close reiteration in Moses' farewell speech from Mount Nebo (Dt 7). All the same thematic elements are present: the demand of obedience, a promise of utopia, the covenant, the sending of Yahweh's terror and the gradual elimination of the nations. In this speech, the closing warning (Dt 7:26) plays on the theme of retributive justice: "Do not bring what has been set under the ban into your house or you yourself will be put under the ban."

The story purpose of the holy war theme is explained in a similar farewell speech by Joshua at the close of the conquest stories. A threat of retribution is transformed into theological principle:

All that Yahweh has promised is now fulfilled; not a single thing has he failed to accomplish. Just as every good thing that Yahweh has promised has been fulfilled, he could as well bring every evil thing, until he has removed you from the land he has given you. (Josh 23:14)

Not only is the future of Israel predicted, but Yahweh controls that future.

If you break the covenant and serve other gods, then Yahweh's anger will burn against you and you will perish from the good land he has given you. (Josh 23:16)

In this patron's absolute demand for loyalty from his client, it becomes clear that the holy war theme is not intent on the killing of Israel's enemies, let alone the indigenous population of Palestine. The nations under the ban—and not least the populations of Jericho and Ai—remain remarkably ethereal. Nor is the patronage demand to be understood as simply obeying or else. It is not even a warning against worshiping the gods of foreigners, though all of these ethnically competitive overtones are used as elements of attraction in the course of the story.[36] The story's audience does not live in the time of Joshua. They never had anything to do with such peoples as these twelve nations. The historical bloodshed that is our story's reference was shed in the real destruction of Samaria and Jerusalem past. The author knows this and therefore knows where his story will end. Nothing he or his audience—and certainly nothing an ancient Israel or Judah—could do would change that conclusion. The narrator, however, uses his story to instruct his own generation, not Joshua's. It is they who need to understand what Joshua's audience had not.

By the close of the conquest of Palestine (Jgs 2:2), the covenant has already been broken. Accordingly, Yahweh will not drive the nations from the land. The nations are now destined to be a snare for Israel. The people respond to this judgment with tears of repentance. This brings forgiveness and sets the basis for serving Yahweh for that generation. This pattern is repeated until Jerusalem falls. Yahweh allows the nations to oppress Israel but is quickly moved by pity for their suffering (Jgs 2:1–19). No longer interested in driving the nations out, Yahweh chooses to test Israel (Jgs 2:21–22) "to learn whether they would obey the commandments which Yahweh had given their ancestors under Moses" (Jgs 3:4).[37] The logic of retribution implied in the command to love Yahweh drives the narrative and creates a debate of considerable irony: the love of the gods of the nations against the love of God.

The motif of Yahweh's terror used to drive the nations from the land pits Israel's fear of God against their fear of the nations and has a related logic of retribution. If they have fear of God—the beginning of wisdom and source of life (Prv 14:27; 15:33)—they do not need to be afraid of their enemies. Conversely, if they fear their enemies, then they will certainly need to be afraid of God.[38] It is in such a debate about the philosophical virtue of humility ("fear of God") that Moses' angel (Ex 23:20–33) becoming Yahweh's terror (Dt 11:25–26) finds its place. If Israel holds to its covenant with Yahweh, he will drive the nations before them. He will bring "fear and terror" over the whole land. This Yahweh embodies what Noah's covenant promised since men first began to imitate gods and giants in eating flesh.

Such violently ironic play on the virtue of the fear of God finds ample illustration in the tragic failure of Yahweh's first attempt to drive the nations from the land (Num 13–14). This wilderness story is introduced by two very short but important tales centered on *murmuring* and *meat*. The first (Num 11) begins with the people loudly complaining about the manna that God gave them for their food. It is too boring. In fact, their hunger for meat is making them want to go back to the famous fleshpots of Egypt. The story echoes the craving for meat—by both men and gods—which first brought fear and terror into the world. Yahweh gives them quail, but his anger promises retribution. They will get so much meat that it will come out their noses. They will vomit it—a prediction that prepares the reader for the story of flesh-eating giants.[39] The second story (Num 12) offers the reader a key for interpreting Yahweh's holy war against the nations and the theme of foreign wives in Ezra. Moses' sister Miriam and his brother Aaron murmur against Moses because he has married a foreigner. They claim that Yahweh speaks through them as well as Moses. While Miriam and Aaron speak in hubris, Moses is described as "humble, more than any man on earth" (Num 12:3). Punishing them for their claim to speak for God, Yahweh strikes Miriam with leprosy: her skin was "like a dead-born child: its flesh eaten away."

The key to the story is flesh, but we are also warned against those who claim to speak for God. The Israelites prepare to attack the *nephilim* (the "fallen ones," Gen 6:4) in the valley of the giants by sending spies to search out the land. After forty days, the scouts return, two of them carrying a single cluster of grapes from the land whose rivers flow with milk and honey. Moses is eager to take the land (Num 13:13–30). The spies, however, refuse. They argue that it is an evil land: *a land that eats its inhabitants*. Its men are giants. They saw the *nephilim* there. The people cry all night in terror. Theirs is not a cry of humility that expresses the fear of God. It is a cry of murmuring and fear of the giants. They are afraid of the *nephilim*. Yahweh's demand endangers their wives and children (Num 14:3). They want to choose a new leader and return to Egypt. Moses and Aaron submit to their demand. Two of the spies, however, object. Caleb and Joshua promise the people to reverse the fate they fear:

> Do not be afraid of the people of the land, for they are our food. Their protection is false [i.e., the empty "shades" of the underworld], while Yahweh is with us. (Num 14:8–9)

The people refuse to obey and the entire generation is condemned to wander forty years in the wilderness, never to see the promised land. Caleb and Joshua are given the savior's role promised by Joshua's name ("savior"). They become the faithful remnant and heralds for a new generation. Not the generation of the Exodus, but a new generation of their children, for whose sake they had feared to obey Yahweh, will come to know the land Israel's fear had rejected (Num 14:31–33). When the people hear their judgment, they decide to attack after all. God, however, is no longer with them and, without God, they are defeated.

The message to the audience is far from a hatred of foreigners, whether *nephilim* or Philistine, as we already know from the introductory tale about the humble Moses' foreign wife. The moral is the *imitatio* of Joshua and Caleb. Unflinching submission to Yahweh's will is demanded. Yahweh will have an Israel of Joshuas: obedient and ready to eat not merely quail and manna, but the flesh of giants if he asks it of them. The retributive logic is designed to undermine the reader's certainty about who falls under the curse and who will be blessed: Israel or the nations. It turns the reader's attention from the surface plotline of a story to its function as parable. The purposes of God are other than that of men (Gen 50:16–21), but one learns of God's purpose through the stories of the past.

None of the stories on holy war in Numbers, Deuteronomy and Joshua gives hope that Israel will ever succeed in fulfilling the demand for perfection that Yahweh has set: to love God with a pure heart. The command of a perfect God is hardly to be obeyed by imperfect men. The wilderness generation is doomed to failure and destruction, while the nations survive. The nations are still around in Solomon's day, when they take up their roles as snares (1 Kgs 9:20–21). The most striking irony of the Bible's use of holy war is that all such stories have their closure in the destruction of Israel. Samaria and Jerusalem are the primary victims of holy war.

Our critical question regarding Yahweh's demand for ethnic cleansing is not complete without a brief reference to the story of Joshua's farewell speech (Josh 23–24). Joshua, the successful general, explains the past to his gathered troops. The victory over the nations of Canaan is Yahweh's. He has driven them out and he will be the one to drive out those who remain (Josh 23:1–5). Israel must be faithful to Moses' teachings, deviating from it neither to the left nor right. They must take care to love God, rather than intermarry with the "remnant of these nations" (Josh 23:10–11). The narrator reiterates the contrast between the love of Yahweh and the love of wife and family to predict Israel's destiny. If they intermarry with the "remnant of the nations" they themselves will play a remnant's role. The logic of retribution in Israel's identification with the people of the land sets the terms for future guilt. As the refusal to fight giants stemmed from fear for their wives and children, so Joshua's story turns to Israel's marriages with the remnant of those nations to bring a new generation under holy war's ban.

That such failure is the implied author's intention is never far from the biblical text. The Torah's impossible demands require the humility of a Moses and his love for the foreigner. In the opening words of Joshua's second address, he describes the destiny to which the story's logic has brought its participants. All the good things that Yahweh promised Israel have come true. But just so, Yahweh can bring every evil, until he has banished them from the land he gave them (Num 23:14–15). Yahweh was the one who had fought holy war. Much like the great emperors of the past, he gave them the land. It was not payment but blessing. They had not worked the land. They had not built the towns nor did they plant the vineyards and olive groves (Josh 24:13; cf. Dt 6:10–11). Joshua paraphrases Yahweh's demand of the people: "Fear Yahweh and serve him with unflinching loyalty" (Josh 24:14). When the people eagerly respond that they will serve Yahweh, Joshua surprises them and the reader. He is not happy with their answer. He warns them that they are not able to fulfill Yahweh's demands. He warns them of hubris and of the danger they put themselves in: Yahweh is a holy God. He is El Qano: a jealous God. He will not forgive disloyalty. He will bring unhappiness and destroy them even as he had been good to them (Josh 24:19–21). Even after this brutal analogy of their divine patron as a murderously jealous husband, the people are unmoved by Joshua's warnings. As one, they repeat that it is their wish to serve Yahweh—as the author makes the whole nation responsible for the coming disaster. Joshua's acquiescence marks the tragedy implicit in his words: "You are witnesses against yourselves. By your own act, you have chosen to serve Yahweh" (Josh 24:22). The scene closes with solemnity as Joshua creates a covenant, as Ezra does in his story for Israel's surviving remnant. Like Moses and Ezra, Joshua fixes statutes and ordinances and writes them in the book of God's Torah. He sets up a stone as a witness *against* them. He dies and his book ends.

On the story's surface, neither Joshua's nor Ezra's sad ambiguity functions as a closure. The stories do not rest—and only a modern assumption about "books" allows us the illusion. The endings, however, do create discomfort. Their authors stand at a distance, while the audience is absorbed in the broader discourse about giants, a jealous God and love. Can the people of Israel love God with a whole heart? Can the remnant of Israel be like Moses and love their foreign wives and Yahweh too? To fight giants, one risks the loss of the wives and children one loves. But in rejecting wives and children, do they love God? However the question is worded, it attempts to link the love of God with the love of the foreigner (Lev 19:32–34).

As this discussion closes, we need to return briefly to the Merneptah stele. The goal of Merneptah is epitomized by his relationship to the "nine bows": objects of Egypt's holy war. Similarly, the Assyrian king goes to war against the twelve kings of Hatti in rebellion. Just so, Yahweh fights against the nations in uproar (Ps 2:1, 12c). The goal of holy war in all three traditions is not the extermination of such nations—but eternal peace. The eightfold song of *shalom* in

Merneptah's song of the nine bows expresses a divine power to turn curse to blessing: nations in uproar into happy subjects of empire:

> The kings lie prostrate, saying *shalom!* Not one raises his head among the nine bows. A desert is Lybia; Hatti is scorched. Plundered is Gaza with every evil; carried off is Ashkelon. Bound is Gezer; Yenoam is one not existing. Israel is laid waste; his seed is no more; Hurru has become a widow for Egypt. All lands are united; they are in peace. Everyone that was in uproar is bound by King Merneptah. They are given life like Re, forever![40]

Merneptah's song is reiterated in the victory song sung by Isaiah about Cyrus as messiah (Is 45:1–8). Isaiah also announces the good news of Yahweh as savior (Is 40:1–11). All three of these victory songs find a close variant in the herald's cry announcing the "happy day" of Ramses IV's birth (Appendix 1, no. 22). Such lasting peace is also illustrated in the *shalom* of Solomon's *(shlomo)* kingdom (1 Kgs 5). *Shalom* is celebrated in the mythic banquet on the mountain of God in the wilderness story, as the seventy elders of Israel "saw God, ate and drank." It is found in the table Yahweh spreads for his flock (Ps 23:5). Such is the peace ever present in holy war themes.

Yahweh's war against the nations (Canaan plus eleven nations: Gen 10:15–19), which echoes Marduk's war against Tiamat and the eleven monsters of the Babylonian creation story, finds its *shalom* in a scene in Ezekiel, which parallels the book of Ezra's story of the temple. In a vision from exile (Ez 40–48) Ezekiel describes a new temple, a new Israel and a new Jerusalem. He draws a picture of a return to paradise and the tree of life. Water springs up from the temple platform (cf. Gen 2:6, 10–14) and becomes a great stream flowing into the Arabah, giving life to every living creature.[41] Fishermen will stand on the banks of the Dead Sea, which will be lined with trees whose leaves do not wither (cf. Ps 1:3). Ezekiel's vision then divides the land in a new inheritance, reversing the disaster of Joshua's covenant. In this division, the vision illustrates the Torah's great command to "Love your neighbor as yourself" (Lev 19:18), reminding us of Moses and his Cushite wife, of Boaz and Ruth, of Abraham, Ishmael, Esau and Joseph and their wives. Ezekiel's land is an inheritance to both Israel and foreigners with their children: "The foreigner among you becomes as one of Israel's sons" to be given his share in the land where he lives (Ez 47:22–23).[42] The ironic critique of Ezra's revision of Ezekiel's temple is implicit. Ezra opens his book by interpreting Cyrus's decree of return as a fulfillment of the prophecy that Jeremiah had written in a letter to the exiles in Babylon, announcing the closure of the exile "when Babylon's seventy years are over" (Jer 29:10). While Ezekiel closes his vision and his book on the note that from the day on which his new Jerusalem will be named: "Yahweh is there," Jeremiah's prophecy opens in a declaration reiterating Moses' promise of the Torah: "You will seek Yahweh your God and you will find him, if you search after him with all your heart and with all your soul" (Dt 4:29). When Israel, accordingly, calls and prays and seeks Yahweh, he will answer and hear and be found by them (Jer 29:12–14). As Jerusalem is under siege and about to be destroyed by the Babylonians, Jeremiah prophesies a new Jerusalem. He identifies the suffering of the people as the path to understanding. In the new Zion, they will be Yahweh's people and he will be their God (Jer 30:22, 31). Their destiny will be turned. They had been scattered but now they will be gathered: mourning will be turned to joy (Jer 31:10, 13). At the center of this prophecy of the new Jerusalem come tears of suffering. First come the mothers, weeping for the dead; but they are comforted; the suffering had purpose (Jer 31:16). Then Ephraim's tears are given as the sign that he has been successfully chastised. Yahweh will receive his prodigal child in love (Jer 31:18, 20).

An even closer variant to Ezekiel's vision comes in the closing songs of Isaiah (Is 64–66), which address the theme of holy war's *shalom* directly. Jerusalem's destiny is determined as Yahweh dissolves his curse of the city with the blessing that Ezra and his people sought in their new Jerusalem. Hatreds of the past are forgotten, to be hidden even from God's eyes. A new earth and a new heaven are created (Is 65:16–17). The garden story's snake is eternally tamed (Is 65:25). With Ezekiel and the book of Revelation, Isaiah gathers all the nations into his new Jerusalem (Is 66:18–21). In contrast, the book of Ezra celebrates no *shalom*, and the Jerusalem that the priest Ezra and the remnant of Israel rebuild is not the new Jerusalem of Isaiah, Jeremiah or Ezekiel. It is the Jerusalem of the past, trapped in a never-ending story.

CHAPTER 9

ᕃ᠖ᕐ

Good King, Bad King

THE PROBLEM WITH THE HISTORY OF KINGS

The central biblical texts of the debate about history and the Bible are no longer the stories of creation, or those about Abraham, Moses, Joshua's conquest or even the stories about a united monarchy or an imperial Jerusalem under David and Solomon. All of these narratives are widely recognized as unhistorical. The history of Palestine of both the Bronze and Early Iron Age has rapidly learned to proceed independently of biblical traditions. Some historians may still wish to speak of a historical David or even a state centered in Jerusalem, but neither such a David nor the state resemble what we find in the Bible.[1] The debate today centers on the books of 1–2 Kings. This is not inappropriate, as this work, unlike most books of the Hebrew Bible, often deals with persons known to be historical—kings such as Omri, Ahab, Joash, Jehu, Menahem, Pekah, Hosea, Ahaz, Hezekiah, Manasseh and Jehoiakin, whose names also appear in cuneiform texts. Historical events are discussed in these narratives in large number—including major military events that radically altered the history of the region, like the campaign of Pharaoh Sheshonk at the end of the tenth century or the conquest of Samaria in the eighth. Also great events of imperial politics that occurred outside of Palestine are discussed, like the assassination of Sennacherib, the king of Assyria.

The tales of Kings are arranged in an order of succession from Solomon to Jehoiakin. Shorter or longer accounts are given for each king's reign in a chain that synchronizes the rulers of Jerusalem with those of Samaria. Some of the stories included have the structure and character of tales, much like those of David or Abraham—for example, the parable of Naboth's vineyard, in which Ahab and Jezebel have an innocent man killed because they want to take his property (1 Kgs 21). Nearly half of the chain of narrative, however, is filled by a stereotyped mock chronicle that judges each king in turn as having done good or evil in Yahweh's eyes. This judgment chronicle has transformed central themes from the myth of the good king to project a divine judgment over the kings of Samaria and Jerusalem. It describes whether the king improved the temple or whether it was plundered, whether other cult places were left standing, whether the worship of other gods was favored and whether the king suffered. The fate of Israel and the house of David is balanced on this ancient scale of justice. The coming day of reckoning, "The day of Yahweh," is decided or delayed by judgments of curse or blessing.

The story of the sevenfold plundering of Jerusalem's temple from Sheshonk to Nebuchadnezzar does not recount historical events. It is a single narrative retold many times that all of David's sons might be implicated in the theft of the gold and wonders of Solomon's temple. The narrative as a whole is structured as a story of hubris and fall from grace. Its content is parabolic rather than historical. The plundering stories of Kings develop a version of the story of the seven-headed dragon in a form that is reiterated in similar literary compositions of early Judaism. The Jewish Roman writer of the first century CE, Josephus, wrote stories about the expansionist policies of the late second century BCE king of Jerusalem, John Hyrcanus, against the Samaritans of Gerizim and against Edom. These tales can be compared in detail with the stories of Josiah in 2 Kings, 2 Chronicles and 1 Esdras. The stories of the reforms of Hezekiah and Josiah, as the stories of the rebuilding of Jerusalem under Zerubbabel and the striving for a true Jerusalem under the Maccabees, reflect a comparable imitative rewriting. Whether we are dealing with themes, like the death of the king, the plundering of the temple or cult reform, or whether we are dealing with stereotypical conflicts between Judah and Edom, Jerusalem and Samaria or the Canaanites and Israel, the point of departure lies in other texts and stories available to the writer, not events of the past. In the complex, patterned stories of Kings, four of Jerusalem's rulers follow in David and Solomon's steps by building up, repairing and reforming the temple: Asa (1 Kgs 15:9–24), Joash (2 Kgs 12), Hezekiah (2 Kgs 18–20; cf. 2 Chr 29–32) and Josiah (2 Kgs 22–23). These are set in sharp contrast to four kings who are assigned roles of antireform. They take part in the plundering of the temple, build high places or worship idols: Rehoboam (1 Kgs 12), Ahaz (2 Kgs 16), Manasseh (2 Kgs 21:1–17) and Amon (2 Kgs 21:17–26). As Manasseh epitomizes all that is evil with kingship, Josiah plays the good king.

He is ever "good King Josiah." Though judged good in Yahweh's eyes, the reigns of Asa, Joash and Hezekiah are flawed. In spite of these reforms, each shared in plundering the temple in efforts to bribe the foreign kings Ben Hadad, Hazael and Sennacherib and find peace. Each in turn also meets his punishment: Asa dies a cripple and Joash is assassinated. Hezekiah, though his death is delayed for the sake of his role as Jerusalem's representative, is condemned to death by Yahweh. In contrast, good King Josiah is blessed with an early death.

THE SWORD OVER DAVID'S HOUSE

Regicide, death in battle or exile is a frequent closure to the lives of the sons of David. Among all the implications of this theme, I limit myself to Josiah's hardly heroic death at the hands of Pharaoh Neco and some of the stories it echoes. In 2 Kings, a single verse suffices to tell the story: "King Josiah went up against him and he killed him at Megiddo when he saw him" (2 Kgs 23:29). In the variant found in the book of Chronicles, the story of the king's death is more substantial:

Neco, King of Egypt, went up to fight at Carchemish on the Euphrates and Josiah went out against him. But he [Neco] sent envoys to him, saying "What have we to do with each other, king of Judah? I am not coming against you this day, but against the house with which I am at war; and God has commanded me to make haste. Cease opposing God, who is with me, lest he destroy you." Nevertheless, Josiah would not turn away from him, but disguised himself in order to fight with him. He did not listen to the words of Neco from the mouth of God, but joined battle in the plain of Megiddo. And the archers shot King Josiah; and the king said to his servants, "Take me away for I am badly wounded." So his servants took him out of the chariot and took him in his second chariot and brought him to Jerusalem. And he died and was buried in the tombs of his fathers. All Judah and Jerusalem mourned for Josiah. Jeremiah also uttered a lament for Josiah. (2 Chr 35:20–25)

Chronicles' story of Josiah's death is a variant of a type scene, which Shakespeare, for instance, gave to Richard II. Chronicles—along with Kings— gives this role to Ahab (1 Kgs 22; var. 2 Chr 18). In this story, Jehoshaphat, Jerusalem's king, and Ahab, the king of Israel, fight against Syria. Their prophets have promised them victory, but the true prophet, Micaiah, cryptically predicts death. Not knowing who the true prophet is, Israel's king tries to hide from his fate by disguising himself. The stakes are raised as the Syrian king instructs his thirty-two captains to fight only the king of Israel. While Ahab hides in disguise, Jehoshaphat is mistaken for him and his life threatened until his true identity is exposed. The plot is finally resolved by an archer who shoots an arrow into the air. Falling and guided by the grace of God, the arrow strikes the king of Israel. He is taken from the battle and dies in his chariot. In the version of this scene in the Chronicles Josiah story, Pharaoh Neco plays the true prophet who warns Josiah. Like Ahab, Josiah refuses to listen to Yahweh's true prophet and tries to hide from his fate by disguising himself, only to be shot by the archers and forced to leave the field. With Yahweh, it does not serve to hide or not to hide. The story closes on the theme of mourning "until this day."[2]

While Chronicles has Josiah die for not listening to Yahweh's true prophet, Kings tells a story of Josiah's violent death *because of* his goodness. Josiah has the same "unique" virtue as Hezekiah. He fulfilled the law of Moses with a pure heart (cf. Dt 6:5) and in goodness, he was also without peer before or since (cf. 2 Kgs 18:5–6; 23:25). Nevertheless, Yahweh's anger and determination to reject Jerusalem and its king rushes Josiah to a fate his grandfather Manasseh had determined (2 Kgs 23:26–27). The behavior or virtue of kings does not determine Jerusalem's fate. It is Yahweh's choice of blessing or curse. Such fateful logic is stressed already at the beginning of David's story in Hannah's prophetic version of the song for a poor man, determining the fate of both king and pauper: "Yahweh kills and he makes live; he brings down to *she'ol* and he raises up (1 Sm 2:6). Hezekiah was the one he raised up, turning not only Ahaz's sundial but history's clock backward fifteen years (2 Kgs 20:4–11).[3]

The plotline of the story of Samuel-Kings also has a narrative reason for Josiah's violent death. As the reiterated motif of failing to listen to Yahweh's prophet determines the story in Chronicles, in Kings a chain of narrative is defined by Solomon's prayer. This prayer pits its irresistible principle—that judgment fall on the guilty one alone (1 Kgs 8:32)—against its unmovable fact: "No man is without sin" (1 Kgs 8:46). The irony and logic anchoring Solomon's prayer is patent: no man can avoid judgment and all are subjects of Yahweh's mercy. Solomon's riddle finds its roots in a matching tale of David's sin (2 Sm 24). Together, they open a discourse on guilt and collective punishment. Tempted to undertake a forbidden census, David measures his own strength in war, rather than trusting in Yahweh (2 Sm 24:9). When a repentant David finally confesses his sin, Yahweh gives him a choice between collective or individual justice: three years famine, three months flight from his enemies or three days plague.[4]

The greater story's turning point had taught David to trust in Yahweh rather than himself. In flight from his son Absalom, abandoned by his friends and in a state of despair, David finally learned to play the role given to him by the

Psalter: he sought his refuge in Yahweh alone and walked in the path of righteousness (Ps 1–2). Climbing the Mount of Olives, where—the text tells us—one is "wont to go to pray" (2 Sm 15:32), he plays the role of piety's representative and illustrates the power of prayer. The role is given to him by Psalm 3 for just this occasion: "When he fled from his son Absalom" (Ps 3:1). "My enemies are many; they rise against me; they say: God will not save him" (Ps 3:2–3). There is nothing left of David's greatness when he sets out to climb to his final refuge on the Mount of Olives, where one is wont to bow before God (2 Sm 15:32). He weeps as he climbs. He is barefoot; his head is bowed; everyone who is with him bows his head and weeps. As David escapes the Jerusalem he himself built, where he no longer has a refuge, he speaks to his friend Zadok ("righteousness," "discernment") and expresses his saving wish. He finds wisdom's key that unlocks his story:

> If I find favor with Yahweh, he will bring me back and let me see the ark and its dwelling place once again. But if he says he does not want me, then here I am; let him do what he pleases with me. (1 Sm 15:25–26)

David is here humanity's representative and Yahweh's servant, climbing his mountain in humility. His prayer heard, he crosses over the mountain with his kingship renewed and returns to Jerusalem, riding on a donkey.[5]

The logic of the census story is subtle. Having been emptied of self-will in his story's climax on the Mount of Olives, David now uses this same "refuge in Yahweh" to his own benefit in an effort to turn his fate from judgment. Preferring Yahweh's mercy to his own never-ending story of flight from the hands of men, he chooses the nation's suffering to his own. On the first day of wrath, however, Yahweh himself is horrified at the terrible plague. As seventy thousand die in a single day, Yahweh reacts as he did in the great flood. He repents of his evil and stops the angel on the threshing floor. Such an angel also appears in Jeremiah's vision of "the spirit of the destroyer," who sends "threshers to thresh" Babylon. The figure of destruction in Jeremiah is a double image: the punishing arm of the thresher stretched out to beat the grain serves the image of judgment and punishment from the angel of death. The threshing also brings salvation, freeing Israel's grain from its chaff. Doubly so, the threshers' *(zarim)* outstretched arms are equally the outstretched arms of the sower, planting grain *(zara')*, preparing a new spring (Jer 51:2; cf. Is 6:3). With the grain threshed on the first day of wrath, Yahweh's repentance transfers itself to David. A repentant king now wishes to take up his more fitting role of shepherd of his people. Horrified as the plague turns toward Jerusalem, David humbly confesses: "I have sinned; I have done wickedly; but these sheep, what have they done?" (2 Sm 24:17a). In the eleventh hour, David finally passes his test and prays for a more fitting judgment: "Let your hand strike me and my father's house" (2 Sm 24:17b).

The census story finds its parallel in the story of Nathan's judgment of David for the murder of Uriah (2 Sm 12:10)—a variant story of David's "only sin" (so 1 Kgs 15:5) and a reiteration of the myth of the god of war Ares, who hated the lame Hephaestus and slept with his wife, Aphrodite. Hephaestus avenged himself with a net so fine it could not be seen and so strong it could not be broken. From this adultery, Harmonia ("peace") was born.

In the biblical version of this legend, judgment follows the logic of retribution. Because David killed his faithful servant by the sword, the sword will never leave David's house. This judgment's reference to Uriah being cut down by the Ammonite's sword creates a typical "blind motif" of traditional narrative. In the story itself, Uriah is shot with an arrow (cf. 2 Sm 11:24; 2 Sm 12:9–10), with resonance from the death of Josiah scene in Chronicles. The sword of retribution in Nathan's judgment is the two-edged sword of Near Eastern holy war tradition: the magic sword given by the gods to their chosen king to use in battle, well-known in Egyptian inscriptions. In the Great Karnak Inscription, Merneptah dreams that the statue of Ptah gives him the "sword that banishes all fear."[6] In a scene on the Cairo column, a god gives pharaoh a sword with which to destroy the chiefs of Libya.[7] The famous Israel stele uses its magic sword as a sign of recognition of Merneptah's role as son of god, sitting on the throne of Shu.[8] Used in obedience to the divine commander of holy war, it defeats every enemy. In the garden story, this magic weapon is a flaming sword that cuts in all directions: invincible (Gen 3:24). In David's story, he receives the sword of wonder when the priest Ahimelek gives him Goliath's weapon, as David flees from Saul (1 Sm 21:9). Because David has used the sword of holy war for his own purposes, however, it turns against its possessor and becomes the eternal fate of his dynasty.

As the sword over David's house takes the form of a leitmotif and casts its threatening shadow over the stories of David's sons, one finds echoes of it in many of the smaller tales and scenes that the David story has attracted. Four quick giant tales are tied to the list of David's thirty heroes (2 Sm 21:18–22) and expanded with tales and anecdotes (2 Sm 23:8–39). One of the best of these uses three of David's heroes to tell a parable. David is thirsty and asks his men for water. Like a spoiled Egyptian princess, with her every whim a precise demand,[9] David does not want just any water. He wants the water from the cistern beside the gate of Bethel. That the gate is in enemy hands is beneath the notice of such a great king. He wants that water! Good soldiers all and wishing only to fulfill their king's least wish, David's faithful heroes break through the Philistine camp and bring him his water. Realizing what his soldiers have done, David is abhorred by his own God-miming hubris, causing his trusty men to risk their lives. He repents, refuses to drink the water lest he be guilty of his own men's blood and offers the water to Yahweh. Having sent his heroes into battle, David owes that holy war booty to his patron (2 Sm 23:13–17).

David's repentance—with the motifs of whim and water and causing a faithful hero to risk his life at the gate—is a reflection on the tale of Uriah. In the stories of the water and the census, David sinned against God. In the story of the murder of Uriah, however, his sin was against man (cf. David's argument against Saul in 1 Sm 26:20–21). His desire for a woman in his water had even greater whimsy than his thirst (2 Sm 11:2–6). When Bathsheba becomes pregnant, David sets her husband—one of his thirty heroes, willing to risk all for his whims (2 Sm 23:39)—at risk that, when he is killed, David might marry Bathsheba. The murder is set in the story of Joab's siege of Rabbah (2 Sm 11–12). It is told to the rhythm of dispatches, received and sent. One brings news of Uriah's death shot by an archer from the city gate (2 Sm 11:21).[10] In the story of David and the woman in the bath, Uriah's lifeblood is bought, like that of the king of Israel and Josiah, by an arrow shot by chance (2 Sm 11:14–21; 2 Chr 35:23; 1 Kgs 22; 2 Chr 18), as he pays a loyal servant's price for his king's whim. The arrow becomes sword when the author sends his reader a dispatch through David: "The sword eats both one and the other" (2 Sm 11:25). This two-edged sword exposes the destiny of David's family to retribution.[11] When David marries the woman from the bath, which the husband's death at "Watertown" (2 Sm 12:27; 13:27) had won, neither his fate nor the sword find rest. Judgment falls, appropriately, from David's own mouth, himself judging Yahweh's parable through the prophet Nathan:

There were two men in a certain city, the one rich and the other poor. The rich man had many flocks and herds, but the poor man had nothing but one little ewe lamb, which he had bought. He raised it and it grew up with him and his children. It used to eat of his small bit and drink from his cup and lie in his bosom. It was like a daughter to him. Now there came a traveler to the rich man, but he was unwilling to take from his own flock or herd to prepare for the wayfarer who had come to him. He took the poor man's lamb and served it to the man who had come to him. (2 Sm 12:1–4; cf. Gen 18)

"As Yahweh lives, the man who would do such a thing must die." King David decrees in anger and his words judge the rich man of Nathan's parable—a man who would steal a poor man's only possession. Such a man was David (2 Sm 12:5). In punishment, fitting the crime, the child of his sin must die, opening a parallel story (2 Sm 12:7–14).

As Sennacherib's death came at the hands of his own son in the Hezekiah story (2 Kgs 19:37), David's punishment comes from his own house as his dynasty is caught in the conspiracies of the great. His wives are taken by the one dearest to him. While David sinned in secret, his wives are taken in broad daylight.[12] The price for the rape of Bathsheba is paid by David's ten wives, raped by his son Absalom. As the story progresses, retribution offers the would-be patricide a similar fate. Escaping a bounty of ten shekels on his head, he has his head caught fast in an oak tree, where—in brutal mockery of a would-be messiah—Absalom finds his "balance between heaven and earth" (2 Sm 18:9; cf. Ps 8:6). The anointed Absalom is murdered by Joab with three arrows to the heart and with the blows of ten armor bearers (2 Sm 18:16), as the story turns retribution into prophecy. The ten northern tribes of Israel, with their ten shares in David (cf. 2 Sm 19:44), are as lost to the great king (2 Sm 20:1–2) as his ten wives, who became "widows of a living husband" (2 Sm 20:3).

Like Ahab in the story of Naboth's vineyard, David coveted the property of his servant by falling in love with the man's wife. After David successfully arranges Uriah's murder, his punishment determines the destiny of his house and the plotline of the larger narrative of 1–2 Kings: a double-edged sword of his own violence. The curse opens a Pandora's box of tales that ultimately destroy all of David's sons—even good King Josiah, whom the author of Kings describes as having "turned to Yahweh with his whole heart and soul and with all his might. . . . but still Yahweh did not turn away from his wrath" (2 Kgs 23:25–26). The first of his house who pays for this crime, as we have seen, was Bathsheba's child. In David's story, repentance and his child's death function to delay Yahweh's wrath in David's lifetime—a motif famously reused in Hezekiah's story to bring peace in his lifetime.

Bathsheba's grief is comforted with a new child, whom Yahweh decides to love. David calls him Solomon ("peace"), but Yahweh names him Jedediah ("Yahweh's beloved"). Yahweh, who loved David (*dwd* "the beloved"), will now love his son, who is again the youngest with seven brothers and will play David to a new generation. In his story in the book of Kings, the grown Solomon will be put to the test by the abundance of Yahweh's blessing: his wealth, women and wisdom. The competition and wordplay over Solomon's name at his birth marks the difference between David's and Yahweh's purpose. David will have peace, but

Yahweh craves a love he would have had from David. The wordplay on David's name also marks the plotline's direction toward the tale of good King Josiah, the son of Jedida (2 Kgs 22:2), in which Yahweh's love for Josiah gathers him to his grave in mercy, his eyes spared from seeing Jerusalem's disaster (2 Kgs 22:20).

THE GREAT PEACE THAT SHOULD HAVE BEEN SOLOMON'S

The relationship between the temple and a king's responsibility for protecting it is not new to the book of Kings. In monumental inscriptions, the good king reverses former suffering by dealing with the gods' anger through temple repair and cultic reform. In Esarhaddon's inscription (Appendix 2, no. 4), the king describes earlier evil days, when the gods were angry and planned evil. Like Yahweh (Jer 25:11–12; 29:10), Marduk cursed Babylon. It became an empty desert and its people were sent into exile for seventy years. Babylon's savior, Esarhaddon is called from among his elder brothers. Also like David, he is chosen by Marduk to rule his empire. While the biblical King Josiah discovered God's will in the law code he found in the temple (2 Kgs 22:8–13), and Hezekiah found equally divine guidance by consulting the prophet Isaiah (Is 37:2), Esarhaddon used oracles. They encouraged him to rebuild and restore the temple of Babylon: Esagila. As in the myth of the good king, he returns the gods to their proper place and frees the enslaved from bondage. In a modest variant of David's prayer to Yahweh after being saved from all his enemies (2 Sm 7:1, 18–29), Esarhaddon prays that his seed, the temple Esagila and Babylon itself would last forever.

In the inscriptions of Babylon's King Nabonidus (Appendix 2, nos. 6–7), the god Marduk was responsible, like Yahweh (Is 37:21–38), for the murder of Sennacherib. Nabonidus also went into mourning for the sins of the Mandeans, much as the repentant Josiah mourned for the sins of Judah (2 Kgs 22:11–13). Nabonidus set himself the task of restoring the temple and true cult to his city. In contrast, his Persian successor, Cyrus, tells a tale of a godless Nabonidus (Appendix 2, no. 8), whose impiety Cyrus contrasts with his own piety. The evil of Nabonidus is reversed by the good king Cyrus, who (like Nebuchadnezzar before him; Appendix 2, no. 5) brought both gods and people back from exile and restored the temple to its proper worship. This same Cyrus, in the story of Ezra, ends Jeremiah's seventy years of exile (Ezra 1:1; cf. also 2 Chr 36:21–23). Like Hezekiah and Josiah (2 Kgs 18:3–8; 23:1–24), Xerxes destroys temples and cults of evil gods and returns the people to the one true worship of the god of heaven, Ahuramazda: "What had been done in a bad way is now done in a good way"

(Appendix 2, no. 9). In Mesha's stele (Appendix 2, no. 21), the Moabite king twice removes elements of Yahweh worship from the cult and returns both cult and shrine to the proper allegiance of his god Chemosh.

Such examples can be multiplied, for the "events" behind the Hezekiah and Josiah stories belong to a cluster of narrative elements with roots reaching as far back as the third millennium tales of Egyptian Pharaohs and, indeed, the Gilgamesh Epic. In an "envelope narrative" closing and opening the long story of the king's adventures, Gilgamesh rebuilds the walls of Uruk and the temple of Inanna.[13] Most royal inscriptions connect themes of temple restoration and cult reform to the celebration of an ideal and often eternal peace, resulting from holy war's success. Biblical narrative sets its building projects into a pattern of cyclical recurrence to better serve a never-ending story. For example, in the Judges cycle of twelve saviors, war comes when Israel does "evil in Yahweh's eyes." Each successive savior has the task of returning Israel to Yahweh's peace. As this cycle continues in the stories of David and his sons, the understanding of such divinely inspired peace is dominated by a single figure, Solomon, and the story of his building the temple in Jerusalem (1 Kgs 5:15–8:66).

In Solomon's story, the temple is constructed in the twentieth year of his reign. Rather than an eternal *shalom,* Solomon's glory serves as prelude and contrast to the reign of sin, which follows, as Solomon multiplies horses, wives, silver and gold in fulfillment of Moses' prophecy:

> When you come to the land, which Yahweh your God gives you, and you possess it and dwell in it and then say, "I will set a king over me, like all the nations round about me," you may indeed set as king over him whom Yahweh, your God, will choose. . . . Only, he must not multiply horses for himself, or cause the people to return to Egypt, since Yahweh has said to you, you must never return that way again. And he must not multiply wives for himself lest his heart turn away. Nor must he greatly multiply silver and gold for himself. (Dt 17:14–17)[14]

The theme of a golden age celebrating the union of God's will with the king ruling as his servant and building him a temple is given to Solomon as a test. The temple's entire floor and its decorations, the inner sanctuary, the altar and the cherubim are covered with gold (1 Kgs 6:15–35).

Solomon's story is controlled by two meetings with Yahweh in visions. The first marks his rise to glory; the second his fall from grace. The first comes at the beginning of his reign, in a dream when he is at Gibeon, after sacrificing at the high place. Yahweh presents Solomon with the classic wonderland test of true wisdom: "Ask what you will; it will be granted" (1 Kgs 3:1–14). The story hangs on what is chosen. Ignoring riches, a long life and the death of his enemy, Solomon wisely asks for discernment of good and evil—that great virtue, eluding mankind since the garden story (Gen 2:9). With an "understanding heart," Solomon would judge over a folk so large they cannot be counted (1 Kgs 3:9). However, just as this story echoes Moses' unsuccessful effort to judge his uncountable folk in the wilderness (Ex 18:13–18), the story of Solomon's wisdom foreshadows the failures of the past in order to begin the tale of the fall of the sons of David. For the moment, the reader is given epitome of a good king's reign: "Solomon loved Yahweh, walking in the path of his father David. He had but a single fault. He offered incense on the high places" (1 Kgs 3:3). Solomon's reign begins a chain of narrative with the leitmotif of a king who does good in Yahweh's eyes yet does not remove the high places. This stereotyped formula, as it is used and reused in the following stories, faults each of David's sons who did right in Yahweh's eyes, except Hezekiah and Josiah.

That Solomon's two visions measure Solomon's rise and fall is also implied by the parable of Solomon's wisdom. The parable presents the positive side of a Janus-faced Solomon, marking the essence of the narrative of 1–2 Kings as a whole. Two prostitutes come to Solomon for judgment. One has a living child and the other, a child dead. Each claims the living child as her own (1 Kgs 3:15–28). In his judgment Solomon shows himself a Hebrew Alexander. He recommends that the living child be divided by his sword. He knows that the true mother can tell the difference between a child and a knot and will surrender her son to her competitor. The parable closes as Solomon restores the child to his mother. Such is the divine wisdom by which Solomon governs his people.[15]

In Solomon's twentieth year, at the midpoint of his career, the king has a second vision (1 Kgs 9:1–9). It comes at the height of his greatness (1 Kgs 9:1–9). The story evokes Moses' prophecy of destruction, when Israel's king no longer does "what is good in Yahweh's eyes" (Dt 4:26; 8:19–20; 28:36; 30:19; 31:28). He pointed ahead to the story of Solomon collecting gods along with his foreign wives. As in the parable of the two whores, Solomon has the whole of Israel as his audience (1 Kgs 8:22–53), especially the failed Israel of the future. He asks that Yahweh forgive the people's sins (1 Kgs 8:34). "No man is without sin" (1 Kgs 8:46), he argues and speaks for all future sons of David. He foresees that Israel will finally turn to God in defeat, having sinned and repented with a pure heart. He prays that the future Israel be allowed to return from exile. The prayer speaks with a voice of a repentant, postdestruction Jerusalem. With the parable of the mothers and its interpretation in Solomon's prayer, the narrative in Kings turns into a never-ending story (cf. 2 Macc 2:17–18).[16]

PLUNDERING THE TEMPLE:
FROM SOLOMON TO ZEDEKIAH

In the story opened by Solomon's prophetic prayer, the theme of plundering the temple fatally undermines the greatness of Solomon's glory. It implicates all of David's sons in Jerusalem's fate. "No man is without sin," declares Solomon, the philosopher. An affront to divine patronage is marked in the stripping of divinely intimate gold from the inner sanctuary. Plundering the temple, we saw in Chapter 5, is a stock element of royal inscriptions. It is used to express the theme of former suffering: past sin that the chosen king's reign reverses. In biblical stories, it is Yahweh's temple that is plundered and the theme serves as one of several that provoke and justify divine retribution. Because Solomon's heart turned away from Yahweh (1 Kgs 11:9ff.), the union of his kingdom was lost long before his son Rehoboam comes to the throne. As in the story of David before him, Jerusalem's fate, though already sealed, is delayed in Solomon's lifetime. Already in preparing for Solomon's coming death, Jerusalem is displaced as the divine center of this world. Yahweh's anger brings Edom and Damascus into revolt against Solomon.

After Solomon's death, Jerusalem becomes and remains a small provincial town. Its glory resides in a failed past. Solomon's son Rehoboam goes to Shechem to be proclaimed king, where "all Israel" asks the new king to lighten their burdens. In hubris, Rehoboam increases their burdens and Israel revolts as God had planned (1 Kgs 11:29–40; 12:24). Solomon's son is left to rule the single tribe of Judah, and that only for David's sake. In an epitome of Jerusalem's corruption (1 Kgs 14:21–31), two scenes are offered as cause and effect. In the first, idols and male prostitutes are brought into the temple where Yahweh's name had been. Yahweh is provoked to jealous anger. In the second scene, Yahweh's anger brings Pharaoh Shishak to plunder the temple. He strips the temple of everything, including the golden shields Solomon had made. King Rehoboam replaces Yahweh's gold with brass, haplessly ordering his captain to guard this "treasure." The king's reign closes on war with Israel.

King Asa's heart was pure (1 Kgs 15:9–24). He reforms Jerusalem's cult, removes idols and prostitutes and—although, like Solomon, leaving high places—gives the temple gifts of gold and silver. With this good king's reign firmly established on a positive note, his enemy, the king of Israel, builds a fortress at Ramah and prepares to besiege Jerusalem. Asa removes the remaining treasure from the temple and sends it to Ben Hadad in Damascus, successfully bribing him to break his treaty with Israel. Ben Hadad forces Israel to lift the siege. Using stones from

Ramah for balance, Asa goes on a building campaign to celebrate the "peace" he has bought. Asa's reign closes on a negative note: "In his old age he was diseased in his feet" (1 Kgs 15:23). Having plundered his patron's temple, this lame man's peace is hardly a peace following holy war. Rather than trusting in Yahweh as David had done, Asa bribed and bought protection from a man.

The plundering of the temple theme dominates a similar story in the reign of another good king who did not remove the high places (2 Kgs 11:1–12:21). Joash had been raised secretly in the temple when a boy and came to power in the wake of a religious reform. The priest leading the reform made a covenant between Yahweh, the king and the people. This story is dominated by the repair of the temple, which is decorated with rich illustrations of the king's honesty. In a closing episode, Hazael of Syria threatens to attack Jerusalem (2 Kgs 12:17). Like Asa before him, Joash fails to seek refuge in Yahweh and instead takes the votive offerings and gold from the temple and bribes Hazael. Unsurprisingly and in implicit retribution, this clay-footed king is killed through a court conspiracy. His son was also a good king, but Amaziah failed to remove the high places (2 Kgs 14:1–20). He begins his story by executing his father's assassins and defeating Edom in war. Peace, however, hardly marks his reign. The king of Israel captures him, destroys Jerusalem's walls and plunders the temple of gold and silver. Fifteen years later, Amaziah is murdered after a conspiracy chases him from the city.

King Ahaz (2 Kgs 16:1–20), like Solomon's first son, Rehoboam, was a bad king who reversed the reforms of the kings before him. In retribution, Syria and Israel together besieged Jerusalem. True to the story's pattern (if not to his God and true overlord), Ahaz takes silver and gold from the temple and bribes the king of Assyria to save him. Echoing the story of Rehoboam's bronze shields, Ahaz replaces the temple's altar with an exact copy of an altar his new patron showed him in Damascus. He dies at peace with the Assyrians as Yahweh prepares himself for war.

In the Kings version of Isaiah's Hezekiah story (Is 36–39; 2 Kgs 18:1–20:21), the theme of plundering reaches its climax. In bringing the Hezekiah story into the Kings narrative, two important scenes are added to Isaiah's story and harmonized with a reference to Samaria's fall to the Assyrian army (cf. 2 Kgs 18:9–11; 2 Kgs 17:5–7, 18). The first scene is a variation on the theme of cult reform (2 Kgs 18:3–6). It is told in the same manner as in the stories of the good kings, Asa (1 Kgs 15:11–14) and Joash (2 Kgs 11:17–18; 12:2–3). Hezekiah surpasses these kings, however. He is the first of Jerusalem's kings to remove the high places. In this brief episode, Hezekiah, like Amaziah before him, obeys Yahweh's Torah. The second scene added to Isaiah's story is told in the pattern of the stories of Ahaz, Asa and Joash (2 Kgs 18:13–16; cf. 2 Kgs 12:18; 15:18–21; 16:7–8). Hezekiah saves Jerusalem by bribing Sennacherib with the gold and silver of the temple. Hezekiah strips the gold from the doors of Yahweh's temple. While the center of Isaiah's story deals with the saving of a remnant Jerusalem under siege through pious tears and prayer, the 2 Kings revision creates irony by having the story's closure echo its beginning.[17] It starts with Hezekiah plundering the temple and closes by having Hezekiah evoke the future plundering of the temple by the Babylonians. A backsliding Hezekiah plays generous host and shows his Babylonian guests from the future his treasure house (Is 39:1–7; 2 Kgs 20:12–19). Hezekiah's flirtation with the great powers of this world hardly presents him in a positive light.

While the closure of Hezekiah's story in the book of Isaiah rushes Jerusalem into exile that the audience might hear the saving cadences of the song of comfort in Isaiah 40 for a new remnant saved, Kings uses the reigns of Hezekiah's son Manasseh (2 Kgs 21:3–18) and his grandson Amon (2 Kgs 21:19–26) to undermine and reverse all of Hezekiah's reforms. The author builds a flattering contrast for the narrative's great reform under Josiah (2 Kgs 23:1–8). Josiah's reign offers an expansive double story of temple repair and cult reform, following the patterns of the stories of Asa and Joash, only to close his tragic story with scenes of destruction and deportation under Jehoiakin and Zedekiah. Nebuchadnezzar is not bribed. Like Shishak (1 Kgs 14:25–26) and Israel's own Joash (2 Kgs 14:14), he strips the temple (2 Kgs 24:10–13) and steals Solomon's ever-plunderable gold. This scene is itself reiterated in the city's final collapse in Zedekiah's reign. Nebuchadnezzar burns the temple and, in a cluster of variable motifs, takes from it all the copper furniture and utensils—even the great pillars Solomon built, and, yes, again, gold and silver (2 Kgs 25:13–17). The episode closes a sevenfold reiteration of Shishak's plundering of Jerusalem's temple treasury, which provides Kings with its dominant narrative structure. The recycled story of Hezekiah becomes its central example of how Judah's kings feared men rather than God. All of David's sons are implicated in the plundering of Yahweh's temple. The Kings story of the tragic fall of the House of David includes no good kings.

The episode of Sennacherib's plundering the temple (2 Kgs 18:14–16) allows Kings to integrate Isaiah's story about Hezekiah (Is 36–39) as part of a sevenfold reiteration of Pharaoh Shishak's theft of Solomon's gold. The Kings story of Josiah not only follows but supersedes the story of Hezekiah (cf. 2 Chr 29–32). This king not only rids Jerusalem of the idolatry of Manasseh and Solomon (2 Kgs 23:12–13), he tears down the altar at Bethel. He successfully undoes the original sin of Jeroboam that had determined the path of Israel and the greater story's plotline since the northern kingdom first refused to follow Solomon's son.[18] This integration of Isaiah's narrative strengthens the good king–bad king structure in Kings with a similar pattern of reform and antireform. Rehoboam builds high places, sacred pillars and poles dedicated to the goddess Asherah. His crime is reiterated by Ahaz, Manasseh and Amon. They are matched by four reform kings: Asa (1 Kgs 15:9–24), Jehoash (2 Kgs 12), Hezekiah (2 Kgs 18–20; 2 Chr 29–32) and Josiah (2 Kgs 22–23; 2 Chr 34–35), striking a climax in the completeness of Manasseh's sin and Josiah's reform.[19]

A similar discursive reiteration of the themes of reform and antireform, of rededication and failure to rededicate and of plundering and desecrating the temple alternates with victory scenes in the books of 1–2 Maccabees. This structure is more than can be discussed here. Under the genre of rewritten Bible, these techniques used by the books of Maccabees are well recognized in recent scholarship. The role of such techniques in biblical narrative, however, is less acknowledged.[20] 1 Maccabees displays a rhetoric similar to that of Kings. Both 1 and 2 Maccabees have seven stories marking Antioch's decline and offer their own version of the seven-headed dragon of Assyria. This sevenfold pattern is matched in 1 Maccabees by a series of reiterations, soaked in biblical allusion. The structure not only creates laments over victim Jerusalem but also presents corresponding resurrection stories, celebrations of Jerusalem's elevation and expansions. In Josephus's retelling of the stories of John Hyrcanus, his sons and grandsons, David and Josiah live once again to fight their battles against Judaism's traditional enemies: Edom and Gerizim.[21]

A Golden Age?

It is commonplace to describe 1–2 Kings as a tragedy centered in explaining the destruction of Samaria and Jerusalem as acts of divine punishment.[22] As such, the story can be seen as part of Israel's greater history and a narrative, which is essentially incomplete. This understanding of Kings confines itself to the surface of the narrative. It looks at the work from a historical context that is imagined sometime after the story closes and understands it as an account of events of the past, perhaps even a distant past. Implicitly added to the story and claimed for its meaning is an undefined future, allowing the modern critic considerable freedom to speculate. Perhaps an exilic—even a postexilic—period might provide us with the context in which the story's implied author stood. When the Chronicler offered his variation, he was quite explicit in closing the narrative in a perspective belonging to the story's future:

In the first year of Cyrus, king of Persia, that the word of Yahweh by the mouth of Jeremiah might be accomplished, Yahweh stirred up the spirit of Cyrus, king of Persia, so that he made a proclamation throughout all his kingdom and also put it in writing: "Yahweh, the God of heaven, has given me all the kingdoms of the earth and he has charged me to build him a house at Jerusalem, which is in Judah. Whoever is among you of all his people, may Yahweh his God be with him. Let him go up." (2 Chr 36:22–23; var. Ezra 1:1–4; also Ezra 6:2–5; Is 45:1–7)

Chronicles happily echoes a famous decree of return related to Cyrus's conquest of Babylon, itself modeled on inscriptions of an Assyrian king, Asshurbanipal (669–c. 630):

Of Nin[eveh], Ashur and also of Susa, of Agade, of Eshnunna, of Zamban, of Meturnu and of Der, up to the borders of Gutium, the cult centers beyond the Tigris, whose [cult] structures had long remained in ruins, I returned to their place the gods who lived there and re-established them for eternity. I gathered all their people and returned their habitations. And the gods of Sumer and Akkad, whom Nabonidus, to the wrath of the lord of the gods [Marduk], had transported to Babylon, I had them, on the order of Marduk, the great lord, joyfully installed in their cella ("rooms"), in a dwelling for the joy of the heart.[23]

Whatever we might decide about the history behind the closure in Chronicles, the closure in Kings has another function in mind and holds its audience outside of time: that the reader's thoughts might return to the beginning and understand eternal truths. The narrative of Kings recounting the reigns of David's sons does not proceed in the pattern of Pentateuch biographies from Abraham to Moses. Nor do its stories begin with the magic of fertility, a hero's birth and his naming. Kings begins rather with the sad story of David's impotence:

Now King David was old and advanced in years, and although they covered him with clothes, he could not get warm. Therefore his servants said to him, "Let a young maiden be brought for my lord, the king, and let her wait upon the king, and be his nurse; let her lie in your bosom, that my lord, the king, may be warm." So they sought for a beautiful maiden throughout all the territory of Israel and found Abishag the Shunammite, and brought her to the king. The maiden was very beautiful and she became the king's nurse and ministered to him; but the king knew her not. (1 Kgs 1:1–4)

This scene at the end of David's reign and the beginning of the story in Kings opens the plot on David's failure to win the wholehearted support of the north (2 Sm 19:23; 1 Kgs 2:1-9) and the humiliation of having his eldest surviving son attempt to usurp the throne (1 Kgs 1: 5–53). This opening projects a template with which each successive tale is stamped until the narrative reaches its closure. It helps create a chain narrative of futility. David's impotence is the theme story of Kings. It links and interprets the great story of David's reign in the books of Samuel by denying David's "biography" its classic closure in *shalom*, although this closure was planned by David in the lasting peace implied in the cue name he gave to Solomon.[24] Yahweh's decision at the close of David's story to destroy Jerusalem with a plague (2 Sm 24:6) is not overturned by David's repentance. It is only delayed. The narrative of David's sons becomes a forty-seven-chapter story of futility. It is the unhappy story of Yahweh, who would be a God of compassion and mercy, but for the sake of the education of kings, accepts the more primitive role of the God of justice.

In the closing chapter of the Kings narratives (2 Kgs 25), Ishmael, a member of the House of David, with a band of ten assassins, kills Gedaliah, the Babylonian-installed governor in Jerusalem, that the murder of Absalom, carried out by David's general Joab with his band of ten assassins (2 Sm 18:14–15), might finally be avenged. This done, all the people of Jerusalem, small and great, fulfill the destiny Moses had predicted in the story's beginning (Dt 28:68). They who do so—and return to Egypt—did not fear God; they "were afraid of the Chaldeans" (2 Kgs 25:26).

In this story's final scene, Jerusalem's king, Jehoiachin, imprisoned for thirty-seven years, is pardoned by Evil-Merodach on the occasion of his ascent to Babylon's throne (2 Kgs 25:27–30). He is given a place in the court higher than any of the other kings who were with him in Babylon. This mercy to the last remnant of David's house reiterates David's invitation to the displaced Mephibosheth, last remnant of Saul's house. Jehoiachin is dressed in new clothes, allowed to eat at the king of Babylon's table and given an allowance from his king and patron every day for life (cf. Jer 52:31–34). Reiterating a metaphor of reversal and peace at the close of the story of Jerusalem's destruction is a stunning use of irony. The last son of David takes his refuge with a man. Evil-Merodach—usurping Yahweh's theological role—frees this son of David from his prison bonds of death. In the end the king of Babylon, not Yahweh, is the son of David's patron. He loves the last of David's sons as the story ends where it had begun.[25]

My reading of this closure as parable is supported by two prophecies. The first is the prophecy of Moses, which is used in Kings to cast the plotline. It has determined the fate of David's sons from the very beginning. Moses speaks to the people of Israel from Mount Nebo just before they enter the promised land. He tells them of Jerusalem's future kings (Dt 17:14–20). He speaks of a time in which they will want to have a king, like other nations. He offers a riddle, warning them of coveting power, love and wealth. If heeded, they will avoid the never-ending story, to which the story chain condemns them. Their future king must not collect horses and cause the people to return to Egypt. He must not collect wives to turn his heart. Nor is he to collect silver and gold. Moses' riddle finds its key early in the Kings narrative (1 Kgs 5:1–14). As soon as we hear of Solomon's divinely inspired wisdom, admired even by the queen of Sheba, and as soon as golden age expectations of Solomon's *shalom* are raised, Yahweh's beloved Solomon collects more than his share of horses, women and gold. He begins with 666 talents of gold to make shields for the house that he has built for Yahweh (1 Kgs 10:14–25), a quantity of gold that is fittingly reused by the author of Revelation as the sign of his beast (Rev 13:1–18). The temple's gold, whether in the form of shields or otherwise used, is repeatedly plundered in the course of the Kings narrative. Solomon also collects horses from Egypt, which become the object of an interesting discourse centered around trusting in Yahweh or in the military powers of this world (1 Kgs 10:26–29; cf. Dt 17:16–17). Finally Solomon collects seven hundred wives and three hundred concubines to fulfill Moses' prophecy and "turn his heart" away from Yahweh (1 Kgs 11:1–8).

David's story provides the template for the tale of Solomon's fall from grace. When he reached the height of his career as Yahweh's warrior at the head of his band of thirty heroes and giant killers, his heart is turned by Bathsheba ("daughter of Sheba"). Similarly, Solomon comes to the height of his glory and fulfills everything he might wish to do. He builds the temple and dedicates it. His test comes with his second vision. Yahweh offers him a choice to determine his destiny. If he walks in the path of David and fulfills all of Yahweh's commandments, his throne will remain forever. Failing that, however, Yahweh will reject his dynasty and destroy Israel from the face of the earth. The temple will lie in ruins. Instead of praise, his house will be met with scorn and derision (1 Kgs 9:4–7). With this choice to make, Solomon goes to meet *his* daughter of Sheba, the queen herself (1 Kgs 10:1–13), who meets him with fatal flattery:

> Blessed are your men and blessed are your servants who always are near you to hear your wisdom. Blessed is Yahweh your God who has delight in you and has set you on the throne of Israel. Because Yahweh loved Israel forever, he has made you king, that you might execute justice and righteousness. (1 Kgs 10:8–9)

So much said, the queen of Sheba leaves Solomon with his gold, horses and wives. No longer gifts of divine favor, they become seductively attractive and play to the king's vanity.

His great wealth in gold, horses and women is now recounted; in fulfillment of Moses' prophecy they draw his heart away from the "righteous path" of David. The queen of Sheba is the first and the last person to describe a son of David with the attribute of righteousness. The first time it is used about David comes from the mouth of Saul, recognizing David's righteousness (1 Sm 24:18).[26] In Psalms and Proverbs, it is linked with the fear of God—the singular virtue of a client's awe before his divine patron. It is also the virtue Moses demands of Israel's future kings. In the closure of the stories about the House of David, the people flee to Egypt. Both they and Jehoiachin have transferred their fear of God to Evil-Merodach.

The implicit author of Kings is in a discourse with the book of Isaiah, from which he borrows his agenda. In Kings, David's sons play the role of Isaiah's Israel as badly raised boys who need a father and teacher's cane to learn their lessons (Is 1:2–6; 3:5, 12). Having taken to heart Solomon's proverb that Yahweh "punishes the child he loves, as a father his son" (Prv 3:12), our author is supported by a stock tradition of wisdom with stories of reward and punishment, so well carried out by Eliphaz's God in the book of Job:

> Blessed is he whom Yahweh reproves. For this reason, one should not despise the punishment of the Almighty. He wounds, but he binds up; he strikes, but his hands heal. (Job 5:17–18)

Isaiah's old Israel—devastated and plundered by Assyria and Babylon—a child to be educated through tears and suffering, plays the role in which the author of Kings casts the sons of David. At the close of their story, they are yet to rise from their ashes (cf. Is 6:11–13). The author awaits his audience's new generation, who, understanding, will take Yahweh as its God and hear the Torah in its heart.

Isaiah calls his audience to *imitatio*. The story about Isaiah and King Hezekiah during the Assyrian siege of Jerusalem, which we discussed above in Chapter 3, is a parable on the theme of humility (Is 36–39). The story takes its departure in the good news of God's presence as expressed in the announcement of salvation through a full eightfold version of the song for a poor man. It announces the new creation, which springs from old Israel's dead stump:

> The retribution of God: he comes to save you. The eyes of the blind will be opened; the ears of the deaf unlocked. The lame will spring like the gazelle,

and the tongue of the dumb shout; for water will spring from the desert and a stream in the wilderness; the baked earth will become a pool and the dry earth a fountain. Where jackals lived will become a marsh: a home to reeds and rushes. There, a way will appear that will be called: the holy way. (Is 35:4–8)

Along that holy way, Yahweh's ransomed return home; their sorrow and sighs have become a child's noise of joy and gladness (Is 35:10; cf. 51:11). Hezekiah's is a tale epitomizing nations in rebellion against Yahweh and his messiah in Psalm 2, which are judged on the day of Yahweh's coming wrath:

Oh, the noise of many nations . . . the peoples roar like the roar of the sea. Behold in the evening: terror; and in the morning: they are nothing. This is the fate of those who plunder us, the lot of those who despoil us. (Is 17:12–14)

This prophetic warning seals the fate of the Assyrian army in the Hezekiah story. The Assyrians are rebuked for their noise (Is 37:24–29), and at night Yahweh visits them with the terror of his plague (Is 37:36). The prophetic message renders both blessing and curse. On the one hand salvation and life is given to Jerusalem's remnant of Judah, which through Hezekiah put its trust in Yahweh and, on the other hand, death and terror to 185,000 of the greatest army on earth in retribution for Sennacherib's hubris. The Hezekiah story and its prophetic songs stand in the discourse of royal creation ideology. Hezekiah's important tears of repentance are also central in this discussion. Yahweh has rejected Hezekiah in his anger and tells him to die. In response, the scene of Hezekiah's prayer (Is 38:3; 2 Kgs 20:3) illustrates and echoes the Psalter's faith that Yahweh will hear the sound of weeping (Ps 6). Hezekiah is the righteous prince who finds his refuge in Yahweh (Ps 2:12). He walks in Yahweh's path (Ps 1), in truth (Psalm 15:2; 51:8; 86:11) and with a pure heart (Ps 15:2; 17:3; 24:4; 27:8; 37:31; 51:12; 84:6; 86:11; 119:10; 138:1). He does what is good in Yahweh's eyes.

It is in Yahweh's response to Hezekiah, however, that the story lends itself to the greater themes of both Kings and Isaiah and comes close to the motif of a new birth in royal ideology. Yahweh responds to Hezekiah's tears with the voice of the Babylonian Akitu festival's high priest (above, Chapter 6). While illustrating one or other of Solomon's proverbs: "Keep my commandments and live; keep my Torah" (Prv 4:2, 4; 7:2), Yahweh allows the king to take up his crown. He renews his reign: "I have heard your prayer; I have seen your tears. Behold, I will add fifteen years to your life" (Is 38:5; 2 Kgs 20:6). The book of Chronicles uses this episode for a story about King Rehoboam (2 Chr

12:1–16). It too stresses the need to test the king for humility. The story begins, "When the reign of Rehoboam was established and strong" (2 Chr 12:1). In his own strength, the king "abandons Yahweh's Torah, and all Israel with him" (2 Chr 12:1b). As in Hezekiah's story, the king's betrayal threatens to cost Rehoboam his life. The punishment is measured by the crime. As he abandoned Yahweh's Torah, so Yahweh will now abandon him into Pharaoh's hand (2 Chr 12:5). Facing death, the king humbles himself and is therefore allowed to take up his rule once again.

> The princes of Israel and the king have humbled themselves. . . . They have humbled themselves and therefore I will not destroy them . . . my anger will not be poured out over Jerusalem by Shishak's hand. (2 Chr 12:7)

Once Hezekiah's humility is demonstrated, Yahweh lifts the siege that Hezekiah might take up his role as king anew. The final scene of the story opens on Yahweh's mockery of Assyria (cf. Ps 2:4). Sennacherib is killed in the temple of his hapless god in Nineveh. The sword of retribution cuts down the Assyrian king, imitating the angel's terror that destroyed the Assyrian army.

Earlier in the Kings chain of narratives, Yahweh promised Solomon that if the king walked in the integrity of his heart and was true to his commandments (1 Kgs 9:4–5), the House of David would continue forever. Now, in the story of the siege of Jerusalem, Hezekiah sought his strength in neither Egypt's broken reed nor in the horses and chariots of great kings. He relied on Yahweh alone, and his humility overthrew the great dragon of Assyria. Is he the implicit savior of Solomon's promise? Challenged by just such a retributive logic in his plotline, the author dashes his readers' hopes by closing his story with understated brilliance. As soon as the shadow on the sundial moves backward ten steps as a sign of Hezekiah's renewed life, the king receives envoys from the king of Babylon. Virtuous Hezekiah, finally given opportunity, shows himself to be just a man. He takes his Babylonian guests from the future and shows them all the treasures of the temple and his palace: "There is nothing in my storehouses which I did not show them" (2 Kgs 20:15). On this note of naïveté, the tragic story of good King Hezekiah in the book of Kings closes where it began: on the sevenfold theme of plundering the temple. Isaiah steps from behind the curtains to explain the fatefulness of Hezekiah's hospitality:

> Behold the days are coming, when all that is in your house, and that which your fathers have stored up till this day, shall be carried off to Babylon; nothing shall be left says Yahweh. And your own sons, who are born to you, they

will be taken away to be eunuchs in the palace of the king of Babylon. (2 Kgs
20:17–18)

THE END OF WAR

As argued in the last chapter, all wars in the ancient world are holy wars, and the
purpose of war is peace. Such ideology is not cynical but pacifist; for no man can
know the will of God. The closure of violent struggle against the nations is both
a utopian and a mythic peace. This has been a staple of royal ideology since long
before Pharaoh Merneptah closed his great victory stele with the announcement
of *shalom* over the nine bows of his world. It is this utopian expectation—that
kings and war can create eternal peace—which supports the theme of Solomon's
fall from grace. It adds a voice of critical irony to the narrative. The king's noble
and transcending role as servant of the divine gives him the task of reestablishing the world as God originally created it. The task of these stories is to expose
the king's humanity and vanity, his wish to remake the world in his own image
rather than God's. Rather than viewing David and Solomon as great figures of a
past golden age, the author implicit in the closure of 2 Kings invites his readers
to judge such sons of David for their pretensions to power. Ever present figures
of prophets lead this choir.

The book of Kings sets its themes of hubris and vanity in prophet stories,
which do not shy from the comic. When successful, the prophet as ironic figure
competes well against the tragic king and creates a peaceful alternative to the
royal path of murder and terror. Although prophets of doom popularly fill the
imagination with a violence of apocalyptic proportion, the violence is neither na-
tionalist nor xenophobic. In both books of Kings and most of the prophets, the
primary victims of holy war are Samaria and Jerusalem. The figure of the
prophet is used as catalyst for a diatribe against Israel's ignorance, disobedience
and rejection of pietism's path of righteousness: "The ox knows its owner and the
ass its master's crib; but Israel does not know, my people do not understand" (Is
1:2–3; cf. Jer 2:1–4; Ez 2:3–5; Hos 1:2–5; Jl 1:2–4; Am 2:4, 6; Mic 1:3–5; Zeph
1:2–4; Zech 1:2–4).

The books of Kings critique the doomsday prophets who fill their pages as
much as bloody kings. It also questions the retribution of their God of justice.
The prophet Elijah sets out on a career of bringing destruction and divine wrath
literally to rain on his enemies. The climax of his story finds the great prophet,
fresh from the slaughter of Baal's prophets on Mount Carmel, hunted by his enemies and running for his life. Then the scene turns comic and ironic. Elijah

finds himself in the desert of Horeb, falling asleep under a tree (1 Kgs 19:5; cf. Jon 4:6). So much is he in fear for his life, he prays to die (1 Kgs 19:4; cf. Jon 4:2–4). The author's irony, with Isaiah's great theme of a generation that hears its prophet but does not understand, now turns to bite the audience of Kings, where the nature of the living God is the theme. Yahweh's prophet Elijah had just won a life-and-death contest with the prophets of Baal over whether God can hear. They called out, but Baal did not hear (1 Kgs 18:26). Yahweh, of course, who once heard his son Ishmael in the desert (Gen 21:1), is a God who hears and so Elijah wins his contest. At Horeb, speaking with Yahweh, Elijah introduces himself as a prophet made in the image of the god who sent him, "filled with zeal for Yahweh the God of armies," destroying altars and killing prophets (1 Kgs 19:10). The story, however, closes with a message that contradicts all that Jonah would have Elijah stand for. God is not in the great storm, earthquake or fire. His voice is "a voice of soft silence"(1 Kgs 19:12).

The books of Kings dethrone both prophet and storm god. They transform the tradition and give it new significance. A silent God mocks the storm god of Carmel who destroyed the prophets of Baal. In this turning point of the prophet stories of Kings, Elijah, seeing and understanding with Moses at the mountain of God, gives way to his successor, Elisha. Inheriting Elijah's mantle, Elisha recovers the power of the spirit that Moses had passed to Joshua. The third of this trilogy of figures who walked dryshod through the sea, Elisha has power to divide the waters of the Jordan. With his double portion of Elijah's spirit (2 Kgs 2:1–22), he is one greater than Elijah. While Elijah brought judgment and war against the house of Ahab because of the murder of Naboth and the theft of his vineyard (1 Kgs 21; cf. 1 Sm 11–12), Elisha is given the role of closing the cycle of violence and bringing peace and reconciliation to Israel.

A small threefold story of Elisha presents Elijah's successor as Samaria's prophet of peace (2 Kgs 6). The first scene is a simple miracle story, illustrating Elisha's double portion of spirit. One of Elisha's disciples has dropped a borrowed ax into the Jordan. As Moses turned bitter water sweet, Elisha cuts a stick of wood and drops it into the water to cause the iron to float (2 Kgs 6:1–7). The second scene is set during Samaria's war with the Arameans from Damascus (2 Kgs 6:8–18). Doubly filled with the spirit as Elisha is, he is able to read the enemy king's mind and repeatedly sends reports to Israel's king, informing him of the Aramean king's strategy against him. Understandably, this upsets Aram's king, who sends his cavalry to surround the town where Elisha is staying. In this second episode, the enemy plays Solomon's role and puts his trust in horses and chariots, while Elisha has his trust in Yahweh. The prophet's servant is terrified at the charge of the cavalry, until Elisha—the man of God—points out that "there are more on our side than on theirs." He prays that his young companion's eyes be opened. With such inspired eyes, the servant sees Elisha—much like Joshua at Jericho—"surrounded by a mountain of fiery horses and chariots." He understands that his tale might offer illustration to Isaiah 6 and open the eyes of a blind generation. The third scene of the trilogy is constructed as the story's closure (2 Kgs 6:18–23). When the Arameans attack, Elisha prays that the enemy be struck—like Isaiah's ignorant generation—with blindness. This done, he tells the blinded soldiers that theirs is not the path. Such a statement, however out of context, opens an exchange that illustrates the Psalter's "theology of the way" and the true path of righteousness.[27] If the reader follows that path as Elisha's story continues, she will find herself at the heart of Torah.

The soldiers—efficient, well trained and as terrifying as they are—are not even in the right town. Elisha offers to lead them along the right path to Samaria. Again, the opening of eyes brings understanding. The enemy soldiers are in the middle of Samaria, surrounded by the king and his army, who, as is the custom of soldiers, are eager to kill them. Elisha rebukes his king and, in a dramatic commentary on the law of Moses, instructs the Samaritans to love their enemy (Lev 19:18, 34): "Let them eat and drink and send them back to their master." The king of Samaria gives a feast before sending the soldiers home. The story closes on a note of lasting *shalom*: that the Arameans did not send their soldiers on raids into Israel again.

Such stories, illustrating obedience to Moses' Torah and, in particular, the command to love the enemy or stranger, have many variants in the Bible.[28] The love of neighbor, foreigner and enemy, the center and epitome of Moses' law, is intentionally played against the politics of war. Beginning with contrasting figures of good kings and bad kings, the book of Kings engages in a thematic contest between violent and peaceful concepts of the divine, represented by the contrasting roles of the doomsday prophet Elijah and his successor, the prophet of mercy and compassion, Samaria's Elisha.

The effort draws characteristics from the ancient form of disputations, fables and didactic tales, found already in the early wisdom literature of Sumer and Egypt. This literature typically sets two contrasting or opposite figures in debate with each other, such as summer and winter, a bird and a fish and a ewe and wheat.[29] Many of the debates are playful and almost all are sharpened with satire and irony. Some are pious, like the debate between a man and his god, which presents the man's argument for pious imitation.[30] Still others are deeply critical of public injustice and shallow piety. The Egyptian story of the eloquent peasant, one of the finest, might justly be taken as a forerunner of Franz Kafka's *The*

Trial.[31] Also unsurpassed is the profoundly ironic dispute between a man and his *ka* (soul) over the benefits of suicide, capped by the *ka*'s closing remarks:

> My soul said to me: Set mourning aside, you who belong to me, my brother! [Although] you be offered up on a brazier, [still] you will cling to life, as you say. Whether it be desirable that I [remain] here [because] you have rejected the West [sunset, the realm of the dead] or whether it be desirable that you reach the West and your body join the earth, I will come to rest after you have relaxed [in death]. Thus we will make a home together.[32]

The Bible is deeply influenced by this form and its rhetoric. Certainly among some of the best-known pieces are the father's contrast between the son who is advised to keep his commandments and avoid the prostitute and adventuress (Prv 6:20–7:5) and the "young man without sense" who seeks out the loose woman (Prv 7:6–23) or the similar contrast between Lady Wisdom and Dame Folly (Prv 8). Best known, of course, are the debates between Job and his three friends over righteousness (Job 4–31) and Abraham's debate with Yahweh over divine justice (Gen 18:22–33). Even more appropriate to the context of Kings is the implicit disputation of the Psalter between the paths of the righteous and the ungodly:

> Blessed is the man who does not walk in the counsel of the wicked, nor stand in the way of sinners, nor sit in the seat of scorners, but his delight is in Yahweh's Torah and on his Torah he meditates day and night. He is like a tree planted by streams of water that yields its fruit in season and its leaf does not wither. In all that he does he succeeds. Not so the wicked. They are like chaff the wind blows away. Therefore the wicked will not stand in the judgment, nor sinners in the assembly of the righteous. Yahweh recognizes the path of the righteous, but the path of the wicked will perish. (Ps 1:1–6)

The illustration of such debates through stories is typical of biblical narratives, parables and other folktales. Such illustration is particularly dominant in the many stories of struggles between nations and brothers.[33]

⟨⟨⟩⟩

CHAPTER 10

The Figure of
David in Story and Song

DAVID'S PREDECESSORS IN THE
ANCIENT NEAR EAST

While the figure of David in the stories of 1–2 Samuel finds its earliest parallels in Syria and Mesopotamia in the stories of Esarhaddon of Assyria and Idrimi of Alalakh (Appendix 2, nos. 4, 13), the closest parallels are perhaps the Greek myths of Hercules and the apocryphal traditions of 1–2 Maccabees. As discussed in Chapter 5, Idrimi's tale offers us early variations of the young adventurer who, like Esarhaddon, is the youngest of his brothers.[1] Many other elements of Idrimi's story parallel David's: the threat to the hero and his flight to the desert; his life with the Hapiru for seven years; the struggle for his kingdom with his band of followers; the thoughts he thinks that no one else does; the threat to his life by his own patron; efforts to negotiate an amnesty and make peace with his king; oaths of allegiance; acknowledgment and love given him; a military campaign ending in his triumphal entry into Alalakh; the building of a house and the regulation of the proper cult in the city and entrusting it to his son. While Idrimi reigned for thirty years, David reigned the biblical forty.

The more mythical aspects of the figure of David in the Psalter and in the songs that structure his story (1 Sm 2:1–10; 2 Sm 1:19–27; 2 Sm 22; 23:1–7) are closely related to a tradition of victory hymns and songs that we know from

Eighteenth Dynasty Egyptian sources such as the Song of Thutmosis,[2] which could well be understood as the earliest known of the saving figures we find in the Psalter. Begotten of Amon-Re, Thutmosis crushes his father's enemies. He is the terror of and subjugator of foreign lands. All are cast under his feet and bound to his patronage. His reign reaches the ends of the earth and his rule is eternal. He has power over the floods of the Nile and is enthroned in Re's house. He is the beloved, the son of Amon-Re, born from his body. Other streams of tradition also influence the development of the figure of David. For example, David's role as musician and singer draws convincingly from an Orphic tradition. On the other hand, as the beloved of his god and great warrior, crushing a world in uproar, few parallels come so close as the inscription of Seti I:

> The good god, potent with his arm, heroic and valiant like Montu, rich in captives, knowing how to place his hand, alert wherever he is; speaking with his mouth, acting with his hands, valiant leader of his army, valiant warrior in the very heart of the fray, a Bastet [lion] terrible in combat, penetrating into a mass of Asiatics and making them prostrate, crushing the princes of Retenu, reaching the very ends of him who transgresses against his way. He causes the princes of Syria to retreat, all the boastfulness of whose mouth had been so great. Every foreign country to the ends of the earth, their princes say: "Where shall we go?" They spend the night giving testimony in his name, saying Behold! Behold! in their hearts. It is the strength of his father Amon that decreed to him valor and victory.[3]

The tale of David's heroic threefold quest to win the daughter of the king as his bride, finally paying two hundred Philistine foreskins (1 Sm 18:20–27), finds a lighter variant in an Egyptian tale, The Prince Who Was Threatened by Three Fates.[4] The story includes many elements also found in Esarhaddon, Idrimi and the tales of David, including the theme of testing in the wilderness. This prince goes to the wilderness to "follow his heart." He tells all that he was the son of an Egyptian officer, who had been driven from Egypt by his wicked stepmother. He came to the land of the Prince of Nahrin, who had a beautiful daughter. Her room had a window, opening 70 cubits (100 feet) from the ground. The prince sent for all the sons of all the princes of the land of Syria: "He who reaches the window of my daughter, his wife she shall be!" For three months the sons of the princes pass their time leaping. When the gaze of the princess falls on the youth, he joins the sons of the princes in their leaping. Finally he reaches the window of the daughter of the Prince of Nahrin, who refuses to give his daughter to a fugitive. He sends his servants to tell the foreigner to go back to where he came from. The daughter of the prince, however, loves the young man and swears that she will die without him. The prince sends assassins to kill the young man, but again the daughter declares that she will die if they harm the youth: "I will not live an hour longer than he." The prince calls the young man and his daughter before him and is so impressed by his appearance that he embraces him, kisses him and declares him his son.

While David's story includes the more important elements of this story, the motifs of flight into the wilderness and the winning of a wife through a heroic deed occur in three other biblical narratives. Abraham was old when he charged his servant to go back to Abraham's country to find a wife for his son Isaac. When the servant arrives in Mesopotamia, he prays to Yahweh, Abraham's God, for success and sets a test:

> I am standing by the spring of water, and the daughters of the men of the city are coming out to draw water. Let the maiden to whom I shall say, "Pray let down your jar that I may drink," and who shall say, "Drink and I will water your camels," let her be the one whom you have appointed for your servant Isaac. By this I will know that you have shown steadfast love to my master. (Gen 24:13–14)

Yahweh passes his test as a beautiful young virgin does eagerly all that the servant had wished, before he asks it of her and moreover invites him to lodge with her family. That the young girl proves to be Rebecca, the daughter of Bethuel, Abraham's own nephew, confirms divine intention. Yahweh's angel went before him and prospered his way (Gen 24:40). A similar story meets Jacob in his quest for a wife. Both fleeing from his brother Esau and—in imitation of Isaac's story—sent by his mother to find a wife from the family of Bethuel, Jacob arrives in the wilderness of Qedem and comes to a well covered by a great stone. Three flocks of sheep are waiting to be watered when the shepherds gather together to move the stone. Rachel, Bethuel's daughter, is just coming with a fourth flock. Knowing that it is not yet time for all the flocks to come together, Jacob goes to the well and, alone, rolls the stone back from the well. Winning his bride with this feat of strength, Jacob kisses Rachel, stays with the family a month and agrees to work seven years to make her his bride (Gen 29:1–14). A third variation of the biblical tale is presented when Moses flees from Pharaoh to the land of Midian and similarly sits down by a well (Ex 2:15–22). His test comes when the seven daughters of the priest of Midian, having come to water their father's flock, are chased away by shepherds. "But Moses stood up and helped them and watered their flock." Invited to eat bread, Moses stays and marries one of the daughters, who bears him a son, Gershom ("a stranger in the land").

The golden age rhetoric of both Samuel-Kings and Chronicles, associated with the figures of David and Solomon, reiterates Near Eastern royal inscriptions. While care of the temple and its cult is a stock element in the role of the good king, it is also an element of Assyrian campaign inscriptions, where it is closely associated with imperial claims of world dominance. Typical rhetoric is found in an inscription of Adad-Nirari, which captures some of the imaginative power the Bible uses so effectively in its stories of David and Solomon:

> Property of Adad-Nirari, great king, legitimate king, king of the world, king of Assyria—a king whom [the god] Ashur, the king of the Igigi [high gods] had chosen [already] when he was a youth, entrusting him with the position of a prince without rival, whose shepherding they made as agreeable to the people of Assyria as the Plant of Life, whose throne they established firmly; the holy priest, tireless caretaker of the temple, who keeps up the rites of the sanctuary, who acts [only] upon the trust-inspiring oracles of Ashur, his lord, who has made the princes within the four rims of the earth submit to his feet from the Siluna mountain of the rising of the sun . . . as far as the Great Sea of the Rising Sun from the banks of the Euphrates . . . as far as the shore of the Great Sea of the Setting Sun, I made them submit all to my feet, imposing upon them tribute.[5]

The central theme of the united kingdom and golden age, which structures both versions of the David and Solomon story—the building of a temple: a house for Yahweh—draws heavily on the ancient Syrian myth of Baal.[6] Having defeated his rival Mot (death), a risen Baal moves to consolidate his power over the gods. Having given promises of rain and fertility, Baal is recognized king over the gods. However, a problem remains: the sons of El still have their refuge in El's palace because Baal has no house of his own, no place to dwell, no court to which he might invite the gods. And so this god without a temple sends a request to his sister Anat to ask El that a house be built for Baal like the houses of the other gods, with a court like the courts of all the sons of 'Athirat. Because Baal sends rain in its season, thunders and sends lightning, he is granted permission to build a house. In seven creative days, Baal builds his house of Lebanese cedar and covers it with silver and gold and precious stones from the mountains. He summons an entire caravan to bring wares to his house, to "build a house of silver and gold, a mansion of purest lapis." He is pleased with his house and invites his brothers and relatives to a feast of oxen and sheep, bulls and fatted animals, yearling calves and many goats. He feeds the seventy sons of 'Athirat with rich meats and wine. Now he alone will rule as king over the gods.

Solomon builds just such a house for Yahweh, a God without a house who wishes to rule exclusively and have all seek refuge in him. The great peace of a golden age waited for Solomon, who, when rebellion against the House of David comes to an end, takes up the task of ending Yahweh's search for a house. He sends for cedars from Lebanon, for skilled craftsmen and all that was necessary. In seven years, the temple was built. He covered it with gold and silver and inlaid precious stones. Solomon then invited the elders and leaders of the tribes to Jerusalem to bring the ark of the covenant to Zion. All the men of Israel came to the feast and sacrificed so many sheep and cows they could not be counted— and Yahweh's glory filled the temple. Solomon's feast of twice seven days closes with his prayer that Yahweh hold to his covenant with Israel: to establish justice, to forgive Israel's sins and return them to the land, to send his rain and to protect them from famine and plague (1 Kgs 5:15–6:32; 7:13–8:66; cf. 2 Chr 1:18–7:10). The biblical writer uses the reechoing structure of the story of Baal's house and of the great feast to celebrate its construction not to present a temple and palace of transcendent grandeur, expressing the highest cultural achievement of Israel's golden age, but to comment on the vanity of human achievement and to introduce the story of the temple being stripped of Solomon's glory as a prelude to its rejection and destruction already determined by Yahweh.

The Motif of the
Messiah in the Hebrew Bible

Much of David's life story, as it is presented in biblical narrative, including the many roles he is called on to fill in both narrative and poetry, clearly belongs to a stream of myth and narrative, long antedating biblical literature. This stream of tradition is closely associated with creation myth, fertility cult and a royal propaganda common to the ancient world. The term "messiah," however, taken from the verb "to anoint," reflects a Jewish reuse of ancient royal ideology. It is hardly a role in its own right and defies comparison with particular roles with which "the anointed one of Yahweh" may be associated, such as "shepherd," "son of God," "chosen one," "savior" and the like, or even "son of David." Part of the difficulty results from the way biblical scholars have attempted to explain the term within a historical evolution with roots in an assumed ancient practice of anointing kings in ritual enthronement ceremonies. The figure of the anointed one, accordingly, draws to itself all of the characteristics and roles associated with kingship—whether or not they have any direct association with anointing, oil or any of its symbolic overtones of strength or power. The difficulties have been increased by the common assumption that the gospels' reference to Jesus as "the messiah" as "the one who is to come" to establish the kingdom of God on earth implies real, historical expectation of the authors and their society: that they expected the messiah to come and establish such a kingdom. Not only does a story's expectation become a historical one, but the expectation creates a concrete role for an otherwise enigmatic figure. As the utopian metaphors of the kingdom of God and divine judgment have been understood as apocalyptic, the narrative's parable has similarly been assumed to reflect historical expectations—even complex political movements—of the Hellenistic and Greco-Roman periods. It is only to be expected that scholars of the Hebrew Bible, who do not take their perspective from such later messianism—whether Jewish or Christian—have reacted by tending to *demythologize* the understanding of the figure of a messiah in their texts and bring it into closer agreement with a historical function of ancient Israel's cult, namely, the storied "event" of the anointing of the king. In this effort to historicize the messiah of the Hebrew Bible, the dynamics of story and metaphor have been generally ignored.

At the first Princeton symposium on Judaism and Christian origins in 1985, for example, the members unanimously endorsed the opinion that the term "messiah" in the Hebrew Bible refers to "a present, political and religious leader who is appointed by God, applied predominantly to a king, but also to a priest and occasionally a prophet."[7] While the term often describes priests, it is also used for a specific figure, such as Yahweh's anointed or "the anointed one."[8] With a single exception of Cyrus (Is 45:1), the term is thought to refer to the contemporary Israelite king and reflect his relationship to Yahweh.[9] The members of the symposium, particularly the Jerusalem scholar S. Talmon, sharply separate the use of the epithet "messiah" in the Hebrew Bible, which is understood to refer to "an actual ruling king or his immediate successor," to later forms of messianism. These had a credal and visionary dimension that went well beyond what the symposium felt was the original meaning of the term.[10] The earliest use of the term "messiah" is drawn from a historical setting in ancient Israel's institution of kingship in the Iron Age, whereas the unique, future-oriented, superterrestrial savior is linked to the Persian, Hellenistic and Greco-Roman periods and culminates in an idealized figure after 70 CE.[11] The argument presents messianism as specifically Jewish in origin and denies the influence of similar ancient Near Eastern figures.[12] Particularly the concepts of anointed, universal salvation and cosmic peace are stressed as reflecting a unique Jewish development.[13] The "custom of anointing" is explained as an effort of the Israelite monarchy to join two elements of leadership: the charismatic leadership of the time of the Judges, characterized by the election of one marked by the divine spirit on the one hand, and the dynastic government of the monarchy, considered to have been devoid of religious or spiritual dimensions on the other.[14] This consensus understands the Bible in terms of "history and realism." It also separates messianism—and the messiah of the New Testament—from the figure of the messiah in the Hebrew Bible.[15]

This understanding of the messiah is vulnerable to the critique of assuming that the "best way to learn about the messiah in ancient Judaism is to study texts in which there is none."[16] The assertion that this epithet in fact refers to a contemporary Israelite king is unfortunately not argued. Apart from the obvious historicizing of the hero tales of Judges, the assertion that dynastic kingship is devoid of religious or spiritual dimension is mistaken. Figures fully comparable to the messiah are well-known from both Egyptian and cuneiform literature from at least the Bronze Age. Already in our earliest texts, the same thematic elements that dominate Jewish messianism of the Persian, Hellenistic and Greco-Roman periods are in place in both ancient Near Eastern and biblical tradition.

The use of the word "messiah" itself is not terribly important in the Hebrew Bible and related literature. Nor is it as common as one might think. However, the myth of the ideal king is ubiquitous. It is the intellectual foundation for the stories of both covenant and eternal reign, including themes of restoration and a golden age. The figure of the king as a holy warrior with the power to determine destiny and rule the world, expressed in stock metaphors of *shalom,* with its blessings of divine patronage and curses of judgment, as well as the king's universal rule, are all aspects of early imperial texts. Moreover, biblical texts do not simply absorb or borrow metaphorical elements from royal ideology as Talmon asserts. They use them specifically to transform Yahweh into a universal and imperial god of an ancient Near Eastern type. The metaphor of the messiah and the related motif of anointing priests, prophets and kings are metaphors and motifs belonging to this greater myth of the king. The messiah is a figure of myth—an element in an ancient story's effort to speak of the transcendent, in which the human world has its reflection. It is used neither as a direct reference to any contemporary, historical king nor to any known *historical* expectations before Bar Kochba (c. 135 CE). The Bible transforms an imperial ideology for theological purposes.[17] The thematic elements cluster coherently around the messiah epithet and reflect a mythic reiteration of Near Eastern royal ideology in an effort to reflect divine immanence. Later Jewish messianism tends to historicize the transcendental and interpret the biblical and ancient Near Eastern tradition by casting its language of myth into an apocalyptic future. But historicizing is only one possible (although unlikely) reading that is particularly attractive to a modernist interpretation.

The collusion of the utopian metaphor of peace, expressive of the transcendent and eternal in well-recognized "apocalyptic" texts, hardly does more than reiterate themes already basic in the Hebrew Bible (e.g., Rev 22:16; cf. Num 24:17; Is 7:14; 9:16; 11:1–8). The eternal future of a universal kingdom of peace is basic to Eighteenth and Nineteenth Dynasty royal ideology, the Baal myth of ancient Ugarit, royal inscriptions throughout the ancient Near East and Assyrian campaign texts. It is used, for example, as a metaphor in Babylonian prophecy:

> He will renovate Uruk. The gates of the city of Uruk he will build with lapis lazuli. The canals and the irrigated fields, he will refill with the plenitude of abundance. . . . After him his son will come as king in Uruk and he will reign over the four regions of the earth. He will exercise sovereignty and royalty over Uruk. His dynasty will last forever. The king of Uruk will exercise sovereignty like the gods.[18]

The thematic elements of a new creation and the maintenance of creation by the king are not uniquely Jewish. They are fundamental to ancient Near Eastern royal ideology. Rather than apocalyptic, they are utopian in their essence. They recreate what had been intended since the beginning of time.

In spite of my strong disagreement with the Princeton consensus, I agree with Talmon that a historically developed "expectation of the Messiah" as an integral aspect of messianism in Judaism is not immediately implied by the biblical tradition.[19] Whether in the Hebrew Bible or in the gospels, the use of messianic metaphor bears a literary perspective of myth and story. The transcendence and immanence of myth renders such stories meaningful. They are not in themselves direct reflections of either past or future-oriented beliefs or expectations related to the world outside the texts. The issues are rather philosophical and theological, literary and intellectual. The development of beliefs and expectations, on the other hand, reflects the responses of readers of the tradition and is strongly influenced by the perception of the written tradition as an authoritative expression of the reader's worldview.

Astonishingly, a reference to anointing in David's song of lament over the death of Saul and Jonathan is raised as the singular exception to the use of the messiah metaphor, and therefore it is seen as irrelevant for understanding the messiah in the Hebrew Bible:

You mountains of Gilboa, let there be no dew or rain upon you nor fields of offerings; for there the shield of the mighty was defiled, the shield of Saul, not anointed with oil. (2 Sm 1:21)[20]

This is one of the few passages in which the metaphorical description of the king *specifically as anointed* carries an interpretive weight in its text. The song begs to be read not as an event but as an interpretation of the meaning of Saul's death for the greater story. Saul himself is the shield, who, without Yahweh's protection, can give none to those who seek refuge in him. The shield metaphor is central to an understanding of the anointment, through which Yahweh protects his messiah. Yahweh is the messiah's shield (Gen 15:1, as in Ps 3:4; 18:3; 28:8; 84:12; 144:2–3), which enables the messiah to be the shield of those who in piety seek their refuge in Yahweh (so, precisely, Ps 5:13; 18:31; 84:10; 91:4). That David's lament over Saul's death deals in messianic themes is confirmed by other imagery of the same song (2 Sm 1:19–27). He is "the hero who has fallen." As with Samaria's destruction, rejoicing must be rejected. Gilboa has become a desert because Israel's glory (mirroring Yahweh's glory) has fallen (2 Sm 1:19; Mic 2:9). In David's lament, there can be no "happy day" of a new creation. In Saul's death, as in Samaria's disaster, the singer prophesies also Jerusalem's undoing (Mic 1:8, 16). This is not a time of *shalom* but of evil (Mic 2:3), a foreshadowing of the exile to come.

The important theme of messianic time is not merely hyperbole. Nor should it be reduced to futuristic and simplistic expectations. It is a central metaphor for expressing control by the transcendent over events in this world. In Daniel 9, the time of exile is calculated as seventy years as in Jeremiah (Jer 25:11; 29:10). As Chronicles explains,: "Until the land has been reconciled for its Sabbaths, because as long as she lay desolate she has kept the Sabbath—to fulfill seventy years" (2 Chr 36:21). This chronology is based neither in realism nor mathematics but theology. The logic determining the time of salvation—for which the return from exile is the Bible's dominant metaphor—is based on the Torah commandment that the seventh year shall be a Sabbath year: a solemn rest for the land (Lev 25:4).[21] The measured time follows the holy war logic of retribution. In an expansion on the first commandment, Yahweh explains that if Israel obeys his commandment, he will grant rains at their time and give them all fertility and security. He will give peace, and their enemies will flee from them (Lev 26:1–13; Josh 23:10). However, if they do not obey, then their destiny will be disastrous (Lev 26:14–33; cf. Dt 32:30). The land will be a desert and its towns will revert to ruins. The land must rest because it wasn't able to rest while they lived there (Lev 26:34–35).

In prayer, Daniel points out that Yahweh's city has become a laughingstock among the nations, and so he should save it for his own sake (Dan 9:15–19). Gabriel tells him that the time of seventy weeks has been set, before eternal righteousness comes and the holy of holies is anointed (cf. Zech 1:12–17). For Daniel, the role of coming at the fullness of time to rebuild the temple is a messianic role given to Yahweh in the Psalter (Ps 102:13–15), where he will rebuild Jerusalem "in the time for showing mercy."[22] In this time of favor Yahweh calls Israel, who had been "despised, detested, a slave of rulers," to restore the land (Is 49:8). As mountains are turned into roads and roads to mountains, the heavens, earth and mountains will shout the good news: Yahweh's mercy to the helpless. The great flexibility of this literary role also allows it to be given to Zion (Is 49:14–21), as Isaiah complains, like the singer in the Psalter, that Yahweh had betrayed his messiah and forgotten him (Ps 89:39–52). In Isaiah, Yahweh denies the charge, arguing that he is like a mother, one who has given birth to Zion and cannot forget. Those who play the royal messiah's role of rebuilding the temple are already hurrying on the way. Such idealized, utopian visions of God's rule on earth stand opposed to a time-ordered world. The fullness of the past is present. Scattered from paradise and destroyed by the return of the waters of chaos in the great flood, God's new creation is scattered from Babylon, to be led back to Zion with Abraham. Sent again into slavery in Egypt, they are returned to the promised land under Joshua. In a never-ending story, the text searches provocatively for a new humanity, a new Israel with a pure heart. Its goal is to return to paradise. In this implicitly utopian quest through every generation, contrasting metaphors of the day of wrath and the day of mercy are used to forecast the story to come, but the ruling principle of messianic sacred time can be epitomized with the axiom that nothing is new under the sun:

> All things are full of weariness; a man cannot utter it; the eye is not satisfied with seeing, nor the earth filled with hearing. What has been is what will be, and what has been done is what will be done; and there is nothing new under the sun. Is there a thing of which it is said: "See, this is new"? It has been already, in the ages before us. There is no remembrance of former things, nor will there be any remembrance of later things yet to come. (Eccl 1:8–10)

This is not a product of historical thinking; nor does it project expectations of future change. It makes sense within the literary and intellectual world in which biblical texts were written.[23]

Linked by theme to the role of the messiah bringing divine mercy at the appointed time, the Torah uses the logic of retribution to bind such timely mercy to the death of Yahweh's messiah. One who has fled to a town of refuge because of unintentional manslaughter must remain there "until the death of the high priest who has been anointed with oil" (Num 35:25). That is to say, the life of the anointed one is the man's protection. While this role and the epithet "messiah" are also given to the Davidic king of the Psalter, in the Numbers narrative the messiah is the high priest, who, of course, dies. It is the office, his role as high priest, that is eternal and transcendent. In ending the exile of one who had been responsible for unintentional manslaughter, Numbers draws on an argument implicit in Isaiah. He addresses Yahweh with reference to the Babylonian exile: "Speak tenderly to Jerusalem. Declare to her that her term of service is over; her crime expiated" (Is 40:2). That this announcement of good news comes at the fullness of time, when the messiah reigns in peace, is implicit in Isaiah's rhetoric. A new creation prepares the return from exile by leveling mountains and straightening valleys (Is 40:3–5; cf. Mal 3:1–7; 4:5), a trope belonging to the reversal of fates and a sign of the kingdom. The expiation for crimes links the role of the priestly messiah in Numbers to the end of exile and the creation of a new Israel.

In related texts of the Pentateuch, the thematic element of reconciliation, linked with the role of the anointed, supports a coherent messiah figure. Both the mythic origins of anointing and the transcendent role of the forgiveness of sin are *secondarily* linked to the classic ancient Near Eastern role of heroic warrior and king. He bears equally mythic roles as savior, shepherd and shield of his people against the powers of chaos. He is typically identified in his role as king as divinely chosen one, son of god and judge over the eternal powers of destiny. The death of the anointed high priest expiating sin in Numbers can also be compared with the priest messiah of Leviticus, who similarly deals with unintended sin (Lev 4:1–21). In the situation in which guilt falls on the anointed priest himself (Lev 4:3), he cannot protect or redeem himself. The guilt is therefore transferred to the people, whom the priest then can represent before God and bring reconciliation. This central text on the theme of corporate guilt clearly marks the role of the messiah as both representative and mediator of the people before God. It also prepares the reader for the role of the messiah as the object of divine wrath. The priest's role also involves mediating the divine for the people. The understanding of the messiah as holy is illustrated in the origin story of the medallion to be worn on the high priest's forehead:

Take a medallion of pure gold and engrave on it, like the engraving of a signet, "Holy to Yahweh." Fasten it on the turban with blue lace, on the front of the turban. It will be on Aaron's forehead and Aaron will take upon himself any guilt incurred in the holy offering, which the people of Israel make holy as their holy gifts. It will always be on his forehead that they be accepted before Yahweh. (Ex 28:36–38)

At the end of the description of the high priest's clothing, Aaron's priesthood is described as "transcendent." With similar rhetoric, Aaron, the altar and its utensils are made holy by being anointed with oil (Lev 8:10–12). They are dedicated to Yahweh and to the temple service, much as Samuel and Samson are in their birth-of-a-hero stories (Jgs 13:7; 1 Sm 1:11). The traditions of Aaron's anointing are paraphrased by Ben Sira, explaining the messiah's function as bound by an eternal covenant to offer sacrifice, make atonement, exercise authority and judgment, teach the testimonies and enlighten with the law (Sir 45:6–17). The high priest is like Moses, equal to the holy ones (Sir 45:1–5). The role of the priestly messiah as representing the divine has a wonderful illustration in the story of Samuel's deathbed declaration of innocence (1 Sm 12:1–5). This story echoes ancient Near Eastern treaties, in which the king calls on the gods to be guarantors of a solemn declaration made in their presence. In Samuel's story, both Yahweh and his messiah are called on to guarantee Samuel's oath.

The coherence of the symbol system implied in this tradition is also apparent in the origin story about the creation of the magic oil for anointing. It is replete with Yahweh's recipe for the oil that makes one holy:

Take the finest spices: of liquid myrrh 500 shekels; of sweet-smelling cinnamon half as much; that is, 250 and of aromatic cane 250, of cassia 500 according to the sanctuary shekel and of olive oil a hin. Make of these a sacred anointing oil blended as by the perfumer: may it be holy anointing oil. (Ex 30:23–25)

Whatever the oil touches will become holy. This will be Yahweh's holy anointing oil through all of Israel's generations. No one may make the like again or use the oil on any other person (Ex 30:22–33). A reiterating gloss assigns the task of making the magic oil to Bezalel (Ex 31:1–11), who is filled with the spirit of God and uses divine knowledge to make the oil. This last detail offers an origin story to the messiah's (and the Nazirene's) association with divine power and spirit (cf. Ex 40:1–16; Num 3:1–4). This association is clearly understood in Qumran's Damascus Code, which speaks of "those anointed with his holy spirit" (CD 1–2).[24]

ETERNAL PROMISES AND THE
FAILURE OF THE COVENANT

The role of the messiah in biblical literature is dominated by the figures of the high priest in the Pentateuch and by the figure of the king in the stories from Joshua to 2 Kings, the books of the prophets and the Psalter, but it is hardly restricted to the figures of priest or king. The "anointed one" also identifies a prophet-like figure through whom divine *presence* is effected, much as is implied in the doubling of the Psalter's admonition: "Touch not my anointed ones; do my prophets no harm" (Ps 105:15; cf. 1 Chr 16:22; 2 Chr 6:40–42). More idealistic and transcendent roles connect the messiah with the divine spirit, announcing the good news to the poor, universal divine judgment (Is 61:1) and world-transforming changes (Jl 3:1; Is 61:1). The role in the Psalter of the king at war against "the nations in uproar against Yahweh and his anointed" (Ps 2:2; 110:5–6) might also be understood as universal and transcendent, since the goal of such war is to make the entire world subject to Yahweh. Foreign kings are also given roles as messiah in the Bible, which suggests that we should understand this term as mythic and theological rather than as a characteristic element related to a historical Israelite kingship. Even more than a Davidic king, foreign kings, in their role as messiah, messenger and bearer of divine patronage, present Yahweh as transcendent ruler of the entire world throughout history. The Aramean king Hazael, the Babylonian Nebuchadnezzar and the Persian Cyrus—messiahs all—bring Yahweh's judgments and blessings to Israel (1 Kgs 19:15–18; 2 Kgs 24:1–2; esp. 2 Chr 27:6–7; Is 45:1).

The interactive roles of the messiah as prophet, king, judge and priest are well-known aspects of the messiah's profile. These roles of illustration struggle constantly to maintain a doorway between transcendent and ephemeral worlds. In the opening chapters of 1 Samuel, which present the origin story of Yahweh's messianic king, recurrently echoing the stories of judges like Gideon (Jgs 6–8), Abimelek (Jgs 9–10), Jephthah (Jgs 11) and Samson (Jgs 13–16), the transference of the role of the chosen one from priest to prophet to king is presented. Playing relentlessly on the ambiguity of the transcendent in its relationship to the house of the messiah, the story establishes one of the central plotlines of the Saul–David chain narrative.

In an expansive variation of the Pentateuch's theme of the office of the high priest as an eternal gift to Aaron and his house (Num 18:1–10), the narrative of 1-2 Samuel expands the story of the rejection of Aaron's eldest sons, Nadab and Abihu, with two variations. Aaron's sons sinned by offering unholy fire in the sanctuary. In retribution, their sin (Ex 30:9) drew holy fire from Yahweh and killed them (Lev 10:1–5). Following the Pentateuch's story pattern of the younger superseding the elder, Aaron's sons are replaced in their office by his younger sons, Eleazar and Itamar (cf. Ex 6:23). In the opening story of the succession of the priesthood from Eli to Samuel, these wilderness stories are reiterated. The priest Eli was old, but "the sons of Eli were worthless; they had no regard for Yahweh" (1 Sm 2:12). They treated the offerings with contempt and they lay with the women who served in the Tent of Revelation. When Eli rebuked them, "they would not listen to their father, because it was Yahweh's will to kill them" (1 Sm 2:12–17, 22–25). Judgment comes in the context of an oracle from "a man of god," as Yahweh regrets his eternal promise to the house of Eli:

> Yahweh the God of Israel declares: "I promised that your house and the house of your father should go in an out before me forever." Now Yahweh declares: "It will not happen; for those who honor me, I will honor, but those who despise me will be lightly esteemed. Behold, the days are coming, when I will cut off your strength and the strength of your father's house. . . . I will raise up for myself a faithful priest, who will do what is in my heart and in my mind. I will build him a sure house and he will go in and out before my messiah forever. (1 Sm 2:30–31, 35)

This story begins a chain of narrative whose theme centers on an interpretation of the eternal promise as conditional. Drawing on the principles of Torah, the narrative transforms and subordinates the office of the messianic high priesthood to principles of justice. As the chain of narrative progresses, this same transformation is used to undermine the role of the king until it reaches Solomon. When David reaches the height of his success in war—with Jerusalem conquered and the Philistines defeated—the prophet Nathan visits him to speak of Solomon, to whom the role of *shalom* has been given. It is Solomon who will build the temple and it is to Solomon that the promise is given: "I will be his father and he will be my son" (2 Sm 7:14). When Solomon sins, Yahweh will beat him with a stock and give him stripes as men do, that he might learn. Yet he will not take his steadfast love from him as he had from Saul. "Your house and your kingdom will be made secure for ever before me; your throne will be established forever" (2 Sm 7:16). This is not a formula to create security. Knowing the story of Solomon's sons, the stock and stripes allusion to Isaiah's call to prophecy for his generation forces the reader to ask, with Isaiah, "How long?" (cf. Is 6:1–13).

Similarly, when Solomon is anointed with the holy oil by Zadok the priest (1 Kgs 1:39), the rule of the sons of David remains conditional. When David dies in the opening of the book of Kings, the eternal covenant dies with him. In his deathbed blessing, he gives the future into Solomon's hands and the conditional clause invites disaster in its wake:

> I go the way of all the earth. Be strong and show yourself a man. Keep the charge of Yahweh your God, walking in his ways and keeping his statutes, his commandments, his ordinances and his testimonies, as it is written in the law of Moses, that you may prosper in all that you do and wherever you turn that Yahweh may establish his word which he spoke concerning me, saying, "If your sons take heed to their way, to walk before me in faithfulness, with all their hearts and all their soul, there will not fail you a man on the throne of Israel." (1 Kgs 2:1–4)[25]

As parable, the story of the eternal covenant illustrates the principle of retribution in divine judgment. The theme is expressed in two songs with which the larger narrative opens and closes. Forming an interpretive frame for their narrative, these songs function much in the manner of Solomon's two visions, marking his rise and fall (1 Kgs 3:1–14; 1 Kgs 9:1–9; cf. above, Chapter 9). The first song is sung by Hannah, wife of Elkanah. It is a thanksgiving song of a barren woman who will be the mother of Yahweh's faithful priest. He will bear the "eternal priesthood" for his generation. It is a song of universal judgment, centered in the ethics of reversal and retribution we have seen in the song for a poor man. Its theme draws on the metaphor of God as holy from the story of Aaron and his sons, giving no room to human pride. Used as an introduction to the figure of Samuel as messiah, it lays stress on a demand for faithfulness and humility and points ahead to the future messiah as king:

> There is none holy like Yahweh; there is none besides you; there is no rock like our God. Talk no more so very proudly; let no arrogance come from your mouth, for Yahweh is a God of knowledge and by him actions are weighed. . . . He will guard the feet of his faithful ones, but the wicked will be cut off in darkness. Not by might will a man prevail. Yahweh's enemies will be broken to pieces; against them he will thunder in heaven. Yahweh will judge the ends of the earth; he will give strength to his king, and exalt the power of his messiah. (1 Sm 2:2–3, 9–10)

The Hannah story deals with Samuel's dedication to Yahweh and continues the holy war chain of heroes of the covenant. Because of the evil of Eli's sons, Yahweh chooses Samuel to be faithful priest instead. Like Samson, he is dedicated to

Yahweh from before his birth, with his mother filled with the Holy Spirit. Samuel was thrice called by Yahweh and answered that call with an obedience comparable to Abraham's (1 Sm 1–2). The narrative, however subtly, transforms Abraham's "walking before Yahweh" to Samuel walking before the messiah. Samuel will "do all that Yahweh wishes and intends, walking before his messiah all his days" (1 Sm 2:35). This understands the messiah in the essential role of the Near Eastern king: as mediator of the divine for his people and as demanding the total allegiance of his ministers. The story of Samuel superseding Eli effectively creates a harmonic bridge in a chain of supersession. As Eli's house is condemned to eternal punishment (1 Sm 3:13), so Hannah sings of the divine power over life and death (1 Sm 2:6). She sets the stage for Saul's (Hebrew *Sha'ul*) fall from grace and descent to Sheol, the realm of the dead. Eli's sons illustrate the Psalter's way of the godless (Ps 1:5–6; cf. 1 Sm 2:12). The supersession of Samuel to the priesthood, in addition to ending Yahweh's eternal promise to Levi, also passes on the high priest's role of bringing reconciliation for his own sin (1 Sm 3:14). In humbly accepting his fate and the fate of his house, Levi defines the role of a king, which Yahweh will play through the rest of the greater narrative: "He is Yahweh; he will do what is good in his own eyes" (1 Sm 3:18).

The second song offering interpretation to the greater story is sung by David at the end of his life. The song confirms the principles of Hannah's song and uses a similar logic of retribution, but applies it to the entire narrative. The fall of the houses of men—Eli, Samuel, Saul and David—serves as parable for the kingdom of God. David's song carefully reiterates the governing principles of Hannah's:

> Yahweh repays me according to my righteousness, according to my purity in his eyes. With the merciful you show yourself merciful; with the upright man you show yourself upright; with the pure you show yourself pure, but with the crooked you wrestle [referring to Israel: Gen 32:24–32]. The afflicted you will save, but your eyes are upon the proud: to bring them down. (2 Sm 22:25–28; Ps 18:25–28)

In contrast to Eli, Samuel stands in the path of righteousness (Ps 1:6). Through his father's cue name, his birth story presents him with the king's title of "son of God" and the role of messiah for the "God of creation" (1 Sm 1:1; Hebrew: *el kanah*: "God creates"). Samuel grew in stature and in favor with Yahweh and men (1 Sm 2:6). When he grows old in his narrative, Eli's story is reiterated. Samuel appoints his sons as judges over Israel, but his sons do not walk in his path. They take bribes and pervert justice (1 Sm 8:1–3).

Yahweh's rejection of Samuel's house quickly gives way to a story of Israel's rejection of Yahweh and the supersession of the priest by the king. The elders of Israel go to Samuel and, pointing out that his sons do not follow in his path, ask him to give them a king "to govern us like all the nations" (1 Sm 8:5). An unhappy Samuel consults Yahweh and is told to accept the request: "For they have not rejected you. They have rejected me from being king over them" (1 Sm 8:7). Yahweh compares this story of Samuel and the people to Moses and the wilderness generation: "Ever forsaking him and serving other gods"—a never-ending betrayal. The scene closes forebodingly with Yahweh's warning of the king's future tyranny and enslavement of the people. When they cry out to Yahweh for help, Yahweh will not answer, for he is no longer their king (1 Sm 8:10–22; cf. Ex 15:18). When the prophet Balaam interprets what Yahweh did in bringing Israel out of Egypt, the image of the people as bearing with them their transcendent king casts the story as fulfillment of the divine plan of the covenant stories:

> Yahweh their God is with them and the voice of the king is among them. God brings them out of Egypt. They have as it were the horns of a wild ox. . . . Now it shall be said of Jacob and Israel, "What has God wrought!" Behold a people! As a lioness it rises up and as a lion it lifts itself. It does not lie down until it devours the prey and drinks the blood of the slain. (Num 23:21–24)

If, in bringing them out of Egypt, Yahweh had provided his people with a king's voice, they will now, in rejecting Yahweh, need to listen to the voice of a man. Yahweh's quest for a people has come to nothing and he must give them to another. The implications of the scene are great: no longer a holy people, they will be a nation like others. They are no longer the people of God but will have a king like others. He—and by implication not Yahweh—will stand in their midst, and he—not Yahweh—will fight their wars.

The premonition of impending disaster such a leitmotif supports is mixed with alternating hopeful scenes of Saul's election, delaying Yahweh's judgment of Saul. Yahweh chooses a king and sends Samuel to anoint him. He has heard the cry of his people and answers (1 Sm 9:16–17). This intimation of hope is doubled when Samuel invites Saul to dine with him and Saul responds with classic humility: Benjamin is the least of the tribes and Saul's the humblest of the families of Benjamin. Invited to dine, a humble Saul is placed at the head of the table and given a portion kept for this "appointed hour" (1 Sm 9:22–24). The story's progress continues, marked with the portent favor of the rising sun. "At the break of dawn," Samuel pours oil over Saul, telling him that Yahweh anoints him as prince to rule over his people and save them from their enemies. The scene of Saul's anointing closes by opening an alternative future. Samuel puts Saul to a simple but fateful test: "I am coming to you to offer burnt offerings and to sacrifice peace offerings. Seven days you shall wait, until I come to you to show you what to do" (1 Sm 10:1–8).

As Saul leaves Samuel, God gives him a new heart and the signs are fulfilled that same day. With the spirit of God, Saul prophesies with the prophets (1 Sm 10:9–13). As Saul now moves toward the crossroads of his fate, warning signals over having a man as king return. The breach of the covenant and apostasy that kingship and nation bring are brought to center stage. When Samuel calls the people together to choose Saul as their king, he tells them that they "have this day rejected your God, who saves you from all calamity and distress" (1 Sm 10:19). With such words, the audience is prepared. However, when Saul stands among the people, there is none like him: Yahweh's chosen one is a head taller than all the others. With this recommendation, they shout, "Long live the king" (1 Sm 10:24). At the close of the greater story, this shout finds a contrasting echo in the submissive shout of David's defeated enemies: "Yahweh lives!" (2 Sm 22:46–47).

In a story with many echoes from the book of Judges, Saul acknowledges that it is Yahweh who has delivered them and learns his messianic role as tool of the divine spirit (1 Sm 11:12–15; cf. Jgs 3:10; 6:34; 11:29–40; 13:25; 14:6, 19; 15:24; 19:22–30; 1 Sm 10–14). Throughout this story of the king and the divine spirit that guides him, the author uses every opportunity to prepare the audience for Saul's coming failure. The author uses the opportunity in Samuel's farewell address (1 Sm 12:1–25) to warn the people, reminding them of their apostasy and preparing his own audience for Saul's threefold test. They chose a man for their king rather than Yahweh, and his appointment is clearly conditional and implicitly threatening (1 Sm 12:14–15).

The story takes great pains to present Saul at the beginning of his reign as committed to his people's welfare and protection. He is well-meaning, ever cast in the role of the good king of ancient Near Eastern inscriptions. Saul's final test comes with instructions from Yahweh to attack the Amalekites. The attack is to fulfill Moses' judgment against this people for attacking Israel in the wilderness story (Dt 25:17–19). As Moses' curse had been to "blot out the memory of Amalek under heaven," they are now placed under the ban, dedicated to Yahweh with an eightfold list for destruction: "Man and woman, child and infant, ox and sheep, camel and ass" (1 Sm 15:3). Saul directs the war against the Amalekites with a good general's integrity, limiting the slaughter in the story's every line. First, he spares the Kenites because they showed kindness to the Israelites when they came out of Egypt (1 Sm 15:6). In his victory, he takes Agag, their king and the best of the livestock, alive. He destroys "only what is worthless."

The figure of Yahweh is cast in contrast. Angry at Saul's mercy, he sends a message to Samuel:

> I repent that I have made Saul king; for he has turned back from following me and has not performed my commandments. (1 Sm 15:11)

Saul does not understand. Great stress is laid on this. When Samuel comes to him with the message of Yahweh's rejection, Saul tells him about how successfully he has "performed Yahweh's commandments" (1 Sm 15:13). Samuel, however, understands what Saul does not: though Saul has spared the best to be sacrificed to Yahweh, he did not obey. Saul denies this again. The best of things devoted to destruction are to be sacrificed to Yahweh at Gilgal (1 Sm 15:17–22). Samuel closes the debate by paraphrasing Jeremiah and the theology of the prophets:

> Has Yahweh as great delight in burnt offerings and sacrifices as in obeying the voice of Yahweh? Behold, to obey is better than sacrifice and to listen than the fat of rams. Rebellion is as the sin of divination; stubbornness as idolatry. Because you have rejected Yahweh's word, he also has rejected you as king. (1 Sm 15:22–23; cf. Jer 7:22–23; also Is 1:11–14; Jer 6:20; Hos 6:6; Am 5:21–23; Mic 6:6–8)

This brings Saul to repent with great humility, confessing his sin and asking for pardon that he might worship Yahweh in a threefold acceptance of his fate. As Saul has rejected Yahweh's word, so Yahweh rejects Saul. Saul takes hold of the fringe of Samuel's robe and begs a second time to be forgiven. Having Samuel answer that Yahweh has given the kingship to "a neighbor" who is better than Saul, the author points ahead to Saul's future efforts to murder David and specifically to the scene in the cave when David cuts this fringe from Saul's robe and—being the neighbor Samuel speaks of—takes the kingdom from him. A third time Saul repents, now asking not for forgiveness but only that he be allowed to worship Yahweh. The scene closes as Saul worships Yahweh.

After this scene of Saul's humiliation and final rejection, Samuel is again instructed to fill his horn with oil. He is sent to Bethlehem to choose a king from among Jesse's sons (1 Sm 16:1). This time, the king is not chosen as a man would choose a king. Yahweh does not see as a man sees, but looks into the heart.

Though Samuel would have chosen Eliab, Yahweh has learned his lesson and does not choose by appearance or by a man's height. Seven of Jesse's sons pass by Samuel, but none of them are chosen. There remains but the youngest, who—with implicit prophecy—is watching the sheep. David is chosen and anointed by Samuel. The spirit comes upon him from that day on (1 Sm 16:6–13). As soon as the spirit that had been with Saul is transferred to David, Saul suffers its replacement: an evil spirit that torments him (1 Sm 16:14).

Beginning a wonderfully illustrative narrative discourse on the Torah's command to love one's neighbor (Lev 19:18, 34), the story of David in the books of Samuel joins forces with the Psalter. David is the neighbor, the "beloved" ("David" in Hebrew). David's skill at the lyre brings Israel's shepherd into Saul's service. He is recommended to Saul with a sixfold of virtue: "skillful in playing, a man of valor, a man of war, prudent in speech, of good presence and Yahweh is with him" (1 Sm 16:18–19). As in the story of Saul's election, David is provided with bread, wine and meat (1 Sm 16:20). Saul loves David, who becomes his armor bearer, and whenever God's evil spirit haunts Saul, David plays his lyre and the evil spirit departs (1 Sm 16:23).

The story of David's entrance into Saul's service is doubled by the heroic legend of the killing of Goliath (1 Sm 17), one who for forty days challenged the Israelites to send a hero to fight him in a duel. The Israelites in fear flee from Goliath. The king promises riches and his daughter as a prize to any man who will fight Goliath. David asks with scorn who this "foreskin man" is, who mocks the living God's army (1 Sm 17:25–26). David, the shepherd boy, takes up the challenge. Like Job, the good shepherd of his people who broke the jaws of evil and ripped its booty from its maw (Job 29:17), a shepherd boy, David tells Saul, is used to fighting lions and bears to save animals from their jaws (1 Sm 17:35). He takes up the challenge and Yahweh is with him (1 Sm 17:37). Little David, of course, cannot move in Saul's armor or fight with Saul's sword and so must take his shepherd's crook and five smooth stones from the brook. The entire scene mirrors the holy war tradition. To Goliath, David is just a boy and he calls David to come on that he might feed his flesh to the birds (1 Sm 17:42–44). David, like Joshua before him who called on Israel to eat giants (Num 14:9), tells his giant that it is Goliath's flesh that the birds will eat. Goliath is ignorant that Yahweh does not save with sword and spear, yet war belongs to Yahweh (1 Sm 17:45–47; cf. Ex 15:3; Zech 4:6). Though he has no sword or spear, David slays his giant and the Philistines flee the battlefield.

As this story also brings David into Saul's service and into the chain narrative, Jonathan also loves David as David's name requires. This opening to a new plotline plays out its role of complicating the plot, which will contrast all the world's love for David to the hatred of Saul and his evil spirit. David's fame spreads to compete with Saul's: "Saul has slain his thousands and David his ten thousands" (1 Sm 18:7). Saul becomes angry and the evil spirit rushes again on him, even though David plays his lyre. Saul tries to kill David with a spear as hatred replaces love (1 Sm 18:10–11).

With Saul now David's enemy, the story turns to the prize David won for his victory over Goliath: the hand of the king's daughter in marriage. Thinking that the Philistines will kill David for him, Saul offers David his eldest daughter, Merab, in marriage on the condition that David will fight Yahweh's battles. David is humble and does not consider himself worthy to be son-in-law to the king. When the time comes for his wedding, Merab is given to another (1 Sm 18:17–19). Michal, however, like her brother Jonathan, loved David and so Saul tries a second time, that the Philistines might kill his enemy for him. David again demurs: he is a poor man,: not one to be son-in-law to a king (1 Sm 18:20–24). Having tied the story once again to the song for a poor man and the Torah's command to love the neighbor—even this stranger and enemy, the story takes up a hero's test in Saul's third offer of a daughter to be David's bride. Saul is now direct in his plan to have him killed by the Philistines. He answers David's poor man's demurral by telling him that the bride-price is a mere one hundred Philistine foreskins. This David can accept. Before the deadline expires, he delivers not one hundred but two hundred Philistine foreskins to the king, in reiteration of the doubling of Jacob's bride price in his story (Gen 30:15–30). David takes Michal for his bride and Saul becomes David's enemy on a daily basis (1 Sm 18:25–29).

In terms of the greater story, Saul's efforts to kill his loyal servant, David, prepare the way for David's later, successful efforts to send his own servant to death in in the guise of holy war. A threefold attempt by Saul to kill David with his spear sends the story into a complex reiteration of the classic hero's flight into the wilderness, which belongs to the myth of the good king. Jonathan and Michal save David in spite of Saul's efforts to kill him. Saul's own children love David and are hated by Saul in return (1 Sm 19–20). David, alone in the wilderness and hunted, seeks asylum with the priest Ahimelek in the town of Nob. He gives him magic symbols: the bread of Yahweh's presence and Goliath's sword (1 Sm 21:1–9). Chased by Saul, David again flees to the Philistine king of Gath, where he feigns madness (1 Sm 21:10–14). According to the Psalter, it is in this scene that David learned to fear God and to sing of the joy of the humble whom Yahweh answered, of the helpless whom Yahweh heard, of the righteous to whom Yahweh's eyes turn and of the brokenhearted whom Yahweh saves (Ps 34:1, 3, 7, 16, 19, 22). Finally David flees to the cave of Adullam, where his father and brothers and all who are in distress, discontent and debt join him. This salvation army of David's heroes of the poor—four hundred strong—turn flight to resistance (1 Sm 22:1–2).

After moving his mother and father to safety, David breathlessly runs into a threefold story of flight and betrayal. The first episode presents Saul, spear in hand, as enemy of Yahweh (1 Sm 22–23). Fighting unholy war, Saul orders an entire city of Yahweh's priests to be massacred in: an ironic reversal of the figure of Saul as the good king, unwilling to destroy what was of value. Men and women, children and infants, oxen, asses and sheep are put to the sword (1 Sm 22:19; cf. 1 Sm 15:3). Abiathar, Ahimelek's son, the lone remnant of this slaughter, escapes and seeks refuge with David. In the following story, Saul lays siege to the city of Keilah, where Yahweh has sent David to fight the Philistines. David is forewarned by Yahweh that the people of Keilah will betray him and he escapes (1 Sm 23:1–14). Saul's ongoing pursuit of David, which dominates the narrative for five chapters (1 Sm 22–26), finds mocking caricature in the wilderness of Maon at the "rock of escape," where Saul chases David around one side of the rock and David escapes around the other (1 Sm 23:15–29).

Finally, informed once again where David hides, Saul returns to close his quest for David's life. The story is told through a tale of two variants. The first is set at En Gedi and the other on the hill at Hachilah (1 Sm 24; 26). In the first story, Saul is told where David is hiding and takes three thousand picked men and resumes his hunt for David. Coming to a cave, he stops to relieve himself, not knowing that David and his men are hiding inside. Seeing Saul at their mercy, David's men tempt David with a citation from the Psalter:

> Here is the day of which Yahweh said to you: "Behold, I give your enemy into your hand. You will do to him as it seems good to you." (1 Sm 24:4; cf. Ps 63:1–2, 10–11)

What "seems good" to David, however, is not Saul's death as his men had thought. Instead, David cuts the fringe from Saul's robe, echoing the scene in which Saul grabbed Samuel's cloak (1 Sm 15:27). David regrets even this impulsive action and repents that he has put his hand against Yahweh's anointed. His argument persuades his men to spare Saul's life, as Saul is allowed to go his way (1 Sm 24:4–7). This scene requires an interpretive gloss. To understand why David reproaches himself for "cutting off" Saul's "fringe" (1 Sm 24:6; *karat et-kanaf*: "emasculate"), the scene needs to be understood with reference to the Egyptian military practice, discussed in Chapter 8, of marking enemy dead by cutting off a hand of those who had been circumcised (i.e., dedicated to a deity), rather than cutting off the penis of one uncircumcised. The testicles—like the hands—signify the soldier's strength. Moreover, as Saul and David both belong to the same deity, David cannot treat him as an enemy, as he does when he symbolically emasculates Saul. Similarly, when Saul gripped Samuel's fringe, begging for another chance, he symbolically clung to the power Samuel had given him. Repenting his act and rejecting his heroes' suggestion that he kill Saul (cf. Mt 26:51–53), David wins recognition as Saul's son and heir to the kingdom.

The song the Psalter has David sing while he is in the cave (Ps 142:1) has several motifs that can be linked to the story in interesting ways. David "pours out his complaint" to Saul and finally "brings his troubles before him" (Ps 142:3; cf. 24:9–15). The "trap in the path where he walks," if attributed to Saul walking into the cave, works very nicely as does the following verse in the mouth of David unseen by Saul: "look to the right" and "there is none who takes notice of me" (Ps 142:4–5; cf. 1 Sm 24:3–5). The trap might yet be in David's path, since David walks in the path of righteousness and his "trap" is this scene's central theme: to kill Yahweh's messiah (1 Sm 24:6–7). In the Psalter's commentary on this story, David cries to Yahweh as his refuge and begs that his cry be heard (Ps 142:2, 5–6). Nevertheless, the most defining prayer for his story's parable is David's final plea that Yahweh intervene in his conflict with Saul: "May Yahweh be judge and judge between you and me and let him see and plead my cause and deliver me from your hand" (1 Sm 24:15). This line intellectually epitomizes David and Saul's conflict. It resolves that conflict and brings Saul finally to recognize David, delivering him and bringing him from his "prison" (Ps 142:7–8; cf. 1 Sm 24:17–18). At the last, Saul goes home while David returns to "his way" with his "righteous" men to the stronghold (Ps 142:8; cf. 1 Sm 24:22).

The plot does not turn on the story's surface conflict between the good David and the evil Saul. Not even that Saul is the great king and David the poor man, the prince of the downtrodden. It turns on their relationship to Yahweh, their true king and patron. That is what drives the plot. David tells his men that he will not kill Yahweh's messiah. As David tells Saul in the closing debate, he did not kill Saul because "he will not put his hand *against Yahweh*" (1 Sm 24:10). To sin against Saul—Yahweh's anointed—is the same as to sin against Yahweh. This pivotal argument was first established at the opening of the chain narrative, when Eli's sons had no respect for Yahweh (1 Sm 2:12). In rebuking his sons for their sin, Eli succinctly exposed the key to a narrative progression that does not close until the confrontation between David and Saul:

If a man sins against a man, God will mediate for him; but if a man sins against Yahweh, who can intercede for him? (1 Sm 2:25)

Eli's proverb, distinguishing a sin against a man from a sin against God, structures the narrative chain. In rejecting Eli's house, Yahweh rejects the high priest's eternal role in reconciling sin through sacrifice. The eternal promise of blessing becomes an eternal punishment (1 Sm 3:13–14). An eternal covenant opens the way to an eternal rejection of those who break it.

In the theme's second movement, which deals with Saul's rejection, the same logic of retribution is reiterated. Because Jonathan, in eating honey, had sinned against man—Saul—his sin could be forgiven and his life ransomed (1 Sm 14:45). Saul, however, in wishing to displace obedience with sacrifice, sinned against God (1 Sm 15:23). *Yahweh is not a man that the sin can be forgiven* (1 Sm 15:29). Finally, in the confrontation between Saul and David, David's decision not to raise his hand against Yahweh breaks the pattern of eternal rejection (1 Sm 24:10). In an interesting reversal of the motif in the variant story, David addresses the issue with an explicit argument addressed to the king for judgment:

If it is Yahweh who has stirred you up against me, may he accept an offering; but if it is men, may they be cursed before Yahweh, for they have driven me out this day that I should have no share in Yahweh's heritage, saying: "Go serve other gods!" Now, therefore, let not my blood fall to the earth, away from Yahweh's presence. For the king of Israel has come out to seek a flea, like one hunts a partridge in the mountains. (1 Sm 26:19–20)

David's self-designation as a flea (in the cave story, "a dead dog, a flea" is used: 1 Sm 24:14) is important, as it underscores his humility, an abiding motif of the entire chain narrative. It is clear from this closing episode that it is not sacrifice as such that is superseded by an ethical reinterpretation and internalization of the Torah, but the use of sacrifice to heal a breach of the covenant—the sin that cannot be forgiven. This was already announced in the story of Moses' covenant of blood that closed with the warning that disobedience to Yahweh's messenger would not be forgiven (Ex 23:21). David and Saul are both clients of the same king—Yahweh. As a client of Yahweh, David owes respect to the anointed one Yahweh has chosen. Therefore, to raise his hand against Saul is a sin against Yahweh. However, Saul is also in Yahweh's service and he cannot usurp the role of the true king by doing what he sees is right (1 Sm 3:18). By hunting David, Saul—as Yahweh's chosen king on earth—chases David from Yahweh's service. He forces him into the service of another god. Saul's sin is against Yahweh. With his argument in place, David declares his subordinate status. A humble flea submits to Saul's judgment as king. Saul acknowledges David as his son and himself a fool (1 Sm 26:21). The story closes with Saul's blessing (1 Sm 26:25).

Saul's closing acknowledgment, echoing Judah's closing judgment that Tamar is more righteous than he (Gen 38:26), is that David is the more righteous. David acted well, while Saul did evil. This not only shares the David story's technique of illustrating the Psalter (1 Sm 24:18; cf. Ps 35:12), but closes the narrative with an echo of Genesis. The story of David and Saul in the cave closes on the theme of David's destiny as king and awaits Saul's death at the close of the book. The story of David and Abishai in Saul's camp in the dead of the night is, however, denied the closure its variant had received. Saul's acknowledgment of David's justice, with its closing blessing of David's success (1 Sm 26:21–25), is undermined in the opening of the next narrative in the chain (1 Sm 27:1).

David does not believe Saul and flees to the Philistines. He and his men spend their time fighting a holy war against the nations left in the land by Joshua. All the while, he tells his Philistine overlord he is killing Judeans (1 Sm 27:8–12). When the Philistines threaten Saul after Samuel dies, he finally fills the potential of his cue name (Hebrew: *Sha'ul*; cf. *she'ol* "realm of the dead"). Saul secretly seeks Samuel's counsel with the help of necromancers (1 Sm 28:8–14). This prepares the reader for his own death and descent to the underworld. Samuel, irritated at being disturbed during his well-earned rest, reminds Saul that Yahweh has become his enemy and has given his kingship to his neighbor (1 Sm 28:16–17). He prophesies that on the morrow Saul will meet his fate at the hands of the Philistines—the destiny he had pressed on David. Forced to leave the Philistines because of their conflict with Saul (1 Sm 29), David hunts the Amalekites with six hundred men. Two hundred of them, however, were too exhausted by the chase to continue. After attacking and defeating the Amalekites, rich with plunder from Philistia and Judah, David collects the spoil and returns to the two hundred he left behind. The wicked and base among his men refuse to share the booty with those who did not fight with them. David rejects their protest, pointing out that Yahweh gave them the plunder and Yahweh preserved them in battle. The spoil belongs to Yahweh. David makes a statute and an ordinance "to this day," as is later illustrated in the gospels, that every laborer shall have the same pay (1 Sm 30; Mt 20:1–16).

The final chapter of the book of 1 Samuel closes on Saul's death at the hands of the Philistines (1 Sm 31). David's song of lament over his death (2 Sm 1:19–27) uses balanced rhetoric to mark the story death with messianic themes. Contrasting Saul's death with the living messiah's horn, ever raised to bring fertility to his land, David calls on the hills of Gilboa to create drought. This is not a time for life (Eccl 3:2–4). The anointed one lies dead. In a contrasting discourse with this song, Jeremiah's Lamentations present the messiah as the very cause of life's breath (Lam 4:20), much as Merneptah in his victory song brought the breath of life to the nations. In David's song, Saul's protection is gone. No longer messiah, he is an unoiled shield. Other themes also cluster. Rather than announce victory over Saul, as, for example, victory over death and the powers of chaos, as had been broadcast to the world at Ramses IV's birth, Saul's death must not be mentioned, lest the Philistines (Ps 2:2, "nations")—those foreskin men of David's scorn, not dedicated to Yahweh—rise in rebellion. David's plaintive lament, the leitmotif of his song, "How heroes have fallen" (2 Sm 1:19, 25, 27), allows the closure to evoke a pale ghost of *shalom*: the absence of war. Weapons are broken (2 Sm 1:27b; cf. 2 Sm 2:4), but are they turned to ploughshares? In David's grieving, he likens Saul and his son to kings and gods at war: "swifter than eagles" and "stronger than lions" (2 Sm 1:23). In this, he echoes ancient Near Eastern metaphors of kings and their gods as wild bulls, lions and birds of prey.[26] Adad, the god of Syria, at war is pictured as a roaring lion and as a deity with thunderbolts. Assur, the god of Assyria, is an attacking eagle in the sky, high above his mirrored image of the king in his chariot.[27] The Lamentations of Jeremiah (4:17–20) draw a refraction of this same trope. Jerusalem's end is near and there is no hope: "Those who pursue us are quicker than the eagles of the sky." The parallel verse holds a lion implicit: "They hunt us in the hills and lie waiting for us in the desert." Meanwhile, an empty messiah (an Israel that could not save) lies dead, caught in the traps laid for him. The tragedy of loss is all the greater, as it was in Yahweh's protective shadow that Israel lived among the nations, sheltered by eagles' wings.

DAVID AND THE ROLE OF ELIJAH

With David's lament over Saul and Jonathan's death in his "Song of the Bow" opening 2 Samuel, the plot of the narrative turns to a cycle of betrayal, murder and vengeance in the outbreak of war between Israel and Judah (2 Sm 2:12–32), reiterating the greater tradition's competition between Samaria and Jerusalem. David becomes king in Hebron (2 Sm 2:1–7), while Saul's son, Ishbosheth ("a man of shame"), is made king over the "whole of Israel" (2 Sm 2:8-11):

> The war between Saul's house and David's house was long and drawn out. David grew stronger and stronger, while Saul's house grew weaker and weaker. (2 Sm 3:1)

The leitmotif of David's innocence from bloodguilt in this civil war, begun already in the story of Saul and Jonathan's deaths, continues in an expansive reiteration of the story of regicide and bloodguilt from the Hittite legend of Telepinu (see above, Chapter 5; cf. 2 Kgs 12:20–22; Jer 31:29–30; Ez 18): first in the assassination of Abner, Saul's general by David's Joab (2 Sm 3:36–39), and then in the brutal murder of Ishbosheth (2 Sm 4:5–12).

Spared such guilt by his astute general, Joab, David becomes Israel's king and takes a Jebusite Jerusalem from "the blind and lame whom David hates" (2 Sm 5:6–12). In a series of quick campaigns, he brings the nations under his rule: the Philistines, Moabites, Ammonites and Arameans (2 Sm 5; 8; 10). Interlaced with these holy war stories are three tales marking David's victory with signs of the peace and transcendence of the kingdom of his God. First David brings the ark to Jerusalem, returning Israel's glory and ending the shame that killed Eli when the ark was taken as booty by the Philistines (2 Sm 6; 1 Sm 4:1-22). In a second tale, the prophet Nathan announces to David that Yahweh is with him and, as Marduk promised Nabonidus (see above, Chapter 5), he will do all that he wishes. Also, like Nebuchadnezzar and so many of the kings of the ancient world, David has his kingdom established for eternity (2 Sm 7:5–17). The third story of peace in his kingdom lays the ground for the theme of reconciliation that dominates and closes the greater narrative. This Elijah role of reconciliation in 2 Samuel parallels Elisha's role of peace and love of the enemy in 2 Kings. David demonstrates the mercy and graciousness of a great king. He invites the sole survivor of the house of Saul, Mephibosheth ("from the mouth of shame": 2 Sm 9), to be his guest at the king's table. Taking up Jacob's role as the crippled Israel (Gen 32:31–32), a twice-lame Mephibosheth reenters Jerusalem and overturns David's curse, which had banished all blind and lame from Jerusalem (2 Sm 5:8).

The theme of David's peace hardly survives these three tales. The story of his adultery and the murder of his faithful servant Uriah opens a new round of violence as David's sword of victory (1 Sm 21:10), which had supported him since his flight from Saul, now becomes the sword of retribution, over David's house (2 Sm 11–19). At the close of this chain of rape, murder and conspiracy, which covers his house with shame and scandal, David once again sings a lament when his beloved son Absalom dies. He too is killed by David's ever-faithful Joab (2 Sm 18:9-18). This second movement of 2 Samuel's narrative, opening with the story of David's great sin (2 Sm 11), presents the tragic fall of David's house. It is highlighted by the stories of his son Amnon raping his daughter Tamar (2 Sm 13:1-20), the murder of Amnon by his brother Absalom in avenging his sister (2 Sm 13:21–39) and Absalom's banishment from Jerusalem and his conspiracy and war against his father (2 Sm 14:1-15,12), which finally drives David from the city and his throne (2 Sm 15:13–16:14). When Absalom becomes the victim of Joab's third assassination, David's heart is broken. He returns to Jerusalem in victory, only to face another revolt. The Benjaminite Sheba, mirroring Absalom—who had taken David's ten wives (whom the returning David condemned to live as widows [2 Sm 16:21–22; 20:3])—now takes from David the ten tribes of Israel. At the center of the story of the fall of David's house is a scene of humility: crying, barefoot and in mourning, David climbs his Mount of Olives to pray. In striking contrast to the story of Saul trusting his own judgment (1 Sm 15:1-35), David accepts a future that not he but Yahweh determines (2 Sm 15:25–26). This acceptance sets the stage for the third movement of the narrative.

Three tales of reconciliation dominate this third movement and close the David story of the books of Samuel. (1) The first story opens with a three-year drought. Yahweh sent the drought as punishment for the bloodguilt Saul incurred when he tried to exterminate the Gibeonites (2 Sm 21:1–2). The Gibeonites demand the death of seven of Saul's sons to revenge their father's war crimes (2 Sm 21:4–9; cf. Gen 4:15). David accepts their demand, and Saul's sons return to the story to be executed on the first days of the harvest as the drought ends (2 Sm 21:9).

This brief story reverses the holy war demand of ethnic cleansing and reconciles Israel with the people of the land. It is followed by a song David borrows from the Psalter, now that "Yahweh has saved him from all his enemies" (Ps 18; 2 Sm 22). Although the entire song is important for the understanding of the messiah as mediator and model for the pious who sing the songs of the messiah in the Psalter, it has its climax in the final three of its seven stanzas (2 Sm 22:31–51), illustrating the Torah epitome of love of one's enemy. The violence and hatred of holy war are reversed in a vision of resurrection and reconciliation. The song's fifth stanza (2 Sm 22:31–37) describes the messiah as holy warrior, born and bred for war, protected and supported by Yahweh. The following stanza (2 Sm 22:38–43) projects a victory scene in battle, in which the pious—who had previously trembled in fear and terror at the war's violence—welcome Yahweh's support and turn on their enemy. The hunted becomes the hunter and remorselessly pursues and destroys his enemies, finally catching and forcing them into submission. This holy warrior's ferocity is remarkable:

Those who hate me, I kill. They call for help, but there is none to help; they cry to Yahweh, but he does not answer. I beat them down as dust before the wind; like offal in the streets, I exterminate them. (2 Sm 22:40–42)

The intensity echoes Yahweh in the flood story, capturing with precision the sectarian fanaticism of a world in black and white. Like the Psalter's godless, those who hate God's warriors will be blown away like chaff or burned.[28]

The messiah of this song plays the role of the three messiahs of Elijah's judgment—Hazael, Jehu and Elisha—to destroy and exterminate. The enemy are dust, which an exile's wind scatters. The final stanza of the song, however, turns back to the fundamental elements of the messiah myth:

> You delivered me from the noise of peoples; you appointed me as ruler over the nations. A people I hated have subjected themselves to me. As soon as they heard, they obeyed me; strangers stretched themselves out on their bellies. The enemy withered; they came shaking from their cave: "Yahweh lives!" Blessed be my rock; may the God of my salvation be upraised. He is the God who has given me retribution and subdued peoples under me, who delivered me from my enemies. Yes, you have exalted me over those who stand against me. You have saved me from men of violence. (2 Sm 22:44–49)

Basic themes of the tradition are reiterated. Especially noteworthy is the noise of rebellion, which is the foundation of Marduk's battle with the monster of chaos in the Babylonian creation story and echoes the roar of the sea in Exodus 15, the noise of Sodom's perfidy (Gen 19) and the noise of singing and dancing in the golden calf story (Ex 32:1–35). As in Psalm 2, where the messiah advises the princes in uproar against Yahweh to kiss with a pure heart and submit themselves to Yahweh's rule, David's song evokes a similar change of destiny. A people unloved—Israel—now learns humility and subjects itself to the kingdom. Strangers, foreigners and enemies subject themselves to the messiah in perfect obedience. The theology of the way in Psalm 1 is reinterpreted in a metaphor of resurrection. Those who are worthless—the godless who walked in the path of sinners, who were remorselessly exterminated and driven into the underworld of the dead—now come shaking out of their caves (graves?). Such "shaking" (2 Sm 22:46) is intentionally ambiguous. They shake not only in fear and humiliation but with an ecstatic shaking of awe for their God. The noise of their rebellion is transformed into a shout: "Yahweh lives!" This is the excited crowd of the Hasidim ("the pious") shouting together. The song closes with an expression of the understanding of the converted pious: the parallel of Isaiah's repentant remnant in the metaphor of Israel as Yahweh's suffering servant. David as the messiah stands with the nations, praising Yahweh. Stranger, foreigner and enemy are reconciled. They become one with the pious: the remnant of Israel is gathered to

Jerusalem in Isaiah 65 from all corners of the world (cf. the motif of desert transformed to fertile land in Is 35 and of transformation in Is 55).

The third and final scene in 2 Samuel begins with Yahweh's anger at Israel. He tempts David into taking a census to measure the strength of Israel and Judah's troops for war (2 Sm 24). Although Joab protests, David insists on making the count. When he learns, however, that there are 800,000 Israelites to his 500,000 Judeans, David repents his mustering of the armies, which would once again have sent Israel and Judah into a disastrous civil war.[29]

For this deed, Yahweh offers David the choice of three years of famine (cf. 2 Sm 21), three months being chased by his enemies or three days of plague (2 Sm 24:13–14). While David chooses the plague because he prefers the mercy of Yahweh to the terror of men, the narrator has other reasons for David's choice. Stories of both famine and pursuit have already been told. Moreover, the Pentateuch's law for census taking (Ex 30:12-16) requires—with a threat of a three days' plague—that reconciliation be paid for every soldier mustered to holy war. The plague Yahweh sends ravages the whole of Israel—from Dan to Beersheva— and kills 70,000 (2 Sm 24:16). When the angel of death approaches Jerusalem, however, Yahweh repents and stays his hand. The remnant saved, David repents his choice of punishment at the threshing floor. The innocent have suffered though the sin was David's, and he asks that the punishment be directed against him and his father's house in order to introduce the story line of 1–2 Kings.

In closing these three stories of reconciliation and the book of 2 Samuel as a whole, David takes on the role of the high priest. Like Noah, Abraham and Moses before him, he builds an altar on the threshing floor—the site of the temple Solomon later builds—and offers a burnt offering in reconciliation, that the plague might be diverted from the people of Jerusalem (2 Sm 24:18–25). In this scene at the threshing floor, David brings reconciliation and marks the place of Jerusalem's future reconciliation. The use of the threshing floor as a place of punishment and redemption returns the reader to Jeremiah's ambivalent metaphor for chaos at the punishment of Babylon on its day of wrath. Yahweh's wind, which blew at the creation (Gen 1:2), blows across the threshing floor of Babylon (cf. Ex 15:10):

> Thus says Yahweh: "Look, I will stir up the spirit of destruction against Babylon, against the inhabitants of Chaldea. I will send to Babylon thrashers and they will thresh here." (*zarim we zeru'a;* Jer 51:2)

The outstretched arm of Babylon's cosmic executioners (the *zarim*), like the outstretched arm of Moses that destroys Egypt and creates Israel (Ex 14:26), also veils a prophecy of hope in the messiah's arm stretched out to sow new seed (*zera'*).[30]

CONCLUSION: *IMITATIO CHRISTI*

Much more can and needs to be said about the construction of the figure of David and how it is used in the Bible. Of course, much can and needs to be said also about the figure of Jesus and its use in the gospels. The present study, which began with questions of the historical Jesus and with assumptions of implied history writing, closes, I hope, as a contribution to intellectual history. Biblical figures such as Adam, Noah, Abraham, Moses, Joshua, David, Elijah and Elisha, Hezekiah, Josiah, John and Jesus—to name only the most famous— are the bearers of Palestine's ancient Near Eastern intellectual life. It is a tradition that lays great weight on such enduring values as justice, compassion, forgiveness and humility. It has a preference for the poor and the oppressed: for others, be they strangers, foreigners or even the enemy. It is also pacifist, reserving to God the eternal plague of blood guilt, revenge, terror and war. It is a tradition of great learning, which shares the deep roots of humanism from the earliest literature of Africa, Europe and western Asia. The themes of the ancient world's royal ideology, I hope, have provided insight into the written traditions of the Bible, whose eventual development in collections of various holy scriptures has provided the earliest intellectual foundations of Samaritanism, Judaism, Christianity and Islam.

If biblical scholarship is able to resolve its questions about the social and historical contexts in which biblical works were written, it needs to step aside from the mythic origin stories that the Bible uses for quite other purposes. Neither the Hebrew Bible nor the gospels tell us directly of the origins of Samaritans, Jews or Christians: not even about Moses, David and Jesus. If this kind of literature can be useful to modern questions of history, I believe it will be because of the many implicit ways literature reflects its authors and their audience. Questions relating to identity seem very important, especially when they imply competition and debate. The importance of Gerizim in the Pentateuch, of Jerusalem in the stories of prophets and kings and the nature of the pietism implicit to the Psalter are far more important than any particular stories we might favor about patriarch, lawgiver, priest or king. Implicit arguments of supersession and sectarian rhetoric are useful clues to the complex history of our tradition. Identifying a given tradition's opponent has the potential of unveiling its author or at least the interests he serves.

Such problems, of course, are best dealt with in a book of their own. In an effort to close my discussion on the myth of the messianic king in the Bible, I wish merely to identify one of a myth's central functions: the education of its audience to a set of values and principles. In this regard, David's role as an ideal figure seems helpful in clarifying the symbol system in which such figures carry out this function. Heroic figures and parables, hymns and prayers educate by evoking imitation.[31] In the history of Christian theology, such imitation—the equivalent of an education in a way of life—has been identified by the practice of *imitatio Christi*. It shares much with what history of religions might identify as the "theology of the way" or "philosophy of the path": a pragmatic pedagogy that instructs its implicit adherent in how one lives. It is more than an incidental foundation for hagiography and biography. Central to this genre is the authorial strategy of capturing the audience and encouraging identification with his hero or model of piety.

The figures of David and Jesus are the most developed figures in the biblical myth of the messiah, though, as we have seen, they are far from the only ones. In what follows, I limit myself to the figure of David as it is the most complex. The transcendent character of David's promise and his role as messiah lives on in the Psalter. As the anointed priest had both represented holiness to the people as well as the petitions of the people before God, the figure of the priest centers on reconciliation and the forgiveness of sin. David, in his role as king, also takes up such an everyman role. In the story of David's anointing (1 Sm 16:1–13), the messiah as a guide to piety is given focus. As we have seen, Yahweh's choice of Saul's successor is not based on appearance, but on the heart of the man (1 Sm 16:7). The Cinderella character of David as the chosen one is also reflected in the Psalter's quest for purity of heart and forms the theological matrix of David's role as everyman.[32] In Chronicles, even greater advantage is taken of David's ideal character. In the Psalter—unhindered by the narrative world's need to present a story—the idealism of David's figure is primary. Its pedagogical function as an *imitatio Christi* ("imitation of the messiah") defines a role that allows his life to provide parable for piety. As David's purity of heart in the story tradition determined the fate of his house and his people, the idealized David of the Psalter provides the pious with their role as David's house and people. Here David is not so centrally a figure of the past. He is a figure of perfection to be imitated by the Psalter's implicit audience. The process of imitation and identity, in which singer and audience recreate the voice of David through their own voices, creates a psychic transfer and identity between the figure of the messiah and an audience which eventually take on roles as David's sons: a new Israel for their generation.

In the colophon of David's "last song" (2 Sm 23:1–7), he is identified as "the messiah of Jacob's God, whom the Most High raised up." He is the darling of Israel's song. Through him, the spirit of Yahweh speaks and finds voice. The continuation of the song attributes to David metaphors that cluster around the motif of the messiah in the Psalter. They also belong to the tradition of ancient Near Eastern royal ideology, expressed in the ritual of the Akitu festival and victory hymns of the New Kingdom we saw in Chapters 5–6. Like the great kings, David rules over men in righteousness and humility. He rules with justice. With Pharaoh, David is likened to the dawn. His rule is transcendent; his is an eternal dynasty. His house and covenant are ordered and secure. Like the rain, his just rule causes grass to grow. All that he hopes for, his every wish flourishes. David's rule as king is presented as that of a new Adam, now ruling as a good king over creation and all who walk in the path of righteousness. It is this way of righteousness that is confirmed by Yahweh. The role-identifying "last words" of David close in messianic judgment: "The godless are like thorns cast away; for they cannot be taken with the hand" (2 Sm 23:6). The judgment recasts the judgment of the godless in Psalm 1. They are chaff, blown from the threshing floor. They cannot be taken by God's hand; they cannot stand in judgment; they perish (Ps 1:4–6). David's final song gives the role of judgment to the good king as representative of the righteous. The man who touches the godless thorns, as Yahweh's holy warrior to cast them into the fire, is armed with iron and the shaft of a spear, that the godless be "wholly consumed with fire."

The pietistic metaphors of David's last words and the context within its audience's piety, within which Psalm 1 structures the Psalter, reflect an imagery that is essentially religious and sectarian. The theology, which interprets the legends of David and his sons and the entire Psalter, presents itself within an antithetic parallelism of great importance.[33] This structure reflects an intellectual world that historians of religion call the "theology of the way." Its purpose is sectarian. It distinguishes a self-identity of belonging to the true Israel from those who reject it. This perspective influences a great part of biblical literature.

The opening words of Psalm 2 take their point of departure from the last words of Psalm 1: "The way of the godless perishes" (Ps 1:6).

> Why are the nations in uproar? Why do the peoples lay plans that cannot succeed? The kings of the earth set themselves and the rulers take counsel together against Yahweh and his messiah. (Ps 2:1)

Whether or not one uses this illustration as an argument that these two songs form a single introduction to the Psalter, it presents this first of the messianic psalms as an illustration of the theology of the way. Those against whom the messiah fights his holy war stand against those who walk in the path of the Torah. Nations in uproar are not the only ones who are identified with Psalm 1's ungodly, like chaff to be blown away (Ps 1:4). We must also include the large cluster of comparable figures filling the Psalter. A contrast is engaged between two mutually exclusive and always implicitly related tropes. The way of the ungodly implies also the way of evil, pain, violence, the flesh, the willful, mankind, all the earth, sinners, fools and many comparable others. These are opposed to the way of Yahweh, of David, the Torah, the spirit, joy, the innocent, pious, wisdom, righteousness, peace, truth, life, and so on. While some of the terms form stereotyped word pairs, such as the way of the wise in contrast to the way of fools, or God's way against the way of evil, the whole cluster of motifs is present implicitly. The way of Yahweh already implies the way of Torah and righteousness, while the way of flesh cannot be a way of peace. It is the way of violence. These two clusters of metaphors are entirely antagonistic to each other. The way of mankind is opposed to the way of God as philosophical principle. This tradition develops a simplistic, black-and-white theology that functions well in folktale, legends and myth.

The myth of the messiah encourages the flight of the pious to their refuge in Yahweh. Kings and messiahs are not themselves the objects of interest. They merely illustrate the piety that they aim to support. In the discussion of the narratives of Samuel, Saul and David, I described three songs from the Psalter, which are placed in David's mouth at different occasions during his flight from Saul. There are thirteen such psalms. They introduce their songs with a stereotypical, mock setting: "A psalm of David when he fled from his son Absalom" (Ps 3:1); "when he sang to Yahweh, because of the Benjaminite Kush" (Ps 7:1) and the like. The three songs we have seen clearly illustrate the close interrelationship of the songs with the tradition of the David narrative. Not only does the story of David give the songs a background and setting in story, they interpret David's life. The technique is very close to the way Hannah's song (1 Sm 2:1–10) and the song David sings "after Yahweh has saved him from all his enemies and from Saul's hand" (2 Sm 22:1) radically direct the story they attach themselves to. They bring David into the theology of the way and present him as everyman for their audience. David's song, set at the close of his contentious, war-torn life, still keeps its historicizing title from the Psalter (Ps 18:1). Clearly this tradition of interpretation takes part in the composition of the David story we have in the books of Samuel. This narrative can hardly claim to be "the original" story of David, which we can recognize from other settings given to these thirteen psalms. Psalm 60, for example, offers a setting full of details, placing the song in David's mouth during his war against the Arameans:

A *miktam* of David, for instruction, when he struggled with Aram-Nahraim and with Aram-Zobah and when Joab on his return killed 12,000 Edomites in the Valley of Salt. (Ps 60:1)

In the story we now have in 2 Samuel 8, however, David fights against Zobah and Aram-Damascus and kills 22,000. On his return, he kills 18,000 Edomites in the Valley of Salt (2 Sm 8:5, 13). Two chapters later Joab fights the Arameans and returns to Jerusalem. David, thereafter, meets a counterattack across the Euphrates and destroys seven hundred chariots and forty thousand horses (2 Sm 10:9–19). Whatever the real or imagined original story—and there are rarely originals of such stories to be known—the setting of Psalm 60 and the narrative of 2 Samuel reflect variant stories of a common tradition.

The headings of these thirteen psalms all refer to one or other situation in David's life, in which he confronts deadly threats. Thematically, these songs have much in common. Not only is the number of thematic elements used very limited. All are closely tied to the opposition and conflict between the way of evil and the way of the Torah. They also share a link to a cosmic holy war against Yahweh's enemies. Their motifs can be grouped in four implicitly related clusters. (1) The righteous, those who are good or innocent and sing praises and bless Yahweh. They keep themselves from evil and the godless and wait in the desert. The singer suffers. (2) Dangers threaten. There are threatening nations, enemies who bring war or rise against Yahweh. There are figures of the unrighteous, the ungodly and evil ones, who must not succeed. (3) Refuge is sought with Yahweh; one prays for or cries out to be saved. God is described as a fortress, as one who protects and strengthens. One depends on, seeks refuge with or trusts Yahweh. Either one has fear of God or one does not fear the enemy. (4) Yahweh answers, saves, protects, guards, strengthens. He mocks, strikes or defeats enemies. He crushes the ungodly and glory comes to the world.

Psalm 7 is particularly interesting, though it has not been possible to identify the setting with any of the narratives we now have in 1–2 Samuel. The thematic elements in this song include motifs of praise to Yahweh as cosmic lord and God of war, who saves his people and messiah. Yahweh is described with all the strength poetically possible. Transcendent war is fought between the righteous and unrighteous. David is the author of this song and takes part in its struggle. The song identifies transcendence with the life of piety.

There are three psalms that well represent the role the pious have in trans-forming messianic war to peaceful purpose. The first-person voice of Psalm 63, for example, the voice of the sufferer, finds his happiness in praising Yahweh. He is opposed to liars whose mouths need stopping. The transference of this song of David to piety is strikingly complete. David becomes the model for and repre-sentative of the life of the soul.

Similarly, the cluster of motifs we find in Psalm 3 all bear a double meaning, depending on whether the singer is David in his story or the pious in the tem-ple. Enemies threaten and mock, while the singer holds to his trust that God will save him and answer from his holy mountain. With the fear of God in his heart, the singer prays for help. Yahweh answers by striking enemies and the godless. Salvation and blessing come from him alone. The transference is relatively sim-ple and examples can be found throughout the Psalter. What is interesting, how-ever, is the situation in which David in his story world is given to sing: "When he fled from his son Absalom." The reference points to the story of David's des-peration after his son Absalom is proclaimed king in Hebron and David becomes once again the fugitive (2 Sm 15:10–12). It is a story of David, as we have seen, in which he is friendless and weeping, as he repents of his sin. Finally David in-structs his friend, priest and adviser, Zadok:

> Carry the ark of God back into the city. If I find favor in Yahweh's eyes, he will bring me back and he will let me see both it and his dwelling place. However, if he says, "I have no pleasure in you," look, here I am. Let him do with me as it seems good to him. (2 Sm 15:25–26)

One can only ask whether Psalm 3's potential for piety adds to the understand-ing of David on the Mount of Olives. Is it not as well that the story's evocation of piety's highest values—the temple, humility and selfless acceptance of what God wills—has encouraged this obvious setting. Certainly the potential of David's words in his submission to Yahweh's will has motivated the gospel writ-ers to set precisely this story, this question and this answer for Jesus in Gethsemane (Mt 26:36–46; Mk 14:32–42; Lk 22:39–46).

For my third and closing example, I choose a psalm that relates to David's great sin against his faithful servant Uriah. Psalm 51 is set with David as sinner, confronted by Yahweh's prophet: "When the prophet Nathan came to him" (Ps 51:1; cf. 2 Sm 12:1–25). It is unusual among our thirteen songs as David is not threatened here by any enemy army or any strong man. His enemy, in fact, is Yahweh on Judgment Day. Nevertheless, the title holds him well to his role as piety's representative. His is the voice of the sinner. The song uses the metaphor of rebuilding Jerusalem's walls as a motif of psychology and the life of the soul. It supports a piety that turns on repentance and transformation. David, who had so much, has taken everything his faithful servant Uriah had. The psalm interprets the story in light of the salvation that comes to the poor because of David's humility. Every motif in the psalm aims at this interpretation, from the beginning prayer for mercy and grace to the final search for the fear of God. It is an instruction for reconciliation and cleansing from sin. With David, the generation of the Psalter's audience is taught understanding and love for truth. The evil of David's sin is transformed to the good, as he prays for a new spirit. Even sacrifice is internalized as a broken spirit and a broken heart teaches him to fear God. David, as representative of the poor and weak, becomes the cornerstone of piety. The association of David, the poor man and heir to the temple, to God's kingdom creates an abiding metaphor for personal salvation.

Appendix 1

Examples of the Song for a Poor Man

Egyptian Examples

1. Inscription of Nefer-Sheshem-Re (Sixth Dynasty)

I judged between two so as to content them; I rescued the weak from one stronger than he as much as he was in my power. I gave bread to the hungry, clothes [to the naked], I brought the boatless to land. I buried him who had no son, I made a boat for him who lacked one. I respected my father; I pleased my mother; I raised their children.[1]

2. Autobiography of Harkhuf (Sixth Dynasty)

I gave bread to the hungry, clothing to the naked; I brought the boatless to land.[2]

3. Stele of Inteft (Middle Kingdom)[3]

I am a friend of the poor, one well-disposed to the have-not. I am one who feeds the hungry in need, who is open-handed to the pauper.

4. Egyptian Coffin Text (Middle Kingdom)[4]

Pray be prosperous in peace! I repeat for you four good deeds which my own heart did for me in the midst of the serpent coil, in order to still evil. . . . I made the four winds that every man might breathe like his fellow in his time. There is one deed. I made the great flood that the poor man might have rights like the great man. That is [one] deed. I made every man like his fellow. I did not command that they do evil; it is their hearts which violated what I said. That is [one] deed. I made their hearts cease from forgetting the West, in order that divine offerings might be given to the gods of the nomes. That is (one) deed. I brought into being the four gods from my "sweat," while men *(romet)* are the tears *(remit)* of my eye.[5]

5. The Instruction of the King Amenemhet (Middle Kingdom)[6]

When you lie down, guard your heart yourself, for no man has adherents on the day of woe. I gave to the beggar; I raised the orphan; I gave success to the poor as to the wealthy.

6. The Eloquent Peasant (Middle Kingdom) lines I.7–8; II.14-III.1[7]

You are father to the orphan, husband to the widow, brother to the rejected woman, apron to the motherless. . . . None hungered in my years; none thirsted in them.

7. Sinuhe (Middle Kingdom), lines 95–97, 1150–155[8]

I let everyone stay with me. I gave water to the thirsty; I showed the way to him who strayed. I rescued him who had been robbed. . . . A fugitive fled his surroundings; I am famed at home. A laggard lagged from hunger, I give bread to my neighbor. A man left his land in nakedness; I have bright clothes, fine linen. A man ran for lack of one to send; I am rich in servants. My house is fine, my dwelling spacious; my thoughts are at the palace.

8. A Hymn to Amon-Re (Middle Kingdom)[9]

Who extends his arms to him he loves, while his enemy is consumed by a flame. It is his Eye that overthrows the rebel, that sends its spear into him that sucks up Nun and makes the fiend disgorge what he has swallowed. Hail to you, O Re, lord of truth, whose shrine is hidden, the Lord of the Gods. . . . who hears the prayer of him who is in captivity. Gracious of heart in the face of an appeal to him, saving the fearful from the terrible of heart, judging the weak and the injured. . . . When he comes, the people live. He who gives scope to every eye that may be made in Nun, whose loveliness has created the light. In whose beauty the gods rejoice; their hearts live when they see him.

9. A Litany of Rejoicing (Middle Kingdom)[10]

How happy are the gods; for you have maintained their offerings. How happy are your children, for you have established their domain. How happy are your fathers who were before, for you have increased their portion. How happy are Egyptians in your strength, for you have protected the ancient heritage. How happy is mankind under your governance, for your mighty power has received their lives unto itself. How happy are the two banks in awe of you, for you have increased their possessions. How happy are your young men of the army, for you have allowed them to prosper. How happy are the old and the venerable, for you have caused them to feel young again. How happy are the two lands in your strength, for you have protected their citadels.

10. The Prophecies of Neferti[11]

I show you the land in turmoil. The weak of arm is [now] the possessor of an arm; one salutes him who [formerly] saluted. I show you the lowly as superior. . . . One lives in the necropolis. The poor man will make wealth; the great one will [pray] to live. The beggar will eat bread; the slaves will be exalted. The Heliopolitan nome will no longer be.

11. The Great Hymn to Osiris (New Kingdom)[12]

They sat themselves down in the court of Geb to offer the legacy to its rightful owner and the kingship to whom it belonged and they determined for Horus, his voice was true; and his father's legacy was given to him. . . . and Nepri helped him nurture the fruits of the earth so that Horus might bring on abundance and give it to all the lands. And everyone was glad, hearts were sweet, thoughts were happy and each face showed joy. . . . They offered this song to the son of Isis; "His antagonist is fallen because of his offense, for evil acts against the criminal. He who commits offense, retribution comes upon him. . . . wrongdoing passes, injustice passes away. The land is at peace under its master. Lady truth stands firm for her master, the back is turned on iniquity.

12. Hymns to the Gods as a Single God (New Kingdom)[13]

The fear of you is for everybody; their hearts turn about to you, good at all times. Everyone lives through the sight of you. Do not widows say; "Our husbands are you", and little ones "Our father and our mother!" The rich boast of your beauty and the poor worship your face. He that is imprisoned turns to you and he that is sick calls out to you. . . . Everyone returns to your presence that they may make prayers to you. Your ears are open, hearing them and taking care of them. O our Ptah, who loves his crafts; herdsman who loves his herds. His reward is a goodly burial for the heart which is satisfied with truth. His love is the moon, as a child to whom everyone dances. When petitioners are gathered before his face, then he will search our hearts. Green plants turn about in his direction, that they may be beautiful, and lotuses are gay because of him.

13. Merikare (New Kingdom)

Do justice, then you endure on earth. Calm the weeper; do not oppress the widow; don't expel a man from his father's property.[14]

14. The Cairo Hymns to Amon-Re; Papyrus Bulaq xvii (New Kingdom)[15]

Atum—who hears the prayer of the one in distress, is kind to whoever calls on him, saves the fearful man from the hand of the insolent, judges fairly between the wretched man and the affluent.

15. Praise of Amon-Re; Papyrus Anastasi II[16]

He is Amun-Re, first to act as king. God of the beginning of time, vizier of the poor. He does not take bribes from wrongdoers, nor speak with one who bears tales, nor regard him who makes easy promises. Amun-Re judges the earth with his finger, and his words shall rest in the heart. He judges the unjust and sends him on to the place of fire; the just man goes to the West.

16. Prayer to Amun of a Man on Trial; Papyrus Anastasi II[17]

Amun, give your ear to one who is alone in court; he is needy and without power. The court extorts him with silver and gold to the recording scribes and clothing for their followers. May it be given that Amun transform himself into a vizier, allowing this humble man to go forth free. And let it be found that the humble man becomes a just man and let the humble surpass the powerful.

17. In Praise of Amun; Papyrus Anastasi II[18]

A pilot who knows the waters; that is Amun, a steering oar for the helpless. One who gives food to the one who has not, who helps the servant of his house to prosper. I do not take myself a great man as protector nor do I mingle with the men of means. I do not place my portion under the strong arm of someone wealthy in a noble household. My lord is my protector. I know his strength.

18. The Book of the Dead, chapter 125 (New Kingdom)[19]

I have given bread to the hungry, water to the thirsty, clothes to the naked, a ferryboat to the boatless.

19. Ramesside Hymn to the Nile (New Kingdom)[20]

The poor are like the highest of the land and the great are like the humble; the man of low degree attains to power, so that he brings forth barley; Emmer is created for him and the hunter hunts for him.

20. The Israel Stele (New Kingdom)

Give him a lifetime like Re that he may answer [on behalf of] him who is suffering because of any country. Egypt has been assigned to him . . . that he might protect his people. Behold as one dwells in the time of the mighty one, the breath of life comes immediately. The valiant one, who causes goods to flow to the righteous man; there is no cheat who retains his plunder. He who gathers the fat of wickedness and takes away the strength of others will have no children. . . . Ptah said about the enemy of Rebu; "Gather together all his crimes, returned upon his [own] head. Give him into the hand of Merneptah Hotep-hir-Maat, that he may make him disgorge what he has swallowed, like a crocodile."[21]

21. Joy at the Accession of Merneptah (New Kingdom)

Be glad of heart, the entire land. The good times are come. A lord—life, prosperity and health—is given to all lands and normality has returned to its place. The King of Upper and Lower Egypt . . . crushes Egypt with festivity . . . All you righteous, come that you might see.

Right has banished wrong; evildoers have fallen on their faces; all the rapacious are ignored. The water stands and is not dried up; the Nile lifts high. Days are long, nights have hours and the moon comes normally. The gods are satisfied and content of heart. One lives in laughter and wonder. May you know it.[22]

22. Joy at the Accession of Ramses IV (New Kingdom)

O Happy Day! Heaven and earth are in joy. They who had fled have returned to their homes; they who were hidden live openly; they who were hungry are filled and happy; they who were thirsty are drunken; they who were naked are clothed in fine linen; they who were dirty are dressed in white; they who were in prison are set free; they who were chained rejoice; the troubled of the land have found peace. . . . The homes of the widows are open [again], so that they may let wanderers come in. Womenfolk rejoice and repeat their songs of jubilation . . . saying, "Male children are born [again] for good times, for he brings into being generation upon generation. You ruler, life, prosperity, health! You are for eternity!"[23]

23. Instruction of Amenemopet (New Kingdom), chapters 25 and 28[24]

Do not laugh at a blind man, nor tease a dwarf, nor cause hardship for the lame. Don't tease a man who is in the hand of the god, nor be angry with him for his failings. Man is clay and straw. The god is his builder. He tears down; he builds up daily; He makes a thousand poor by his will; he makes a thousand men into chiefs, when he is in his hour of life. . . . Do not pounce on a widow when you find her in the fields, and then fail to be patient with her reply. Do not refuse your oil jar to a stranger; double it before your brothers. God prefers him who honors the poor to him who worships the wealthy.

MESOPOTAMIAN AND SYRIAN EXAMPLES

24. The Babylonian Theodicy, II, XVII, XXII, XXV and XXVI (Akkadian)[25]

When you survey teeming mankind all together, the poor man's son advanced, someone helped him get rich. Who did favors for the sleek and the wealthy? He who looks to his god has a protector. The humble man who reveres his goddess will garner wealth. . . . The son of a king is clad [in rags]; the son of the destitute and naked is dressed in [fine raiment]. The maltster [can pay in] finest gold, while he who counted red gold bears a [debt?]. He who made do with vegetables [sates himself] at a princely banquet, while the son of the eminent and wealthy has only carob to eat. The man of substance is fallen, [his income] is removed. . . . As for the rascal whose good will you wanted, the [gap in text] . . . of his feet will soon disappear. The godless swindler who acquires wealth; a deadly weapon is in pursuit of him. Unless you serve the will of a god, what will be your profit? He who bears a god's yoke shall never want for food, though it may be meager. Seek after the favorable breeze of the gods. What you lost for a year, you will recoup in a moment. . . . Pay attention my friend, learn my next response; consider the well-chosen diction of my speech. They extol the words of an important man who is accomplished in murder. They denigrate the powerless who has committed no crime. They esteem truthful the wicked to whom truth is abhorrent. They reject the truthful man who heeds the will of god. They fill the oppressor's stronghold with refined gold. They empty the beggar's larder of provisions. They shore up the tyrant whose all is crime. They ruin the weak, they oppress the powerless. And as for me, without means, a parvenu harasses me. . . . Enlil, king of the gods, who created teeming mankind, Majestic Ea, who pinched off their clay; the queen who fashioned them, Mistress Mami, gave twisted words to the human race. They endowed them in perpetuity with lies and falsehood. Solemnly, they speak well of a rich man. "He is king," they say, "he has much wealth." They malign a poor man as a thief. They lavish mischief upon him; they conspire to kill him. They make him suffer every evil because he has no [gap in text] . . . They bring him to a horrible end; they snuff him out like an ember.

25. Dialogue Between a Man and His God (Akkadian)[26]

I am your god, your creator, your trust. My guardians are strong and alert on your behalf. The field will open to you its refuge; I will see to it that you have long life; So, without qualms, you anoint the parched, feed the hungry, water the thirsty. But he who sits there with burning eyes, let him look upon your food, melt, flow down and dissolve. The gate of life and well-being is open to you . . . make straight his way, open his path. May your servant's supplication reach your heart.

26. Counsels of Wisdom (Akkadian)[27]

To your opponent, do no evil. Recompense your evildoer with good. To your enemy, let justice [be done]. . . . Give food to eat; give date-wine to drink; honor, clothe the one begging for alms. Over this, his god rejoices. This is pleasing to the god Shamash; he rewards it with good. Be helpful, do good. A maid in the house, do not. . .

27. Hammurapi Code (Old Babylonian)[28]

I, Hammurapi, the perfect king, was not careless or neglectful of the black headed people, whom Enlil had presented to me. . . . I overcame grievous difficulties; I caused light to shine on them. . . . I rooted out the enemy above and below; I made an end of war. I promoted the welfare of the land; I made the people rest in friendly habitations. I did not let them have anyone to terrorize them. . . . I always governed them in peace; I sheltered them in my wisdom, in order that the strong not oppress the weak, that justice might be dealt the orphan and the widow. . . . I set [my stele] up to administer the law of the land, to prescribe the ordinances of the land, to give justice to the oppressed.

28. Hymn to Telepinus (Hittite)[29]

Whatever you say, O Telepinus, the gods bow down to you. Of the oppressed, the orphan and the widow you are father and mother; the cause of the orphan and the oppressed you, Telepinus, take to heart.

29. *Great Hymn to Marduk (Middle Assyrian)*[30]

You support the weak; you give the wretched room. You bear up the powerless and shepherd the meek. O Marduk, you extend your benevolence over the fallen. The weakling takes his stand under your protection; you pronounce recovery for him. . . .

30. *Hymn to Marduk (Middle Assyrian)*[31]

You are the one who, like the sun, illumines their darkness. Each day you give justice to the oppressed and abused; you administer the destitute, the widow, the wretched and the anxious. . . . You are merciful; you rescue the weak from danger and hardship; you look upon the exhausted and desperate, the one whom his god punished. . . . You release the captive; you take by the hand and raise the injured from his bed. You make the captive in darkness and prison, the hostage, see light.

31. *Hymn to Ishtar (Middle Assyrian)*[32]

At your command, O Ishtar, humankind is governed. The sick man who sees your face revives; his bondage is released; he gets up instantly. At your command, O Ishtar, the blind man sees the light, the unhealthy one who sees your face, becomes healthy.

32. *To Nabu (Middle Assyrian)*[33]

I am a guardian of truth. Do not destroy the truth I have guarded. May the lonely one not die; who has called up to you, O Lord. O Nabu, take the hand of the fallen one, who attends your divinity. Spare the life of the weakling, whom ill-wishers hemmed in, whom baleful witches have splashed with conjured water. Let the dead man revive by your breeze; let his squandered life become gain.

33. *Hymn to Ninurta; Protector of the King (Middle Assyrian)*[34]

You judge the case of mankind; you do justice to the wronged, the powerless, the destitute girl. At your command, O Ishtar, the blind man sees the light, the unhealthy one who sees your face, becomes healthy. You promptly reconcile the man whose god or goddess is angry with him.

34. *Esarhaddon (Seventh-Century Assyrian); Prism Bu*[35]

As for the enslaved Babylonians, who had been the feudatories, the clients of Anu and Enlil, their freedom I established anew. The "capitalists" who had been brought into slavery, who had been apportioned to the yoke and fetter, I gathered together and accounted them for Babylonians. Their plundered possessions I restored. The naked I clothed and turned their feet into the road to Babylon. To resettle the city, to rebuild the temple, to set out plantations, to dig irrigation ditches, I encouraged them. Their clientship which had lapsed, which had slipped out of their hands, I restored. The tablet of their freedom I wrote anew. Towards the four winds of heaven, I opened up their way; so that, establishing their tongue in every land, they might carry out their thoughts.

35. Nebuchadnezzar II (Babylonian)[36]

[Lebanon], over which a foreign country was ruling and robbing its riches—its people were scattered and had fled to a far away region. Trusting in the power of my lords Nebo and Marduk, I organized my army for an expedition to the Lebanon. I made that country happy by eradicating its enemy below and above. All its scattered inhabitants, I led back to their settlements. I did what no former king had done: I cut through steep mountains, splitting rocks; opening passages, constructing a straight road for the transport of the cedars.

36. Lament to Ishtar (Neo-Babylonian)[37]

O deity of men, goddess of women, whose delights no one can conceive, where you look one who is dead lives; one who is sick rises up. The erring one who sees your face goes straight. . . . Drive away the evil spells of my body [and] let me see your bright light. How long, O my lady, shall my enemies look at me; in lying and untruth, plan evil against me? Shall my pursuers and those who exult over me rage against me? How long, O my lady, shall the crippled and the weak seek me out? One has made for me long sackcloth; thus have I appeared before you. The weak have become strong, but I am weak!

37. Kalamuwa Inscription[38]

A young woman was given for a sheep and a young man for a garment. . . . I am Kalamuwa, son of Hayya; I sat upon the throne of my father. Before the former kings, the *Mushkabim* were living like dogs. But I was to some a father, and to some a mother, and to some I was a brother. Now whoever had never possessed a sheep, I made lord of a flock; and whoever had never possessed an ox, I made owner of a herd and owner of silver and lord of gold. Whoever from his childhood had never seen linen, now in my days wore byssos.

38. Azatiwada Inscription[39]

I humbled strong lands in the West, which no king who was before me ever humbled, but I, Azatiwada, have humbled them. I brought them down. I settled them in the far regions of my borders in the East. I settled the Danunians there. They were in my days on all the borders of the Plain of Adana from the East to the West, even in places which formerly were feared, where a man feared to walk the road. In my days, mine, a woman can walk alone with her spindles by the grace of Ba'al and the gods. Now there was in all my days abundance and luxury and good living and ease of heart for the Danunians and for all the plain of Adana.

39. Darius (Susa; Se 001)[40]

Much of the evil that had been committed, I turned into good. The countries that fought each other, I fixed, by the grace of Ahura Mazda, so that their people did not kill each other and I restored each one to its place. And, faced with my decrees, they respected them in such a way that the strong did not strike nor despoil the poor.

EXAMPLES FROM THE HEBREW BIBLE

Exodus	4:10–12; 22:20–26; 23:3–9
Leviticus	19:9–18, 33–34
Deuteronomy	10:17–19; 14:29; 15:4, 7–11; 16:11–12; 24:14–15, 17–22; 26:3–13;[41] 27:18–19; 28:47–48
1 Samuel	2:1–10[42]
2 Samuel	1:21, 27
1 Kings	8:41–43
1 Chronicles	29:14–15[43]
Job	1:20–21; 5:8–26; 12:13–25; 19:13–15; 22:5–11, 29–30; 24:1–12; 29:7–17; 30:25–31; 31:16–23[44]
Psalms	9:8–9, 18–19; 10:2, 12–18; 14:5–6; 18:25–30; 35:10–14; 37:9–11, 14–15, 28–29; 38:12–15; 39:13; 68:6–11, 19; 69:8–10, 33–34; 70:6; 72:1–8, 12–14; 74:19–21; 76:3–10; 79:11–12; 82:1–8; 86:1–2; 102:18, 21–22;[45] 107:9–16, 33–38, 41;[46] 109:5–17, 31; 112:9–10; 113:5–9; 119:18–20; 126:1–6; 132:13–18; 146:3–9;[47] 147:5
Proverbs	3:33–34; 10:3; 14:20–21, 31; 17:5; 19:17; 22:2; 23:10–11; 25:21–22; 26:21; 28:27–28; 29:7, 13, 23; 30:21–23; 31:4–9
Ecclesiastes	10:6–7
Isaiah	1:17–20, 23; 5:13–17, 20–24; 6:9–10; 9:17; 10:1–4; 11:3–9; 13:9–13; 14:1–23; 24:21–23; 29:6–10, 17–21;[48] 30:25–26;[49] 32:1–8; 35:1–10; 41:17–20;[50] 42:5–7, 13–16, 18–23;[51] 43:8; 44:3–4; 47:8–9; 49:8–13, 24–26; 54:1, 4–5; 55:1–3; 56:3–8; 58:6–11; 59:9–11; 61:1–4; 65:13–14, 17–20, 25[52]
Jeremiah	5:21, 27–29; 7:5–6; 22:3–5; 31:7–20;[53] 49:10–11
Lamentations	3:1–9;[54] 4:4–10; 5:2–18
Ezekiel	3:25–27;[55] 16:49; 18:5–13; 22:6–7; 24:27;[56] 34:17, 20–31; 37:12–14; 47:21–23
Hosea	2:4–7
Micah	4:3–4, 6–7; 7:16–17
Zephaniah	1:17–18; 3:19–20
Haggai	1:6
Zechariah	7:9–14; 12:4–5
Malachi	3:1–2, 5

Examples from the
Nonbiblical Dead Sea Scrolls

40. *The War Scroll (1QM, col xi.7–9.11–14)*[57]

By the Hand of your anointed ones, seers of decrees, you taught us the times of the wars of your hands, to [fight] / to cover you with glory / with our enemies, to fell the hordes of Belial, the seven nations of futility, by the hands of the poor, those you saved, with the strength and the peace of your wonderful power. . . . From of old you foretold the moment of the power of your hand against the Kittim "Ashur will fall by the sword of no-one, the sword of a no-body will devour it" [Isa 31:8]. For you will deliver into the hands of the poor the enemies of all the countries, and by the hand of those prone in the dust, you shall fell the powerful ones of the peoples, you shall give the wicked their reward, on the head of . . . you shall carry out justice by your truthful judgment on every son of man, gaining everlasting renown for yourself among the people.

41. *The War Scroll (1QM, col xiii.13–15)*[58]

Who is like you in strength, God of Israel? Your mighty hand is with the poor! And which angel or prince is like you for aid? Since ancient time you determined the day of the great battle . . . to assist truth and destroy wickedness, to demolish darkness and increase light.

42. *The War Scroll (1QM, frags 8–10, col.1)*[59]

He has gathered an assembly of nations for destruction with no remnant. In judgment he has lifted up the melting heart; he has opened the mouth of the dumb to sing God's marvels. The hands of the frail he has trained in war. The knees that shake he gives strength to stand up-right. And he girds the kidneys of those with broken backs. Among the poor in spirit . . . to a hard heart. For the perfect ones of the path all the wicked nations shall be destroyed. None of their heroes will remain standing. Only we the remnant of your people.

43. *4Q Isaiah Pesher (4Q163, frags 18–19)*[60]

. . . without darkness or gloom the eyes of the blind will see. The oppressed will return to re-joice in the Lord and the poorest of men will delight in the Holy One of Israel. Because the tyrant is destroyed, the skeptic finished off and all those alert for evil will be obliterated and those who are going to seize another in speaking and the one who defends in the gate with snares and, for nothing, engulf the innocent.

44. *4Q Psalms Pesher (4Q171, col ii)*[61]

And the poor shall inherit the land and enjoy peace in plenty [Ps 37:11]. Its interpretation concerns the congregation of the poor who will tolerate the period of distress and will be res-cued from all the snares of Belial. Afterwards, all who shall inherit the land will enjoy and grow fat with everything . . . of the flesh. The wicked plots against the just person, grinding [his teeth] aga[inst him]; Yahweh laughs at him because he sees that his day is coming [Ps 37:12–13]. Its interpretation alludes to the ruthless ones of the covenant who are in the House of Judah, who plot to destroy those who observe the law, who are in the community council. But God will not surrender them into their hands. The evildoers unsheath the sword and discharge their bows to bring down the poor and the humble, to murder those on the correct path. Their swords shall pierce their own hearts and their bows shall break [Ps 37:14–15]. Its interpretation concerns the wicked of Ephraim and Manasseh who will attempt to lay hands on the priest and the members of his council in the period of testing which will come to them. However, God will save them from their hands and after they will be delivered into the hands of the dreadful nations for judgment.

45. *4Q Psalms Pesher (4Q171, col iii)*[62]

The wicked asks for a loan but does not pay, while the just man is sympathetic and gives. For those who are blessed by him shall inherit the earth, but those who are cursed by him shall be cut off [Ps 37:21–22]. Its interpretation concerns the congregation of the poor [for of them is] the inheritance of the whole wor[ld]. They will inherit the high mountain of Israel [and] delight [in his] holy [moun]tain, but those who are [cursed] by him will be cut off. These are the ruthless ones of the co[venant, the wicke]d men of Israel who will be cut off and exterminated forever.

46. *4Q Psalms Pesher (4Q 171, col iv)*[63]

Wait for Yahweh and observe his path and he will promote you, so that you inherit the earth and you will see the destruction of the wicked. Its interpretation concerns the community of the poor who will see the judgment of evil and with his chosen one will rejoice in the true inheritance.

47. *4Q Apocryphon of Joseph (4Q 372)*[64]

In all of this, Joseph was delivered into the hands of foreigners, consuming his strength and breaking all his bones up to the time of his end. And he shouted and his call summoned the powerful God to save him from their lands. And he said, "My father and my God, do not abandon me in the hands of gentiles, do me justice, so that the poor and afflicted do not die. You have no need of any people or of any help. Your finger is bigger and stronger than any there are in the world. For you choose truth and in your hand there is no violence at all. And your tenderness is great and great is your compassion for all who seek you."

48. *4Q Psalmsᶠ (4Q88, col ix)*[65]

. . . may they praise the name of Yahweh. Because he comes to judge all things, to obliterate evil-doers from the earth; the sons of wickedness will find no rest. The heavens will give their dew, and there will be no corrupt dealing with the frontiers. The earth will give fruit in its season, its crops will not fail. The fruit trees . . . of their vineyards and their springs will not deceive. The poor will eat and those who fear Yahweh will be replete.

49. 1Q Hymns (1Q Hodayot, col xiii.12–20)[66]

In the distress of my soul, you heard my call; you identified the outcry of my pain in my complaint and saved the soul of the poor man in the lair of lions, who sharpen their tongue like swords. And you, my God, you closed their teeth so that they would not rip up my soul of the poor and wretched; their tongue has been drawn in like a sword into the scabbard, so that it would not destroy the soul of your servant. And to show your greatness through me before the sons of man, you did wonders with the poor, you placed him like gold in the crucible, under the effect of fire like purified silver in the furnace of the jeweler to be refined seven times. The powerful wicked hustle me with their harassment and the whole day they crush my soul. But you, my God have changed my soul to a calm and have freed the soul of the poor like . . . from the power of the lions. Be blessed Lord, because you did not desert the orphan, nor have you slighted the wretch.

50. 4Q427 (4Q Hodayot*, frag 7, col ii)[67]

Proclaim and say; Great is the God who works wonders, for he brings down the arrogant spirit without even a remnant; and he raises the poor from the dust to an eternal height, and extols his stature up to the clouds and cures him together with the divinities in the congregation of the community.

51. 4Q Sapiential Work (4Q413, frag 2, col iii)[68]

From poverty he lifted your head and seated you among the nobles. Over an inheritance of glory he has given dominion to you, always seek his will. If you are poor, do not say "I am poor and can not seek knowledge." Bend your shoulder to all discipline and in all . . . refine your heart and in much knowledge your thoughts. Investigate the mystery of existence, consider all the paths of truth and examine all the roots of evil. Then you will know what is bitter for man and what is sweet for a man. Honor your father in your poverty and your mother in your steps.

52. 4Q Messianic Apocalypse (4Q521, frag 2, col ii)[69]

The heavens and the earth will listen to his Messiah and all that is in them will not turn away from the holy precepts. Be encouraged, you who are seeking the Lord in his service! Will you not, perhaps, encounter the Lord in it, all those who hope in their heart. The Lord will observe the devout and call the just by name and upon the poor will he place his spirit, and the faithful will he renew with his strength. For he will honor the devout upon the throne of eternal royalty, freeing prisoners, giving sight to the blind, straightening out the twisted. Ever shall I cling to those who hope. In his mercy he will judge and from no one will the fruit of good deeds be delayed and the Lord will perform marvels such as have not existed, just as he said. He will heal the badly wounded and will make the dead live. He will proclaim good news to the meek, give lavishly to the needy, lead the exiled and enrich the hungry.

53. *4Q Wisdom Text with Beatitudes (4Q525)*[70]

Blessed is the one who speaks the truth with a pure heart and does not slander with his tongue. Blessed are those who adhere to his laws and do not adhere to perverted paths. Blessed are those who rejoice in her and do not explore insane paths. Blessed are those who search for her with pure hands and do not importune her with a treacherous heart. Blessed is the man who attains wisdom and walks in the law of the Most High and dedicates his heart to her ways and is constrained by her discipline and always takes pleasure in her punishments and does not forsake her in the hardship of his wrongs and in the time of anguish does not discard her and does not forget her in the days of terror and in the distress of his soul does not loath her. For he always thinks of her and in his distress he meditates on the law and throughout his whole life he thinks of her and places her in front of his eyes in order not to walk on paths of evil. . . . together and on her account casts away his heart . . . and with kings it will make him s[it] . . . with his scepter over . . . brothers. . . .

54. *4Q Bless Oh my Soul* (4Q434, frag 1, col i)[71]

Bless, my soul, the Lord for all his marvels, for ever. And blessed be his name, because he has saved the soul of the poor. The needy he has not despised and he has not forgotten those oppressed. He has opened his eyes upon the oppressed and has heard the cries of the orphans and has paid attention to their entreaties. In the abundance of his mercy, he has favored the needy and has opened their eyes so that they see his paths and their ears so that they hear his teaching. He has circumcised their hearts and has saved them by his grace and has set their feet firm on the path. In their many sorrows he did not forsake them and did not deliver them into the hands of violent men, nor did he judge them with the wicked.

55. *4Q Bless Oh my Soul* (4Q436, frag 1)[72]

Knowledge to strengthen the downcast heart and to triumph in him over the spirit, to console those oppressed in the époque of their anguish and his hand will lift the fallen to make them receptacles of knowledge and to give knowledge to the wise and increase the instruction of the upright.

NEW TESTAMENT EXAMPLES

Matthew	5:3–12, 43–45; 11:4–6; 13:14–17; 18:1–5; 20:25–28, 33–34;[73] 23:8–12; 25:31–46
Mark	2:10–12; 4:2–9; 7:32–37; 8:22–26;[74] 10:21–27
Luke	1:46–55, 76–79; 3:5–6; 4:18–19; 6:20–27; 7:21–23; 10:29–37; 14:7–14; 17:11–18;[75] 18:2–8; 18:9–17; 19:2.5–10[76]
John	7:37; 8:12; 9:39
Romans	12:14–21.
James	2:15–16; 4:6, 9–10, 12
1 Peter	5:5–7
Revelation	7:16–17; 21:1–4, 6–8; 22:17

❦ APPENDIX 2 ❦

Testimonies of the Good King

THEMATIC FUNCTIONS

De *Dedication* of memorial

Le Statement of *legitimation*

Pa Declaration of the king as *chosen by the gods* or as servant of the divine patron

Pi Declaration of *innocence, piety or virtue* in office

Su Description of *past evil, rebellion* or the anger of the gods

Di Recognition of *divine participation* as the primary cause for change

Vi Declaration of *strength and victory* over hardship, suffering, evil or enemies

Re The *reversal of destinies* and the power over fate

Na Establishing a *name*

Bu *Building* or repairing temples or cities

Go *Fullness of time* or reference to sudden, transcendent *good news.*

Sha Creation of a utopian *shalom*

TEXT PARAPHRASES

1. In the seventh-century story of Sargon of ancient Akkad,[1] the king presents himself in the first person (**De**). The text refers to his family (**Le**) to present Sargon's birth as the birth of a hero (**Na**). His mother is a priestess (a virgin); his father unknown (**Pa**). He is born in secret, and put into the Euphrates in a basket of rushes (**Su**), whose door is sealed with pitch. He is saved by a laborer, who rears him (**Vi**). He was Ishtar's lover and her father's gardener (**Pi**). He was king over Akkad for four years. He conquered mountains; he scaled the heights and walked

in the valleys (**Re**) and circled the sea three times (**Go/Sha**), capturing Dilmun and going up to the great Der to destroy Kazallu (**Vi**). He calls on the kings who follow to do likewise (**Na**).

2. Written in a third-person voice, the inscription of Yahdun-Lim (**De**)[2] is dedicated to the god Shamash as king of heaven and earth and overlord of Mari (**Pa**). The king is described as digger of canals, builder of walls, erector of steles and provider for his people (**Pi**). He is a mighty king and a famous hero (**Na**) who writes his stele when Shamash listened to his prayer (**Pa**). The king, who is identified as the son of Yaggid-Lim (**Le**) is described as the first king to reach the Mediterranean (**Vi**) since Shamash built Mari (**Di**). He entered the mountains, did battle, made his name and proclaimed his power (**Na**). He united the entire region under him, and imposed a permanent tribute (**Sha**). The same year, three kings rebelled (a list) and conspired against him (**Su**). He defeated them, made a massacre, razed their cities and annexed their land (**Vi**). He repaired the embankment of the Euphrates and built a temple to Shamash with perfect construction (**Bu**). He prays for a long and happy rule (**Di**). A curse follows for anyone who neglects the temple, stops the offerings or erases Yahdun-Lim's name (**Na**).

3. The inscription attributed to Assurbanipal II[3] opens in a first-person (**De**) description as high priest, favorite of the gods and king of the world (**Pa**), son of Tukulti-Ninurta, son of Adad-Nirari (**Le**), a hero (**Na**) who follows the instructions of the gods and is therefore without rival (**Pi**). He is the shepherd of all, unafraid, and irresistable flood (**Pi**). He makes the unsubmissive submit and rules all humanity (**Re**). He has personally conquered all lands from beyond the Tigris to Lebanon and from the source of the Subnat river to Urartu (**Vi/Sha?**). Asshur, himself, chose him (**Na**) and proclaimed his power (**Di**). In wisdom and knowledge he rules Calah (**Pi**). He then describes building the palace, including painted scenes to tell his heroic deeds (**Na**) and his establishment of proper cult in Calah (**Pi**). He describes his "garden of happiness," with rare trees from all the countries through which he marched, listing some forty varieties (**Sha**). He erects temples and established festivals (**Bu**). He made a statue of himself in gold and placed it before Ninurta (**Pa**). He resettled abandoned tells (**Re**). Ninurta and Palil who love him (**Pi**) ordered him to hunt (**Di**); so he heroically kills large numbers of animals (**Na**). He organizes herds of wild animals and adds land and people to Assyria (**Sha**).

4. The Esarhaddon inscription[4] is a first-person (**De**) inscription identifying Esarhaddon as king of the universe, king of Assyria and other titles (**Le**), worshiper of Nabu and Marduk (**Pa**). Before him there were evil days, factions and rebellions (**Su**). The gods, plundered, were angry and planned evil. Babylon was flooded and the people went into slavery (**Su**). Seventy years of desolation was appointed (**Go**), but merciful Marduk turned fate about and ordered restoration (**Re**) in the eleventh year (**Go**). Esarhaddon was called from among his older brothers (**Na**), his foes were slain and he was entrusted with the rule of Assyria (**Pa**). At the beginning there were favorable signs (**Go**). He was hesitant about the commission and prostrated himself (**Pi**), but the oracles encouraged him to rebuild Babylon's walls and restore Esagila (**Bu**). He restored the gods to their places, freed the enslaved from their slavery (**Re**). A variant of this inscription[5] reiterates the narrative as above. After the restoration, Esarhaddon prays that his seed, Esagila and Babylon endure forever (**Go/Pr**), that he be like the plant of life to the people (**Sha**), and that he rule in justice (**Pi**) to a ripe old age. He prays for the blessings of life and fertility for himself and his land (**Sha**), a secure rule, a happy spirit and that he might walk his bright path (**Sha**), including a conquering hand against his ene-

mies **(Vi)**. He speaks of having made memorial steles and foundation inscriptions, writing his name, of writing of the deeds he accomplished and of his works **(Na)**. He blesses whoever among his sons succeeds him to read and anoint his inscription and states that Marduk will hear his prayer. One who destroys his name and shatters the inscription, however, is cursed **(Na)**. The inscription closes: Year of accession of Esarhaddon, king of Assyria.

5. The first-person inscription of Nebuchadnezzar II[6] **(De)** introduces him as servant of Marduk **(Pa)**, a wise ruler, who causes Babylon to become the foremost country in the world **(Pi/Na)**. The god wants timber from Lebanon **(Di)**, which is controlled by foreigners and robbers, its people scattered **(Su)**. Nebuchadnezzar's role is of a royal savior **(Na)**. He eliminates the enemy and makes everyone happy **(Vi)**. He breaks the mountains and makes a straight path to deliver the people, return them to their homes **(Re)**, where they live in safety undisturbed **(Go/Sha)**. He is established as eternal king **(Na/Go/Sha)**. He blesses the destiny of those who protect his inscription and asks for a name **(Na)**, long life, fertility and an eternal dynasty.

6. The first of the Nabonidus' inscriptions[7] is in the first person **(De)** and begins speaking of Sennacherib and his crimes against Babylon and of Marduk's anger **(Su)**. When the time was full **(Go)** and Marduk appeased **(Re)**, the deity remembered Esagila and Babylon, and caused Sennacherib to be murdered by his sons, who had earlier destroyed Babylon by Marduk's command **(Di)**. The Mandeans destroyed the temples of Assyria and the towns and cult-centers of Akkad **(Su)**. The king of Babylon was innocent and went as in mourning **(Pi)**. The king of Akkad rebuilt the temples and restored the cults **(Re)**. Nabonidus was made king by the rule of Marduk **(Na/Pa)**. He will obtain all that he wishes **(Vi)**. He is successor to Nebuchadnessar and Neriglissar and his purpose is to carry out their will **(Le)**. Nabonidus reports a dream, predicting for him a long life: a permanent throne **(Go)** and enduring rule **(Sha/Na)** in which Marduk will hear him **(Sha)**. He asks Marduk to allow him to rule long years if that is his wish. He promises to care for the sanctuaries. He describes improvements, including the rebuilding of the temple **(Bu)**.

7. The second Nabonidus text,[8] written in the first-person **(De)**, announces a great miracle **(Go)**, in a dream calling him to kingship **(Pi)**. He was an only son, one alone in the world **(Na/Le)**, who did not seek kingship **(Pi)**. The gods chose him to rebuild the temple in Harran **(Bu)** and to give him "all the lands" **(Pa)**. The people and administrators of the cities of Babylonia did evil and sinned **(Su)**. They ate each other, caused disease and starvation and the god Sin decimated the land **(Di)**. Nabonidus is forced by Sin to leave his city and wander in the desert for ten years **(Go/Su)**. Sin appointed gods to watch over him **(Di)**. Ishtar caused all hostile kings to send messages of friendship **(Sha/Di)**. Nergal broke the weapons of his eternal enemies in Arabia **(Sha/Di/Vi)**, and they submitted to Nabonidus' patronage and Shamash caused the hearts of the people to turn again to him **(Sha/Pa)**. The time the divine crescent[9] had appointed falls on the seventeenth of Tashritu, a day on which Sin is gracious **(Go)**. A prayer of praise and recognition of Sin as his patron is given **(Pi)**. The gods who had fled Babylon returned **(Re)**. He rewards his supporters generously and returns home unchanged **(Sha)**. He builds a temple to Sin and restores the gods **(Bu)**. Whenever he has fought a war, it was to carry out the command of the divine crescent **(Pa)**. He instructs his successor to visit the sacred places of Sin and find support in battle.

8. The Cyrus inscription[10] begins in the first person, with the problem of the bad former king, Nabonidus, who had removed the images of the gods from their thrones and replaced

them with fakes; used wrong rituals and prayers and set the people under corvée without relief **(Su)**. The gods withdraw from the city and leave their temples empty **(Di/Pa)**. The people become like the living dead, without the breath of the gods **(Su)**. Marduk hears their plaint and repents of his anger, showing mercy **(Di)**. He finds the righteous Cyrus **(Pi)** and names him to rule the whole world **(Na/Pa)**. Both Guti and Manda submit to Cyrus's just patronage **(Vi)**. The inscription's second part presents Cyrus in the first-person **(De)** and reiterates the themes of the first part. Marduk is his friend **(Na/Pa)** and makes him attack Babylon **(Di)**, where his soldiers enter without a battle **(Sha)**. Godless Nabonidus is defeated **(Vi)**. Sumer and Akkad rejoice at Cyrus's patronage **(Go)**, which brings them back from the dead **(Go/Re)**. Cyrus is king of the world **(Sha/De)**, like his father and grandfather **(Le)**, whom the gods love. He forbids terror, corvée **(Sha)** and improves housing **(Pi)**, reversing the people's plaint **(Re)**. All recognize his patronage and bring tribute **(Na)**. Gods and people return from exile **(Sha)**.

9. The Xerxes inscription[11] begins in a third-person voice **(De)**, declaring that Ahuramazda made Xerxes the sole great king **(Pa)**. Xerxes then speaks in the first person as ruler over all countries and languages **(Na)**. He is the son of Darius **(Le)**. Under Ahuramazda he is king over thirty great regions from Media to Kush **(Pa)**. There is a rebellion **(Su)**. With Ahuramazda's help **(Di)**, Xerxes's reestablishes the rebels' status as clients **(Vi)**. Some of these had worshipped evil gods **(Su)**. Xerxes reform destroys their temples, forbids the services, and reorients all religious services to Ahuramazda and the cosmic order **(Re)**. What was done in a bad way, is now done in a good way **(Pa/Re)**. Xerxes teaches the audience: All should live according to God's law and serve him alone **(Pi)**. Xerxes prays for protection from evil.

Inscriptions from Anatolia

10. The very long story of The Manly Deeds of Suppiluliuma, the Great King, the Hero **(Na)**[12] is told by his son Mursili II **(De)**. The author refers to Suppiluliuma as "my father" who met the Kashka enemy **(Le)**. The gods stood by him **(Pa)** and he was successful **(Vi)**. Suppiluliuma bravely asks to be sent to battle **(Pi)** in his sick father's stead **(Su)**. The first campaign is to the land of Hatti. Outnumbered, the enemy surrenders **(Vi)** and goes home in peace **(Sha)**. The grandfather is well and joins the father to attack Masha and Kammala **(Vi)** and the gods again go before him **(Pa)**. There is rebellion **(Su)** and all enemies die **(Sha)** when it is put down **(Vi)**. The gods marching in front create victory **(Di)**.

In fragment 18, the story proceeds with recurrent resistance matched by reiterations of near success. For example, there is a rebellion but the towns are not returned **(Su)**, Suppiluliuma sends his commander, who is taken by surprise and defeated **(Su)**. Suppiluliuma lays siege to Mount Tiwatassa **(Vi)**. When the enemy refuses to fight, Suppiluliuma abandons the siege and chases the enemy, fighting from town to town **(Vi)**. He challenges the king of Mitanni, but the Mitanni king mocks him **(Su)**. A plague breaks out in his army and the towns of Kashka **(Su)**. The gods march in front and the enemy die en masse **(Di/Vi)**. All fear Suppiluliuma **(Sha/Na)**. Further extensions of the story are created within a cycle of winters at home and springs on campaign. When the enemy see him, they fear him **(Na)** and make peace **(Vi)**. All the lands make peace **(Sha)**. But Carchemish does not make peace and lays siege to his town Murmuriga **(Su)** and his father with the gods' help **(Di)**, defeats them **(Vi)**.

The narrative is further expanded with an Egyptian conspiracy **(Su)**. Having heard of Suppiluliuma's attack on Amqa, they become afraid **(Na)**. Thutmosis's widow offers to marry one of Suppiluliuma's sons. Suppiluliuma is suspicious of a conspiracy **(Su)**. Suppiluliuma lays siege to Carchemish for seven days and takes it in "a terrific battle on the eighth day" **(Go/Vi)**. He fears the gods of Carchemish and honors them **(Pa)**, taking booty only from the lower town **(Pi)**. Captives brought to the palace were 3,330, while those his troops took were "beyond counting" **(Sha)**. In considering the Egyptian offer, the king calls for the "tablet of treaty," as proper precedent for making a treaty between Egypt and Hatti **(Pi)**. The seventh tablet of the inscription opens with news of the murder of Suppiluliuma's son Zannanza **(Su)**. Suppiluliuma makes a lament. The gods help him **(Di)**. In reiterating cadence, he destroys one town, spends the night and goes on to the next **(Vi)**. He comes to Timuhala, "a place of pride." They humble themselves and he accepts them as clients of Hatti **(Re)**. The story continues, but the colophon tells us that the text is incomplete.

11. A short first-person narrative of Tudhaliya IV[13] **(De)** relates the taking of booty from Cyprus **(Vi)**. Tribute is listed in the order of the gods to whom it is dedicated **(Pa)**. The text closes with a statement of Suppiluliuma, informing us that his father had not made the statue **(De)**, but Suppiluliuma had, who is son of Tudhaliya and grandson of Hattushili **(Le)**. He declares that he has engraved true exploits **(Pi)**. He built a mausoleum and put the statue in it **(De)**.

12. Separated from the foregoing with a double line,[14] a narrative of Suppiluliuma speaks in the first person **(De)**. He declares his heroic status **(Na)** and lists his titles with references to his father and grandfather **(Le)**. With an uncertain reference to his father, he speaks of crossing the sea to Alashiya. Ships meet him in battle three times, whom he defeats and burns **(Vi)**. On coming ashore, large numbers of enemies attack **(Su)** whom he defeats **(Vi)**. The rest of the narrative is lost. The text closes with the reiteration that his father did not make the statue, but that Suppiluliuma had and had built a mausoleum for it **(De)**, including assigning villages for its support **(Pi)**. The gods who recognized Tudhaliya's kingship **(Pa)** will punish anyone changing the arrangements.

INSCRIPTIONS FROM SYRIA

13. The first-person voice **(De)** of the Idrimi inscription[15] identifies the king as "son of Ilimilimma **(Le)**, servant of Adad, Hepat and Ishtar" **(Pa)**. The narrative begins with the report of a hostile act in Aleppo, causing his family to flee to Emar **(Su)**. Idrimi is the younger brother **(Na)** who thinks thoughts that no one else thinks **(Na/Pi)**. He goes into the desert and spends the night with Suteans **(Su)**. He goes to the land of Canaan, where, because of his family ties **(Le)**, he becomes chief of the town Ammiya **(Vi)**. He lives among Hapiru for seven years **(Su)**, where he studies birds and divination **(Pi)** and discovers that Adad turned to him **(Go/Pa)**. He built ships, took aboard soldiers and traveled north. His land hears of him **(Na)** and Alalakh and three other cities bring gifts and his allies make a treaty with him **(Vi)**. For seven years Barratarna, the Hurrian king, was hostile **(Su)**. Idrimi writes him declaring his family's traditional vassal status **(Le)**. Idrimi is king in Alalakh **(Sha)**. Kings rise up against him on the left and right **(Su)** and Idrimi puts an end to the warfare **(Vi)**. He goes to war and destroys a list of Hittite vassal cities **(Vi)**. He did as he pleased **(Re)**. With his

booty from Hatti, he builds a house and a throne, and shares his kingship with his brothers, sons and friends **(Sha)**, and settles those who are settled in his land in better houses, and makes the nomads live in houses **(Re)**. He reestablishes the proper cult of his ancestors **(Re)**. Idrimi calls on the gods to curse those who would steal, change or erase the statue or its inscription and asks the gods to bless the scribe who has written it. On the right cheek of the statue is added: "I was king for thirty years **(Go/Sha)**. I wrote my achievements **(Na)** on the statue **(De)**. Let people [read it] and ble[ss me]."

14. The Kalamuwa inscription[16] begins in the first person **(De)**, with identification of the writer as son of Hayya **(Le)**. The narrative begins in the former times when the Mushkabim lived like dogs **(Su)**. Kalamuwa was, however, father, mother and brother to some **(Pi)**. There follows a variant of the poor man's song **(Re)** to show that Kalamuwa protects the Mushkabim and that they love him **(Sha)**. The text closes with curses and the wish that the gods punish successors who damage the inscription or erase it **(Pa/Na)**.

15. The Azatiwada inscription[17] begins in the first person **(De)**, identifying Azitawada as blessed **(Na)**, servant of Baal **(Pa)**. The speaker is empowered by Awariku the king of the Danunians **(Le)**. He is father and mother to the Danunians, giving them life **(Pi)**. With Baal's grace, there was prosperity in his day **(Di)**. The (former) Rebels and all evil **(Su)** were destroyed **(Sha)** and he caused his patron to reign on his father's throne **(Pa)**. Because of his righteousness **(Na)**, he established peace with every king **(Vi/Pi)**. He built fortresses **(Bu)** and offers a form of the poor man's song: he makes evil men subject **(Re/Sha)**; he humbles the strong land of the West and resettles them in the East. Where there had been insecurity he established security **(Re)**. Commissioned by the gods **(Pa)**, he builds and names the city of Azatiwadaya, and establishes offerings for Baal **(Bu)**. The inscription closes with the hope for blessings, prosperity, long life, strength for every king, fertility and piety. Any who removes his name or gate **(Na)**, may the gods erase that king and kingdom **(Cu)**.

16. The inscription of Yehawmilk[18] begins in the first person **(De)** with identification as son of Yeharbaal and grandson of Urimilk **(Le)**, made king by Baalat of Byblos **(Na/Pa)**. He called to the goddess **(Pi)** and she heard his voice **(Su)** and gave peace **(Sha/Di)**. He built an altar and temple to Baalat **(Bu)**. A prayer in the third-person asks the mistress of Byblos to lengthen his days **(Pr)**, for he is righteous **(Pi)** and to give him favor before the gods and the people **(Pr)**. He orders that any later work on the altar bear his name **(Na)**, but if anyone removes his name or changes the foundation, Baalat should cause him and his seed to rot before the gods.

17. The Zakkur inscription[19] begins in the first person **(De)**. He was raised by Baal Shamem **(Na/Pa)**, who stood by him and made him king of Hazrach **(Na/Pa)**. Bar-Hadad of Aram, together with seventeen kings, conspired against him and laid siege to Hazrach **(Su)**. He prayed to Baal Shamem who answered him **(Di/Pa)**, saying through seers and diviners that he should not be afraid **(Pi)**. Baal will save him **(Di)**. He built Hazrach and its defenses. He built shrines **(Bu)** and wrote his achievements on this monument **(Na)**. The inscription closes with the prayer that any who erases his deeds **(Na)** or removes the monument be cursed by the gods.

18. The Hadad inscription[20] begins in the first person **(De)**, identifying Panamuwa as son of Qarli, king of Y'dy **(Le)** who erected this statue to Hadad in "my eternal abode" **(Pa)**, that is, his tomb. The gods supported him and gave him dominion **(Di)**. Whatever he took up or asked of the gods, they granted **(Pi)**. He restored the lands fertility and prosperity **(Re)**. He

reigned on the throne of his father and he eliminated war and slander **(Su/Vi)**. The people of Q'dy were prosperous **(Sha)**. He built towns and villages **(Bu)**. He made offerings to the gods and they were delighted in him **(Pa)**. He prays that whichever of his sons succeed him maintain his memory with the gods **(Pr)**. He also prays that he remember his name **(Na)**, or that Hadad reject him and give him sleepless nights and terror. He closes with the wish that his successor not act in violence and that no one be put to death. He then offers a discourse on treachery **(Pi)**.

19. The Panamuwa inscription[21] begins in the first person **(De)**, identifying the statue as one that Bar Rakib set up for his father, Panamuwa, king of Y'dy **(De/Le)**. The gods of Y'dy delivered Panamuwa **(Pa/Di)** from the destruction that was in his father's house **(Su)**. A damaged part of the inscription states that his father Barsur was assassinated with his seventy brothers **(Su)**. Panamuwa mounted a chariot and escaped **(Vi)**. The usurper filled prisons and created ruins more numerous than towns **(Su)**. Panamuwa's resistance creates inflation **(Su)**. Panamuwa brings a gift to the king of Assyria **(Pi)**, who makes Panamuwa king over his father's house **(Pa)**. He then "kills the stone of destruction **(Vi)**," and gives a short form of the "poor man's song" **(Re)**. He organized proper government **(Pi)** and was esteemed among kings **(Na)**. He was rich, wise and loyal. He lived and Y'dy also lived **(Sha)**. He was at the Assyrian king's side in war **(Na)** and transported the people of the east to the west and profited more than all others **(Re)**. He died in the service of the king of Assyria **(Pi)**, who, with his relatives and all the Assyrian camp, wept **(Na)** and brought his body from Damascus to Assyria **(Vi)**. In a postscript, Bar Rakib states that, because of his father's loyalty **(Le)**, Tiglathpileser caused him to sit on his father's throne **(Pa)**. The inscription closes, asking that the gods show him favor.

20. The Bar-Rakib inscription[22] begins in the first person **(De)**, with the statement that he is son of Panamuwa, king of Sam'al, servant of Tiglath Pileser **(Pa)**, who, because of his loyalty, gave him the throne **(Le)**. The land prospered **(Sha)** and he was with the Assyrian king in war **(Pi)**, along with powerful, rich kings **(Na)**. He took control of his father's house and made it better than that of the powerful kings **(Pi)**. The text closes with reference to building his palace **(Bu)**.

21. The Mesha inscription,[23] in the first person, identifies the king **(De)** as son and successor of Chemosh-[uncertain reading], king of Moab, who reigned for thirty years **(Go/Le)**. It is set up in a sanctuary dedicated to Chemosh **(Bu)** because he delivered him from all his enemies **(De/Pa)**. Mesha recounts that Omri, king of Israel, had long oppressed Moab because Chemosh was angry **(Su)**. This oppression was intensified by his successor **(Su)**. Mesha, however, has triumphed and Israel was totally destroyed **(Vi)**. The narrative is reiterated: Omri lived in Madeba in his time and half the time of his son: forty years **(Go/Su)**,[24] but Chemosh lives there in Mesha's time **(Re/Pa/Sha)**. Mesha builds Baal Meon and Kiriathaim **(Bu)**. The Gadities were indigenous to Ataroth and the king of Israel built the city **(Su)**. Mesha captured the city **(Vi)** and dedicated the population as a sacrifice to Chemosh **(Pa/Pi)**. He returned the Arel [uncertain reading][25] to Kemosh **(Re/Bu)** and settled there the people of Sharon and Maharith **(Re)**. Chemosh instructed Mesha to take Nebo from Israel **(Di)**. He marched by night and fought from dawn until noon **(Go)**, took the city **(Vi)**, and killed the people (7000) for Ashtar-Chemosh **(Go/Pa/Pi)**. He took from there the [uncertain reading] of Yahweh and brought it before Chemosh **(Re/Bu)**. The king of Israel had built Jahaz **(Bu)** and dwelt there **(Su/Pa)**, but Chemosh drove him before Mesha **(Di)**. With two hundred

men (Go) Mesha took the town (Vi). He built Karchoh, Aroer and the road in the Arnon (Bu). He rebuilt Beth Bamoth and Bezer, which had been in ruins (Re). All Diban is subject to him and he is king over one hundred towns (Go/Sha). A campaign was taken against Horonaim, apparently also occupied by Israel (Su). Chemosh sent Mesha against the city (Di). The town was taken (Vi) and Chemosh has returned to the city (Pa). . . . The closure of the text is lost.

✑ NOTES ✑

PREFACE

1. Th. L. Thompson, *The Bible in History: How Writers Create a Past* (London: Cape, 1999); Thompson, *The Mythic Past: Biblical Archaeology and the Myth of Israel* (New York: Basic, 1999), xv–xvi; Thompson, "Historiography in the Pentateuch: Twenty-Five Years After Historicity," *Scandinavian Journal for the Old Testament* 13, no. 2 (1999): 258.

2. L. L. Grabbe, *Can a History of Israel Be Written?* European Seminar on Historical Methodology 1 (Sheffield: SAP, 1997); Th. L. Thompson, "Can a History of Ancient Jerusalem and Palestine Be Written?" in *Jerusalem in Ancient History and Tradition* (London: T&T Clark, 2003), 1–15.

3. Here one might consider two important recent works: N. Silberman and I. Finkelstein, *The Bible Unearthed: Archaeology's New Vision of Ancient Israel and the Origin of Its Sacred Texts* (New York: Free Press, 2001); and M. Liverani, *Oltre la Bibbia: Storia antica di Israele* (Rome: Laterza, 2003), which will appear in English shortly. For a general review of the problems of writing history, see N. P. Lemche, *Prelude to Israel's Past: Background and Beginnings of Israelite History and Identity* (Peabody, Mass.: Hendrickson, 1998); Lemche, *The Israelites in History and Tradition* (Louisville: Westminster, 1998).

4. Biblical citations usually use the Revised Standard Version (1946) or the Jerusalem Bible (Jerusalem: Koren, 1992), both slightly adjusted to fit better the Hebrew, Aramaic or Greek. Occasionally the translations are my own.

5. I. Hjelm, *The Samaritans and Early Judaism: A Literary Analysis* (Sheffield: SAP, 2000); Hjelm, *Jerusalem's Rise to Sovereignty: Zion and Gerizim in Competition* (London: T&T Clark International, 2004).

CHAPTER ONE

1. For a summary of the current debate, we have some excellent discussions in German, especially G. Theissen and A. Merz, *Der historische Jesus: Ein Lehrbuch* (Göttingen, 1996),

and J. Schröter and R. Brucker, eds., *Der historische Jesus: Tendenzen und Perspektiven der gegenwärtigen Forschung*, BZNW 114 (Berlin: De Gruyter, 2002); in Danish, T. Engberg-Pedersen, ed., *Den historische Jesus og hans Betydning* (Copenhagen, 1998) is recommended. In English, the bibliography is large and often stridently tendentious. J. P. Meier, *A Marginal Jew: Rethinking the Historical Jesus*, 3 vols., Anchor Bible Reference Library (New York: Doubleday, 1991), is an easily accessible introduction. Briefer but hardly superficial is the discussion in B. D. Ehrman, *Jesus: Apocalyptic Prophet of the New Millennium* (Cambridge: Oxford University Press, 1999).

2. A. Schweitzer, *Geschichte der Leben-Jesu Forschung*, 2nd ed. (Tübingen: Mohr-Siebeck, 1913; *The Quest for the Historical Jesus*, 1910).

3. J. G. Eichhorn, *Einleitung in das Alte Testament*, 3 vols. (Göttingen, 1780–1783; *Introduction to the Study of the Old Testament*, 1888); Eichhorn, *Einleitung in das Neue Testament*, 2 vols. (Göttingen, 1804–1827).

4. W. M. L. de Wette, *A Critical and Historical Introduction to the Canonical Scriptures of the Old Testament* (1817; Eng. trans. with notes by T. Parker, 1843), 38–39. De Wette's understanding of myth found a modern restatement in R. Otto, *The Idea of the Holy* (1951).

5. Two studies are most important: D. F. Strauss, *Das Leben Jesus kritisch bearbeitet*, 2 vols. (1835–1836; *Life of Jesus*, 1906); and Strauss, *The Christ of Faith and the Jesus of History: A Critique of Schleiermacher's Life of Jesus* (1864; Philadelphia: Fortress, 1977).

6. L. Feuerbach, *Das Wesen des Christentums* (1841; *The Essence of Christianity*, 1854).

7. J. Weiss, *Jesus' Proclamation of the Kingdom of God* (1892; Philadelphia: Fortress, 1971).

8. W. Wrede, *Das Messiasgeheimnis in den Evangelien: Zugleich ein Beitrag zum Verständnis des Markusevangeliums* (1901; *The Messianic Secret in the Gospels*, 1971).

9. B. D. Ehrman, *Jesus: Apocalyptic Prophet of the New Millennium* (Cambridge: Oxford University Press, 1999).

10. I am using this term in the sense of E. Said, *Orientalism* (New York: Pantheon, 1978).

11. For a fine discussion of the nature and function of Q in New Testament scholarship, see J. S. Kloppenborg Verbin, *Excavating Q: The History and Setting of the Sayings Gospel* (Edinburgh: T&T Clark, 2000).

12. This theory was first proposed by James Robinson, "'Logoi Sophon': On the Gattung of Q," in J. Robinson and H. Koester, *Trajectories Through Early Christianity* (Philadelphia: Fortress: 1971), 71–113; see also H. Koester, "Apocryphal and Canonical Gospels," *Harvard Theological Review* 73 (1980): 105–130.

13. Robinson associated Q with Thomas as an example of early collections of wisdom literature, much as in Egyptian literature. However, J. Kloppenburg, in a critical evaluation of Robinson's thesis, related such wisdom collections to Greek literature as well, particularly Hellenistic "handbooks of instruction," with which he identified several blocks of the sayings in Q. He went on to argue that the "earliest levels" of Q were wisdom sayings, which only later were organized around the apocalyptic theme of judgment. J. Kloppenborg, *The Formation of Q: Trajectories in Ancient Wisdom Collections*, Studies in Antiquity and Christianity (Fortress: Philadelphia, 1987); Kloppenborg, *Q Parallels: Synopsis, Critical Notes and Concordance* (Sonoma, Calif.: Polebridge, 1988).

14. Among the many projects of this seminar related to research into the historical Jesus is the publication of an annotated edition of Q as if it were an existent text. See Kloppenborg, *Excavating Q*.

15. R. W. Funk and R. W. Hoover, *Five Gospels, One Jesus: What Did Jesus Really Say?* (Sonoma, Calif.: Polebridge, 1992).

16. For a discussion of the debates of the seminar with the publication of the proposed text of Q, see the multivolume summary of commentaries and discussions in J. M. Robinson, P. Hoffmann, and J. S. Kloppenborg, *Documenta Q: Reconstructions of Q Through Two Centuries of Gospel Research: Excerpted, Sorted, and Evaluated* (Leuven: Peeters, 1996).

17. Ehrman, *Jesus,* chap. 7.

18. M. Borg, *Conflict, Holiness, and Politics in the Teachings of Jesus,* Studies in the Bible and Early Christianity 5 (Toronto: Mellen, 1984).

19. M. Borg, "A Temperate Case for a Non-Eschatological Jesus," *Forum* 2 (1986): 81–102.

20. R. A. Horsley, *Jesus and the Spiral of Violence: Popular Jewish Resistance in Roman Palestine* (San Francisco: Harper & Row, 1987; Horsley, *Sociology and the Jesus Movement* (New York: Crossroad, 1989); and Horsley, with J. S. Hanson, *Bandits, Prophets, and Messiahs: Popular Movements in the Time of Jesus* (New York: Seabury, 1985).

21. The writings of E. J. Hobsbawm, especially *Primitive Rebels* (New York: Norton, 1965); Hobsbawm, *Bandits* (New York: Delacorte, 1969); and E. R. Wolf, *Peasants* (Englewood Cliffs, N.J.: Prentice Hall, 1966), have been particularly influential in biblical scholarship.

22. The bibliography is large, but the pioneering studies in biblical scholarship include G. Theissen, *The Miracle Stories of the Early Christian Tradition* (1972; Philadelphia: Fortress, 1983); Theissen, *Sociology of Early Christianity* (Philadelphia: Fortress, 1978); and N. K. Gottwald, *The Tribes of Yahweh: A Sociology of the Religion of Liberated Israel,* 1250–1050 B.C.E. (New York: Maryknoll, 1979); Gottwald, *The Politics of Ancient Israel* (Louisville: Westminster, 2001).

23. The problems of such harmonized reconstructions are quite common in biblical studies. A thorough criticism of these methods can be found in Th. L. Thompson, *The Historicity of the Patriarchal Narratives: The Quest for the Historical Abraham,* 3rd ed. (Berlin: De Gruyter, 1974).

24. Horsley, *Bandits,* 48–87; J. D. Crossan, *The Historical Jesus: The Life of a Mediterranean Jewish Peasant* (Edinburgh: T&T Clark, 1991), 137–206.

25. See especially the critique of M. D. Goulder, *Midrash and Lection in Matthew* (London: SPCK, 1974).

26. Amenemopet's collection is described as the Teaching of Life. It is attributed to the Egyptian overseer, "Amenemopet, the son of Ka-nakht the triumphant one of Abydos, for his son . . . Horemmaakheru." For the text, see the anthology of J. B. Pritchard, *Ancient Near Eastern Texts Related to the Old Testament* (Princeton: Princeton University Press, 1969), 421–425. Hereafter referred to as *ANET.*

27. *ANET,* 421.

28. Besides the *Historical Jesus* mentioned above, one should also consult J. D. Crossan, *Sayings Parallels: A Workbook for the Jesus Tradition* (Philadelphia: Fortress, 1986).

29. B. Mack, *A Myth of Innocence: Mark and Christian Origins* (Philadelphia: Fortress, 1988); Mack, *The Lost Gospel: The Book of Q and Christian Origins* (San Francisco: Harper, 1993).

30. J. D. Crossan, *The Historical Jesus: The Life of a Mediterranean Jewish Peasant* (Edinburgh: T&T Clark, 1991), 227.

31. Crossan, *Historical Jesus*, 227–228. Crossan discusses the considerable and confusing variation of meaning given the term "apocalyptic" on page 238.

32. H. Koester, *Introduction to the New Testament* (Philadelphia: Fortress, 1982), 2:121–122, on 1 Corinthians 7; S. Davies, *The Gospel of Thomas and Christian Wisdom* (New York: Seabury, 1983), 83; and Kloppenborg, *Formation of Q*, 244–245.

33. For a discussion on the segmented nature of biblical literature, see Th. L. Thompson, "4Q Testimonia and Bible Composition: A Copenhagen Lego Hypothesis," in *Qumran Between the Old and New Testaments*, ed. F. Cryer and Th. L. Thompson, Copenhagen International Seminar 6 (Sheffield: SAP, 1998), 261–276.

34. In this, Crossan, *Historical Jesus*, 238–239, follows Marcus Borg, "A Temperate Case for a Non-Eschatological Jesus," *Forum* 2 (1986): 81–102.

35. Crossan, *Historical Jesus*, 239–240, referring to the visions of Daniel in chapters 7–9 and 10–12 and to 1 Enoch 46:1–4, an understanding that Mogens Müller disputed in his Tübingen dissertation. M. Müller, *Der Ausdruck "Menschensohn" in den Evangelien* (Leiden: Brill, 1984).

36. A related effort with the writings of Paul has been developed by T. Engberg-Petersen, *Paul and the Stoics* (Louisville: Westminster, 2000), esp. 33–44.

37. Mack, *Lost Gospel*, 237–243.

38. Mack, *Lost Gospel*, 219.

39. A. Clarke Wire, *Holy Lives, Holy Deaths: A Close Hearing of Early Jewish Storytellers* (Atlanta: SBL, 2001).

40. M. Parry and A. Lord, *Serbo-Croatian Heroic Songs*, 2 vols. (Cambridge: Harvard University Press, 1960); A. Lord, *The Singer of Tales* (Cambridge: Harvard University Press, 1960); J. M. Foley, *The Theory of Oral Composition* (Bloomington: Indiana University Press, 1988); Foley, *The Singer of Tales in Performance* (Bloomington: Indiana University Press, 1995); also the study of oral forms by A. Jolles, *Einfache Formen* (Halle: Niemeyer, 1929); D. E. Bynum, *Daemun in the Wood: A Study of Oral Narrative Patterns* (Cambridge: Harvard University Press, 1978); A. Dundes, "Text, Texture, and Context," *Southern Folklore Quarterly* 20 (1965): 251–261; D. Ben-Amos, "Narrative Forms in the Haggadah," Ph.D. diss., Indiana University, 1967; Ben-Amos, *Folklore in Context: Essays* (New Delhi, 1982).

41. Clarke Wire, *Holy Lives*, 10–11.

42. Clarke Wire, *Holy Lives*, 6.

43. D. Gunn, *The Story of King David* (Sheffield: SAP, 1978); Gunn, *The Fate of King Saul* (Sheffield: SAP, 1980); D. Irvin, *Mytharion: The Comparison of Tales from the Old Testament and Ancient Near East* (Neukirchen, 1978); Th. L. Thompson and D. Irvin, "The Joseph and Moses Narratives," in *Israelite and Judean History*, ed. J. Hayes and J. M. Miller (Philadelphia: Westminster, 1977), 147–212; Th. L. Thompson, "A New Attempt to Date the Patriarchal Narratives," *Journal of the American Oriental Society* 98 (1978): 76–84.

44. Clarke Wire, *Holy Lives*, 84–85.

45. For a discussion of these tales and their theological function, see Th. L. Thompson, *The Bible in History: How Writers Create a Past* (London: Cape, 1999; Thompson, *The Mythic Past: Biblical Archaeology and the Myth of Israel* (New York: Basic, 1999), 337–352.

46. N. Wyatt, "Arms and the King," in *Und Moses schrieb dieses Lied auf* (Neukirchen, 1998), 833–881; Wyatt, "The Mythic Mind," *Scandinavian Journal for the Old Testament* 15

(2001): 3–56; Th. L. Thompson, "Kingship and the Wrath of God: Or Teaching Humility," *Revue biblique* 109 (2002): 161–196.

47. *ANET,* 589–591.

48. W. G. Lambert, *Babylonian Wisdom Literature* (Oxford: Clarendon, 1960), 21–56; *ANET,* 596–601.

49. *ANET,* 601–604.

50. *ANET,* 426–27.

51. *ANET,* 427–430.

52. Both the proverbs collected and the figure of Sennacherib exerted a powerful influence on wisdom literature well into early Christian times. A. Harrak, "Tales About Sennacherib," in *The World of the Arameans,* ed. P. M. Michèle Daviau (Sheffield: SAP, 2001), 168–189.

53. *ANET,* 410.

54. W. Anderson, *Kaiser und Abt: Die Geschichte eines Schwanks,* Folklore Fellows Communications 42 (Helsinki, 1923).

55. S. Thompson, *Motif Index of Folk Literature,* 6 vols. (Bloomington: Indiana University Press, 1955–1958).

56. Th. L. Thompson, "4Q Testimonia and Bible Composition: A Copenhagen Lego Hypothesis," in *Qumran Between the Old and New Testaments,* ed. F. C. Cryer and Th. L. Thompson (SAP: Sheffield, 1998), 261–276.

CHAPTER TWO

1. For example, E. P. Sanders, *Jesus and Judaism* (Philadelphia: Fortress, 1985); Sanders, *The Historical Figure of Jesus* (London: Penguin, 1993); B. Ehrmann, *The New Testament: A Historical Introduction to the Early Christian Writings* (New York: Oxford University Press, 1997); Ehrmann, *Jesus: Apocalyptic Prophet of the New Millennium* (New York: Oxford University Press, 1999).

2. Ehrmann, *Jesus,* 33.

3. Especially in contrast to the single use of the kingdom motif in John's gospel (Jn 3:3–5); see Sanders, *Historical Figure of Jesus,* 68–70.

4. Such a conflict with historical contexts is particularly troublesome in Bart Ehrman's otherwise interesting discussion of apocalyptic figures waiting for the end of time, in *Jesus,* chap. 1.

5. J. Taylor, "The Coming of Elijah, Mt 17,10–13 and Mark 9,11–13: The Development of the Texts," *Revue biblique* 98 (1991): 107–119.

6. So M. Müller, *Kommentar til Mattæusevangeliet,* 383–385, and most commentaries.

7. For birth stories in the Bible, see Th. L. Thompson, *The Bible in History: How Writers Create a Past* (London: Cape, 1999); Thompson, *The Mythic Past: Biblical Archaeology and the Myth of Israel* (New York: Basic, 1999), 323–374, esp. 350–352. For this theme's earlier ancient Near Eastern context, see Th. L. Thompson and D. Irvin, "The Joseph and Moses Narratives," in *Israelite and Judean History,* ed. J. H. Hayes and J. M. Miller (Philadelphia: Westminster, 1977), 149–212, esp. 181–209; for further comparisons of this theme, see A. Clark Wire, *Holy Lives, Holy Deaths: A Close Hearing of Early Jewish Storytellers,* Studies in Biblical Literature 1 (Atlanta: SBL, 2002), 25–101; R. Laurentin, *Les évangiles de l'enfance du Christ; Vérité de Noël au-delà des mythes* (Paris, 1982); R. E. Brown, *The Birth of the Messiah:*

A Commentary on the Infancy Narratives in Matthew and Luke (Garden City, N.Y.: Doubleday, 1993); R. A. Horsley, *The Liberation of Christmas: The Infancy Narratives in Social Context* (New York: Crossroad, 1993); and O. Davidsen, *Christi Fødsel: Tekster og tolkninger år totusind* (Hovedland: Højbjerg, 2000).

8. Thompson, *Bible in History,* 353–374.

9. Thompson, "How Yahweh Became God: Exodus 3 and 6 and the Center of the Pentateuch," *JSOT* 8 (1994); Thompson, "From the Mouth of Babes, Strength: Psalm 8 and the Book of Isaiah," *JSOT* 16 (2002): 226–245.

10. O. Loretz, *Ugarit und die Bibel* (Darmstadt, 1990), 163–164.

11. On chain narratives and their patterned introductions, see Th. L. Thompson, *The Origin Tradition of Ancient Israel* (Sheffield: SAP, 1987), 155–189.

12. The enduring importance of this story in the world of ancient Judaism can be traced in the illustrative paintings on the walls of the early synagogue at Dura Europos, in which the story of the woman and the son Elisha raised from the dead is captured in the motif of Madonna and child and coupled with a resurrection scene of the messiah as the new Israel.

13. See the discussion on "designated outsiders" in G. Jackson, *"Have Mercy on Me,"* Copenhagen International Seminar 10 (Sheffield: Sheffield Academic Press, 2002), 61–70.

14. *ANET*, tablet VI.68–70.

15. For more on this theme, see I. Hjelm, *Jerusalem's Rise to Sovereignty: Zion and Gerizim in Competition* (London: T&T Clark International, 2004), 276, 284.

16. See I. Hjelm, *The Samaritans and Early Judaism: A Literary Analysis* (Sheffield: SAP, 2000), 125.

17. Thompson, *Bible in History,* 317–322.

18. See, on the issue of supersessionism in early Judaism, Hjelm, *Samaritans and Early Judaism,* 120–123; Hjelm, *Jerusalem's Rise to Sovereignty.*

19. This discussion of Isaiah's children and the Assyrians follows Hjelm, *Jerusalem's Rise to Sovereignty.*

20. Mythic overtones are ascribed to those who give birth painlessly (implicitly in Ex 1:19 and explicitly in Is 66:7–11; cf. Gen 3:16), as to those whose births are stopped (Gen 20:17–18; Is 37:3).

21. On this trait of the Abraham stories, see Th. L. Thompson, *The Origin Tradition of Ancient Israel* (Sheffield: Sheffield Academic Press, 1987), 158–160.

Chapter Three

1. Crossan, *Historical Jesus,* 265–271.

2. For a very different view, see A. Wire, "The Structure of the Gospel Miracle Stories," *Semeia* 11 (1978): 83–113.

3. See Crossan, *Historical Jesus,* 310–313; however, Crossan interests himself in a possible chain of tales prior to Mark's use of the stories. See also R. T. Fortna, *The Gospel of Signs: A Reconstruction of the Narrative Sources Underlying the Fourth Gospel* (Cambridge: Cambridge University Press, 1970); P. Achtemeier, "Toward the Isolation of Pre-Markan Miracle Catenae," *Journal of Biblical Literature* 89 (1970): 265–291; Achtemeier, "The Origin and Function of the Pre-Markan Miracle Catenae," *Journal of Biblical Literature* 91 (1972):

198–221, tries to reconstruct a collection of miracle stories existing prior to Mark's gospel; B. L. Mack, *Mark and Christian Origins: A Myth of Innocence* (Philadelphia: Fortress, 1988), 216–223.

4. Asking the demon for his name, "legion"—a large unit of the Roman army—creates a balance between symbols of uncleanness: foreigners, tombs and pigs.

5. Hjelm, *Jerusalem's Rise to Sovereignty,* 221–230.

6. Crossan, *Historical Jesus,* xxvii–xxxiv.

7. Crossan, *Historical Jesus,* xxxiii.

8. Crossan, in *Historical Jesus* (xxi), classifies his sayings in four chronological strata: 30–60, 60–80, 80–120 and 120–150 CE.

9. Crossan, *Historical Jesus,* xxxiii and 436.

10. In contrast, A. Clark Wire places many of the story types and sayings found in the gospels in the more general context of early Jewish storytelling: *Holy Lives, Holy Deaths: A Close Hearing of Early Jewish Storytellers,* Studies in Biblical Literature 1 (Atlanta: Society of Biblical Literature, 2002).

11. So Crossan, *Historical Jesus,* 266–267.

12. Such as Albert Huck/Heinrich Greeven, *Synopsis of the First Three Gospels: With the Addition of the Johannine Parallels,* 13th ed. (Tübingen: Mohr, 1981), 176–179.

13. Hjelm, *Jerusalem's Rise to Sovereignty,* 93–168.

14. F. J. Stephens, "Prayer of Lamentation to Ishtar," in J. B. Pritchard, *Ancient Near Eastern Texts Relating to the Old Testament* (Princeton: Princeton University Press, 1969), 384, lines 54–60. Hereafter *ANET.*

15. Hjelm, *Jerusalem's Rise to Sovereignty,* 83–84, 238–239.

16. In the sixth-century Samaritan tradition, *Kitab al Tarikh of Abu'l-Fath,* the Samaritans refer to the Jerusalem temple as the house of shame. The first century CE writer Josephus referred to an event during the reign of Herod early in the first century, when Samaritans scattered human bones in the courtyard of the temple (Josephus *Antiquities.*xviii.29–30). Whether history or a retaliation for the story of the shaming of the shrine at Bethel-Gerizim, Josephus's story suggests an early basis for the scornful description of the temple. On this issue, see Hjelm, *Samaritans and Early Judaism,* 251.

17. In this connection, Mogens Müller finds support in the Dead Sea scrolls (*Kommentar til Matthæusevangeliet,* 439).

18. Thompson, *Bible in History,* 323–374.

19. Tablet I.ll.80–84.

20. A similar function of the first person is found in Lam 3, which transposes the first person in Psalm 23 to a voice for Jerusalem: see P. J. P. van Hecke, *Lamentations 3:1–6: An Anti-Psalm 23* (forthcoming).

21. For the holy war motif of the gift of breath, see I. Hjelm and Th. L. Thompson, "The Victory Song of Merneptah," *Journal for the Study of the Old Testament* 27 (2002): 3–18.

22. This story is found in the Bible in three variations: Isaiah 36–39; 2 Kings 18–20 and 2 Chronicles 29–31. For the origin of the Hezekiah story in Isaiah, see Hjelm, *Jerusalem's Rise to Sovereignty.*

23. *Kitab al-Tarikh of Abul'Fath,* trans. Paul Stenhouse, *Studies in Judaism,* vol. 1 (Sidney: University of Sidney Press, 1985), 115–116.

24. For a discussion of Mark's presentation of Jesus as teacher, see the interesting study done by V. K. Robbins, *Jesus the Teacher: A Socio-Rhetorical Interpretation of Mark* (Minneapolis: Fortress, 1992), esp. 75–107.

CHAPTER FOUR

1. Mack, *Lost Gospel,* 155.

2. Mack, *Lost Gospel,* 86.

3. J. S. Kloppenborg Verbin, *Excavating Q: The History and Setting of the Sayings Gospel* (Edinburgh: T&T Clark, 2000), 68–109; Mack, *Lost Gospel,* 83; J. D. Crossan, *The Historical Jesus: The Life of a Mediterranean Jewish Peasant* (Edinburgh: T&T Clark, 1991), 270–274.

4. *ANET,* 379.

5. *ANET,* 378–379.

6. The implied reference is to G. E. Wright, *The Old Testament Against Its Environment* (London: SCM Press, 1950).

7. *ANET,* 602–604.

8. (1) Songs of the kingdom in Is 1–12; (2) songs of judgment in Is 13–35 (seven songs cursing the nations in Is 13–21, 23, and seven songs cursing Samaria and Jerusalem in Is 22, 24–35); (3) the book's central story of good king Hezekiah in seven scenes in Is 36–39; (4) seven songs of return from redemption from exile to Yahweh's covenant with the New Jerusalem in Is 40:1–55:13; and (5) seven songs of peace from the song of the temple for all peoples to the song of a new heaven and a new earth in Is 56:1–66:24.

9. The Hebrew of this verse is unclear. The entire poem (Is 35:1–10) is dominated by the motif of the desert becoming fertile as a sign of divine glory.

10. Hjelm and Thompson, "Victory Song of Merneptah," 6.

11. F. Garcia Martinez, *The Dead Sea Scrolls Translated: The Qumran Texts in English* (Leiden: Brill, 1994), 203–205.

12. Garcia Martinez, *Dead Sea Scrolls,* 337–338.

13. Garcia Martinez, *Dead Sea Scrolls,* 384–385.

14. Garcia Martinez, *Dead Sea Scrolls,* 394.

15. On the knowledge of and distribution of biblical literature in the Dead Sea scrolls, see J. Vanderkam, *The Dead Sea Scrolls Today* (Grand Rapids, Mich.: Eerdmans, 1994).

16. Garcia Martinez, *Dead Sea Scrolls,* 303–304; 365.

17. Garcia Martinez, *Dead Sea Scrolls,* 189.

18. Garcia Martinez, *Dead Sea Scrolls,* 116–117. The theme of holy war and its ironies is discussed in Parts 2-3 below.

CHAPTER FIVE

1. For the creation of such complex chains, see Th. L. Thompson, *The Origin Tradition of Ancient Israel* (Sheffield: SAP, 1987), 155–189.

2. This problem plagues New Testament studies, as in the analyses of Q and the Gospel of Thomas in the Jesus Seminar (Kloppenborg, *Excavating Q;* Mack, *Lost Gospel;* Crossan, *Historical Jesus*), and has been particularly bothersome in Old Testament research of the prophetic books. R. Carroll, *The Wolf in the Sheepfold: Bible as Problematic for Theology* (London: SCM Press, 1991).

3. In *Origin Tradition,* I discuss the difficulties in understanding the diversified collection of Abraham stories as stories related to a coherent personality. Abraham's travels, so to speak, moved the figure of Abraham from place to place, that he might be attached to ever new stories (199–200).

4. Thompson, *Origin Tradition,* 51–59.

5. Compare 1 Sam 13 and 15; 2 Kgs 18:2–7; *ANET,* 159b.

6. *ANET,* 6a–8a; 10b–11b; 253a–253b.

7. *ANET,* 365–367.

8. *ANET,* 365–367.

9. Hjelm and Thompson, "Victory Song of Merneptah."

10. See M. Liverani, *Prestige and Interest: International Relations in the Near East: ca 1600–1100 BC,* History of the Ancient Near East 1 (Padua, 1990); Th. L. Thompson, "Kingship and the Wrath of God, or Teaching Humility," *Revue biblique* (109) 2002: 161–196; Hjelm and Thompson, "Victory Song of Merneptah"; N. Wyatt, *Myths of Power: A Study of Royal Myth and Ideology in Ugaritic and Biblical Tradition,* UBL 13 (Münster, 1996).

11. The results of this study are presented in Th. L. Thompson, "A Testimony of the Good King: Reading the Mesha Stele," in L. L. Grabbe, *European Seminar for Historical Methodology* (forthcoming).

12. M. Liverani, "Partire sul carro, per il deserto," *AION* 32 (1972): 403–415; J. Sasson, "On Idrimi and Sarruwa the Scribe," in *Nuzi and the Hurrians,* ed. D. Owens (Winona Lake, Ind.: Eisenbrauns, 1981), 309–324.

13. Hjelm and Thompson, "Victory Song of Merneptah."

14. On such parallels with Syrian and Assyrian stories, especially those of Idrimi and Esarhaddon's with David's stories, see M. Liverani, *Prestige and Interest: International Relations in the Near East* (Padua, 1990); B. Oded, *War, Peace and Empire: Justifications for War in Assyrian Royal Inscriptions* (Wiesbaden, 1992); Hjelm, *Jerusalem's Rise to Sovereignty,* esp. 130–142.

15. See already A. Hermann, *Die ägyptische Königsnovelle* (Glückstadt, 1938); and especially B. Albrektson, *History and the Gods: An Essay on the Idea of Historical Events as Divine Manifestations in the Ancient Near East and in Israel* (Lund, 1967); see, more recently, H. W. F. Saggs, *Encounter with the Divine in Mesopotamia and Israel* (London, 1978).

16. Th. L. Thompson, "Kingship and the Wrath of God: Or Teaching Humility," *Revue biblique* 109 (2002): 161–196.

17. The hymn of Thutmosis III can be found in *ANET,* 373–375. The inscription involves themes that are reused in the inscriptions of Amenophis III, Seti I and Ramses III. For the Amenhotep III inscription, see *ANET,* 375–376; that of Seti I can be found in J. Breasted, *Ancient Records of Egypt,* vol. 3 (London, 1906–1907), sec. 116–117; and the Ramses III variant can be found in J. A. Wilson, *Historical Records of Ramses,* vol. 3, SAOC 12 (Chicago: University of Chicago Press, 1936), 111–112. For the Merneptah hymn, see *ANET,* 376, and

W. W. Hallo, *The Concept of Scripture*, vol. 2, *Monumental Inscriptions from the Biblical World* (Leiden: Brill, 2000), 40-41.

For a discussion of these inscriptions in the context of royal ideology, see Thompson, "Wrath of God"; and Hjelm and Thompson, "Victory Song of Merneptah."

18. Th. L. Thompson, "He Is Yahweh; He Does What Is Right in His Own Eyes: The Old Testament as a Theological Discipline II," *Tro og Historie, Forum for Bibelsk Eksegese 7* (Frederiksberg: Museum Tusculanum, 1996), 246–262.

19. Th. L. Thompson, "From the Mouth of Babes: Strength, Psalm 8,3 and the Book of Isaiah," *JSOT* 16 (2002): 226–245; Thompson, "Historie og teologi i overskrifterne til Davids salmer," *Collegium Biblicum Årbog,* 1997, 88–102.

20. M. Liverani, "The Ideology of the Assyrian Empire," in *Power and Propaganda,* ed. M. T. Larsen (Copenhagen, 1979), 297–317; Oded, *War, Peace and Empire,* 155–157; Hjelm, *Jerusalem's Rise to Sovereignty,* 133.

21. Ahlström, *History of Ancient Palestine,* 755.

22. The attribute of fear or terror as a divine quality is seen in the nearly ubiquitous self-description of Assyrian kings as USUM.GAL, "the great dragon," a description that first appears on the Hammurapi stele (*ANET,* 276); Thompson, "Wrath of God."

23. Tablet 1.i.8–10.16–19.

24. Tablet 11.304–308.

25. Jeremiah 25:8–31; Dan 9:1–8; compare the converse use of significant numbers for peace as in Jgs 5:31, in which the land has peace for forty years.

26. Cf. Jer 29:10–14; Ezra 1:1; Dan 9:8–19.

27. Ten years of suffering or exile, as in the second Nabonidus text. The eleven years of Esarhaddon involve a scribe's pun of reversing the sixty plus ten of the seventy years of suffering to ten plus one, creating a numerical pun that draws on the cuneiform similarity of the numbers sixty and one; cf. Hallo, *Context of Scripture,* 2:306.

28. For similar use of particularity, compare the announcement of the utopian *shalom* on the birthday of Ramses IV (*ANET,* 378–379), which bears the same function.

29. Thompson, *Bible in History,* 217–227.

30. Hallo, *Context of Scripture,* vol. 1, *Canonical Composition from the Biblical World* (Leiden: Brill, 1997), 477–478.

31. See the discussion in C. J. Gadd, "The Harran Inscriptions of Nabonidus," *Anatolian Studies* 8 (1958): 35–92; T. Longman, *Fictional Akkadian Autobiography,* 97–103; Hallo, *Context of Scripture,* 1:477–478; *ANET,* 311–312, 560–562.

32. H. Hoffner, "Propaganda and Political Justification in Hittite Historiography," in *Unity and Diversity: Essays in the History, Literature and Religion of the Ancient Near East,* ed. H. Goedicke and J. J. M. Roberts (Baltimore: Johns Hopkins University Press, 1975), 49–62; Hallo, *Context of Scripture,* 1:194–198.

CHAPTER SIX

1. See, for example, H. Niehr, *Der höchste Gott, BZAW* 190 (Berlin: De Gruyter, 1990); Th. L. Thompson, "The Intellectual Matrix of Early Biblical Literature: Inclusive

Monotheism in Persian Period Palestine," in *The Triumph of Elohim: From Yahwisms to Judaisms,* ed. D. Edelman (Kampen: Pharos, 1995), 107–126.

2. E. Meyer, *Geschichte des Altertums* (Berlin, 1913), 2:282–285; J. Van Seters, *In Search of History: Historiography in the Ancient World and the Origins of Biblical History* (New Haven: Yale University Press, 1983); Van Seters, *Prologue to History: The Yahwist as Historian in Genesis* (Louisville: Fortress John Knox, 1992).

3. G. Garbini, *History and Ideology in Ancient Israel* (London, 1988), 151–152.

4. Th. L. Thompson, "Conflict Themes in the Jacob Narrative," *Semeia* 15 (1979): 5–26; Thompson, *The Origin Tradition of Ancient Israel* (Sheffield: SAP, 1987), 51–59, 97–99, 104–116.

5. J. B. Pritchard, *Ancient Near Eastern Texts Related to the Old Testament* (New Haven: Yale University Press, 1969), 60–72, 501–503. Hereafter *ANET.*

6. *ANET,* 3.

7. N. P. Lemche, "The Old Testament: A Hellenistic Book?" *SJOT* 7 (1993): 163–193.

8. For a discussion of some of these variations, see Th. L. Thompson, "Historiography in the Pentateuch: Twenty-Five Years After Historicity," *SJOT* 13 (1999): 258–283.

9. The reiteration of this motif is central in understanding the threefold reiteration of Israel's emptiness in the stories of the House of Baasha (1 Kgs 15:33–16:7), the extended story about the fall of the House of Omri (1 Kgs 16:23–2 Kgs 10:30) and in the story of Samaria's fall. Hjelm, *Jerusalem's Rise to Sovereignty: Zion and Gerizim in Competition* (London: T&T Clark, 2004), 36–37.

10. *ANET,* 60–72; additions to tablets V-VII: *ANET,* 501–503; W. W. Hallo, *The Context of Scripture,* vol. 1, *Canonical Compositions from the Biblical World* (Leiden: Brill, 1997), 390–402.

11. W. G. Lambert, "The Great Battle of the Mesopotamian Religious Year: The Conflict in the Akitu House," *Iraq* 25 (1963): 189–190; T. Jacobsen, "Religious Drama in Ancient Mesopotamia," in *Unity and Diversity,* ed. H. Goedicke and J. J. M. Roberts (London, 1975), 65–97; also J. A. Black, "The New Year Ceremonies in Ancient Babylon: 'Taking Bel by the Hand' and a Cultic Picnic," *Religion* 11 (1981): 39–59.

12. *ANET,* 8 n. 6.

13. *ANET,* 104–109, 512–514.

14. A variant of a story found in 1 Kings 14:21–31. The association of the Hezekiah story with the 2 Chronicles story of Rehoboam's humbling himself is discussed in I. Hjelm, *The Samaritans and Early Judaism: A Literary Analysis,* CIS 7 (Sheffield: SAP, 2000), 148–152.

15. *ANET,* "Deliverance of Mankind from Destruction," 10–11.

16. A text from Middle Kingdom Coffin Texts, found in chapter 108 of the Book of the Dead, whose mythic themes are often cited in Egyptian texts. When the sun barge enters the evening, it is threatened by an evil dragon. Seth's task is to bind the snake and make her harmless. See *ANET,* 11–12.

17. *ANET,* 275–287.

18. Tablet I.80–84.

19. For a discussion of these and related birth tales, see Th. L. Thompson and D. Irvin, "The Joseph and Moses Narratives," in *Israelite and Judean History,* ed. J. H. Hayes and J. M. Miller (Philadelphia: Westminster, 1977), 181–209. The Sargon birth story, long associated with the story of Moses' birth, can be found in both Neo-Assyrian and Neo-Babylonian

versions (*ANET*, 119). For the story of Oedipus, the central figure in the Theban cycle of sagas, see the Loeb Classical Library edition of Sophocles: F. Storr, *Sophocles: With an English Translation*, Loeb Classical Library, 20–21 (London: Heinemann, 1912).

20. *ANET*, 557–558.

21. On the Cyrus story, see K. Stott, "Herodotus and the Old Testament: A Comparative Reading of the Ascendancy Stories of King Cyrus and David," *Journal for the Study of the Old Testament* 16, no. 1 (2002): 52–78.

22. In the Greek version of Psalm 110 (Greek Ps 109), however, special emphasis is given to the birth of the king by Yahweh himself. The transcendent birth of a divine king is set in a cosmic context with an independent solar metaphor of the king as the dew at dawn, born on Zion's hill (Ps 110:2): "On the holy mount I have given birth to you like dew from the dawn's womb."

23. For text, see B. Lafont, "Le Roi de Mari et les prophètes du dieu Adad," *RA* 78 (1984): 7–18; For a discussion of the biblical parallel, see A. Malamat, "A Mari Prophecy and Nathan's Dynastic Oracle," in *Prophecy: Essays Presented to G. Fohrer, BZAW* 150 (Berlin: De Gruyter, 1980), 68–82.

24. Seen at the Museum of Fine Arts in Boston on November 16, 1999, in a display entitled *Pharaohs of the Sun: Akhenaton, Nefertiti, Tutankhamen*, cat. no. 25: catalogue edited by R. E. Freed, Y. J. Markowitz and S. H. D'Auria (Boston: Bulfinch, 1999), 56–58, 208–209.

25. *Pharaohs of the Sun*, p. 204, cat. no. 12.

26. The Hymn to the Sun God is also called the Great Hymn to Aten. The song is preserved in five variants from tombs of the period, the best of which comes from the tomb of Ay, the commander of Akhenaton's chariotry during Akhenaton's reign and also pharaoh from 1322 to 1319, after the death of Tutankhamen (Freed et al., *Pharaohs of the Sun*, pp. 26, 99). English translations can be found in J. H. Breasted, *The Dawn of Conscience* (New York: Doubleday, 1933), 281–286; *ANET*, 281–286; and W. W. Hallo and M. Lichtheim, "The Great Hymn to the Aten," in *Context of Scripture*, 1:44–46. For the chronology, see W. J. Murnane, "The History of Ancient Egypt," in *Civilizations of the Ancient Near East*, ed. J. M. Sasson (New York: Doubleday, 1995), 2:712–714.

27. Compare the opening lines of The Instruction of King Amenemhet in *ANET*, 418–419.

28. *ANET*, 281–286.

29. Already, Breasted, *Dawn of Conscience*, 366–370; P. Auffret, *Hymn d'Egypte et d'Israel: Etudes de structure litteraires, OBO* 34 (Freiburg: Universitätsverlag, 1981).

30. *ANET*, 446–447.

31. *ANET*, 447 n. 16.

32. J. H. Breasted, *Ancient Records of Egypt: Historical Documents*, vol. 3 (New York, 1906), sec. 511, p. 218.

33. Breasted, *Ancient Records*, vol. 3, sec. 534, p. 225.

34. English translation: The Hymn of Victory of Thutmosis III, in *ANET*, 373–375. This rather common epithet is found in inscriptions of the Eighteenth and Nineteenth Dynasties, for example, Amenhotep III (*ANET*, 375), Merneptah (*ANET*, 376–378) and Ramses IV (*ANET*, 379).

35. See Appendix 1, variously no. 11 to no. 23.

36. See, for example, G. L. Mattingly, "The Pious Sufferer: Mesopotamia's Traditional Theodicy and Job's Counsellors," in *The Bible in Light of Cuneiform Literature: Scripture in Context,* vol. 3, *Ancient Near Eastern Texts and Studies,* ed. W. W. Hallo (Lewiston, N.Y.: Mellon, 1990), 305–348. See also the just sufferer compositions in Hallo, *Context of Scripture,* 485–495, 575–578; also *ANET,* 589–591.

37. Dated to the Neo-Babylonian period by A. Ungnad, *Die Religion der Babylonier und Assyrer* (Jena, 1921); for English translation, see *ANET,* 383–385.

38. *ANET,* 384.

39. I. Hjelm and Th. L. Thompson, "The Victory Song of Merneptah: Israel and the People of Palestine," *Journal for the Study of the Old Testament* 27 (2002): 3–18.

40. Breasted, *Ancient Records,* vol. 3, sec. 582, p. 245.

41. Breasted, *Ancient Records* vol. 3, sec. 594, p. 253.

42. Breasted, *Ancient Records* vol. 3, sec. 612–613, pp. 261–262.

43. *ANET,* 377.

44. Appendix 1, no. 22; *ANET,* 378.

45. Breasted, *Ancient Records,* vol. 3, sec. 613, p. 262.

46. Breasted, *Ancient Records,* vol. 3, sec. 614, p. 262. For the structure of the hymn in three major movements, see G. Fecht, "Die Israelstele, Gestalt und Aussage," *Fontes atque Pontes: Eine Festgabe für Hellmut Brunner,* Ägypten und Altes Testament 5 (Wiesbaden: Harrassowitz, 1983), 106–138.

47. Breasted, *Ancient Records,* vol. 3, sec. 614, p. 262.

48. See J. H. Breasted, *The Dawn of Conscience* (New York, 1933), 366–370; text from *ANET,* 369–371.

49. Papyrus Sallier I. Compare R. A. Caminos, *Late Egyptian Miscellanies* (Oxford: Clarendon, 1954), 323–325; *ANET,* 378.

50. Appendix 1, no. 23; *ANET,* 379.

51. *ANET,* 370–371.

52. Fecht, "Israelstele," 129.

53. Hymn of Victory of Thutmosis III, *ANET,* 373–375, citing from 374. Compare Breasted, *Ancient Records,* vol. 2, sec. 655–662, pp. 262–266.

54. In Merneptah's soliloquy in the Great Karnak Inscription, not only does the king bring unity among his subjects, but he fights against conspiracy. The Libyans Plotting Evil Things Against Egypt in Breasted, *Ancient Records,* vol. 3, sec. 591, pp. 251–252; compare also the victory hymn of Thutmosis III, *ANET,* 373–375.

55. Breasted, *Ancient Records,* vol. 2, sec. 890–892, pp. 360–362; *ANET,* 375–376.

56. D. B. Redford, *Egypt, Canaan and Israel in Ancient Times* (Princeton: Princeton University Press, 1992), 137, 201.

57. Breasted, *Ancient Records,* vol. 3, sec. 490, p. 210: "husband of Egypt, rescuing her from every country." See Breasted, *Ancient Records,* vol. 3, 264 note a. A similar motif is found in the accession speech of Ramses III, in Breasted, *Ancient Records,* vol. 4, sec. 63: "I surrounded her, I established her by my valiant might. When I arose like the sun as king over Egypt, I protected her, I expelled for her the nine bows." In the Great Karnak Inscription, pharaoh is the father who keeps his children alive (Breasted, *Ancient Records,* vol. 3, sec. 580, p. 243).

58. Th. L. Thompson, *The Bible in History: How Writers Create a Past* (London: Cape, 1999); Thompson, *The Mythic Past: Biblical Archaeology and the Myth of Israel* (New York: Basic, 1999), 280.

CHAPTER SEVEN

1. For the rewriting of scripture in Matthew's gospel, see J. Jeremias, *Die Abendmalsworte Jesu* (Göttingen, 1935); W. D. Davies and D. C. Allison, *A Critical and Exegetical Commentary on the Gospel According to St Matthew* (Edinburgh: T&T Clark, 1997), 3:472–473; and esp. M. Müller, *Kommentar til Matthæusevangeliet* (Århus: Universitetsforlag, 2000), 529–533.

2. On the sacrifice story in Exodus 12, see especially J. D. Levenson, *The Death and Resurrection of the Beloved Son: The Transformation of Child Sacrifice in Judaism and Christianity* (New Haven: Yale University Press, 1993), 43–52.

3. For a recent discussion of these myths, see T. Mettinger, *The Riddle of the Resurrection: "Dying and Rising" Gods in the Ancient Near East,* Coniectanea Biblica, no. 50 (Stockholm: Almqvist & Wiksell International, 2001).

4. For text and commentary, see F. O. Hvidberg-Hansen, *Kana'anæiske myter og legender* (Århus, 1990), 1:101–120; O. Loretz, *Ugarit und die Bibel: Kanaanäische Götter und Religion im alten Testament* (Darmstadt, 1990), 110–115; J. B. Pritchard, *Ancient Near Eastern Texts Related to the Old Testament* (Princeton: Princeton University Press, 1969), 129–142. Hereafter *ANET.*

5. This is clearly demonstrated in a wonderfully clear study, shortly to appear in English: H. J. Lundager Jensen, *Gammeltestamentlig religion: En indføring* (Frederiksberg, 1998).

6. A wide spectrum of stories about Dumuzi or Tammuz is known. Some few are collected in, for example, *ANET*: "Dumuzi and Enkimdu": *ANET,* 41–42; "A Vision of the Netherworld": *ANET,* 109–110; "Dispute Between the Date Palm and the Tamarisk": *ANET,* 410–411. Among the very earliest are the Sumerian tales: "Inanna's Descent to the Nether World," *ANET,* 52–57; "Dumuzi and Inanna," *ANET,* 641–644, as well as a series of Sumerian songs that refer both explicitly and implicitly to the Dumuzi tradition: "Lettuce Is My Hair," *ANET,* 644; "Life Is Your Coming," *ANET,* 644–645; "The Honey-man," *ANET,* 645; and "Set Me Free, My Sister," *ANET,* 645. The reference in the Gilgamesh Epic can be found in tablet VI, lines 45–47 (*ANET,* 84); see also S. N. Kramer, *The Sacred Marriage Rite: Aspects of Faith, Myth, and Ritual in Ancient Sumer* (Bloomington: Indiana University Press, 1969).

7. See especially *ANET,* 52–57, 641–644.

8. *ANET,* 644–645.

9. On this metaphor, see K. Nielsen, *For a Tree There Is Hope* (Århus: Universitetsforlag, 1989).

CHAPTER EIGHT

1. L. Feuerbach, *The Essence of Christianity* (New York: Harper, 1956).

2. J. B. Pritchard, *Ancient Near Eastern Texts Related to the Old Testament* (Princeton: Princeton University Press, 1969), 8, n. 6. Hereafter *ANET.*

3. Given by the might of Nanna according to the true word of Utu: *ANET*, 523–525; here p. 523; for the Code of Hammurapi, given to the king by the god Shamash, see *ANET,* 163–180; cf. Ex 20:1–23:33.

4. The Narcissus motif is widespread in the ancient world. In a much older Egyptian story, the goddess Hathor, having set out to destroy mankind, comes to a field filled with red-colored beer that the god Re, in an effort to save mankind, had colored red with ochre to give the appearance of human blood. When the goddess looked into the lake, she saw her own beautiful face in the beer. Drinking it, Hathor falls asleep and forgets her plan to kill mankind. For the text, see *ANET,* 10–11.

5. *ANET,* 99: Mami is called "the mother-womb, the one who creates mankind"; for Ishtar, 111–112; and for Asherah, 131.

6. The structure of theological debate in Cain's story is described in Th. L. Thompson, *The Bible in History: How Writers Create a Past* (London: Cape, 1999); Thompson, *The Mythic Past: Biblical Archaeology and the Myth of Israel* (New York: Basic, 1999), 330–337.

7. Mirroring the Samaritan/Jewish competition between the Gerizim and Jerusalem temples: I. Hjelm, *Jerusalem's Rise to Sovereignty* (London: T&T Clark, 2004).

8. For further discussion of the Cain story and its relation to the biblical tradition of violence, see R. Schwartz, *The Curse of Cain: The Violent Legacy of Monotheism* (Chicago: University of Chicago Press, 1997).

9. This is recognized by Luke. In setting the genealogy of Jesus from Joseph backward through the biblical tradition, he does not close with "son of Adam" but takes his genealogy of son to father back to "son of God," marking all humanity as "sons of God" (Lk 3:23–38).

10. J. C. VanderKam, *Enoch and the Growth of the Apocalyptic Tradition,* Catholic Biblical Quarterly Monograph Series, no. 2 (Washington, 1984).

11. H. S. Kvanvig, "Gen 6,3 and the Watcher Story," *Henoch* 25 (2003): 1–20; F: Garcia Martinez and E. J. C. Tigchelaar, *The Dead Sea Scrolls Study Edition* (Leiden: Brill, 2000), 403, 405.

12. *ANET,* 42–44, 93–97, 104–106.

13. The implicit reference is, of course, 2 Chr 36:21 and the seventy years of Sabbath rest that will be given to the land in fulfilment of Jeremiah's prophecy (Jer 25:11).

14. Citation is from the Gilgamesh story in *ANET,* 94–95.

15. On this rich, complex system, see M. Liverani, *Power and Propaganda* (Copenhagen, 1979); Liverani, *Prestige and Interest: International Relations in the Near East, ca. 1600–1100 BCE* (Padua, 1990).

16. I am following the reading in the Samaritan Pentateuch for verses 5–6.

17. B. Maader, "Ares," in *Lexikon des früh-griechischen Epos,* vol. 1, col. 1246–1265. The double reference of Yahweh's bow was first suggested by my colleague N. P. Lemche.

18. For the external structure of the Abraham stories, see Th. L. Thompson, *The Origin Tradition of Ancient Israel* (Sheffield: SAP, 1987), 158–160.

19. See I. Hjelm and Th. L. Thompson, "The Victory Song of Merneptah: Israel and the People of Palestine," *Journal for the Study of the Old Testament* 27 (2002): 14–15.

20. Mt 22:34–40 cites Dt 6:5 as the great and first commandment and then likens it to Lev 19:18. Mark and Luke reiterate Dt 6:5's epitome in a fourfold form. Luke does not separate Deuteronomy from Leviticus but presents a coherent epitome in a fivefold formula.

21. There are very important social and political goals at stake in both the development of holy war stories and their scholarly interpretation: issues explored, for example, in M. Prior, *The Bible and Colonialism: A Moral Critique*, The Biblical Seminar, no. 48 (Sheffield: SAP, 1997); Prior, "The Moral Problems of the Land Traditions of the Bible," in *Western Scholarship and the History of Palestine* (London: Melisende, 1998), 41–81; R. Schwartz, *The Curse of Cain: The Violent Legacy of Monotheism* (Chicago: University of Chicago Press, 1997); Hjelm, *Jerusalem's Rise to Sovereignty*.

22. Th. L. Thompson, *The Historicity of the Patriarchal Narratives, BZAW* 133 (Berlin: De Gruyter, 1974), 326–330.

23. See the classical studies of R. Labat, *Le caractère religieux de la royauté Assyro-Babylonienne*, vol. 2, *Etudes D'Assyriologie* (Paris: Librairie D'Amerique et D'Orient, 1939); B. Albrektson, *History and the Gods* (Lund, 1967); H. W. F. Saggs, *Encounter with the Divine in Mesopotamia and Israel* (London, 1978); Saggs, "Assyrian Prisoners of War and the Right to Live," *Archiv für Orientforschung* 19 (1982): 85–93. Unfortunately the dominant historicizing tendency of Sa-Moon Kang's Hebrew University dissertation, *Divine War in the Old Testament and in the Ancient Near East, BZAW* 177 (Berlin: De Gruyter, 1989), limits this ambitious work's usefulness in either literary or religio-historical analysis of the divine war theme, in spite of its numerous useful references to relevant ancient Near Eastern texts. Similarly tendentious problems plague the studies of P. D. Miller, *The Divine Warrior in Early Israel, HSM* 5 (Cambridge: Harvard University Press, 1973), and of P. D. Miller and J. J. M. Roberts, *The Hand of the Lord: A Reassessment of the Ark Narrative* (Baltimore: Johns Hopkins University Press, 1977). Less problematic in this respect is F. M. Cross, *Canaanite Myth and Hebrew Epic* (Cambridge: Harvard University Press, 1973).

24. *ANET,* 164; lines 1–40.

25. H. Niehr, *Der höchste Gott, BZAW* 190 (Berlin, 1990).

26. Thompson, *Bible in History*; Thompson, *Mythic Past*, 317–322.

27. L. W. King, *Chronicles Concerning Early Babylonian Kings* (1907), 2:87–96; *ANET,* 119; see also P. Jensen, "Aussetzungsgeschichten," in *Reallexikon der Assyriologie* (1928), 1:322–324.

28. *ANET,* 378.

29. *ANET,* 373–375.

30. Cf. Genesis 15 and 2 Sam 7 with the last paragraph of Thutmosis' song: *ANET,* 375.

31. Such stereotypical oppositions often describe the single change in status from enemy to client. See further, B. Oded, *Mass Deportation and Deportees in the Neo-Assyrian Empire* (Wiesbaden: Harrassowitz, 1979), 19, 28–30; for the impact of such policies on ancient Israel and Judah, see Th. L. Thompson, *The Early History of the Israelite People*, 3rd ed. (Leiden: Brill, 2001), 339–351.

32. *ANET,* 376–378.

33. Such as those of Esarhaddon (*ANET,* 534–541), and especially clauses 37–106, where the king plays the role of determining the destiny of the vassal and the prosperity of his land. See also the epilogue to Hammurapi's code, *ANET,* 177–180.

34. J. B. Breasted, *Ancient Records*, 3:16–22; especially sections 26, 30, 38 and 44. In terms of literary metaphor, one moves from the twelve kings in uproar in the Assyrian texts to the twelve sons of Jacob in Genesis and in the Pentateuch's illustration of the twelve tribes of Israel in uproar against Yahweh.

35. The Assyrians play both sides of this metaphor by describing the Assyrian king himself as USUM.GAL, "the great dragon." See, for example, this reiterated motif in the inscriptions from the reigns of Shalmaneser II and Shalmaneser III in *ANET,* 276–281, but also the allusions to the plant of life and the cosmic battle that are engaged in the description of Adadnirari III's campaign against Palestine (*ANET,* 281). The nearly ubiquitous self-description of Assyrian kings as "great dragon" first appears on the Hammurapi stele (*ANET,* 276).

36. For elements of attraction in narratives, see Th. L. Thompson, "Conflict Themes in the Jacob Narratives," *Semeia* 15 (1979): 5–26.

37. The thread continues in Judges 8:27 and esp. 17:5–6, where it is linked to the chain of origin stories of the monarchy: Judges 18:1; 19:1; 21:25, and so on.

38. For a different discussion, see P. E. Dion, "The 'Fear Not' Formula and Holy War," *CBQ* 32 (1970): 565–570.

39. Psalm 78:26–33 also interprets the story of the quail in light of Numbers 14.

40. Hjelm and Thompson, "Victory Song of Merneptah," 10.

41. As in Akhenaten's long hymn to the Aton: J. H. Breasted, *The Dawn of Conscience* (New York, 1933), 366–370; *ANET,* 369–371.

42. See also the "new song" (Ps 149:1), which has been placed as a chiastic response to the war against the "nations in uproar" in Psalm 2. It is sung in the utopian context of Jerusalem's resurrection (Ps 147:2–6), where the "nations" and the "kings of the world" are bound and chained under a universal and divine patronage of blessing.

CHAPTER NINE

1. Th. L. Thompson, *The Bible in History: How Writers Create a Past* (London: Cape, 1999); Thompson, *The Mythic Past: Biblical Archaeology and the Myth of Israel* (New York: Basic, 1999); Thompson, ed., *Jerusalem in Ancient History and Tradition* (London: Continuum, 2003); N. P. Lemche, *Prelude to Israel's Past: Background and Beginnings of Israelite History and Identity* (Peabody, Mass.: Hendrickson, 1998); Lemche, *The Israelites in History and Tradition* (Louisville: John Knox, 1998); I. Finkelstein and N. A. Silberman, *The Bible Unearthed: Archaeology's New Vision of Ancient Israel and the Origin of Its Sacred Texts* (New York: Free Press, 2001).

2. Another variation on Josiah's death—close to the story in Chronicles—is offered by 1 Esdras 1:30–33.

3. In the narrative, the fifteen extra years are first granted Hezekiah. As a sign that he will be healed, Yahweh moves the shadow of the sun dial backward ten steps.

4. I. Hjelm, *Jerusalem's Rise to Sovereignty* (London: Continuum, 2004), 235–239.

5. For a discussion of parallels with the New Testament story of Jesus, see Th. L. Thompson, "If David Had Not Climbed the Mount of Olives," in *Virtual History and the Bible,* ed. J. C. Exum (Leiden: Brill, 2000), 42–58.

6. J. H. Breasted, *Ancient Records of Egypt: Historical Documents* (New York: Russell & Russell, 1906), 3, sec. 582, p. 245.

7. Breasted, *Ancient Records,* 3, sec. 594, p. 253.

8. Breasted, *Ancient Records,* 3, sec. 612–613, pp. 261–262.

9. See Th. L. Thompson and D. Irvin, "The Joseph and Moses Stories," in *Israelite and Judean History*, ed. J. H. Hayes and J. M. Miller (Philadelphia: Westminster, 1977), 157–212.

10. Ironic reference is made to a parallel story (2 Sm 11:21; Jgs 9:53–54) in which the hero, Abimelek, was struck by a millstone thrown by a woman from just such a gate. Abimelek begs his weapon bearer to kill him with the sword, that the reader not mock his death at the hands of a woman.

11. The woman in the bath killed David as surely as Abimelek's woman killed him at the gate. Yet, unlike Abimelek, David does not find death's mercy. He has already murdered his faithful servant—one who might have played his armor bearer to release him from his shame.

12. Merneptah visits a similar fate on the king of Lybia: Hjelm and Thompson, "Victory Song of Merneptah."

13. Tablet 1.i.8–10.16–19; tablet 11.304–308; see J. Pritchard, *Ancient Near Eastern Texts Related to the Old Testament* (Princeton: Princeton University Press, 1969), 73, 97. Hereafter *ANET.*

14. On Solomon's three temptations, see Thompson, *Bible in History*, 65–66.

15. This enduring parable finds its darker mate in the stories of Elisha. Its theme is not wisdom but horror and its ownership. Set in a scene of starvation during the siege of Samaria (2 Kgs 6:25–31), the story tells of a gruesome pact of two mothers to eat their own children. On the second night, the mother of the living child repents her pact and hides her child, while her betrayed covenant mate seeks justice from a far from Solomonic king. If Yahweh will not help, how can he? Hardly a figure of wisdom, he is so overcome with the horror of the siege that he would kill the prophet who brought him to despair. This horrible variant of two mothers seeking justice is tied to its parallel through the leitmotif of the sword, cutting and dividing the sons of David's house. It will return as the reference of a proverb about a mother forgetting her child, while the tradition protects it hidden away for Yahweh to remember.

16. E. Jensen, *Die unendliche Geschichte* (Stuttgart, 1979).

17. Hjelm, *Jerusalem's Rise to Sovereignty*, 93-159.

18. Hjelm, *Jerusalem's Rise to Sovereignty*.

19. While the theme of Kings strikes its climax in the completeness of Manasseh's sin and Josiah's reform, the parallel narrative in the books of Chronicles integrates these themes within its own theology and speaks with its own independent voice. G. Auld, *Kings Without Privilege: David and Moses in the Story of the Bible's Kings* (Edinburgh: T&T Clark, 1994).

20. L. H. Schiffmann, *Reclaiming the Dead Sea Scrolls: The History of Judaism, the Background of Christianity, the Lost Library of Qumran* (Philadelphia: Jewish Publication Society, 1994); J. A. Goldstein, *I-II Maccabees: A New Translation with Introduction and Commentary*, Anchor Bible 41 (Garden City, N.Y.: Doubleday, 1977); E. Nodet, *A Search for the Origins of Judaism: From Joshua to the Mishnah* (Sheffield: SAP, 1997), 140–147; Hjelm, *Jerusalem's Rise to Sovereignty*, 254–293.

21. Hjelm, *Jerusalem's Rise to Sovereignty*, 254–293, deals comprehensively with the problem of the rhetoric of 1–2 Maccabees.

22. F. A. J. Nielsen, *The Tragedy in History*, Copenhagen International Seminar 4 (Sheffield: SAP, 1997).

23. P. Briant, *From Cyrus to Alexander: A History of the Persian Empire* (Winona Lake, Ind.: Eisenbrauns, 2002), 43f.

24. Hjelm and Thompson, "Victory Song of Merneptah," 3–18.

25. Hjelm, in contrast, reads this same closure as a sign of promise; *Jerusalem's Rise to Sovereignty*, 87, 108.

26. On the motif of righteousness in Samuel and Kings, see Hjelm, *Jerusalem's Rise to Sovereignty*, 165.

27. See Thompson, *Bible in History*, 237–244.

28. One of the best known is recounted in the work of the Chronicler (2 Chr 28) and also centers on a good Samaritan story. This time, they have captured 200,000 Jews in battle. Showing love instead of hatred and turning war into peace, they give kindness to enemies. Instead of killing them, the Samaritans clothe the Jews and, like King David before them and Jesus after, they anoint them, set them on donkeys and send them home to the City of Palms. For a similar conflation of Jericho with Jerusalem, see the Qumran manuscript 4Q Testimonia. Th. L. Thompson, "4Q Testimonia and Bible Composition: A Copenhagen Lego-Hypothesis," in *Qumran Between the Old and New Testaments*, ed. F. H. Cryer and Th. L. Thompson, CIS 6 (Sheffield: SAP, 1998), 265.

29. W. W. Hallo, *The Context of Scripture* (Leiden: Brill, 1997), 1:575–588.

30. Hallo, *Context of Scripture*, 1:573–575.

31. *ANET*, 407–410.

32. *ANET*, 405–407.

33. I. Hjelm, "Brothers Fighting Brothers," in *Jerusalem in Ancient History and Tradition*, ed. Th. L. Thompson (Sheffield: SAP, 2003), 197–222.

CHAPTER TEN

1. M. Liverani, "Partire sul carro, per il deserto," *AION* 32 (1972): 403–415; J. Sasson, "On Idrimi and Sarruwa the Scribe," in *Nuzi and the Hurrians*, ed. D. Owens (Winona Lake, Ind.: Eisenbrauns, 1981), 309–324; M. Dietrich and O. Loretz, "Die Inschrift der Statue des Königs Idrimi von Alalah," *UF* 13 (1981): 201–268. More recently, N. P. Lemche, *Prelude to Israel's Past: Background and Beginnings of Israelite History and Identity* (Peabody, Mass.: Hendrickson, 1998), 157–165.

2. J. B. Pritchard, *Ancient Near Eastern Texts Related to the Old Testament* (Princeton: Princeton University Press, 1969), 373–375. Hereafter *ANET*.

3. *ANET*, 253–254.

4. M. Lichtheim, *Ancient Egyptian Literature*, vol. 2, *The New Kingdom* (Berkeley: University of California Press, 1976), 200–203.

5. *ANET*, 281.

6. F. O. Hvidberg-Hansen, *Kana'anæiske myter og legender* (Århus, 1990), 1:81–99; for an English translation, see W. W. Hallo, *The Context of Scripture*, vol. 1, *Canonical Composition from the Biblical World* (Leiden: Brill, 1997), 255–264.

7. J. H. Charlesworth, ed., *The Messiah: Developments in Earliest Judaism and Christianity* (Minneapolis: Fortress, 1987), xv; J. J. M. Roberts, "The Old Testament's Contribution to Messianic Expectations," in Charlesworth, *The Messiah*, 39–51.

8. It is used as an adjective for priests in Ex 28:41; 30:30; 40:15; Lev 4:3, 5, 16; 6:15; Num 3:3; 35:25; or as a figure, "Yahweh's anointed," in 1 Sm 24:7, 11; 26:9, 11, 16, 23;

2 Sm 1:14, 16; 19:22; Lam 4:29; "the anointed of the God of Jacob" in 2 Sm 23:1; and "his," "my" or "your anointed" in 1 Sm 2:10, 35; 12:3, 5; 16:6; 2 Sm 22:51; Is 45:1; Hab 3:13; Ps 2:2; 18:51; 20:7; 28:8; 84:10; 89:39, 52; 132:10, 17; 2 Chr 6:42.

9. However, Hazael of Syria is also to be anointed by the prophet Elisha (cf. 1 Kgs 19:15–16). See further below.

10. Talmon, "Concepts of *Mashiach* and Messianism in Early Judaism," in Charlesworth, *The Messiah*, 79–115; here 80.

11. Talmon, "Concepts of *Mashiach* and Messianism," 81–83; see further Talmon, "Kingship and the Ideology of the State," in *King, Cult, and Calendar in Ancient Israel* (Jerusalem, 1986), 9–38; Talmon, "Types of Messianic Expectation at the Turn of the Era," in *King, Cult, and Calendar*, 202–224.

12. Talmon, "Concepts of *Mashiach* and Messianism," 84. In making this claim, Talmon attempts to give historical support to Martin Buber's essentialist theological understanding of messianism as one of the foundation pillars of Judaism's originality. M. Buber, *Drei Reden über das Judentum* (Frankfurt, 1911), 88–91.

13. Talmon, "Concepts of *Mashiach* and Messianism," 84. On the motif of anointed, Talmon objects particularly to the conclusions of J.-G. Heintz, "Royal Traits and Messianic Figures: A Thematic and Iconographical Approach (Mesopotamian Elements)," in Charlesworth, *The Messiah*, 52–66. On the more generic concepts of universal salvation and cosmic peace, Talmon seems to be arguing within a context of comparative religion, specifically opposing the legitimacy of well-known comparisons with cargo cults. See, further, S. Talmon, "Der Gesalbte Jahwes—biblische und frühnachbiblische Messias und Heilseerwartung," in *Heilserwartungen bei Juden und Christen* (Regensburg, 1982), 27–43.

14. Talmon, "Concepts of *Mashiach* and Messianism," 85.

15. J. H. Charlesworth, "From Messianology to Christology: Problems and Prospects," in *The Messiah*, 3–35; here 3: "For the most part, I am convinced, Jewish Messianology developed out of the crisis and hope of the non-messianic Maccabean wars of the second century, BCE." Also P. D. Hanson, "Messiahs and Messianic Figures in Proto-Apocalypticism," in Charlesworth, *The Messiah*, 67–75.

16. W. S. Green, "Introduction: Messiah in Judaism: Rethinking the Question," in *Judaisms and Their Messiahs at the Turn of the Christian Era*, ed. J. Neusner, W. S. Green, and E. S. Frerichs (Cambridge: Cambridge University Press, 1987), 1–13; here 6. This critique is also appropriate to the article by de Jonge, "Messiah," in *Anchor Bible Dictionary*, 4: 777. After reiterating the realism thesis of the Princeton Symposium, de Jonge uses two-thirds of the article to deal with motifs that are taken up in a purportedly later messianism.

17. Th. L. Thompson, "The Intellectual Matrix of Early Biblical Narrative: Inclusive Monotheism in Persian Period Palestine," in *The Triumph of Elohim: From Yahwisms to Judaisms*, ed. D. Edelman (Kampen: Pharos, 1995), 107–124; Edelman, "Historiography in the Pentateuch: Twenty-Five Years After Historicity," *SJOT* 13, no. 2 (1999): 258–283.

18. From the reign of Nebuchadnezzar, 604–562 BCE: J.-G. Heintz, "Royal Traits," in Charlesworth, *The Messiah*, 64.

19. Talmon, "Concepts of *Mashiach* and Messianism," 113, against, for example, A. Laato, *A Star Is Rising: The Historical Development of the Old Testament Royal Ideology and the Rise of the Jewish Messianic Expectations*, University of South Florida International Studies in Formative Christianity and Judaism (Atlanta: Scholars, 1997), 236–260, who discusses in

considerable detail an understanding of the rise of such expectations in early Judaism. See also his discussion of the messiah in relationship to the Hezekiah story in A. Laato, *"About Zion I Will Not Be Silent": The Book of Isaiah as an Ideological Unity,* Coniectanea Biblica, Old Testament Series 44 (Lund: Almqvist & Wiksell, 1998), 121–123.

20. So Roberts, "The Old Testament's Contribution" (p. 40), for example, dismisses this passage as relevant to a discussion of the messiah in the Old Testament on the grounds that it refers to the oiling of a shield.

21. Thompson, *The Bible in History: The Mythic Past,* 217–225.

22. Although Isaiah casts Cyrus, Yahweh's shepherd, in precisely this messianic role of re-building the temple (Is 44:28–45:4), his song about "the time for showing mercy" and his "day of salvation" gives the role of Cyrus to the birth of a new Israel. Yahweh's servant, Jacob, is called from his mother's womb (Is 48:20–49:3) to restore Israel's remnant.

23. On the very different understanding implicit in Jewish and Islamic messianism, see the interesting discussion of Sadik J. al-Azm, *Islamic Fundamentalism Reconsidered: A Critical Outline of Problems, Ideas, and Approaches,* South Asia Bulletin, Comparative Studies of South Asia, Africa, and the Middle East (Durham, N.C.: Duke University Press, 1995), 40–41.

24. F. Garcia Martinez, *The Dead Sea Scrolls Translated* (Leiden: Brill, 1994), 34. Such messiahs are recounted in CD 3. They are the men of renown—like Samson—on God's side. CD 6:1 has "the holy anointed ones" to refer to prophets. L. H. Shiffman, "Messianic Figures and Ideas in the Qumran Scrolls," in Charlesworth, *The Messiah,* 116–129, here 117.

25. Alter, *The David Story: A Translation with Commentary of 1 and 2 Samuel* (New York: Norton, 1999), appropriately suggests that 1 Kgs 2:11 and the scene of David's death consti-tute the closure of David's story.

26. See I. Hjelm, *Jerusalem's Rise to Sovereignty* (London: Continuum, 2004).

27. Heintz, *Messiah,* 63. For this type of metaphor, particularly involving the analogy of the roar of thunder, bulls and lions, see also Num 23:24; 24:8–9; Dt 33:17; Ps 18:14; 22:13–14; 29:3–9; Job 16:9–10; Amos 3:8, 12; a perhaps competitive use of the lion as a metaphor for Judah can be found in Gen 49:9.

28. For a discussion of the sectarian voice of the Psalter, see Thomas, *Bible in History,* 237–244.

29. See Hjelm, *Jerusalem's Rise to Sovereignty,* 241.

30. Thompson, "Twenty-Five Years after Historicity," *JSOT* 1999.

31. The term is used in anthropology and is discussed by C. Geertz, *The Interpretation of Cultures* (New York, 1973), 91–99.

32. See further, Th. L. Thompson, "If David Had not Climbed the Mount of Olives," in *Virtual History and the Bible,* ed. J. Cheryl Exum (Leiden: Brill, 2000), 42–58.

33. For an earlier discussion of this theology, see N. P. Lemche, "Because They Have Cast Away the Law of the Lord of Hosts—or We and the Rest of the World: The Authors Who Wrote the Old Testament," *Scandinavian Journal for the Old Testament,* 1999.

Appendix i

1. M. Lichtheim, *Ancient Egyptian Literature* (Berkeley: University of California Press, 1975), 1:17.

2. Lichtheim, *Ancient Egyptian Treasure,* 1:24.

3. Lichteheim, *Ancient Egyptian Treasure,* 1:122, l:16.

4. J. B. Pritchard, *Ancient Near Eastern Texts Related to the Old Testament* (Princeton: Princeton University Press, 1969), 7–8. Hereafter *ANET.*

5. Th. L. Thompson, "Jerusalem as the City of God's Kingdom; Common Tropes in the Bible and the Ancient Near East," *Islamic Studies* 40 (2001): 634–635.

6. Lichtheim, *Ancient Egyptian Treasure,* 1:136.

7. Lichtheim, *Ancient Egyptian Treasure,* 1:172.

8. W. W. Hallo, *Context of Scripture* (Leiden: Brill, 1997), 1:77–82.

9. Papyrus Bulaq 17, stanza 4, in *ANET,* 365–367.

10. J. L. Foster, *Hymns, Prayers, and Songs: An Anthology of Ancient Egyptian Lyric Poetry* (Atlanta: Scholars, 1995), 135–136.

11. Hallo, *Context of Scripture* 1:109, lines 54–57. The reversal of destinies is viewed negatively. The variant here is part of a threefold development of the theme "That which has never happened, has happened."

12. Foster, *Hymns, Prayers, and Songs,* 48–53; Stele of Amenmose, Louvre no. 286.

13. *ANET,* 371–372.

14. Hallo, *Context of Scripture,* 1:62, col. 2.

15. Foster, *Hymns, Prayers, and Songs,* 58–65.

16. Foster, *Hymns, Prayers, and Songs,* 149–150.

17. Foster, *Hymns, Prayers, and Songs,* 151.

18. Foster, *Hymns, Prayers, and Songs,* 151–152.

19. Lichtheim, *Ancient Egyptian Treasure,* 2:128.

20. Foster, *Hymns, Prayers, and Songs,* 118–122.

21. *ANET,* 377.

22. *ANET,* 378.

23. *ANET,* 378–379.

24. Hallo, *Context of Scripture,* 1:115–122.

25. B. R. Foster, *From Distant Days: Myths, Tales, and Poetry from Ancient Mesopotamia* (Bethesda: CDL, 1995), 316–323; Hallo, *Context of Scripture,* 1:492–494; *ANET,* 602–604.

26. Hallo, *Context of Scripture,* 1:485.

27. *ANET,* 426.

28. *ANET,* 177–178.

29. *ANET,* 397.

30. B. R. Foster, *Before the Muses* (Bethesda: CDL, 1996), 2:521–524, lines 12–15.

31. Foster, *Before the Muses,* 2:589.

32. Foster, *Before the Muses,* 2:578–579.

33. Foster, *Before the Muses,* 2:606.

34. Foster, *Before the Muses,* 2:617.

35. The inscription appears in several copies or close variations; cf. D. D. Luckenbill, *Ancient Records of Assyria and Babylonia* (Chicago: University of Chicago Press, 1927), 2:253, par 659E.

36. *ANET,* 307.

37. *ANET,* 384.

38. Hallo, *Context of Scripture,* 2:147f.

39. Hallo, *Context of Scripture,* 2:148–150.

40. The citation is taken from P. Briant, *From Cyrus to Alexander: The History of the Persian Empire* (Winona Lake, Ind.: Eisenbrauns, 2002), 166.

41. A confession of innocence. Compare the Inscription of Nefer-Sheshem Re; Harkhuf and Book of the Dead, chap. 125.

42. This classic expression of the poor man's song in the story of Samuel's heroic birth has countless parallels, particularly regarding the power over life and death (Dt 32:39; Ps 71:20), the reversal of the fate of the oppressed (Ps 75:8) and his power over potency (Ps 132:17).

43. Similar to Leviticus 19:23–24; 1 Chronicles 22:2; 2 Chronicles 2:17 both deal with a census of the foreigners for courvée labor on the temple; 1 Chronicles 29 resolves the sin of the story in 1 Chronicle 21:1–7 of David's census of Israel through a storyteller's retributive logic.

44. Here the poor man tradition is referred to in the form of an oath, in a longer declaration of innocence (Job 31:1–40) that is a common trope of ancient literature. The closing reference to the divine terror marks the context of judgment (see below).

45. A narrative version of this royal accession motif is found in 2 Kings 25:27–30; compare also Psalm 106:46.

46. The entire psalm of thanks, which opens the fifth book of the Psalter, is oriented to this theme. It begins with a short series of examples of the suffering whose fate has been reversed when they called on Yahweh for help; the hungry and thirsty in the desert whom he led by a straight path to a city where their needs were satisfied (v.4–9). Those sitting in the darkness of prison (v. 10–16); those sick unto death (v. 17–22); those in a storm at sea (v. 23–32), all who cried out to Yahweh and were saved. This sets the context for the closing stanza, which goes back to the figures of the thirsty and hungry in the desert and brings them to the city the song promised. The desert is turned into the new Jerusalem.

47. This psalm includes an eightfold list of Yahweh's blessings (v. 7–9) as marks of those who are happy or "blessed" (v. 5; cf. Ps 40:5; Ps 1; Jer 17:7). Close variations of some of these motifs are found in Ps 145:14.

48. Compare also Isaiah 29:9–11. This poem is structured in double sixfold reversals, first positive and then negative, reflecting a transition to the theology of the way. Note the coming day of divine judgment with which the poem opens, with its association of the themes of fertility, turning the fate of the oppressed and justice. This is reiterated in Isaiah 32:15–18, where the change from desert to fertility is a mark of eternal peace.

49. A cosmic scene of the day of judgment where the crippled and wounded are healed of the strokes given by Yahweh.

50. Combining the reversal of fortune of the poor with changing the arid desert to fertile land, much as in the examples from Isaiah 30; 35.

51. Yahweh plays the role of the conqueror who gives the people breath to live by and the task to create his kingdom. The second half of chapter 42 (v. 13–17) offers a reversal of the poor man's song as Yahweh plays a warrior's role, while the third portion of the song turns didactic (v. 18–25).

52. See a more expansive version in no. 104.

53. This song of the reversal of Yahweh's judgment against Israel and reverses Rachel's fate cast in the story of Genesis 35:16–20. A similar song is sung for Jerusalem in Zechariah 8:1–8, while Hosea 11:8–12 speaks similarly of Ephraim's return from exile.

54. This is the reverse of the poor man's song, using some of the same motifs to structure a lament. Compare Psalm 23.

55. Compare Isaiah 6.

56. The theme is taken up again in Ezekiel 33:22.

57. F. Garcia Martinez, *The Dead Sea Scrolls Translated: The Qumran Texts in English* (Leiden: Brill, 1994), 104–105.

58. Garcia Martinez, *Dead Sea Scrolls,* 108–109.

59. Garcia Martinez, *The Dead Sea Scrolls,* 116–117.

60. Garcia Martinez, *Dead Sea Scrolls,* 189.

61. Garcia Martinez, *Dead Sea Scrolls,* 203–204.

62. Garcia Martinez, *Dead Sea Scrolls,* 204.

63. Garcia Martinez, *Dead Sea Scrolls,* 205.

64. Garcia Martinez, *Dead Sea Scrolls,* 225.

65. Garcia Martinez, *Dead Sea Scrolls,* 303–304.

66. Garcia Martinez, *Dead Sea Scrolls,* 337–338.

67. Garcia Martinez, *Dead Sea Scrolls,* 365.

68. Garcia Martinez, *Dead Sea Scrolls,* 384–385.

69. Garcia Martinez, *Dead Sea Scrolls,* 394.

70. Garcia Martinez, *Dead Sea Scrolls,* 395.

71. Garcia Martinez, *Dead Sea Scrolls,* 436.

72. Garcia Martinez, *Dead Sea Scrolls,* 437.

73. Parallel stories are in Mark 10:42–52 and in a different order and context in Luke 18:35–43; 22:25–27.

74. A similar tale is found in Mark 10:46–52.

75. Compare the same theme in the story of the centurion in Luke 7:1–10.

76. Compare the similar parable in Luke 18:18–30, which has parallels in Matthew 19:13–15; Mark 10:13–16.

APPENDIX 2

1. L. King, *Chronicles Concerning Early Babylonian Kings* (London, 1907), 87–96; B. Lewis, *The Sargon Legend, ASORDS* 4 (Missoula, 1980); W. W. Hallo, *The Book of the People, BJS* 225 (Atlanta: Scholars, 1991), 130–131; *ANET,* 119; W. W. Hallo, *Context of Scripture* (Leiden: Brill, 1997), 1:461.

2. G. Dossin, "L'Inscription de Fondation de Yahdun-Lim, roi de Mari," *Syria* 32 (1935): 1–28; A. Malamat, "Campaigns to the Mediterranean by Iahdunlim and other early Mesopotamian Rulers," *AS* 16 (1965): 365–372; *ANET,* 556–557.

3. Luckenbill, *Annals of Sennacherib,* 116; D. J. Wiseman, "A New Stela of Assur Nasirpal II," *Iraq* 14 (1952): 24–44; *ANET,* 558.

4. D. D. Luckenbill, *Ancient Records of Assyria and Babylonia,* vol. 2 (Chicago: University of Chicago Press, 1926–1927). Hereafter Luckenbill, vol. 2.

5. Luckenbill, vol. 2, sec. 647–659. Longer and shorter variations on this narrative can be found in Luckenbill, vol. 2, sec. 659A–E and 660–665. In an inscription intended for the statue of the king and clearly written to serve a similar narrative function (Luckenbill, vol. 2, sec.

666–677), many of the thematic elements of this story are reiterated to mark Esarhaddon as chosen by Assur and Marduk as the restorer of temples and services throughout the empire.

6. F. H. Weissbach, *Die Inschriften Nebukadnezars II im Wadi Brissa und am Naahr el-Kelb* (Leipzig, 1906); *ANET,* 307.

7. *ANET,* 308–311.

8. C. J. Gadd, "The Harran Inscriptions of Nabonidus," *Anatolian Studies* 8 (1958): 35–92; W. Röllig, "Erwägungen zu neuen Stelen König Nabonids," *ZA* 22 (1964): 218–260; *ANET,* 562–563.

9. In central Arabia in the Hellenistic period, the crescent represents the divine *Wd,* (*d'wd* "the beloved"), the protector of the poor and needy.

10. *ANET,* 315–316.

11. *ANET,* 316–317.

12. Hallo, *Context of Scripture,* 1:185–192. It survives only in its preliminary composition on clay tablets, used prior to inscription in bronze as explained in the colophon of fragment 28 A. Hallo, *Context of Scripture,* 1:190b: "Seventh Tablet, not complete. Not yet made into a bronze tablet." For an early discussion of the quality of Hittite narrative as heroic story and the following three narratives' relationship to biblical story, see esp. H. Cancik, *Mythische und historische Wahrheit*; Cancik, *Grundzüge der Hethitischen und alttestamentlichen Geschichtsschreibung* (Wiesbaden: Harrassowitz, 1976).

13. Hallo, *Context of Scripture,* 1:192–193; R. H. Beal, "Kurunta of Tarhuntassa and the Imperial Hittite Mausoleum," *Anatolian Studies* 43 (1993): 29–39; S. Heinhold-Krahmer, "Zur Bronzetafel aus Boghazköy und ihrem historischen Inhalt," *Arkiv für Orientforschung* 38–39 (1991–1992): 138–158.

14. H. Hoffner, "The Last Days of Khattusha," in *The Crisis Years: The Twelfth Century BCE: From Beyond the Danube to the Tigris,* ed. W. A. Ward (Dubuque: Kandall Hunt, 1992), 46–52; Hallo, *Context of Scripture,* 1:192–193.

15. S. Smith, *The Statue of Idrimi* (London, 1949); J. Sasson, "On Idrimi and Sarruwa the Scribe," in *Nuzi and the Hurrians,* ed. D. Owens (Winona Lake, Ind.: Eisenbrauns, 1981), 309–324; M. Dietrich and O. Loretz, "Die Inschriften der Statue des Königs Idrimi von Alalah," *UF* 13 (1981): 201–268; *ANET,* 557–558; Hallo, *Context of Scripture,* 1:479–480.

16. S. Parker, *Stories in Scripture and Inscriptions: Comparative Studies on Narratives in Northwest Semitic Inscriptions and the Hebrew Bible* (Oxford: Oxford University Press, 1997), 76–83; J. Tropper, *Die Inschriften von Zincirli,* ALASP 6 (Münster: Ugarit Verlag, 1993), 27–46; W. W. Hallo, *The Context of Scripture,* vol. 2, *Monumental Inscriptions* (Leiden: Brill, 2000), 147f.

17. M. L. Barré, "An Analysis of the Royal Blessing in the Karatepe Inscription," *Maarav* 3 (1982): 177–194; K. L. Younger, "The Phoenician Inscription of Azatiwada: An Integrated Reading," *JSS* 43 (1998): 11–47; Hallo, *Context of Scripture,* 2:148–150.

18. S. Moscati, *The Phoenicians* (New York: Abbeville, 1988), 305; Hallo, *Context of Scripture,* 2:151–152.

19. J. Greenfield, "The Zakir Inscription and the Danklied," *Proceedings of the Fifth World Congress of Jewish Studies* (Jerusalem: World Union of Jewish Studies, 1972), 1:174–191; B. Otzen, "The Aramaic Inscriptions," ed. P. J. Rijs and M. L. Buhl (Copenhagen: Nationalmuseet, 1990), 267–318; Hallo, *Context of Scripture,* 2:155.

20. Tropper, *Inschriften*, 54–97; H. Niehr, "Zum Totenkult der Könige von Sam'al im 9. Und 8. Jh.v.Chr.," *SEL* 11 (1994): 58–73; Hallo, *Context of Scripture*, 2:156–158.

21. Tropper, *Inschriften*, 98–139; K. Younger, "Panammuwa and Bar-Rakib: Two Structural Analyses," *JANES* 18 (1986): 91–100; Hallo, *Context of Scripture*, 2:158–160.

22. Tropper, *Inschriften*, 132–139; Younger, "Panamuwwa," 100–103; Hallo, *Context of Scripture*, 2:160–161.

23. R. Doussaud, *Les monuments palestiniens et judaiques au Musée du Louvre* (Paris, 1912), 4–22; H. Donner and W. Röllig, *Kanaanäische und Aramäische Inschriften*, text 181; J. Gibson, *Textbook of Syrian Semitic Inscriptions* (Oxford, 1971), 1:71–83; E. Ullendorf, "The Moabite Stone," in *Documents from Old Testament Times*, ed. D. W. Thomas (New York, 1958), 195–197: W. F. Albright, "The Moabite Stone," *ANET*, 320–321; K. A. D. Smelik, "The Inscription of King Mesha," in Hallo, *Context of Scripture*, 2:137–138.

24. My classification is based on the parallelism between Omri and Chemosh, suggesting a motif of hubris as in the Rabshakeh's speech of the Hezekiah story in Isaiah 36:7.

25. The association of *Arel* with *dwd* in the Mesha story is much discussed. See now the dissertation of G. Athas, *The Tel Dan Inscription: A Reappraisal and a New Interpretation*, CIS (Sheffield: SAP, forthcoming). The possible occurrence of the theophoric epithet *dwd* in Transjordan is interesting as the name of the divine *wd* (Arabic *dwd*: "the god") with crescent and star, marking the Nabatean god of love and care of others, similar to the Samaritan understanding of Yahweh, occurs in two inscriptions found at the Nabatean caravanserai of Qaryat al Faw in the Hijaz (courtesy of the museum of Imam Mohammed ibn Saud Islamic University in Riyadh).

༻ BIBLIOGRAPHY ༺

Achtemeier, P. "The Origin and Function of the Pre-Markan Miracle Catenae." *Journal of Biblical Literature* 91 (1972): 198–221.

_____. "Toward the Isolation of Pre-Markan Miracle Catenae." *Journal of Biblical Literature* 89 (1970): 265–291.

Ahlström, G. W. *The History of Ancient Palestine.* Sheffield: SAP, 1999.

Al-Azm, S. J. *Islamic Fundamentalism Reconsidered: A Critical Outline of Problems, Ideas and Approaches.* South Asia Bulletin, Comparative Studies of South Asia, Africa and the Middle East. Durham, N.C.: Duke University Press, 1995.

Albrektson, B. *History and the Gods: An Essay on the Idea of Historical Events as Divine Manifestations in the Ancient Near East and in Israel.* Lund: Gleerup, 1967.

Alter, R. *The David Story: A Translation with Commentary of 1 and 2 Samuel.* New York: Norton, 1999.

Anderson, W. *Kaiser und Abt: Die Geschichte eines Schwanks.* Folklore Fellows Communications 42. Helsinki, 1923.

Athas, G. *The Tel Dan Inscription: A Reappraisal and a New Interpretation.* Copenhagen International Seminar 12. Sheffield: SAP, 2003.

Auffret, P. *Hymn d'Egypte et d'Israel: Etudes de structure litteraires.* OBO 34. Freiburg: Universitätsverlag, 1981.

Auld, G. *Kings Without Privilege: David and Moses in the Story of the Bible's Kings.* Edinburgh: T&T Clark, 1994.

Barré, M. L. "An Analysis of the Royal Blessing in the Karatepe Inscription." *Maarav* 3 (1982): 177–194.

Beal, R. H. "Kurunta of Tarhuntassa and the Imperial Hittite Mausoleum." *Anatolian Studies* 43 (1993): 29–39.

Ben-Amos, D. *Folklore in Context: Essays.* New Delhi, 1982.

_____. "Narrative Forms in the Haggadah." Ph.D. diss., Indiana University, 1967.

Black, J. A. "The New Year Ceremonies in Ancient Babylon: 'Taking Bel by the Hand' and a Cultic Picnic." *Religion* 11 (1981): 39–59.

Borg, M. *Conflict, Holiness and Politics in the Teachings of Jesus.* Studies in the Bible and Early Christianity 5. Toronto: Mellen, 1984.

_____. "A Temperate Case for a Non-Eschatological Jesus." *Forum* 2 (1986): 81–102.

Breasted, J. H. *Ancient Records of Egypt: Historical Documents.* Vol. 2. New York: Russell & Russell, 1907.

_____. *Ancient Records of Egypt: Historical Documents.* Vol. 3. New York: Russell & Russell, 1906.

_____. *The Dawn of Conscience.* New York: Doubleday, 1933.

Briant, P. *From Cyrus to Alexander: A History of the Persian Empire.* Winona Lake, Ind.: Eisenbrauns, 2002.

Brown, R. E. *The Birth of the Messiah: A Commentary on the Infancy Narratives in Matthew and Luke.* New York, 1993.

Buber, M. *Drei Reden über das Judentum.* Frankfurt, 1911.

Bynum, D. E. *Daemun in the Wood: A Study of Oral Narrative Patterns.* Cambridge: Harvard University Press, 1978.

Caminos, R. A. *Late Egyptian Miscellanies.* Oxford: Clarendon, 1954.

Cancik, H. *Grundzüge der Hethitischen und alttestamentlichen Geschichtsschreibung.* Wiesbaden: Harrassowitz, 1976.

_____. *Mythische und Historische Wahrheit.* Stuttgarter Bibelstudien. Stuttgart, 1970.

Carroll, R. *The Wolf in the Sheepfold: The Bible as Problematic for Theology.* London: SCM Press, 1991.

Charlesworth, J. H. "From Messianology to Christology: Problems and Prospects." In *The Messiah: Developments in Earliest Judaism and Christianity,* 3–35. Minneapolis: Fortress, 1987.

Charlesworth, J. H., ed. *The Messiah: Developments in Earliest Judaism and Christianity.* Minneapolis: Fortress, 1987.

Clarke Wire, A. *Holy Lives, Holy Deaths: A Close Hearing of Early Jewish Storytellers.* Atlanta: SBL, 2001.

Cross, F. M. *Canaanite Myth and Hebrew Epic.* Cambridge: Harvard University Press, 1973.

Crossan, J. D. *The Historical Jesus: The Life of a Mediterranean Jewish Peasant.* Edinburgh: T&T Clark, 1991.

_____. *Sayings Parallels: A Workbook for the Jesus Tradition.* Philadelphia: Fortress, 1986.

Davidsen, O. *Christi Fødsel: Tekster og Tolkninger År Totusind.* Højbjerg: Hovedland, 2000.

Davies, S. *The Gospel of Thomas and Christian Wisdom.* New York: Seabury, 1983.

Davies, W. D., and D. C. Allison. *A Critical and Exegetical Commentary on the Gospel According to St Matthew.* Vol. 3. Edinburgh: T&T Clark, 1997.

De Jonge, J. "Messiah." In *Anchor Bible Dictionary,* 4:777–779. Garden City, N.Y.: Anchor, 1992.

De Wette, W. M. L. *A Critical and Historical Introduction to the Canonical Scriptures of the Old Testament.* Original German, 1817; English translation with notes of T. Parker, 1843.

Dietrich, M., and O. Loretz. "Die Inschrift der Statue des Königs Idrimi von Alalah." *Ugaritische Forschungen* 13 (1981): 201–268.

Dion, P. E. "The 'Fear Not' Formula and Holy War." *Catholic Biblical Quarterly* 32 (1970): 565–570.

Donner, H., and W. Röllig. *Kanaanäische und Aramäische Inschriften.* Vols. 1–3. Wiesbaden: Harrassowitz, 1964–1968.

Dossin, G. "L'Inscription de Fondation de Yahdun-Lim, roi de Mari." *Syria* 32 (1935): 1–28.

Doussaud, R. *Les monuments palestiniens et judaiques au Musée du Louvre.* Paris, 1912.

Dundes, A. "Text, Texture and Context." *Southern Folklore Quarterly* 20 (1965): 251–261.

Ehrman, B. D. *Jesus: Apocalyptic Prophet of the New Millennium.* Cambridge: Oxford University, 1999.

_____. *The New Testament: A Historical Introduction to the Early Christian Writings.* New York: Oxford University Press, 1997.

Eichhorn, J. G. *Einleitung in das Alte Testament.* 3 vols. Göttingen, 1780–1783. Also published as *Introduction to the Study of the Old Testament,* 1888.

_____. *Einleitung in das Neue Testament.* 2 vols. Göttingen, 1804–1827.

Engberg-Pedersen, T. *Paul and the Stoics.* Louisville: Westminster, 2000.

Engberg-Pedersen, T., ed. *Den historische Jesus og hans Betydning.* Copenhagen: Museum Tusculanum, 1998.

Fecht, G. "Die Israelstele, Gestalt und Aussage." In *Fontes atque Pontes: Eine Festgabe für Hellmut Brunner.* Ägypten und Altes Testament, 5:106–138. Wiesbaden: Harrassowitz, 1983.

Feuerbach, L. *Das Wesen des Christentums.* 1841. English translation: *The Essence of Christianity.* New York: Harper, 1956.

Finkelstein, I., and N. A. Silberman. *The Bible Unearthed: Archaeology's New Vision of Ancient Israel and the Origin of Its Sacred Texts.* New York: Free Press, 2001.

Foley, J. M. *The Singer of Tales in Performance.* Bloomington: University of Indiana Press, 1995.

_____. *The Theory of Oral Composition.* Bloomington: University of Indiana Press, 1988.

Fortna, R. T. *The Gospel of Signs: A Reconstruction of the Narrative Sources Underlying the Fourth Gospel.* Cambridge: Cambridge University Press, 1970.

Foster, B. R. *Before the Muses.* Vol. 2. Bethesda: CDL, 1996.

_____. *From Distant Days: Myths, Tales and Poetry from Ancient Mesopotamia.* Bethesda: CDL, 1995.

Foster, J. L. *Hymns, Prayers and Songs: An Anthology of Ancient Egyptian Lyric Poetry.* Atlanta: Scholars, 1995.

Freed, R. E., Y. J. Markowitz and S. H. D'Auria, eds. *Pharaohs of the Sun: Akhenaton, Nefertiti, Tutankhamen.* Boston: Bulfinch, 1999.

Funk, R. W., and R. W. Hoover, *Five Gospels, One Jesus: What Did Jesus Really Say?* Sonoma: Polebridge, 1992.

Gadd, C. J. "The Harran Inscriptions of Nabonidus." *Anatolian Studies* 8 (1958): 35–92.

Garbini, G. *History and Ideology in Ancient Israel.* London, 1988.

Garcia Martinez, F. *The Dead Sea Scrolls Translated: The Qumran Texts in English.* Leiden: Brill, 1994.

Garcia Martinez, F., and E. J. C. Tigchelaar. *The Dead Sea Scrolls.* Study ed. Leiden: Brill, 2000.

Geertz, C. *The Interpretation of Cultures.* New York, 1973.

Gibson, J. *Textbook of Syrian Semitic Inscriptions.* Vol. 1. Oxford: Clarendon, 1971.

Goldstein, J. A. *I-II Maccabees: A New Translation with Introduction and Commentary.* Anchor Bible 41. Garden City, N.J.: Doubleday, 1977.

Gottwald, N. K. *The Politics of Ancient Israel.* Louisville: Westminster, 2001.

_____. *The Tribes of Yahweh: A Sociology of the Religion of Liberated Israel.* New York: Maryknoll, 1979.

Goulder, M. D. *Midrash and Lection in Matthew.* London: SPCK, 1974.

Grabbe, L. L., ed. *Can a History of Israel Be Written?* European Seminar on Historical Methodology 1. Sheffield: SAP, 1997.

Green, W. S. "Introduction: Messiah in Judaism: Rethinking the Question." In J. Neusner, W. S. Green and E. S. Frerichs, eds., *Judaisms and Their Messiahs at the Turn of the Christian Era,* 1–13. Cambridge: Cambridge University Press, 1987.

Greenfield, J. "The Zakir Inscription and the Danklied." *Proceedings of the Fifth World Congress of Jewish Studies,* 1:174–191. Jerusalem: World Union of Jewish Studies, 1972.

Gunn, D. *The Fate of King Saul.* Sheffield: SAP, 1980.

_____. *The Story of King David.* Sheffield: SAP, 1978.

Hallo, W. W. *The Book of the People.* BJS 225. Atlanta: Scholars, 1991.

_____. *The Context of Scripture.* Vol. 1, *Canonical Compositions from the Biblical World.* Leiden: Brill, 1997.

_____. *The Context of Scripture.* Vol. 2, *Monumental Inscriptions from the Biblical World.* Leiden: Brill, 2000.

Hanson, P. D. "Messiahs and Messianic Figures in Proto-Apocalypticism." In J. H. Charlesworth, ed., *The Messiah: Developments in Earliest Judaism and Christianity,* 67–75. Minneapolis: Fortress, 1987.

Harrak, A. "Tales About Sennacherib." In P. M. Michèle Daviau, *The World of the Arameans,* 168–189. Sheffield: SAP, 2001.

Heinhold-Krahmer, S. "Zur Bronzetafel aus Boghazköy und ihrem historischen Inhalt." *Arkiv für Orientforschung* 38–39 (1991–1992): 138–158.

Heintz, J.-G. "Royal Traits and Messianic Figures: A Thematic and Iconographical Approach to Mesopotamian Elements." In J. H. Charlesworth, ed., *The Messiah: Developments in Earliest Judaism and Christianity,* 52–66. Minneapolis: Fortress, 1987.

Hermann, A. *Die ägyptische Königsnovelle.* Glückstadt, 1938.

Hjelm, I. "Brothers Fighting Brothers: Jewish and Samaritan Ethnocentrism in Tradition and History." In T. L. Thompson, ed., *Jerusalem in Ancient History and Tradition,* 197–222. London: T&T Clark International, 2003.

_____. *Jerusalem's Rise to Sovereignty: Zion and Gerizim in Competition.* London: T&T Clark International, 2004.

_____. *The Samaritans and Early Judaism: A Literary Analysis.* Sheffield: SAP, 2000.

Hjelm, I., and T. L. Thompson. "The Victory Song of Merneptah: Israel and the People of Palestine." *Journal for the Study of the Old Testament* 27 (2002): 3–18.

Hobsbawm, E. J. *Bandits.* New York: Delacorte, 1969.

_____. *Primitive Rebels.* New York: Norton, 1965.

Hoffner, H. "The Last Days of Khattusha." In W. A. Ward, ed., *The Crisis Years: The Twelfth Century BCE: From Beyond the Danube to the Tigris,* 46–52. Dubuque: Kendall Hunt, 1992.

———. "Propaganda and Political Justification in Hittite Historiography." In H. Goedicke and J. J. M. Roberts, eds., *Unity and Diversity: Essays in the History, Literature and Religion of the Ancient Near East,* 49–62. Baltimore: John Hopkins University Press, 1975.

Horsley, R. A. *Jesus and the Spiral of Violence: Popular Jewish Resistance in Roman Palestine.* San Francisco: Harper & Row, 1987.

———. *The Liberation of Christmas: The Infancy Narratives in Social Context.* New York, 1993.

———. *Sociology and the Jesus Movement.* New York: Crossroads, 1989.

Horsley, R. A., with J. S. Hanson. *Bandits, Prophets and Messiahs: Popular Movements in the Time of Jesus.* New York: Seabury, 1985.

Huck, A., and H. Greeven, *Synopsis of the First Three Gospels: With the Addition of the Johannine Parallels.* 13th ed. Tübingen: Mohr, 1981.

Hvidberg-Hansen, F. O. *Kanaʾanæiske myter og legender.* Vol. 1. Århus: Universitetsforlag, 1990.

Irvin, D. *Mytharion: The Comparison of Tales from the Old Testament and Ancient Near East.* Neukirchen: Neukirchner Verlag, 1978.

Irvin, D., and T. L. Thompson. "The Joseph and Moses Narratives." In J. Hayes and J. M. Miller, eds., *Israelite and Judean History,* 147–212. Philadelphia: Westminster, 1977.

Jackson, G. *"Have Mercy on Me."* Copenhagen International Seminar 10. Sheffield: SAP, 2002.

Jacobsen, T. "Religious Drama in Ancient Mesopotamia." In H. Goedicke and J. J. M. Roberts, eds., *Unity and Diversity,* 65–97. London, 1975.

Jensen, E. *Die unendliche Geschichte.* Stuttgart, 1979.

Jensen, P. "Aussetzungsgeschichten." *Reallexikon der Assyriologie,* 1:322–324. Berlin: De Gruyter, 1928.

Jeremias, J. *Die Abendmalsworte Jesu.* Göttingen, 1935.

Jolles, A. *Einfache Formen.* Halle: Niemeyer, 1929.

Kang, S. *Divine War in the Old Testament and in the Ancient Near East,* BZAW 177. Berlin: De Gruyter, 1989.

King, L. *Chronicles Concerning Early Babylonian Kings.* Vol. 2. London, 1907.

Kloppenborg, J. *The Formation of Q: Trajectories in Ancient Wisdom Collections.* Studies in Antiquity and Christianity. Philadelphia: Fortress, 1987.

———. *Q Parallels: Synopsis, Critical Notes and Concordance.* Sonoma: Polebridge, 1988.

Kloppenborg Verbin, J. *Excavating Q: The History and Setting of the Sayings Gospel.* Edinburgh: T&T Clark, 2000.

Koester, H. "Apocryphal and Canonical Gospels." *Harvard Theological Review* 73 (1980): 105–130.

———. *Introduction to the New Testament.* Vol. 2. Philadelphia: Fortress, 1982.

Kramer, S. N. *The Sacred Marriage Rite: Aspects of Faith, Myth and Ritual in Ancient Sumer.* Bloomington: Indiana University Press, 1969.

Kvanvig, H. S. "Gen 6,3 and the Watcher Story." *Henoch* 25 (2003): 1–20.

Laato, A. *"About Zion I Will Not Be Silent": The Book of Isaiah as an Ideological Unity.* Coniectanea Biblica, Old Testament Series 44. Lund: Almqvist & Wiksell International, 1998.

_____. *A Star Is Rising: The Historical Development of the Old Testament Royal Ideology and the Rise of the Jewish Messianic Expectations.* University of South Florida International Studies in Formative Christianity and Judaism. Atlanta: Scholars, 1997.

Labat, R. *Le caractère religieux de la Royauté Assyro-Babylonienne.* Etudes D'Assyriologie 2. Paris: Librairie D'Amerique et D'Orient, 1939.

Lafont, B. "Le roi de Mari et les prophètes du dieu Adad." *Revue d'Assyriologie* 78 (1984): 7–18.

Lambert, W. G. *Babylonian Wisdom Literature.* Oxford: Clarendon, 1960.

_____. "The Great Battle of the Mesopotamian Religious Year: The Conflict in the Akitu House." *Iraq* 25 (1963): 189–190.

Laurentin, R. *Les Évangiles de l'enfance du Christ: Vérité de noël au-delà des mythes.* Paris, 1982.

Lemche, N. P. "Because They Have Cast Away the Law of the Lord of Hosts—or We and the Rest of the World: The Authors who Wrote the Old Testament." *Scandinavian Journal for the Old Testament* 17 (2003): 268–290.

_____. *The Israelites in History and Tradition.* Louisville: Westminster, 1998.

_____. "The Old Testament: A Hellenistic Book?" *Scandinavian Journal for the Old Testament* 7 (1993): 163–193.

_____. *Prelude to Israel's Past: Background and Beginnings of Israelite History and Identity.* Peabody, Mass: Hendrickson, 1998.

Levenson, J. D. *The Death and Resurrection of the Beloved Son: The Transformation of Child Sacrifice in Judaism and Christianity.* New Haven: Yale University Press, 1993.

Lewis, B. *The Sargon Legend.* American Schools of Oriental Research Dissertation Series 4. Missoula, Mont.: Scholars, 1980.

Lichtheim, M. *Ancient Egyptian Literature.* Vol. 1, *The Old Kingdom.* Berkeley: University of California Press, 1975.

_____. *Ancient Egyptian Literature.* Vol. 2, *The New Kingdom.* Berkeley: University of California Press, 1976.

Liverani, M. "The Ideology of the Assyrian Empire." In M. T. Larsen, ed., *Power and Propaganda,* 297–317. Copenhagen, 1979.

_____. *Oltre la Bibbia: Storia antica di Israele.* Rome: Laterza, 2003.

_____. "Partire sul carro, per il deserto." *AION* 32 (1972): 403–415.

_____. *Prestige and Interest: International Relations in the Near East: Ca 1600–1100 BC.* Vol. 1 of *History of the Ancient Near East.* Padua, 1990.

Longman, T. *Fictional Akkadian Autobiography.* New York, 1988.

Lord, A. *The Singer of Tales.* Cambridge: Harvard University Press, 1960.

Loretz, O. *Ugarit und die Bibel: Kanaanäische Götter und Religion im alten Testament.* Darmstadt, 1990.

Luckenbill, D. D. *Ancient Records of Assyria and Babylonia.* Vols. 1–2. Chicago: University of Chicago Press, 1926–1927.

_____. *The Annals of Sennacherib.* Oriental Institute Publications 2. Chicago: University of Chicago Press, 1920.

Lundager Jensen, H. J. *Gammeltestamentlig religion: En indføring.* Anis: Frederiksberg, 1998.

Maader, B. "Ares." In *Lexikon des früh-griechischen Epos,* vol. 1, col. 1246–1265.

Mack, B. *The Lost Gospel: The Book of Q and Christian Origins.* San Francisco: Harper, 1993.

_____. *A Myth of Innocence: Mark and Christian Origins.* Philadelphia: Fortress, 1988.

Malamat, A. "Campaigns to the Mediterranean by Iahdunlim and Other Early Mesopotamian Rulers." *Assyriological Studies* 16 (1965): 365–372.

_____. "A Mari Prophecy and Nathan's Dynastic Oracle." In *Prophecy: Essays Presented to G. Fohrer,* 68–82. BZAW 150. Berlin: De Gruyter, 1980.

Mattingly, G. L. "The Pious Sufferer: Mesopotamia's Traditional Theodicy and Job's Counsellors." In W. W. Hallo, ed., *The Bible in Light of Cuneiform Literature,* 305–348. Vol. 3 of *Scripture in Context.* Ancient Near Eastern Texts and Studies 8. Lewiston, N.Y.: Mellon, 1990.

Meier, J. P. *A Marginal Jew: Rethinking the Historical Jesus.* 3 vols. Anchor Bible Reference Library. New York: Doubleday, 1991.

Mettinger, T. *The Riddle of the Resurrection: "Dying and Rising" Gods in the Ancient Near East.* Coniectanea Biblica 59. Stockholm: Almqvist & Wiksell, 2000.

Meyer, E. *Geschichte des Altertums.* Vol. 2. Berlin: Topelmann, 1913.

Miller, P. D. *The Divine Warrior in Early Israel.* Harvard Semitic Monographs 5. Cambridge: Harvard University Press, 1973.

Miller, P. D., and J. J. M. Roberts. *The Hand of the Lord: A Reassessment of the Ark Narrative.* Baltimore: Johns Hopkins University Press, 1977.

Moscati, S. *The Phoenicians.* New York: Abbeville, 1988.

Müller, M. *Der Ausdruck "Menschensohn" in den Evangelien.* Leiden: Brill, 1984.

_____. *Kommentar til Mattæusevangeliet.* Århus: Universitetsforlag, 2000.

Murnane, W. J. "The History of Ancient Egypt." In J. M. Sasson, ed., *Civilizations of the Ancient Near East,* 2:712–714. New York: Doubleday, 1995.

Niehr, H. *Der Höchste Gott.* BZAW 190. Berlin: De Gruyter, 1990.

_____. "Zum Totenkult der Könige von Sam'al im 9. und 8. Jh.v.Chr." *Studi epigrafici e linguistici* 11 (1994): 58–73.

Nielsen, F. A. J. *The Tragedy in History.* Copenhagen International Seminar 4. Sheffield: SAP, 1997.

Nielsen, K. *For a Tree There Is Hope.* Århus: Universitetsforlag, 1989.

Nodet, E. *A Search for the Origins of Judaism: From Joshua to the Mishnah.* Sheffield: SAP, 1997.

Oded, B. *Mass Deportation and Deportees in the Neo-Assyrian Empire.* Wiesbaden: Reichert Verlag, 1979.

_____. *War, Peace and Empire: Justifications for War in Assyrian Royal Inscriptions.* Wiesbaden: Reichert Verlag, 1992.

Otto, R. *The Idea of the Holy.* 1951.

Otzen, B. "The Aramaic Inscriptions." In P. J. Rijs and M. L: Buhl, eds., *Hama* 2:267–318. Copenhagen: Nationalmuseet, 1990.

Parker, S. *Stories in Scripture and Inscriptions: Comparative Studies on Narratives in Northwest Semitic Inscriptions and the Hebrew Bible.* Oxford: Oxford University Press, 1997.

Parry, M., and A. Lord. *Serbo-Croatian Heroic Songs.* 2 vols. Cambridge: Harvard University Press, 1960.

Prior, M. *The Bible and Colonialism: A Moral Critique.* Biblical Seminar 48. Sheffield: SAP, 1997.

_____. "The Moral Problems of the Land Traditions of the Bible." In M. Prior, ed., *Western Scholarship and the History of Palestine,* 41–81. London: Melisende, 1998.

Pritchard, J. B. *Ancient Near Eastern Texts Related to the Old Testament.* Princeton: Princeton University Press, 1969.

Redford, D. B. *Egypt, Canaan and Israel in Ancient Times.* Princeton: Princeton University Press, 1992.

Robbins, V. K. *Jesus the Teacher: A Socio-Rhetorical Interpretation of Mark.* Minneapolis: Fortress, 1992.

Roberts, J. J. M. "The Old Testament's Contribution to Messianic Expectations." In J. H. Charlesworth, ed., *The Messiah: Developments in Earliest Judaism and Christianity,* 39–51. Minneapolis: Fortress, 1987.

Robinson, J. "'Logoi Sophon': On the Gattung of Q." In J. Robinson and H. Koester, eds., *Trajectories Through Early Christianity,* 71–113. Philadelphia: Fortress, 1971.

Robinson, J., P. Hoffmann and J. Kloppenborg. *Documenta Q: Reconstructions of Q Through Two Centuries of Gospel Research: Excerpted, Sorted and Evaluated.* Leuven: Peeters, 1996.

Röllig, W. "Erwägungen zu neuen Stelen König Nabonids." *Zeitschrift für das Assyriologie* 22 (1964): 218–260.

Saggs, H. W. F. "Assyrian Prisoners of War and the Right to Live." *Archiv für Orientforschung,* 1982, 85–93.

_____. *Encounter with the Divine in Mesopotamia and Israel.* London, 1978.

Said, E. *Orientalism.* New York: Pantheon, 1978.

Sanders, E. P. *The Historical Figure of Jesus.* London: Penguin, 1993.

_____. *Jesus and Judaism.* Philadelphia: Fortress, 1985.

Sasson, J. "On Idrimi and Sarruwa the Scribe." In D. Owens, ed., *Nuzi and the Hurrians,* 309–324. Winona Lake, Ind.: Eisenbrauns, 1981.

Schiffmann, L. H. *Reclaiming the Dead Sea Scrolls: The History of Judaism, the Background of Christianity, the Lost Library of Qumran.* Philadelphia: Jewish Publication Society, 1994.

Schröter, J., and R. Brucker, eds. *Der historische Jesus: Tendenzen und Perspektiven der gegenwärtigen Forschung.* BZNW 114. Berlin: De Gruyter, 2002.

Schwartz, R. *The Curse of Cain: The Violent Legacy of Monotheism.* Chicago: University of Chicago Press, 1997.

Schweitzer, A. *Geschichte der Leben-Jesu Forschung.* Tübingen: Mohr-Siebeck, 1906; English translation: *The Quest for the Historical Jesus,* 1910.

Shiffman, L. H. "Messianic Figures and Ideas in the Qumran Scrolls." In J. H. Charlesworth, ed., *The Messiah: Developments in Earliest Judaism and Christianity,* 116–129. Minneapolis: Fortress, 1987.

Silberman, N., and I. Finkelstein, *The Bible Unearthed: Archaeology's New Vision of Ancient Israel and the Origin of Its Sacred Texts.* New York: Free Press, 2001.

Smith, S. *The Statue of Idrimi.* London, 1949.

Stenhouse, P. *Kitab al-Tarikh of Abu l'Fath.* Translated into English, with notes. Studies in Judaism 1. Sydney: University of Sydney Press, 1985.

Storr, F. *Sophocles: With an English Translation.* Loeb Classical Library 20–21. London: Heinemann, 1912.

Stott, K. "Herodotus and the Old Testament: A Comparative Reading of the Ascendancy Stories of King Cyrus and David." *Journal for the Study of the Old Testament* 16 (2002): 52–78.

Strauss, J. F. *The Christ of Faith and the Jesus of History: A Critique of Schleiermacher's Life of Jesus*. Philadelphia: Fortress, 1977.

_____. *Das Leben Jesu kritisk bearbeidet*. 2 vols. 1835–36. English translation: *Life of Jesus*, 1906.

Talmon, S. "The Concepts of *Mashiach* and Messianism in Early Judaism." In J. H. Charlesworth, ed., *The Messiah: Developments in Earliest Judaism and Christianity*, 79–115. Minneapolis: Fortress, 1987.

_____. "Der Gesalbte Jahwes—biblische und frühnachbiblische Messias und Heilseerwartung." In *Heilserwartungen bei Juden und Christen*, 27–43. Regensburg, 1982.

_____. "Kingship and the Ideology of the State." In *King, Cult and Calendar in Ancient Israel*, 9–38. Jerusalem, 1986.

_____. "Types of Messianic Expectation at the Turn of the Era." In *King, Cult and Calendar in Ancient Israel*, 202–224. Jerusalem, 1986.

Taylor, J. "The Coming of Elijah, Mt 17,10–13 and Mark 9,11–13: The Development of the Texts." *Revue biblique* 98 (1991): 107–119.

Theissen, G. *The Miracle Stories of the Early Christian Tradition*. Philadelphia: Fortress, 1983.

_____. *Sociology of Early Christianity*. Philadelphia: Fortress, 1978.

Theissen, G., and A. Merz. *Der historische Jesus: Ein Lehrbuch*. Göttingen, 1996.

Thompson, S. *Motif Index of Folk Literature*. 6 vols. Bloomington: Indiana University Press, 1955–1958.

Thompson, T. L. *The Bible in History: How Writers Create a Past*. London: Cape, 1999. Also published as *The Mythic Past: Biblical Archaeology and the Myth of Israel*. New York: Basic, 1999.

_____. "Can a History of Ancient Jerusalem and Palestine Be Written?" In *Jerusalem in Ancient History and Tradition*, 1–15. London: T&T Clark, 2003.

_____. "Conflict Themes in the Jacob Narrative." *Semeia* 15 (79): 5–26.

_____. *The Early History of the Israelite People from the Written and Archaeological Sources*. Studies in the History of the Ancient Near East 4. Leiden: Brill, 1992.

_____. "From the Mouth of Babes, Strength: Psalm 8 and the Book of Isaiah." *Scandinavian Journal for the Old Testament* 16 (2002): 226–245.

_____. "He Is Yahweh: He Does What Is Right in His Own Eyes: The Old Testament as a Theological Discipline." *Tro og Historie*, 2:246–262. Forum for Bibelsk Eksegese 7. Frederiksberg: Museum Tusculanum, 1996.

_____. *The Historicity of the Patriarchal Narratives: The Quest for the Historical Abraham*. 3rd ed. London: Trinity Press International, 2002.

_____. "Historie og teologi i overskrifterne til Davids salmer." *Collegium Biblicum Årbog*, 1997, 88–102.

_____. "Historiography in the Pentateuch: Twenty-Five Years After Historicity." *Scandinavian Journal for the Old Testament* 13, no. 2 (1999): 258–283.

_____. "How Yahweh Became God: Exodus 3 and 6 and the Center of the Pentateuch." *Scandinavian Journal for the Old Testament* 8 (1994).

_____. "If David Had Not Climbed the Mount of Olives." In J. C. Exum, ed., *Virtual History and the Bible*, 42–58. Leiden: Brill, 2000.

_____. "The Intellectual Matrix of Early Biblical Literature: Inclusive Monotheism in Persian Period Palestine." In D. Edelman, ed., *The Triumph of Elohim: From Yahwisms to Judaisms,* 107–126. Kampen: Pharos, 1995.

_____. "Jerusalem as the City of God's Kingdom: Common Tropes in the Bible and the Ancient Near East." *Islamic Studies* 40 (2001): 632–647.

_____. "Kingship and the Wrath of God: Or Teaching Humility." *Revue biblique* 109 (2002): 161–196.

_____. "A New Attempt to Date the Patriarchal Narratives." *Journal of the American Oriental Society* 98 (1978): 76–84.

_____. *The Origin Tradition of Ancient Israel.* Sheffield: SAP, 1987.

_____. "4Q Testimonia and Bible Composition: A Copenhagen Lego Hypothesis." In F. C. Cryer and Th.L. Thompson, eds., *Qumran Between the Old and New Testaments,* 261–276. Sheffield: SAP, 1998.

Thompson, T. L., ed. *Jerusalem in Ancient History and Tradition.* London: T&T Clark International/Continuum, 2003.

Tropper, J. *Die Inschriften von Zincirli.* ALASP 6. Münster: Ugarit Verlag, 1993.

Ullendorf, E. "The Moabite Stone." In D. W. Thomas, ed., *Documents from Old Testament Times,* 195–197. New York, 1958.

Ungnad, A. *Die Religion der Babylonier und Assyrer.* Jena, 1921.

VanderKam, J. C. *The Dead Sea Scrolls Today.* Grand Rapids, Mich.: Eerdmans, 1994.

_____. *Enoch and the Growth of the Apocalyptic Tradition.* Catholic Biblical Quarterly Monograph Series 2. Washington, 1984.

Van Seters, J. *In Search of History: Historiography in the Ancient World and the Origins of Biblical History.* New Haven: Yale University Press, 1983.

_____. *Prologue to History: The Yahwist as Historian in Genesis.* Louisville: Fortress, 1992.

Weiss, J. *Jesus' Proclamation of the Kingdom of God.* 1892. Reprint, Philadelphia: Fortress, 1971.

Weissbach, F. H. *Die Inschriften Nebukadnezars II im Wadi Brissa und am Naahr el-Kelb.* Leipzig, 1906.

Wilson, J. A. *Historical Records of Ramses.* Vol. 3. SAOC 12. Chicago: University of Chicago Press, 1936.

Wire, A. "The Structure of the Gospel Miracle Stories." *Semeia* 11 (1978): 83–113.

Wiseman, D. J. "A New Stela of Assur Nasir-pal II." *Iraq* 14 (1952): 24–44.

Wolf, E. R. *Peasants.* Englewood Cliffs, N.J.: Prentice Hall, 1966.

Wrede, W. *Das Messiasgeheimnis in den Evangelien: Zugleich ein Beitrag zum Verständnis des Markusevangeliums.* 1901. English translation: *The Messianic Secret in the Gospels,* 1971.

Wright, G. E. *The Old Testament Against Its Environment.* New York, 1955.

Wyatt, N. "Arms and the King." In *Und Moses Schrieb dieses Lied auf,* 833–881. Neukirchen: Neukirchner Verlag, 1998.

_____. "The Mythic Mind." *Scandinavian Journal for the Old Testament* 15 (2001): 3–56.

_____. *Myths of Power: A Study of Royal Myth and Ideology in Ugaritic and Biblical Tradition.* UBL 13. Münster, 1996.

Younger, K. L. "Panammuwa and Bar-Rakib: Two Structural Analyses." *Journal of Ancient Near Eastern Studies* 18 (1986): 91–100.

_____. "The Phoenician Inscription of Azatiwada: An Integrated Reading." *Journal of Semitic Studies* 43 (1998): 11–47.

❧ Index of Biblical Citations ❧

～ SUBJECT INDEX ～